P9-CDF-586

Iowa City Community Theater
P. O. Box 827
Iowa City, Iowa 52244

GEORGE S. KAUFMAN AND HIS FRIENDS

GEORGE S. KAUFMAN

AND HIS FRIENDS

by Scott Meredith

DOUBLEDAY & COMPANY, INC., GARDEN CITY, NEW YORK

Excerpts from this book originally appeared in Playboy.
Copyright © 1974 by Playboy

Library of Congress Cataloging in Publication Data

Meredith, Scott.
George S. Kaufman and his friends.

Bibliography: p. 681
1. Kaufman, George S., 1889–1961—Biography.
I. Title.
PS3521.A727Z75   812'.5'2   [B]
ISBN 0-385-01566-6
Library of Congress Catalog Card Number 73-22632

Copyright © 1974 by Scott Meredith
All Rights Reserved
Printed in the United States of America

TO HELEN,
of course

Contents

CONTENTS

List of Illustrations

[ix]

Introduction

IF IT'S TRUE that a man can best be judged by the way his friends and relatives remember him after he's gone, when the force of his personality is no longer present to blur an objective appraisal, then George S. Kaufman may well have been one of the best-liked and most-respected men of his time. The willingness, even eagerness, with which busy and important people rushed to help me when I asked for information about him was both heartening and startling.

I talked at length to a great many people about Kaufman: Marc Connelly, Max Gordon, Howard Dietz, Arthur Marx, Franklin Heller, Clare Boothe Luce, and many, many others. It was interesting, and rather touching, how often people told me that they still missed him, so many years after his death, and how often people stressed the fact that there'd never been anyone else like him, with his complete honesty, his quiet but constant generosity, and his special knack of illuminating every day with the quick, flashing brilliance of his humor. It was this feeling for Kaufman, clearly, which caused people to give so much time to our discussions, though some of them were so pressed that they were also doing six other things while they were talking to me about him.

But it was in correspondence that Kaufman's friends really showed their respect and affection for him. Early in the course of my research, I sent out about a hundred letters to people who had been associated with Kaufman during his lifetime, asking for comments and recollections. And then, almost immediately, I regretted doing so, because the letters I sent out were identical, Xerox copies of a form letter, and I suspected that some people might consider my approach too impersonal. I needn't have worried. Within a few days, the mailbags at my office were jammed with warm, anecdote-filled reminiscences, some of these of astonishing length and detail.

Charles Martin, the motion picture producer, who once wrote a play called *The White Haired Boy* with Beatrice Kaufman and lived for nearly a year with the Kaufmans while writing the play, sent me two letters totaling nearly thirty pages, full of marvelous writing and fascinating detail. Irwin Shaw sent me a very short letter, which didn't surprise me at all at first look because his writing pay is probably over a dollar a word, and this was for free. But the short letter was just to say that there'd be a long letter soon, and, true to his word, a huge, helpful letter followed. Morrie Ryskind, Kaufman's collaborator on *Of Thee I Sing*, sent two long letters packed with useful information; and other long letters came from Harold Rome, Harry Ruby, Frank Sullivan, Mrs. James Thurber, Gertrude Tonkonogy Friedberg, George Jessel, George Oppenheimer, Charles Friedman, Roger Bower, Don Mankiewicz, and many, many others.

Groucho Marx wrote to say he was unable to help. "George was a nice man and a very close friend of mine," he wrote, "and I'd like to write you a nice long confidential letter, but I've just graduated from two different hospitals." But then he told his son, Arthur, about the situation, and Arthur Marx followed up a few days later with a long, thoughtful letter giving me all the information his father had been unable to provide.

And not one of the people resented the questions with which I sometimes came back, though, once or twice, I was impelled to apologize myself for the nature of some of these. Shortly after a meeting with Marc Connelly, I wrote him, "You agreed to answer any further questions I might have, but I don't believe you expected them to be as weird as the one which follows." And then I asked my question, which stemmed from the fact that I'd become fascinated at the realization that George Kaufman had had so much hair and Mr. Connelly has so little. (I thought I might be able to develop an interesting description of the two contrasting physical types working together.) "Can you tell me," I wrote, "when you began to lose your hair—and if you were already losing it when you began working with George Kaufman?"

The wonder of it is that I got an answer at all, but I did, and a friendly one. "Biography has reached a new depth when people are asked about their hair," Mr. Connelly replied. "But I'll go down there with you—and say that by exercising great self-control in Atlantic City when I was twenty and never letting fresh water touch my locks after spending most of my daytime hours in the sea, I managed to be bald by the time I was twenty-one." Then he added, and no one can argue the point: "When I began to collaborate with George Kaufman, I was quite reconciled to his having enough hair for both of us."

The interviews and letters were of tremendous value to me for many reasons, of course, the most important of which is that they enabled me to track down and pin down hundreds of facts which were not available in published sources. There was another important reason: they also helped me to determine what I hope and believe are the true origins of some of the classic Kaufman stories and classic stories about the other people in his life. Famous stories have a way of changing in the telling and retelling, getting pinned to people who seem more appropriate to the anecdote than the people to whom the events actually happened, getting expanded or shortened or improved, or suddenly beginning to include the narrator as participant. To give just one example among many, I found one funny story told in *eleven* different ways (involving varying people, occurring at varying points in history, happening in varying places). The way the stories are told in this book are the way that the strongest evidence indicates they really happened, and I apologize in advance if you've heard some of them told differently, and perhaps better, elsewhere.

This, then, is to express special thanks to George S. Kaufman's friends, who confirmed in the clearest possible way the feeling I had about my subject when I first decided to write this book. Moss Hart apologized a little, in his eulogy at Kaufman's funeral, for the complimentary things he said about his friend and collaborator; he said he could picture Kaufman peering over his glasses and telling him that his speech needed cutting. Kaufman, true enough, was not a man who admired sentimentality. But I think that, this time, if he were able to listen to his friends and relatives and read their letters, he would not mind the things he read and heard.

SCOTT MEREDITH

GEORGE S. KAUFMAN AND HIS FRIENDS

1. THE WIT

Iowa City Community Theater
P. O. Box 827
Iowa City, Iowa 52244

UNLIKE DOROTHY PARKER, who seems to have been credited with every witticism uttered by every woman in the United States between 1920 and 1970 but actually said only a few of them, George S. Kaufman was the genuine author of virtually all the funny, sardonic, and wise comments and *bon mots* attributed to him. There is, in fact, only a single famous Kaufman story which should be removed from the archives, and that is the one concerning the advice Kaufman is supposed to have given Alfred Bloomingdale, the producer and member of the department store family, when Bloomingdale was in trouble in Boston with a musical called *Allah Be Praised*.

According to the story, Bloomingdale had hired Kaufman, who worked frequently as a doctor on other people's plays when he wasn't writing or directing one of his own, to take a look at the musical, which had drawn bad reviews following its tryout opening. The producer confronted Kaufman eagerly right after the performance.

"Well," he asked, "what do you think?"

"Here's what I'd suggest," Kaufman is supposed to have answered. "Close the show and keep the store open nights."

It's a funny line, but it isn't Kaufman's; it was said by another play doctor named Cy Howard, more recently the director of the very successful film, *Lovers and Other Strangers*. The authority for this is Bloomingdale himself, who finally wrote a letter to the New York *Times* correcting the attribution when he saw it credited to Kaufman for perhaps the hundredth time in a memorial article published shortly after the playwright's death on June 2, 1961. Despite this, the story survives as genuine Kaufmaniana, to the point where longtime friends and associates of Kaufman's continue to insist that he really said it, some of them even stating that they were present at the Ritz Hotel in Boston when the incident took place. They may indeed have been present at the Ritz Hotel that night, but Kaufman wasn't; he was on a European vacation when *Allah Be Praised* was trying out and failing in Boston.

But it's easy to understand why people continue to think of the story as a Kaufman story. It's the kind of thing Kaufman did say all the time, typical of his lifelong habit of viewing the world and its inhabitants, including himself, with worry and a certain amount of sadness, but always making his sometimes devastating comments in humorous terms. He was a painfully shy man who rarely looked directly at his companion when he spoke, preferring instead to look down at the carpet in the hope that he could see a piece of lint he could pick up and throw away, or down at his plate at mealtimes, or down at his long-fingered, nervous hands. The things he said so quietly, however, were noted and remembered.

It *was* Kaufman, for example, who deflated Raymond Massey when the actor had scored a huge success playing Abraham Lincoln and began to grow more and more Lincolnesque in his manner, speech, and clothing off the stage. "Massey," Kaufman said, "won't be satisfied until somebody assassinates him." It was Kaufman who deflated Charles Laughton when Laughton, commenting on his own performance as Captain Bligh in *Mutiny on the Bounty*, said pompously that he was probably so effective in the role because he came from a long line of seafaring men. "I presume," Kaufman said, remembering Laughton's equally excellent performance as Quasimodo, "that you also come from a long line of hunchbacks." And it was also Kaufman who took care of an actor with the unfortunate name of Guido Nadzo by commenting, "Guido Nadzo is nadzo guido."

Kaufman's comments were aimed with deadly accuracy, but he wanted them to make their point and nothing more, and he became upset and contrite if damage resulted and seemed to be growing permanent. When, for example, his line about Nadzo achieved such widespread currency that the actor began to find it difficult to get work, Kaufman went from friend to friend until he found a job for him, and he continued to get him jobs until Nadzo himself decided that Kaufman had been right in the first place and left the stage.

Actors were a favorite target of Kaufman's, partially because they caused him constant agonies by forgetting, rewording, playing badly, or otherwise failing to do justice to the brilliant lines he wrote for them. The Marx Brothers, for whom he wrote two plays, *Animal Crackers* and *The Cocoanuts*, and a movie, *A Night at the Opera*, were particularly painful to him because of their practice of changing lines at every performance and even trying to throw each other off balance by suddenly speaking lines which weren't in the play at all, stealing these from other plays or making them up on the spot. Once, in despair, Kaufman walked up onto the stage in the middle of a rehearsal of *Animal Crackers*. "Excuse me for interrupting," he said, "but I thought for a minute I actually heard a line I wrote." He was less gentle when he felt that the lines replacing his weren't as good as his own; he once argued for hours about a bit of business Groucho Marx had invented and wanted to insert in a play, insisting the bit just didn't work. Marx finally gave in, but said gloomily, "They also laughed at Robert Fulton." "Not," said Kaufman, "at matinees."

He used humor all the time to bring his associates and others back into line when he felt they were straying too far, employing every device from notices on backstage bulletin boards—"11 a.m. rehearsal tomorrow morning," he once noted on a call board, "to remove all improvements inserted in the play since the last rehearsal" —to telegrams. Once he dropped in to view his Pulitzer Prize-winning play, *Of Thee I Sing*—it was the first musical in history ever to win the prize—after it had been running for many months, and was depressed to observe that William Gaxton, who played the principal role of John P. Wintergreen, had grown bored and was speaking his lines routinely and mechanically. Kaufman left the theatre, went to a nearby Western Union Office, and sent Gaxton a wire: WATCHING YOUR PERFORMANCE FROM THE LAST ROW. WISH YOU WERE HERE. He also used a telegram to tell another actor that he didn't admire his slipshod habit of forgetting his part and substituting speeches which were approximate rather than exact, and not nearly as good as written. YOUR PERFORMANCE MAGNIFICENT AND IMPROVING EVERY DAY, he wired the man. SORRY I CAN'T SAY SAME ABOUT LINES. But he needed no telegram to cool down an actor who kept blowing his lines and blaming the script. "It doesn't flow," the actor said. "It flows, all right," Kaufman said. "*You* don't."

Kaufman wrote mostly with collaborators; the reason he gave was that it was good to have company when you were locked in a room with a blank piece of paper. There was a great deal more to it than that, of course. He worked extremely hard at everything he undertook, giving every script and every directing job the absolute limit of his immense abilities, and he lived his life the same way, conducting himself so honorably that his spoken word became an absolute guarantee and he rarely had formal contracts with his business associates. But he was so insecure and so unsure of himself that he needed collaborators because he never believed that his best was very good.

This attitude remained with him all of his life: he was absolutely convinced that each new work was terrible, the beginning of the end of his career, until the critics finally came along and told him otherwise. The period before the opening of each play was a nightmare for him; he ate almost nothing for days before the opening date, walked around blindly and as though he were at death's door, and staggered into the theatre hours before curtain time but stayed

[4]

backstage moaning to himself instead of watching the play. It was said around Broadway that Moss Hart was his favorite collaborator because Hart was much the same way; Hart managed to eat a little more than Kaufman before openings, but then spent his opening nights in bathrooms giving it all back.

Sometimes people associated with Kaufman used reminders of his misplaced gloominess to win arguments with him. When Michael Todd talked Kaufman into directing *The Naked Genius*, a third-rate comedy written by Gypsy Rose Lee, Kaufman began the assignment with his customary skill and dedication, but quickly realized that the play didn't have the necessary ingredients and would be destroyed by the critics if brought to Broadway. As time passed, the author herself came to agree with him, and Kaufman went to Todd and pleaded with him to close the play out of town. Todd, however, was unwilling to do this. He suspected that his director and his author were probably right, but he'd made a complicated movie deal which would bring him much more money if the comedy played Broadway, even for a short run. He managed to keep Kaufman on the job by reminding him that he'd also begged Sam H. Harris, the producer of the vastly successful *The Man Who Came to Dinner*, to close *that* play while it was still trying out.

Others tried to distract Kaufman from his miseries with attempts to take his mind off the play currently under the gun. When one of Kaufman's plays was doing extremely poor business in an Atlantic City tryout, grossing only $94 at a matinee, the play's stage manager, Clifford Hayman, heard that the thermometer had passed the 100° mark that day, and, in desperation, mentioned this. "I've got the only play in history," Kaufman said, "where the temperature is higher than the gross." The same sort of thing happened to Howard Teichmann, who collaborated with Kaufman on *The Solid Gold Cadillac*. The day of the opening, Teichmann came over to Kaufman's apartment to try to cheer him up. Kaufman's responses were so melancholy and his manner so funereal that the conversation soon lapsed into a silence which lasted over an hour. Finally, Teichmann walked to a window, stared outside, and blurted, "Nice day." "It was a nice day," Kaufman said, "when they burned Joan of Arc at the stake."

He was exactly the same when it came to plays he directed

rather than wrote. The first play on which he received formal director's credit was *The Front Page*, written by Ben Hecht and Charles MacArthur. Even though he had had a hand in the direction of some of his own plays before that, he managed to convince himself as rehearsals went along that he knew nothing about directing. His wife, Beatrice, was traveling in Europe at the time, but his letters and calls to her finally became so piteous that she hurried home to comfort him and assure him that he wasn't messing up the play as much as he thought. *The Front Page*, of course, became a huge hit, and he went on to direct many other hits after that, but he was still as worried as ever when, nine years later, Beatrice read a new book called *Of Mice and Men*, and urged him to tie up the stage rights and direct the property as a play on Broadway. This time Kaufman had a new fear: he had never before been involved with a totally serious work. He did eventually tie up the rights, and there is strong evidence that he wrote most or perhaps even all of the play version in addition to directing it, but he was convinced of the play's certain failure until that one, too, won the Pulitzer Prize.

His insecurity manifested itself in a great many other ways. He was dramatic editor of the New York *Times*, a job more prestigious than profitable when, in 1921, he and Marc Connelly wrote their first hit, *Dulcy*. And, though he and Connelly followed up with such other hits as *To the Ladies*, *Merton of the Movies*, and *Beggar on Horseback*, and he then wrote the tremendously successful *The Butter and Egg Man* on his own, and such other great hits as *The Royal Family* with Edna Ferber and *June Moon* with Ring Lardner, he continued to hang on to his steady job until 1930. This was long after his plays were earning more for him in an hour than the *Times* paid him per month.

He refused to fly, breaking the rule only on the rarest of occasions, such as when his adopted daughter, Anne, suddenly became seriously ill, and he rushed home from Hollywood to be at her bedside. He never learned to drive, so he and Beatrice often used public transportation when they were first married, and then, after he became rich and famous, chauffeurs. He was a light, unenthusiastic, and extremely finicky eater, the constant despair of the cooks at his various homes and of the chefs at the midtown restaurants he patronized. And, because his mother had lost another son before he was born, and as a result surrounded him with excessive health precautions when he came along, he grew up with an extreme and abnormal fear of illness and death which remained with him nearly all of his life.

He also had a phobia about shaking hands and other physical contacts, a phobia he managed instantly if temporarily to overcome whenever his rather spectacular sex life was involved. He and Beatrice were a very affectionate, devoted couple, and he was absolutely shattered when, after more than twenty-eight years of marriage, she died very suddenly on October 6, 1945, at the age of fifty-one. But their closeness did not extend to their sexual relationship. Beatrice told several friends and relatives, after she and Kaufman had been married only a couple of years, that the two of them were physically incompatible, and thereafter they decided to go their separate ways as far as physical love was concerned. Both were extremely successful, even though Beatrice was more sophisticated-looking than beautiful, and Kaufman was anything but handsome.

He was, in fact, rather ugly by ordinary standards. He was fairly tall, 6'1", and rather thin, weighing about 165 pounds; he walked with a perpetual slouch; he wore glasses; his hair was thick and always appeared unruly and uncombed; and his nose was so big that a writer doing a piece about him in 1932 compared it to Jimmy Durante's. But his visible strength of character, and his reliability and honesty, made him astonishingly attractive to women, and he had an unending history of taking one beautiful woman after another, most of them actresses, to dinner, the theatre, and, nearly always after that, to bed. His most publicized extramarital romance was with Mary Astor—then, in 1936, a fragile and beautiful young movie actress. But this was only because she wrote some purple and detailed passages about Kaufman in her diary, and the diary got into the hands of her husband, Dr. Franklyn Thorpe, with whom she was having a bitter court battle for the custody of their daughter, and from Thorpe into the hands of the press. Statistically, however, she was only one among dozens.

Kaufman's romances often started quickly and frequently grew pretty fiery, but they were just physical things to him, replacements for the one element of life not available to him at home. When they ended, they ended, and he never looked back with regret. This was not always the case with his former flames, who sometimes brooded about the injustice he had perpetrated on them by moving on. Once, in an apartment building, he ran into one such girl, accompanied by her new friend and attempting to console herself with him, but still smarting over the fact that Kaufman no longer found her appealing. "This," said the girl, sensing a possible opportunity to lord it over the playwright, "is Mr. Phillips. He's in cotton." Kaufman regarded the couple calmly. "And them as plants it is soon forgotten," he said, and entered an elevator.

Kaufman's second and final marriage, to Leueen MacGrath in 1949, was very much in the pattern of his multiple romances. Leueen was an actress who had come to the United States from England to appear in *Edward, My Son* with Robert Morley. She was slim and delicate, and she was unquestionably beautiful—so much so that the New York critics, in reviewing *Edward, My Son* and the plays in which she appeared after that, devoted as much space to her looks as to her undeniable talents as an actress. John McClain, writing in the *Journal-American*, called her "fragile and attractive" in one review and "lovely" in another; William Hawkins, in the *World-Telegram*, called her "one of the most attractive women in the theatre"; and Walter Kerr, also writing at that time in the *Herald Tribune*, called her "most attractive" and said she had an "absolutely perfect waistline" for the clinging clothes of 1915 she wore in the play he was reviewing. Even the irascible George Jean Nathan, reviewing *Edward, My Son*, made note of both her talent and her beauty. He muttered fretfully that she had "an abundance of the looks which usually persuade the younger critics and more susceptible older ones that a great deal of histrionic ability must inevitably accompany them," but then conceded that she was "nevertheless impressive."

She was also very young compared to Kaufman. Her more recent biographical sketches give her date of birth as July 3, 1919, and the earlier ones as July 3, 1914. The latter is probably the accurate date; either way, she was thirty or thirty-five when they were married, and he was nearly sixty. The marriage was not a successful one, and they were divorced in August 1957. But even after that, they remained good friends; they had written two plays together during their marriage, *The Small Hours* and *Fancy Meeting You Again*, and they continued to write together and see a lot of each other. And when Kaufman became ill and entered the final year of his life, his ex-wife turned down all acting jobs to remain with him and keep him company.

Lifelong associations were the rule with Kaufman. He collaborated with many writers in the course of his long career—in addition to Hart, Connelly, Lardner, Teichmann, Edna Ferber, and Leueen, he also worked with, among others, Alexander Woollcott, Robert E. Sherwood, John P. Marquand, Dorothy Parker, Morrie Ryskind, Howard Dietz, Laurence Stallings, Herman J. Mankiewicz, Nunnally Johnson, and Abe Burrows, and with such composers as George Gershwin, Irving Berlin, and Harold Rome—and, contrary to the history of most collaborations, remained friends with every one of them to the end of his life or theirs. He and his collaborators stopped working together for various reasons. Sometimes one partner or the other wanted to work on a solo project or with someone else, and sometimes the reasons were personal, as when Ryskind began to veer to the right politically and Kaufman remained strongly liberal, but the friendships remained intact.

There were times when the friendships remained too intact. Moss Hart became so attached to Kaufman and so dependent on him, making so much of a father figure of him—the two men were only fifteen years apart in age, but Kaufman often acted as though he were a hundred years older than his ebullient collaborator—that Hart finally had to undergo psychoanalysis to convince himself that he could also write on his own again. And Edna Ferber was clearly in love with Kaufman. Kaufman, unfortunately, just didn't feel the same way about her, and this was one of the reasons she remained unmarried until her death in 1968 at the age of eighty-two.

Part of Kaufman's talent for friendship stemmed from the same quality which attracted all the young actresses to him, his absolute honesty and reliability; a substantial part undoubtedly stemmed from his great generosity. He was always generous, but never ostentatiously so, sometimes hardly even visibly so. He was an easy touch on Broadway, his handouts to unemployed actors and others totaling tens of thousands of dollars over the years, but usually given in a roundabout way so that the people would not know the money came from him. He harassed his business partners like Max Gordon into giving bigger salaries and bigger Christmas bonuses to office boys and other employees. And when former associates like George C. Tyler, who had produced some of his early plays, fell on hard times, he arranged for Tyler to receive a regular but indirect check, so that Tyler would not be embarrassed by his situation, and worked unceasingly to get many of Tyler's other old friends to do the same thing in the same way.

He was equally generous when it came to giving credit to his collaborators, an area in which many otherwise kind and gentle writers stop being kind and gentle and become cannibalistic. He was clearly the dominant figure in every one of his many collaborations, even considering the massive talents of some of the people with whom he collaborated, but he fought to the death every attempt to pin this on him. His curtain speech, following the opening of *Once in a Lifetime*, the first Kaufman-Hart collaboration, was brief and typical: "I would like the audience to know that eighty per cent of this play is Moss Hart." Hart quickly corrected his statement, saying it was possibly even the other way around, but Kaufman went right on saying it, adding, "I very quickly knew, when I met Moss, on which side my bread was buttered." He also said the same thing about Marc Connelly and a lot of other people, and saw to it that his collaborators got extra credits whenever possible, as when he worked with Howard Dietz on *The Band Wagon*. Because Dietz was just starting out and needed credits, Kaufman arranged for the program booklets to carry an impressive line: *Entire production supervised by Howard Dietz*.

Kaufman felt absolutely no envy about anybody else's success in the theatre. On the contrary, he had a favorite saying, "One hit begets another," and the logical theory that every success helped everyone else in the business because it gave more and more people the habit of going to the theatre. So he went right on deprecating his own contributions, even to the point of denying it when critics stated in their reviews, as they often did, that certain plays directed by Kaufman but written by others had obviously had the benefit of the addition of some Kaufman-created lines. Kaufman said No, even on plays like *My Sister Eileen*, *The Doughgirls*, and *Over 21*, where the Kaufman touch stood out a mile, and everybody in the theatre knew that an experienced writer-director like Kaufman could no more resist adding a brilliant gagline than he could resist picking up those invisible pieces of lint he was always picking up.

He even said it in print when he felt it was needed. When the Pasadena Playhouse in California ran a festival of George S. Kaufman plays throughout the summer of 1941, Kaufman groaned under the weight of a festival bearing his name when everybody ought to be aware that eighty per cent of the plays were someone else's. He commented on this in the *Times*:

> *When I come to write that book on playwriting—which I never will—the first twenty-six chapters will be concerned with How to Pick a Collaborator. Because I don't mind telling you that's where I excel. The eight plays that make up the current festival . . . involved the labors of Miss Edna Ferber, Mr. Connelly and Mr. Moss Hart. All three of these are persons who never have shown the slightest sign of talent except when they wrote with me. The only things Miss Ferber ever wrote by herself were eight or ten novels like* Show Boat *and* Cimarron, *and not more than two or three hundred short stories. Mr. Connelly, it is true, wrote* The Green Pastures *by himself, but it only ran five years. And Mr. Hart, pathetically laboring without me, is in a nasty fix with* Lady in the Dark. *It seems the cast may die of old age.*

Generous, in short, perhaps to a fault, making sure his friends were cut in even on the fun of having a festival, ignoring such obvious things as the fact that, for example, the only reason *The Green Pastures* was able to run so long was that Kaufman helped get it produced after Connelly had many turndowns. But his generosity did not cause anyone, least of all his friends and collaborators, to forget that the other side of him was always present, the honest, hard-working, steely-eyed Kaufman to bring them to heel if they did anything unworthy.

Hart came under the Kaufman gaze when he began to break out in all directions as money rolled in. Kaufman viewed most of it tolerantly because he knew that Hart had come from an extremely poverty-stricken background and took unusual joy in all that cash. But when Hart, born in Brooklyn, turned up in a rhinestone-studded cowboy suit which had cost him a thousand dollars, Kaufman felt he had moved too far into the realm of the *nouveau riche*. He reminded Hart of this with a simple two-word greeting: "Hiyo, Platinum!"

He also had to perform a similar service for Connelly, though Connelly's crime was far more heinous by Kaufman's standards. Connelly grew lazy and stopped writing for a very long period; he kept promising to write, and kept talking about writing, but he never actually wrote anything. As it happened, Connelly's period of non-production took place at the same time that the New York publishing firm, Simon and Schuster, discovered a forgotten Charles Dickens manuscript called *Life of Our Lord* and published it. They also arranged for the work to be run serially, and the dual publication created a lot of attention.

Kaufman used the event to give Connelly a gentle reminder. "Dickens writes more dead," he told Connelly, "than you do alive."

2. THE FAMILY

WHEN GEORGE KAUFMAN (the S. was added much later to give rhythm and balance to his byline) was fourteen years old, in 1903, he collaborated with another youngster named Irving Pichel on a play, a serious drama about a man who disowns his son. The play was called *The Failure*, but the title was not prophetic. *The Failure* was a smash hit when the two youngsters performed it repeatedly for an audience of one, Kaufman's younger sister Ruth, and the enthusiastic reception prompted the boys to join, not long afterwards, Rabbi J. Leonard Levy's Dramatics Club at the Rodeph Sholom Community House in Pittsburgh, Pennsylvania. Levy, an Englishman who had made a permanent move to the United States, was a towering figure in Reformed Judaism and a much-respected community leader who encouraged creative activity in the youngsters of the town, and he, too, admired the boys' dramatic talents. He once, in fact, cast Kaufman as the lead in a play called *A Pair of Spectacles*, and was so impressed with his performance that he urged Kaufman's father to see to it that the boy pursued a career as an actor.

The impression that there was a future in theatrical circles for the two boys was an accurate one. Pichel, following graduation from Harvard, was first a pioneer in the little theatre movement throughout the country, then a very successful actor both on Broadway and in Hollywood—among many other roles, he played the part of Fagin in the silent film version of *Oliver Twist* and the prosecuting attorney in the silent film version of *An American Tragedy*—and finally the director of such films as *The Moon Is Down*, *The Dark Mirror*, *The Pied Piper*, *Colonel Effingham's Raid*, and *Mr. Peabody and the Mermaid*. And Kaufman became the most successful playwright and director of his time, second only to Shakespeare in the number of appearances and revivals of his plays throughout the United States and much of the rest of the world.

The road to the theatre was an unplanned one for both Kaufman and Pichel. They wrote *The Failure* only because they were frequent and awed spectators at the melodramas showing in local theatres, and felt a typical urge to emulate what they watched so often on the stage. Nor did either boy come from a family with any kind of theatrical background or leanings, though both their sets of parents, like most of the people living in their upper-middle-class Jewish section of Pittsburgh, were enthusiastic theatregoers and frequent visitors to playhouses like the Nixon Theatre, then a major Pittsburgh showcase for important plays and players on tour. Pichel's father was a newspaperman; young George's father, Joseph Kaufman, was a businessman who was fairly successful in a whole series of firms and jobs until he became bored with each one in turn.

Kaufman's father and his mother, born Henrietta Myers but always called Nettie, came from similar backgrounds. Both the Kaufman and Myers families were German Jews; both families came to the United States early in the nineteenth century; and both families settled in Pittsburgh and prospered immediately. They were also related in a complicated sort of way: Nettie's father was Joseph's father's uncle.

Joseph's father came to America in 1848 and eventually opened one of the first pants factories in the United States; he started his business by hiring tailors all over Pittsburgh and putting them to work in their own homes making ready-to-wear pants for him at low rates. And later, as he began to pursue the then-novel idea of developing a whole range of stock sizes, he opened his own plant and moved many of the tailors there. Joseph's mother came to America on a sailing ship and immediately met tragedy. Her father and mother and four of her brothers and sisters died during a cholera epidemic which developed on board the ship, and her grandmother, a strong and remarkable woman who lived to the age of 106, took over and raised the remainder of the family.

Joseph, born on December 29, 1856, was one of ten children, several of whom became rich or famous or both. One of his brothers, Sol, followed their father into the pants business, but also invested money in tin-plate stock and became a millionaire when the tin-plate company was taken over by National Steel. (Sol had tried to convince Joseph to buy the stock, too, but Joseph, who showed a consistent talent for avoiding success, refused.) Another brother, Sidney, was one of the early developers of the typewriter. And a third brother, Gustave, was co-founder and co-owner of the eminent engineering firm of Ferris and Kaufman, which built many of the country's bridges. (He also invented the Ferris wheel, but named it after his partner because he and his family were ashamed of it. He continued to be ashamed of it for the rest of his life. When he died and the *Times* listed the wheel among his achievements, his widow wept with embarrassment at the association of the frivolous invention with the Kaufman name. Most of the Kaufmans were touchy, anyway, about the dignity and usage of the family name. The name had originally been Kaufmann, but Joseph's father made it less German, upon his arrival in the United States, by dropping one of the n's. He also Anglicized the sound of it a little by pronouncing it as though it were spelled Koffman. Thereafter, that was the family preference, and throughout his life George Kaufman corrected people who pronounced his name in the German manner, as though it was spelled Kowfman, even when he was introduced that way on radio or television.)

The Myers family made their money in the meat-packing business, also one of the first of its kind in the country, and lived in plush opulence on the swank north side of town. Their wealth diminished, abruptly, in the late 1870s. Nettie's father kept virtually all of his money in unregistered and negotiable government bonds, and the bonds were kept in several tin boxes in his basement. He threw a large party one evening for some relatives who were visiting from Baltimore, and several well-dressed thieves drove up in a carriage, were assumed to be guests and were let into the house, and promptly proceeded to chloroform and tie up the family and their guests and servants, nearly killing one of the servants by giving him too much chloroform. Then, clearly in possession of inside information, the thieves did a thorough job of cleaning out the house and loading everything onto their carriage. They took all of the Myers's bonds, all of the family's silver and other valuables (even though many of these things were hidden under the carpeting and floor of a study), and stripped every person present of every piece of jewelry. The thieves made a clean and total getaway, presumably heading into the still-wild West, and, in those pre-insurance days, the Myers family changed overnight from plutocrats to people in merely comfortable circumstances. Fortunately, the family business continued to flourish, enabling the family to maintain their big house pretty much as before, and eventually Nettie and Joseph were married there.

Joseph had a very pleasant childhood; the Kaufman home was on a wide and lovely street, Cedar Avenue, and Joseph later reminisced about sitting on the curbstone outside his house in 1862 and watching a parade in which Abraham Lincoln was a participant. When he grew up, he shunned his father's field, left school at an early age—though he eventually educated himself and became extremely well-read and knowledgeable, owning a huge library which included about forty volumes by his favorite author, Voltaire, and works by Darwin, Huxley, Spencer, Tyndall, and many others, all of which he read and reread—and undertook a series of exciting jobs and adventures. He fought against the Ute Indians, worked for three years in Leadville, Colorado, at Haw Tabor's famous silver mine, and finally returned to Pittsburgh, and, now a tall, lean, sun-tanned, broad-shouldered man of twenty-eight, met and courted Nettie and married her on January 7, 1884.

Nettie, at twenty-five, seemed pretty special. Whereas the Kaufmans laughed and joked a lot, the members of the Myers family tended toward aloofness, and Nettie was slim, cool, and elegant. Nettie had been educated at an Ursuline convent, the best school in town for girls of all faiths, and had even won two medals there, one for excellence in music and the other for excellence in scholarship. (She gave both medals many years later to her daugher Ruth. The music medal, which was shaped like a harp, was stolen one day, but the other is still owned by the family, its engraved testament to Nettie's scholarship, dated June 1876, still readable.)

Nettie's regal air was inherited from her mother, a woman so queenly and demanding that, as the years passed and Nettie sometimes became overexacting herself, her children could occasionally make her smile at herself by saying blandly, "Is there anything else, Frau Myers?" But despite the rare and reluctant smiles, Nettie remained imperious throughout her life, and examples were regular and deadly. Once Ruth was being courted by a scion of an eminent and ancient Portuguese-Jewish family, and the boy told Nettie that the family was very old-fashioned and it had been necessary to get approval for the courtship of a girl from a German-Jewish family. He added, however, that this had been given readily. "Very generous of them, I'm sure," Nettie said coldly.

Another time, after George Kaufman had become famous, Nettie was at a health resort and was told by a mutual friend that George Gershwin's mother was there, too, and wanted to meet her. "I don't know her," Nettie said. "My God," the friend said, "Gershwin's probably the most successful composer in the world today. And he's collaborated with your son." "My son," Nettie said, "collaborates with all kinds of people."

The Kaufmans were married on a crisp, snowy Monday night and moved into a house in Allegheny, Pennsylvania. It was a very modest house because they had almost no money, and that remained their financial condition much of the time through the years. "When I was born," George said later, when an interviewer asked him if his boyhood had been rich or poor, "I owed twelve dollars."

This was mostly due to Joseph's practice of abandoning each job not long after mastering it, an eccentricity he never discarded. He had a theory that one business was very much like every other business, that, for example, manufacturing nuts and bolts was really not very different from manufacturing pianos or shoes, and he spent his lifetime proving this. The trouble was that, once he had proven it, the challenge was no longer there, and his working day grew tedious and he moved on to something else.

As a result, the financial status of the Kaufman family was both ever-changing and unpredictable. Sometimes they lived in big, impressive houses with several servants; sometimes they lived in small places and ate in nearby boardinghouses. It all depended on the job or business Joseph was in at the time, and he went through a great many of them.

Early in the marriage, he had a particularly good job. He was Crucible Steel's first superintendent, working directly under Charles Schwab, and for a while he labored hard and happily, because he'd never run a steel business before and it interested him. In very short order, he had the plant running smoothly, introducing innovation after innovation and doing a lot of other things. He even named the town in which the mill was located, calling it Aliquippa, an Indian name he'd once heard, a name the town still bears.

But then he formed a friendship with Samuel Gompers, the pioneer labor leader. Steelworkers were then working twelve hours a day, and the two men decided to see Schwab and suggest that this be reduced to ten hours. Schwab's response was immediate; he told Kaufman and Gompers that they were radicals and troublemakers, and fired Kaufman on the spot. "You'll see the day," Joseph told Schwab, "when Gompers will be considered a conservative." Events, of course, proved him right, but he was jobless after that meeting.

But there were other jobs and businesses, even if one didn't live too well between them, and nothing in the world could stop him from being innovative and ahead of his time—at least until he grew bored. He formed a business called Vulcan Machine and Foundry Company and introduced an astonishing number of new methods and procedures, and continued to introduce new methods and procedures until the business was running so well that he began to ignore it and it failed. He went to work as manager of a firm called Columbia Ribbon Company, and had been there only six months when he designed and introduced a new loom which worked substantially better than the looms that had been in use for years. And it was still the same with the final firm with which he was associated, an organization he bought called the New York Silk Dyeing Company, which dyed raw skein silk. He was one of the first in the field to introduce the forty-hour week, and, when he died in 1940, he left the firm to his employees rather than to his family. His belief, which he'd often expressed, was that there would be no militant employees if employers behaved decently, and he felt that the business really belonged to the people who had worked so hard with and for him.

Surprisingly, the frequent financial crises had no deleterious effect whatever on the marriage; Nettie, and later the Kaufman children, learned to live as events and bank balances dictated. But finances were only part of the picture, and, as time passed, other parts of the picture grew increasingly bleak. Two aspects of Nettie's character, in particular, showed up which made Joseph's life miserable much of the time and had an even more profound and permanent effect on their son George. They were things which were to affect both his personal and professional life in massive ways.

The first of these manifested itself because of a tragedy in Joseph's and Nettie's own lives. Their first child, Helen, born on October 6, 1884, grew up and lived to a happy old age, but they were not as lucky with their next child. A son, Richard, was born in 1886, but he was dead two years later.

This was a time when the second summer of a child's life was considered the most dangerous period of all; one child in seven died during that summer. Relatively few children died during their first year of life because they were protected by inborn immunities, inherited antibodies and the like, but these immunities had begun to fade and weaken by the time the second summer came. Then many succumbed to the various causes of death all around them: milk wasn't pasteurized, bottles weren't truly clean, there was a great deal of typhoid, food spoiled in the summer heat and became poisoned.

Richard died of an intestinal infection. It was called dysentery, but it wasn't really that; he died, in effect, of dehydration. If hydration had been understood at that time, he might possibly have been saved, but scientific knowledge in that area was still very sketchy.

Nettie's reaction to her first son's death was excessive. The event was a terrible one, and Joseph, a sensitive man, felt it deeply, too; he had also grown to love their small son. But he was a realist, and knew that death was a part of life and must on occasion be faced and lived with. Nettie never came to feel that way.

Nettie had always been almost abnormally apprehensive about illness and death, so much so that, when Helen once became ill, and had convulsions, it was Joseph who had to take over and nurse the first Kaufman child back to health. Now, with Richard's death, Nettie's horror of these things became even stronger. And when her second son, George, was born a year later, she was ready to protect him and fight for his life and make absolutely sure he would survive and flourish as Richard had not.

She started imposing on her household in general, and on George in particular, every health and safety measure she could remember or invent. Milk sometimes made children sick, so she excluded milk entirely from the Kaufman table. Water taken straight from the tap sometimes made people sick, too, so she required that all water be boiled before being drunk. Children sometimes got hurt playing games, so George played few games. She followed this up by warning George against all the other things in life which might hold hidden dangers. And that included almost everything: high places, low places, rivers, lakes, swimming pools, and especially close contacts with other people who might have diseases.

Her attitude toward George became unchangingly neurotic, and at times perhaps even psychotic. And the result, inevitably, was that, exactly opposite to her intentions, he grew up to be thin, pale, sickly, and plagued with phobias which remained with him and disabled him as long as he lived.

As mentioned, he developed an overwhelming horror of being touched. (When he became famous, many interviewers mentioned his amusing habit of greeting people by lifting a casual finger and saying, "Hi." It wasn't casual at all; it was a quick move to greet people that way before they tried to shake hands with him.) He became a total hypochondriac, certain he had every new disease which appeared over the horizon. He was so much in the grip of his fears that when his nephew, Allan Friedlich, became a physician and visited him one day, the young doctor found more than thirty bottles of medicine on Kaufman's night table which were unneeded and could be swept into the wastebasket, some of them years old and potentially dangerous for self-medication. He ate unenthusiastically and sometimes worriedly. Even when he moved to New York, and had many of his meals at the best restaurants in the world, he ordered simple foods and would not allow sauces to be used because he couldn't see with his own eyes what they contained. He developed so great a fear of death that he was often afraid to go to bed because he feared dying in his sleep. Sometimes he even hesitated to open doors because of fear of some vague and uncertain menace which might be waiting on the other side.

He also, because Nettie's method of getting her son to avoid things like strenuous sports was to convince him that he couldn't perform well in them anyway, developed in his early years the self-doubts which continued to assail him throughout his career. As a boy, he was always certain that he would do badly in his schoolwork and in his tests, even though he invariably ended up doing well; as an adult, the manifestation was the certainty that everything he wrote would later be torn to bits by the critics. He was held so tightly in the grip of his self-doubt that by critics he meant anybody: not just the people who wrote for the newspapers and magazines, but *anybody*, anybody at all who saw one of his plays. He was once depressed for days because his laundress happened to mention that her daughter had seen *Of Thee I Sing* and hadn't cared much for it.

"George Kaufman was a mess," Dorothy Parker told a reporter who asked her about him, and, as far as his phobias were concerned, she was undoubtedly right. The relationship between the playwright and the lady, however, remained a casual one throughout their lives, even though they met occasionally at the Algonquin Hotel's famous Round Table and also worked together for a brief period on a movie short. People who knew Kaufman better felt differently about him. This was not only because the attractive aspects of his character more than counterbalanced his eccentricities, but also because, even where the phobias were concerned, he managed to control them and keep them from getting in the way when something really important was at stake.

A good example of this was his distaste for physical contacts; obviously, this had to be put aside when it came to the more intimate moments in his many romances. Typical was the time when, as he was wining and dining a girl in a Manhattan restaurant, she expressed curiosity about the soup he was eating. Then, as he watched in stunned silence, she used the spoon from her own soup to take a sampling of his.

Kaufman immediately summoned a waiter and ordered another bowl. "But that's unnecessary," the girl protested. "I just wanted a taste."

"The bowl," Kaufman said, "is for me."

Later, however, Kaufman took the girl home to her apartment, and she failed to respond when he kissed her because she was still offended by the incident in the restaurant. "I see," she said, "you're not so worried about my germs now."

Kaufman's quiet answer won her back. "I've been looking at you all evening," he said, "and I've decided it's worth the risk."

He was, in short, able to cope where necessary, but this was less true with the after-effects of Nettie's second area of odd behavior. These were acts which, unlike the safety and health measures, were not even aimed directly at him. Their effect on him, however, was even stronger and deeper than the effects of the phobias; they created a major defect thereafter in the way he lived and in everything he wrote. Nettie began to throw frequent emotional tantrums, and Kaufman found the scenes so horrifying that he was never able afterward to tolerate a show of emotions in his own life, or write an emotional scene in his plays.

Nettie's *crises de nerfs* ran along classic lines. She became jealous about her husband, she became jealous *of* her husband, and she surrounded herself with family attention by developing one ailment after another, usually feigned. The way in which she differed from other wives with similar patterns of behavior was degree. Her emotional scenes were lengthier, more extended, than those of most other women.

She accused Joseph, her voice cold and complaining, of having affairs with every woman with whom he came in contact. One particularly unpleasant scene occurred when Joseph received a postcard from his manicurist informing him that she had moved from one barber shop to another. Joseph pointed out that the card was printed and that the manicurist would hardly have done this just to arrange an assignation with him, but Nettie continued to rage. She accused women who were long-time friends of really being interested only in Joseph, and she wept self-pitying tears at her certainty that people found her boring and remained friends only because they liked Joseph so much.

Joseph, a fairly modest man, always denied this last accusation, but there was probably a degree of truth in it. Nettie had more formal education than he had, but her schooling had all the narrowness and limitations of a convent education of her period. She learned the piano and became technically expert, but played sentimental little pieces by Ethelbert Woodbridge Nevin and shunned Brahms because she considered his music too modern. She was also surprisingly slow on the trigger at times. Her son once bought her a share in one of his new plays, but warned her not to expect quick profits because the production had been an expensive one. The action, he reminded her, took place in a lot of different rooms. "But that shouldn't be expensive," Nettie said. "The rooms are all in the same house."

In addition, she was limited in most of the ways typical of Victorian women. She would not read a novel which she considered in any way daring, and required both her daughters to undress for bed, even in the privacy of their rooms, underneath their nightgowns.

Joseph, on the other hand, was hungry for knowledge and for expansion of his tastes, and would read and listen to anything. He was also, as typified by his romantic early adventures and his final gesture of giving his business away to his employees, capable of expansive actions which were totally foreign to someone like Nettie. A member of the posh Engineers Club in his later life, he was approached by another member, General Brian Somerville, a one-time cabinet officer and war hero, who poured out a tale of woe to the effect that his daughter was thinking of marrying an artist. The artist, furthermore, was unsuccessful and had never even sold a painting. Joseph did not agree with Somerville's view that the artist's lack of success was sufficient reason for breaking up the romance, and went to the gallery which represented the artist and bought two paintings so that the artist would no longer be non-selling. In this way, Joseph felt, he was enabling Somerville's daughter to make her decision about the artist as a man, without consideration of his financial condition.

In time, few days passed without Nettie's complaints or accusations of infidelity, and Joseph began to disappear at the first signs, walking the streets of Pittsburgh until he was fairly sure that Nettie had finally stopped talking. The children stayed and suffered, George most of all. He was a dutiful and loving son, despite everything. Sometimes, he'd protest, but only very mildly; if Nettie would ask him if he'd like to run upstairs and get her glasses, he might say, "Do I have to like it?" But then he'd run right up and get them.

There were times when things were very bad, when Nettie's demands were so constant or her imaginary illnesses so severe that nurses were brought in, and at the very end of her life they were psychiatric nurses. Her family, in the tradition of Jewish families, never deserted her. Nettie and Joseph were still together in 1934, fifty years after their marriage, and George threw a big 50th Anniversary party for them, attended by more than 125 guests, at the Savoy-Plaza ballroom. They were still together when they died within five months of each other in 1940. But the incidents took their toll.

For George, Nettie's heritage to him was the lifetime of phobias and imagined illnesses, and painful shyness so severe that even Jed Harris, one of the world's most self-centered men, noticed it. Harris, who produced Kaufman's and Edna Ferber's *The Royal Family*, went on a two-week vacation to Florida with Kaufman, and commented wonderingly afterwards that Kaufman was so embarrassed about his thin body that he refused to put on a bathing suit and walked the beaches in street clothes.

Kaufman's other inheritance, his dread of emotions, resulted in the one area of his career in which he was not hard-working and totally dedicated. In all other ways, he worked unceasingly. Sometimes he spent a full day rewriting and polishing a single line. But when it came to love scenes or other scenes of emotion, he turned these quickly and gladly over to his collaborators, and seemed anxious to be confronted as little as possible afterward by the scenes. "That's fine, that's fine," he would say hurriedly, after a collaborator would read him an emotional scene he'd just written, and then move on to something else.

"Some scars don't show on the skin," Kaufman once said. He was not, but could have been, talking about himself.

3. THE BREAKTHROUGH

KAUFMAN WAS BORN on a Saturday morning, November 16, 1889, at 6230 Station Street, a fashionable Pittsburgh street because Joseph was then doing well. The original intention was to name him after the physician and close family friend who delivered him, John Cooper. But Nettie decided at the last minute that John Cooper Kaufman was no name for a nice Jewish boy. She chose George instead because she liked the sound of it.

Aside from the million phobias and health strictures, his boyhood was a relatively normal one. He rarely engaged in sports himself but was an enthusiastic Pittsburgh Pirates fan. He kept tabs on batting averages and usually saddled his little sister, Ruth, born on his seventh birthday and the last of the Kaufman children, with the chore of going to the local cigar store and bringing back details on the late scores posted there. He also participated in the usual run of juvenile moneymaking enterprises. The most successful of these was a partnership with a boy named Freddie Gravenstein, in which the two youngsters went periodically to Howe Spring on nearby Shady Avenue, and filled milk cans with sparkling water. Kaufman, of course, was never permitted to drink personally, but sold the water to a route of neighborhood spring-water lovers. He also, like most boys, abhorred washing. He was caught on several bath nights sitting on the floor of the bathroom and reading *Argosy* magazine, running his free hand around the filled bathtub to simulate the sounds of bathing. And, when Nettie insisted that he cut out that nonsense, he used some of his savings to subscribe to a clipping service and presented her with a sheaf of news stories about bathtub accidents. It didn't do any good.

It was during his early boyhood that he also began a lifelong love affair with Mark Twain. In addition to great admiration for Twain's special brand of humor, Kaufman discovered many similarities in their lives. Twain's hair was also an unruly mop. Both had fathers who failed in business and mothers who feared they'd die as infants. Twain also had a phobia about touching people. Kaufman revealed how much he was trying to pattern himself after Twain in an inscription he wrote in a Twain book he sent to his sister Helen as a birthday gift: "Not Twain yet but doing my damnedest." His admiration for Twain never left Kaufman. Moss Hart remembered seeing an engraving of Twain hanging on the wall of a bedroom in Kaufman's town house at 158 East 63rd Street, and a later collaborator, Howard Teichmann, saw the same picture on the wall of Kaufman's bedroom in his apartment at 1040 Park Avenue.

Kaufman's schooling was normal, if truncated. He entered Liberty School, a public elementary and junior high school, when he was six, and transferred to New Castle Elementary School, another public school, when Joseph decided that his future lay in tool steel and formed the Vulcan Foundry and Machine Company in nearby New Castle. Joseph rented a big house at 28 Croton Avenue, but when Vulcan began to falter, and then failed, the family headed back to 6102 Walnut Street in Pittsburgh. And George returned to Liberty School.

George entered Central High School in September 1903. Joseph managed to stay afloat with a series of jobs, and put aside enough money so that college remained a possibility. Writing, at this stage, was not a serious ambition for the future playwright. He began to write stories, essays, and poems for the high school literary magazine, trying a few of them out first on the magazines and newspapers in New York and gathering a big pile of rejection slips. But he did not consider writing for a living any more seriously than he took the advice of several of his teachers who saw him play the title role in a school drama called *The Queen's Messenger* and thought, echoing Rabbi Levy, that he could succeed as an actor. As far as he was concerned, he had seen in his father's career what could happen to a man who pursued one visionary means of livelihood after another. He wanted no life of feast or famine, a big house and three maids one day and a couple of rooms in a boardinghouse the next, for himself. He chose the solid, sober profession of the law, and in September 1907 entered Western University of Pennsylvania's law school.

He lasted exactly three months; he had just arrived at Blackstone on Torts when he became ill with pleurisy. Dr. Cooper had died and been replaced by Dr. Clarence Rinehart. The physician, a brother of the Dr. Stanley Rinehart who later married a young nurse named Mary Roberts and saw her become one of America's most popular mystery writers, thought the young clerk needed more fresh air and advised an outdoors job.

Kaufman went along with the advice, though he should have known better. He had had one previous experience with the great outdoors, when, aged fifteen, he was sent to spend the summer on a ranch owned by a friend of Joseph's because Joseph felt his son needed building up via a lot of horseback riding and piles of buckwheat cakes for breakfast. Kaufman looked at one horse and never went near another for the rest of his life; he ate one buckwheat cake and never again ate another; he got through one day walking around the hot, arid countryside and spent the rest of the summer inside the cool bunkhouse reading *Argosy*. But Dr. Rinehart was, after all, the family physician and a man he respected, and he took a job as "chainman and transitman" with a surveying gang.

He didn't know what a chainman and transitman was when he

took the job, but soon learned that it involved carrying around an immensely heavy iron chain which the rest of the surveying gang used for their own mysterious purpose. He was, he later reported, the world's worst surveyor; he came home from a work trip one week and admitted to Joseph that it was entirely because of his errors that the town of McCullom, West Virginia, would henceforth be situated on a plain three feet lower than the site for which it had been intended. But he lasted through the summer and regained his health, though otherwise he left the job just as he had come to it: over six feet tall but weighing only 130 pounds.

That fall of 1908, happily back indoors again, he entered business school, took a crash course in typing and stenography, worked for a while as window clerk at the Allegheny County tax office, and then got a job as stenographer to the comptroller of the Pittsburgh Coal Company. He didn't know what a comptroller was, either, but in time he found out. "A comptroller," he told a friend, "is a man who starts dictating letters at a quarter to six." The job, though, was a lot easier than carrying around heavy chains, and, since he had already begun to develop his lifelong preference for city sidewalks, was pleasant because it was located right in town instead of in some suburb overrun by things like grass and trees. He decided to remain with the job until some major opportunity or change came his way.

The change came in the form of a new opportunity for Joseph. Joseph's Pittsburgh jobs were all pretty mediocre, and he'd been busily applying for other positions—all kinds of jobs in all kinds of fields, telling owners and managers of firms from coast to coast about his theory that every business was essentially like every other business. The owners of the Columbia Ribbon Company accepted the theory, and offered Joseph the job of manager of their plant in Paterson, New Jersey. Joseph moved his family to Paterson in the summer of 1909, settling more permanently in Passaic that fall because Passaic had a better school for Ruth.

George stayed on alone in Pittsburgh for a while, living in the same boardinghouse which the whole family had occupied before their move to New Jersey; it was run by a woman named Smith, and the only thing George remembered about it afterward was that the food was awful, consisting in large part of what he called XYZs—

alphabet soup. Then Joseph got him a job as salesman for Columbia Ribbon, selling ribbons and leather goods both in the firm's sales office and on the road, and he moved eastward too.

At first, he was even worse as a salesman than he'd been as a chainman and transitman, making at least one extended sales trip in which he failed to bring back a single sale, but in time he became fairly good at his job. This was far more the result of necessity than of aptitude. He became determined to hang on at Columbia Ribbon because the firm's sales office was in New York City, and New York City was the center for what had previously been only a casual interest for him, his writing, but was suddenly and all at once becoming the most important thing in his life.

He'd been doing almost no writing at all at the time he moved to New Jersey. In fact, he'd begun to wonder if people might not have been right about his histrionic abilities, and the first thing he did when he arrived on the eastern seaboard and gathered together a little money was enroll in a Saturday morning acting class at a second-rate but inexpensive establishment called the Alveine School of Dramatic Art. He also tried out for an acting job: he met a friend of a playwright-producer named Charles Klein, learned that Klein had written and was about to put on a play called *The Gamblers*, and got the friend to give him a letter of recommendation describing him as a "promising amateur."

Klein, furthermore, found him interesting and promised him a job—only a walk-on, of course, Klein said, but at least it would be a foot in the door—and told him he'd receive a postcard giving him the date of the start of rehearsals. But the card never came. Klein sent it out as promised, but it was lost in the mails, and both men assumed the other had changed his mind. Kaufman returned to his typewriter, and later commented on the incident with his usual deadpan delivery. "If that card had arrived," he said, "I'd almost certainly have become an actor instead of a writer. And then Eugene O'Neill would have been the most important playwright in the United States."

His new hometown, Passaic, had a newspaper called the *Herald*, and he began to send them a steady stream of humorous essays and poems. To his pleasure and surprise, they were accepted; the *Herald* didn't pay for the pieces, but at least they ran them. And he was, at last, an author published in a professional publication.

And so, thus encouraged, he turned his eyes toward the big time, New York City, and felt the strong determination to keep the job which took him into the city. Because New York contained a newspaper named the *Mail*, and a column called *Always in Good Humor*, and, most important of all, a man named Franklin Pierce Adams.

Adams, possessor of the most celebrated set of initials in the country, had been running his column in the *Mail* since 1903. He was a man very much like Kaufman in many ways. Despite his WASP name, he was also Jewish; his writings and his literary ambitions, like Kaufman's, centered entirely around the field of humor; and he was noted for the same kind of brilliant, quick wit for which Kaufman later also became famous. He even looked a little like Kaufman, despite the fact that he was sparse on top and had a mustache, and with Kaufman it was just the opposite. Both men had the same tall, thin, long-necked, pleasant kind of ugliness. "My God," Irvin S. Cobb once said, walking into a club and seeing a moose head on the wall, "they've shot Frank Adams!"—and that summed it up nicely.

Adams was eight years older than Kaufman almost to the day— he was born on November 15, 1881—and he had a strong headstart in the direction in which Kaufman now wanted to go. Dozens of things he said were quoted all the time in smart circles throughout the country. His humor ran the full spectrum. He was famous for a wise kind of humor—things like, "ninety-two per cent of the stuff told you in confidence you couldn't get anybody else to listen to anyway" and, "Every time we tell anybody to cheer up, things might be worse, we run away for fear we might be asked to specify how" to, "When politicians appeal to all intelligent voters, they mean everyone who's going to vote for them." He was capable of punnish black humor, as when there was a theatre fire in the Basque section of Spain and a lot of people were crushed and killed trying to get out of the single door of the theatre. "Don't," he said, "put all your Basques in one exit." And he was most devastating of all, exactly in the manner of the later George S. Kaufman, when it came to commentary on his friends and neighbors.

One of his most-quoted lines was his sorrowful report about an acquaintance who, though notorious for his stinginess, had become engaged and was, surprisingly, reported to have given his fiancée a ring. "I hear he's had a terrible accident," Adams said. "He was out shopping for the ring, and he got his fingers caught between two pushcarts." Another famous Adams line concerned Alexander Woollcott, who once, as Adams watched, picked up one of his own books at a friend's house, looked inside at the copyright page, and said, "Ah, what is so rare as an Alexander Woollcott first edition?" "An Alexander Woollcott second edition," Adams said. (Woollcott later wrote two plays in collaboration with Kaufman, *The Channel Road* and *The Dark Tower*, and found himself receiving exactly the same kind of treatment from his collaborator. At a run-through of *The Dark Tower* one morning, the two authors were sitting together when an actor in the play, whose role required him to enlarge himself with padding, approached them to complain about it. "I hate to walk out on the stage with a big paunch," he said. Kaufman jumped to his feet. "You've grossly insulted Alexander Woollcott," he said. Then, with his instinctive and impeccable timing, he waited a moment or two, and added, "And for that, you'll receive a gold medal.")

Sometimes, of course, Adams was on the receiving end himself, as when he told Neysa McMein, the artist, "You really ought to do my portrait. I have the face of an old Greek coin." "You have the face," Miss McMein said, "of an old Greek waiter." But most of the really celebrated ripostes were chalked up on Adams's side, increasing his fame with each new one. He won, for example, an argument with Reginald Birch, the small-statured but ferocious editor of the humor magazine, *Judge*, with one shattering line. "If you were half a man," he said to Birch, "—and you are." And he was equally brief, much later, when Harold Ross, the brilliant and eccentric editor and founder of *The New Yorker*, became a friend of Adams's and Kaufman's, and Kaufman heard one day that Ross, an unathletic man who normally shunned sports, had taken up tobogganing. "Does he look funny tobogganing?" Kaufman asked. "Well," Adams said, "you know how he looks *not* tobogganing."

Famous lines, all of them, but the thing which really brought

Adams nationwide celebrity, and deservedly, was his newspaper column. Adams, born in Chicago, had started out as an insurance salesman, after a year at the University of Michigan, but switched to writing when he went one February morning to sell a policy to George Ade, the humorist. Ade was having strawberries for breakfast when Adams arrived at his house. Adams decided that any profession which could enable a man, in those days before frozen foods, to afford strawberries in February was the line of work for him, and managed to get himself a job on the Chicago *Journal*. He moved to New York in 1903, started a column called *Always in Good Humor* in the *Mail*, and stayed on the *Mail* until 1914, when he moved over to the *Tribune* and changed the column's heading to its better-remembered title of *The Conning Tower*.

Adams did not pay for contributions to his daily column of "wit and wisdom in prose in verse"; the only tangible remuneration was a gold watch given once a year at a banquet to the writer who had appeared most frequently in the column in the preceding twelve months. He, usually, gave the prize for quantity, as he explained to a contributor who asked why he didn't give the watch for quality, for the *best* contribution of the year, because every contribution he accepted was a gem. The column sparkled and shone, and was unhesitatingly named by all experts as the best column appearing in any newspaper in America, and perhaps in the world, so an appearance in *Always in Good Humor* or *The Conning Tower* was really its own reward. Adams received so many contributions, was so tough a judge, and was so unerring in his taste that many of his contributors soon went on to bigger and more profitable things, or started to make big money elsewhere while they continued to contribute to the column.

Among the writers who made their first, or at least early, appearances in print in FPA's columns were Sinclair Lewis, Edna St. Vincent Millay, Newman Levy, Arthur Guiterman, Deems Taylor, Dorothy Parker, who later told people that Adams had raised her from a couplet, and four of the people who subsequently wrote plays with Kaufman: Woollcott, Edna Ferber, Ring Lardner, and Moss Hart. In the fall of 1909, Kaufman himself joined the club.

He made his first contribution at just about the same time as Woollcott, a recent graduate of Hamilton College and a plump, brash young man much more confident of his own future in the field of letters than Kaufman, was wangling himself a job as a cub reporter on the New York *Times*, and at about the same time as Kaufman's first collaborator, Irving Pichel, was entering Harvard. Kaufman, conscious of his personal lack of formal education, and unaware that Adams's formal education wasn't much better, sent in his contribution timidly in the mails. He was also nervous about the fact that the piece, an untitled poem, was visibly imitative of the work of another of his idols, W. S. Gilbert. It couldn't have been all that unoriginal; Adams accepted it at once and asked for more. Kaufman sent more and Adams accepted these, too.

Most contributions to *Always in Good Humor* and *The Conning Tower* were signed with initials or pseudonyms, a practice which had started because many of the well-known contributors wanted to avoid the trouble of having to explain to other editors their reasons for insisting on large fees from them while being willing and even eager to write for FPA for nothing. Kaufman used G.S.K., and the initials appeared more and more frequently in Adams's column. By spring of the next year, Kaufman was so regular a contributor that Adams invited him to New York and to lunch so that he could have a look at him.

The two men hit it off immediately, not startling in the light of their similarities to each other in so many ways. Kaufman was still working as a salesman for the Columbia Ribbon Company, but his job gave him sufficient freedom of movement and time so that he was able to write short pieces frequently and see Adams now and then for lunch and dinner. Then, one day, he answered a *Billboard* magazine advertisement for a company manager inserted by a stock company in Troy, New York. In place of experience, the ad said, the company would be willing to accept a man who could put $100 into the company to help keep it going. Kaufman scraped up the hundred, said farewell to ribbons, and left for Troy. The theatre turned out to be a dismal affair on the second floor of an office building, with no money, no talent, and no audience. At the end of the first week, Kaufman wired home for train fare. His telegram to his father said: LAST SUPPER WITH ORIGINAL CAST WOULDN'T DRAW IN THIS HOUSE.

He returned to Columbia Ribbon, but in November 1912 Frank A. Munsey, the publisher, approached Adams and asked him to recommend a bright but cheap young writer to do a humor column for the Washington *Times*. Adams recommended Kaufman immediately. Both Munsey's approach to Adams and Adams's recommendation of Kaufman were extraordinary, in a way. Munsey, in addition to being the proprietor of a great many newspapers and magazines, was also a virulent and unashamed anti-Semite. Kaufman reasoned it all out some days later and told his theory to his family. As for Adams, Munsey either didn't know he was Jewish, or knew it but was interested only in getting some free advice from a man noted for his impeccable taste in writers. As for himself, Kaufman decided in his self-deprecatory way, Adams had suggested him less for his abilities than for the mischievous fun of seeing Munsey's face when he proposed someone with a clearly Jewish name.

If that was Adams's notion, it didn't work. Munsey accepted Kaufman without comment and offered him $20 a week, requiring him to do columns every day except Sunday for that price. Kaufman, though now earning $3 more per week than that amount at Columbia Ribbon, leaped at the chance. He left his job, moved to Washington, and his first column, under the title of *This and That and a Little of the Other*, appeared in the Washington *Times* on December 9, 1912.

Kaufman modeled his column after *All in Good Humor*, an amalgam of short pieces by the conductor of the column and contributions by other people, and it, too, sparkled and shone. A few months later, the *Times*'s editor asked Kaufman to extend the appearances of the column to seven times weekly and raised his salary to $25. The column also began to attract attention all around the country, with many other newspapers running excerpts and giving admiring credit to the source.

Everything might have continued smoothly and indefinitely if Kaufman had not also adopted another of FPA's practices. Adams had a theory that the success of published material stemmed as much from its attractiveness to the eye as its content—or if not as much, he said, then certainly in part. Because of this theory, he insisted that his columns be set in a variety of types, changing from paragraph to paragraph and sometimes from line to line, and he selected the typefaces himself and delivered each column personally to the composing room and remained there to make sure the final product was exactly as he wanted it. Kaufman began to do the same thing with his column, and it was on one of his trips to the *Times* composing room that he ran—literally—into Munsey.

Munsey had been having a hard day. He had been called to Washington because the paper was suddenly developing a whole series of problems, among them a labor dispute with some members of the composing room, and he was in no mood for annoyance when Kaufman came hurtling toward him. Kaufman, of course, knew nothing of this; he was hurrying because his column was a little late that day, and he hit Munsey so hard that the publisher was thrown to the floor.

Munsey rose slowly and painfully to his feet, and there was a long, tense silence as he looked first into Kaufman's mild brown eyes and then settled his gaze on Kaufman's long nose. Then he turned to one of his assistants, hovering nervously nearby.

"Who," he asked, "is that Jew in my composing room?"

Kaufman's attitude toward his religion had, up to this point, been rather ambivalent. He had inherited this ambivalence from his parents, since Nettie, on the one hand, was enthusiastic enough about Judaism to encourage her son to attend the local synagogue and become involved in Rabbi Levy's various projects, whereas Joseph, on the other hand, was an assimilationist who felt that creeds separated people rather than brought them together. "Whether it's God or Allah or Buddha," he said, "we're all talking about the same thing." Joseph was sufficiently detached from a sense of his own religion so that he sometimes became irritated when friends talked about "one's duties and responsibilities as a Jew," saying, "I don't like putting people in pigeonholes," but he became even angrier when he heard someone attempting to ascribe unpleasant traits like excessive business shrewdness to the Jewish people. He was quick to point out that, as head of Vulcan Machine and Foundry, he often sold his products to distinctly non-Jewish manufacturers whose business methods were considerably sharper than the norm. "People who complain about sharp Jewish practices," he said, "have never tried doing business with New England Yankees."

Later in life, George Kaufman was able to regard his origins and his religion with calmness. He took serious things seriously, refusing to allow his plays to be shown in Germany from the time of the rise of Nazism to the day of his death, but he turned away milder anti-Jewish slurs and too-WASP posturing with one or another of his quiet-voiced quips. When a man at dinner one night boasted too long and too loudly about his strictly Christian background, tracing his ancestry all the way back to the tenth century, Kaufman got up and left the table, but not before assuring the man that he, too, had an ancestor who had gone on the Crusades—Sir Roderick Kaufman. Then he added, "As a spy, of course." And when Woollcott, who was not anti-Semitic at all, but whose eagerness to seek out his opponents' more vulnerable points in arguments sometimes caused him to overlook the precepts of good taste, punctuated an Algonquin lunchtime debate with Kaufman by calling him a Christ-killer, Kaufman again got to his feet. "This is the last time," he said, "that I am going to sit here and listen to my religion being slurred. I am going to walk away from this table and out of this room and out of this hotel." And then, inevitably, he turned to Dorothy Parker, who was Jewish only on her father's side. "And I hope," he said, "that Mrs. Parker will walk halfway out with me."

But that day in Washington, aged twenty-four and still an innocent, he listened to Munsey's words in stunned silence, suffused with all the feelings of Jewishness his ancestors had felt as they, too, had faced savage and unwarranted anti-Semitic cruelty.

"That's George Kaufman," the assistant said. "He does the—"

"I don't care what he does," Munsey said. "Get rid of him."

The column had been running in the *Times* for just under a year. Later that day, Kaufman was told to prepare his final column for the December 1, 1913, editions.

During his year in Washington, his father had moved the Kaufman family to New York City. Joseph had heard of an opportunity to buy the New York Silk Dyeing Company and had done so, undaunted, in his usual way, by the fact that he knew nothing about silk dyeing. He had taken over the firm's plant at 22–26 119th Street, in the College Point section of the Borough of Queens, and had rented an apartment at 241 West 101st Street in Manhattan. The apartment had nine rooms, and when George left Washington and moved in again with his family, he was out of the writing business and prepared to ask his father for a job as an apprentice silk-dyer, whatever that involved.

4. THE GIRL

IT WASN'T NECESSARY. Frank Adams, continuing his amiable and benevolent role as Kaufman's guardian angel, got him a job as a dramatic reporter on the New York *Tribune*.

Adams had just come over to the *Tribune* himself after eleven years on the *Mail*, wooed there by the combination of a much higher salary and the *Tribune* owners' contention, with which Adams was inclined to agree, that their newspaper was a far more stable operation than the rather low-circulation *Mail*. The acquisition of FPA and his column, now changed to *The Conning Tower* because Adams wasn't allowed to take *Always in Good Humor* away with him, was a considerable coup for the *Tribune*, since many people believed the column had been the *Mail*'s principal drawing card. The *Tribune*'s editors, therefore, were only too happy to oblige Adams when he asked for a job for his friend and protégé.

New York, in the second decade of the century and the beginning of the third, was a curiously unlucky place for people named Kaufman, judging by current newspaper stories, especially if the various spellings of the name were included. A man named Harry Kaufman was arrested for sending black-hand letters to two sisters. A woman named Mrs. Joseph Kaufman—not Nettie, of course—was reported as having shot herself. A girl named Gladys Kaufman was arrested on a charge of attempted robbery; a man named Meyer Kaufman was arrested on a charge of highway robbery. A man named Jacob Kauffman was arrested and held without bail, accused of burglary; a man named Joseph Kauffman made the newspapers when he was arrested on suspicion of forgery; and a man named Louis Kauffman was reported held for assault on a woman. There was also Nathan Kaufmann, arrested for larceny, and Harry Kaufmann, arrested for stealing an automobile.

But George Kaufman knew none of these people, and New York presented a very different face to him. He was, in fact, entering one of the happiest and most important periods in his life.

His boss in the drama department was a big, rumpled, crumpled bear of a man, eventually to become famous as a columnist himself: Heywood Broun. Broun, born in Brooklyn on December 7, 1888, had become a newspaperman in 1912, after graduating from the posh Horace Mann School but failing to get a degree from Harvard because he was unable to master elementary French. Broun's life was an encyclopedia of the unexpected. He was first a rewrite man on the *Tribune* and then a baseball writer, and seemed one of the least qualified men on the paper when the dramatic critic died and the post became available, but talked his way into the job and became one of the most outstanding critics in newspaper history. He was the son of a rich printing-plant owner but became a strong voice for organized labor and the original new left, and a founder and president of the American Newspaper Guild. He fought openly with his publishers in a period when few other newspapermen dared to do this. When he began to write his column, *It Seems to Me*, and moved from the *Tribune* to the *World*, the *World* suppressed two of his columns, charging that they were written with "the utmost extravagance" and were "contrary to the policies of the paper." Broun responded immediately by saying, "I contend that in a column headed *It Seems to Me* and signed Heywood Broun it is Heywood Broun speaking and not the *World*." And he followed this up with an article in *The Nation* in which he stated that there was no truly liberal paper in New York, and that the *World* attempted liberality but never really attained it—for which the *World* immediately fired him.

It was no problem getting another job; Broun's column resumed in the *Telegram* almost at once. He continued to be full of surprises and to espouse unpopular causes. His first wife, Ruth, was an ardent member of the Lucy Stone League, an early women's lib organization whose platform was that women should not subordinate themselves to their husbands and should therefore continue to use their maiden names. Broun supported this and introduced his wife as Ruth Hale throughout their marriage. (Harold Ross did the same thing with his wife, Jane Grant, another Stoner. The fact that both marriages failed may or may not prove something). Broun was one of the first to cry out in horror at the recommendations made by the panel of aged men in the Sacco-Vanzetti case, and his protest is still quoted: "We have a right to beat against tight minds with our fists and shout a word into the ears of old men. We want to know, we will know, 'Why?'"

He was always emotional about political causes, but casual and philosophical about most other things. Once he came to the Algonquin Hotel in a rainstorm and ordered a glass of wine. He didn't care for its quality, but drank it contentedly. "Any port in a storm," he said. Another time he revealed his marital philosophy. "The only real argument for marriage," he told a friend, "is that it's still the best method of getting acquainted." He could also be the butt of a quip without feeling offended about it. General John J. Pershing was inspecting troops one day during World War I and suddenly came upon Broun, probably the sloppiest soldier in the Army. "What happened?" Pershing asked. "Did you fall down?" Broun thought it was one of the funniest lines he'd ever heard, and went around repeating it for years.

Even the end of his life, when it came at the early age of fifty-one, on December 19, 1939, had its share of the unexpected. He had argued against religion for years, calling it restrictive and oppressive, but converted to Catholicism in the last year of his life and was given a High Requiem Mass at St. Patrick's Cathedral. He was so big and strong-looking that it appeared that he might never grow old or ill, but he caught a cold, and in four days it had turned into pneumonia and he was dead. The newspaper to which he had moved the same day he grew ill, the *Post*, provided the final twist to his life: its pages trumpeted the appearance of his "very first column." It also turned out to be his last.

Broun made every day's work, every new assignment, more interesting and exciting than the last for Kaufman. Kaufman was sent to interview actors and actresses and producers and directors, and sometimes even to review new dramatic and musical plays and variety shows. Most significant of all, he was being introduced—not as an onlooker, but as an instant insider because of his job on an important paper—to a new world, the world of Broadway and Times Square. He knew almost from the first day that it would thereafter be the only world for him.

Kaufman's job on the *Tribune* lasted only about a year—he joined the paper on February 14, 1914, and left the following February—but he was never again really comfortable when he was away from the rialto, a usage which, incidentally, he himself coined. Circumstances in later years took him away from midtown Manhattan from time to time, such as when he went to Hollywood to work on a picture, or to London for the opening of one of his plays, or when he became for a time a country squire with a big house and considerable acreage in Bucks County, Pennsylvania. But it was clear to everyone who knew him well that he was simply marking time until he could be back again mingling with theatre people and walking along playhouse-lined streets.

Voluntary departures became such a rarity that his sister Ruth once stared at him in disbelief when he told her that, without any business reason and entirely through his own choice, he'd gone away from the midtown area. "You went on a trip?" she echoed, shocked. "I certainly did," Kaufman said. "I threw some things into a bag and went up to 92nd Street."

His friend Irving Pichel was just then graduating from Harvard, but Kaufman was so happy on the *Tribune* that he no longer felt any sense of loss for his own shortened education. He even turned it to advantage, using his personal history to make his first magazine sale. He wrote a satirical piece, *On the Value of a College Education*, and sold it to the Princeton University magazine, *Princeton Tiger*, which then occasionally paid for outside contributions. And other sales followed quickly after that—short humor pieces and poems for *Puck*, the same kinds of things he'd written for the Passaic *Herald* and for Frank Adams, but now for pay.

He was beginning to make it; he was becoming a pro. And then, on September 24, 1914, he took one more step in the direction he was going to follow for the rest of his life: he began an evening course in Dramatic Composition under Professor Harvey Hatcher Hughes at Columbia University.

He intended nothing significant or monumental; he told his family and friends that he wanted to see what school felt like again, and half believed it, requesting and receiving academic credit for the course. His real reason, however, was that, as he wandered around theatrical circles and saw more and more professional plays, some excellent and some awful, he had begun to wonder how he'd do if he tried writing a play or two himself.

The chance to try didn't come immediately. Professor Hughes's course was completed satisfactorily on January 28, 1915, and Kaufman also used his work in the theatre to sell an article about a new hit, *"Kick-In" Scores Field Goal at Republic Theatre*, to a magazine called *Gotham Weekly Gazette*. But then FPA came along with a brand-new opportunity for him.

The opportunity, to Kaufman's surprise, was on the *Mail*. There had been a certain amount of hard feelings when Adams had left the paper, but this had dissipated and disappeared with the passage of time. Now the *Mail*'s editor, after trying two other writers who'd proved to be not very good, had come to Adams and asked if *he* knew anybody who might be talented enough to take over his old spot.

Adams had a ready answer: the young man who'd done such an excellent job with *This and That and a Little of the Other* on the Washington *Times*. The *Mail* editor respected Adams's judgment—"so," Adams told Kaufman, "the job is yours if you want it."

[43]

Kaufman hesistated only very briefly. It was true that the job would take him away from the theatre, but it was an opportunity to have a column byline on a New York paper, and it paid so well that he could go on seeing plays even if he now had to pay for them himself. His first column, under the title of *Be That as It May*, appeared in the *Mail* on February 5, 1915.

The column was popular at once, drawing heavy fan mail. The newspaper's editors were satisfied with it, too, so much so that they asked Kaufman to change the title to something with the name of the newspaper in it—something which would identify it more specifically with the paper. Kaufman pondered until June and came up with *The Mail Chute;* the editors approved; and the first column appeared in the June 29 editions. It looked as though he might be settling in for a long stay.

The stay proved instead to be a very short one. The *Mail* had been up for sale for many months, and in July it was suddenly sold. The new owners made a lot of changes in the paper, and one of the things they decided was that Kaufman's column was dead as of July 16. He was once again jobless, and once again Adams came to his rescue and got him back into the drama department of the *Tribune*.

Kaufman was disappointed, but only mildly. He settled back into his former, pleasant routine, and on September 30 he began a second course at Columbia, this one on Contemporary Dramatic Literature and given by Professor Clayton Hamilton. He made one more decision as he did so, giving up forever the idea of further education with a view toward a degree, and he enrolled as a special non-matriculating student. He was becoming more and more serious about the idea of trying to become a playwright, and he took the course strictly for its own sake, to help him learn what he had begun to hope would one day be his trade.

In the meantime, he continued to write and sell more pieces to the magazines. Two of these appeared in the first month of the new year, 1916: *Wringing in the New Year* in the January 1 issue of *Harper's Weekly* and *Point and Counterpoint* in the January 23 issue of *Musical America*. But 1916 became a banner year for him for two far more important reasons. That year, he wrote his first play since *The Failure*

—and he met a tall, slim, dark-eyed, dark-haired, nineteen-year-old Rochester girl named Beatrice Bakrow.

The play he wrote was a one-act farce called *Going Up*, and dealt with the special criminal art of check-raising. This involves taking a legitimate check written by a solvent individual for, say, one hundred dollars, adding a zero or two in what appeared to be the same handwriting (this was before check amounts were required to be written out as well as written in figures), and managing to get the check cashed for the improved amount. Kaufman wrote the play because a young man named Henry R. Stern invited him to do so.

Stern was the son of the owner of the Joseph W. Stern Music Company, a major and progressive publishing organization. One of the first things he did upon entering the family firm was to look around for new ways to make money, offshoots of the basic business. He got the idea for a new kind of play brokerage. This was not to be the usual business of representation of established playwrights, which would have been difficult to establish because virtually all of the top people were tied up elsewhere, but the discovery and development of good new people who'd be willing to pay a higher commission, 20 per cent rather than the usual 10 per cent, for the Stern Company's help. He hired several readers, and asked the man he appointed chief play-reader to submit a list of promising young writers. The man was Burns Mantle, later to become reviewer for the New York *Daily News* and editor for twenty-seven years of the highly regarded *Best Plays of the Year* series of books. And Mantle, who didn't know Kaufman personally but had admired his column in the *Mail*, put his name first on the list.

Going Up was a pretty derivative piece of work, Kaufman later admitted, very similar to a lot of other curtain-raisers being shown around town, but he gave it the same kind of meticulous care he was eventually to give to his more famous plays. He rewrote the farce fifty-five times, subjecting each word and each sentence to the sort of microscopic examination and study which later caused Moss Hart to give the Kaufman-Hart collaborations the rueful and affectionate name of "Days of Terror." (It was Kaufman who first put into words a fact which in time became an axiom of the theatre. "A play," he said, "isn't written. It's rewritten.") Sometimes the revisions on *Going Up* were based on Stern's and Mantle's suggestions, and more often the changes were Kaufman's own idea. When they all finally agreed it was ready, Stern and Mantle were confident that they'd make a quick deal.

They were wrong. The play didn't sell. It ran into trouble immediately when Stern found out that Frank Craven, a prominent stage actor and producer, already had a play called *Going Up* set for production, a musical version of an earlier hit named *Too Many Cooks*. And though the young broker quickly assured people that it would be no trouble at all to change the title of the Kaufman play, provided there was real interest, every producer who read the play returned it on the grounds that it just wasn't fresh enough to put on. Stern ran through the complete list of possibilities and finally, with real reluctance, returned the script to Kaufman.

Kaufman shrugged, marked the play down as a failure, and tossed it into a desk drawer; he had already begun to feel the first stirrings of his recurring conviction that everything he wrote was no good, anyway, and this seemed to be confirmed on *Going Up*. He was overreacting on the one-acter just as he would later overreact on so many of his other plays. The truth was that nearly every producer and producer's reader who looked at *Going Up* liked it, though not enough, and there was one man who took particular note of what was obviously a major comedic talent. This was John Peter Toohey, the chief playreader for George C. Tyler.

Toohey, born in Binghamton in upstate New York, was a bright, brash young man with a quick, intuitive mind; one of his most notable achievements was giving, nine years later, the name to a new magazine then being started. The magazine's founder and associates were baffled but the choice seemed to Toohey to be obvious. "You keep saying it'll be a magazine about New York," he told his friend Harold Ross. "Why don't you, for crissakes, call it *The New Yorker?*"

Toohey was equally quick in his judgment on *Going Up*. He knew at once it was not for Tyler; Tyler was then, and for many years to come, the foremost play producer in the country, the man who had presented such plays as *Mrs. Wiggs of the Cabbage Patch*, Booth Tarkington's *A Gentleman from Indiana*, George Arliss's *Disraeli*, and a great many others (he produced or managed over 350 plays in his lifetime). Kaufman's little farce just wasn't first-rate enough for a man of his stature. But Toohey felt that Kaufman's basic talent *was* clearly first-rate enough so that Tyler might well want to make use of him in some way one day, and he told Tyler to be sure to read the short play.

Tyler read the play and was interested, but only in a casual way; he sometimes hired young playwrights to do small revisions for him, things like adding a few comedy lines or a scene or two to his productions, but he had no job of that sort on hand just then. He told Toohey to make a note of the young man's name and promptly forgot him.

Kaufman, unaware of Toohey's interest, also had his mind on other things. He was about to leave for Buffalo on a vacation cruise on a steamer plying the Great Lakes—a package-deal type of vacation then very popular with young New Yorkers because it lasted only one week, which was all the vacation time given to most young employees, and because it was very inexpensive. He was also looking forward to stopping en route in Rochester and seeing his sister Ruth and her new husband.

Kaufman had always been closer to Ruth than to his other sister, Helen. Helen was, after all, five years older than he was, a distance of a million miles when the elder sibling was a girl. This was particularly true when the girl was, like Helen, busy with her own interests, painting and becoming a much-admired ceramist. She had also married and left the family circle when Kaufman was only eighteen, moving with her new husband, Frank Gordon Lieberman, to Georgia. (Kaufman once said about Lieberman, "You know the way everybody has a relative in the insurance business? Well, the relative in my case is Frank. He has a regular pattern. He goes into the insurance business, insures me, and then goes out of the insurance business." His brother-in-law was also the subject of Kaufman's first recorded "reverse-word," his trick of taking a common word and using its never-used opposite. The most famous example of this is Kaufman's one-line review in the New York *Times* of a very bad play: "I was underwhelmed." He also used this advice in reprimanding two stand-by actors who had rehearsed each other so much at home that they were now speaking their lines as mechanically as a telephone operator. "You're not understudies," Kaufman said. "You're overstudies." His comment on Lieberman was similarly pointed. "Frank," he said, "is a very painsgiving man.")

But the situation was entirely different where Ruth was concerned. Kaufman had always been the prototype protective big brother to Ruth; he had, it is true, sometimes told her Edgar Allan Poe stories and then left her trembling and alone in her darkened bedroom, but in all other ways he'd always regarded her with considerable affection. Now she had, on June 6, married a young Rochester man, Allan Friedlich, and would soon be moving with him to Des Moines, Iowa, where he was entering his family business. (Much later, Friedlich took a position which was important but had a description which amused Kaufman enormously: he became a troubleshooter for the American Molasses Company.) Kaufman wanted to be sure to see them both before they wandered off, perhaps forever, to the kind of town into which, as the most chauvinistic kind of New Yorker, the adopted kind, he was fairly certain he would never venture.

He arrived in Rochester on July 8, which was a Saturday, and that gave Ruth and Allan Friedlich an idea: they'd entertain their visitor by taking him, the next morning, on a Sunday drive to Niagara Falls, a distance of about ninety miles. Kaufman would, of course, need a girl to make up a foursome, and they decided to invite Beatrice Bakrow. Beatrice, as it happened, was engaged to a local rabbi, but that didn't matter; this wasn't going to be anything more than a casual day's drive through the pretty countryside.

Kaufman was then four months short of his twenty-seventh birthday, and his distinctive physical and mental characteristics were already pretty much formed. Physically, he already looked, as the novelist Irwin Shaw described the later George S. Kaufman in a letter to a mutual friend, "like a small schooner built in a local New England shipyard by a boatwright with noble intentions but rough tools . . . and in action like the same craft with a few tattered sails flying in a force eight wind." Mentally, too, he was the same mixture of order and disorder, symmetry and imbalance, which both attracted and disturbed his friends all of his life.

[48]

He had long since achieved his full height of six feet one inch, but he looked much taller because he was so lean; despite a passion for fudge and chocolate bars, two rare examples of foodstuffs he really enjoyed, he never weighed over one hundred and sixty-five pounds. He was generally neat, preferring dark suits and dark, rich ties, but his neatness stopped at his hairline; he had a fear of losing his hair, and washed and brushed it constantly, but he wore it high and wild and tended to comb it mostly with his fingers. (The man who later became his friend and Toohey's, Harold Ross, also wore a pompadour so high that Ina Claire, the actress, once expressed a desire to walk through Ross's hair with her bare feet. But Ross's pompadour was nothing compared to Kaufman's.)

He was also already unendingly plagued by his wide-ranging collection of phobias, and many of these caused physical and visible side effects. He was so nervous that he veered between bursts of rapid speech and periods of shy and total silence; he sometimes, when walking alone and about to face some grueling test of courage like taking an elevator to a high floor or crossing a heavy-traffic thoroughfare, talked encouragingly out loud to himself; and he was often so tense when he worked that his head bobbed stiffly up and down as he typed. (One woman reporter, working at a desk across from his when he subsequently joined the New York *Times*, wondered why he kept nodding courteously to her so often, and why he never tried to follow through when she smiled and nodded encouragingly in return.)

He was not, all things considered, with his thinness and his wild hair and his big nose and glasses and his nervous, jerky movements, the most appealing blind date the Friedlichs could have turned up for a lady, even in view of the fact that the lady was engaged to someone else and it was all just to fill a sunny Sunday. Beatrice was almost ready to back out; she did not do so, finally, only because it would have been an open affront to her friends. And Kaufman, aware of this with his usual quick sensitivity, became even more shy and nervous and more unattractive.

There was an added reason for his nervousness: his response to her was the exact opposite of hers to him. Beatrice thought Kaufman awkward and unappealing; he thought she was the loveliest creature he had ever seen in his life. He had gone through nearly twenty-seven years of virginal existence, dating girls occasionally but mostly concentrating on trying to find himself and trying to develop a writing career. Now, every other interest in his life went out of the window as he looked at the cool, dark-eyed girl who was already committed elsewhere.

Beatrice was not really beautiful, then or later; her nose was a fraction too long, her mouth a shade too wide. But she already had the passion and the tremendous, shining charm which made many men in her home town stop and look at her on the street, and which, later on, made her the proprietress of one of New York's great literary and theatrical salons and caused many famous actors and writers to fall in love with her, or come to her constantly for counsel, or both. Alexander Woollcott was one of these men, and, surprisingly, his feeling for her was far stronger than the usual platonic relationship he developed with many of his other women friends; he had had a severe case of mumps as a boy which had lost him his sexual abilities, and this ordinarily made him avoid all talk of marriage, but he became so fond of Beatrice and mentioned marriage so often that she finally had to tell him to behave himself. The young Oscar Levant was also in love with her, even though she sometimes grew irritated with him and introduced him to people as "undiscovered and deservedly so." And, though she was much older than Moss Hart, his feeling toward her was a kind of love-for-mother mixed strongly with romantic love, so that at times he followed her around like a lovesick puppy but other times called her up three or four times a day to ask for advice about other women.

At this point in her life in Rochester, she had also shown her freedom of spirit and her defiance of dull convention by getting herself thrown out of Wellesley. This had occurred because, while having tea at the Copley Hotel in Boston with some classmates, she had allowed herself to be picked up and taken for a drive by a man who was almost as famous for his way with women as he was for his voice: Enrico Caruso. Clearly, nothing very much happened on the drive, since Beatrice was almost certainly still without sexual experience at the time of her marriage, but the authorities at Wellesley were so shocked at the basic fact that she had gone out alone in an automobile with the notorious tenor that they expelled her immediately. Beatrice had then transferred to the University of Rochester, attended classes there in a desultory manner for two years, and was now doing charity work in a settlement house and waiting for the day of her marriage to come around.

The drive to the Niagara Falls took a little over two hours, and the two couples arrived at the American-Canadian border at around noon. They decided to have lunch at a restaurant Allan Friedlich knew, a little place on the Canadian side. It was a monumental decision for George Kaufman and Beatrice Bakrow, and changed both their lives completely, because, in the restaurant, Kaufman had one of his celebrated run-ins with a waiter.

Kaufman's lifelong war with waiters and taxi drivers became, in time, world famous; there is virtually no biographical sketch in existence which does not devote considerable space to it, though nobody seems to know why it was or how it started. In all other things, he was the most gentle and understanding of men; he avoided arguments at all costs with friends, family, and business associates, always willing to help but nearly always unwilling to fight. Even with actors, who gave him many causes for fury, he was what Irwin Shaw calls "the whispering type of director"; he would, Shaw says, "take an offending actor off to one side and quietly, out of the hearing of anybody else, pass on his instructions." But, for some mysterious reason, it was entirely different with waiters and taxi drivers. He seemed to feel that they were the most stupid and incompetent of human beings, and they brought out the animal in him.

Part of it stemmed from his nervousness and impatience; he was nearly always in a hurry to get through dinner at restaurants, and even more in a hurry to get to his destination when he was in a taxicab, telling the drivers constantly which streets to take and which turns to make. Sometimes, as in an incident recalled by his collaborator Morrie Ryskind, this turned to disaster; once, hurrying through a rainstorm to the docks to see an aunt off to Europe, his arms loaded with going-away presents, he berated the driver so fiercely for making a couple of wrong turns that the cabbie finally pulled up at the curb and forced him out into the rain, packages and all. Most of the time, however, it was Kaufman himself who made the decision to leave the taxi, and nearly everyone who knew him experienced or observed at least one such incident, and sometimes many. It happened so often that this was true even of people who did not know him well. Frank Sullivan, the humorist, was one of these; he never visited the Algonquin Round Table because he worked late mornings and afternoons on the *World* in those years and didn't stop for lunch, and he spent most of his evenings at speakeasies rarely frequented by the almost-teetotal Kaufman. But he still managed to share a cab with Kaufman one day and watch the playwright—right in the middle of a ride which Sullivan thought was proceeding uneventfully—blaze into sudden fury and stalk out of the cab and into the distance.

It was exactly the same with waiters. They incensed Kaufman so much that, much later, he finally wrote a piece about it, a hilarious satire which appeared in the August 2, 1947, issue of *The New Yorker* and revealed that waiters took courses in avoiding customers' eyes, captains took courses in interrupting to ask for orders just as a customer got to the point of a joke, and headwaiters took courses in asking idiotic questions like, "Two?" as two people walked into a restaurant.

The waiter in the Canadian restaurant gave the party from Rochester considerable cause for anger. He was maddeningly slow, failed to observe the normal amenities like bringing glasses of water, and was consistently wrong on nearly every item ordered. Kaufman said nothing throughout the meal, but when it was over and the bill was brought, he took it and rose slowly to his feet.

"Back in New York," he said, between his teeth, "I am known as a rather generous tipper. But I also believe in tipping in relationship to the quality of the service." He paused and looked over his glasses, right into the waiter's glazing eyes. "You'll note," he went on, "that I'm putting down on the table the exact amount of the bill and not one cent more."

Beatrice watched the scene in fascination as the waiter seemed about to reply, changed his mind as Kaufman towered over him, and finally picked up the money and moved soundlessly away. Her lips were parted and her eyes were bright with admiration; she had never seen anything like this before. Everyone else she knew was cowed by waiters; everyone else she knew would have left a tip, possibly even—because that was the way most people seemed to react to bullying and bad treatment—have overtipped. When the four young people left the restaurant, she tucked her arm into Kaufman's and was looking at him in a new way.

Kaufman, warmed by the change in her, began to open up and converse in his quiet, funny way. There was no conversation like Kaufman conversation when he was at his best; Groucho Marx summed it up once by saying that his notion of an ideal date was a girl who looked like Marilyn Monroe and talked like George Kaufman. By the time the four returned to Rochester, Kaufman and Beatrice had an appointment to go driving again the next day; and when they returned from that drive, a long one in Beatrice's Buick, the rabbi was jilted and they were engaged.

The Bakrows were not overwhelmed with joy at the news. They were a rich and prominent family who, with their relatives, the Adlers, owned one of the largest clothing-manufacturing businesses in the East, and their sparkling young daughter was throwing herself away on a penniless and rather eccentric newspaperman. The Adlers may have felt the same way when their daughter, Sarah, married Jules Bakrow, who was a traveling salesman from Kentucky. But Jules had the redeeming factor of being business-oriented and entered the family firm, Adler Brothers and Company, which had been founded as a clothing-manufacturing company before the Civil War. The firm was proud of having been one of the companies which made "Union Blue" uniforms for the Grand Army of the Republic. The family was also proud of the fact that its members were not new immigrants, but had been in the United States since 1848.

Later the fortunes of the Bakrows and the Adlers were to change. A family named Levy emigrated from Europe and opened the same kind of business in Rochester. The established firm sneered at the Levys for being so peasant-like and working so hard, but the Levys ended up absorbing the older firm and Kaufman became the most successful member of the clan. But at this stage, it didn't look like a very marvelous match.

It didn't matter. Beatrice brushed off her parents' disapproval as casually as she had ignored her classmates' horror at her date with Caruso; she told her parents that she was going to marry George S. Kaufman and that was all there was to it. The Bakrows capitulated, and the couple were married in a big, conventional Jewish wedding on March 15, 1917, at the Rochester Club. Frank Adams drove up from New York City to act as Kaufman's best man. Beatrice was attended by her best friend, Dorothy Michael, who later married Robert Nathan, the novelist. Beatrice and Dorothy had once cemented their relationship by forming the Two Spooner Club, whose symbol of friendship was that both girls ate from the same ice cream dish, and the two women continued to see each other occasionally for the rest of Beatrice's life.

The Bakrows were so sure Kaufman couldn't support their daughter properly that they provided her with $100 a week to buy clothes. Since they were in the clothing business, they put great emphasis on personal appearance—which was another thing that made them shudder as they looked at their new son-in-law. Kaufman also offended them a little by joking at his own wedding. Noting the headlines about the upheaval in Russia, he told Beatrice, "Well, it took the Russian Revolution to keep our wedding off the front pages."

The Kaufmans moved into an inexpensive one-bedroom apartment at the Majestic Hotel on West End Avenue. Their preparation for the sexual side of marriage was Kaufman's membership in a celibate boys' club and Beatrice's surreptitious reading of Balzac's *Droll Stories*. Her father had kept the book in a locked case, but Beatrice found the key.

Frank Adams and his wife had taken to Beatrice at once, and the four became close friends, going to plays and other places together and frequently having dinner at each other's apartments. Adams showed his affection for his friend's new bride by making her the occasional subject of his sardonic jokes. Once she sat down in a fragile chair and plunged right through the wicker seat, stuck helplessly with her behind hanging down. "Beatrice," FPA said gravely, "I've told you a hundred times that that isn't funny." He also lured her into a trap one time by asking her if she knew whose birthday it was that day. Beatrice made the obvious guess. "Yours?" she asked. "No," said Adams, "but you're getting warm. It's Shakespeare's."

It was a pleasant time, and in September it grew more pleasant. Adams heard about an opening in the dramatic department of the

New York *Times* and told Kaufman about it. Kaufman applied at once and was hired at a starting salary of $36 a week. Three years later, his was raised to $48 a week.

Kaufman started on the *Times* on September 17, 1917. In December, George C. Tyler called him suddenly and asked him to come over for a talk.

5. THE BEGINNING

TYLER HAD BEEN reminded about Kaufman by John Peter Toohey. Kaufman didn't walk to the appointment; he ran.

The producer was a man who, by all the laws of stereotype and type-casting, should have been an object of amusement rather than an impressive figure to sophisticated theatre people. He was not a rough, tough product of city streets, like so many other producers of that period; he had been born in the sleepy rural town of Chillicothe, Ohio, on April 13, 1867. He had no formal education or theatrical heritage; he had started out in life as a tramp printer, moving from job to job on freight trains, worked his way up from there to reporting and editorial jobs on a number of Ohio newspapers, and had drifted into the theatrical field by going to work for James O'Neill, the actor and father of Eugene O'Neill, who was then appearing in *The Count of Monte Cristo*. And he was hardly impressive physically. He was short, squat, and pink-faced, and the most noticeable thing about him was the fact that his legs were so bowed that the lower half of his body resembled the letter O.

Nevertheless, he had become, since his arrival in New York in 1897, the most important producer in the business, and the people who worked for him regarded him with a mixture of respect, reverence, and fear. Helen Hayes, who got her first important roles in Tyler productions, adored him but was also desperately afraid of him; she later commented in her memoirs that she regarded his word as law, his slightest suggestion as an edict, and his disfavor as too terrible to contemplate, and added that she sometimes felt she and Tyler were playing the father and daughter in *The Barretts of Wimpole Street*. She never complained about the notoriously small salaries he paid, and even read faithfully the uplifting books he handed her from time to time.

Nearly everyone else felt the same way about him, and even the few people who tried to oppose him were quickly routed. One of these rare few was Lynn Fontanne, not yet the regal personage she later became, but already, as a young actress newly arrived from England, self-possessed enough to brush past his secretary without an appointment and try to get her salary improved. It took one Tyler look from under his heavy eyebrows to quell her. "Well?" Tyler said irritably, around his cigar. "Well? What do you want?" The young actress found herself stammering out her thanks for his many kindnesses, added her thanks for the fact that he was allowing her to remain in America, and retreated.

Tyler's track record, and his willingness to innovate, unquestionably merited the respect he received. He was the first producer to present George Bernard Shaw's plays in the United States. He introduced the distinguished Irish actors, the Abbey Theatre Players, to American audiences. He brought to New York stages such major names as Sarah Bernhardt, Eleanora Duse, Mrs. Patrick Campbell, Minnie Maddern Fiske, William Faversham, Arnold Daly, and William S. Hart, and introduced, in addition to Helen Hayes and Lynn Fontanne, such other talented newcomers as Alfred Lunt, John

Barrymore, and Jeanne Eagels. This was the man now becoming interested in Kaufman.

The project about which he wanted to see Kaufman was one of his less important productions: a four-act play called *Among Those Present*. *Among Those Present* wasn't much of a play; it was a fairly simple-minded melodrama-comedy about a society type named J. Percyval Glendenning who tries to do his World War I bit by writing and presenting a play with the proceeds to go to a fund for fighting men, and uses, as a stunt to publicize his play, a famous necklace as a prop, causing a gentleman crook named Jimmy Burke to decide to steal the necklace. But Tyler had considerable faith in plays about gentlemen crooks named Jimmy. One of his greatest successes had been a play based on an O. Henry story and written in three days in a room at the Algonquin by a man named Paul Armstrong: *Alias Jimmy Valentine*.

Among Those Present, however, had not been following the successful path of the earlier play. It had premiered at the Academy of Music in Richmond, Virginia, on November 12 and received good local and national reviews—the critic for *Dramatic Mirror*, for example, called it a play of merit and charm and said it was admirably mounted—but it had gone on to do poor business. And business had been equally slack when the play moved to the Broad Street Theatre in Philadelphia.

Tyler was now faced with the grave possibility, since *Alias Jimmy Valentine* had had its success back in 1909, that plays about gentlemen crooks had grown passé; audiences, he had to admit, had become considerably more sophisticated in the intervening eight-year period. But he also thought he had the solution. "I think we can skim through if we add more comedy," he told Kaufman, "and the way to do it is by building up a part I have in mind. I've got the perfect actress to play the part—a British kid named Lynn Fontanne." He was killing two birds in making the arrangement: he had felt, ever since Lynn Fontanne had come over from London with Laurette Taylor's company to do *The Harp of Life*, that she was ready for bigger things, and here was his opportunity to try this out and save his play at the same time.

Among Those Present had been written by two men, Larry Evans and Walter C. Percival, but neither was really capable of doing the repair job Tyler needed. Evans was gravely ill with tuberculosis, and would never write another play; he would linger on for another eight years, bedridden and supporting himself by writing sports fiction in longhand for magazines, and finally succumb to the disease in 1925. Percival was healthy enough, but he was a part-time writer and part-time actor who didn't have much talent in either field. Even a close friend of Percival's, when Tyler asked him if he thought Percival could add the necessary comedy, replied bluntly, "Let's face it. Walter's a hell of a nice fellow, but he's no writer."

Tyler, looking at Kaufman, wasn't sure he was the perfect choice, either. Toohey was certainly enthusiastic about him, but the position he occupied in Tyler's own mind was that of that funny-looking guy from the *Times* who dropped in occasionally to get paragraphs for the paper. But time was extremely short, and Tyler said reluctantly, "How about it? Do you want to do the job?"

The appointment with Tyler had taken place ten o'clock at night. "When do you need the rewrite?" Kaufman asked.

"I need it," Tyler said, "by ten o'clock tomorrow morning."

Kaufman turned green. He wasn't a rapid writer, and, as he had done on *Going Up*, he liked to rewrite his material again and again until he was reasonably satisfied with it. But it was a foregone conclusion that evening at Tyler's office; he couldn't pass up an opportunity like this one. He accepted the assignment, fleeing into the street and managing to avoid noticing Tyler's outstretched hand. His own hand was too moist with panic, and anyway he was already deep into his phobia about touching or being touched by people. He went home to work all night.

One of the things which helped him to accept Tyler's offer, though he would undoubtedly have accepted it even if his mind had been a total blank, was that he already had an idea for the part to be played by Lynn Fontanne. There was a very funny character named Dulcinea, called Dulcy for short, created by his friend Frank Adams and quoted all the time in Adams's column. Dulcy was a woman who spoke almost totally in clichés, but there was an underlying element of wisdom in everything she said, and it seemed to Kaufman that a part developed along similar lines might be exactly right for the young British actress.

He didn't stop to ask Adams's permission; he relied upon his friend's unfailing kindness toward him to secure him forgiveness for the appropriation. The socialite, Glendenning, was given a Dulcy-like wife, and Kaufman delivered the pages to Tyler promptly at ten o'clock. Tyler read them at once, found himself laughing aloud, and looked at the young man from the *Times* with new respect.

The play reopened at the Blackstone Theatre in Chicago on Sunday, February 10, 1918. Lynn Fontanne did not go into the cast immediately—she was being saved for New York, and the part was played by another young actress, Ethel Dane—but some big guns were added at once for protection. The part of Jimmy Burke had been played in the earlier run by Shelley Hull, but it was now taken over by H. B. Warner, already an important star and later to become even more famous as Jesus in the film, *King of Kings*. Two Broadway standbys and eventual movie character-role favorites, Dudley Digges and Robert Barrat, were also added to the cast. And there were two other men in the cast destined to become better known: Sidney Toler, who later became one of the screen's most durable Charlie Chans, and Hassard Short, who turned to directing after a while and staged such hits as *Sunny*, *As Thousands Cheer*, *Carmen Jones*, and a great many others. (Short, an Englishman whose real name was Hubert Hassard-Short, later directed a Kaufman musical, *The Band Wagon*, written with Howard Dietz, and made theatrical history by trying out for the first time an idea of Dietz's: a stage which revolved. He also later revolutionized stage lighting when, in 1930, in *Three's a Crowd*, he turned out the footlights and hung a row of spots in their now familiar position across the front of the balcony. The actors in the play screamed, but the new method of lighting was so much more effective that it became standard.)

The revised play did much better business, but the important thing for Kaufman, even more than his share of royalties, was that he finally had his name on a play headed for Broadway: the authors' credits on *Among Those Present* now read, "By Larry Evans, Walter Percival, and George S. Kaufman." Percival had dropped his middle initial because he decided his name sounded better that way, and Kaufman gave a lot of thought to reverting to his original initial-less name, too, but finally left it in for the same reason that he'd put it in years before. His name, it seemed to him, just sounded better with an S in it than without it.

Kaufman grew, in time, very protective toward the initial. He told people who inquired that the S. stood for nothing. But if they persisted and asked "Then why is it there?" he had a prepared speech ready for them. "Listen," he said, "if Al H. Woods, Charles B. Dillingham, Henry B. Harris, George C. Tyler, William A. Brady, Sam H. Harris, Jake J. Shubert, A. L. Erlanger, H. H. Frazee, Sam S. Shubert, and George M. Cohan can't get along without a middle initial, why should *I* try?"

The play opened in New York at the Knickerbocker Theatre on September 9, with Lynn Fontanne playing Mrs. Glendenning and with a new title, *Someone in the House*. The actress' performance and the lines Kaufman had written for her drew many good notices. The *World* said, "The play is rich in situations and most of the situations are surrounded by humor"; the *Times* said, "The play is filled with lively humor"; and even *Harper's Weekly*, which didn't like the play and called it "slow-moving" and "a dull evening," admitted that Lynn Fontanne and her role enlivened that evening. It looked as though the play might have at least a fighting chance.

Unfortunately, there was a villain lurking in the wings: the flu epidemic of 1918. It hit the New York area with savage suddenness, and a great many people died. The frightened residents of the city began to avoid public places, where they might find themselves standing or sitting next to a carrier of the disease, and one of the places they found easy to avoid was the Knickerbocker Theatre. Attendance began to drop, and quickly dropped almost to nothing.

Kaufman, characteristically, tried to cover his concern and disappointment with humor. "Let's change the title to *No One in the House*," he told Tyler. "Or perhaps we ought to run a series of ads emphasizing the advantages of the play. You know, things like *Avoid Crowds—See* Someone in the House! Or *Want to Be Alone with Your Girl? See* Someone in the House!" Tyler was not amused. But then, truth to tell, neither was Kaufman.

The play had run fifteen tryout weeks out of town; it ran less than five weeks in New York, closing after thirty-two performances. Kaufman remarked later that that was less performances than revisions. After the New York opening, Tyler had eyed the dwindling audience and kept Kaufman constantly rewriting and rewriting in the hope of saving the play; when the curtain finally went down for the last time, Kaufman emptied his desk of thirty-five different versions.

H. B. Warner was bitter about the closing and, temporarily, about the theatre in general; he had been in few flops and didn't care for the feeling. He turned to Ruth Friedlich, who was then in New York on a brief visit and had been invited to the closing party, and said, "I trust this will discourage your brother from any further playwriting."

Kaufman was standing nearby and overheard the remark. He wasn't in any mood to argue with it. He went wearily back to giving his full attention to his duties on the *Times*.

Many years later, Kaufman was asked if he could summarize his boss on the *Times*, Alexander Woollcott, in a single word. Kaufman found it easy. "Improbable," he said.

Woollcott was certainly that. He was a fat little man with an owl's face, an enormous paunch, and a wisp of a mustache; he looked like nothing and became one of the great celebrities of his time. He was loved fiercely by some and despised by others. His taste was eccentric—some people insisted that "non-existent" was a more accurate description—but he became the strongest influence in the country on the taste of the general public; his writing style was awful, florid and purple and described by one critic as "loaded with sweetness to the point of being diabetic," but he became one of the highest-priced and most successful writers in the world; and his voice was high, squeaky, unpleasant, and almost effeminate, but he became one of radio's most popular commentators.

He was the darling of the women's clubs and other dignified and fervently cultured organizations, yet his humor was sometimes primitive and frequently scatological. One of his most quoted reviews, for example, was his two-line comment on a play called *Number Seven:* "*Number Seven* opened last night. It was misnamed by five." And he was equally earthy in another review when a woman wrote a mediocre and pretentious book of poetry called *And I Shall Make Music*. Woollcott's review this time was only one line long: "Not on *my* carpet, lady."

The Marx Brothers loved him, as well they should have; they had just escaped from vaudeville and were appearing in their first Broadway play, *I'll Say She Is,* still billed as Julius H., Leonard, Arthur, and Herbert Marx rather than Groucho, Chico, Harpo, and Zeppo, when Woollcott saw the show and trumpeted their praises so steadily and enthusiastically that they became famous and rich. James Hilton loved him, as well he should have; his novel, *Good-bye, Mr. Chips,* was a quiet failure when Woollcott happened on it, loved it, and began to plug it so unceasingly that the novel became a best-seller and Hilton became a wealthy and successful author. Fred Astaire loved him, too; Astaire was an obscure hoofer appearing on a third-rate vaudeville bill when Woollcott saw the show, thought Astaire was great, and told so many major producers that they ought to take a look at that kid that the dancer soon moved into the big time. So, too, did Will Rogers, who was still thought of only as a man who did rope tricks when Woollcott began to talk him up as a humorist and urge people to see him; it was also Woollcott who first gave Rogers the idea of writing his stuff down instead of just talking it, and who then went to Harold Ross, at that time the editor of *Judge,* and convinced him to publish the stuff after Rogers wrote it.

But it wasn't only the people he championed who flocked around him. He became, in time, so powerful a personage, so integral a member of the in-group, that he acquired all the accoutrements of a super-celebrity: he was a frequent guest at the White House; he had a drink named after him, the brandy Alexander; and he was constantly in the company of the world's most famous names, people like Noël Coward, W. Somerset Maugham, Paul Robeson, and the luminaries of the Round Table like Kaufman, Dorothy Parker, Robert Benchley, and all the others. Kaufman and Hart were exaggerating only slightly when, in *The Man Who Came to Dinner,* they had their Woollcott-like character, Sheridan Whiteside, receive calls in rapid succession from H. G. Wells, Felix Frankfurter, and Dr. Allan Roy Dafoe, the physician for the Dionne quintuplets, and then plan a radio broadcast to include his friends Jascha Heifetz, Katharine Cornell,

Schiaparelli, the Lunts, Dr. Alexis Carrel, and Haile Selassie as his guests.

Not all of the people who spent a lot of time with him, inviting him to their parties and going to his, loved him, of course. Some stayed close to him strictly because he was so well-known and attracted so many other well-known people wherever he went; others liked him for a time, began to hate him when they fell victim to his waspish tongue, and sometimes found themselves liking him again when his bitchy mood vanished and he turned on his considerable charm. It split down the middle, pretty evenly divided between people who liked him for his humor, his strong enthusiasms, and his genuine kindness at times, and people who felt the opposite and considered him small, discourteous, and even dishonest because he tended to give good reviews to bad things written by or starring his friends.

It broke down into about the same percentages in things written about him—and many, many things were written about him. There were two full-length studies of Woollcott published, one by Samuel Hopkins Adams and the other by Edwin P. Hoyt, and both of these were adulatory, as were many of the references to Woollcott in other books. Typical of these was this summary by George Oppenheimer, the critic, playwright, and screenwriter, in his book, *The View from the Sixties:* "I found him, with all his crotchets, a fascinating character. He spoke the English language with all the style of a prose writer; his wit was devastating and original; he was a man of great but deviating loyalty to his friends; and, if he chose, could make an evening come brightly to life." On the other hand, William Faulkner, asked what he thought of Woollcott after their first meeting, said in his slow Southern drawl, "When I came to New York, I didn't know I'd have to sit and listen to a fat man talk all night." Tallulah Bankhead said, in her autobiography, *Tallulah:* "He was petty, shockingly vindictive in a feminine fashion, given to excesses when expressing his preferences or his prejudices. He probably endorsed more second-rate books than any man of his time." John Mason Brown called his behavior "unhousebroken." And Bennett Cerf said, "I disliked him intensely. The charm that he turned on for people he considered important was singularly lacking when he was dealing with people he considered his social inferiors. This is not my idea of the way a gentleman acts."

Gentleman and no gentleman, friend and enemy, sometimes all at the same time. "Louisa M. Woollcott" was what Howard Dietz called him, and James Thurber's name for him was "Old Vitriol and Violets"—but Eleanor Roosevelt thought he was brilliant, Ruth Gordon thought he was one of the kindest men of all time, and Harpo Marx said simply, after his death, "There was no one better." Improbable is clearly the right word.

His childhood was equally improbable; he was born on January 19, 1887, the son of Walter and Frances Grey Bucklin Woollcott, in an eighty-five-room house which was all that was left of a partially Socialistic, partially aesthetic, and partially religious commune which his grandfather had helped found in Phalanx, New Jersey. The commune had failed long before Woollcott was born, but the family used it as a kind of permanent address, returning there each time the Woollcotts were low on funds, which was often; Walter Woollcott was a rolling stone and had no fixed occupation. In the late 1890s, while the family was living in Philadelphia, the elder Woollcott finally rolled off permanently, and, though young Alexander's mother and three brothers and sister returned to Phalanx, the future *Times*-man remained on alone in Philadelphia, attending Central High School and supporting himself by doing book reviews and other odd jobs for the *Evening Telegraph and Record*.

At Central High School, he managed to get himself a scholarship to Hamilton College in upstate Clinton, New York. It was at Hamilton that Woollcott first began to shine; he was editor of the college magazine, founder and director of the drama club, winner of a Phi Beta Kappa key in his junior year, and a much-pointed-out eccentric who walked around the campus wearing a turtle-neck sweater, corduroy trousers, and a red fez. He also became friendly with a distinguished Hamilton alumnus, Samuel Hopkins Adams, the very successful author who later wrote the book about him; Adams became interested in him in the way, later on, another Adams became interested in Kaufman, and gave him a letter of introduction to an influential friend on the New York *Times*.

Woollcott presented the letter immediately upon his graduation from Hamilton, but was not hired at once; he had to work for a while as a $15-a-week clerk at the Chemical Bank before the *Times* found a spot for him as a cub reporter. He did not become a reporter of Richard Harding Davis quality: according to his near-namesake Wolcott Gibbs, who later did a long piece about him for *The New Yorker*, "He was not exactly hostile to facts, but apathetic about them." Nevertheless, he managed to hang onto his job, and when, in 1914, the *Times*'s drama critic, Adolph Klauber, married Jane Cowl, the actress, and left the paper to become a producer, Woollcott took over the dramatic department.

Woollcott was on military leave when Kaufman joined the *Times*. Kaufman was not touched personally by the war; he was rejected almost at once as too nervous to make a good soldier. Woollcott, too, was rejected, though for overweight rather than nervousness, but he persisted, pulling every string within reach to get the rejection overturned. He took the rejection as a slur on his manhood, and this was an area in which he was particularly sensitive because many people were beginning to suspect and hint, as they did all through his lifetime, that he was a homosexual. He was not a homosexual; he was non-sexual because of his destructive siege with the mumps. But in those days, long before the present era of sexual freedom in which most people do what they want and talk openly about it, sexual deviation was regarded as a matter of shame, a criminal act more heinous than many other criminal acts. Woollcott managed to get into the Army and was sent as a private to France, ending up as a sergeant on the staff of the military newspaper, *Stars and Stripes;* the editor was Harold Ross and the supervising officer was Captain Franklin Pierce Adams.

Woollcott returned to the *Times* shortly after the end of the war, which was shortly after the end of *Someone in the House,* and he and Kaufman, drawn together by their jobs and their mutual friendship with Frank Adams, quickly developed a bristly but affectionate friendship of their own, full of comradely insults tossed back and forth. He touched on his relationship with Kaufman in a profile called *The Deep, Tangled Kaufman*—the title was a twist on the title of one of Kaufman's plays, *The Deep Tangled Wildwood*—which he wrote for *The New Yorker* in 1929. His piece described Kaufman's running war with waiters and taxi drivers and others of similar ilk, but quickly made it clear that Kaufman was no bully who confined his attacks to underlings. "I think it only fair to add, in his behalf," Woollcott wrote, "that he is equally severe with overlings. As one who was his abashed chief at the *Times* for several years, I can testify that he was always careful to treat me like dirt, and I am sure that Mr. Ochs and all the executives at the *Times* have had to struggle along, even unto the present day, without so much as a conciliatory smile."

Later, Woollcott expanded on his theme in *That Benign Demon George S. Kaufman,* a piece he wrote in 1933 for the *Times* to plug one of his own two collaborations with Kaufman, *The Dark Tower,* which had opened a week previously. He wrote: "In my days (or rather nights) as a dramatic critic I had at one time or another ten assistants, of whom several were shot from under me. These lucky ten varied widely in character and origin. One ran a hay-and-feed store on the side in the Bronx. One was a personable and chronic bride who was given to weeping in taxis. One was an elderly clown from St. Louis. Another (seriously) was a belted Earl. He had inherited the title in mid-season, rushed home to be inducted into the House of Lords and returned breathless to resume his more interesting duties in a field where the only important bills were not legislative matters at all, and the only Palace was far more interesting than the one called Buckingham . . . Of these ten George S. Kaufman was the most alarming. I was his uneasy chief for three years from 1919 to 1922 and he was never really satisfied with me. Throughout that period he smiled only once. That was when I told him an old joke I had read long before in an almanac. It was about a cat hospital where they charged $4 a weak purr. Imagine my surprise when I came across this veteran quip included among Kaufman's contributions to *Life.* This painful incident was settled by his paying me $2.50."

Woollcott added: "I remember a night when I decided to knock off work early and go home to bed. I paused at the office door to express the hope that despite this defection he wouldn't think any the worse of me. He looked up from his typewriter only long enough to say 'I couldn't' and then went on with his work."

The picture of Kaufman at his desk, scowling and tossing off insults, is a deceptive one. The scowls were frequently present, but they were more often concentration than irascibility, and the insults were simply one aspect of his wide-ranging lexicon of humor. The truth of the matter was that, though he wasn't the type to smile at passersby and whistle as he worked, he was enjoying his job hugely and was extremely happy.

He liked the work; it had been fun wandering around the theatrical area as the man from the *Tribune*, but it was even more fun covering the same territory as the man from the pre-eminent *Times*. He liked the atmosphere; nothing suited a man with his kind of temperament and nervous energy more than the frantic atmosphere of a newspaper office, and the *Times* office—the staid appearance of its product notwithstanding—was very frantic in its constant determination to get out the most accurate and complete newspaper in the country. And he even, despite his mania for neatness, came to like his dingy, dusty desk in a third-floor cubicle; he grew so used to it that, when his plays were successful and Beatrice turned one of the rooms of their apartment into a luxuriously furnished study, he tried the study a few times and then hurried back to write his plays after working hours on his rattly typewriter at his dingy desk.

He had the habit of walking in his office with his hands behind his back, his head bent forward, and his body slightly stooped in deep concentration. His concentration was so intense that one day he banged his head, with a clang, against a fire extinguisher. He'd also sometimes send Sam Zolotow, then an office boy and later the *Times*'s stage-news columnist, out to get some clippings, and then he'd become so absorbed in his work that he'd forget he sent Zolotow and bawl him out for his long absence, complaining that phones had been ringing and that he'd had to answer them personally. The *Times*'s Louis Calta, who was then also an office boy and is now a cultural-news reporter on the paper, says that Kaufman was the fastest writer he's ever seen, and that Kaufman put paper in the typewriter and immediately began typing as fast as his fingers could move, never hesitating until the page was finished, then fed in another sheet and did the same. Calta compares him to Clive Barnes, the *Times*'s reigning drama critic, who also writes excellent prose at top speed.

Curiously—perhaps because his success as a playwright and director overshadowed his work as a newspaperman—Kaufman is usually left out of stories which list eminent *Times* alumni. In Gay Talese's best-selling, 555-page study of the *Times, The Kingdom and the Power*, for example, Kaufman is mentioned only once, and then obliquely, as part of a list of a particular *Times* editor's circle of acquaintances. But the fact is that Kaufman accomplished important things in his years on the newspaper. When he first came to work on the *Times*, the theatrical page was a dull compendium of press agents' handouts; almost singlehandedly, Kaufman changed it to a fresh, colorful page of real news stories and interesting theatrical gossip. Before his arrival, it was common knowledge that any flack could get a plug printed in the *Times:* all he had to do was buy one of the boys in the dramatic department a meal or hand him a few bucks. Kaufman turned this completely around; he was so scrupulously honest that the only people who found cause to complain were the producers with whom he was friendly rather than those with whom he wasn't. George Tyler, for instance, later complained that the closer he and Kaufman grew, the more difficult it became to get one of his productions mentioned in the *Times*.

Kaufman also brought humor to the theatrical page. The Sunday listing of current shows was like a railroad timetable; nearly every listing was followed by an asterisk, dagger, or other symbol, calling attention to a forest of footnotes below giving information like *Matinees Wednesdays and Saturdays* and *Extra Performance Sunday for Actors' Fund*. When *Strange Interlude*, which ran nearly five hours—right through and beyond the dinner hour—appeared on the list, Kaufman satirized the maze of symbols and footnotes, and commented at the same time on the excessive length of the O'Neill play, by adding an additional symbol and an additional footnote. "Sorry," the footnote said, "does not carry dining car."

Kaufman remained on the *Times* for thirteen years, leaving, finally, on August 16, 1930, only because the Depression had arrived and he was making so much money with his plays that he could not in conscience hang onto a job which could otherwise go to someone in need. Most of his reason for staying as long as he did was his insecurity; even as he left, though he was already one of the most successful playwrights in the world, he said nervously to Sam Zolotow, "The playwriting business is not like putting up a building. In my case, a big hole is often dug and then nothing happens." But there was another reason he stayed on at the *Times.* He would never have put it in so sentimental a manner himself, but it was because he really—*really*—liked the place.

Around the middle of 1919, George C. Tyler re-entered Kaufman's life. Actually, he had never left it; he had been quite impressed with Kaufman's work on *Someone in the House,* despite the failure of the play, and had been looking around for something else to give him to do. He found something, finally, in *Jacques Duval,* an international opus which was about a French doctor, was written by a Danish dramatist, Hans Muller, and was then playing in the German language in a Berlin theatre.

Tyler was working very closely at the time with the frozen-featured British actor, George Arliss, and the principal role seemed exactly right for what *Variety,* in reviewing *Jacques Duval* later on, called "Arliss's glacial art." And it seemed to Tyler that Kaufman, who spoke and read German fairly well because of his parents' and grandparents' background, was the perfect man to translate the play into English and make all the necessary changes to adapt it to American tastes.

The play was not exactly Kaufman's cup of tea; it was a gloomy melodrama with no humor whatsoever. In real life, a cure for tuberculosis was still many years off, but the play dealt with a doctor who discovers a serum which defeats the disease, but has been so single-minded and dedicated in his research that he neglects his wife, Marie, thrusting her into the arms of an attractive young neighbor, Henri, Marquis de Charvet. The plot was equally predictable beyond that point: Henri catches a cold from his habit of standing outside the house mooning up at Marie's window; the cold develops into tuberculosis; Henri requests and receives a shot of Duval's serum, but dies instead of being cured; a jealous colleague accuses Duval of unprofessional conduct and he is tried by the local medical board; but fortunately, in the big climactic scene, Marie whips out a letter from Henri, and the letter reveals that he has decided to kill himself with an overdose of heroin because he realizes that Marie is still in love with her husband and his own love is hopeless. So it wasn't Duval's serum, after all, which did him in, and Duval is exonerated and reunited with his wife.

Not, in short, precisely the calibre of *Hamlet*, but Kaufman leaped at the opportunity. He was anxious to do more work in the theatre; it was an opportunity for a very visible credit because Tyler had decided to ignore the original author and not even mention him in the ads or on the programs; and it was also a considerable honor to be involved in a vehicle for Arliss, because Arliss had been a great hit a few years before in *Disraeli* and had become enormously popular.

The play opened at the Blackstone Theatre in Chicago on Monday, November 10. It was distinguished by the big credit Tyler had promised—the credit line said simply, "Adapted by George S. Kaufman," with no mention of the author from whose work he had adapted it—and by an interesting if unflattering bit of casting. Dr. Nada Anastova, Duval's lady-doctor assistant and chief consolation when Marie is discovered to have strayed, was played by a young actress, Fernanda Eliscu, while Florence Arliss, the actor's wife, played Duval's mother.

Unfortunately, the reviews were not good. *Variety*, the country's most important barometer on out-of-town openings, misspelled Kaufman's name, and made the error of assuming he'd adapted the play from the French because of the Gallic characters, but was reasonably kind to him. "George S. Kauffman," the reviewer said, "did a good clean-cut job of playwriting." But, the review went on, "He was helpless in his efforts to introduce through the heavy air of ether and iodoform . . . one single breath of natural, fresh air . . . If it is true that Mr. Arliss gave up Molière for this play, it was a mistake of judgment. . . ."

The play limped along for a while in Chicago, and then played Toledo, Ohio, and Boston, but it was never brought in to New York.

It was another failure for Kaufman, but better things were coming. At the same time Tyler was keeping an interested eye on Kaufman, he had been keeping his other eye on another young newspaperman who had come to New York from Pennsylvania. The man, who came from McKeesport, only a short distance from Kaufman's home town of Pittsburgh, was also in the dramatic department of a newspaper, covering the Broadway beat for the *Morning Telegraph*. His name, soon to be linked to Kaufman's on one credit line after another, was Marcus Cook Connelly.

6. THE HIT

MARC CONNELLY WAS once spending an evening at one of his favorite saloons, Tony's, when an acquaintance, hoping to get a big laugh, wandered over to his table and ran a hand over the gleaming expanse of Connelly's big bald head. "You know," he said, "that feels just like my wife's behind."

Connelly regarded the man calmly for a moment, then moved his own hand over his baldness. "I'll be damned," he said. "You're absolutely right. It does."

The instant retort was unsurprising; the fact that Connelly had been bald all of his adult life had long since inured him to the attentions of the endowed. For this reason, he was not, in the winter of 1917, either surprised or perturbed when, standing in the rear of the auditorium of the Hippodrome Theatre in the hope of getting an item or two for the *Telegraph*, he was suddenly conscious of eyes focused unblinkingly on him. He looked around to see another young man staring in apparent alarm at his head. It was Kaufman, worrying that the same thing might one day happen to *him*.

Connelly ignored the stare and greeted the other man cordially, and the cordiality increased when he learned that Kaufman was a fellow newspaperman also on the prowl for items. They talked for quite a while at that first meeting; neither was in any particular hurry to leave the theatre because it was bitterly cold outside, with heavy snow falling. It developed that they had many other things in common. They were almost the same age; Connelly was just a year younger, born December 13, 1890. They had reminiscences to swap about Pittsburgh; since McKeesport was within commuting distance of the larger town, Connelly's first jobs—after he left Trinity Hall, a military school in Washington, Pennsylvania—had been as a reporter on the *Gazette-Times* and other Pittsburgh papers. They had both transferred to New York not too long before, Connelly in 1916. Most important, it developed that Connelly also had the strong ambition to succeed as a playwright.

Connelly walked Kaufman home that night, the snowfall forgotten, and their talk continued in the hallway of Kaufman's apartment building long after they reached it; they had both already gotten the notion that they ought to try writing something together. The walks home continued in the months that followed, and became easier and more convenient when, early in 1918, the Kaufmans took advantage of the larger *Times* salary and moved to a better, two-bedroom apartment on West 80th Street between Amsterdam and Columbus avenues, directly across town from Connelly's apartment in the East 80s. It was still quite safe in those days for one man to walk the other home and then cut across Central Park to his own place.

The months of conversation, trying out ideas and plot twists on each other, were fine with Connelly, but, after a while, the passage of time became upsetting to the more nervous Kaufman. He finally said, in despair, "Do you think we'll ever actually *write* anything?" But Connelly calmed him down, and in time they did move to the typewriter.

[74]

The play they began to write was a musical comedy called *Miss Moonshine*, and they hoped to interest Irene Franklin, a leading star of the musical stage, in doing it, feeling they could easily secure a leading producer if they brought her along as part of the package. The idea of being involved in a musical comedy had worried Kaufman a little, at first; he enjoyed listening to music but didn't feel very knowledgeable or comfortable about the subject, telling a friend once, "I don't know the difference between Handel's *Largo* and—well, Largo's *Handel*." (The tepid quality of his interest in music remained the same throughout his life. When he was working on *Face the Music*, which he co-directed with Hassard Short, the play's composer, Irving Berlin, stopped talking to him for weeks because he gave his typically total attention one afternoon to the first reading of the book, and then walked absent-mindedly out of the theatre as Berlin started to play the music he'd just written for the show. Kaufman subsequently apologized, pointing out that the reason he'd been hired only as director of the book, while Short had been engaged as general director, was that he was no expert on music and his opinion didn't mean much anyway. But Berlin was not quick to forgive him.)

Connelly prevailed on Kaufman to work on *Miss Moonshine* by telling him that he knew Irene Franklin well and could guarantee an interested and sympathetic reading. Connelly himself was much more comfortable with musical comedies; he had, in fact, broken into the theatre in that area. He had written the lyrics for a musical called *The Amber Princess*, and when the play was sold and opened on Broadway on September 19, 1916, he had moved to New York to enjoy what he hoped would be the fruits of its success. There were no fruits; the musical closed quickly. But Connelly had remained in New York, supporting himself with newspaper work and making it a point to meet people who might help in what he considered his real career. He convinced Kaufman that *Miss Moonshine* might do what *The Amber Princess* had not done, and, once started, work moved quickly.

Irene Franklin read the completed script at once and liked it very much, but there was one major snag. The musical comedy star said she'd do the play only if a manager she particularly admired, Charles B. Dillingham, would produce it, so Dillingham would now have to be approached, and would have to read and like the play, too. Kaufman secured an interview with Dillingham, but reported afterward to Connelly that it had been an extremely brief one, consisting of one question and one answer. "Would you be interested," Kaufman asked, "in producing a musical comedy that a friend and I have written—with Irene Franklin in the leading role?" "No," Dillingham said, and turned away.

That was that. Irene Franklin dropped out, a lot of unsuccessful attempts were made to sell the play without her as part of the package, and *Miss Moonshine* was sadly put aside. It was finally done seven years later under the title of *Be Yourself*, opening at the Harris Theatre with Queenie Smith in the leading role, but was not successful.

Kaufman and Connelly continued to walk home together now and then after the script went into the trunk, but for the most part went their separate ways. And the separation grew wider as Kaufman became busy with *Someone in the House* and *Jacques Duval*, and with his work on the *Times*. He also broke into the *New York Times Magazine and Book Review*, then one combined section of the Sunday paper rather than the two separate sections they later became, with a long and serious piece about theatrical labor problems, *Collective Bargaining for Actors' Wages*, which appeared in the July 13, 1919, edition.

Early in 1920, Tyler called with news of an unexpected bonanza: Metro had bought the film rights to *Someone in the House*. He also told Kaufman that he'd just given a job to Connelly. He was planning, in association with William Farnum, to revive an old comic opera named *Erminie*, and had hired Connelly to revise the play and bring it up to date.

The theatre was undergoing a nostalgia wave in the years after the First World War, and *Erminie*, which had originally played New York in 1886, was Tyler's choice to cash in on the trend. The basic play was even older than that; the 1886 comic opera was the musical version of an earlier play called *Robert Macaire* which had been in the repertoire of Henry Irving and other noted actors years before the musical version had been written. As *Erminie*, it had been a smash hit, playing over 500 performances. It had also zoomed to stardom an actor named Francis Wilson, and Tyler now planned to emphasize the nostalgia appeal by bringing Wilson out of retirement to play the same role again. He was also hedging his bet by adding an extremely popular actor, De Wolf Hopper, as co-star, and getting a hot young stage designer named Norman Bel Geddes to do the sets.

A few days later, Kaufman and Connelly ran into each other, as they did from time to time, inevitably, since they covered the same beat and knocked on the same doors. Connelly congratulated Kaufman on the movie sale, and Kaufman congratulated Connelly on the assignment. Then Kaufman said, "I'm going to be doing a piece on *Erminie* for the *Times Magazine*. I suggested it and got an okay."

Connelly looked at him hopefully, sensing the possibility of a big, friendly plug. He should have known better; he was about to be confronted with the same kind of rigid honesty which Tyler and other friends of Kaufman's found so frustrating. When the piece appeared on January 2, 1921, under the title of *Erminie: Thirty-Five Years Later*, it included, among a lot of other miscellaneous information, the fact that Francis Wilson's weekly salary had jumped from $125 to $600 in the course of the original musical production, that an English low comedian named Harry Paulton had done the adaptation, and that a lady anxious to see the play in 1886 had had to pay a speculator the sum of $1.50 for her ticket. But Connelly was not mentioned in the article at all.

Connelly was not offended by Kaufman's rigidity. He was already a strong admirer of Kaufman's, going around telling people that as a collaborator Kaufman was like Old Faithful in the way he could be depended upon to come up with great gag lines whenever needed. He was also already an awed admirer of Kaufman's humor in ordinary conversation, particularly what he called Kaufman's "disappearing gun" technique—the way Kaufman had of standing in silence, suddenly emerging with something devastatingly funny, and instantly retreating into silence again. Connelly said only, "You know, we ought to do something else together."

Kaufman nodded in agreement. "As a matter of fact," he said, "I have a sort of idea." He paused, and there was a look on his face which Connelly was able to remember vividly fifty years later:

Kaufman, always insecure, always half fearful of rejection, was trying to decide if Connelly was serious about another collaboration or was just being polite. Connelly made it clear with his own expression that he was completely serious, and after a moment Kaufman went on, "I've been thinking about the fact that the reviewers all said such good things about that character that Lynn Fontanne played in *Someone in the House*—the one I based on Frank Adams's character, Dulcinea. And I thought we ought to try a complete play about Dulcinea this time."

Tyler liked the idea of the play, but wasn't as enthusiastic about the notion of a Kaufman-Connelly collaboration. He thought that, if Kaufman felt like working with a collaborator, he ought to tie up with someone far more experienced than Connelly. Kaufman did feel like working with a collaborator; he nearly always felt like working with a collaborator from that point onward. He had enjoyed working with Connelly on *Miss Moonshine*, having someone on whom he could bounce off lines and who could try out lines on him. He told Tyler that he appreciated his viewpoint but felt comfortable with Connelly and wanted him as his collaborator on this particular play, and he persisted until Tyler agreed. The two young playwrights got busy.

The film based on *Someone in the House* was released as a six-reeler on November 22 and got fair reviews. *Erminie* opened a month and a half later, on January 3, 1921, to similar reviews. Clearly, neither production was going to bring the collaborators world-wide fame, and they continued to work hard on their play. This time, there was no casual free use of Adams's character, slightly altered. They secured formal permission to use the actual character and name and arranged for Tyler to pay Adams 10 per cent of their take. And they decided to call the play, simply, *Dulcy*.

At the *Times* office, Woollcott began to notice a stranger showing up every night and hanging around, a benign-looking young man with a shining bald head. He seemed to be a friend of Kaufman's. But there was something suspicious about him: he kept looking over at Woollcott as though he was eager to see him leave.

There was clearly something odd going on, and Woollcott decided

HELEN, RUTH, AND GEORGE KAUFMAN
Mark Twain and baseball scores.

KAUFMAN AS TWO ARTISTS SAW HIM

Kaufman by Miguel Covarrubias, left; Kaufman by George Hughes, right

(Covarrubias drawing Copyright 1929, 1957 by The New Yorker Magazine, Inc. Used by permission. Hughes drawing used by courtesy of George Hughes and Reader's Digest © 1967.)

FRANKLIN PIERCE ADAMS

Who discovered Kaufman (and just about everybody else).

FRANK MUNSEY

A Jew in the composing room.

GEORGE C. TYLER

Kaufman ran.

Culver Pictures, Inc.

BEATRICE

A surly waiter started it.

JULIA HAY AND ROBERT HUDSON IN A SCENE FROM
SOMEONE IN THE HOUSE

How to avoid an epidemic.

MARC CONNELLY

Dickens was more prolific.

MARION DAVIES AS *DULCY*

(In the first screen version, now called Not So Dumb.*)*

ROLAND YOUNG IN A DREAM SEQUENCE FROM
BEGGAR ON HORSEBACK

It's dated.

o put the question to Kaufman bluntly and openly. "Who's that fel-
ow who keeps hanging around here?" he asked. "And what does he
vant?"

Kaufman answered somewhat evasively. "He's an associate of
nine," he said. "A dramatic reporter from another paper." He
eemed to be trying to suggest that he and Connelly were getting
ogether for professional talk, useful to the *Times,* the pooling of
rade secrets.

"What paper?" Woollcott asked.

The *Morning Telegraph* was not a publication to boast about; it
vas given over mostly to horse-racing news and similar matter. But
he actual situation was even worse: Connelly had recently left the
Telegraph and made an even less impressive association. Kaufman
hrugged uncomfortably. *"Garment News,"* he said.

"Well, what does he want here?" Woollcott demanded. "Why does
ie keep staring at me as though he's waiting for me to leave?"

Kaufman didn't answer for a moment. "Well, to tell you the truth,"
ie said finally, "he is. We both are. We're writing a play, and we've
)een using your typewriter. It's the best one in the building."

Woollcott understood, and thereafter left his desk the moment his
lay's stint was completed. The work on *Dulcy* moved more swiftly
ifter that.

Dulcinea had originally been created by Adams for two reasons:
ie was looking for something to help fill his columns on arid days,
and he also needed a brief regular feature to serve as a separation between contributions from other people. It struck him one morning
that the presentation of that young woman, saying what she said with
such wide-eyed delight that it was obvious she thought she was making up the stuff, might be a pretty funny feature. The series might
also have additional appeal to his readers because they'd recognize the
truth of the statements despite the staleness of their wording. Adams's
columns soon began to bristle with Dulcinea's quotations: *It never
rains if you have your umbrella. When you need a policeman, you
can never find one. Juries don't usually convict good-looking women.
Most people don't start functioning until they have a cup of coffee in
the morning.* They were all familiar statements expressed in a familiar
way, but, as Kaufman emphasized to Connelly in explaining his idea

[79]

for the play, clichés become clichés because they express popular truths or beliefs, and Dulcinea's comments made her a quick favorite with Adams's readers.

Kaufman and Connelly took the character forward from there. They gave her a last name which was also a cliché, Smith, and made her the wife of a young jewelry manufacturer who is in financial difficulties and invites an older and far more successful competitor and his wife and daughter over for the weekend in the hope of arranging a merger of their two companies. Smith's intention is to keep the weekend quiet and devoted to business talk. But the collaborators envisioned Dulcy as a well-intentioned meddler as positive in her actions as she is in her comments, and she decides that her husband's plans will be more likely to work if she turns the weekend into a fashionable party. So she hires a butler who also happens to be an ex-con, and loads her house with a lot of ill-assorted types she's met at other parties: an egomaniac screenwriter, a brash advertising man, and a presumed millionaire socialite who actually turns out to be an escaped lunatic.

The idea of setting up disparate types in a confined setting and allowing them to react to each other was one which continually fascinated Kaufman. He did it again in *The Man Who Came to Dinner*, contrasting Sheridan Whiteside and his celebrity friends with the small-town people with whom they come in contact when Whiteside breaks his leg during a lecture tour and is confined to a house in Mesalia, Ohio, and again in *You Can't Take It with You*, which deals with a household which includes one man who makes firecrackers in the cellar, another who spends his time playing the xylophone and operating a printing press, a woman who writes plays, another woman who practices ballet, and so forth. In both these plays, the uneasy mixtures explode into chaos, and it was the same plan for *Dulcy*. The rich jewelry man hates the screenwriter and his daughter elopes with the man, the butler is revealed as a felon and a string of pearls disappears, and the one man who has impressed everybody, the alleged millionaire, is led off by a keeper. But, of course, as in the other plays, everything ends happily when it turns out that the tycoon's daughter has really decided to marry Dulcy's brother, a young man as levelheaded as his sister is impulsive, and that the butler has merely put the pearls away for safekeeping to avoid presenting temptation to other servants who may not have learned the advantages of honesty as he has. And Smith gets his merger and financial salvation.

The play fell into place with startling speed. Kaufman and Connelly discussed the characters and plot in three or four walks home after their papers had gone to bed at night, and then went to Woollcott's typewriter and in a few days had tapped out a complete and detailed twenty-five-page synopsis. The procedure they followed after that was one they continued to use throughout all their collaborations: they divided up the scenes, each man taking those he thought he could write best, and then getting together at regular intervals and going over, line by line, the scenes which had been written since the last meeting. Kaufman, predictably, refused to write any of the love scenes, but Connelly had no objection to taking those on. (In later collaborations like *Merton of the Movies* and *Beggar on Horseback*, Connelly suggested that Kaufman should at least *try* writing some of the love scenes, but desisted when he saw that the suggestion literally made Kaufman look sick.) They ended up writing just about the same number of scenes apiece, using their own typewriters and then meeting at Woollcott's for rewrites and final drafts.

As they worked together, the collaborators' admiration for each other continued to increase. Kaufman was impressed with Connelly's sure touch with construction and plot twists, and Connelly was delighted with Kaufman's quick humor; he said afterward, "George's wit sparkled on everything we did." This did not, however, prevent each man from attacking mercilessly each scene presented by the other. Once in a great while, a scene was approved exactly as it came out of the typewriter, and was allowed to stand, but most scenes were written and rewritten and then rewritten again a few more times. Despite this, they worked together so well and so rapidly that they completed and delivered *Dulcy* less than thirty days after they'd begun it.

Tyler approved the play enthusiastically and decided to produce it in association with H. H. Frazee, a flamboyant man who owned two of the theatres into which Tyler wanted to book the play: the Cort in Chicago and a New York theatre which had once been called the

Harris but which Frazee had recently and matter-of-factly named after himself. This was all, of course, provided Frazee also liked the play; he was extremely unpredictable and it was difficult to tell which direction he might take in any matter.

Frazee's start had been rather similar to Tyler's; he, too, had come from a small town—he'd been born in Peoria, Illinois, on June 29, 1880—and, after going to work as an usher and box-office man in a Peoria theatre at the age of sixteen, had, like Tyler, been an advance man for a road company for a while. But the two men had taken opposite paths once they both reached New York. Tyler tended toward the dignified and what he hoped was the safe; Frazee built the cornerstone of his fortune by unorthodox show business ventures, things like taking two heavyweight boxing champions, James J. Jeffries and James J. Corbett, and sending them out to box each other on theatre stages across the country. Throughout the rest of his career, a sadly short one because he developed Bright's disease and died suddenly on June 5, 1929, at the age of forty-eight, his interests were divided equally between the theatre and the world of sports. His most spectacular success in the theatre was *No, No, Nanette*, which was a total flop when he first opened it in Chicago in 1925, but which he turned into an international hit by ignoring, in his typically maverick fashion, all the advice to close the play which came to him from expert after expert. He continued to revise the play until it was strong enough to run for years, and even strong enough to become a hit all over again when it was revived recently. He probably made even more money, however, from such sports ventures as his ownership of the Boston Red Sox, which he bought in 1916 for under $400,000, and sold in 1923, after turning it into a championship team, for more than $1,500,000, and from his then-unprecedented (and generally considered outrageous) practice of building up new ballplayers and selling them to rival teams at huge profits.

In 1921, Frazee was particularly well-heeled: in addition to his plays and his theatres—he also owned the Lyric in New York, the Arlington in Boston, and had recently built another New York theatre called the Longacre—he had a few months before sold a youngster named Babe Ruth to the Yankees for $125,000, the highest price ever paid for a ballplayer up to that time. Tyler, realizing that Frazee could help finance *Dulcy* as well as house it, awaited his decision with considerable anxiety. He was soon able to relax. Frazee liked the play as much as Tyler did, if not more.

Tyler had one further idea. He wanted to open the play and give it a week of tryouts in a rather unexpected city. Kaufman and Connelly listened to his proposal in dismay. "*Indianapolis?*" Kaufman echoed hollowly. "For God's sake, why?" But the playwrights agreed when Tyler explained his reason. Indianapolis was the home of Tyler's distinguished friend, Booth Tarkington, whose *A Gentleman from Indiana* Tyler had produced, and an opening in Indianapolis would enable the young authors to secure Tarkington's advice on revisions before the play moved on to Chicago.

Tyler then went on to assemble a really brilliant cast. Lynn Fontanne, who had been so marvelous in her small but similar role in *Someone in the House*, was signed for the lead. The ad man was played by Elliott Nugent; Nugent was a talented young actor and playwright who subsequently wrote *The Male Animal* in collaboration with James Thurber. Dulcy's brother was played by Gregory Kelly, a sardonic actor married at the time to Ruth Gordon and subsequently to play the lead in another Kaufman play, *The Butter and Egg Man.* And Tyler's choice for both the director of the play and the part of the screenwriter was another excellent young actor, Howard Lindsay.

Lindsay eventually teamed up with Russel Crouse to form a hugely successful playwriting team: they wrote, among other plays and musicals, *The Sound of Music, Call Me Madam, State of the Union,* which won a Pulitzer Prize in 1946, and *Life with Father,* and he also played the title role in the latter play during most of its record-breaking seven-year, 3,224-performance run. At the time of *Dulcy,* he was still an unknown quantity; his experience had been limited to acting and direction on very minor projects, mostly silent movies, tent shows, burlesque, and vaudeville, so his dual assignment as both director and performer was both unusual and chancy. Fortunately, he proved excellent in both jobs. He seemed to have an instinctive understanding of Kaufman's and Connelly's brand of comedy and characterizations, and he brought out the best in his own role and the roles of the other actors.

[83]

Lynn Fontanne responded particularly well to Lindsay's direction, which was a lucky thing for the play. The young British actress was then living in a theatrical boardinghouse run by a shrewd-eyed, gray-haired woman who was called Dr. Rounds because of her habit of telling long and detailed stories about her operations and other medical experiences. Alfred Lunt also lived in the same boardinghouse, and so did another ambitious actor, Noël Coward. The three young people talked constantly about their future and their dreams, Lunt and Lynn Fontanne already having decided to form a permanent team both matrimonially and professionally—but when she was given the leading role in *Dulcy*, the British actress became terrified. She was constantly sick to her stomach and certain that she would flop, despite Lunt's assurances that she would be great, and Coward's statement that he had recently met the Kaufmans at a party, had been overwhelmed by Kaufman's wit, and was absolutely certain the part was the break of a lifetime. Lunt and Coward tried everything; they took the actress for walks and bought her an endless stream of Cokes and chocolate sodas to try to soothe her stomach. But it was Lindsay's calm manner and businesslike, professional direction which finally brought her around and enabled her to give a memorable performance.

The play opened at English's Opera House on Monday, February 14, 1921, and the reviews were uniformly excellent, doing much to help Kaufman overlook the fact that several of the reviews ran his name with two n's. "The play is unqualifiedly good," one reviewer said. "It has a humanness, a sharpness, and a good humoredly sophisticated, civilized viewpoint. . . . There is no straining to be either funny or dramatic and the play is both . . . There are lines of delicious writing in it." The reviewer then went on to report that there had been at least twenty curtain calls. Another reviewer said: "For once, here we have a heroine who gushes platitudes and bromides that are intended to be laughed at. Commonly, the heroine's bromides and platitudes are expected to be taken seriously. The distinction indicates in Dulcy's creators a civilized and grownup point of view somewhat rare in the theatre . . . The same intelligence is shown elsewhere in the play. No skulls are cracked to get a joke over. There is hardly a gag line in the piece. The humor, in fact, is human, natural, and sly, and all of it comes out of character, not out of vaudeville."

The best tribute of all came from Booth Tarkington, greatly respected by Kaufman and Connelly both for his plays and his other writings, including such novels as *Monsieur Beaucaire, Penrod, Seventeen,* and *The Magnificent Ambersons.* Tyler, despite the glowing reviews, had begun to worry a little about the play's rather simple plot, and he went to Tarkington for the advice the Indiana writer had promised to give if the play opened in his town. Did Tarkington, Tyler asked, think the play needed more complexity, more plot twists?

Tarkington shook his head. "There's no advice to give," he said. "All those young men need from now on are a couple of typewriters. And to be left alone."

Tarkington's comment was relayed to Kaufman and Connelly, and Connelly said, beaming, "I think we've got a hit, George." To Connelly's surprise, though he was later to grow used to this kind of reaction, Kaufman merely looked gloomy. "This isn't Chicago," he said. "There are forty-four theatres in Chicago. That means forty-three other shows to help people ignore ours."

By the time the play opened at the Cort in Chicago, on Sunday, February 20, Kaufman had worked himself into a state of almost total despair. "We've been kidding ourselves," he told Connelly at dinner just before the opening, "and we might as well admit it."

Connelly wasn't ready to admit it at all. He was, true enough, in a euphoric state because he had fallen in love with a beautiful young actress named Margalo Gillmore who had scored a success the year before in a play called *The Famous Mrs. Fair,* and, though she kept spurning his offers of marriage, she had at least agreed to attend the opening at the Cort with him. But the facts more directly related to the play were equally inspiring. *Dulcy* had done absolutely marvelous business in Indianapolis, making the authors more money in royalties than they'd ever seen before in their lives; and the actors had grown perceptibly in their parts with each performance, drawing bigger and bigger laughs.

Connelly tried to point this out to Kaufman, but Kaufman was inconsolable. He slouched off by himself after dinner, and was not in sight, either backstage or at the back of the theatre, at the opening.

It was obvious throughout the first act that the play was going to be an even bigger hit in Chicago than it had been in Indianapolis. The audience, including some of the toughest critics in town, began to laugh helplessly almost from the first lines, and the laughter continued without pause; there were even laughs at lines which the producers had admired but which had been laughless in Indianapolis.

At the end of the act, Connelly and Margalo Gillmore went to look for Kaufman to point *this* out to him, but he was still nowhere to be found. He was still not backstage or in the back of the theatre, and the Cort's doorman hadn't seen him all evening. Connelly and Miss Gillmore returned, worried, to their seats, but soon forgot everything else in their enjoyment of the way the play was going and the way the audience was responding to it. It was really sensational; the laughs during the second act were even longer and harder than during the first, and the curtain applause even more enthusiastic.

When the second act was over, Connelly and his date, worried again about Kaufman, went backstage and talked to the actors, and found them exhilarated at the audience reaction. But they hadn't seen Kaufman either. Now Connelly and Margalo Gillmore were really worried, and they broadened their search, looking for Kaufman in places where he couldn't possibly be, or could he? They finally found him. He was, astonishingly, huddled against a rusty pipe in the dusty, dirty, deserted scene dock, the area back of backstage where the theatre stored old sets and props. He was staring blankly at the floor and running his fingers through his thick hair. He looked, Connelly later told people in describing the incident, almost numb with agony.

He looked up as Connelly and Miss Gillmore approached. "Listen," he said, "we tried. Nobody can deny that we tried."

"What on earth are you talking about?" Connelly said. "The play's a smash so far."

"It's a failure," Kaufman said. "It's running an hour too long."

Connelly spoke patiently. "George," he said, "the play is running ten minutes longer than it ran in Indianapolis. And that's because we're getting a lot of new laughs and a lot of longer laughs."

"The play's artificial," Kaufman said.

"George," Margalo Gillmore said, "it's a darling play. Everybody loves it."

"Well," Kaufman said, "nobody can deny that we tried."

He would not return to the front of the theatre with them for the final act, even though Connelly reminded him that the third act contained many of their strongest scenes and assured him that the audience would receive the act well. It turned out even better than that. The third act drew the best laughs of all, and the applause at the play's conclusion seemed endless.

The critics, later that night and the next morning, were equally enthusiastic. The town's leading and toughest critic, Percy Hammond of the *Tribune*, called the play a happy satire, said it was friendly as well as amusing, and added that the acting deserved "anthems and hat-waving." And another tough critic, Amy Leslie of the *News*, wrote a review which was headlined *Lynn Fontanne Scores Triumph; Fine Play Admirably Presented*, and said, "It is caviar and its appeal is to the intellectual and exquisitely cultivated . . . The play ripples with honest laughter; it has deliciously accentuated speed and an irresistible surface fun which captivates . . . Certain episodes have Rabelasian depths of satire, and the characters are drawn with superb correctness of color and technique. As for the cast provided by Mr. Frazee and Mr. Tyler, it achieves perfection."

"Well?" Connelly said to Kaufman.

"Not so terribly well," Kaufman said. "Chicago isn't New York. Do you know how many theatres there are in New York?"

"George," Connelly said, "if you're going to keep on talking that way, I'm just not going to listen."

Dulcy scored its biggest triumph of all in New York City, opening at the Frazee Theatre on Saturday, August 13. The play had been eagerly awaited because of the notices in Indianapolis and Chicago, and nobody misspelled Kaufman's name now.

Kaufman's and Connelly's friends, not surprisingly, gave the play good reviews. Woollcott, covering *Dulcy* in his review and in a subsequent Sunday piece in the *Times*, called it "a deft and diverting comedy of character—a gay piece written by and for the sophisticated" and described Lynn Fontanne as "an actress of extraordinary gifts." Kaufman's old boss on the *Tribune*, Heywood Broun, said, "Stout Cortez was silent when he saw the Pacific, but if he had lived long enough to discover authentic satire in a Broadway theatre he would have shouted with the rest . . . *Dulcy* is an ingenious trick play and the patter which introduces the legerdemain is even better than the stunts." Burns Mantle, now a reviewer on the *Mail*, called it a bright comedy and said Dulcinea set the house "rocking with laughter." And Leo A. Marsh in Connelly's alma mater, the *Telegraph*, said, "If there are more entertaining, scintillating plays extant than *Dulcy*, we have yet to hear about them."

But all the other critics were equally enthusiastic, or even more so. The headlines above the reviews told the whole story; it wasn't even necessary to read the reviews themselves, though of course Kaufman and Connelly read them thoroughly and avidly. *Dulcy a Clever Satirical Play*, said one review, adding in a sub-head, *Work of Kaufman and Connelly Well Received at the Frazee Theatre Saturday Night. Dulcy Sweetens Summer Show List*, said another, and, its sub-head went on, *Lynn Fontanne Wins Honors in Title Role. Dulcy Should Fill the Frazee Until Spring*, said a third, adding, to Connelly's mild irritation, *New Play by George Kaufman, of the Times, Scores Hit.* (Kaufman, too, was mildly irritated—by the lack of the S.) Alfred Lunt and Noël Coward, seated in the least expensive seats on opening night, nudged each other knowingly. Lynn Fontanne, returning from Chicago, had been even more nervous than when she'd gone out to the Midwest, fearing that the applause at English's and the Cort might well end abruptly when she faced a far tougher audience at the Frazee, but they'd told her she'd be even better at her real test. She was, right from the moment she swept in for her first entrance. And at another performance of the play, a very young James Thurber watched *Dulcy* with his eyes bright with admiration and told people afterward that the brilliant satire of the play was what had inspired him to begin writing his own special brand of humor. (In the same way, nearly a decade later, another youngster, Moss Hart, sat bright-eyed and entranced at another Kaufman play, *June Moon*, Kaufman's sole collaboration with Ring Lardner, and went home to begin writing the first draft of *Once in a Lifetime*.) Kaufman later came forth with one of his most famous lines in discussing satire, which the dictionary describes as "the use of irony, sarcasm, ridicule, etc., in exposing, denouncing or deriding vice or folly"—as opposed to comedy, which the dictionary defines as "simple humor of a happy and cheerful nature." "Satire," Kaufman said cynically, but with considerable accuracy, "is what closes Saturday night." *Dulcy*, however, like nearly all of the Kaufman plays, was a blend of all the various branches of humor, all of the words which are really just synonyms for "funny"—satire, comedy, nonsense, parody, wit, and all the rest. And though it did indeed close on a Saturday night, it was a Saturday night which marked its 246th performance, a great run for the time.

The play went on tour after its New York run, with Lynn Fontanne continuing to play the lead but with some changes in the rest of the cast. A small part was played on the road by a little-known actor named George Abbott, still six years away from his first directing assignment, and one of the leads was taken over by Jimmy Gleason, later an even bigger success in the movies.

The British actress and the Irish actor quickly developed a strange kind of love-hate relationship which Abbott watched with fascination and subsequently described in his memoirs. "Gleason," he said, "was a thorough professional . . . with very little sense of humor. Lynn was a hoyden, a fey girl who exaggerated her eccentricities because they were charming." The young actress quickly noted Gleason's unyielding seriousness and began to drive him crazy with generalities said with smug certainty, rather in the Dulcy manner.

"All policemen," she told him one day, "wear red underwear."

This was a statement especially calculated to infuriate Gleason, because it was nonsense about a subject he knew well; he had a lot of cops in his own family. "That's ridiculous," he said angrily. "They do not!"

Miss Fontanne smiled at him. "All policemen," she said again, "wear red underwear. *Everybody* knows that."

Gleason began to choke with rage. "And I'm telling you they don't," he said. "I ought to know. I've got a lot of relatives who are policemen."

The actress shook her head pityingly. "You don't know," she said. "You're just not the observant type. All policemen *do* wear red underwear." And she walked quickly away, leaving him in a towering fury for hours.

But they liked each other generally, when she wasn't baiting him, and they admired each other professionally. The road company acted well together and the tour did excellent business.

Some months later, Mantle, who was already well into his series of books, selected *Dulcy* for *The Best Plays of 1921–22*, and shortly afterward Joseph M. Schenck bought the movie rights. The play was eventually filmed three times: in 1923 with Sidney Franklin directing and with Constance Talmadge in the Fontanne role; again in 1930, under the title of *Not So Dumb*, with King Vidor directing and Marion Davies in the lead this time and Elliott Nugent supporting her; and for a third time in 1940, once again called *Dulcy*, with Ann Sothern as the star.

Even Kaufman, watching the money pouring in, was finally convinced, though he did not miss the opportunity to tell Connelly gloomily that it was probably all a fluke and they'd never be able to do it again. Connelly threw up his hands and left the room in stony silence, but Beatrice followed a more practical path in showing that she had strong faith in her husband's abilities even if he didn't. Not long after *Dulcy* opened as a smash hit in New York, she persuaded Kaufman to give up their small apartment and take a far bigger and more lavish place at 200 West 58th Street, complete with a cook and two maids.

7. THE GROWTH

NOW THAT HE had suddenly become a success and even a celebrity, though in his opinion merely a temporary one, Kaufman discovered that a new kind of phenomenon was developing. He had, in the past, ignored most people and in turn been ignored by them. But now all kinds of people, people he knew and people he'd never seen before in his life, famous people and people who served him in restaurants and sold him things in stores, were coming over to him and giving him advice on playwriting. *Dulcy* had drawn few critical and constructive suggestions in its reviews around the country, most reviewers simply being content with saying that the play was just about perfect and leaving it at that, but now Kaufman found himself on the receiving end of detailed and sometimes even technical commentary from people who were mostly not in the business at all.

People with faces absolutely new to him came up and told him that *Dulcy* was a great little play, but; people approached him on his way to the men's room in restaurants and told him that *Dulcy* wasn't such a great little play but could have been, if; and people sidled up to him as he was getting in or out of cabs, or leaving the *Times* or his apartment, and told him specifically what he and Connelly should or should not write next.

Kaufman later described the phenomenon in an article called *A Playwright Tells Almost All*, which appeared in the *New York Times Magazine* on September 17, 1944. "Having listened for many years to the dramatic opinions of all kinds of persons," he wrote, "I would like to suggest a basic change in the manner of printing the phone directory, so that this generally secondary profession may receive recognition. 'Baldwin, Walter J.,' I would have it say, 'furs and dramatic critic.' 'Stuffnagel, Rufus W., garbage collector and dramatic critic.'"

He was more surprised and flattered by this kind of constant occurrence than irritated by it; the men and women who approached him were, after all, showing interest rather than indifference, and they were the people who bought those tickets and brought in those royalties. But the truth was that he didn't really need the advice on *Dulcy* and on what to write next. *Dulcy*, in the manner of all things, had in time begun to wear down: the play, after its out-of-town tour, had come back to do a run around the subway circuit, the local theatres in Brooklyn and Queens and the other boroughs, but it did only fair business. Tyler, after some thought, decided to close the play; it had been a tremendous success and he made the decision without regret. He even derived some final benefits from the closing. He decided to avoid the cost of storing *Dulcy*'s eighty truckloads of scenery by giving the sets away to amateur theatrical groups and anyone else who wanted the stuff, and he got over a hundred applications and a lot of good newspaper publicity. And he also continued to receive royalties for years afterward from those amateur groups and others. In those days, as in these, high school and college and other non-professional groups constantly put on performances of plays, buying piles of paperback copies of the plays published by firms like Samuel French, Inc., and paying both for the books and for the right to give performances. Sometimes the income from these sources was astonishing. Occasionally, thousands and even tens of thousands of dollars poured in, and, now and then, producers and authors shared more money from amateur rights than the play had earned on Broadway and on tour.

And as for the next play, Kaufman and Connelly already had their own ideas about that. They had filled some of their writing time after *Dulcy*'s opening by contracting with *Life* to do a monthly feature called *Life's Calendar*, and the feature, illustrated by the leading comic artist of the twenties, John Held, Jr., ran through the entire year of 1922. But at the same time as they started writing the *Life* feature, they began to work on a new play which they eventually called *To the Ladies*.

The feature for *Life* didn't require all that much effort. It appeared, at first glance, to be a legitimate almanac, a compilation of real events: items like *January 9, First shot fired in Civil War, 1861*, and *July 16, Printing invented, 1451*. But interspersed with the straight items, or adding to them, were example after example of the quick humor which seemed to flow so effortlessly from the typewriters of the two collaborators, and particularly from Kaufman's. It was looking up the occasional real items, Connelly said afterward, which took a certain amount of time. The rest was easy.

Some of the items memorialized events which had received little prior publicity, but which—there is no reason to doubt—probably actually happened, like the one which led off the January calendar: *14,276 recipients of unexpected New Year's cards sent out 14,276 New Year's cards, dating them December 29.* Or the one for September 25: *"My, but you're tan!" was said 25,736,987 times to 2,837,752 returned vacationists.* Some items were of more dubious authenticity, such as the item for February 3: *Man remembers to buy razor blades the day he runs out of them, 1917.* Or the items for March 3, *Grocer, when asked if eggs are fresh, answers "No," 1903*, and August 18, *User of coin-box telephone, on completing conversation, doesn't put finger in return slot, 1919*, and October 14, *Loser in poker game quits early because he is sleepy, 1889.* The truly unlikely items were relegated to the future: *March 20: Toupee fools someone, 1973; December 15: Hotels stop starching towels, 1956;*

July 18: Actor, playing scene over telephone, pauses long enough to create illusion of someone speaking on the other end, 1926. And, inevitably, there was a future-dated item to further Kaufman's favorite feud: *June 24: Taxi driver polite on a rainy night, 1960.*

There were also straight items followed by pointed comments. *Post Office established by Congress, 1789* is the item for March 12; it is followed by *First complaint about service, 1789.* The item for May 26 is *Last Confederate Army surrenders, 1865.* The follow-up: *Writers begin work on first movie in which Northern lieutenant falls in love with proud Southern Beauty, 1865.* This format was also used for the item which was probably their best in the entire twelve-month series, a bit of commentary well advanced for its time. It said, simply: *February 26: Fifteenth Amendment giving Negro full rights as citizen adopted, 1869. Negroes still trying to get them, 1922.*

They did one other quick magazine piece, *A Christmas Carol,* satirizing the Dickens classic, which appeared in *The Bookman* for December 1922; then they concentrated totally on their new play. The writing of *To the Ladies* came a bit harder.

It started out with a single idea: it was to be the story of a young clerk who is one of two men being considered for an important promotion by his firm. He goes out and buys a book of prepared speeches—one of those books which gives suggested complete texts, including a funny opening line and all the rest—because he has learned that the promotion will be given to the man who makes the better speech at the company's annual banquet. He picks a good speech, one which starts with the line, "I am feeling at this minute exactly like a man who is about to be seasick," memorizes it, and sits confidently at the banquet awaiting his turn. But his confidence turns to horror as his rival is called upon and gets up and says, "I am feeling at this minute exactly like a man who is about to be seasick . . ."

There was, of course, much more needed than that, particularly since Tyler, with his remarkable instinct for major talent, now had his sights focussed on another young actress who he felt could achieve quick stardom. His eye this time was on a twenty-two-year-old girl who had received excellent notices a few years before when she played William Gillette's daughter in *Dear Brutus,* an actress from Washington, D.C., named Helen Hayes. Since that time, she had appeared in a number of flops, the most recent being her first appearance in a Tyler play, *Golden Days*. The play had closed after four weeks in New York and two weeks on tour despite excellent notices again for Miss Hayes and equally strong notices for a young actor who had recently come over from England, Leslie Howard, but Tyler was certain that the girl from Washington could carry a really good play and help make it a success.

Kaufman and Connelly took a week to come up with a plot outline which satisfied them. To build a starring role for Helen Hayes, a more down-to-earth type than the ethereal Lynn Fontanne, they decided to make their feminine lead the exact opposite of Dulcinea: a woman who is visibly smarter than her husband, and who runs both her household and her husband although she does it subtly enough so that he isn't really aware of it. And that gave them a strong finish for the play, to take place after their hero sits numbly listening to his rival giving the exact speech he had selected and memorized himself. As Kaufman now visualized it, the husband is completely lost and non-functioning, so their heroine, whom they decided to call Elsie Beebe, gets to her feet when the rival is finished, explains that her husband has laryngitis and she'll have to give his speech for him, the speech he'd planned to give himself, and proceeds to give a charming, extemporaneous talk which captures all hearts and gets her husband the promotion.

It would require a character who was a long distance beyond the simpler, cliché-loving Dulcinea, but they felt they might be able to bring it off if the young actress could handle the role. As soon as they had their first two acts in rough draft, they went to see her and look her over.

Miss Hayes was living with her mother in a lovely duplex on East 19th Street which had formerly been the Astor family's carriage house. It was a beautiful place, but the problem was that the utilitarian rooms—two bedrooms, dining room, and kitchen—were upstairs, and the downstairs area had been converted into one huge living room, over forty feet long, which was practically unfurnished. The Hayes ladies just hadn't had the money to buy furniture; *Golden Days* had had too short a run, and even part of that had been at reduced salary. The young actress was in panic, terrified at the prospect of a visit to that big, empty barn of a room by the two men who had become, with a single play, the most successful playwrights in town, but she made the best of it. She lit the fireplace at the far end of the room, grouped her four pieces of furniture—a refectory table, two Italian chairs, and a small settee—around the fire, and hoped that Kaufman and Connelly would regard the emptiness through which they'd walk to get to the grouping as, in its own impressive way, the world's largest foyer.

Kaufman and Connelly didn't comment on the room; they knew that young actresses were rarely rich, and anyway they were more interested in how she'd do in their play than in how she furnished her home. One thing particularly important to them was that they had made their hero, Leonard Beebe, an employee of a piano company, and it was necessary to the plot that the heroine play a few selections. "You do play the piano, don't you?" Kaufman asked.

The actress had taken three years of piano lessons as a child, but hadn't been near a piano since and didn't remember a thing she'd learned. "Of course," she said casually, ignoring the fact that her mother was looking at her in alarm.

"We've also," Kaufman said, "made our heroine a sort of southern belle. I'm sure you can manage the accent, but Elsie also has to sing a couple of Negro spirituals. You do sing, don't you?"

"I've sung spirituals," said Miss Hayes, "all my life." Since Mrs. Hayes had the feeling that her daughter may never even have *heard* a spiritual before, her gaze changed from alarm to horror.

But Kaufman and Connelly were apparently satisfied and started to read the play, and the actress and her mother loved it. Like nearly all the Kaufman plays to come, it contained far more than its relatively simple plot; it was also a penetrating and hilarious exposure of the Babbittry of big business. This was so much the case, in fact, that, when Sinclair Lewis later approached them and suggested that they adapt his novel, *Babbitt*, into a play, they were interested but finally declined because they decided they had already done too similar a job in *To the Ladies*.

The moment Kaufman and Connelly left the big, empty room, the young actress put on her hat and told her mother to do the same.

"Where are we going?" her mother asked. "To rent a piano, of course," she said.

The two women went directly to Wurlitzer, where the clerk talked them into buying a piano for $750 rather than renting because the installments would be the same as the rental fee and they'd eventually own it. Mrs. Hayes, however, put her foot down firmly when the clerk said it was customary to pay a third on signing; she told him that she'd pay $50 and not a cent more. The clerk accepted, and the actress' mother wrote a check, keeping her thumb over the balance figure so that the clerk could not see that they only had $150 to their name.

The piano helped fill the living room, but the sight of it kept upsetting Mrs. Hayes; she pointed out that $750 could have completed furnishing the entire apartment. Her daughter remained calm. "Those men from Pennsylvania," she said, "are going to make me rich and famous," and she hired a piano teacher. She also solved the problem of the singing by getting the woman who cooked for them to teach her the lilt and style of Negro spirituals while her mother took over the cooking for a week or two.

By January 15, 1922, the authors had their first two acts polished and in final form, despite an incident which might have halted a less determined man than George S. Kaufman. One afternoon, Kaufman took the draft of the second act with him to the *Times*, hoping to look it over on company time if the day was a light one. But the day was jammed, and he didn't even finish his regular duties until after midnight. He read the act through on his subway ride home, but he was so exhausted that he left the script on the subway. It was the only copy.

The next morning, Kaufman appeared for an appointment with Connelly looking slightly red-eyed but saying nothing about what had happened. When, however, Connelly read over the two acts and made no comment, merely looking satisfied, Kaufman confessed. He had stayed up nearly all night writing the second act over again from memory. It was, if anything, Connelly later recalled, even a shade better than the version which had been lost.

Tyler sped them up with a matter-of-fact pronouncement which reminded them forcibly that they didn't have a word of their third act written. "We begin rehearsals," he said, "on the twenty-seventh. And we open at the Lyceum in Rochester on February 13. You fellows better get busy."

Tyler had picked Rochester deliberately for the play's tryout because it was known as a tough theatre town, with a reputation for turning ugly if the local citizens didn't like a play. Many years later, talking about Boston as a tryout town, Kaufman said, "It's the strangest thing. The town seems to take it personally if you bring in a bad play, and you become an outcast. Even the pigeons snarl at you as you walk along the Common." The equivalent comment could have been made about Rochester in 1922. But Tyler realized that second plays, like second novels, are often failures—usually because authors are overconfident and don't work as hard the second time around, or because critics expect even more of them. And he wanted to make sure these authors worked at top level because of the realization that they'd have to please particularly demanding audiences.

Kaufman and Connelly were all too well aware of the town's reputation; Kaufman in particular was familiar with everything about the place because, in addition to marrying Beatrice there, he had occasionally returned with her to Rochester to visit her family. He described to Connelly a statement made by a Rochester resident to a theatrical manager: "Yes, I guess this is just about the coldest town in the country, so far as new plays are concerned. If a show will go here it will go anyplace. The town is famous for being a hard spot— even the actors say so. But mind you, it's a good theatre town for a good show; just ask anybody. They'll go to see it, all right, when it's something they want to see. But they're discriminating. By the way, how's *your* show doing? That so? Well, don't be discouraged—this is a tough town. I know people like it—everybody says so—but they're funny in this town. They'd rather go to the movies or something."

As Tyler had intended, Kaufman and Connelly began to work even more carefully. The third act came hard. Their original intention had been to have Leonard Beebe, disgusted by the big business antics all around him, abandon his ambitions and end the play content to remain a clerk. But the addition of the Hayes character changed that; the play had to be restructured so that it ended just after Elsie's speech, with Beebe achieving success and accepting it happily. The original conception, with everything pointing to a final spurning of the promotion, kept getting in the way as they worked, and they finally ended up with an uncertain third act which was an anthology of funny lines and little more. When they delivered the pages to Tyler, he tossed it right back to them. "This is no act," he said. "One man comes on and says his lines and goes off, then another man comes on and says his lines and goes off, then a third man comes on and says his lines and goes off, and so on. That's no good. If you want your play to work, your people have got to interact with each other, *affect* each other with what they say and do." It was sound, basic advice, and Kaufman and Connelly realized that they should not have lost sight of it. They went back to work, and next time delivered a third act which worked, an act in which all the lines and movements were meaningful and advanced the plot and characterizations.

Even then, Tyler remained tough, requiring many changes right up to the Rochester opening and all through the run there. His instinct was certain, even when he was forcing them to throw away something they particularly liked, such as the way the play ended during the Rochester run. This was something which later became a cliché, but which was very fresh then: a scene in which Elsie says to her husband, "Dear, we have more than enough money for two, but I've been wanting to tell you—" "Yes? Yes?" Beebe says eagerly, and she tells him that she thinks they need an automobile. "It's funny," Tyler said, "but it isn't working." And when the authors asked why it wasn't, he explained. "Because the audience likes Beebe and his wife and likes the fact that they're in love with each other—that's one of the most important things in the play. So they're not really amused when they think Elsie's talking about having a baby and find out she's only talking about buying a car. They're disappointed because they *want* her to have a baby." He was right; the scene was cut and the third act was much more effective.

Helen Hayes proved to be as much of an asset as Tyler had said she would be. Offstage, Kaufman and Connelly learned when they got to know her better, she was a kind of Mrs. Malaprop. Once, telling about a time she was in a taxi which hit another taxi, she said, "The drivers hurled the most horrible epitaphs at each other"; another time, told about a woman who'd married a man for his money, she said, "Don't you think she's horrid to be so mercantile?" And when she decided to give something away, she said, "Anybody who wants it is willing to it." (To which Kaufman replied, "That's very seldom of you, Helen.") But onstage she was as sure as if she were sixty-two rather than twenty-two.

There were other problems before the play opened in New York on February 20 at the Liberty Theatre. Tyler was notorious for his stinginess when it came to sets and costuming—Connelly once accused him of staging all of his plays with old flats and wings from *Uncle Tom's Cabin, Ben-Hur,* and the like—and had thrown quite a tantrum during rehearsals of *Dulcy* when he learned that Lynn Fontanne had bought all of her onstage dresses at the most expensive shop in town, Bouet Soeurs, and had sent him the bill. He later admitted grudgingly that her attractive appearance in the dresses had probably contributed to the success of the play, but he was penurious all over again with *To the Ladies.* Connelly finally had to go out to the five-and-ten and buy a pair of lampshades to replace a pair which looked as if they'd come from one of the earliest sets to be lighted by electricity. "With our compliments," he said, when he saw Tyler watching suspiciously as the stage manager put on the new shades. "Now it looks as if human beings live there." Tyler slapped himself emotionally on the forehead. "My God, another Clyde Fitch!" he said, naming another playwright who was then known as the most demanding man in the theatre.

But these remaining problems were all rather good-natured. The reviews in Rochester were very good, with Helen Hayes getting much the same kind of raves that Lynn Fontanne had gotten in *Dulcy,* and all of the participants except one moved along with the comfortable feeling that they probably had a hit. The exception was Kaufman, who was certain that the play would fail, even with the clearly remarkable Helen Hayes in the cast and with the nearly-as-excellent Otto Kruger playing Leonard Beebe. Kaufman, as usual, was merely overanxious. "This *To the Ladies,* the bright, bubbling comedy at the Liberty," said Alexander Woollcott, "is hereby recommended as an uncommonly refreshing entertainment," and *Variety* said, "Helen Hayes has not had very much luck in the allotment of roles that came her way.

But all that is gone, and with the opening of *To the Ladies* there is no further cause to worry on her part for a long time to come . . . *To the Ladies* looked like a knockout opening night. The ticket speculators seemed to concur in that opinion." All the other reviews were equally enthusiastic, and Helen Hayes played in *To the Ladies* for 128 performances on Broadway and then toured in it around the country for an additional two years.

There was also a successful production at the Embassy Theatre in London, and it was also filmed twice, in 1923 by Famous Players-Lasky, and again in 1934 by Paramount. The second production was released as *Elmer and Elsie*, with Leonard Beebe's name changed to Elmer Beebe to achieve that awful purpose, and with George Bancroft and Francis Fuller playing the Beebes.

Kaufman and Connelly now had their second hit, and this confirmed it: they were accomplishing it on their own talents and not because colleagues and well-wishers were lending a helping hand by giving good reviews, as some people hinted. The truth was that, as Tyler once complained bitterly, it was lucky for him that the *Times* had Woollcott as well as Kaufman in the dramatic department or the Kaufman-Connelly plays might never have been mentioned at all. Certainly *Dulcy* had received fewer mentions in the *Times* during its run than most other current plays, and it was even worse with *To the Ladies*. Tyler's press agent, aware that it was Kaufman's strict sense of morality which was keeping out most of his releases, finally went to see Kaufman when the playwright, wearing his newspaperman's hat, killed a story about Helen Hayes which the flack was certain that the *Times* would otherwise have run. "For God's sake, George," he said, "what do I have to do to get your own star's name in the paper?" "Shoot her," Kaufman said firmly.

Two things related to the play, however, did manage to achieve a great deal of publicity in other papers, if not in the *Times*. The first was a bit of type-casting of a kind which has since been done in other plays, but was then unique. There was a bootblack in the play, and Kaufman and Connelly insisted, to everybody's astonishment, on hiring an actual bootblack, Paolo Grosso, whom everybody called Garry as a diminutive for Garibaldi, and who had been shining shoes in the theatrical district for thirty years. Garry was paid $25 a week to shine the shoes of one of the characters in one scene, and was a big hit, but returned to shining shoes when the play left New York. His popularity grew even greater, however, as producer after producer called him in so that they could tell people that they'd always *said* they'd have an actor shining their shoes one day.

Kaufman and Connelly's other well-publicized action was the result of their solemn promise to each other never to grow bigheaded enough to rush onstage on an opening night and make a curtain speech; they had a treaty that, if either attempted this, the other had permission to fire a pistol at him from a box. But there was still a question of what to do when people started to shout, "Author! Author!" as they often did in those days, and Kaufman vetoed Connelly's suggestion that they go onstage followed by seven or eight actors representing their landlord, grocer, butcher, tailor, and the like, and say, "We owe it all to them." Their final resolution was simple. When the call came for the authors, long and strong, the curtain lifted and revealed a pair of clothing-store dummies seated onstage.

It was time for a failure, considering the law of averages, and Kaufman and Connelly got it later that year with *The 49ers*. The unexpected thing about it was that it mowed down a great many of the other bright new talents then emerging on the New York scene.

The genesis of *The 49ers*, in a sense, was a Russian importation called *Chauve Souris*, a variety show produced by Morris Gest, who was David Belasco's son-in-law and a sort of forerunner of Sol Hurok, specializing in bringing in cultural shows from other countries. *Chauve Souris* was at the 49th Street Theatre and had become one of the hottest tickets in town, and it occurred to Kaufman and Connelly that it might be fun to take over the theatre for one Sunday night, when the house was ordinarily dark, and put on a satirical counterpart of the Russian play, calling it—since the Russian play was pronounced something like "show soree"—*No Sirree*. Their notion was that their show would be mostly for the amusement of theatre people, most of whom worked in plays themselves Mondays through Saturdays and so didn't get to see many other shows, and would be written *and performed* mostly by reviewers and other riters—with assists by well-known performers in small and ordinarily unacceptable roles. As an example of the latter plan, they hought they might get someone like Jascha Heifetz to provide incidental music, and they did; he played offstage, unseen, and off-key.

No Sirree played the night of April 30, 1922, and featured Heywood Broun as master of ceremonies, since he resembled, at least in irth, the distinguished host of the Russian presentation, Balieff. roun, as always, was dressed in the same kind of rumpled suit which aused one acquaintance to compare him to an unmade bed and nother to describe him as a one-man slum. The show included a ketch in which Robert E. Sherwood—the gentlemanly, six-foot-even-inches-tall critic for Life who later wrote three Pulitzer Prize-inning plays, Idiot's Delight, Abe Lincoln in Illinois, and There hall Be No Night, and a Pulitzer Prize-winning book, Roosevelt and Iopkins—appeared surrounded by Tallulah Bankhead, Lenore Ulric, Ielen Hayes, and six other ingénues. There was also a sketch in vhich Frank Adams played an Irish cop, a parody of a Eugene)'Neill play in which Kaufman, Connelly, and Woollcott appeared as eamen, and a show-biz sketch in which Beatrice Kaufman, Dorothy 'arker, and most of the rest of the cast played bad-mannered first ighters.

The evening also marked the first appearance anywhere of the ketch which eventually became Robert Benchley's best-known iece of writing and acting, The Treasurer's Report. Benchley, a native of Worcester, Massachusetts, was born on September 15, 889, the son of a Worcester city official. He was an amiable man vho edited the Harvard Lampoon but otherwise had an unspectacu-ir career at the school, was then employed for a while as a social vorker, and afterwards came down to New York to work on Vanity 'air, the World, and Life. He was noted for the gentleness of his heatrical reviews for Life—and later on, when he went to work here, for The New Yorker—even when he hated a play. His most iolent comment on record, about a play he considered oversexy, was hat it was "too obstetric for my taste," and a typical comment bout a play he didn't like at all was that it was "one of those plays 1 which all the actors unfortunately enunciated very clearly." Bench-y's appearance was not even listed in the No Sirree program be-ause he'd promised to contribute a sketch but had failed to deliver

anything by the time the program went to press. But he finished hi
sketch in time to read it onstage that night, and it led to a contrac
to do the sketch nightly in *The Music Box Revue*, and eventually to hi
career in movie shorts and feature films.

All reviews of the show were written by performers, and arrange
ments were made for the reviews to appear in the columns normall
filled by people appearing in the show. The *Times* review, which re
placed Woollcott's regular piece on the morning following the show
was written by Laurette Taylor, the gifted comedienne in whos
company Lynn Fontanne had first come to America, and whose ow
career came to an abrupt halt later on when her husband died an
she turned recluse with only a bottle for company, resuming whe
she finally emerged and said calmly, "Well, that was the longest wak
in history, wasn't it?" Her review was unenthusiastic, but tongue-in
cheek. She used all of the stale phrases which had become standard i
theatrical criticism, saying that some people were competent an
some were adequate and some were their usual selves, mentioned–
again in the manner of some critics–that unfortunately she'd arrive
late and hadn't been able to stay until the end, and dismissed the outstanding Benchley monologue with a story of her own. "Rober
Benchley," she wrote, "came out and read, as far as I could understand it, the multiplication table, or perhaps it was a time table. It pu
me in mind of my checkbook the time I accused the bank of being
short some $1900, and after many arguments the President, whom
knew personally, went over my account and pointed out the fact that
I had added in the date."

Wilton Lackaye's review in the *World* was also carefully cool. He
also mentioned that he'd come late and left early, and said that the
best sketches were probably those he'd missed. But these were just
what theatrical people later came to call roasts, and it was clear that
the real reaction to the show was one of almost unbridled admiration.
This–unfortunately, as it turned out–gave Kaufman and Connelly
another idea. If their show had proved so successful on a one-time
basis, why not cook up a similar show for more permanent presentation?

The show they put together was *The 49ers*, given that name because it, too, was scheduled to appear on 49th Street, but at a much

smaller house, the Punch and Judy Theatre. It opened on November 7.

Kaufman and Connelly quickly found out that they'd failed to take into account three factors which later seemed so obvious that they couldn't understand why they hadn't thought of them. The first was that all authors had contributed their services free to *No Sirree*, but wanted fees for a professional revue like *The 49ers*, and their fees weren't low. This fact, plus the limited number of seats at the Punch and Judy, forced the management—George C. Tyler again, though a very reluctant participant this time—to charge a top of $5, very high for 1922. And even though the top was quickly dropped to $3 after the first week, it didn't help. The second mistake was Kaufman's and Connelly's assumption that the special, inside kind of humor which had appealed so much to *No Sirree*'s audience of theatre people, men and women who were in a relaxed, mellow mood and eager to be entertained themselves instead of doing the entertaining as they normally did, would appeal just as much to the ordinary theatregoer. And the third mistake was the choice of master of ceremonies. Instead of someone with the commanding presence of a Balieff or even the casual informality of Heywood Broun, Tyler made a rare misjudgment and insisted Kaufman and Connelly hire May Irwin, an old-time comedienne who he thought might punch up the show. As it turned out, the comedienne ignored the lines the playwrights had written for her, told a lot of old jokes everybody had heard a hundred times before, and was completely out of tune with the sophisticated revue being attempted. She was so bad that, in desperation, Tyler finally asked Kaufman and Connelly to appear onstage with her, pointing out that they'd both done bits in *No Sirree* and had been pretty funny. Kaufman refused immediately, but Connelly went on and appeared side by side with the old actress for a few performances. This didn't help, either.

The 49ers was loaded with talent. The writers of the sketches, in addition to Kaufman and Connelly, included Ring Lardner, Dorothy Parker, Sherwood, Benchley, Broun, Montague Glass, Howard Dietz, Morrie Ryskind, and others. Howard Lindsay directed the show and also appeared in it, and the cast also included Roland Young, Sidney Toler, Beryl Mercer, and a lot of other good people. But the wild, offbeat comedy either bored people or bewildered them. Even a sophisticate like Frank Crowninshield, the publisher of *Vanity Fair*, watched one actor dressed as Cardinal Richelieu sit onstage and play solitaire without ever uttering a word, and two other actors dressed as Grant and Lee appear suddenly and exchange swords, and said helplessly to his companion, "Maybe I'm missing the point, but is it all supposed to be taking place in an insane asylum?" The play closed after two weeks of feeble business. About $11,000 a week was needed to break even, but neither week came within half that figure.

8. THE CONTINUED GROWTH

KAUFMAN AND CONNELLY were not broken-hearted about the closing. Kaufman, in fact, looked almost relieved, causing Connelly to ask him crossly if he was pleased now that one of his dire predictions had finally come true. "Well," Kaufman said, "you've got to admit we've made a lot of people happy." He was referring to a cynical comment he had made to Connelly and a group of other people at a theatrical party not long before. "How many people," Kaufman had said, "even among your best friends, really hope for your success on opening night? A failure is somehow so much more satisfying all around." And Connelly, reminded of this, and never one to remain irritated for long anyway, smiled and agreed.

But the real reason for their fortitude was that they had put together *No Sirree* and *The 49ers* almost in their spare time. They were also busy on three major new projects, two plays and a musical, all of which ended up doing them good in one way or another.

The first play was *Merton of the Movies*, which became an even bigger success than *Dulcy* and *To the Ladies*. The second was *The Deep Tangled Wildwood*, a near-miss which closed quickly but drew generally favorable reviews and further enhanced their growing reputations. And the musical was *Helen of Troy, New York*, which was more failure than success; it ran a solid 181 performances but ended up losing money because it was such an expensive production and had such a large cast. But it, too, was beneficial to their careers. Few people knew about *Miss Moonshine* because it was then still unproduced, and *Helen of Troy, New York* showed critics, producers, and the general public for the first time that Kaufman and Connelly were capable of working in areas of the theatre other than straight, small-canvas comedies.

It was Connelly who first realized that *Merton of the Movies*, which started out as a comic novel, would make a good play; he read it while it was running serially in *The Saturday Evening Post* and mentioned the possibility to Kaufman and Tyler. Connelly had long considered the magazine a good source for play material. His first attempt to become a playwright, in fact, when he was seventeen, had been connected with a *Post* story. The story was *Putting on the Screws* by Gouverneur Morris, a sentimental vignette about an old actress who is both wealthy and in good health, but pretends that she's ill and broke in order to test the true feelings of her relatives. Connelly thought the story would make a good play, and wrote Morris, asking for the dramatic rights, but Morris, obviously sensing Connelly's youth and inexperience, replied with a good-natured but businesslike letter expressing regret that the rights were already gone.

The attempt to acquire the stage rights to *Merton of the Movies* was more successful. The author of the novel was the popular humorist, Harry Leon Wilson, and Tyler knew him well; he had produced a play on which Wilson had collaborated with Booth Tarkington, *The Man from Home*. Tyler got in touch with Wilson at his home in Monterey, California, and had the rights sewed up before the serial had finished running in the *Post*.

The story was a simple one: it was about Merton Gill, a grocery clerk who endures his dull life by dreaming about becoming a great movie star, eventually gets to Hollywood and in pictures but is a terrible actor and a dismal failure, ending up as a success only when someone gets the bright idea of releasing his serious film as a comedy. Kaufman and Connelly wrote the dramatization quickly, and Hugh Ford was brought in as director. Ford was a soft-spoken, absent-minded man who once admitted to an interviewer that he didn't know where he lived, because he and his wife had moved that morning and he'd failed to write down the address, so he was hanging around the Lambs Club in the hope that his wife would call him there. Another time, he was returning from a business trip to Hollywood and got on the train with only ten cents in his pocket, arriving in New York so wild with hunger that he rushed to the Lambs Club, where he had credit, and ordered three dinners served simultaneously. But he had directed *The Squaw Man* and *The White Sister* and a lot of other hits, and was considered by many to be the best director in the business, and Tyler offered him 50 per cent of the play to come in. The generous offer proved worth it. Ford suggested Glenn Hunter, a gentle, wistful-looking young actor, for the difficult part of Merton Gill, and Hunter played the role with a sensitivity which, as hoped for, kept audiences laughing at him but, at the same time, rooting for him. Ford's touch was equally sure with the rest of his casting and direction, putting strong people in all the other roles and bringing out all the nuances of the Kaufman-Connelly script. As always, the authors had included biting satire about their subject —the burgeoning movie industry this time—along with their story-line.

Merton of the Movies rehearsed and then opened for tryouts at a theatre in Brooklyn; in interesting contrast with the present day, with newspapers constantly running advance tips about plays headed for Broadway from places as distant as London and Paris, not a single critic took the subway ride across the river to cover it. But when the play had its official opening at the Cort Theatre on Monday, November 13, the critics were all present, and they all raved. John Corbin, a *Times* second-stringer, for example, called the play "a credit to all concerned, not excepting the audiences that catch every shift and shading in its satire of the silver screen and unlock their hearts to the very human and touching story it unfolds." Corbin, in addition to being a writer of rather purple prose, was also a bigot who later turned on Kaufman and wrote an anti-Semitic piece, *Drama and the Jew*, for *Scribner's Magazine*, which called Jews names like "Yids" and accused Kaufman and other Jewish writers and actors of taking over the American theatre and ruining it by making it, as the magazine's blurb summarized it, "corrosive, vitriolic, and animated by the spirit of a separate minority." But his review of *Merton of the Movies* stated the majority opinion, and even the generally tough *Theatre Magazine* called the play "an engaging, entertaining, and otherwise excellent comedy."

The play ran 248 performances, was picked by Mantle for *The Best Plays of 1922–23*, and was then made into a film by a director as highly regarded in the movie industry as Ford was on Broadway, James Cruze, who had leaped to prominence with his direction of *The Covered Wagon* and another film about the movie business, *Hollywood*. Cruze hired Hunter to play the role again in the picture, and, following the film's release by Famous Players-Lasky, the unsigned review in the *Times* was even more enthusiastic than the paper's review of the play. It called the film "a brilliant pictorial effort which draws laughter with a lump in one's throat and makes one smile through tears," added, "It is only too rare that one sees a celluloid gem like this one," and concluded, "It is such a good picture that we intend seeing it again at the first opportunity we have." The film was remade with equal success by Paramount-Publix in 1932, under the title of *Make Me a Star*, with Stuart Erwin playing the lead, and made for a third time less successfully under its original title—because Red Skelton played Merton in this version and played it too broadly—by M-G-M in 1947.

To top it all off, even Harry Leon Wilson, the author of the work that producers call, casually, "the underlying property," was satisfied. Tyler found this out when he sent a copy of the playscript to Wilson for his autograph, doing it nervously and to test the water because he knew that authors of books and stories are often bitter about the plays or movies adapted from their material. (The author of a book or story on which a play or film is based is, of course, compensated for this use, and the compensation, depending on his reputation and the success of his published work, can range from interesting to immense. In the case of a film, sometimes the rights are bought for as little as a thousand dollars, and there have been a few instances in which the price paid for film rights to a book has been as much as a million dollars. And on important properties, the author sometimes also receives a percentage of the net—meaning a percentage of the film's earnings after deduction of costs and expenses; there have also been a few instances in which authors have received a percentage of the gross—meaning a piece of *every* dollar the film brings in. In the case of published works converted into plays, the original author generally receives a very modest advance, or down payment, of no more than a few thousand dollars, but he then goes on to receive a percentage—anywhere from one per cent up—of the weekly box-office gross of all companies of the play. And if the play is a hit and grosses many thousands of dollars weekly for years, it can amount to a fortune. All this, naturally, enriches the author, but he often still winces as he observes what has been done to his creation. It's a case of singing as the money comes in but crying at the realization of what's bringing it in.)

Harry Leon Wilson, however, returned the signed script at once and said in an accompanying note, "The copy of *Merton* has been duly enhanced with my name and returned today, though I felt it to be a mere formality. True, I wrote the book, but you people did the play. I merely bought a cheap lot and sold out at an enormous profit after the town grew—me sitting around playing checkers while it was growing."

Ford was also signed to direct *The Deep Tangled Wildwood*, but had little to do with the play's quick demise. The real problem, many critics said, was that the play, underneath its humor, was basically a love story, and cried out for added romance and love scenes. Kaufman, naturally, wouldn't touch that with a mile-long pole, and Connelly was just being asked too much to be expected to provide that essential element all by himself.

Tyler later developed an additional theory for the failure of the play. The comedy was about a successful Broadway playwright who grows bored with the brittle urbanity of the New York scene and returns to his home town, Millersville, where the people are real and honest, only to discover that civilization has penetrated the hinterlands, too, and the people there are drinking and wearing sophisticated clothes and engaging in artificial social conversation like everywhere else. As it turns out, the only really honest person he meets is a girl who is also escaping from New York, and the play ends with the couple marrying and agreeing to spend their honeymoon in the Broadway area. Tyler theorized that the play offended a large portion of theatre audiences—those people from the hinterlands who attended plays when the shows were on tour, and, for that matter, made up a substantial percentage of Broadway audiences by attending plays in New York while on vacation or business trips.

He had first begun to wonder about all this, Tyler said, when he had produced the Tarkington-Wilson play, *The Man from Home*, which was about a small-town American's travels abroad. "I'd rather," the character said at one point, "have our state insane asylum than the worst ruined ruin in Europe." It was a line which was intended to emphasize the lead's narrow chauvinism and provincialism, but in some places, Tyler noticed, people didn't laugh at the line as they were supposed to do; they looked upon the character's homespun simplemindedness as Lincolnesque and applauded the line as patriotic. Tyler felt that there was sometimes the same sort of reaction, and even more strongly and frequently, to the Kaufman-Connelly plays: too many people missed the satire entirely and were bored, taking things like the banquet scene in *To the Ladies* seriously because they often attended similar banquets themselves and took those seriously, or caught the satire and were angered because they didn't enjoy scornful amusement directed at sacred institutions. And Tyler felt that perhaps *The Deep Tangled Wildwood* represented the problem at its worst: people either couldn't see what was so funny or so surprising about the fact that small towns were just like big towns, or were offended because they realized that Kaufman and Connelly weren't simply saying that small towns were just like big towns. They were saying that small towns were just as bad as big towns.

There was probably a good, legitimate point in Tyler's theory, particularly when considered from the short-range point of view; no one could dispute box-office reports which showed that touring Kaufman-Connelly plays sometimes did poorly in some areas where less subtle comedies did well. But the thing Tyler did not realize was that, legitimate point or not, Kaufman and Connelly were not willing to make it a major consideration, a guideline for their present and future work. For one thing, they really believed the conclusion they were presenting in *The Deep Tangled Wildwood:* that the country was no longer, or at least would soon no longer be, a place divided into areas with city slickers and areas with gape-mouthed rubes, but was changing rapidly and becoming a country where small-town people would soon be as sophisticated and aware as people in the metropolitan regions. And even more important, the truth was that Kaufman and Connelly didn't give a damn about the fact that there would always be people who would not like or understand their brand of humor; they just weren't going to write down to catch the moron audience.

The other theory, the critics' suspicion that *The Deep Tangled Wildwood* failed because it was a love story with insufficient love in it, made far more sense to them. They weren't prepared to abandon something integral to their personalities and character, like subtlety in humor, just for the sake of picking up the boob vote, but they *were* prepared to understand a basic fact of play construction, the fact that a play in which an essential ingredient is lacking is likely to fail no matter how strong or good the play's other elements may be. This didn't, of course, necessarily mean that they determined then and there to master every kind of play technique; Kaufman's subconscious response to the problem with *The Deep Tangled Wildwood*, in fact, was very probably that, if certain kinds of plays demanded emotional love scenes, he had better never again write those kinds of plays.

Tyler never really understood Kaufman's and Connelly's point of view about *his* theory. It was a viewpoint which kept Kaufman writing at his own high level because he was certain that there were enough people around to enjoy it and make it as profitable as writing at a lower level, a viewpoint which enabled Connelly to be enough his own man to listen carefully to friends' warnings that many people would be offended by the fact that God and the angels in *The Green Pastures* were black—and then calmly ignore the warnings. Some years later, long after Tyler's association with the two playwrights had ended, he pointed out triumphantly in his autobiography that Kaufman had finally accepted his reach-for-the-basement philosophy; Tyler had gone to see *The Band Wagon* and noted that the humor was broad and obvious, and Kaufman, he said, had admitted to him, "I can't help it. They won't get it any other way." Tyler just didn't realize that this was a temporary aberration, a manifestation of Kaufman's ever-present insecurity and uncertainty, a brief surrender which would soon be abandoned forever; Kaufman's next musical was the subtle and brilliant *Of Thee I Sing*. And it was this dichotomy of basic intention, this bifurcation of the right way to go, at the time of *The Deep Tangled Wildwood*, which eventually led to the end of the relationship between the producer and the writers.

Tyler's dismay over Kaufman's and Connelly's intellectualism had not, of course, prevented him from producing the play; he merely expressed the hope that there would be enough people around to understand it and moved ahead. The play, in fact, had been put into the works far ahead of *The 49ers* and *Merton of the Movies;* it didn't actually open in New York until late in 1923, on Monday, November 5, but Frank Adams was plugging it in his column as early as May 30, 1922, saying he'd seen the play in tryout in Stamford, Connecticut, and had loved it.

He may well have been one of the very few who felt that way, because the play was a headache from the start, going through scores of changes before Tyler, Ford, and the two authors decided it was probably, or at least possibly, ready for Broadway. Connelly later speculated that the constant changes might have been one of the reasons for the failure of the play; he and Kaufman had become so nervous over the realization that they'd achieved the near-impossible, with two hits out of two in *Dulcy* and *To the Ladies,* that they decided to play it safe on the third one, listening to and following the advice of everyone associated with the play in every capacity, everyone who had any notion at all on where the play was going right or wrong. Even the title became the subject of conference after conference; the play was called *Little Old Millersville, West of*

Pittsburgh, and *The Old Home Town* before the producer, director, and authors settled on the not-especially-inspired final title. And all that accomplished was to cancel out all advance plugs like the one in Adams's column: the play was called *West of Pittsburgh* when he mentioned it, and people who made a note didn't necessarily connect it with the subsequent *The Deep Tangled Wildwood.*

But whether the problem was Connelly's too-many-cooks theory, or Tyler's theory of too much sophistication and subtlety, or the fact that the play didn't pull together because of the missing love scenes, the hard work didn't really matter in the end. The Frazee Theatre, in which the play finally opened in New York, was dark again after only sixteen performances, despite the presence of the very popular Jimmy Gleason in the lead, and despite the fact that the critics expressed considerable admiration for the authors' humor even if they didn't admire the lack of romance in their souls. And not a single movie company came forward with an offer to extend the play's life on celluloid.

The play might have been forgotten permanently and totally except for two peripheral events. Neither event put money in the playwrights' pockets, but, Kaufman later told a friend philosophically, at least it reminded a *few* people that there had once been a play called *The Deep Tangled Wildwood.* The first was that Irving Berlin borrowed the title and used it in one of his songs, *Lazy;* the line goes, "I wanna peep through the deep tangled wildwood, counting sheep till I sleep like a child would." The second was that the show's quick death caused an actor named Denman Malley, who had a small part in the play, to employ a unique device to get himself new work. Malley's stunt created great amusement around Broadway, got him more jobs than he could handle, and is still remembered with smiles by many old-timers in the business. He accomplished all this by sending a simple engraved card to every producer and agent in New York.

The card read:

MRS. DENMAN MALLEY
ANNOUNCES
THE IDLENESS OF HER HUSBAND
DENMAN MALLEY

The Deep Tangled Wildwood was the last Kaufman-Connelly play produced by George C. Tyler. The end of the relationship did not spell the end of activity for Tyler any more than it did for the two authors: he went on to produce such notable plays as *The Constant Nymph* in 1926, *The Plough and the Stars* in 1927, *Becky Sharp* in 1930, and *The Admirable Crichton* in 1931. Nor did it mean the end of his friendship with Kaufman, which turned out to be a fortunate thing for the producer. Tyler was as free with his money away from business as he was tight with it in his productions; he had been a pioneer "automobilist," the first man to cross the Balkans in a car and one of the first to attempt to drive across the Sahara Desert, he had an irresistible compulsion to buy every beautiful car which came under his gaze, and he also spent money recklessly on all other available luxuries. The result was that, when his career began to limp to a halt in the middle 1930s, Tyler was stunned to find himself suddenly almost destitute, almost completely without funds. It was then that Kaufman got his idea of sending Tyler a regular check, and then that he wrote quietly to George Arliss, Mrs. August Belmont, Tarkington, and others to do the same.

It was a painful task for Kaufman; he was never one to ask people for favors, even favors for someone else. It was particularly painful in this instance, because there was resistance. Kaufman asked Arliss to send $300 a year, and Arliss sent the first check, but complained, "I need not say I am in full sympathy with your suggestion, but I cannot pledge myself to a regular allowance. I have more commitments of this kind already than I can afford. You see, I get it coming and going—England and the U.S." And Eleanor Belmont responded querulously that she'd already sent Tyler $250 on her own, adding, "This year, it is impossible for me to do anything more. But certainly I want to be counted among those who will continue to help—as far as my steadily diminishing income will permit." But Kaufman persisted, and Tyler was able to live in relative comfort until his death, at the age of seventy-eight, on March 16, 1946.

The break in the ranks had actually begun while *The Deep Tangled Wildwood* was still being revised again and again. The big, basic differences in attitude and approach, on the compromises a writer had to make to satisfy his public, had been visible almost

from the start of the relationship between Tyler and the two playwrights, and the situation became exacerbated severely, around the
end of 1922, as Tyler began to worry more and more loudly about
the new play. At that point, with *The 49ers* and *Merton* already produced and *The Deep Tangled Wildwood* still not ready to go, Kaufman and Connelly were ripe for an additional association. They
seized the opportunity when a man named Rufus LeMaire approached
them and asked if they'd be interested in writing a musical for him.

The title was all that LeMaire had at that point. Kaufman and
Connelly thought the title, *Helen of Troy, New York*, was corny,
and they weren't wild about LeMaire, either. LeMaire had produced
one earlier hit, *Broadway Brevities*, and that was pretty much the
extent of his producing experience; he functioned most of the time
as an agent. He was a good one—he handled business affairs for
Arliss, among other people—but he was also a rabid yet inexpert
crapshooter and had a reputation for being frequently broke. But he
also represented a chance for Kaufman and Connelly to move off in
another direction without giving pain or embarrassment to Tyler.
Tyler did not ordinarily produce musicals, and LeMaire, after all,
had approached them, not the other way around. In addition, Le-
Maire already had two good people doing the music and lyrics,
Harry Ruby and Bert Kalmar. They agreed to do the book.

Kaufman and Connelly soon found out that the things they'd
heard about LeMaire's finances were all true. Connelly handled the
original negotiations because Kaufman was busy at the *Times* that
day, and he demanded an advance of $3500; LeMaire looked stunned
but managed to come up with a down payment of $1000, stunning
Connelly in turn by handing him a thousand-dollar bill instead of a
check. Kaufman and Connelly learned afterward that the first investors in the play were bootleggers, which explained it. Bootleggers
dealt strictly in cash. The remaining money, however, was much
slower in coming; LeMaire kept telling the authors that it was on its
way, that he was doing something about it, but it never seemed to
arrive.

The thing he was doing was trying to promote two additional
bootleggers and a more successful gambler than himself, Nick the
Greek, into putting a lot of money into the play. It was a desperate

time for LeMaire: in addition to the money he owed Kaufman and Connelly, he also owed Kalmar and Ruby another thousand dollars which he didn't have, and he was actually so broke that he'd just been locked out of his office. But he was certain things would improve soon. The bootleggers had promised him $50,000 as soon as their next shipment came in and they received payment, and Nick the Greek had also promised to make a big investment soon.

LeMaire felt that all he needed was time. He went to a close friend, George Jessel, then an up-and-coming young stage and night-club comedian, and asked Jessel to help him pin things down by sending a fake telegram agreeing to invest in the show and signing it with a distinguished-looking name. Jessel sent the telegram, and it worked; the bootleggers and the gambler confirmed their promise to invest. A few days later, however, LeMaire was sunk even more deeply in despair. Nick the Greek had had a terrible run of luck and was now broke himself, and the bootleggers' shipment had been hijacked.

LeMaire finally returned to Jessel and began to tell him fervently how good a play he had, extolling the virtues of Kaufman, Connelly, Ruby, Kalmar, and the musical's catchy title. He also showed Jessel a telegram he'd just received, an enthusiastic promise to invest. When he finished talking, Jessel gave him $10,000, his total savings, and it was only later, after the oratory had worn off, that Jessel realized that the telegram had been worded in a manner suspiciously similar to the one he himself had sent.

The $10,000 was used mostly to hire a lot of actors and chorus girls and give them salary advances, and LeMaire was soon broke again. He began to beg Jessel to go around and try to get investments from rich people he knew. Jessel went to see a lot of manufacturers in the garment district, but it didn't work; the country was in a recession, and the manufacturers weren't feeling very rich. Jessel gave the bad news to LeMaire, and the two men went for a glum breakfast the next morning at the Automat, the best they could afford.

They talked sorrowfully for a while, and were about to abandon the whole project when Jessel picked up a discarded copy of the *Times* and saw an item which he pointed out to LeMaire. LeMaire became red-faced with excitement. The item said that Wilmer and

Vincent, who owned a lot of theatres through Pennsylvania, were interested in producing plays on Broadway, especially dramas.

"Go see them," LeMaire pleaded. "You're a well-known guy. You'll impress them!"

Jessel was dubious. "How can I talk experienced theatre men like them into putting up money?" he asked. "Our musical's still in the early stages. And anyway, it says they're looking for dramas."

"Try anyway," LeMaire said. "Try and switch them."

Jessel finally agreed to see Wilmer and Vincent, but he remained doubtful; he decided to go only because he had an ulterior motive. He had recently seen a play at a little theatre in Greenwich Village, a powerful drama called *Dry Rot*, and knew he could acquire the rights cheaply. It seemed to him that that play could make a lot of money on Broadway and might well interest the Pennsylvania theatre owners.

His judgment was accurate; the play was subsequently brought to Broadway by Earl Carroll, who changed its title to *White Cargo*, and it grossed more than a million dollars. But when Jessel described the drama to Wilmer and Vincent, never even mentioning *Helen of Troy, New York*, the showmen found the description unappealing. Disappointed, Jessel got up and was turning to leave when Wilmer asked casually, "What's around with music in it?"

Jessel turned back and began to talk fast. The following morning, he was handed Wilmer and Vincent's check for $100,000.

That same night, LeMaire and Jessel received another unexpected break. LeMaire's office had been reopened, and a big man with a strong Southern accent came in and asked for directions. He explained that he was the head of a group which had just built a beautiful new theatre in Fairmont, West Virginia, and he wanted to find the Shubert office to arrange for a good new play to try out there. At the end of his explanation, he suddenly recognized Jessel, whom he had seen not long before doing his act at the Winter Garden, and greeted him with cries of admiration. Jessel and Le-Maire returned the enthusiastic greeting and told the man there was no necessity to go over to the Shubert office. Before the West Virginian left, he had signed an agreement to pay the show's

expenses to come down to Fairmont, and had guaranteed a profit o
$15,000, paying half that amount on the spot.

The Fairmont Theatre's program for the show glows with the loca
civic pride which had caused the building of the playhouse. Th
program devotes a total of about three pages to facts concernin
Helen of Troy, New York, and about five to the conception, build
ing, and facilities of the theatre. The theatre had been conceive
because Fairmont's Chamber of Commerce had noticed that, in ever
report made available to them by corporations considering buildin
plants in their area, there had been significant mention made of th
fact that Fairmont lacked sufficient amusement facilities. A committe
had been formed in June 1920 to consider the building of a theatre
had been stalled for a while by poor business conditions, and actua
construction had started in June 1922. The theatre, which wa
planned for use both as a legitimate theatre and a movie house, con
tained 800 seats in the orchestra and 500 in the balcony, nine dressin
rooms, three property rooms, and such modern conveniences as ic
water in every drinking fountain, a cooling device which brought i
fresh air and made the theatre fifteen degrees cooler than outside
and what the program called "retiring rooms for both sexes" on a
floors.

Kaufman and Jessel sat opposite each other on the train comin
down to Fairmont for the musical's out-of-town opening on June 4
1923; Connelly and others were in other cars. This was happen
stance because the two men were not very friendly at this point
Jessel felt, as some critics did five months later about *The Dee
Tangled Wildwood*, that the musical was essentially a love stor
lacking in love. The book was about a secretary who is fired by he
boss because the boss's son falls in love with her, but she gets the boy
anyway when she builds a successful rival factory and the two firm
merge. Jessel considered it disappointing and unsatisfying becaus
the lovers never once clinched throughout the entire play. He also, a
Tyler had begun to feel about the Kaufman-Connelly plays in gen
eral, feared that much of the humor was too cerebral and elevate
for the average audience. He had expressed these views in emphati
terms to Kaufman, who peered silently at him for a moment over hi
glasses and thereafter ignored him. The silence continued on th
train ride, with both men looking out of the window and not at eac

other, until Jessel, who was feeling extremely uncomfortable about it all, happened to see a decrepit little shack on the road. The only sign of life at the shack was a pair of ladies' drawers, flaming red, hanging on a clothesline. Jessel nudged Kaufman. "Let's get off the train," he said, "and go into that shack and forget." The suggestion broke Kaufman up. The two men began to talk, and they remained friends for the rest of Kaufman's life.

Opening night was not an unqualified success, not precisely the kind of theatre magic which the town fathers had hoped would attract industry to Fairmont. The theatre was not wholly finished despite the fact that construction had begun a year before, and not all the electrical work was complete. A sudden rainstorm knocked out the lights a few minutes after the beginning of the first act, making it necessary to light the stage for a while with flashlights and candles, and the lights went on and off three more times during the act. Then trouble developed with the principal comedian, Tom Lewis, who was a man of about seventy and was having trouble remembering his lines. At one point, he was supposed to say, "Jennings is a thief"; instead, he looked confused for a moment and then said, "Jessel is a thief," a line which would have fractured a New York audience but merely baffled the people in Fairmont. Later, Lewis created an even more awful incident. Toward the end of the first act, Lewis forgot his lines completely and floundered in total silence for three long, dragging minutes, never hearing the prompter shrieking his next line to him. Finally, just for the sake of saying something—anything—Lewis launched into an old vaudeville monologue he had done for years before moving into the legitimate theatre. The monologue had nothing whatever to do with the play, and it lasted for twenty minutes.

But the main problem was that Jessel had been right about the oversophistication of the lines, at least for the Fairmont audience. The audience was a particularly unhip one, presumably because most of them had never before seen a play or even a movie. This innocence was perceptible right from the start because the orchestra had forgotten to have an overture arranged and had to fake choruses of *April Showers* and *Kiss Me Again*, and the audience applauded enthusiastically, apparently under the impression that the songs were brand-new. LeMaire and Jessel were also sure that the play would run long, and Jessel even made a little opening speech, promising the audience pajamas and toothbrushes if the action onstage continued until morning. But this was because they were counting in the usual laughtime, and there were virtually no laughs. Suddenly and unexpectedly, the play was all over at 10:30, a full forty-five minutes short even with Lewis's unplanned vaudeville routine. And Kaufman and Connelly, in one of the few such instances in modern theatrical history, found themselves adding material for the Fairmont run instead of cutting.

They were glad to get out when the run was over, and the musical went on to do some further shaking down at the Broad Street Theatre in Newark, New Jersey. The play was in much better shape when it opened in New York at the Selwyn Theatre on Tuesday, June 19. The critics were generally kind: the *Herald* called it "the perfect musical comedy," the *Telegram* called it a gem, the *American* said, "Don't miss it," and Percy Hammond said enthusiastically in the *Tribune*, "It seems improbable that I shall ever again be asked if there exists in New York any musical plays in which bare legs and barer jokes do not abound." The play settled in for a long run, staying at the Selwyn until the fall, moving to the Times Square Theatre for a while, and then touring in Boston, Allentown, Pennsylvania, and other places.

As always, Kaufman had continued rewriting and touching up right to the last minute, continuing long after Connelly had pronounced himself satisfied and stopped. Even a gag line in the program kept being changed. In the Fairmont program, the line read, "Owing to the unimportance of the prologue, latecomers will positively be seated at all times." By the time the play reached Newark, the line read, "Owing to the utter unimportance of the 1st Act, latecomers will positively be seated at all times." And in New York, the final version read, "Owing to the utter unimportance of the plot, latecomers will positively be seated at all times during the play." Minor touches, but the sort of thing which helped turn a disaster into a hit.

Ironically, Wilmer and Vincent did not make any money on the play, nor did Jessel; the huge cast of sixty ate up profits and the show ended in the red. But Kaufman and Connelly did all right, with their royalties coming right off the top, and Kaufman also later used his experiences with the musical to write a hit play about the frenzied finances of the theatre, *The Butter and Egg Man*. Rufus LeMaire did all right, too. He sold out his interest just after the show opened and used the money to move to the West Coast, where he became a top executive at Universal.

Helen of Troy, New York also brought Kaufman and Connelly, in addition to their first credit for a musical, and their first experience with a producer other than Tyler, another thing which was brand-new to them: a lawsuit which accused them of plagiarism. The lawsuit was so specious that Connelly regarded it with disdain, but the experience created alarm and even horror in Kaufman. Lawsuits became, in time, the item which headed his list of those aspects of life he hated most, surpassing even waiters, taxi drivers, and people who insisted on shaking hands.

Kaufman and Connelly had had an earlier brush with the law, but that was different because it was remote; and, anyway, they were on the other side of the fence in that one. The Kaufman-Connelly plays had begun to have occasional foreign productions, with *To the Ladies* achieving a good run at the Embassy Theatre in London and *Merton* doing even better at the Shaftesbury in the same city, and *Merton* had also had a French production. It was André Rivollet, the producer of the French version, who introduced the playwrights to the world of the litigious; he claimed that a Marcel Pagnol play, *Le Schpountz*, was a direct steal from *Merton*, similar in plot and even in some of the dialogue, and threatened a suit. Pagnol retorted hotly that that was libelous nonsense, that his play was about three real people easily recognizable in French film circles, and threatened a countersuit. Like many Gallic feuds, there was considerable passion but apparently not much substance, and the controversy eventually petered out. There is no record of whether or not Pagnol's defense caused the three people involved to sue him for invasion of privacy.

The suit on *Helen of Troy, New York* was far more involving for Kaufman and Connelly: they, along with LeMaire and others, were suddenly slapped with a Supreme Court action by a woman named Elaine Sterne Carrington, who alleged that the play had been stolen from her. She had, she said, three specific reasons for her allegation. The first was that the plot of her play somewhat resembled the plot of

the Kaufman-Connelly musical. The second was that she had give
her play to an agent, Julia Chandler, whose office was in the Empir
Theatre Building, and she swore that, by chance, she had entered th
building shortly afterward and seen Kaufman coming out with he
play under his arm. She recognized it, she said, by the color of th
binder. And, she concluded triumphantly, her final point was th
most damning of all. Her play had the *very same title, Helen of Troy
New York*.

The suit was another irony connected with the play, because Kauf
man and Connelly had, of course, accepted the title glumly, anc
though they were reasonably fond of some of their individual line
and comedy bits, they were never really enthusiastic about thei
over-all script. *Variety*, in fact, had commented on this in its initia
report on the play, saying, "*Helen of Troy, New York* is a debutting
musical comedy for two firms, LeMaire & Jessel, its producers, an
Kaufman & Connelly, its writers. Both went to it with trepidation
The producers because they liked the book but needed a bankroll fo
its production, and the writers because they didn't like their ow
book." But the Carrington claims had to be answered, and the play
wrights' lawyers went to work.

The lawyers got the stuff about Kaufman and the script under hi
arm thrown out immediately; Kaufman and Connelly said bluntl
that they had never heard of Elaine Sterne Carrington or her pla
before the lawsuit, and the judge agreed that the story about th
chance encounter and the binder color was not evidence. The clair
of similarities was also set aside; the two plays proved to be not ver
similar at all, and the Court apparently agreed with Kaufman's sar
donic comment, "If we were going to steal, we'd have stolen some
thing a lot better." That left only the fact that the two plays ha
the same title, and the lawyers really tore that one to pieces.

They did some research, and found, in addition to the Kaufman
Connelly and Carrington plays, seven other literary works with th
same title. One of these was by Robert Benchley's older brother,
graduate of West Point who had written and produced a schoo
play with that title at the military institute; two of these were i
The Saturday Evening Post, which repeated itself, forgetfully, b
running two different stories under that same name. Elaine Stern

Carrington's suit was thrown out, and she went on to become a leading writer of radio and television soap operas, in which field, of course, fantasies are more appreciated.

The Carrington suit was the first of a long series of similar actions throughout Kaufman's lifetime. He and his collaborators were sued so often—at least one lawsuit per success, or so it seemed—that he once talked wistfully about a favorite daydream. He would like, he said, to give a big dinner for all of the people who had sued him, a really lavish affair with white wine for the fish and red wine for the meat and all the rest. In that way, he said, he would lull his guests into thinking he had forgiven and forgotten. But then, after dinner, he would approach each one in turn and ask each man or woman a simple question which he hoped would not only ruin the evening for them, but their sleep and their self-esteem for many months afterward as well. "You wrote *The Man Who Came to Dinner*," he'd say to the man who had sued him on that play. "What have you written since?" "You wrote *You Can't Take It with You*," he'd say to the woman who had sued him on that play. "What have *you* written since?" He never gave the dinner, but he thought about it a lot.

It sometimes seemed to Kaufman that he was always winning one lawsuit just in time to find himself involved in another. Most of them were so wildly specious that the judges were often irritated; they felt the courts were being clogged senselessly. Federal Judge John C. Knox, in dismissing an action brought by a woman named Virginia Gordon on *You Can't Take It with You*, which she said was stolen from her own unproduced play, *Rash Moment*, said coldly, "The absence of copying is so obvious that I don't consider an argument in support of my conclusions to be necessary," and assessed her with costs plus $500 in counsel's fees. The same was the situation on a suit brought by Vincent McConnor, a radio writer who had co-authored a play called *Sticks and Stones*, on *The Man Who Came to Dinner*. McConnor's claim was based almost solely on the fact that his play, too, dealt with a character similar to Alexander Woollcott, and the two other collaborators on the play, James and John Monks, refused to have anything to do with the action. The trial memorandum for the case written by the defendants' lawyer, Howard E. Reinheimer, was almost contemptuous in its language. "Neither Hart nor

Kaufman copied so much as a punctuation mark from *Sticks and Stones*," Reinheimer wrote. "The two plays are as foreign to each other as *Gone With the Wind* and *David Copperfield*." The judge agreed and angrily dismissed McConnor's suit.

But the suits went on and on, as long as Kaufman lived. He and Hart were once even sued by the Chock Full O' Nuts Company. In *The Fabulous Invalid*, there was a line which mourned the decline of the New Amsterdam Theatre, mentioning sadly that 42nd Street, once deluxe, now housed a flea circus, an Army and Navy store, and a Chock Full O' Nuts coffee shop. The coffee company brought suit, claiming the reference was derogatory and made it difficult for them to rent space for future shops. Kaufman explained in court that he and Hart functioned as satirists and that the line was fair comment. "Have you ever held anyone else up to ridicule?" the judge asked. "Yes," said Kaufman, thinking of *Of Thee I Sing* and *Let 'Em Eat Cake*, "the President of the United States, the Vice-President, and the Supreme Court." The judge turned to Hart. "And have *you*," he asked, "ever held anyone up to ridicule?" "Yes," said Hart, thinking of *Jubilee*, "the King and Queen of England." The judge then asked, "And none of these people sued you?" "No," Kaufman answered. "Only Chock Full O' Nuts." The suit was thrown out.

All of the suits, ultimately, were thrown out, with one exception. A girl who had taken Edna Ferber to the Rehearsal Club, a residential hotel for young actresses, brought an action claiming that this had given Miss Ferber and Kaufman their idea for *Stage Door*, and there was merit in that claim. The case was settled out of court.

Kaufman's principal attorney through the years was a brilliant and highly respected man named Howard E. Reinheimer, but he was sometimes involved in so many legal actions at once, and needed so many subsidiary lawyers in addition to Reinheimer, that he became, in a wry way, rather apologetic about it. "It sounds a little grand, I know, to say 'my lawyers' in the plural," he once told Jack Paar, when he was a guest on Paar's television show. "It didn't start out that way. I started with one lawyer, but you know what happens. One moves in and pretty soon there are seven, all in the same office. They get together all day long and say to each other, 'What can we

ostpone next?' The only thing they don't postpone, of course, is
reir bill, which arrives regularly."

Kaufman summed it all up in a speech he made at Yale on March 4,
939. The speech consisted mostly of advice on writing techniques
or the budding playwrights in Yale's famous drama school, but
Caufman's legal troubles were obviously also, as they usually were,
n his mind. "Be a little suspicious, if you're a playwright, of play
leas," he said. "The important thing really is not that first idea, but
ne subsidiary ideas that support it. Unless the original notion brings
vith it a little flood of material, unless it has a beginning and a middle
nd an end, or at least two of those things to start with, be careful.
'eople are always ready to give you ideas for plays, and they're worth
othing. Watch out for that true story that somebody brings you—
've never known it to be worth a nickel. You know—the fellow
vho says, 'The darnedest thing happened to me the other night. You
:ould make a great play out of it. I was walking along the street and
met a fellow I hadn't seen in ten years. What do you think of
hat?'" Kaufman concluded bitterly, "Of course all you have to do is
ake that idea, put two and a half hours of stuff after it, and you've
ot a play. It's a cinch. And then you get sued for plagiarism."

9. THE PARTING

THE NEXT KAUFMAN-CONNELLY play, *Beggar on Horseback*, made a profound impression on audiences viewing it, possibly because it was so innovative and experimental. Throughout the rest of his lifetime, long after the play had been imitated and possibly even bettered, and long after the play was no longer fresh in either idea or execution, Kaufman was constantly being approached by people who had an urge to see the play again. "You know which play you ought to revive?" people always began. Kaufman developed an automatic response. "It's dated," he would say, cutting them off and moving away. The play *was* finally revived a few years ago at Lincoln Center, and the critics agreed with Kaufman. Kaufman himself was gone by that time, but Connelly and Ruth Friedlich were present, and Connelly asked Ruth sentimentally, "Don't you just love it?" Ruth replied, "It's good to see *you* looking so well, Marc."

Beggar on Horseback was based on a German play, originally produced in 1912, with a jaw-breaking name, *Hans Sonnenstoesser's Hohlenfahrt*. The play's author was Paul Apel, and the title can be roughly translated as *Hans Sonnenstoesser's* (or *Johnny Sunstormer's*) *Trip to Hell*. It was about a young artist who is unable to support himself and decides to marry the daughter of a *nouveau riche* millionaire in order to continue his work, after which he falls asleep, dreams a series of fantastic dreams about the horrors of life with the vulgar, materialistic family into which he'll be marrying, and changes his mind. The play created great controversy in Germany. William Lyon Phelps was present at opening night, in Munich, and recalls in his memoirs that so many new millionaires were in the audience and tried to drown out the play with derisive laughter that a dignified man finally stood up and shouted, *"Es ist eine Roheir zu lachen!* It's brutal to laugh!"

The play had been kicking around for years at various New York producers' offices; it had been rejected by the Theatre Guild and a great many others as unsuitable for American audiences when the rights were offered to Winthrop Ames. Ames, a cultured and sensitive producer-director who came from a distinguished Boston family (his wife was a Cabot), had enough money so that his first interest was quality rather than a play's commercial prospects. He had built a showcase theatre, the Booth, and had presented, among other things, a series of Shakespeare plays done in the original manner, Galsworthy's *Strife*, and Maeterlinck's *Sister Beatrice*.

Ames's feeling about the Apel play was that it was indeed hopeless for the American market as written—because, as Ludwig Lewisohn later pointed out in his review of *Beggar on Horseback* in *The Nation*, "The German *Philister*, though blood brother to the American Babbitt, differs from the latter very radically in both mentality and manner." But it seemed to him that a very good play for the New York stage could be written if a first-rate American satirist took the basic idea and went to work, substituting American excesses and vulgarities for the German variety. The logical choice was the team of Kaufman and Connelly, and Ames phoned them and asked them to come around and see him.

Kaufman and Connelly accepted the assignment at once; *The Deep Tangled Wildwood* had still not opened in New York, but the only work remaining was touch-up. They liked the idea of the Apel play, and the offer also represented another opportunity to leave Tyler, make the break final, without hurting him more than necessary. Ames, after all, like LeMaire, had come to them. They did not even read *Hans Sonnenstoesser's Hohlenfahrt*, though Kaufman could have done so, with his knowledge of German; Ames had described the play to them in great detail, and that was all they needed. In effect, they threw the German play in the wastebasket and started from scratch.

The play they eventually delivered, and which Ames directed personally, was billed as a "fantastic comedy," and it was certainly that. Kaufman and Connelly made their hero a writer of serious music, and gave him a fairly standard name, Neil McRae, but the ordinary ended right there. In every other way, the play was completely innovative, the authors trying every experiment which occurred to them. It was a chance particularly welcomed by Kaufman, who was no traditionalist. He always preferred looking forward to looking backward, and once told a man who talked too long about the glories of the past, "My friend, nothing is more responsible for the good old days than a bad memory."

Since most of the play dealt with the nightmarish things that McRae dreams after he decides to marry the rich girl for her money, Kaufman and Connelly worked hard to give their play a fantastic quality, writing their scenes and their set suggestions to give the play that mixture of the logical and the absurd which so often make up the fabric of nightmares. The millionaire's house—a huge palace of a place—has endless corridors, dozens of mirrors which reflect each other and blister the eye, and furniture which looks both expensive and in horrible taste. The servants are an army; when McRae rings for the butler, four butlers appear, and then eight. When McRae is told that he's going to be taught the newest dance steps, ten dance instructors appear, all dressed identically and all looking like the same man repeated *ad infinitum*. The millionaire walks around the house dressed in golf clothes, and with a telephone strapped to his big belly; the phone is a direct wire to his office. And the millionaire's wife and daughter behave with dignity when they remember to do so, but lapse constantly into gaucheries; they dance with a waiter and often interrupt the action to turn somersaults. It was all a totally different concept for the American stage.

There were two other things in the play which had never, or rarely ever, been done before. The first occurs around the middle of the play: when McRae, told that he must attend to business and write no more music, goes berserk and kills everybody in sight with a paper knife. The instant he does this, newsboys appear and rush down the theatre aisles handing every member of the audience a four-page newspaper giving details of McRae's crime and of his forthcoming trial. It has now become almost a commonplace to involve the audience in a play's action, with plays from *Hellzapoppin* to *Hair* doing it throughout every act, but it was a startling innovation for 1924. The newspaper also lent an added dimension to the evening in the theatre; it was both a brilliant parody of a tabloid newspaper, fun to read for itself, and a great souvenir to be taken home in addition to the usual, commonplace program.

The newspaper, which was called *THE MORNING-EVENING, With Which Has Been Combined THE EVENING-MORNING, Retaining the Best Features of Each*, a title commenting on the proclivity of American newspapers to merge, was quite hilarious from front page to last. In addition to the usual tabloid interview with the murderer—"'I killed them,' said Neil McRae enthusiastically"—the newspaper also included political stories—"'What this country needs,' said Senator Gabrilowitch, 'I've got'"—and other news stories of various kinds, plus typical ads, like one for a walk-up clothing firm which says, "Climb sixty flights and save." There was even a play review full of stock and carefully-middle-of-the-road phrases, and an equally temporizing headline: NEW PLAY MAKES HIT OR DOES NOT.

The other surprising innovation was the inclusion in the play of a long, serious, and quite beautiful ballet, for which the music was written by Deems Taylor. This was really a departure from the norm, since, to the traditionally inclined in the theatre, the rule was simple: musicals had music and straight plays didn't. But this was a straight play which really cried out for music. Since the theme of the play is, essentially, art versus commercialism, the logical culmination of the dream sequences would be a scene in which the judge trying to determine if there is any justification at all for McRae's crimes, asks to hear his music in order to see whether or not his work is likely to be of lasting value. So *Beggar on Horseback* got music and a lovely seventeen-year-old girl named Grethe Ruzt-Nissen, who later simplified her name to Greta Nissen and became an important screen star, danced the ballet.

The play opened at the Broadhurst Theatre on Tuesday, February 12, 1924, with Roland Young playing Neil McRae, George Barbier who later played the pompous rich man in every picture filmed in Hollywood in the '30s and '40s, or so it seemed, playing the millionaire here, too. Osgood Perkins appeared as the millionaire's son, beginning a theatrical dynasty which is now being continued by his son Tony, and a small part went to an actress who also later became one of the busiest people in films, Spring Byington. There was even more than the usual amount of fear and trembling in the ranks this time. Kaufman was certain that the play would fail so badly that it would mean the end of all their careers, and told friends earnestly that his one consolation was that he still had his job on the *Times*. Connelly and Ames were concerned over the fact that the play was so offbeat that the critics just might not get it at all.

The critics, to their credit, got it completely. Corbin's review in the *Times* was typical; he called the play "quite mad, utterly delightful and inerrant in touching off our mundane fads and follies" and "intelligently witty and inspired throughout by the richest and most varied good taste" and said that "the authors' phantasmagoria is of the here and now, and it ranges the entire field of arts and letters, of politics, crime, and the newspapers, touching everything as it passes with the witches' fire of fancy and the dart of deadly satire." He also commented, "There are no beggars in this new Kaufman-Connelly comedy and indeed no horsebacks. There is not really anything here that has ever been in a play before. That was one reason why the audience rose to it from the very start. The reason why it kept on rising with ever-increasing delight was that the play bristles with sly and caustic satire, brims with novel and richly colored theatric invention, and overflows with inconsequent humor and the motley spirit of youth."

The interesting thing is that this proved true of all kinds of audiences, from tired businessmen out for an evening's relaxation to more cerebral types. John Galsworthy, visiting the United States, devoted most of one interview to talking about two American plays he particularly admired: *Anna Christie* and *Beggar on Horseback*. He talked more about the Kaufman-Connelly play than the O'Neill play, saying he considered it "absolutely American, something no other country could reveal or picture." He continued, giving the play a defense it didn't really need, "Of course it's satire, but it's satire with a quality of genius in it. That is why I liked it so much. I consider satire good and healthy. It keeps a nation on an even keel. We must all be prepared to be laughed at a little." Ordinary citizens, though less widely quoted, expressed the same kind of admiration for the play. So many people came up to Kaufman and told him that they'd seen the play three or four times that he finally developed a stock response for that situation, too. "Is that so?" he'd say innocently. "Didn't you get it the first time?"

Beggar on Horseback ran for 144 performances at the Broadhurst, toured for a while, and then returned to New York, opening again at the Shubert on Wednesday, March 25, 1925, for another good run. It also opened in London on May 7 of the same year with similar success; the *Telegraph* called the play "a very distinguished piece of stagework, interesting from beginning to end and containing beauty, wit, satire, and humor," and the other London papers were equally kind. The play also was included in *The Best Plays of 1924–25.*

Beggar on Horseback was Kaufman's and Connelly's most successful collaboration, and, except for an abortive attempt to renew their relationship nearly forty years later, their last. Just as they had decided to move quietly away from George C. Tyler, they now decided to get away from each other as well.

When the break was announced, there were persistent whispers that the fault was Connelly's—that he was too rigid in his opinions, falling in love with certain lines and insisting that they stay in, even when they didn't advance the plot or characterizations, until Kaufman had been unable to stand it any longer. *Variety* even came right out and stated flatly that the reason for the break was Connelly's excessive rigidity. Like many rumors, however, this was all based on a misapprehension. It wasn't that Connelly was so rigid; if anything, he was far more relaxed about his work than Kaufman, and sometimes urged that a line be left in because he felt it was good enough, which created agony in Kaufman because Kaufman drove himself constantly and *never* agreed that good enough was good enough if it could be made better. The charge of rigidity might more accurately have been leveled against Kaufman. Kaufman sometimes argued for a work session when Connelly, with his more casual attitude toward his career, wanted to take the evening off; and anybody might have found it wearing to be part of a five-hour or six-hour stretch of work devoted to forty or fifty rewrites and final perfection of a single line.

There was no question about the fact that the men were entirely different types, and many years later, in a piece called *High Jinks in the Twenties*, John Mason Brown, a very perceptive critic, looked back and summarized the mental and physical differences between the two. "Kaufman and Connelly," Brown wrote, "were Broadway's favored Siamese twins, collaborators as linked in the public mind as Gilbert and Sullivan or, for that matter, as Kaufman and Moss Hart were to be in the thirties. But although thought of during these budding years as if they were one person because of the deceptive blend their comedies seemed to be, they were actually glaringly dissimilar.

"Kaufman was all nerves and concentration, as lean and tense as an exclamation point. His face was long, his patience short. His black hair rose like a cliff from his expansive forehead, his chin had cement in it, his nose was large and imperious, his cheekbones were as high as an Indian chief's, and his dark eyes burned behind his tortoise-shell glasses like coals banked deeply in a grate. A tireless worker, he was a craftsman who labored over the fashioning of a line or scene until both functioned with the accuracy of precision instruments. Connelly, on the other hand, was a plump, Pickwickian man, already

bald, whose nose rose from his face like a pointer on a sundial. He
was a Winnie-the-Pooh, protean within himself and protean in what
he could become. Inhibitions did not shackle him nor audiences
large or small dismay him. An author who contained an actor, he
was an actor who enclosed a professor. Radiantly gifted as a mimic,
as good at improvising as at remembering, he could, without bothering about props or costumes, be Spartacus at one moment and the
next be Barbara Frietchie waving her rebel flag. He could lift a
party as few could and drop it when the 'Herr Doktor' in him took
over or he arrived too fresh from a reading of the encyclopedia. He
worked rapidly and well, once he got started, but his imagination
was such that he could mistake the intention to work for work
already done. Woollcott, who later came to respect him hugely,
called him 'an infuriating blend of poet, peacock, and procrastinator.'
Connelly was more than that, far more, but very, very different
from his partner."

All of these factors, all of these differences, weighed, of course,
into the decision to separate. But the main reason for the parting was
far more simple than all this. The two men had had their first hit
together and worked their laborious way up to the top together, and
now felt the need for a change, the need to see what it felt like to
work again on their own or with others.

There were still some loose ends to be tied up. For one thing,
S. Jay Kaufman, unrelated to George S. but also in newspaper work—
he wrote a popular column called *Round the Town* for the *Telegraph*—had asked them, a few months before *Beggar on Horseback*
opened, to contribute a sketch or two to a revue which he was
putting together and which was going to have the same name as his
column. The request became impossible to refuse when Herman
J. Mankiewicz joined the project as co-producer. The *Telegraph*
columnist wasn't especially popular with the two playwrights—
George Kaufman called him, derisively, "the *nice* Kaufman" because
he was a glad-hander and back-slapper—but both men liked Mankiewicz tremendously. Mankiewicz was then, at twenty-seven, an assistant of George Kaufman's in the dramatic department of the
Times, a wild, irresponsible, and utterly charming and endearing
man who later wrote a play in collaboration with his boss, *The*

Good Fellow, moved to Hollywood and won an Academy Award for his screenplay for the memorable *Citizen Kane*, and died tragically at the age of fifty-six. The project itself wasn't all that appealing, either; it sounded like *The 49ers* all over again, with most of the sketches to be written by newspapermen and other wits around town, and with possible appearances by Heywood Broun and Robert Benchley. But Mankiewicz was in it, so Kaufman and Connelly did their bit.

Significantly, *Round the Town* was the first public preview of their coming separation, the first time since they had joined forces that their bylines were divorced. They wrote one sketch together which was a parody of their own current play, and which they called *Beggar off Horseback*, but Connelly also wrote a second sketch on his own, *The Girl from W.O.R.*, and Kaufman wrote a sketch in collaboration with Mankiewicz, *Moron Films, Educational, Travel and Topical*. Kaufman also wrote the lyrics for a song, *If One of Us Was You, Dear*, in collaboration with Jay Velie, a song-and-dance man signed to appear in the show. None of the contributions were on view or audible for very long. Benchley did his famous monologue, *The Sex Life of the Polyp*, while the revue was trying out at the Shubert Theatre in Newark, but local critics called the monologue dirty and he dropped out of the show; Broun stayed in, but someone talked him into wearing a tuxedo and combing his hair, and both out-of-town and Broadway critics panned him, complaining that that just wasn't the real Heywood Broun up there on the stage. The revue opened at the Century Roof on Wednesday, May 21, 1924, with an eleven o'clock curtain, hoping to pick up the after-theatre crowd, people with an appetite for still more entertainment, and with Jack Haley, Gloria Foy, and Harry Fox backing up Broun. But receipts were terrible—less than $9000 for six performances—and the show soon folded.

The other item of unfinished business was *Miss Moonshine*, the first Kaufman-Connelly collaboration, still languishing on a shelf. Wilmer and Vincent, the Pennsylvania theatre men who had bankrolled *Helen of Troy, New York*, solved that one by telling Kaufman and Connelly that they were undaunted by the fact that they'd made no money on *Helen* and asking if they had anything else. The playwrights dusted off *Miss Moonshine*, retitled it *Be Yourself*, and it opened at the Sam H. Harris Theatre on Tuesday, September 24, 1924.

The newly titled musical had a chance. The book was a fairly funny one about a man named Matt McLean who travels through Tennessee mountain country and finds himself in the middle of the long-standing Brennan-McLean feud, realizing at the same moment that he's deep in Brennan territory. Jack Donahue, a popular performer whom Ray Bolger later called America's greatest dancer, played McLean, and Queenie Smith was his love interest. The music and lyrics were written mostly by a good, reliable team, Lewis Gensler and Milton Schwarzwald, and five additional, outstanding lyrics were contributed by a young writer who was so unsure of himself that he had previously worked only under a pseudonym, Arthur Francis, but now used his real name, Ira Gershwin. But unfortunately, Jack Donahue became ill and missed many performances, and it was also too apparent to the reviewers that Kaufman and Connelly had come a long way since *Miss Moonshine; Variety* called the play "obvious and conventional" and other critics echoed the sentiments. The *Variety* reviewer was particularly prophetic: he ended his review, "Queenie Smith and Jack Donahue might send it along for a few weeks, say 12." After exactly twelve weeks, ninety-three performances, the play folded in New York, went on tour to Boston and other cities for a while, and then died completely. And the long, successful collaboration of George S. Kaufman and Marc Connelly was over.

It was not the end of their friendship, any more than the friendship between Kaufman and Tyler had ended when they stopped working together. Kaufman and Connelly continued to see each other occasionally for the rest of their lives, and their respect for each other remained undiminished. And it was Kaufman, as stated, who was responsible for the production of *The Green Pastures*. Connelly had read Roark Bradford's stories, *Ol' Man Adam and His Chillun*, and had immediately acquired the dramatic rights, seeing a great play in the stories and feeling confident that he would have no trouble arranging for a production once he did the dramatization. But it hadn't worked out that way. Arthur Hopkins liked the play but passed because he couldn't make up his mind about how to stage it; Jed Harris liked it but said he'd contract to produce it only if he was allowed to make changes without consultation or approval, which was unacceptable to Connelly; Crosby Gaige liked it, too, but was afraid of it; and, at the Theatre Guild, Lawrence Langner and Theresa Helburn voted to produce it, but Philip Moeller and Helen Westley considered the play cheap and sacrilegious and talked them out of it.

Connelly was almost ready to give up when a Wall Street financier named Rowland Stebbins decided he wanted to produce some plays and hired a man named Charles G. Stewart to scout properties for him. Stewart phoned Kaufman and asked if he had anything available. Kaufman said that he didn't have anything himself, but added that Connelly had a really great play which was still available, and Stewart read the play and immediately urged Stebbins to make a deal for it. Stebbins had one question about the play with a black Lawd and all those black angels: "Can we get away with it?" Stewart consulted Bishop Herbert Shipman of the Episcopal Diocese of New York, who read the play and said simply, "The play will serve as one of the greatest sermons man will ever preach." A theatrical agency for Negro actors in Harlem was put to work, the cast was hired within a week, and the play was put on. And Kaufman had the pleasure of watching Connelly read and reread the really extraordinary reviews and say over and over again, his voice husky, "Silly fellows! Silly fellows!" Kaufman also predicted the play's future that night: he said that the play would achieve one of the longest runs in history and win the Pulitzer Prize, which was exactly what happened.

But the two men never worked together again; the closest they ever came to it was when, at the very end of Kaufman's life, they talked for a while about collaborating on a play about a character like Jimmy Hoffa, to be called *Labor Leader*, a play which never materialized because of Kaufman's final illness and death. Even when *Beggar on Horseback* was bought for filming by Paramount, and the movie company asked that a film short on a business theme be written to be shown in theatres as a kind of lead-in or preamble to the feature, Kaufman wrote the short, *Business Is Business*, with Dorothy Parker rather than with Connelly.

Mrs. Parker was born Dorothy Rothschild in West End, New Jersey, on August 22, 1893. She was educated at Miss Dana's School in Morristown, New Jersey, and the Sacred Heart Convent in New York, and her first publishing job came in 1916 when *Vogue*, to which she had submitted some poems, offered to hire her as a picture-caption writer at $10 a week. Two years later, she moved to *Vanity Fair*, where her co-editors were the men to whom she occasionally referred as "the two Bobs," Sherwood and Benchley. She was fired in 1920 by *Vanity Fair* when three theatrical producers protested that her reviews were too tough; the most vehement complaint came from Florenz Ziegfeld after Mrs. Parker said that Ziegfeld's wife, Billie Burke, tried to convey girlishness in a show by playing her lighter scenes as if she were giving an impersonation of Eva Tanguay. Sherwood and Benchley resigned immediately, feeling that the magazine should not have yielded to the pressure. Sherwood went on to *Life*, and Mrs. Parker and Benchley rented and shared an office for a while, trying to survive as free-lance writers. The office was so tiny that Mrs. Parker said afterward, "If we'd had to sit a few inches closer together, we'd have been guilty of adultery." (The well-known story that they grew lonely and tried to lure company by having the word MEN painted on their office door is, unfortunately, apocryphal. It would also not have worked, since men entering the room would have had other things on their minds.)

The collaboration was the only time Kaufman and Dorothy Parker worked together. Kaufman and the lady knew each other because they moved in much the same circles, and they'd brushed shoulders because Dorothy Parker had also contributed to *Round the Town* and *The 49ers*, but they were very much the opposite of a mutual admiration society. There was a certain amount of rivalry between them: Kaufman once said gloomily, "Everything I've ever said will be credited to Dorothy Parker." The dark-haired, pretty writer was also well-known for lines like, "If all the girls at Smith and Bennington were laid end to end, I wouldn't be surprised," and, "One more drink and I'd have been under the host," which Kaufman conceded were funny but which he really didn't consider ladylike. And Mrs. Parker, as mentioned, cast a cold eye at Kaufman's phobias.

As would always be the case, however, Kaufman consistently

brought out the best in his collaborators and worked well with them no matter what their relationship might be away from the typewriter. The film version of *Beggar on Horseback*, directed by James Cruze, and with a screenplay by Walter Woods and Anthony Coldeway which stuck closely to the play, was released with Edward Everett Horton in the lead and was a hit. The short, in which Kaufman had a direct hand, was applauded even more.

10. THE PACT

THINGS WERE NOT going as well in the boudoir as they had begun to go at the typewriter. Almost from the first night of their marriage, George and Beatrice Kaufman became convinced that they were sexually mismatched.

Beatrice's early comment, that she and George were physically incompatible, was probably not meant literally; there is no evidence, from the occasional worried discussions she had with feminine friends and relatives in the early years of the marriage, that either partner in the marriage was abnormal in size, shape, or general construction. More likely, Beatrice meant that their first attempts at marital relations had been fumbling and unsatisfactory, and that the relationship, instead of improving with experience and experimentation, as so often happens in young marriages, had steadily worsened.

Given the facts of the case, it isn't at all surprising. There was no such thing as sex education in the schools of Pittsburgh and Rochester in the period in which the young couple were growing up, and, with a few scattered exceptions, none in the homes, either. Nor is it likely that the elder Kaufmans or the Bakrows, for all their modern thinking in some areas, were among the enlightened exceptions in this one. Nettie, with her own education in a convent, had undoubtedly been instilled with the notion that it would be anathema to discuss a subject like sex with one's children; and, with her health fears for her family, it's logical to assume that, if she ever discussed sex with George at all, it would have been solely for the purpose of filling him with terror for the sex act so that he would not try it with an obliging neighborhood girl and come down with one of the dreaded social diseases. Joseph would not have been of much help, either: a discussion on the subject of sex with his son would have been exactly the kind of responsibility he'd have avoided. And the Bakrows would undoubtedly not have done much better for their eager young daughter. The stern European heritage of all four parents, in fact, could be counted upon to have caused them to bring up their children with the same self-satisfied feeling that they, at least, unlike a few other parents they'd heard about, weren't going to dirty their children's ears and minds with talk about what men and women sometimes did in bed.

The sanctimonious and stupid attitude was typical rather than uncommon; it was shared by most or all of the other parents in the Kaufmans' and Bakrows' social sets in the two cities, and probably caused temporary or permanent injury to most or all of their children. In George Kaufman's youth, he belonged to a group called the Black and White Club, given that name because the members put down their beliefs in black and white. Later the name was changed to the Galahads. The club was made up of boys who were not at all the scions of what the newspapers of the day liked to call "the ignorant poor"; in addition to Irving Pichel and Kaufman, some of the other members were Ferdinand Weil, son of a prominent judge, Bill Frank, son of a millionaire financier, and Carl Kaufmann, whose family owned Pittsburgh's largest department store. (The Kaufmanns were not related to George's family, even though some later biographers became confused by the similar names and credited him with being part of

he wealthy family of merchants.) It was the kind of club where boys
f more daring upbringing might have spent time exchanging porno-
raphic postcards, the little cartoon books—showing favorite comic-
trip characters in sexual activities—which were then so popular, hard-
ore pornographic novels or at least magazines like *The Police Gazette*
vhich showed women in suggestive poses, the names of girls at school
vho had the reputation of being willing, and similar items. Instead,
Kaufman and his friends devoted many meetings to creating a set of
y-laws which ended up consisting of one long and repetitious vow of
celibacy. Their pious reason was that, since they would never marry
girl Who Did That, and since a double standard was clearly un-
air, they wouldn't do it, either, until they married. People who knew
he boys are convinced that many of them kept the vow, and their
esulting inexperience probably blighted many of their eventual
narriages.

Kaufman later commented on this with typically oblique bitter-
ess. He was in a poker game with Raoul Fleischmann, who financed
he birth of *The New Yorker*, when Fleischmann remarked that he
vas fourteen years old before he became aware that he was a Jew.
"That's nothing," Kaufman said. "I was sixteen before I realized I
vas a boy."

Because of their backgrounds, the young Kaufmans came to their
narital couch filled with innocence and ignorance. Both George and
Beatrice told people that they were virgins when they were married,
and there seems to be no reason to doubt it. George undoubtedly embraced his bride with the subconscious, guilty feeling that he should
not try to enjoy it too much because, after all, sex was really for pro-
creation and not for fun, and with neither the knowledge of how to
perform byplay nor the realization of how essential it was. And
Beatrice—when, as probably was the case, the sex acts were too brief
—was undoubtedly both disappointed and ashamed of herself for being
so wanton as to wish the lovemaking had been better and more prolonged.

The relationship did not grow better, and might have settled into
one of those unfortunate marriages, all too common, where couples
made love all their lives but never really learned to enjoy themselves
and each other. But then an event occurred which was the beginning

[143]

of the death knell for their sex life together: Beatrice became pregnant
The young people were delighted. Their bedroom activity might no
have turned out to be the joyful experience that some people had told
them it would be, but at least it was having the result that their parent
had emphasized was the *raison d'être* of it all, and they would soon
be a family.

It was not to be; the experience became instead the most terrible
one of Beatrice's young life. When her time came, her labor pains were
long and agonizing. And when the baby arrived, the doctor told her
his voice gentle with sympathy, that the infant, a son, had been still
born.

A few days later, Beatrice told her husband that sexual relation
were finished between them. She had thought it over thoroughly
she said; she couldn't help the way she felt and was certain her feel
ings would never change. The sexual side of their marriage was
permanently associated in her mind with feelings ranging from un
pleasantness to excruciating pain, and she wanted no more of it. She
suggested that perhaps they might be able to keep their marriage to
gether if they worked out an agreement to have no further sexual
relations, at least with each other, but added that she realized he might
consider this both unfair and unacceptable, in which case she would
not oppose a divorce.

Kaufman was stunned. He hastened to the comforting conclusion
that Beatrice's decision was neither genuine nor permanent, but merely
a temporary irrationality caused by deep postbirth depression. He
had heard that some mothers who gave birth to completely normal
children became deeply depressed for weeks after delivery, so surely
it was logical that a girl who had lost her child might become even
more so. But weeks passed, and then months, and Beatrice's attitude
did not change. She was clearly fond of her husband, and their relation
ship remained normal in every other way, but she would not let him
get near her in bed.

It was a time of agonizing decision for Kaufman. He was a
normal and healthy young man who needed sex, less than satisfactory
though he had found it thus far, but the realization that he would have
to seek it elsewhere was more than just unacceptable to him—it was
appalling and even repellent. Aside from the standards which made the

whole idea of extra-marital sex ugly and immoral in his mind, he was deeply in love with Beatrice; satisfying or not, he wanted sex but wanted it only with her. The desirability of his young wife, so close to him and yet unreachable, made life almost beyond endurance. He continued to hope, and made several clumsy attempts at changing her mind, trying to take her into his arms when they were in bed together. But he was always repulsed—until his shyness and his insecurity, his terror of rejection, finally made him stop trying. And he realized then, at last, that his choice was either life without Beatrice or life with her but without her sexual partnership.

The thing he knew immediately, the moment he finally faced the realization, was that he could never bear to lose her completely. There was more to his feeling for her than just loving her—he also *liked* her. He looked forward to seeing her again whenever he was away from her, looked forward to spending time with her. She had a quick smile which warmed him whenever he saw it, and a quick mind which he had come to admire more and more. She had, he knew, begun to change him perceptibly, even in the brief period of their marriage, and they were changes he rather liked. He had been an indifferent dresser before they met, with little sense of clothes or knowledge of things like matching shirts and ties to suits, and it was Beatrice who helped him pick his clothes, and eventually gave him his taste for beautifully cut suits and dark, rich ties, making him in time one of the best-dressed men in town. He had no social instinct and knew he never would have, and it was Beatrice who cemented the relationships with people whose company they both enjoyed. And he liked her sense of humor, as free-flying and bullet-swift as his own. He had even begun to enjoy the fact that their apartment was becoming a sort of salon visited by the most interesting and amusing people in town; his shyness warred with his enjoyment at the parties Beatrice had started to give, but enjoyment won out because the people were so entertaining.

Beatrice had even become extremely important to him in his work. He had fallen into the habit of showing her everything he wrote, and was astonished at the quick, certain, accurate way she was able to point out the things he'd done wrong and the things he'd done right. He became, very quickly, dependent on her comments and judgments. So, when he stopped to consider it, there was really no question about the way his decision would have to go. He loved her, he liked her, and he needed her. He had to have her, even if it meant the pain of not having her sexual love and, perhaps, of being aware that others were having it. Because she had never said that her sex life would end, only that it must end with him.

He told her reluctantly one day, "Let's try it and see."

Probably he still hoped that things would change; if so, his hopes were never realized. Though the Kaufmans lived together for twenty-eight years, until Beatrice died suddenly on October 6, 1945, and their affection for and dependence on each other deepened with each passing year, they never again had sex together—"Not even once," Kaufman told a close friend sadly, "just to see if things might have changed between us." He suggested this to Beatrice now and then, but Beatrice simply said, gently but in a way which made him realize that there was no room for argument, that she could no longer accept him in that role. And in time they both formed sexual relationships with other people.

Ironically, they both became as successful in their extra-marital sexual pursuits as they had been unsuccessful in their own relationship, even though neither of them was outstandingly good-looking in the classical sense. Beatrice formed many friendships with extremely handsome and well-known men in the course of her life, and slept with many of them; there were constant instances where men-about-town spurned lovely actresses and chorus girls to be with Beatrice Kaufman. And clearly, they came to admire her wit and her mind as much as her favors, since all of them remained friends and admirers long after the passion had subsided. The situation was the same with Kaufman. His business brought him into contact with hundreds of beautiful women, and he succeeded with every one he pursued. He became, after a while, so constant a sexual partner, never without an attractive girl to take to bed, that Max Gordon, who produced most of the later Kaufman plays, once chided him for spending so much time on his romances and called him "a male nymphomaniac."

It didn't happen all at once; it evolved slowly. The first *affaires de coeur* were furtive relationships for both of them; despite their clear understanding, they behaved like cheaters, telling little lies to each other about where they had been and where they were going, and meeting their friends and lovers in out-of-the-way places. Gradually, they became more open about it, and all of their friends, and many of their casual acquaintances and business associates, knew the situation even though the Kaufmans rarely discussed it with others, and it was never discussed by others in their presence. In time, it became a standard facet of their life that, whenever they moved, there were always "his" and "her" phones installed along with their regular phones; any call which came in on one of those phones was never answered by the other or inquired about. And, though they went out together all the time and enjoyed each other's company more and more, they also learned to understand and accept the situation when one told the other, without explanation, "I'm going out," and left alone.

There are people around, close friends of the Kaufmans during their marriage, who viewed their arrangment on its simplest level, as a civilized understanding giving the couple the best of all possible worlds. Some of them still feel that way, saying enviously, "No accusations, no recriminations, loving each other but yet not tied to each other. What a great way to live!" The evidence is that it wasn't at all. It was a way of life to which they were driven by necessity, Beatrice because, through a twist of reasoning she could not control, she could no longer tolerate the thought of a physical relationship with her husband no matter how much she loved him otherwise, the playwright because it was the price he was forced to pay to keep Beatrice as his wife. But neither of them was fooled for a minute into thinking that their marriage was ideal; they were intelligent, sensitive people who knew the ideal life was one where two people enjoyed each other on all other levels and also enjoyed each other in bed and never gave a second thought to straying. Since this just wasn't possible in their case, they accepted the situation because they had to accept it, but each partner's observation of the other's love affairs was never really free of pain.

Their most sensitive friends, of course, realized the way it really was. Ruth Gordon, talking about the Kaufmans in one of her books, used only first names but summarized their love life as though it were a fun game: "They were married, but they both had a lot going. George was crazy about Myra, who liked him but only had eyes for

Harpo, who liked her but that was all. And Evelyn had her friends worried she'd jump out the window because she was crazy about George. On the distaff side, things were about the same." But a more trained observer like Clare Boothe Luce saw how things were beneath the surface.

The playwright's celebrated romance with Mary Astor, in 1936, became famous, as stated earlier, not so much because it was the most passionate and longest-lasting in Kaufman's lifetime—there were many others which burned longer—but because the actress had written a diary full of extremely explicit and admiring comments about Kaufman's sexual prowess, and the diary was mentioned in the court and in the press during her divorce from Dr. Franklyn Thorpe. Beatrice's public posture toward the journalistic revelations was extremely calm; she was in Europe when the stories began to appear, and told reporters who interviewed her in London, "I knew all about this case before it caught the limelight. I know Mary Astor. I know her well. My husband met her just about this time a year ago. I was in Honolulu. He was working in Hollywood. They had a flirtation. I can't see any terrible harm in that. Is it unusual for a husband to flirt with an actress? We've been married twenty years. We're adults, leading our lives in adult fashion."

It was just cover-up for the press; the romance, as more and more details emerged from the diary, was far more than just a flirtation. "And underneath," Mrs. Luce said in a recent conversation, remembering the event, "Beatrice was totally shattered. It wasn't just the embarrassment of the public revelations, either; she could live with that. It was being forced to come face to face with the emptiness of that aspect of their life together." Mrs. Luce also commented on Beatrice Kaufman in a very brief description, summing her up, despite all the romances, despite the glamour of some of the men in Beatrice's life. The summary took only three words: "Lonely and sad."

It required a perceptive mind to realize this, because Mrs. Luce was not really part of the Kaufmans' intimate circle, and Beatrice's loneliness and sadness were essentially inward. Many people knew the real situation, but it is not surprising that others, judging things by outward appearances, assumed that life for the playwright and his wife was a

absolute ball, one long, unending party totally free of problems. The
Kaufmans' enjoyment of each other's company, apart from the marital
couch, was obviously genuine, and their public look of total together-
ness, which had begun so promisingly when Kaufman brought his
bride down from Rochester and saw her receive quick acceptance
from the Frank Adamses and from Woollcott, became even more so
when both were welcomed with equal enthusiasm at the most-publi-
cized social phenomenon of the day: the Round Table at the Algonquin
Hotel.

The Round Table, as is usually the case with that sort of thing,
was unplanned and developed gradually. Its genesis can be traced to
the fact that John Peter Toohey, the man who first spotted Kaufman's
talents in *Going Up,* became a theatrical press agent in 1920, with
Eugene O'Neill as one of his clients, and wanted to try to plant a
story about O'Neill in Woollcott's influential column in the *Times.*
Toohey didn't happen to know Woollcott personally and appealed to
another publicity man, Murdock Pemberton, who was the brother
of Brock Pemberton, the producer, and knew everybody. Pemberton
set up a lunch date for the three of them, choosing the Algonquin
because the hotel happened to have an especially celebrated pastry
cook named Sarah. Pemberton was aware that Woollcott's corpulence
didn't spring from austerity of diet, and hoped that Sarah's famed deep-
dish apple pie would put the critic in a receptive mood for Toohey's
pitch.

Woollcott was already familiar with the Algonquin in a casual
way; he had lived for a while at the City Club, which was located
right next door, and he knew the Algonquin's manager, Frank Case,
because Case had previously been the manager of one of Woollcott's
favorite haunts, the Lambs Club. But none of Woollcott's precious
visits to the Algonquin had been the spectacular success that the
lunch with Toohey and Pemberton turned out to be. Woollcott
thought the food was marvelous, and also enjoyed himself hugely
because he began to reminisce at great length about his experiences
on *Stars and Stripes,* and the two press agents listened in respectful
silence and never interrupted him.

The lunch was so successful that Toohey got his plug and Pemberton got an idea for cementing his own relationship with the

Times man and with other important theatrical people and writers who were friends of Woollcott's: he arranged another and much bigger luncheon for Woollcott at the Algonquin. Pemberton took one big chance: he had a wild, mischievous sense of humor and couldn't resist a gag once he thought of it, so the invitations he sent out were in the form of an agenda of speeches to be given at the luncheon, with every speech being a wartime reminiscence and every speaker being Alexander Woollcott. Furthermore, knowing Woollcott's fury whenever his name was misspelled, the program never spelled Woollcott's name right; one speech was to be by Alexander Wolcott, another by Alexander Woolcott, a third by Alexander Woollcot, and so on. But Woollcott, not unexpectedly, enjoyed the attention, and the other participants were people he liked especially, among them Frank Adams, Robert Benchley, Heywood Broun, Ruth Hale, Brock Pemberton, and George and Beatrice Kaufman. Woollcott was even more lavish this time in his praise of the food and the hotel.

The second luncheon was the beginning of the formation of the Round Table group. Woollcott was now so taken with the Algonquin that he began to drop in for lunch more and more frequently, bringing his famous friends with him or inviting them to meet him there. Other people joined the original recipients of Murdock Pemberton's invitations: Harold Ross, who was the editor of a civilian counterpart of *Stars and Stripes* called *Home Sector* when he joined the group, and still some years away from organizing *The New Yorker;* Herbert Bayard Swope, the red-headed, dynamic executive editor of the *World;* John V. A. Weaver, a former Chicagoan who had known Frank Adams in that city and had been introduced around by Adams when he moved to New York to become literary editor of the Brooklyn *Eagle;* Peggy Wood, Weaver's wife and an up-and-coming actress who later played the matriarch in *I Remember Mama;* Tallulah Bankhead, whose aunt had chosen the Algonquin when she and Miss Bankhead moved to New York because the hotel was also the New York headquarters of the dignified chief of the Salvation Army, Commander Evangeline Booth; Marc Connelly; Harpo Marx; Laurence Stallings, a *World* book reviewer who had lost a leg in the war and later collaborated with a *World* editorial writer, Maxwell Anderson, to write a great anti-war play, *What Price Glory?;* Neysa

McMein, a beautiful young artist who painted covers for all the leading magazines; Alice Duer Miller, a writer for the same magazines, and who later wrote *The White Cliffs of Dover;* Ring Lardner; Herman Mankiewicz; Dorothy Parker; Robert E. Sherwood; and Edna Ferber, who wangled her way into the group by writing plaintively to Woollcott, "Could I maybe lunch at the Round Table once?" After a while, the lunches at the Algonquin became a daily ritual, attended by every member of the group who was in town and not tied up elsewhere, and grew famous because of the celebrity of the participants and the sparkle of their conversation and wit.

The table was not round at first; Case just threw together a couple of ordinary rectangular tables to accommodate the total number of people Pemberton had invited. But Case was a man with an overwhelming admiration for theatrical people, writers, editors, and other artistic types; he disdained more mundane theories about the hotel's great food and service and credited, in an almost mystical way, the Algonquin's popularity among people in the arts to his visible enthusiasm for artists of all types, saying, "If a man should stand in Times Square with his heart simply bursting with love for bricklayers, I don't doubt that in time the bricklayers would sense it and gather round." He was also an astute businessman. He had started out merely as manager of the hotel, going to work for the man who had just built it, and showed immediate foresight by convincing his boss to drop the original choice for the name of the place, the Puritan, which Case felt conjured up only pictures of tepid and dull respectability, and give it a more action-oriented Indian name like the Algonquin instead. By 1927, Case had gathered together enough savings to buy the hotel, and, both as manager and owner, he recognized the value of the group to the Algonquin, since the members' quips were always being mentioned in columns, and the hotel was nearly always mentioned, too. He began to set aside the most prominent table in the room, a big, round one, for the group's exclusive use at lunchtime.

There were no freeloaders at the table; checks were separate, and even the women paid their own tabs or turned them over to their husbands. The strict rule also applied to other prominent people who were not regulars, but showed up at the table now and then. Harpo Marx, who was sometimes as silent when he wasn't working as he was onstage because he was painfully embarrassed about his brief education, which had ended at grade school, once sat at the table for eight solid hours listening in awe to Bernard Baruch discoursing to him. Whenever Baruch paused for breath, Herbert Bayard Swope took over, and Marx kept thinking ecstatically, "If only Miss Flatto could see me now!" Miss Flatto had been his grade-school teacher. But when he tried to make some payment for all the wisdom by seizing the other men's checks, he was frowned down.

The group was held together by its members' mutual gift for great conversation and quotable wit; the same might be given as the reason that the group, at least at the time they first began to gather together at what they liked to call the Algonk, were already nearly all famous members of New York's smart set, even though some of them had not yet written or appeared in anything of prominence—and a few never did. Certainly they didn't have a great deal in common otherwise.

Adams was a home-loving type whose idea of a good time, as he frequently reported in his columns, was to wake up a few close friends like the Kaufmans and have breakfast with them. (George Kaufman's late-evening writing sessions and nighttime theatrical beat for the *Times* had already given him the habit of sleeping until eleven o'clock or noon if he wasn't awakened, a habit he retained all his life.) Woollcott was a party-lover and a lion-hunter, seeking more and more important people as friends as he himself grew more famous. Benchley was a lovable man who rarely said anything nasty to or about anybody. Dorothy Parker was a cute girl but hardly lovable; her forte was criticism which really stung. (It was Dorothy Parker who, commenting on an early and uninspired performance by Katharine Hepburn, in a Broadway play, *The Lake*, said that the actress "ran the gamut of emotions from A to B"; it was also Dorothy Parker who, feeling dislike for Countess Margot Asquith because the Countess had written a book which seemed too narcissistic, took care of her by commenting, "The romance between Margot Asquith and Margot Asquith will live as one of the great love affairs of literature," and adding that the book was "in four volumes, suitable for throwing." She also dealt with a drama called *The House Beautiful* by calling it "the play lousy," and, during the period in which she reviewed books under the pseudonym of Constant Reader, disposed of a book by A. A. Milne, whose cuteness and whimsy she abhorred, by writing, "Tonstant Weader fwowwed up.")

Ring Lardner was so quiet that other people at the Round Table frequently shook him by the shoulder and asked if he'd fallen asleep; Swope was a bundle of energy who stopped speaking only when outtalked by someone like Baruch. Robert E. Sherwood was so impressive in height that Benchley once touched the ceiling and said he'd known Sherwood since he was that high; Sherwood was also unfailingly polite. Oscar Levant, who occasionally joined the group, was short and unfailingly impolite; he worked so hard at being unpopular that Kaufman once offered him a sure-fire business proposal. "We'll both walk through the main thoroughfare of Bucks County," Kaufman told Levant, "and you'll have blueprints in your hand, and this will lead people to think that you're going to build and settle down. The inhabitants will become panic-stricken and real estate will go down. Then we'll buy, you won't build, and we'll clean up." (Kaufman presented an even more outré business proposition to George Oppenheimer, when the two men were walking near Central Park one afternoon. "Let's build a pay toilet in the park," Kaufman said, "and charge thirty-five dollars." "Thirty-five dollars!" Oppenheimer echoed, startled. "Who'd pay thirty-five dollars to use a pay toilet?" "Someday," Kaufman said, "somebody will come along who'll *have* to pay it.")

A typical example of the strong differences between members of the Round Table can be seen by taking a comparative look at Kaufman and Herbert Bayard Swope. Swope, born in St. Louis on January 5, 1882, and so admired a newspaperman that Lord Northcliffe once guaranteed that he'd get him a knighthood if he moved to England and joined the Northcliffe papers, was a flamboyant man who was habitually late for appointments and never gave a thought to time; Kaufman was overcome with embarrassment if he was two minutes late for an appointment. (Swope once called Kaufman at 9:30 in the evening and asked him, "What are you doing about dinner?" "Digesting it," Kaufman replied.) Swope was never on time for opening nights; Kaufman hated people who came late to plays, and, upon learning that the Swopes would be attending the opening of one of his plays, wrote Swope coaxingly: *Curtain time is eight o'clock, and the whole plot is in the first thirty-six seconds. After that the play goes steadily downhill.* Kaufman wasn't much on conversation, confining the openings of his mouth at the Round Table to his food and to the quick delivery of an occasional and marvelously funny line; Swope, who was described by Woodrow Wilson as having "the fastest mind with which I have ever come into contact," was admired by the group because he could speak brilliantly on virtually any subject but had relatively little gift for comedic invention. Swope realized this himself and wrote apologetically to Kaufman when a mild joke which Kaufman had invented, "A Lucy Stone gathers no boss," was credited to him. Kaufman replied politely. "If you'll meet me at my lawyer's," he wrote, "I'll be happy to deed over to you all rights in and to and against that joke about Lucy Stone. I doubt if this transaction will really stand up in law because (a) I don't know if I really said it, and (b) I don't think it's much of a joke anyway."

But short or tall, polite or impolite, punctual or tardy, they were never uninteresting, and some of their comedy lines have become classics. Woollcott has occasionally been credited with a famous line said after being caught in a sudden rainfall, but it was actually Benchley who said it: "I'd like to get out of this wet suit and into a dry martini." Benchley was also responsible for the inspired reply to the statement that liquor was slow poison: "Who's in a hurry?" He also invented the autobiographical statement which has often been credited to various actors and actresses, but Benchley actually said it about his writing career: "It took me fifteen years to discover I had no talent, but I couldn't give it all up because by that time I was too famous." Much of Benchley's humor was self-deprecating. He hated to write and was often late on delivery of scripts, once turning in an article called *I Like to Loaf* two weeks late with the explanation, "I was loafing"; he also brushed aside a suggestion from Case, to whom he had complained that he wasn't getting much writing done because people kept dropping in on him, that he take a room at the Algonquin and instruct the desk not to let people come up. "But how," Benchley asked, "will that keep me from coming down?"

Dorothy Parker's quips were not confined to her reviews, either. Once a feminine visitor to the Round Table boasted of her marriage and said coyly, "I've kept him for seven years." "Keep him long enough," Mrs. Parker said, "and he'll come back in style." One of her most famous lines was said when she was told that Calvin Coolidge was dead. "How can they tell?" she asked. She once got up suddenly at the Algonquin. "Excuse me," she said. "I have to go to the bathroom." Then she added: "I really have to telephone, but I'm too embarrassed to say so." She also once dropped a much-appreciated line about her poetry. "I'm always chasing Rimbauds," she said. And another time she heard that two acquaintances, a man and a woman who had lived together for a long time, had finally gotten married. She went out and sent them a telegram. The wire asked: WHAT'S NEW?

Lardner, in his laconic way, did his part. He had worked as a collector of bad debts before turning to writing, and he commented to his neighbor at the Round Table, "I just thought of something. Have you ever heard of a *good* debt?" Another time, he reported to the assemblage, "The President and I saw *The Merry Widow* on Broadway last night. But not together." He was also once an unwilling listener while someone read a terrible poem by a man who had died years before. "Did he write that," Lardner asked, "before or after he died?" Another example of Lardner's quiet, morose style of humor occurred when Spencer Tracy, then a young stage actor, appeared in a play called *Dread*. One day he ran into Lardner, who asked what he was doing. "I'm going to Brooklyn with *Dread*," Tracy said. "Is there any other way?" Lardner asked.

Woollcott, in his more florid way, did his part, too. One of his least favorite actresses was Elsie Ferguson, and he used that fact when he remembered that it was George and Beatrice Kaufman's fifth wedding anniversary. "I've been looking around for an appropriate wooden gift," he wrote them, "and am pleased to present you with Elsie Ferguson's performance in her new play." He once watched in stunned silence as Harpo Marx pulled up in an ancient Model T Ford, then asked, "What's that supposed to be?" "That's my town car," Marx said. "What town?" Woollcott asked. "Pompeii?" He invented the classic line, "Everything I like is either illegal, immoral, or fattening." And he coined descriptions of Dorothy Parker and Harold Ross which stuck with them throughout their lives. "Dorothy," he said, eying her lovely and angelic face and remembering some of her devastating commentary, "is a mixture of Little Nell and Lady Macbeth." His word picture of Ross was equally apropos. "Ross," he said, "looks like a dishonest Abe Lincoln."

The usual roll call at the lunches numbered about ten, most of them famous, and they became even more famous after they'd been conducting the daily meetings for a while and began to work harder and harder to outdo each other. Not all of the gags were spontaneous. Peggy Wood, for example, once attended a Round Table lunch while she was in rehearsal with a new play, and left the lunch by saying, "Well, back to the mimes." But she admitted afterward that she'd thought of the line the previous evening and had hardly been able to wait for the next day to spring it. Whether the quips were spontaneous or pre-planned, however, they were repeated all over town, and repeated again and again in innumerable magazine and newspaper pieces and books. Frank Case's daughter, Margaret Case Harriman, who grew up to become an author of gracefully written profiles for *The New Yorker* and other magazines, wrote one such book, calling it *The Vicious Circle*, and Robert E. Drennen wrote another one, *The Algonquin Wits*. The group also found themselves in a best-selling novel. Gertrude Atherton, in her novel about rejuvenation, *Black Oxen*, published in 1923 by Boni and Liveright, called the group The Sophisticates and changed their names, but they were recognizable. They also almost got another name during the Ouija Board craze. When a waiter named Luigi was assigned to the table, someone suggested that they start calling their lunches The Luigi Board.

Not everybody remained a regular or even an irregular; some people tried one lunch at the Round Table and didn't like it. One of these was Clare Boothe Luce, who found the lunches "too competitive. You couldn't say, 'Pass the salt,' without somebody trying to turn it into a pun or trying to top it." Some people just couldn't seem to get in, like Morrie Ryskind, even though he later became closely involved with Kaufman.

Ryskind finally started a rival Round Table at the hotel, but Case found Ryskind's group too noisy and evicted them. And some people were often mentioned as Round Table lunchers but rarely or never had the opportunity to attend. One of these was Frank Sullivan, as mentioned, who said recently in answer to a question about his participation in the group, "I can't remember ever having once lunched at the Round Table. I knew nearly all the members but it was not at the Algonquin that I saw them. My routine didn't include the Algonquin or any other place at lunchtime, because I didn't lunch. In those days I was on the *World* and usually didn't leave the *World* until ten or eleven at night. I then made straight to the speakeasy belt for my recreation—Tony Soma's or Dan Moriarty's or the Artists and Writers Club (in those days known simply as Bleeck's). At Tony's I was apt to find Bob Benchley, or Thurber or Mrs. Parker, congenial souls and serious drinkers with whom I was delighted to while away the hours until we all got thrown out."

There were also those who condemned the Round Table as an unhealthy influence on American letters, a powerful log-rolling society whose members used up so much valuable newspaper and magazine space applauding and supporting their friends that there was insufficient space left over to bring more important and more talented authors to public attention. The loudest of these opposition voices were George Jean Nathan, the terrible-tempered and argumentative theatre critic for *The American Mercury*, and Burton Rascoe, the equally irascible book critic for the *Tribune*. Both these men, seen in retrospect, seem a bit suspect, because they both tried to get into the group and were not made too welcome—Nathan because he had an abrasive personality, and also because he had a yellow-journalism tendency to espouse causes which would draw headlines even when the causes were clearly without merit, and Rascoe because he had right-wing leanings and nearly all the Round Table lunchers were liberal. Nathan and Rascoe made a lot of noise at the time, however, and this comment from Rascoe's book, *We Were Interrupted*, is typical (and interesting because of its clear tinge of jealousy): "I was particularly annoyed and aggrieved at the 'Algonquin crowd' because they were making such ill use of their talents and of their power to influence the taste of a great many readers . . . It was, of course, unreasonable of me to expect this group to perform a cultural service that their jobs did not require. Adams was a conductor of a column of wit and humor, Woollcott and Benchley were drama critics and contributors to *Vanity Fair*, and Broun had a column in the *World*, in which he wrote about anything that came into his head, and contributed to *Vanity Fair* and *College Humor*. But it was the very latitude of expression they enjoyed which gave me an acute sense of their abusing it, or at least not making the most of it.

"I considered the influence of the 'Algonquin group' to be a pernicious one, unfortunate in its effect upon the standards of the period, and, therefore, I determined to undermine it in so far as I was able to do so, not only by what I wrote myself but also by attracting to the *Tribune*'s book pages writers who were part of the main stream of contemporary literature and could be counted upon to write with liveliness and effectiveness . . . I knew I could not compete with the 'Algonquin group' for popular attention and influence. The thing I decided, then, was to become *apparently* as self-centered and personal as Broun, Adams, and Woollcott, and to be in the 'Algonquin crowd' but not precisely of it; I would not only jest at their pretensions and their enthusiasms for trivial writers and trivial notions but beat drums for writers they disdained or ignored whom I considered more worthy of attention."

As it turned out, Rascoe never became much of an influence on American arts and letters. He never got in or of the Algonquin crowd, either.

On the reverse side of the coin, there were a few people who dismissed the Round Table members as too inconsequential for consideration, agreeing with the whole group's tendency to share Benchley's habit of self-deprecation. "I'm potentially the best writer in America," Woollcott said, "but I never have anything to say." Ring Lardner described himself as a hack and a second-rater; Adams labeled himself a newspaper columnist and nothing more; Kaufman called himself "a play doctor who got lucky"; Benchley often referred to himself as a failure; and Dorothy Parker made her own decisive estimate of herself as a poet: "I was following in the exquisite footsteps of Miss Edna St. Vincent Millay, unhappily in my own horrible sneakers." A little of this was tongue-in-cheek, and in a case or two probably fishing for disagreement. But some people seconded the motion and dismissed the group, and there are some studies of literary movements of the period which mention none of the Round Table members at all.

There was enough derision so that, in later years, a few of the Round Table's most faithful participants became defensive or scornful themselves about the luncheons. Kaufman had always regarded the log-rolling accusations with amusement, noting, as he often did, that for every critic who gave him, out of friendship, a more favorable review than he perhaps deserved, there were always two who were much tougher than they might otherwise have been, just to show that *they* weren't being influenced by friendship. "Sure there was back-scratching," he said once. "I've still got the scars on my back to prove it." But he also wrote a relatively serious piece on the subject in *The Saturday Review of Literature*'s issue of August 11, 1945.

"It is about time, I think," he wrote, "that someone laid at rest the myth of the Algonquin Round Table. The legend persists that here was a tight little group of critics, playwrights, and novelists, all intent upon praising each other to the skies and rigidly damning the work of any upstanding outsider. Just recently I read intimations to this effect in the columns of John Mason Brown and George Jean Nathan, among others. Perhaps there is some mild excuse in the case of Mr. Brown, for he rose to fame in the post-Algonquin days and inherited the legend. But Mr. Nathan is old enough to know better. Older. The truth is, of course, that the Round Table was made up of a motley and nondescript group of people who wanted to eat lunch, and that's about all. They had no power at all over the literature of the day, and it seems to me that the least thought on the part of the accusers would convince them of that fact. How in God's name could they wield any such power? How could any group wield such power in the critical world as it is made up today, and as it was made up then? The Round Table

[159]

members ate at the Algonquin because Frank Case was good enough to hold a table for them, and because it was fun."

Dorothy Parker was even more vehement. In her last years, she became a sad and embittered old woman, taking cannon shots at most of the things, and many of the people, she had embraced so enthusiastically in her youth. "It was no Mermaid Tavern, I promise you," she told an interviewer for the Associated Press. "There were no giants. Think of who was writing in those days—Lardner, Fitzgerald, Faulkner, Hemingway. Those were the real giants." This was a curious comment, since the man who led her list was a Round Table regular, but the reporter did not comment on this, and she went on. "The Round Table was just a lot of people telling jokes and telling each other how good they were . . . I think of the Round Table and I really get sick at all that fuss about them now . . . Those people at the Round Table didn't know a bloody thing. They thought we were fools to go up and demonstrate for Sacco and Vanzetti." And that, too, was a curious statement, in view of the fact that Broun had been so much in the forefront of the fight to make the public aware of the injustices in the case.

All things considered, looking back at it from the vantage point of a half century later, it's difficult to see any real logic or merit in the comments of the detractors, original or eventual. Mutual admiration society or not, the amount of attention given to the members of the Round Table was far less than the total received by their more serious colleagues like Fitzgerald and Hemingway. And if the Algonquin Hotel was no Mermaid Tavern—it unquestionably spawned no Shakespeare and few Jonsons and Marlowes—it was nevertheless more than just a place where people met for lunch and had fun. The Round Table was also a kind of obstetrics ward and testing and developmental laboratory for some of the best humor and best humorists the United States has ever produced. A lot of people would agree that that is *raison d'être* enough.

11.   THE GAMES

SATURDAYS WERE SPECIAL at the Round Table. Unlike the other lunches, which were generally leisurely and ended with the members going their separate ways, the male participants at the Saturday sessions hurried through their meal, got rid of their wives and girl friends, and moved upstairs to a small second-floor suite provided for them, free of charge, by Frank Case. The suite was the site of a weekly poker game.

The poker players, who eventually began to call themselves The Thanatopsis Literary and Inside Straight Club, usually got down to business about five o'clock in the afternoon and played until the small hours of Sunday morning. Sometimes, when the game was fairly even and there was no big winner who developed a sudden case of exhaustion, or what Adams called "winner's sleeping sickness," the game continued all day Sunday and into Monday morning. (Adams also had a name for the opposite illness. He called it "loser's insomnia, or Broun's disease.")

The name of the card-playing group has been erroneously credited by some historians to John Peter Toohey, probably because he was so quick in coming up with the right name when *The New Yorker* was being organized, but the title was actually Adams's invention. The most famous use of "thanatopsis" is, of course, as the title of William Cullen Bryant's classic poem, written in 1811, but Adams's concentration on the word resulted from a more recent use. He came across the word in Sinclair Lewis's novel, *Main Street*, looked it up because he wasn't sure of its meaning, and discovered that it meant "contemplation on death." (Thanatos is a figure out of Greek mythology, the personification of death, and "opsis" means "sight or view.") The word seemed to be appropriate to poker because, as Adams explained to the other people at the Round Table, you often contemplate dying hopes when you pick up your hand and see the terrible cards you've been dealt, so he began to call the poker group the Young Men's Upper West Side Thanatopsis Literary and Inside Straight Club. This was later shortened to the permanent name.

The game was the direct descendant of an earlier poker group which had begun when Adams, Woollcott, and Ross were working on *Stars and Stripes* and eating at a tiny Paris restaurant named Nini's, located on Place du Tertre. The little restaurant contained only two long tables, located at opposite ends of the room, and three small tables in the center of the room, but the food was excellent, particularly after the three men began to slip the proprietor their ration tickets. They usually went to the place only on Saturdays because it was located at the top of Montmartre, all the way across town from the *Stars and Stripes* office, but stayed on all day and sometimes all night, eating, drinking, and gambling. Sometimes the game was dice, and sometimes the proprietor produced a *chou* and set up a game of *chemin de fer*, but most of the time it was poker.

Other people began to join the game, nearly always brought there by Adams, Woollcott, or Ross because the bistro was so far off the beaten track that few Americans discovered it on their own.

Steve Early, then an AEF captain and later Franklin Delano Roosevelt's press secretary, was a frequent player, as was Grantland Rice, the sportswriter, then an Army lieutenant, Richard Oulahan, who had given up his post as the *Times*'s Washington Bureau Chief to serve as a war correspondent, and Private John T. Winterich, later an editor and expert on rare books. George T. Bye, who worked for a civilian news service but contributed occasionally to *Stars and Stripes*, was also part of the group. He later became an immensely successful literary agent who confined his client list to twelve people, and would not take on a new client unless one of the twelve left him or quit writing or died; Eleanor Roosevelt was one of the people he represented. Jane Grant, in Paris for the YMCA, was allowed to watch but never to play, and caused considerable grumbling because Ross became so interested in her that he occasionally neglected his game. Broun and Lardner also showed up now and then; Broun had convinced the *Tribune* to give him a stint as a war correspondent, and Lardner was doing pieces on the war for magazines and newspaper syndicates.

After the war, Ross and Winterich shared an apartment for a while on West 11th Street, and the game continued there on an irregular basis. The apartment was given up when Ross married Jane Grant and Winterich decided he couldn't afford the place on his own, but the Rosses then took a small apartment at the Algonquin and invited the players over there every once in a while. That, too, didn't work out for long because the games were infrequent, and too many players, filled with card-hunger, showed up whenever there was a game. Toohey, now a popular member of the group, came up with a solution: he suggested a regular Saturday game and offered the players the hospitality of his own large apartment on West 114th Street. He had his reasons for suggesting his own place; his wife was beginning to object strongly to his absences for poker sessions, and wanted him where she could watch him and make him quit if he started to lose too much. The games at the Toohey apartment were the real start of the Thanatopsis group, which soon included Kaufman. The other players gave Toohey the title of Our Beloved Founder and formed the habit of standing up and bowing gravely in his direction whenever he entered the room, and the games continued on West 114th Street until Case offered the Algonquin suite.

The Thanatopsis sessions quickly revealed some new and unexpected eccentricities in some of the players. Woollcott, who would have sneered at a display of superstition on the part of anyone else, became the victim of a weird superstition of his own. He developed a strange compulsion about the king of clubs; he became convinced, for some reason he was never able to explain himself, that the card was a winning portent if it showed up early in his own hand, and sure death for him if it turned up in somebody's else's. As a result, if he was dealt the king of clubs as his first or second face-up card, he immediately raised and continued to raise to the limit; conversely, if the game was stud poker and one of the first two open cards dealt to someone else was the king of clubs, he immediately folded. Since he sometimes drew the king of clubs when the rest of his hand consisted of a five of hearts, an eight of spades, and a three of diamonds, and since he sometimes folded three aces when the opponent who had drawn the king of clubs had nothing to go with it, he was a fairly constant loser at the games. Kaufman, an otherwise skillful player who had learned the game from experts when he was on the Washington *Times*, playing at the National Press Club, where the game continued twenty-four hours a day and seven days a week with ever-changing players, had one strange weakness, too. The most diffident man in the world when it came to assessing his own abilities as a writer, he became overconfident to the point of madness, every now and then, no matter what cards happened to show up in his hand. On those occasions, he bet a pair of tens as though they were a royal flush, and was genuinely surprised when someone else turned up a pair of jacks.

He put a bright face on it all. "Like the Arabs," he said the night the jacks topped him, "I fold my tens and silently steal away," and he summarized a hand in which he'd been hoping for high cards and gotten instead a two and three by saying, "I've been treydeuced." But it was easy to see that he felt betrayed when a hand didn't hold up.

The oddest oddity of them all, however, was Broun's. Broun was normally the most generous and trusting of men; he gave money to causes to the point where he sometimes found himself without funds for his own needs, and he had the reputation for being one of the world's softest touches for anybody who asked him for a loan. But at the poker games—despite the fact that he was playing with the people he knew and liked best in the world—he became almost psychotically suspicious and distrustful, in agony if another player lost more than he had in cash and offered to pay off with a check. He tried at all costs to avoid taking the check, sometimes settling for the other player's cash even when the available cash was much less than the amount owed and the check would certainly have been good.

One particularly soul-scarring incident occurred when Woollcott began to invite Harpo Marx to the games, and Harpo began to invite his brother Chico, and Chico lost $1200 to Broun. Chico started to write a check, but Broun didn't want a check; he told Chico he'd settle for a thousand dollars in cash. "I haven't got a thousand with me," Chico said. Broun hesitated, and then said, "All right, I'll settle for $750." Chico admitted that he didn't have $750, either. Broun was now extremely nervous. "How much *do* you have?" he asked. Chico pulled out his wallet and counted his money. "Eighteen dollars," he said.

Witnesses to the incident insist that Broun actually considered accepting the $18 in full settlement, but finally decided that that was too much of a drop even for him. He accepted the check, and was at Chico's bank at nine o'clock Monday morning. His worst fears were justified; the bank told him there weren't sufficient funds in Chico's account to cover the check. Broun rushed over to see Chico—"roaring," Harpo said in telling the story, "like a wounded bear." Chico reassured him. "Put the check through again tomorrow," he said. "But not before noon." The check bounced again, and again Broun came shouting to Chico. "For God's sake," Chico said, "I told you to wait until twelve o'clock." "I did!" Broun said. "I did! I even waited until *five after* twelve." "That," Chico said, "was too late." Chico eventually made the check good, but Broun never really recovered fully from the effects of the occurrence.

Thereafter, Kaufman, a more trusting type, served as the group's banker, accepting and cashing all checks.

Depending on how the cards ran, the games were sometimes bad and sometimes good, but the conversation was always good. Bob Benchley once showed up late for a game. He was quite an energetic lover despite his mild appearance; his close friends were not surprised when the leading madam of the day, Polly Adler, who wrote her autobiography under the title of *A House Is Not a Home*, kept mentioning that one of her most active customers was "a writer named Bob" and the writer turned out to be Benchley. Benchley was then involved with a young actress named Helen Walker. "Where've you been?" Adams asked. "I've been cuing Helen Walker," Benchley said. "Please!" Adams said. "No baby talk at the table." One of Kaufman's most famous puns was also coined at a Thanatopsis game: "One man's Mede is another man's Persian." And another classic line was born when, shortly after *The Green Hat* had become a success on Broadway, with Katharine Cornell starring, Woollcott brought its author, Michael Arlen, to a game. Arlen, who was an Armenian despite his ultra-British mannerisms (his real name was Dirkan Kouyoumdjian) proceeded to win nearly every hand for hours. Herman Mankiewicz, seated next to Arlen, regarded him sourly. "Let's start kittying out for the Turks," he suggested.

The Thanatopsis group often had trouble with strangers and irregulars. One such was Prince Antoine Bibesco, the Minister from Romania, who came from Washington to play in a game, admitting shyly that he wasn't a very good poker player and sometimes wasn't even sure whether two pair were better than three of a kind. He proceeded to clean out the game and was never invited again; the regulars didn't mind a winner, but they hated a phony, even a royal one. Another was an actor, Herbert Ranson, who embarrassed the regulars because his expressions were so easy to read. His joy at receiving good cards and his gloom at receiving bad cards were so obvious that Adams, Kaufman, and the others never lost to him because they knew exactly when to stay in or drop out. Adams finally suggested a new rule for the club. "Anybody who looks at Ranson's face," he said, "is cheating."

Swope didn't come very often because the games were too tame

or him; he was only a salaried employee on the *World*, but he
had a lot of important friends in financial circles and was getting
ome good stock tips, so he'd begun to play poker for astronomical
igures—sometimes for amounts even beyond his skyrocketing in-
ome. He played in one game with Samuel Goldwyn in which
Goldwyn won $155,000, but, in a game two weeks later, Goldwyn
ost $169,000. Swope's gaming became so heavy that, one year, he
ept a meticulous diary of his wins and losses and discovered that,
ven after making the gentlemanly gesture of deducting his wife's
osses of $11,795, he was still ahead $186,758. The biggest game in
vhich he ever played was a four-man session in Palm Beach with
Florenz Ziegfeld, then raking in money constantly with one success-
ul *Ziegfeld Follies* after another, Joshua S. Cosden, an oil millionaire
vho was worth $75,000,000 and owned a three-hundred-acre estate
n Long Island with its own eighteen-hole golf course, and J. Leonard
Replogle, another millionaire. The game went so well for Swope
hat he told himself he'd quit when he was $150,000 ahead, but, be-
fore he knew it, he was ahead more than that. When the game was
finally over, he had won $470,300. And even though $294,300 of
his amount was owed by Ziegfeld, and the producer reneged and
ventually died broke with the debt remaining unpaid, it was still a
air night's work.

All this made the Algonquin games kid stuff for Swope, but he
till showed up now and then because he liked the company and
he quick wit. This was true even when the wit was used to deflate
ome of his pretensions, such as his effort to appear more and more
WASPish even though he was Jewish. "Did you know," he once
emarked at a game, "that I've got a little Jewish in me?" The
nan across the table from him was Paul Robeson, another oc-
asional player. "Is that right?" Robeson said. "Did you know I've
ot a touch of the tar brush?" Another time, Swope asked Adams,
vho was an enthusiastic gardener, how his flowers were coming
long. Adams answered tartly, because he suspected that Swope
vas not really interested, but was just using the personality-course
rick of talking to the other fellow about *his* interests. "Well,"
Adams said, "my peonies are doing fine because I've been keeping

my eye on them. And I've discovered that if you watch you peonies, your dahlias take care of themselves."

Situations often started at the card table and ranged outward around the world. Once Woollcott, Broun, and Harpo Marx shared a taxi going home from a game, and Woollcott and Broun continued in so animated an argument about the game that they were still quarreling when the cab reached Harpo's apartment and the driver looked inquiringly at him for further instructions. "Take my friends," Harpo said, "to Werba's Flatbush." The theatre he named was a broken-down burlesque house a dozen miles away in Brooklyn, and it was a winter night with the roads icy and heavy snow falling but the driver shrugged and proceeded on his way. Harpo learned afterward that Woollcott and Broun didn't notice what was happening until the car had crossed the bridge and was entering Brooklyn. He also learned that the taxi had broken down on the return trip, and the two men, neither of them sylphlike, had had to trudge for miles through the arctic weather before they could find another cab. Harpo was awakened at six o'clock the next morning by a phone call; a voice, unmistakably Woollcott's, said savagely, "You son of a bitch!" and hung up. But he was forgiven by the time the next game rolled around.

On another occasion, two publishers, Bennett Cerf of Random House and Harold Guinzburg of The Viking Press, showed up for a game. This time the shoe was on the other foot for Broun he lost $1500 to Cerf and Guinzburg and had neither enough cash nor a check to give them, and they were leaving the next morning for a tour of Russia. The publishers decided to make Broun's life miserable by berating him via telegraph for his failure to settle a legitimate debt, and they sent him a page-long cable every day of their trip. Broun was properly chastened, but was also certain looking at the length of the cables, that the publishers had taken leave of their senses. The thing he didn't know was that, because of the favorable position of the dollar at that time in relationship to the ruble, the cables were costing Cerf and Guinzburg only about thirty-five cents apiece.

There was also the occasion when Crosby Gaige, a leading producer of the period, thought he saw an opportunity to make Woollcott

ose some of his cool. He lost $3500 to Woollcott at one of the
Thanatopsis games, but was only able to pay him $2500 that night,
nd promised to pay the additional thousand at "first opportunity."
He made sure the opportunity occurred when Woollcott, in his capacity as critic for the *Times*, arrived at a theatre to review Gaige's
newest production. Gaige waited until Woollcott was surrounded by
people, and then approached him and, ostentatiously and leeringly,
handed him a thousand-dollar bill. The ploy didn't work. Woollcott
calmly tucked the bill into the ribbon of his hat, and left it there, with
the amount showing, for the remainder of the evening.

A more prolonged situation was that one which might be called the
case of Dave Wallace and his mysterious middle initial. Wallace was a
publicity man who was very popular with the group because he knew
every young actress in town and was always ready to arrange introductions for any Thanatopsis member who expressed a desire to meet a
particular actress or just any actress. But the players found themselves piqued with curiosity when it developed, during a desultory
card-game conversation, that Wallace had a middle initial but, for
some reason, was apparently as ashamed of it as Kaufman was proud of
his adopted S. After some investigation, it was learned that Wallace's
middle initial was H., leading to rumors that he was embarrassed about
the initial because it stood for either Horatio or Hepzibah, but this was
never proven. Nevertheless, the players were spurred on by Wallace's
insistent secrecy to publicize the neglected initial, and this became
easy after Ross founded *The New Yorker*. The magazine didn't come
up with the idea of using funny typographical errors from other
magazines and newspapers and books as fillers until later, so every
column which ended short was filled with a pointless quote credited
to Wallace's full name. "As David H. Wallace says," ran one filler,
"tea and coffee are good to drink, but tennis is livelier." "David H.
Wallace, the monologuist, convulsed his set with a good one the other
evening," ran another filler. " 'It seems there were two Irishmen,' Mr.
Wallace began, but could not go on for laughing." Unlike Wallace,
the fillers went on and on, making his middle initial one of the most
famous in New York. They stopped appearing only after Wallace
admitted at a game that he was growing fond of the H.

It was mostly good-natured, even when things were outrageous, such as when Adams, whose first marriage had failed, married again and was given a beautiful poker set, complete with ivory chips, as a wedding present—but only on condition that he and his bride come to the Algonquin directly after the ceremony and spend their first night at the poker game. Adams and his new wife, Esther, met the condition and showed up, but were so amiable about it that they were released at about 2 A.M. to go on to better things. Sometimes there was a brief flare-up, as when a temperamental player like Marc Connelly became so incensed at the cards he was getting that he seized the deck and tore it to pieces. But more serious disputes were so rare that the only one on record is a fistfight between Broun and a stock-broker named Joe Brooks.

Broun and Brooks happened to take seats next to each other at one of the games, which was unfortunate because ten minutes of conversation revealed that they disagreed on every imaginable subject. By the time both men had left the game, they had argued bitterly about everything from politics to the theatre to women, but it might have ended there if Broun had been able to fall asleep when he got home. He was so agitated that he tossed and turned for hours, and he finally told his wife that he was getting dressed and going over to punch Brooks in the nose. His wife tried to talk him out of it; she made some disparaging remarks about the protuberance above his belt, pointed out that Brooks had no such protuberance, and added that Brooks had been an All-American football player. Broun would not allow himself to be dissuaded. He dressed quickly, took a taxi from his house on West 85th Street to Brooks's apartment on East 10th Street, leaned on the doorbell until Brooks opened the door, and hit him.

The stockbroker immediately hit him back. The fight lasted only a few minutes, and Broun got the worst of it. Brooks received only superficial bruises, but Broun got two black eyes, and he was rolled around the floor so much that his clothes were literally torn to bits. He had to go home in a suit borrowed from Brooks. The night, however, ended triumphantly for him after all. He found Brooks's address book in one of the pockets of the suit, meticulously kept and containing the names and phone numbers of every one of Brooks's girl friends, and he spent the rest of the night pulling out page after page and ripping each page into shreds.

Women were rigidly banned at first from the Thanatopsis games, except for special occasions like the command appearance of Esther Adams on her wedding night. Adams, who felt strongly on the subject, wrote a long article about it, calling it, unequivocally, *Women Can't Play Poker*. Women, he pointed out, lost all sense of mathematical reality when it came to poker; if a woman was winning $22 and her husband was losing $218, she invariably insisted that they call it a night, because she was so blinded by her small victory that all she saw was that they were ahead $22, not down $196. He also expressed the view that women could never remember the value of the various colors of chips, that women were never satisfied with conventional forms of poker and varied the game more and more until male players became unsure as to whether an ace was a good card or a bad card, and took wild risks. Woollcott, he said, had even coined a name for Esther Adams's particular folly, which was her habit of holding two cards of the same suit in the hope of drawing three more; he called a hand with two cards of the same suit an Esther flush. And most heinous of all, Adams concluded, was the fact that women always told the truth. If they won or lost $72, they actually *told* people they had won or lost $72. Men, as every man knew, were a much more civilized sex. If you asked a man about a game's outcome, you could always count on being told that he'd ended up even, and you'd never have to worry about feeling either envy or pity.

Kaufman also wrote something along similar lines: he wrote a devstating one-act play called *If Men Played Cards as Women Do* which was played at the Booth Theatre on Sunday, February 11, 1923, for the benefit of the Girls' Service Club. The one-acter was also revived years later in the Paramount film, *Star-Spangled Rhythm*, where it was performed by Ray Milland, Fred MacMurray, Franchot Tone, and Lynne Overman, and was easily the funniest thing in the film. But nothing could halt progress. After a while, a few women were allowed to attend the games as spectators, and eventually Beatrice Kaufman, Esther Adams, Neysa McMein, Jane Grant, Margaret Swope and others were permitted to participate as players.

The Thanatopsis games continued for about a decade, most of this time in the second-floor suite at the Algonquin. There were occasional temporary departures. Case provided the suite free but assumed that, if the players paused to eat, they would order their food from the hotel He was mildly irritated to see that, instead, the group either sent one of the players around the corner to pick up sandwiches and beverages at a Sixth Avenue delicatessen—or, if Swope happened to be in the game, phoned the Colony and asked them to send over some of their expensive delicacies. Case's irritation grew stronger when, one hot summer evening, the poker players brought in a freezer of strawberry and pistachio ice cream from an outside caterer, and some of the ice cream melted and made stains all over the carpet. The next the group met, they saw that Case had tacked an ironic sign on a wall of the suite:

Basket Parties Welcome

The players were amused at first, regarding the sign as a convenient place to jot down phone numbers or do little sums to figure out their winnings or losses. And then, as they thought about it, they became offended. They moved over to the Colony, where the restaurant owner, Gene Cavallero, provided them with a private room. The Colony was tremendously expensive, so much so that Harpo Marx finally asked, plaintively, "Isn't there anything here you can get for fifty cents?" "Sure," Kaufman said. "A quarter." So after two months, they were back in the more familiar and more comfortable surroundings of the Algonquin suite. And though they returned to the Colony for an occasional game, played in various members' houses now and then, and at least once played by invitation at Alice Brady's house—during which the young actress served pheasant and champagne, and then joined the game and lost steadily, causing some worry about her financial well-being until Dave Wallace mentioned that she'd just signed a movie contract paying her $4000 a week —the action remained mostly at the Algonquin.

The poker games finally slowed to a halt for two reasons. The first was that, as the players became more and more successful, they became more mobile and far-flung. Woollcott began to tour all over the country giving lectures, and began to move around the world on various social pursuits. The Marx Brothers went out to the Coast to make some pictures, and eventually settled there. Kaufman, Connelly, and Sherwood began to spend more and more time on out-of-town tryouts of their plays. And suddenly there were some Saturday evenings when not enough people showed up to make a game.

The second reason was economic: the games began to grow too expensive. The stakes never achieved the dimensions of those in Swope's games, but they kept mounting until they became too rich for many of the players, even those whose income was rising at the same time. Ross, struggling to make *The New Yorker* a success and not drawing too large a salary, lost nearly $30,000 one night, and had to arrange to pay it in installments over a long period of time. Harpo Marx came into town and *won* $30,000; he later denied this, saying he never won over a thousand or two in a Thanatopsis game, but other people insisted they had been present at the game and the big score really happened. John V. A. Weaver wrote a moderate best-seller, *In American*, and lost all his royalties in a single game.

The Thanatopsis players tried a little self-deception. To keep the game looking the same, they allowed the chips to remain valued as before, but paid half as much for them and received half as much when they cashed in. But this didn't work, either; Ross won $450 at the end of one game, and spent the rest of the night complaining bitterly that he'd have picked up $900 if it had been the week before. And after a while, though the men and women continued to see each other at lunches and other places, they stopped gathering together around a card table.

There were other games, too. Woollcott became an avid croquet player, and when a lot of other people followed suit, so, to everybody's astonishment, did Kaufman. This was immensely surprising because Kaufman ordinarily had no interest whatsoever in athletics. His boyhood enthusiasm for the Pittsburgh Pirates had not carried over into his adult life, and he never watched baseball games, or, for that matter, football games or basketball games or boxing or wrestling. He never played golf or tennis, either, and his credo was plain enough: "Ring Lardner," he said, "once told me that the only exercise he got was when he took the cuff links out of one shirt and put them in another. That goes for me, too." But Beatrice, Swope, Frank Adams, Harpo Marx, Kathleen Norris, the novelist, Mrs. Nelson Doubleday, wife of the publisher, and others began to play croquet all the time and seemed to be enjoying it tremendously, so Kaufman joined the game and gave it the same kind of single-minded concentration he gave his playwriting. And he became, in Woollcott's words, "unexpectedly powerful and precise"—one of the best players in the group.

The group became so fanatic about the game that they played everywhere and under all conditions. They secured a special permit from the city and played in Central Park, despite the presence of gaping bystanders who sometimes multiplied into gaping crowds. They played at Swope's estate at Sands Point, Long Island, becoming so involved in the game that once, when Swope's butler came to report that Al Smith was on the telephone, Swope asked Smith to hold on because it was his shot, and kept the governor waiting twenty minutes while he made three wickets. They played at Otto Kahn's estate, engaging in so wild a game that they knocked over garden furniture, broke greenhouse windows, and sent so many balls whizzing past the heads of servants and other guests that Kahn himself finally fled to his yacht and stayed there until the game was over. They played at night, illuminating the court by surrounding it with their cars and turning on their headlights, continuing to play until all their batteries had run down. They once even played in a snowstorm, hiring a crew of eight men to stand by and keep clearing the court with snowplows and shovels.

The games grew pretty emotional at times. Swope, who defied tradition by rarely losing his temper despite his red hair, lost his temper regularly at croquet games. He argued so bitterly and constantly with Woollcott about obscure rules of the game that the two men finally decided to put up $500 apiece and have a grudge match; Woollcott won the match and the money, but that didn't stop their arguments. Another time, Swope turned on his partner and began to berate him for making a bad shot. "That's the worst shot I've ever seen in my life!" he screamed. "It's a shot worthy of a moron with ten thumbs!" His partner, a two-star general with a reputation for being one of the toughest men in the Army, listened meekly and did not respond.

Richard Rodgers was another calm man who occasionally became anything but calm on the croquet court. Like Kaufman, he had been militantly non-athletic until croquet entered his life, ignoring even a game like golf, which was played by nearly all of his friends, but

SAM H. HARRIS

He refused to stop talking.

GROUCHO MARX AND MARGARET DUMONT IN
THE COCOANUTS

A preference for apes.

THE ORIGINAL FIVE

(Left to right, Gummo, Groucho, Harpo, Chico, and Zeppo Marx.)

Culver Pictures, Inc

HEYWOOD BROUN

"Did you fall down?"

KAUFMAN AS ABRAHAM LINCOLN AT A MASQUERADE PARTY
John Drinkwater offered him a job.

ROBERT BENCHLEY READING *THE TREASURER'S REPORT*
Out of a wet suit.

Fabian Bachrach

HAROLD W. ROSS

He carried his idea around for years.

JAMES THURBER AND FRIEND
He thought Kaufman was the spirit of comedy.

roquet quickly became one of his great enthusiasms. "Dick takes
roquet more seriously than anything outside his work," his wife
nce said. "At a party he's the soul of effortless charm, but on the
roquet field he can be as stern and as unyielding as granite. He gets
nad at himself, his opponents, the wickets, a passing breeze. He can
ompose music with all hell breaking loose around him, but let one
eaf move within his peripheral vision during a shot and he explodes."
This couldn't always be counted upon by his opponents, however.
Despite all the *sturm und drang*, croquet lasted even longer than the
passion for poker, and in 1953, Kaufman was still playing the game
nd, with Moss Hart, challenged Rodgers and his wife, who lived
n Connecticut, to a Bucks County versus Nutmeg State competition.
During the games, Kaufman and Hart tried all sorts of distractions,
ncluding whistling several Rodgers tunes off-key, but the Connecticut
eam still won.

Most of the other games Kaufman played were more sedentary.
Charades were becoming a popular pastime in the '20s, and Kaufman,
despite his shyness, became one of the best players at that game, too,
reminding people who expressed admiration for his pantomime that he
had, after all, entered the theatrical world with ambitions of becoming
n actor rather than a writer. Another favorite was Twenty Questions
n all of its myriad forms and variations. One particularly frenzied
game occurred when George Oppenheimer, who started his professional life in the publishing field and founded The Viking Press in
ssociation with Harold Guinzburg, tried out some questions from
a book Viking was about to publish, *Ask Me Another*. "Who wrote
The Virginian?" he asked Beatrice. That was easy, and Beatrice
nswered quickly. "Owen Wister," she said. But the next one wasn't
quite so easy. "Who wrote *The Virginians?*" Oppenheimer asked.
Beatrice hesitated for a long time, then finally answered. "Owen
Wisters," she said. Kaufman was equally gifted at stalling when he
didn't know the answer to a question. "What's the longest river in
South America?" Oppenheimer asked him that same day. Kaufman,
oo, was silent for a long time with—clearly—nothing emerging. Then
he asked, craftily, "Are you sure it's in South America?"

But the game which Kaufman enjoyed most of all, after poker and
croquet, was another card game: bridge. Like poker, bridge interested

him because it was possible to develop complex skills and sciences in playing it, and he became in time an expert at the game. Howard Dietz, who played bridge three times a week with Kaufman for a number of years, once corrected an interviewer who said he'd heard Kaufman was an "incredible player," saying, "Not incredible—but damn good." But Ely Culbertson, himself one of the greatest bridge professionals the world has ever known, felt Kaufman was even better than that; he said several times in articles that he considered Kaufman the best amateur bridge player in the United States.

Kaufman first learned the game as a boy in Pittsburgh, playing with his father and mother and others. He quickly became impatient with the game played by Nettie, whom he considered a terrible player, but respectful about the game played by Joseph, who was almost as good as he was. Kaufman became so good so early that Ruth refused to allow him to teach her the game when, around her tenth birthday he offered to do so. She didn't want him to become impatient with her, too, if she turned out to be as bad a player as their mother, and she first learned the game when she attended a bridge school nearly thirty years later.

Kaufman played bridge with great seriousness and watchfulness, studying his opponent's actions and reactions as carefully as a good poker player watches for spots of color and other signs of emotion in other players' faces. "I'd like a review of the bidding with the original inflections," he said during one game. The calibre of his game may be judged by the fact that one of his favorite opponents was Fred Schwed, the brilliant financier whose son, Peter, is now the equally brilliant chairman of the editorial board of Simon and Schuster. The financier was a genius in the stock market and at nearly every other form of gaming; the calibre and size of *his* usual play can be demonstrated by an incident which took place when, in 1919, Schwed and a group of friends hired a private railroad car to take them to the Dempsey-Willard fight in Toledo, Ohio.

The travelers had originally planned to play high-stakes bridge to pass time on the trip, but an insufficient number of good bridge players showed up, so the game became dice instead. Dice was not a game Schwed enjoyed, but that didn't keep him from being good at it, and at one point he found that it had grown quite late and he was

$300,000 ahead. This presented a dilemma: he couldn't quit the game abruptly when he was so far ahead, but he was also very tired and knew he wouldn't enjoy the fight if he didn't get some sleep.

He finally offered a proposition. "Look," he said, "this game can go on all night—and then none of us will enjoy the fight. How about finishing up by letting me toss a coin twice? If I lose either toss, you've got your money back; if I win both tosses, you people will owe me a million two hundred thousand dollars. I think that's a fair proposal. You know what the odds are against my winning two tosses in a row."

The other players examined their resources and agreed to the proposal, and the financier tossed a coin into the air. "It would be nice," Peter Schwed says, telling the story now, "to be able to report that my father won the million two hundred thousand dollars—or even to be able to prolong the suspense by saying that he won the first toss. But he didn't. The first toss was against him, and he went to bed. Anyway, he got a good night's sleep, and he enjoyed the fight." It was one of the few times in his life that the financier did not end up ahead. The other exceptions were often when he played against Kaufman.

It was a bridge game, incidentally, which enabled Kaufman to bring forth one of his most famous lines. It occurred when he was teamed with Herman Mankiewicz, and he watched in horror as Mankiewicz played one of the dumbest games he'd ever seen in his life. He finally exploded. "I know you learned the game this afternoon," he said. "But what *time* this afternoon?"

Kaufman was equally caustic with another poor player. His partner could tell from Kaufman's glower that he was not pleased. Defensively, he said, "Okay, George, how would *you* have played that hand?" "Under an assumed name," Kaufman said.

This may have been the same partner who got up one day, excusing himself to go to the men's room. Kaufman gave him a sour look and said, "This will be the first time today that I'll know what's in your hand."

12.   THE DISTAFF SIDE

FOR BEATRICE, THE YEARS continued to be—apart from the essential emptiness of her romantic and sexual relationships—relatively happy and busy ones. New York remained the most exciting city in the world to her all of her life, and she was always active in the center of the excitement. It was made possible because, as she once explained, "When George became a successful playwright, a whole new world opened for both of us. We were instantly invited into the homes of the great and the near-great."

Her own homes, increasing in elegance as her husband became more and more successful, soon became places to which it was quite an honor to be invited; nearly every interesting man and woman on the New York scene dined or came to a party at the Kaufmans' at one time or another, and some came frequently. And when she and her friends

[178]

began to accompany Woollcott on his trips abroad, she also became an intimate of members of the international set—people like Lady Mendl, Otis Skinner and his daughter Cornelia, George Bernard Shaw, W. Somerset Maugham, Irene Castle, Mary Garden, Frank Harris, and Grace Moore, most of whom spent a lot of time with her whenever they were in New York.

Although she was very much a member of the smart set of her day, she never lost her awe of the famous people with whom she associated. She loved to drop names, as a letter to her mother, written in 1935, indicates. She wrote: "It's like old home week; the Swopes arrived yesterday and Oscar Levant is coming on Wednesday. The party at the Donald Ogden Stewarts was great fun the other night and my evening was made for me when Chaplin sat down beside me and stayed for hours. Or did I write that; I can't remember. Paulette Goddard was there, too—very beautiful; everyone says they are married. So were Joan Bennett, the Fredric Marches, Dotty Parker, Mankiewiczes, etc."

She also developed an astonishingly accurate eye for emerging talent. She told her husband that Hart and Levant were major talents—at a time when he felt that all the votes were still not in on the two young men. William Saroyan received an early invitation to one of her dinners, back in the days when he was still so young and naive that he stared in bewilderment at a dish of soft-shelled crabs. Ruth Friedlich was seated next to him, and he whispered to her urgently, "What in God's name are those? Spiders?" At the same dinner, Saroyan tried to hide his nervousness by demonstrating a parlor trick which involved tapping a dish with a spoon, unaware that the dish he was using was an almost priceless piece of fine china. He tapped the dish so hard that, as he looked down in horror, it shattered into tiny pieces, and he again turned his agonized whisper toward Ruth, asking, "What do I do now?" Ruth knew that her sister-in-law was too perfect a hostess ever to humiliate a guest by berating him in public, however much pain she might be feeling, particularly when the guest was someone as callow and unsure of himself as Saroyan. "You just say, 'I'm sorry,'" Ruth told him, "and you forget it."

Saroyan also attended one other party at which Kaufman was present, and still remembers with deep appreciation a Kaufman line connected with the event. The party took place in May 1935 and was given by Bennett Cerf for Gertrude Stein, who had come to the United States to try to improve her image after a flurry of amused and derisive articles about her work had appeared in the American press. Miss Stein had begun her visit by embarking on a long lecture tour around the country, and the tour was very successful and increased tremendously her popularity with the general public. She was now leaving in triumph for a home she'd recently bought in Italy. "I was wandering around," Saroyan recalled recently, "while Gertrude was boring the shit out of God, while two dozen male and female boobs sat at her feet, and came upon Kaufman also wandering and said, 'How you doing?' To which he replied, 'I just broke even.' Which," Saroyan says in conclusion, "was perfect."

Another youngster Beatrice noticed early was Noël Coward, whose career she helped further by introducing him to Woollcott outside a theatre one day. Woollcott asked Coward what he thought of the play showing at the theatre, and the young actor answered, in his languid way, "Teejus." Woollcott was delighted with the capsule comment, became a close friend of Coward's, and began to push and plug him in every possible way.

Every passing week and month also saw Beatrice functioning more and more as her husband's best editorial adviser. She was also his most enthusiastic fan; she saw some of his plays as many as thirty times, and became helpless with laughter at the funny lines every time. But Kaufman knew at once if there was something she didn't like, and he relied upon and trusted her judgment absolutely. "If she grimaced over certain scenes," a friend of the Kaufmans said recently, "he wouldn't even question her; he'd move to the typewriter and rewrite. Her expression told him everything, and she was just simply never wrong." Beatrice later began to deny it when the press referred to her as "George Kaufman's North Star"; she told one interviewer, "Sometimes he listens to me, sometimes he doesn't." But this was just modesty or unwillingness to take anything away from her husband. The truth was that he always listened to her.

A big name was not an instant key to a Kaufman dinner or party. Beatrice had a strong instinct about people and what they were really like, and didn't leap to accept them because they were *haute monde* or reject them because they weren't. The people had to have some special quality which appealed to the Kaufmans, or at least to one of them. One of the men on whom the Kaufmans disagreed was Billy Rose, who horrified Beatrice at dinner one night by describing the way he treated his father when the elder Rose came to ask for money. "I never see him personally," said Rose, who hated his father. "I keep him waiting for an hour or more, and then I send a servant out with a few dollars. And I tell the servant to *throw* the money at him." Beatrice later expressed her views to her husband. "The man's an utter bastard," she said. "How can you possibly stand him?" "I think he's interesting," Kaufman said mildly, and that was enough for the invitations to continue.

That was the key. A man or woman didn't have to be a paragon of virtue, and didn't really have to be world-famous or even a little bit famous, but absolutely had to be interesting to make it at the Kaufman household. There is a dissenting opinion here; Harry Ruby, the songwriter, insisted in an interview that more than that was required, that a man or woman also had to be important, that Beatrice was really a secret snob who judged people on the basis of their status on the New York scene. He told the interviewer, "She had certain ways that made it evident—to me, at least—that she was a bit snobbish, that she showed a definite preference for people she considered more important, socially and otherwise. On two occasions, I had appointments with the lady—once to have lunch or dinner, I forget which, and once to go and see a show. On both occasions the dates were called off. I found out later that she dropped me to be with others who, in her opinion, were more important. It was so obvious it was funny." Other people who knew the Kaufmans even better, however, contradict this firmly, insisting that the comment would have been accurate only if Ruby had substituted "interesting" for "important." "Not that Harry Ruby wasn't an interesting man," one friend said after hearing about the comment. "He was, very. But people strike other people in different ways, and probably he just wasn't very interesting to Beatrice. Maybe all Harry wanted to do was talk about baseball." Ruby was a baseball fan so dedicated that, when his life was immortalized in a film some years ago in which he was played by Red Skelton, much was made of the fact that he often had to be dragged away from the baseball diamond in order to be persuaded to write some songs—and that may well be the answer. Except for croquet, Beatrice was no more a sports fan than her husband, and there seems to be no record of her having snubbed anyone else.

Beatrice also became, very quickly, a fashion leader, employing her unerring taste, the same instinct for color and clothing combinations which enabled her to help her husband become so well-dressed, to select outstanding wardrobes for herself as well. Margaret Case Harriman, growing up at the Algonquin, later described Beatrice as one of the best-dressed women at the hotel every time she appeared there, adding "which is saying quite a lot." Ring Lardner also commented on Beatrice's sartorial splendor when he wrote an alleged biography of Beatrice for a magazine, a wild and funny piece he called *Dante and—,* saying, "Three times daily a trusted employee of Pol Roger, Inc., calls at her apartment to measure her for a new gown or suit. It is her modest boast that she is never seen in the same costume twice and generally not even once." The piece was satire, but it was not a total departure from the truth.

Beatrice went in for taliored effects and was one of the first women in New York to wear slacks; "trousers for women" were regarded with disapproval when they first began to be seen around town, and became acceptable at a lot of places only because word got around that Beatrice was going to continue to wear them no matter how many people objected. In time, her influence on popular fashions became considerable. This was so much the case that, when she stopped wearing hats for a while, the town's leading milliners, John and Frederic, came to her and pleaded with her to start wearing them again, fearing that, if she did not, bareheadedness might become the style and injure their business. But Beatrice had grown tired of wearing hats and would not agree, and the effects of her abstinence were indeed soon visible at hat shops around town.

A lot of people who helped Beatrice to set her fashion pace were her friends, and some of them were even more princely than other of her friends who were leaders in the arts and in society. Once Ruth's daughter, Katie, then aged sixteen, spent a few days with the Kaufmans and watched in awe one morning as a man in striped trousers and tails entered the apartment and began to wander casually around the living oom. He seemed so ambassadorial that Katie felt he should not be gnored and left all alone that way, so she approached him and ntroduced herself. "Good morning," she said. "I'm Mrs. Kaufman's iece, Katie Friedlich." "Good morning," the man said. "I'm here to lo Mrs. Kaufman's hair."

Right from the start, Beatrice was able to fit in comfortably with ll kinds of people. Two of her closest friends were girls from very prominent Social Register families, but, significantly, both were not t all overimpressed with their own importance and subsequently noved out of their own set to marry show business people. One was Marjorie Oelrichs, heiress to a huge fortune, who married Eddy Duchin, the bandleader and pianist, and became the mother of another popular piano-playing entertainer, Peter Duchin. The other was Ellin Mackay, daughter of one of the richest men in America, Clarence Mackay, who headed Postal Telegraph; Mackay was bitterly opposed, ooth on religious and financial grounds, when Ellin announced that he was going to marry Irving Berlin, the Coney Island singing-vaiter turned songwriter. But the wedding took place anyway, be-came one of the most blissfully happy marriages on record, and Berlin nded up almost as rich as his father-in-law. And a third good friend vas Alice Duer Miller; better known as a novelist, but also a prom-nent member of society. She was, in fact, Ellin Mackay's aunt; Ellin's mother was a Duer.

On the other hand, another of Beatrice's closest friends was Neysa McMein, who was anything but fashionable or Social Register. The beautiful artist, who had been born Marjorie Moran McMein to a niddle-class family in Quincy, Illinois, on January 25, 1890, but ater changed her name to Neysa when a numerologist suggested he name and said it would bring her luck, got only as far as high school in Quincy, moved to Chicago to study for a while at the Chicago Art Institute, and then got a job sketching hats at $15 a veek for the Gage Brothers Department Store. She came to New York a little later to try to develop a career as a free-lance artist, made her first sale with a pastel fashion drawing to *Designer* at $75, two years later sold her first cover to *The Saturday Evening Post*, and eventually worked up to the point where she was receiving as much as $2500 per painting from *McCall's, Collier's, Woman's Home*

[183]

Companion, and other magazines. She also became a leading portrait painter. Her first portrait was a study of Gyp the Blood, the notorious gunman who was later executed for the murder of an equally notorious gambler, Herman Rosenthal, but she was subsequently invited to the White House to paint Presidents Harding and Hoover, and she also secured commissions to paint Chief Justice Charles Evans Hughes, Anne Lindbergh, Jascha Heifetz, Beatrice Lillie, Dorothy Thompson, and other well-known people.

The slim, blond artist was as untidy as she was lovely. Since she worked mostly in pastels, her face and hair were nearly always sprinkled with pastel dust; she was also so casual about her dress that she once answered a knock at her studio door with her bloomers hanging down because, unnoticed by her, the elastic on one side of the undergarment had snapped. Her studio was similarly disorganized. Discarded sketches and paint jars and tubes covered the floor, and things on the walls were put up by whim and without plan, with a cartoon torn from the morning paper pinned up next to an original drawing or painting by a major artist. Once Heifetz wandered into the studio and began, idly, to strike chords on the piano, wondering why the instrument sounded so funny. He discovered the answer when he lifted the top and saw that a half dozen caramels had fallen inside and melted on the strings. Another time, the artist invited a lot of people to dinner, and then had to go searching for her maid when the maid failed to appear to begin serving. She found the maid almost in tears and baffled about how to start. "We don't have any soup plates," the maid explained. "The people downstairs that we've been borrowing them from for the past seven years moved out today."

Like all friends of the Kaufmans, Neysa McMein met the all-important criterion: she was never uninteresting. She was also never a phony: she remained endearingly ingenuous and unsophisticated all of her life. The act which first brought her into the Algonquin group was typical. She was a great admirer of Frank Adams's column, and so, when she first arrived in New York, she dropped in casually at his newspaper office to tell him so, bringing with her a large bunch of sweet peas. Adams, who had never before been given flowers by anybody, was both amused and pleased; he took her to lunch at the

Round Table, and she soon became one of the most popular members of the group. Her cheerful, wide-eyed attitude toward life did not change as she became more prosperous and famous. She accepted every invitation to take part in every event which sounded like fun, from judging bathing beauties at Coney Island to helping open an opulent new movie house in Toronto; she was quick to take part in anything which seemed worthwhile, contributing dozens of drawings without charge to the *Times* for its One Hundred Neediest Cases campaign; and she never became stuffy about her work, taking on an assignment to do a painting for a soap ad as enthusiastically as she undertook a presidential portrait.

Her happy acceptance of life as it came, plus the fact that she had the ability to work at her easel while activity swirled all around her, made her studio almost as much of a salon as the Kaufman apartment. George Gershwin played *Rhapsody in Blue* there before he introduced it to the general public. Charlie Chaplin was a frequent visitor, as was Feodor Chaliapin, and Mary Pickford, and Father Duffy. Charlie MacArthur met Helen Hayes at a party there, offering her peanuts and saying, "I wish they were emeralds." And when, years later, MacArthur presented Helen Hayes MacArthur with a string of emeralds, saying, "I wish they were peanuts," he didn't do so at the studio, but Neysa McMein was one of the first people to whom his excited wife rushed to show the gift.

Beatrice was also very close to Ruth Hale and Jane Grant, though she didn't share their Lucy Stone ideals at all; she said frequently that she was quite happy to be called Mrs. George S. Kaufman. Another particular friend was Herbert Bayard Swope's wife, Margaret, a woman with so acerbic a manner and so sharp a tongue that Beatrice, after spending a weekend at the Swope estate, gave her the cable address *Sourpuss* as a bread-and-butter present. Margaret Swope's wit was often as cold and pointed as an icicle. Once she became angered when a dinner guest brought along a companion who was clearly a lady of the night, and told him, "Everyone who comes here must have a visible means of support." Another time, someone commented about a mutual acquaintance who was not a mutual friend, "She's a charming woman, but somewhat free with her body." "Well," Mrs. Swope said, "that's the only way she can dispose of it."

[185]

She never had anything mean to say about Beatrice, however; the two women liked and respected each other completely.

There was one other special woman friend, also named Margaret. This was Margaret Leech, born in Newburgh, New York, on November 7, 1893, a writer whose first two books, *The Back of the Book* and *Tin Wedding*, were novels, and who then turned to non-fiction, collaborating with Heywood Broun on a biography, *Anthony Comstock: Roundsman of the Lord*. The two collaborators wrote the book in a peculiar fashion; instead of working together page by page in the usual manner of collaborations, they contributed alternating chapters and stayed apart throughout the writing of the entire book. The reason they gave was that they both liked the subject but didn't care much for each other. (The collaboration also brought forth another striking example of Broun's untidiness. Broun admitted one day that he'd lost a valuable research file, and Miss Leech was tremendously upset. George Oppenheimer, who knew Broun well, told her not to worry. He went over to Broun's apartment, crawled under Broun's bed, and found the file—along with twenty or thirty other things.)

Peggy Leech was another slim blonde with a faint resemblance to Neysa McMein, but she was closer in temperament to Margaret Swope. Adams called her "Vinegar Nell" because of her brittle manner. She startled him constantly with some of the things she said; one typical incident occurred when she and Adams were both weekend guests at a country estate, and Adams returned one morning from playing tennis with his shirt open at the throat and the curly black hair on his chest peeping through. "Well, Frank," she said, "I see your fly is open higher than usual today." In 1928, she married Ralph Pulitzer, the owner and editor of the *World*, and son of the creator of the Pulitzer Prize, a wedding which was rendered unique by the fact that, at the very moment the ceremony was being performed, a fire was breaking out at the Pulitzer home and destroying Pulitzer's collection of first editions valued at $30,000. She also won two Pulitzer Prizes herself, both for history, the first in 1941 for *Reveille in Washington* and the second in 1960 for *In the Days of McKinley*. The marriage was a happy one, and the Pulitzers did a lot of traveling, going on African safaris and hunting tigers and black panthers in India and the like. But Beatrice and Peggy Leech still managed to see a lot of each other, and, when Beatrice decided to write a play herself, it was Peggy Leech with whom she collaborated.

Beatrice's male friends, some of whom were also her lovers, were equally numerous. Aside from the men like Woollcott, Adams, and Connelly, who were friends of both the Kaufmans, and the constant seekers of advice like Hart and Levant, there were two other men with whom she formed especially close relationships. One of these was Charles Martin, with whom she collaborated on her second play.

Martin, a handsome young radio director and writer from Bridgeton, New Jersey, started out as a sort of child prodigy, beginning school at the age of three, studying the violin at the age of four, writing and selling a newspaper serial at fourteen, and earning a B.A. degree at New York University in three years. He then drifted into radio, producing and directing fourteen dramatic shows a week for a while for a local New York station, WMCA, and giving a lot of work at $50 per show to a young actor just breaking in, Orson Welles.

At the time Martin and Beatrice met, Martin was twenty-six years old and writing and directing a number of network shows, among them *The Tallulah Bankhead Show* and *The Philip Morris Playhouse.* He was introduced to Beatrice by a literary agent who knew that Beatrice was seeking a collaborator, and also knew that Martin, too, had a yen to write a Broadway play. Beatrice and the writer-director hit it off at once, and Martin eventually moved into the Kaufman household, then located in Bucks County, living there for nearly a year while he and Beatrice worked on their play, and commuting constantly to New York to work on his shows. When the play failed, Beatrice was willing to write another one with him, but this never materialized; Martin became involved with *The Gertrude Lawrence Show,* a weekly radio super-show in which the star was paid the astronomical figure of $10,000 per week, and which also featured big-name guest stars like James Cagney and Ray Milland. Martin eventually moved to Hollywood, where he was frequently photographed squiring Joan Crawford and other movieland lovelies to parties and previews, and he is now a film producer and president of a firm called Forward Films.

The other special friend was Charles Friedman. Friedman began his career as a director and scenic designer for shows in the Catskills, and rose to prominence as the director of *Pins and Needles*, the International Ladies Garment Workers Union presentation which became a long-running Broadway hit. He subsequently directed and co-authored *Sing Out the News*, which was produced by Kaufman and Hart in association with Max Gordon, directed the libretto for *Carmen Jones*, directed *Along Fifth Avenue* and other plays, and also worked for a time in Hollywood on *Sun Valley Serenade*, starring Sonja Henie, and other pictures. His friendship with Beatrice was a long one, ending only at her death.

The interesting, entertaining friends did much to fill the voids in Beatrice's life; she enjoyed their company tremendously, and they felt the same way about her. There were exceptions, of course. As she became a bit older, Beatrice grew capable of displaying considerable dignity and strength on occasion, and this made a few people nervous now and then. Franklin Heller, who later became a very successful television director, directing, among many others, one CBS hit show *What's My Line?*, for seventeen years, started his career as assistant stage manager for *You Can't Take It with You* and other Kaufman-Hart shows; he never got to know Beatrice well, but saw her occasionally, describing her as "so regal she scared the hell out of me." She knew her own mind and could be quite stubborn about things. Frank Adams mentioned in his column of November 22, 1921, that he had come home the previous night and found the Kaufmans waiting for him, and that Beatrice had been wearing a velvet bandeau around her head. He added, affectionately but pointedly, "I said I liked it. G. said he did not, but she kept it on." Max Gordon once got into a minor business argument with Kaufman, with Beatrice present, and, when Beatrice interjected a number of opinions into the discussion, Gordon told her mildly that he preferred to hear the decisions from George. Beatrice closed that line of conversation by saying coolly, "I'm the boss, and don't you forget it." And her husband did not contradict her.

But most people—and that meant nearly everyone who knew her well—considered her an utter delight and were quick to say so. Bennett Cerf called her "the core and connecting link of scores of people in every walk of life who owe some of their success to her ever-ready counsel and sympathy when the going was roughest," adding, "Part of the fun of doing things is telling Beatrice about them." Frank Sullivan called her "a love" and described her as "easy to know and to like, a generous, kind, sweet woman of many friendships. All of her friends were intensely loyal to her and she to them." Howard Teichmann called her "stunning, clever, wise and knowledgeable." Woollcott admired her "common sense, shrewd literary judgment, and sometimes ruthless wit." "She was sensitive, warm, kind, and generous," Charles Martin said. "She loved parties and loved people and loved to laugh. And everybody loved her."

And Kaufman himself was not silent and not an avoider of sentiment when it came to his wife. "When Beatrice is away on a trip or something," he said, "I find it hard to get through the day."

She was not away all that often. Woollcott was a master at talking people into accompanying him on some of his European trips and joining him on some of his other projects, and when he sailed for Naples on the *Roma* on May 19, 1928, planning to go on from Naples on a leisurely motor trip to Rome, Perugia, Siena, Florence, Milan, and Maggiore, and eventually settle for the summer in Antibes, he persuaded Beatrice, Alice Duer Miller, Harpo Marx, and others to come along with him. And when he opened a "country estate" at Katonah, New York, from October 5, 1933, through June 1934, a place where all of his friends were welcome provided they chipped in for their share of costs during their stay, the place appeared to be Woollcott's alone, but was actually owned by Woollcott in partnership with Beatrice, S. N. Behrman, and others—and Beatrice spent a certain amount of time up there. But most of the time, partly because Kaufman hated so much to tear himself away from the midtown area, and partly because the city had come to represent everything Beatrice loved in life, she stayed at home. New York had become totally satisfying to her without too frequent necessity for change and getting away.

The city even came to represent to Beatrice, in a way, the pleasures of a trip back home without the necessity of actually going there, because New York City was so much the first choice of vacationers in the '20s and '30s that she found herself constantly running into friends and relatives from her home town. Once she went for a walk on Fifth Avenue and met so many people she knew from Rochester that she returned home and reeled off a long list to her husband. "Everybody from Rochester," she said, "must be in New York this week." Kaufman, of course, had a quick response for that. "What a fine time to visit Rochester," he said. But he knew that the encounters had pleased her and softened the comment with one of his rare, rather endearing smiles.

There was one other important factor which helped make New York seem to Beatrice to be the most perfect city in the world in which to live. That was the city's almost limitless job and career opportunities. Right from the start of their marriage, Beatrice was proud of being George S. Kaufman's wife and general adviser to him and a lot of other people, but she also felt the need to accomplish some things on her own. And so, almost from the first day of her arrival in the big city to the last day of her life, she worked at a steady series of demanding and important jobs, and was good at every one of them.

Her first three jobs had additional motivation; she took them when her husband was earning only his modest salary on the New York *Times* and had not yet hit as a playwright, and the extra money came in handy. The first of these jobs gave her the dubious distinction of joining all the other people who suffered the agonies of confrontation with Kaufman's rigid code of ethics.

The job was as assistant to the man who handled publicity for two young sisters who were rapidly becoming important stars of the silent screen, Constance and Norma Talmadge, and Beatrice quickly cooked up a long story about the Talmadges and handed it to her husband, certain that she'd see it in print in next morning's paper. "Not a chance," Kaufman said, handing the press release right back to her, and she soon came to realize, along with all of Kaufman's other relatives and friends, that George Kaufman's presence on a newspaper made the paper the hardest of all to crack, not the easiest. This fact became so frustrating that, after a while, she left the publicity job and went to work reading plays for two producers, first for Al H. Woods and then for Morris Gest.

By 1924, Kaufman had hit with *Dulcy*, *To the Ladies*, and all the others, so the motivation was no longer economic. Beatrice began to ook around very carefully and this time took a job she really wanted, a job in the editorial department of the book publishing firm of Boni and Liveright. She started as a first reader and ended as head of the editorial department. She was with the firm eleven years in all and discovered many of their most successful books, occasionally having to lift her voice and insist the company take on manuscripts which her superiors considered dubious commercial prospects. One such was *The Story of Mankind* by Hendrik Willem Van Loon. The decision-makers at Boni and Liveright thought the manuscript was technical and not of general interest, but Beatrice insisted the book be published, and it became one of the great best-sellers of the period. Another book which was even more difficult to push through was *The Common Sense of Music* by Dr. Sigmund Spaeth, an obscure musicologist whose only previous manuscript had been his doctoral dissertation. There was even some suspicion of prejudice here, at least on the part of people unfamiliar with the Kaufman ethical code, because the Kaufmans and the Spaeths were friends and often played bridge together; others simply felt that there was too little interest in a book on serious music, even a book which avoided technical terms and attempted to approach the subject from a layman's point of view. Beatrice almost lost the battle; she finally won her argument only because the firm's sales manager, Richard Simon, was leaving to form his own company with his friend Max Schuster, and said he would publish the Spaeth book if Boni and Liveright didn't want it. This, belatedly, nudged the acquisitive instinct of Beatrice's employers, who were unaware that Spaeth would not have gone with Simon anyway, because he'd heard that Simon and Schuster were going to start their publishing program with a pretty undignified project, a crossword puzzle book, and therefore felt that the new firm had no real future. Boni and Liveright published *The Common Sense of Music*, it became another huge best-seller, and Spaeth went on from there to become world famous, if not beloved by songwriters, for his practice of examining current popular song hits, assumed to be entirely original, and pointing out where many or all of their musical phrases were identical to those in musical works of the past.

There were other interests for Beatrice, of course; while she continued working and helping her husband and having her occasional romance, she also did many other things. Woollcott came up one day with the idea of becoming a night-club entrepreneur by taking over a big, unused ballroom at the Berkshire Hotel, located at Madison Avenue and 52nd Street. He even had a name for the place, the Elbow Room, and a special purpose: it would be a club where VIPs would never be bothered by autograph fiends. As was so often the case, he asked Beatrice to become his partner, and she did. They got Norman Bel Geddes to decorate the room, and he did the job all in blue mirrors and blue glass, making the room so ornate that one of the club's first guests, Gerald Murphy, president of the Mark Cross leather stores, took one stunned look and said, "Just let in the water and it'll make a great swimming pool." The night-club failed because Woollcott got the idea of setting prices very high and keeping out the seamier elements, but he made the mistake of setting prices so high that he also kept out the upper crust. It also became clear that VIPs were staying away because they *liked* being bothered by autograph fiends. The two partners agreed, though, that it was fun while it lasted. Woollcott also got another idea; his wartime buddy, George T. Bye, lived in New Canaan, Connecticut, where there was a rather successful newspaper being published, the New Canaan *Advertiser*, and Woollcott suggested to Beatrice that the two of them acquire the paper jointly and turn it into a high-level periodical to be read by the entire country, rather like William Allen White's famous Kansas newspaper, the Emporia *Gazette*. His plan, he said, would be for Beatrice to cover books and fashions, Deems Taylor to write about music, Broun to write about sports, and people like FPA, Christopher Morley, Kaufman, and himself to contribute occasional pieces on other topics. Beatrice agreed that it was a great idea, but one huge flaw developed when they went to New Canaan to acquire the paper. The owner told them that he was not interested in selling, had never been interested in selling, and would not sell in his lifetime, adding grimly that he intended to live forever. Eventually Broun, remembering Woollcott's idea, did start a local paper of his own along similar lines, *Connecticut Nutmeg*. But though people still remember it as being very good, it lasted only a year and lost money.

Beatrice also tried her hand now and then as a producer, but the problem was that no plays ever got produced. On December 23,

1935, she announced that she was forming a play-producing organization with two of the Marx Brothers, Harpo and Gummo. Gummo was the one brother who had never had ambitions of becoming an entertainer; he was currently the head of the New York office of a theatrical agency owned by another brother who *had* been a performer but had given it up to become an agent, Zeppo. Gummo promised in press releases that he'd soon begin to devote a substantial portion of his time to the new company. The releases also stated that the firm's first production would probably be a play called *Hell Freezes Over*, of which Beatrice and Harpo each owned 10 per cent. But the play was never put on, nor was any other, and the company was eventually dissolved. Three and a half years later, Beatrice tried again with Charles Friedman, with whom she had done some nonprofessional producing for a semi-charitable organization called the Refugee Artists Group. This firm evaporated, too, when the partners were unable to find a play which seemed worth bringing to Broadway.

Mostly, however, Beatrice confined her jobs to editorial positions with established companies. When she finally grew tired of Boni and Liveright and left the firm, she held similar jobs for brief periods at two other book houses, Coward-McCann and The Viking Press, and then worked for a little over a year, from September 16, 1935, to November 27, 1936, as fiction editor at *Harper's Bazaar*, the Hearst fashion magazine. She left *Harper's Bazaar* when an even more interesting job appeared on the horizon. Samuel Goldwyn had decided to employ story editors on both coasts; he hired Thomas B. Costain, an editor for *The Saturday Evening Post* who also later became a leading writer of historical novels, for the West Coast job, and offered Beatrice the East Coast job. After considerable hesitation, she accepted.

The hesitation was because Goldwyn was one of the few people in the world with whom Kaufman had had a business fight. It had happened in 1933, when Kaufman and Robert E. Sherwood were hired by Goldwyn to write the screenplay for a film which would star Eddie Cantor, *Roman Scandals*. The experience was so bad that both men worked as little as possible for the movie industry after that. Kaufman and Sherwood turned in a fresh and hilarious screenplay which is still funny even when read today, but Goldwyn was not satisfied and brought in other writers to do more work, among them William Anthony McGuire, who was one of Ziegfeld's top writers, Arthur Sheekman, Nat Perrin, and a number of Cantor's own gag writers. Goldwyn also refused to pay the remaining fee of $25,000 still due Kaufman and Sherwood. The writers sued, and finally, three years later, on August 25, 1936, settled for $20,000, a lot of which disappeared in paying all the legal bills.

Beatrice reminded Goldwyn of the incident when he approached her. "The thing to do," Goldwyn said, "is pretend it never happened. And then it never happened." He turned away from her and then wheeled back, his eyes opened wide to feign innocence. "What's this," he said, "about a fight with your husband? It *never* happened!" Beatrice was so amused by the histrionics that she took the job, and she spent a happy ten months scouting properties for the Goldwyn studio, resigning on September 20, 1937.

She had one other important editorial job after that, as assistant to the publisher of the unusual and experimental New York newspaper, *PM*, in 1942. The newspaper was not a success; too many readers considered its format, features, and left-wing politics too radical for it to make money. But many other people considered it a brilliant and innovative publication, and many of its best innovations were suggested by Beatrice.

In her first years in New York, Beatrice showed no interest at all in doing any writing of her own, other than things as part of her job like publicity releases. "The only things she wants to create are sweaters," Kaufman told Adams. "She knits fourteen lines a day, like any sonneteer." But then, little by little, Beatrice began to try her hand at her husband's line of business.

She started out in a very small way: by writing a few brief pieces for magazines, and then a few more. It wasn't until 1934, however, that she told Kaufman that she was taking a shot at the big time by writing a play herself, in collaboration with her friend Peggy Leech.

Her reasons for undertaking the project were a trifle obscure, even to the people with whom she discussed her plans at the time. By then, she had been married for seventeen years to the man who was probably America's hardest-working playwright, and so could hardly have suffered from the illusion that writing a successful play was a simple task. It was true that her husband's habit patterns included one item which is a traditional part of every daydreamer's fantasies about the ideal life: he frequently, as mentioned, got out of bed around noon. But Beatrice knew that that was because he had usually worked so late the night before, and she also knew that, when he did get out of bed and returned to his typewriter, he worked harder and under greater, if self-imposed, pressure than almost anyone else among their many friends and acquaintances. Very clearly, a job which sometimes required the relentless pursuit of a single word or line for many hours, and which carried with it the experience of sometimes writing frantically for days or even weeks and then throwing out every single word written, was no cinch. In all likelihood, Beatrice's reason for writing her first play, which she and Peggy Leech eventually called *Divided by Three*, was a simple one, or a group of simple reasons. Beatrice had helped her husband often enough to feel that she had absorbed the rudiments of playwriting herself; her collaborator had considerable experience as a professional writer, even if in other fields; and they both felt they had a pretty good idea for a play.

The play, which they first called *Three Loves*, was to be the story of a strong-willed and beautiful woman who finds, as she enters her forties, that she has been living a double lie. The lesser lie is that her husband, who gives the appearance of being rich and successful, really isn't either; he is frequently in financial difficulties and has to turn to his wife for help, and she helps with funds earned at an art gallery she runs, a gallery which people think is run strictly for fun but which is actually a necessity. The major lie is that she has taken a lover, an automotive tycoon who knows the woman's true financial situation and makes sure, in kind and secret ways, that the gallery is always profitable. And the whole thing blows up and nearly turns into tragedy when the heroine's sensitive young son, just out of college and about to marry a girl who is jealous of his deep affection for his mother, is told the truth about his mother's secret life by the girl. The revelation almost destroys him.

It was a daring idea for the time, particularly since the heroine's adultery was treated with sympathy and understanding; probably

Beatrice was thinking of the sad twists and turns of her own romantic life. And the play nearly made it; certainly it was bought quickly enough once the authors had completed it. There were the expected whispers that the quick sale had been helped by the fact that one author was the wife of George S. Kaufman and the other was the wife of Ralph Pulitzer, but the truth seems to be that that barely entered into it. The play's producer, Guthrie McClintic, was an elegant, tough-minded man noted for his discerning taste, and, though he may have been influenced by the authorship of *Divided by Three* to the extent of giving it a personal reading, and a quicker one than it would have gotten if it had been by unknown authors and slid in over the transom, he would never in a million years have been influenced by the identity of the authors into agreeing to produce a play he did not really like. He told people in his cool, direct way that he'd decided to produce the play because it seemed to have a good chance of making money, and those appear to be the facts.

One weird coincidence occurred just after the two women began work; their close friend Alice Duer Miller, aware that they were working on a play but not knowing at all what it was about, suggested an almost identical idea to Kaufman for his own use. "I'm enclosing an idea I've had for a long time for a play," she wrote him on August 2, 1934, "in the hope that someday when you are out of a job and need an idea, you may think it worth a try . . . I should never write it as a play myself, because I am always too busy doing something I know how to do to stop and experiment with something I obviously don't. I cannot write it as a story because the impropriety of the main thesis—the mother who takes a lover—would stand out and be shocking in a story—but needn't, I think, in a play. The great advantage of the story is that everyone in it could be a sympathetic and understandable character." Kaufman showed the letter to Beatrice, and the startled collaborators rushed to phone and tell their friend that she had come just a little too late.

McClintic proceeded, in his usual way, to give his production of *Divided by Three* the best of everything. Judith Anderson, whom he engaged to play the lead, was already at the top of her profession. Hedda Hopper, who was hired to play the heroine's sophisticated and understanding sister, was another leading actress, still years away

rom abandoning her profession to become a gossip columnist; and
he young son was played by James Stewart, who, though not long
out of college himself, was an extraordinary actor. McClintic directed
the play personally, and the sets, which John Mason Brown, in his review in the *Post*, called "superlatively beautiful . . . among the most
tasteful and effective settings which have been seen on a New York
stage in recent years," and Brooks Atkinson in his *Times* review described as "drenched in luxurious and ravishing beauty," were designed by Donald Oenslager.

Judith Anderson, as always, got excellent reviews when the play
previewed at the Shubert Theatre in New Haven, Connecticut,
through September and then opened at the Ethel Barrymore Theatre
on Tuesday, October 2, 1934, and Hedda Hopper drew good reviews, too. The strongest notices, however, were given to Stewart,
who had already received enthusiastic critical comment the year before, when he played a young Irish soldier who sacrifices himself by
becoming a human guinea pig in Sidney Howard's *Yellow Jack*. He
stole that play, and he did the same in *Divided by Three*. Atkinson
called his performance "a minor masterpiece of characterization, completely free of hackneyed affectation," Brown called him "as excel-
ent as in *Yellow Jack*," and *Theatre Arts Monthly* said he played
"the lighter moments amusingly and the serious ones with more
feeling and dramatic power than one has the right to hope for from
an actor of no long experience." He was so outstanding that Hedda
Hopper recommended him to Rufus LeMaire, Kaufman's producer
on *Helen of Troy, New York*, and at that point a producer at
M-G-M. LeMaire promptly signed Stewart to a contract and started
his long and successful movie career.

Unfortunately, all of the plusses—the outstanding cast, the opulent
production, the fresh play idea, and the play's daring attitudes—just
weren't enough. The problem might be summed up by something
Kaufman once said in another context, a wry remark he made
when, despite his reputation at the time for being able to serve as a
play doctor and fix up other people's plays, one of his own plays was
ailing. "What this play needs," he said, "is George S. Kaufman." That
was certainly true of *Divided by Three*.

The difficulty with the play was that its execution just did not match up to its conception. Atkinson was reasonably kind, saying that "the point of view is wise and the style is luminous," and he also called the play "tenderly moving." But the other reviewers were much less enthusiastic and stated bluntly that Beatrice and her co-author just didn't compare to Beatrice's husband in freshness of dialogue and general writing ability. *Theatre Arts Monthly* said flatly, "Careless or inexpert writing has been the barrier to success in much of the output this month, of which *Divided by Three* is an example." "Their play, however modernistic," said another critic, Gilbert W. Gabriel, "has a soft filling of pensive, patient, far from lively, faintly banal morals . . . It is, I fear, another of those plays in which the scenery wins out. And maybe mercifully." "It prattles on in drawing-room terms," said Brown. The other reviewers had similar things to say, and the play closed after thirty-one performances.

Beatrice did not try again for nearly six years. Then she got the idea for another play, to be called *The White-Haired Boy* and to be a study of a new-wave playwright, rather like Saroyan or Clifford Odets, who is surrounded by sycophants but turns out to have few real friends. She passed the word around that she was again seeking a collaborator, and eventually began to work with Charles Martin.

Unfortunately, it was another near-miss—despite the fact that the play again seemed to have everything, including, this time, George S Kaufman, who helped rewrite it and contributed about twenty-five sparkling lines. It also had considerable advance publicity, since both Saroyan and Odets decided the play was about them, were flattered by the idea, and went around telling everybody all about the play But it still didn't work out; Beatrice, who had so many other triumph in her brief lifetime, just wasn't destined to have a hit play.

Like *Divided by Three, The White-Haired Boy* was bought by the first producer to whom it was shown, Herman Shumlin—and Shumlin, exactly like McClintic, was also well-known for his distinguished discerning, excellent taste. In an indirect way, however, this eventually brought about the play's demise, because Shumlin, who later produced most of the Lillian Hellman dramas and many other serious and important plays, was no hurrier, no pusher-through of quickies He was busy with other things, but he would not have hurried with his casting and staging of *The White-Haired Boy* even if that had been his only project. That was just not his style; he was a meticulous

an with very high standards, and he worked in a slow, careful man-
er.

Regrettably, Beatrice did not share his patience; she wanted the
lay *on*, and she wanted it on quickly. Kaufman, who had read and
eread the play many times in addition to retouching it and supplying
is lines, felt it had a strong chance, and so did everybody else who
ead the play. And the enthusiastic talk grew stronger and stronger,
ith more and more people predicting that the play, possibly about
real person, would have the same kind of success as the Kaufman-
Iart play of a year before about a real person, *The Man Who Came
o Dinner*. But still Shumlin would not be rushed; he continued to
ove in his precise way, and the weeks and months began to pass.

Beatrice discussed the matter with Martin, but the truth was that
Iartin really didn't care. He wanted to see the play on Broadway,
oo, but the play wasn't his only project, as it was Beatrice's; between
ving in Bucks County with the Kaufmans and rushing constantly to
Jew York for his radio shows, he was frantically busy. "I'll leave it
p to you," he told Beatrice. Beatrice did nothing for a while, just
ontinuing to fret over Shumlin's slow pace. And then George Ab-
ott entered the picture.

Beatrice had known Abbott for a long time, going back to the days
hen he had traveled with the touring company of *Dulcy*. He was
ow an extremely successful producer and director, and he had heard
ll the good things about *The White-Haired Boy*. He asked to read
ıe play, and Beatrice gave him a copy. Shortly afterward, he came
o see her. "If you can get Herman to release the play," he said, "I'll
uarantee to have it in rehearsal within two weeks."

Shumlin was deeply disappointed when Beatrice asked him for a
elease, but he was very much a gentleman, and he agreed. Abbott
hen proceeded to live up to his word. He hired Keenan Wynn as the
laywright, and Betty Garde, Philip Loeb, Joan Tetzel, and Leopold
tokowski's daughter Sonia for other important roles. He also hired
tobby Griffith, who later produced *Pajama Game* and a lot of other
its in association with Hal Prince, as stage manager, and put on the
nowledgeable Carl Fisher as business manager. Then he quickly
laced the play into rehearsal.

Wynn was tremendously enthusiastic about the play; he told Mar-
in, "I'm grateful for this play. It'll be a hit when we open in New

York." So were all the other people associated with the play, many of whom took long-term leases on Manhattan apartments. Martin became a bit nervous; he looked at the large cast and all the other people working on the play and said to Beatrice, "Did we start all this? Look how many lives are involved." Beatrice laughed and told him not to worry.

It looked, indeed, as though there was no cause for concern, and this was apparently confirmed when the company held a dress rehearsal at a Broadway theatre prior to leaving to try the play out in Boston. The tough invited audience screamed with laughter throughout the play, and, when the comedy ended with repeated curtain calls, Beatrice and her collaborator embraced and were in turn embraced by Abbott.

The first hint of trouble came when the play opened in Boston at the Plymouth Theatre. The laughter and applause were not nearly as loud, and the reviews were kind but fairly mild. Surprisingly, in view of what happened next, it was Abbott who reassured the authors. "I'm not at all worried," he told them. "This is typical of Boston audiences. They're always cold. Once we hit New York, we're up and away." And to confirm his confidence, he began to place ads offering tickets for the play's run at the Biltmore Theatre in New York.

Martin went back to New York to do some radio work. He was unprepared for the bombshell which came a few days later in the form of a call from Beatrice, and he was stunned to realize that Beatrice was weeping. "Abbott's changed his mind," she said. "He's decided not to bring the play in to New York." She added, through her tears, "Perhaps he's right. Perhaps we *don't* have a play."

Martin was speechless for a moment. Then he said, "But your husband believes in the play . . ."

"Maybe George is just being kind," Beatrice said. "Anyway, it doesn't matter. Abbott says he just won't risk the additional money for a Broadway opening."

It was too late to wonder what might have happened if they had let Shumlin keep the play; *The White-Haired Boy* was dead. Martin went on with his radio work and then moved into films, and became too busy to collaborate on another play with Beatrice, even though she suggested several times that they do so. And Beatrice never wrote another play on her own or with anyone else.

13. THE DAUGHTER

KAUFMAN SOMETIMES TENDED to deride family relation-
ships, and occasionally expressed the blunt opinion that kinfolk were
a pain and who needed them? "The trouble with incest," he once said
to Groucho Marx, "is that it gets you involved with relatives." But
he was not as far removed from the need for such relationships as he
tried to appear, and, as the years passed after he and Beatrice had
agreed to end their sexual relationship, the Kaufmans both began to
be more and more deeply troubled by the fact that they would never
have children.

It started out merely as a wistful thought: Beatrice remarked one
day that it was a shame that their sex life was not as normal as the rest
of their life together, so that they could complete the family circle by
having at least one child. It became, however, and very quickly, almost an obsession. The fact that there was no chance of their becom-

ing what their parents would have called a *real* family was a realization which filled them with severe feelings of regret and guilt; they were both still motivated, in many ways, by their old-school Jewish backgrounds despite their newfound sophistication. And after a while, they found themselves talking about little else.

Kaufman suggested the obvious solution, proposing again that they have another try at a normal sexual relationship. But Beatrice rejected this at once; she did it gently and without rancor, but with absolute finality, saying again that this was no longer possible for her. Then she proposed a new idea which had just come into her mind— that they give some thought to adopting a child.

This, too, began some months of discussions, because it was, at first, a rather alien notion to both of them. They had been brought up to believe that people adopted children only when they were physically unable to have children of their own, and the Kaufmans, of course, had no reason to believe that, if things had been otherwise, they might not have been able to have a dozen. In time, however, they faced the truth: that their mental problems prohibited them as surely from having children as a couple who discovered that one or both of them were barren. The result was that, a few mornings later, they went over to see the people at the adoption center associated with the Stephen Wise Free Synagogue.

The choice was a surprising one in one respect: the center had the reputation of being very severe and searching in the religious requirements it imposed on people who came to adopt a child. Its interviewers insisted, for example, that the potential parents agreed to attend religious services regularly and saw to it that the child did the same. This was hardly the Kaufmans' pattern; neither was religious at all, and neither had been inside a synagogue since childhood. But Kaufman said, "I'll handle that," and proceeded to do so when the interviewer stated that one condition of adoption was that the child would have to be given a Jewish education. "I'll bring the child up any way I want," Kaufman said, directing at the interviewer the same kind of piercing stare over his glasses which was later to bring terror to so many collaborators on occasions when they were conscious that they'd suggested some poor lines. There was a brief silence, but then the interviewer smiled weakly and said, "Well, okay."

Beatrice said afterward that her heart had stopped beating for a moment when her husband had said what he'd said, and she had three theories for the interviewer's quick capitulation. The first was that George had scared the poor man so much that he was afraid to argue. The second was that he hadn't really taken George's statement seriously, accepting it as an example of the increasingly famous Kaufman brand of humor. The third was that would-be adoptive parents of her husband's eminence, capable of fulfilling a child's every need and more, were relatively rare, and the interviewer had decided that an applicant of that kind should not be passed up. In all likelihood, it was a combination of all three, but it didn't really matter; the important thing was that the interviewer was okaying them.

The Kaufmans had decided that they wanted a little girl, and the interviewer told them that the center had exactly the right child for them, a beautiful and responsive infant, just a few months old. In accordance with standard adoption center procedure, he would tell them nothing about the little girl's parents, but the Kaufmans understood the reasons for the ask-no-questions policy and were completely willing to accept it as a condition of the deal, in the same way that the interviewer had shown willingness to accept Kaufman's religious recalcitrance as a condition on the playwright's side. On a summer morning in 1925, the Kaufmans took the baby home.

Anne Kaufman, whose name is now Anne Schneider, is in her late forties today, but even the people who have known her virtually all her life are still not in complete accord on the kind of person she is. All agree that she is complex, and the evidence certainly confirms this. Of six people who talked about her recently, one described her as utterly charming, a second as lacking in charm, a third as lovable, a fourth as unlovable, a fifth as gracious, and a sixth as devoid of the social graces. The answer seems to be that it depends on when and how you strike her.

As with her adoptive parents, a lot of it can be traced back to her childhood development, some of which was handled as clumsily and thoughtlessly as some of the Kaufmans' own upbringing. She was spoiled at times and ignored at other times, and held too tightly in check in some areas and given too free rein in others, with the result that her adult life has not been a total picture of well-adjusted happiness or a complete panorama of thoughtfulness toward others. On the other hand, she has never been in trouble nor involved in any of the excesses sometimes associated with the children of the rich, either. A realistic summary is that she turned out to be neither the dream daughter that the Kaufmans had hoped for nor the disaster that some people fear in secret when they adopt a child whose antecedents are unknown to them.

She was certainly a charmer as a child. Frank Adams, growing acquainted with her in the months after the Kaufmans brought her home, commented on this in reporting on his day's activities in his column for Saturday, December 12, 1925. (Adams's Saturday columns were always diaries written in the style of Samuel Pepys.) "Up," he wrote, "and so for a ride in my petrol-waggon through the city, and fetched up at G. Kaufman's, and played with his little adopted daughter, Anne, as sweet a child of five months of age as ever I saw, and ever in merry mood and laughing, as unlike George as well might be." Anne also, as she grew older, developed a sense of humor rather like her father's, partially because Kaufman refused to treat her like a child. He never talked down to her, and he conversed and joked with her in exactly the same manner and language he used with his friends at a Round Table luncheon.

Once Anne told him that a girl who lived in the neighborhood had left school and gotten married. "I see," Kaufman said. "She put her heart before the course." Anne became equally quick in her responses, some of them acerbic enough to cause Kaufman to peer fondly at her and smile. She once went to see *Pride and Prejudice*, which was at the Plymouth Theatre, directly across the street from the Music Box, where *First Lady*, which Kaufman had written with Katharine Dayton, was showing. As Anne left the Plymouth at the end of the play, she noticed that only three people were leaving the Music Box, and she told her father what she'd seen and asked if, as it appeared, attendance had fallen almost to nothing at *First Lady*. Kaufman explained that it wasn't that at all. *First Lady*, he said, was fifteen minutes longer than *Pride and Prejudice*, so the final curtain came down fifteen minutes later. "Oh," said Anne. "So they're starting to walk out on you before the finish, are they?"

Father and daughter became deeply attached. Because of Kaufman's phobia, which made it painful for him to touch people, there was little of the hugging and kissing so commonplace in most parent-child relationships, but he showed his love for her in every other way. He gave her a nickname, Poky. It was a diminutive for Slow-poke because she was sometimes late for lunch or dinner or other family appointments, but the name was affectionate rather than remonstrative; Kaufman's stern and rigid rules about punctuality became considerably more flexible when they applied to the new lady in his life. He returned with gifts almost every time he left home, even when he went out for just a few hours, and, to the astonishment of his friends, he took Anne constantly to children's shows. It wasn't totally unselfish. Like many humorists whose own brand of comedy tended toward subtlety, he enjoyed slapstick and other types of broad humor when perpetrated by others, and Anne noticed that he laughed as hard as she did at Laurel and Hardy comedies like *Babes in Toyland*. But he took her as readily to shows which were miles below his level of enjoyment if he felt that she would like them.

In addition, in keeping with his insistence that he would never patronize her merely because of her youth, he also took her to see many adult shows. He once even took her to see *The Eternal Road*, an extremely frank and serious drama. Anne learned afterward that one of the reasons was that he had a girl friend in the show, but she felt certain that he'd have taken her even if that hadn't been the case—because it was a good play and he wanted her to learn to appreciate good things. He was always taking her to unexpected places; sometimes he even took her to the Regency Bridge Club and let her sit and watch him play his expert brand of the game for hours. It wasn't surprising that Anne learned a lot from some of the more unlikely sorties. The thing that really surprised her was that she always enjoyed the trips wherever they went.

Kaufman's indulgence of his daughter sometimes stopped when it ran afoul of his prudish sense of morality. Ruth Goetz, his friend and Bucks County neighbor, later remembered the time his fifteen-year-old daughter wore a daring bathing suit down to their pool. Kaufman exploded when he saw the tiny bra and brief panties. "Get back in the house and put on something decent!" he said. Mrs. Goetz felt the bathing suit was perfectly acceptable and that Anne looked charming in it.

With Anne, Kaufman either had to order her to do something or let her have her own way. He was no good at persuasion or at employing child psychology. Anne went to a succession of private schools: Walden, Lincoln, Todhunter, Dalton, and Holmquist. Then, in her last year of high school, she decided that she wanted to attend the University of Chicago. Kaufman sent her a long letter stating that he had talked to Edna Ferber, who knew a lot about the university. He said that the school was "disordered in its program and had no campus life." Then, after adding that the weather in Chicago was "frightful," he asked, "What about Wisconsin? It is apparently a fine school. I'm not trying to sell it to you—look over some of the others. But don't deliberately pick the worst one."

Anne elected to go to the University of Chicago, and Kaufman eventually accepted it and wrote her philosophically: "Well, Poky, I hear you got into Chicago. I thought of sending you, by way of congratulations, a copy of my letter telling you why you shouldn't go there, but maybe you remember it. At least I have discovered how to get you to do anything—just write a strong letter the other way."

Anne could always depend on his eventual support, even in trivial things like the time she entered a Ping-pong tournament aboard ship when she and Kaufman were returning from a European trip. When she went to the table to play her round, Anne was startled to see Kaufman and Hermione Gingold, the British comedienne, waving homemade banners and pennants to cheer her on.

Kaufman demonstrated his feelings for Anne in significant ways. As mentioned, he was in California once on a writing assignment when he learned that Anne had become seriously ill and had been rushed to a hospital. Kaufman was terrified of flying and even hated the sight of airplanes on the ground, but he did not hesitate at all. He abandoned his assignment and boarded a plane for New York. Kaufman's friends were very much aware of his deep affection for his daughter despite his natural reticence and avoidance of sentimentality. "He reserved his deepest love for his daughter Anne," Irwin Shaw said once, and Charles Martin echoed this, saying, "The great love of his life was his daughter."

Anne's love for her father was equally strong. A reporter who interviewed her a few years ago felt that she was telling him, "Let's face it. I've really always loved Daddy best of all"—a fact which, if so, must have disconcerted her husband, Irving Schneider, who sat nearby during the interview. She even, after she became old enough to write, began to send her father little thank-you notes, some for birthdays and some for no occasion at all. A typical letter came to Kaufman in 1940 on his fifty-first birthday, when Anne was approaching sixteen. "Well, sir, here we are again," she wrote. "Every year at this time I want to write you a *really* nice letter, and every year I'm just as much at a loss as I was the year before. In between times I can make up gobs of them—I remember things we do together; funny things you say; but those aren't reasons for writing people birthday letters—those are just a few reasons for liking you. Others are hard to say—hard even to define in thinking terms to oneself. I'm growing up a little every year—but not enough to make you feel any older. In six years I'll still be flunking the same math test I flunked last year—so that is unchanged. And I still can't fold letters and put them into envelopes—I won't even try with this one. Happy birthday, Daddy, *lots of love*, Poky."

The best thing about it all, Anne later told people, was that it was fun so much of the time; her father was sort of crazy in a wonderful way and so were many of his friends. Would any adult outside of the Kaufman circle, for example, behave as her father's friend Alexander Woollcott had behaved? The Kaufmans had applied to send Anne to a rather exclusive school, giving Woollcott as one of their references, and the school's headmistress sent Woollcott the usual form letter requesting confirmation of the good character of parents and child. The ordinary stuffy grown-up, Anne was sure, would have answered routinely, but not Woollcott. "I implore you," he wrote in reply, "to accept this unfortunate child and remove her from her shocking environment." He then went on to invent a series of lurid stories detailing the nightly orgies which took place at the Kaufman household. The headmistress, knowing the reputation of the members of the Round Table, merely smiled and wrote the Kaufmans, accepting Anne for her school. And Anne herself was nearly overcome with laughter and affection for her father and his lunatic friends when she heard about it.

The relationship which developed between mother and daughter was not as idyllic. In an extraordinary interview which Anne gave many years later to a writer named John Gruen, and which appeared in the New York *World Journal Tribune* on November 13, 1966, Anne said coldly that she "didn't much like" Beatrice. Part of this may have stemmed from the fact that Beatrice, though yearning for a child and deciding to adopt one, had also decided firmly that she would not allow the new arrival to disrupt too much the smooth and long-established routine of the household. Kaufman's frequent practice of sleeping late would, clearly, be difficult or even impossible to maintain with tiny feet pattering around the apartment. With this in mind, the Kaufmans, who were then living in their big apartment at 200 West 58th Street, rented a small apartment next door and turned it into a suite for Anne and the governess they hired for her. This gave Anne a tremendous amount of privacy—the kind for which some children of less wealthy parents, forced to share their bedrooms with one or more brothers or sisters, yearn endlessly—but it also gave her a feeling of isolation, separation, and exclusion, and she developed strong resentment toward Beatrice about this. It wasn't a fair or logical reaction, since the decision to rent the adjoining apartment had been both her parents' rather than just Beatrice's, but Anne was sometimes less than logical when it came to adoring her father and resenting her mother.

Another thing which may have helped to widen the chasm between Beatrice and Anne was that Beatrice, in her eagerness to be a modern mother and avoid some of the old-fashioned mistakes made by her own parents, embraced a theory which was considered up-to-the-minute and farsighted in the '20s and '30s, but which has fallen pretty totally into disuse and even disgrace since that time. This was the theory that a mother should not "interfere" too much with her children, but leave as much of their upbringing as possible to professionals, meaning people like teachers and, if the family can afford it, governesses. The feeling is pretty much the reverse today, that love and strong interest in the child should be felt and shown as much as possible, but this was a different time, and the Kaufmans were in a financial position where they were able to follow the tenets of the period. Anne, therefore, grew up served by a whole procession of governesses, most of them French or German. The result was that she was trilingual by the time she was ten, but she also thought a lot about the fact that she spent more time with her current governess than with her mother and often felt unloved.

The fact that she was surrounded by luxury and given the best of everything didn't really help, at least not a lot. Anne, for example, often found herself taken to places like local shops and the movies by chauffeurs and in limousines. It was the kind of experience which might well have been the secret dream of other little girls whose familiarity with that sort of thing was limited to seeing it in the movies, but Anne would probably have enjoyed it more if economics had, as is more usually the case, made Beatrice the family chauffeur. The same applied to the swank schools to which Anne was sent; it got her the best education money could buy, but it also meant more separation from her parents than was perhaps the best idea. When, for example, the Kaufmans bought their estate in Bucks County, in 1936, the best school available for Anne was in New York City, so Anne remained in New York and came to Bucks County on weekends. But it would probably have been better if a school or tutor had been found for her in Bucks County during the times when the Kaufmans stayed there for long periods.

Anne was twenty when Beatrice died in 1945, but she never grew close to her mother; she was not even noticeably sorrowful at Beatrice's funeral. The only visible change in Anne caused by her mother's death was that she became even closer to her father. Not too long before Kaufman's own death, she made two trips with him to Europe—by ship, of course—and subsequently described the trips as among the happiest times of her life. "He was courtly, cozy, fun to be with, and not at all fatherly," she said. "We invented private games—guessing what people did and why—and we laughed a lot. It was really, really marvelous." And a while before that, when Kaufman, recovering from Beatrice's death, met Leueen MacGrath and asked her to marry him, it was Anne who arranged the details of the wedding. Anne admitted that she was a little jealous of the beautiful woman who was not too much older than she herself was, but the British actress was obviously making her father happy. "He was very changed," she remembered later, "very gay, and he simply adored her. She could do no wrong—and her every whim was given in to." So Anne went ahead and arranged the wedding details and did a good job of it.

Unfortunately, charmer though Anne may have been as a child, a few of her adult activities have been a shade less charming. Certainly several gave her father considerable pain, and several others would have pained him equally if he had been alive to be aware of them.

The earliest of these was Anne's first marriage, which took place in 1943, when she was eighteen. The marriage is almost forgotten today; members of the family can't even remember the groom's first name, referring to him as "that Booth boy who was part of the family that owned the Schulte Cigar Store chain." They do recall that he was "a very nice boy." The groom's name was John Booth. He was a graduate of Lawrenceville School and Columbia University, and was a young soldier at Fort Dix, New Jersey, at the time of the marriage. Despite Anne's insistence on going to the University of Chicago, she dropped out of school permanently to marry Booth. The wedding, a substantial affair, was held at the Cottage Room of the swank Hampshire House in New York.

The Kaufmans were not against the marriage because Anne was only eighteen, since a lot of girls married at that age; they were against the marriage because it was clear to them that Anne did not really love the boy. Anne almost, but not quite, came right out and admitted it. Her attitude was never one of "I can't live without him"; it was, fairly openly, "I'll bet the other girls at school never thought I'd be the first to marry." Both parents tried to talk her out of it, in arguments that grew bitter at times, but Anne was unshakable in her intentions. "I'll marry him with your consent or without it," she said, a statement rather similar to the one Beatrice had made to her own parents, and the Kaufmans had no choice other than to go along. The inevitable followed. Anne's young husband went off to war, and not long afterward, Anne told him that the marriage was over.

Anne's second marriage was no more successful than her first, and once more caused Kaufman considerable anguish because he saw no real promise of permanence in the second marriage, either, when Anne told him in 1947 that she was planning to marry again. The Kaufmans were then living at 410 Park Avenue, and Anne's new fiancé, a young editor named Bruce Colen, lived in the same building; the two young people met when they began to notice and smile at each other in the elevator.

Colen, Kaufman felt, was another nice young man, but the same thing bothered him this time as last time: there didn't seem to be any special compatibility between the couple or any deep love on Anne's part for her neighbor. It appeared to him that Anne was just growing tired again of living at home, and that her feeling for Colen was much closer to liking than love. And that just wasn't a strong enough basis on which to build a marriage. But, once again, Anne was absolutely determined, and the marriage took place.

Kaufman was right. Anne's second marriage lasted longer than her first, over five years, and achieved one happy result: Anne's only child, a little girl who was named Beatrice at Kaufman's request because by this time the elder Beatrice was gone. (Anne has never called her daughter by her full name; she always calls her Betsy.) But in 1953, without fuss and by mutual consent, the Colens separated and were then divorced.

Anne didn't marry again for seven years. Then, aged thirty-five, she met Irving Schneider, an assistant to Irene Mayer Selznick, the daughter of Louis B. Mayer and first wife of David O. Selznick, who had begun to produce plays and films. Anne and Schneider were married on April 7, 1960, in a brief ceremony in the study of Rabbi David J. Seligson of the Central Synagogue in New York City. This one stuck; the Schneiders are reported to be very happy, dividing their time between an apartment in the East 60's in New York City and a house in Quogue, Long Island, which a newspaper story described a while ago as "a small turn-of-the-century masterpiece."

Kaufman approved of Schneider far more than Anne's two previous husbands. He was ill and could not attend the wedding, but he subsequently showed his approval by shaking hands with Schneider when the most his closest friends usually got was the uplifted finger. Later Kaufman told a friend, "I hope this one takes like a vaccination." This hope did not keep Kaufman from finding occasional fault with his newest son-in-law. Once while visiting Kaufman's Bucks County farm, Schneider made a half-hour phone call at a time when Kaufman was expecting a call of his own. Finally Kaufman interrupted, saying, "From the length of your conversation, I gather nothing's new." He also sometimes found Anne's new marriage painful. She had spent a lot of time with him after he and Leueen were divorced; now most of her time was taken up with her own family. In June 1958, Kaufman had only three years to live; he was ailing, very lonely, and looking forward with great eagerness to a promised month-long visit by the Schneiders. One day, very casually, Anne phoned and canceled out. Kaufman later mentioned the fact in a letter to Ruth. "Anne, contrary to what I thought," he wrote, "will not be with me in July—Irving Schneider will have a house on the beach, and I don't blame her in the least for preferring the water to me." Typically, he tried to state things lightly, but the hurt showed through.

Kaufman's faint disappointment with his daughter, as he grew older, did not, of course, alter his love for her. He gave her some pretty lavish gifts along with the smaller ones, one of these being all of his rights to *You Can't Take It with You,* a gift similar to giving someone the Hope Diamond. And when he died, he left her, after some relatively small bequests to others, half of his estate, leaving the other half to Leueen MacGrath. The will also gave the two women joint ownership of the estate's future income, meaning a half interest apiece in all royalties from showings of the play around the world and in all other income. In contrast, Kaufman's sisters, Ruth and Helen received a flat $50,000 each, and Kaufman's favorite organization, the Dramatists Guild, was left only $1000.

Anne talked at length about her father and mother in the interview she gave to John Gruen in 1966. Gruen's article is called *The Season's Hottest Playwright* because a number of Kaufman's plays, among them *Dinner at Eight, The Butter and Egg Man,* and *You*

Can't Take It with You, were just then being revived all at once. Anne's description of her father is pleasant enough: "He was, in his black way, a dazzling sort of guy. He was like a stern, Victorian vicar, but he could be terribly funny, immensely witty . . ." The Gruen article, however, is the one in which she says that he never really liked her mother; she also describes Beatrice as having "co-authored two horrible flops." Then she describes her parents' mixed-up marital relationship. "Daddy *must* have had something to turn the ladies on," she says, "because throughout his life he had dozens of mistresses—almost as many mistresses as Mummy had lovers." She adds, "It was a very complicated household, what with 'his' and 'her' private phones being installed wherever we lived, and a lot of unexplained comings and goings, arrivals and departures."

She goes on to talk about Leueen. "I must confess I did find it a bit strange," she says, "that she just happened to leave a book behind when she got to know Daddy at a party. Especially when the book was called *Friends and Lovers* and had her name, address, and phone number in it." She also comments on her father's famous wars with taxi drivers and others, implying that they were caused by snobbery. "Everybody knows," she says, "how much Daddy disliked actors—he really hated them. Still, he was scrupulously polite, and never embarrassed them. This, God knows, cannot be said of his treatment of waiters, taxicab drivers, or persons subservient to him. It was his one hideous fault. The outbursts, the rudeness, his cruelty were almost too much to bear." The interpretation of snobbery is one with which absolutely no one else who knew Kaufman seems to agree. Frank Sullivan sums up the majority opinion by saying, "He just didn't suffer fools gladly."

Anne later came to regret the interview. And when Gruen put together the Kaufman story and a number of other interviews in a book called *Close-Up,* he added a postscript describing what had happened after his piece was published. "When this interview appeared," he wrote, "the congenial, sympathetic, and co-operative Mrs. Schneider suffered a most devastating change of heart. I received a special-delivery letter that fairly oozed with venom. In it she accused me of having distorted every fact she had given me, of having put words in her mouth, and of having degraded her mother, her father, and her husband Irving and herself." But Gruen was a careful reporter who had only written down what he had heard. "The fact of the matter," his postscript continues, "is that Mrs. Schneider is not used to being interviewed, although she seems to have great ambitions in that direction. In my reply, I explained to her how differently things look in print and how accurately she had, in fact, been quoted." He concludes ruefully, "Through this article I lost what I had thought was a friend."

The relationship today between Anne and her relatives is not very good. The Schneiders have not visited or been visited by some close relatives in years.

14. THE SECOND COLLABORATOR

THERE ARE NO records available to prove or disprove it, but several people who were close to Edna Ferber, Kaufman's next collaborator and the author with whom he wrote a number of his best and most successful plays, say that it was because of unrequited love for him that she lived and died a spinster. She was a reasonably attractive woman, so it was not for lack of opportunities; it was, they say, just that, having met Kaufman and fallen in love with him, she remained for the rest of her long life rather uninterested in other men.

On the basis of an obvious fact or two, the statements seem dubious, or at least exaggerated. When Edna Ferber came to know Kaufman well enough to fall in love with him—which was in 1924, the year they wrote *Minick*, their first play together—she was no starry-eyed girl of seventeen or eighteen, about whom an old-fashioned story of blighted love followed by a nun-like existence might just barely be believed. She was a woman of thirty-eight, nearly thirty-nine, when she first began to work with Kaufman, and had reached an age where a woman interested in being wedded would have accomplished it years before. But by her own testimony, she had never even had a serious romance up to that point. So it must be recognized that, even if it is true that she rarely again looked at another man after falling in love with Kaufman, she had also done very little looking at other men *before* falling in love with him.

Her reason, she said many times, was that she realized early in life that, however successfully other women might be able to combine the writing life with family life, her personal makeup was such that she could not; it had to be one or the other. "As a young woman," she said, "there was the alternative: write or marry-and-live-happily-ever-after—but without the satisfaction of writing." She had unhesitatingly chosen writing over marriage. "It's wonderful to be a writer," she explained. "I couldn't be anything else. Life can't ever really defeat a writer who is in love with writing, for life itself is the writer's lover until death—fascinating, cruel, lavish, warm, cold, treacherous, constant; the more varied the moods the richer the experience." She added, "Being an old maid is like death by drowning. It's a really delightful sensation after you cease to struggle."

But important choices are rarely made for simple reasons, and that is certainly the case here. She was always ready to give her quick explanation, her story about the two choices, whenever people were indelicate enough to ask her why she had never married. But she never once explained what it was about her that made her different from all the other women writers, so that she had to choose instead of attempting both writing *and* marriage. She would not, in fact, even respond when that question was asked. A strong clue, however, may well be found in something else she once said about the writing life.

"The entire output of my particular job depends on me," she said. "By that I mean that when I put the cover on my typewriter, the works are closed. The office equipment consists of one flat table, a sheaf of yellow paper and one of white. All the wheels, belts, wires, bolts, files, tools—the whole manufacturing process—has got to be contained in the space between my chin and my topmost hairpin. And my one horror is that some morning I'll wake up and find that space vacant and the works closed down, with a metal sign over the front door reading: 'For rent, fine, large, empty head; inquire within.' Still, even if that should happen, I would probably turn over and say, 'Well, what a grand time I've had.'" She added that nothing could separate her from a script once she had started it. "Clothes are unimportant," she said. "Teeth go unfilled. Your idea of bliss is to wake up on a Monday morning knowing you haven't a single engagement for the entire week. You are cradled in a white paper cocoon tied up with typewriter ribbon."

The significance lies in her long and almost defiant statement of her self-sufficiency, the description proclaiming how little she needs anyone else, and in the way she summarizes the writing life with words like "cradled" and "in a . . . cocoon." All too clearly, her writing was her shield and her retreat, both perhaps desperately needed. There is considerable evidence that she was terrified from girlhood on of the task of attracting a man, and what better way to handle that than to tell herself that she had to choose between writing and marriage, and that writing was the more desirable choice? She had a strange image of herself throughout her lifetime, seeing herself as an unappealing woman, big-nosed and ugly; and she simply never believed it when people told her truthfully that she was not unappealing at all, and that her nose suited her strong, high-cheekboned face more than a tiny snub nose. She finally went out one day and got herself a nose job, one of the earliest operations of that kind on record, but it didn't help. Even after that, she continued to think of herself as ugly.

She was also the world's toughest negotiator, and feared no man on earth when it came to business matters related to her work, but changed abruptly if the man with whom she was dealing suddenly developed a romantic interest in her, or if she felt similar stirrings toward him. She became so fluttery and weak-willed that she had to back off and allow someone like her trusted friend and lawyer, Morris Ernst, to finish the negotiation.

As an example, Leland Hayward, the producer, often said that the ulcer which plagued him much of his life started when, back in the days when he was still an agent, he brought her a huge film deal on one of her books, and she turned it down simply because she felt that he had proceeded without proper authorization from her. But this was because there was no romantic relationship between them; contrast it with the fact that she had to be rescued fairly often by Ernst because she was about to sign a bad contract with a man who had shown a romantic interest in her. It was even true of her relationship with Kaufman. They began their work together by fighting about many aspects of literary technique, but mutual friends noticed that, after the lady started to look at her collaborator through different eyes, they continued to quarrel "but not nearly so often or so hard."

Perhaps her terror of real romance was in itself one of the reasons she became interested in Kaufman; she surely sensed that, even if he returned her interest, it could never develop into anything permanent because he would never, not in a million years, part from Beatrice. She may even have sensed that Kaufman would not return her interest because she probably knew, as so many people did, that a large percentage of Kaufman's romances away from Beatrice were strictly physical and confined to empty-headed chorus girl types. (She was right; he never developed a romantic interest in her.) There is no doubt that *she* was in love with Kaufman, because she said so, openly, to several people, and even said so, a few times, to Kaufman himself, embarrassing him enormously. But part of the attraction may have been that she realized it would be a nice, safe, uninvolving love.

The remainder of the attraction was not one of opposites; in this case, it had to be the attraction of mirror images, because they were startlingly alike in a great many respects. Edna Ferber was four years older than Kaufman, born on August 15, 1885 (though she sometimes, in a rare example of vanity, gave the year of her birth as 1887), but their backgrounds were otherwise astonishingly alike. Like Kaufman, she was Jewish, and quick to counterattack anyone she suspected of anti-Semitism, but, just as he was, she was also non-religious. When she died, the services, held at the same funeral parlor as Kaufman's, were non-sectarian in accordance with her known wishes. Like Kaufman, she grew up in a relatively small-town atmosphere; she was born in

Kalamazoo, Michigan, and spent her early years there and in Appleton, Wisconsin. Like Kaufman, her education was modest; she went only as far as graduation from Ryan High School in Appleton. Like Kaufman, she started out as a newspaper writer, getting her first job as a reporter on the Appleton *Daily Crescent*. And her first ambition, like his, was to go into acting rather than writing: she grew up hoping to attend the School of Elocution at Northwestern University, but her father just couldn't afford to send her. For the rest of her life, she referred to herself as "a blighted Bernhardt."

She even shared some of Kaufman's phobias, such as his great fear of germs and illness. One of the more terrible moments of her life occurred when she was having dinner with Oscar Levant and unthinkingly expressed interest in the spaghetti he was eating. With typical mischievousness, Levant, who knew how she felt about things like that, wound up some spaghetti on his fork and handed it to her. He had her trapped; he realized that she would be horrified at the prospect of using another person's utensil, but would also be too polite to say so. He watched with amusement as she ate the spaghetti, trying to get it into her mouth without touching the fork with her lips, and handed the fork back to him. Then he turned toward the waiter and spoke loudly. "Waiter," he said, "bring me another fork."

She was already a vastly successful and popular writer when she began to work with Kaufman. That year, in fact, was a banner year for her. It was the year in which her publishers brought out her novel, *So Big*, which sold 300,000 copies, an incredible amount in those days before the arrival of paperbacks, won the Pulitzer Prize for 1924, and became required reading at high schools and colleges all over the country. She had begun writing fiction when she moved from the Appleton *Crescent* to the Milwaukee *Journal*, writing and selling a novel about a Milwaukee newspaperwoman, *Dawn O'Hara*. She then decided to approach the writing business seriously, bought a used typewriter for $17 and wrote a story about a fat, homely girl who weighed two hundred pounds but had "the soul of a willow wand," and sold it to *Everybody's Magazine*. Her first big break came when she wrote a story about a young traveling saleswoman named Emma McChesney, who moved around the country with a line of underwear, and sold that one to *The American Magazine*. The story was supposed to be a single, isolated piece, but Emma McChesney proved so popular that magazine after magazine began to ask for more stories featuring the same character, and she ended up writing thirty of them. The McChesney appeal was so widespread that when, in 1904, Miss Ferber was covering the political convention at which Theodore Roosevelt was the candidate, Roosevelt stopped his politicking long enough to come over to her and urge her to write more Emma McChesney stories.

She also had some play experience. Her first play, written in collaboration with George V. Hobart, was a dramatization of one of the McChesney stories, *Our Mrs. McChesney*, which was produced in 1915 with a slim and beautiful Ethel Barrymore in the title role. Her second dramatization was a one-act play, *The Eldest*, which she wrote under unusual circumstances in 1920. She happened to see an announcement in the *Times* to the effect that a one-act play called *The Eldest* was scheduled to be performed at a small theatre in Greenwich Village, the Provincetown Theatre. Since she had once written a short story with the same title, she called the theatre's director James Light, and asked him to synopsize the plot of the play for her. Light proceeded to tell her the plot of her own story; it developed that a young woman had stolen the plot in every detail, written it as a one-act play, and sold it to Light as an original. This placed her in a dilemma because she didn't want to destroy the plans of the Provincetown people, who were all set to go, but she wasn't willing to allow the pirated version to be used, either. She solved the problem by writing her own one-act version of her story in one night, delivering it the next morning to Light for the theatre's use.

Her third play, also produced in 1920, was *$1200 a Year*, written in collaboration with Newman Levy. But none of her plays had been especially successful, and when Kaufman, sharing honors with Connelly as the hottest playwright in town, wrote her one day and said he'd read one of her short stories, *Old Man Minick*, thought it would make a good play, and wondered if she'd be interested in collaborating with him on it, she replied promptly and told him to come over and discuss it. She said later, "If George had approached me with the idea of dramatizing *McGuffey's First Reader*, I'd have been enchanted to talk about it."

Edna Ferber knew Kaufman slightly; she'd met him a few times at Round Table lunches and other places around town and rather liked him, and liked even more his strong reputation as a play constructionist. She had her doubts, however, about whether or not her story would make a successful play. *Old Man Minick* was a bittersweet story, funny in places but essentially rather sad; it was about a widower of seventy who comes to live with his son and daughter-in-law, and is well-meaning but upsets their lives by showing up at his son's office on busy days, messing up his daughter-in-law's social events by appearing suddenly with a lot of his friends from a nearby old age home, and changing things around in their apartment. He finally realizes that it just won't work and goes off again to his own lonesome way of life. Miss Ferber felt that she had said all there was to say about Minick in her 6000-word story; she also doubted that sophisticated Broadway audiences would be interested in the sad little story of an old man whose efforts to ingratiate himself with two young people alienate them instead, even though they're as anxious as he is to get along.

She told this to Kaufman when they met, urging on him instead another of her stories, *The Gay Old Dog*. "There's a story that would make a marvelous play," she told him. She wasn't, she said afterward, derogating *Old Man Minick*; she felt it was one of the best short stories she'd ever written, with a theme that was touching and universally recognizable. But it seemed to her to lack the necessary dramatic importance to make it a popular success. Kaufman's response was to throw her a quick, quelling look. "Don't worry," he said. "I think there's a good play in the story."

It's probable that Edna Ferber first began to fall in love with Kaufman at that moment; she confided to several people later on that his instant assumption of command should have angered her, but instead made her heart flutter a little. "Okay," she said. And, though her interest in Kaufman grew more and more personal as time passed, and Kaufman's interest in his new collaborator remained strictly business in the twenty-four years in which, off and on, they worked together, the relationship remained a totally satisfying one for both of them.

Kaufman learned that Edna Ferber was the same kind of indefatigable worker that he was, and that she sometimes even surpassed him. Throughout her entire adult life, she made it an absolute point to work 350 days a year, spending time at the typewriter even while on a trip. And, when she was working on a novel or short story, she tried to write at least a thousand words a day. He found that she was nearly always willing, as he was, to put work before other considerations, and when once, on New Year's Eve, he suggested rather hesitantly that the two of them send Beatrice and the others in their party off and start a new play, because it would be more fun than watching a lot of people get drunk, she agreed immediately and enthusiastically. He was also pleased to note that she felt exactly the same way about being punctual as he did. When, for a while, the writing of one of their plays was going so well that Kaufman decided to extend their work period by getting up at the unusually early hour of ten in order to appear at her place at eleven, she was always ready for him. He invariably showed up just as her clock was striking the first of eleven tones, and she was there at the typewriter and all set.

He also confirmed with relief an impression received from her books and stories: that she had a sharp, and sometimes biting, sense of humor, an important criterion for Kaufman in judging the people in his circle. He heard, with pleasure, that she had once put down their friend Noël Coward, who sometimes needed putting down. Edna Ferber enjoyed wearing tailored suits, and was wearing one when Coward met her and objected to her appearance. "You look almost like a man," he said. "So," said Miss Ferber, "do you." She once joined one of the Round Table group's European jaunts, and told reporters at the pier that she was hungry for solitude. "I don't intend to talk to another human being on the trip," she said. "I'll just talk to Aleck Woollcott." She often feuded with Woollcott, but she was equally willing to shower her disfavors on others. Louis Bromfield was a friend of hers, but she did not admire his habit of talking endlessly of his life of the earth and of farming while he was engaged in more sophisticated pleasures. She cut him off abruptly when, while he was lunching with her at a fashionable New York restaurant, he began to describe his raising of pigs. "For God's sake, Louis," she said, "brush the caviar off your blue jeans."

She took a strong dislike to a novelist named Tess Slesinger, who also wrote poetry which was glaringly imitative of Dorothy Parker's work. She was in a bookstore when Miss Slesinger came in and asked a salesclerk if he had a copy of the new Slesinger book of poems. Miss Ferber reached over and handed her a copy of Dorothy Parker's *Enough Rope*.

She was equally willing to take on critics when she felt this was necessary. She was pleased about her Pulitzer Prize, but, like many Pulitzer Prize-winning authors, she was a little envious of winners of the even more prestigious Nobel Prize. She once expressed her irritation with critics who seemed to feel that Nobel Prize-winners could do no wrong. "The trouble with those critics," she said, "is that they're awed by the Nobelity." She also once wrote to Harold Ross in some anger when *The New Yorker* reviewed a bad movie based on a Ferber novel and gave the impression that the fault was hers rather than the screenwriter's. "Will you kindly inform the moron who runs your motion picture department," she wrote, "that I did not write the movie? Also inform him that Moses did not write the motion picture entitled *The Ten Commandments*." Kaufman particularly liked that one.

He also, however, occasionally found himself on the receiving end. Edna Ferber once threw one of her barbs at him when she discovered, not long after they began to work together, that, as he paced around the room throwing out lines for her consideration, he had the habit of picking up every piece of paper on her desk and elsewhere in the room and gazing distractedly at it. It was a practice compounded as much of nervousness as of curiosity, cousin to his habit of swooping down suddenly on pieces of lint on the rug and carrying them over to her wastebasket. She still didn't like the fact that every document in her possession came, sooner or later, under his scrutiny. To combat this, she sent herself a telegram one day and left it lying face down, knowing that Kaufman would not be able to resist picking it up and turning it over. He did so within a few minutes after arriving the next morning, and read the message: GEORGE KAUFMAN IS AN OLD SNOOP. For the record, the ploy failed to accomplish its purpose. Kaufman, who was struggling with a particularly difficult line at the time, merely smiled wanly, and, a minute later, picked up and examined a letter which lay a few inches away

But most of their time was spent on the more serious business o writing the play, for which Kaufman suggested Winthrop Ames a producer. Ames, he felt, would be ideal because he would give th production the delicacy and sensitivity it required. He described th story and the general plan for the play to Ames, and had a firm dea within minutes. Then, since Miss Ferber had never met Ames, Kauf man introduced them.

It turned out to be a case of love at first sight—not romantic love of course, since Ames was happily married and Edna Ferber wa beginning to have eyes only for Kaufman, but tremendous mutua respect and affection. Ames turned out to be a great Ferber fan familiar with most of her work, and Miss Ferber found Ames to b one of the nicest men she'd ever met in her life. She later describe him in a way that was almost rhapsodic. "If *Minick* had brought m nothing more than the friendship of Winthrop Ames," she said, "I' have been overpaid for my work, time, energy, or creative effor spent on it. No one could have been more completely unlike the accepted type of theatrical producer than Winthrop Ames. A figur of elegance; tall; slim; the long sensitive hands of an artist; the fine dolichocephalic head of creative intelligence. Boston-born and -bred descendant of the first Massachusetts settlers, all of whom seemed to become governors on attaining their majority, it is difficult to describe him without using the words culture, wit, whimsy, taste, all of which are trite and none of which is good enough for him. Stage struck. Perhaps that will have to do. He cared as deeply about the theatre as George Kaufman and I did. Nobody could be more love-bemused than that. The Massachusetts Ameses had made their millions in the manufacture of hand-turned tools. His bluenosed governor ancestors must have turned purple in their tombs to behold Winthrop pouring a goodly portion of the Ames millions into the vast ravenous maw of the theatre. Or perhaps they weren't bluenoses after all, but free spirits who had fled England because they thought that Shakespeare was more important than either Cromwell or Charles . . . I wish there were a thousand like him."

She was much heartened by the fact that Ames seemed to share Kaufman's confidence in the potential of the project, even though she herself still had her doubts. She did not let her doubts slow her down, however, and the work went very quickly. In two weeks, working some days in Kaufman's apartment and some days in Miss Ferber's apartment on Central Park West, they had the first two acts finished. And then, because there'd been a lot of phone calls and other interruptions at both apartments, they took rooms in a decrepit old American-plan hotel in White Plains to finish up.

The food was awful and the service was worse, but the work went even more quickly without the interruptions. They finished the final act of the play in four days.

Ames's office was located above the Little Theatre on West 44th Street. He had built the Little Theatre himself in reaction to an earlier Ames project which had failed, the gigantic and luxurious Century Theatre on Central Park West; it had had to close down because it was so big that it proved impossible to fill no matter how popular an attraction was presented there. Ames did most of his work, however, in a secret suite located behind the office, a beautifully furnished apartment consisting of a living room, bedroom, kitchen, and bathroom, and served by a white-coated butler who was always on hand to prepare sandwiches and drinks. Only Ames's closest friends and business associates knew about the suite, but Kaufman had been there often. And when the play was finished, he and Edna Ferber made an appointment to come to the apartment one evening and go over it.

The title of the play at this point was still the same as the story; it was shortened during tryouts to *Minick* when people convinced them that the words "Old Man" were depressing and therefore commercially unwise. The authors later commented on this in their introduction to the published version of the play. "It seems," they wrote, "that there is a large and growing class of playgoers who become frightened at the prospect of seeing an old man on the stage, and run and hide in cellars. We rather thought—basing our guess on *Lightnin'* and *The Music Master* and *Rip Van Winkle* and some others—that the opposite would be the case. But when we heard of gay dinner parties shuddering with horror at the merest mention of a play with 'Old Man' in the title, and when, in the early days on the road, whole towns remained steadfastly away from the theatre in which the play was being acted, we weakened and agreed to the change. After all, even collaborators must live."

In most other ways, the play followed the story very closely. There were, of course, some necessary changes. One important scene in the story took place when Minick met and talked in a park with his friends from the old age home; this was shifted indoors because it seemed pointless to add an additional set for no real purpose. The authors felt, anyway, that park sets always looked too artificial. The son's name in the story was George, and Kaufman changed this to Fred because he didn't want to appear to be building any characters in his own image. And where, in the story, Minick decides to leave after he overhears his daughter-in-law tell a friend that she'll never have a baby while the old man is continually stalking around the apartment, this was changed in the play merely to one of the many contributing factors in his departure.

The third act was originally written to center around what the authors came to call, in capitals, The Baby, but it just didn't work. An eavesdropping or overhearing scene onstage is even more artificial than a park set, even though the play's scenic designer, Woodman Thompson, tried to compensate for this by setting the dining room at an angle so that the daughter-in-law and her friend could sit and sip coffee without noticing the old man wandering in. But the scene still looked stagy and overacted when it was tried out, because the actor signed to play Minick, O. P. Heggie, had to walk in and appear startled and then stand there self-consciously in a listening position.

The thing that finally killed the use of The Baby as the principal and conclusive factor in Minick's decision to leave was that Kaufman suddenly realized that it was also bad play construction. The first two acts had been developed to show that the old man was hopelessly out of place in his new surroundings, where there was really no place to entertain his friends, and where all his efforts to be helpful to his children worked against him and made him seem merely a nuisance. So it was simply wrong to bring in a new and dramatic event to drive him away; he had to come to his decision as the culmination of all the past events of the play. And that, after the collaborators had written four more versions of the third act during tryouts, was the way it was finally set.

There was also a question about "the pillows," a memorable device which Miss Ferber had used in the story to demonstrate Minick's basic incompatibility with his son and daughter-in-law: the old man insists throughout the story on having two pillows on his bed, a demand with which the children comply in some bewilderment because he always throws one of the pillows on the floor the minute he gets into the bed. This didn't make its point too well when acted, either, but Kaufman and Miss Ferber decided to leave it in. They really had little choice; nearly everyone with whom they discussed the play, including Ames, said, "Be sure to leave in the stuff about the pillows."

Kaufman read the play to Ames when they met at his apartment, doing it so well that Edna Ferber later said affectionately, "He's very good at this. He made *Minick* sound much better than it was." Ames was delighted with the play. He told the authors he would begin casting at once and would schedule rehearsals for August.

Miss Ferber, exhausted, went off to Europe, where she had a pleasant time walking in pine woods and drinking the waters and getting herself massaged at Carlsbad. Kaufman, who, as always, preferred the New York scene, stayed at home and worked; he was still doing some touching-up, with Connelly, on *Be Yourself*, and he was beginning to think a little about the play which became his only solo effort, *The Butter and Egg Man*. Meanwhile, Ames got busy on *Minick*.

He started by issuing two startling and innovative orders. The first of these was to authorize Thompson to design and build his sets at once, instead of waiting, as was the customary practice, until the show was almost ready to move out of town on tryouts. This had never been done before; the producer always waited, frugally, until he was sure that the play was working and would actually be put on, and actors had to settle for rehearsing on bare stages. But Ames had the theory that *Minick* would jell better if his actors could rehearse on the actual sets they'd be using throughout the run, so he put Thompson and his carpenters right to work. He was right; *Minick* went into tryout as one of the smoothest plays in history. Ames's second instruction was even more surprising: he ordered that a black actress be hired to play the younger Minicks' Negro maid. This, too, had almost never been done before. New York, in 1924, was as biased in some ways as the deep South; white and black actors ordinarily did not mix. Black actors appeared in all-black plays, and a black part in a white play was nearly always performed by a white actor or actress in blackface. Ames was too elegant to say, "The hell with that," but it was what he meant, and an excellent black actress named Emma Wise was hired for the role.

The casting was less inspired for the crucial title role. O. P. Heggie was a popular and talented performer, but he was only in his forties, and he was never entirely convincing, even with heavy make-up, as a man of seventy. He was also British and spoke with a fairly strong accent, which didn't help, either; Minick was supposed to be a man from a small town in downstate Illinois and the action of the play took place in Chicago. But the rest of the casting was good. Minick's daughter-in-law was played by Phyllis Povah, a skillful young actress whose last name always sounded to Miss Ferber as though it should have been the name of a Jewish holiday, the son was played by a very good actor named Frederic Burt, and the part of the daughter-in-law's friend was performed by the scintillating actress for whom the Tony awards were later named, Antoinette Perry.

Rehearsals went smoothly: Ames had the pleasant habit of sending his butler and chauffeur over around lunchtime with baskets containing sandwiches, salads, fruit, and coffee. This was another startling departure from the usual practice of producers, who ordinarily gave actors nothing but scorn. The play then tried out in three towns in Connecticut. The response at the first two, New Haven and Hartford, was fair; the third, New London, was a catastrophe. New London was not ordinarily used for tryouts, and an old theatre owned by the Shuberts was opened and dusted off for *Minick*. The townspeople weren't used to plays, and only enough of them showed up the first night to fill half the theatre. But the real horror developed when all the lights were turned on and people had begun to settle in their seats. Unknown to anybody, the theatre's gallery, dome, and chandeliers had become a residence for hundreds of bats, and they suddenly began to swoop down into the theatre and onto the stage.

Most of the audience ran screaming into the street, but the actors, somehow, managed to remain onstage and complete the performance. They even, astonishingly, kept in mind the main purpose of tryouts, and succeeded in further smoothing-out of their roles.

Minick opened in New York at the Booth Theatre on Wednesday, September 24, 1924. As it turned out, both Kaufman and Edna Ferber were proven right. Kaufman had been right when he said that the short story could be turned into a good play, because nearly all the critics agreed that the bittersweet comedy at the Booth *was* a good play. But Miss Ferber, too, had been right when she said she couldn't see *Minick* as a substantial hit. The play was only a moderate success; it failed to fill the Booth at all performances, and had to move to a smaller theatre, the Bijou, and it ran 141 performances in all in New York. Then it moved to Chicago, where it was expected to do better because it was set in that town, but did even less well there, and ended up on tour in Boston and other towns.

But the play was also picked by Mantle for *The Best Plays of 1923–24*; it had a good run in London, where it was revised and made more British by a writer named Laura Leycester; and it also brought in a substantial additional amount of money by selling to the movies. Famous Players-Lasky bought it, and it was directed by James Cruze and released on May 15, 1925, under the title of *Welcome Home*, with Warner Baxter playing the son, Lois Wilson playing the daughter, and Luke Cosgrave as the old man. The picture was awful; the type of thinking which surrounded it can be demonstrated by the fact that the producers, fearing that Minick sounded too Jewish and might offend some anti-Semitic rednecks, changed the family name to Prouty. It was also remade in 1939 by Warner Brothers under the title of *No Place to Go*, another poor picture.

Curiously, the worst review received by the play in New York was written by the man with whom Edna Ferber fought constantly but whom she also considered a close friend, and who was also a close friend of the Kaufmans, Alexander Woollcott. He attacked *Minick* so violently, calling it "utter trash" and "a total waste," that Miss Ferber complained about it. Woollcott had every right not to like the play, she said, but pointed out that he had "loosed vials of vitriol out of all proportion to the little play's importance." All the other reviews were pretty fair. *Theatre Magazine* described the play as "three short but delightful acts." The acid-tongued George Jean Nathan complained that it was not as interesting as it might have been, and described Heggie as "a very likeable and often ingratiating performer whose actual talents are decidedly second-rate," but admitted that the play over-all was "intelligently planned and sympathetically written" and that "its observations and humor are authentic." And Mantle, surveying the play's record afterward, said, "Anyone who has followed the theatre closely must be surprised to find it counted with the minor, rather than the major, comedy successes of the year."

The play also brought Miss Ferber an unexpected dividend, and an extremely valuable one. It resulted from a mild attempt made by Ames to cheer up the cast and other participants about the disastrous first night in New London. The men and women were assembled in Ames's hotel for the usual after-show postmortem, looking tired and disconsolate, and Ames said, trying to lighten the mood, "Never mind. Next time, we won't bother with tryouts. We'll all charter a show boat and we'll just drift down the rivers. We'll play all the towns as we come to them, and we'll never get off the boat."

Miss Ferber had never before heard of anything like that. She asked casually, "What's a show boat?"

"A show boat's a floating theatre," Ames said. "They used to play up and down the Southern rivers, especially the Mississippi and the Missouri. They'd come downstream, calliope tooting, and stop at the town landing to give their show. The actors lived and slept and ate and worked right there on the boat. The country people for miles around would hear the calliope screeching and they'd know the show boat was in town."

Miss Ferber had been slumped dispiritedly on a cushion on the floor; she sat up as suddenly as if she'd been given an electric shock. When her work on *Minick* was over, she spent a solid year traveling through the South, interviewing people who could tell her things about show boats, reading everything she could find on the subject, and making a mountain of notes and outlines. She learned that there were still a few show boats in operation, playing small Southern owns, and drifting along rivers in North Carolina, Louisiana, and Ohio. She also visited a few of them.

Her research resulted in her classic and vastly successful novel, *Show Boat*. The novel made her rich, and she became even richer when it was turned into the famous musical produced by Florenz Ziegfeld, with book and lyrics by Oscar Hammerstein II and music by Jerome Kern. It was subsequently filmed three times. The second and third films, however, did *not* enrich her, since motion picture companies nearly always acquire the right to remake films as often as they wish without further payment. The experience of watching her creation made into two additional, successful films—for free—infuriated Miss Ferber. She discussed the matter with Morris Ernst, insisting that her next contract for film rights be on a time-limit or lease basis—with all rights to revert to her after a specified period. Ernst managed to push this through on the next Ferber deal, perhaps for the first time in motion picture history. He thereby established an ideal arrangement for authors which all good agents and attorneys try to achieve in offering film rights to very important properties.

Kaufman and Edna Ferber did not work together again for nearly three years. When they decided to collaborate once more, in 1926, it was a happy decision. They were about to write one of the most famous and successful plays of the twentieth century, *The Royal Family*.

For the rest of their lives, Kaufman and Miss Ferber continued to insist that the characters in their play were fictitious, or at least composite, and not based on members of the Barrymore family. If anything, Kaufman told several people, the characters had been inspired by an earlier theatrical family, the Davenports. It was a waste of breath: most people felt the portraits were too accurate. Lionel, everybody said, was left out because he was a relatively colorless member of the Barrymore clan, but the three principal characters in the play—the matriarchal head of a flamboyant theatrical dynasty, her beautiful and regal daughter, and her wild and eccentric son, always in trouble with women and finances—were unmistakable. They simply had to be—there was just no question about it—Mrs. John Drew and her grandchildren, Ethel and John Barrymore.

The second collaboration began exactly like the first one, with a hundred arguments which Kaufman invariably won. It was always that way when they began a collaboration. "Not doing much," he wrote to Ruth one day, "except fighting with Ferber. That takes up most of my time—some nights I don't get to bed until two or three o'clock." But they both—even the habitually gloomy Kaufman—sensed almost from the first hour of their new collaboration that they might be on to something big.

At the very beginning, but only at the very beginning, it *was* true that the new project was not intended as a specific portrait of the Barrymores. In fact, the original plan was to do a play which was not about the theatre at all; it was to do a play about a frantic, fantastic household rather like Herbert Bayard Swope's. Swope, it seemed to them, would lend himself rather well to a larger-than-life portrait in play form: they felt they could do quite a lot with a man so bold that he once cut in on the Prince of Wales at a party at Clarence Mackay's house, so regal himself that every member of his household was expected to rise whenever he entered a room, and so well-liked by the celebrity set that big names by the dozens were his house guests every month of the year. It was an idea which probably eventually germinated, in altered form, into *The Man Who Came to Dinner*, but the final decision in 1926 was that it was not for the team of Kaufman and Ferber. After much thought, they abandoned the idea on the grounds that, even if they reported things accurately and without exaggeration, it would all seem so incredible and unreal that people would simply not believe it. And from there, they moved to the idea of doing a play about a theatrical family.

Even then, the notion of focusing on the Barrymores did not come to them at once. It would be fun, they thought, to write a play about the crazy world of the theatre and some of the more flamboyant, egocentric types who worked in it, and their original plan was to base their characters on an assortment of actual actors and actresses—people who weren't, of course, related in real life—and simply call them members of the same family in their play. At that point, the only Barrymore considered for use was John, because they wanted to include one character who was an amusing rogue. And the obvious way to handle this was to make the character what John Barrymore was in real life, a likeable ne'er-do-well, always in trouble while he was a stage star, who had deserted the stage for the wilder and more insane world of films and, inevitably, found himself embroiled in even weirder troubles there.

But almost immediately, the notion of using John Barrymore expanded into the idea of using the entire Barrymore clan, and if, as Kaufman and Miss Ferber continued to swear even after all the evidence was clearly against them, the decision to do this was never a conscious one, it was so close to it that it didn't matter. The Barrymores were so tailor-made for the new play that the temptation was undoubtedly irresistible.

As they started to work out their plot, they found they needed a matriarch who was so much a *grande dame* of the theatre that she could be allowed to die onstage in the play without appearing unintentionally comic or lapsing into bathos, and nobody in the real theatre fit that description better than Mrs. John Drew, maternal grandmother of Lionel, Ethel, and John, and as grand a *grande dame* as ever lived. The play would also feature the matriarch's daughter, a woman hovering around the age of forty, who was the reigning queen of the American stage and was becoming more and more imperious every day in her public actions, but was considerably less sure of herself in her private life. Ethel, who was born on August 15, 1879, was a little older than that, but the description was otherwise a fair summary of her life. She had gotten better and better roles since playing Emma McChesney back in 1915, and she *had* risen to the height of her profession by 1926. She was now so regal that, when she went to a party and entered in time to catch Tallulah Bankhead imitating her, she punished the act of lese majesty by slapping the other actress sharply across the face. She was also so supremely self-confident as an actress that she undertook the role of Shakespeare's fourteen-year-old Juliet when she was forty-three, and performed the part magnificently. But her private life was much less majestic. She married a playboy, Russell Colt, in 1909, and they had three children together, but the marriage became more and more unhappy with the passage of time, and they were divorced after fourteen years. She did not marry again, and she was thereafter extremely nervous and uncertain about personal relationships.

As for the rest of the main characters, the amiably lunatic movie star really had to be John, nobody else, and the other important character, the theatrical family's manager, was not a Barrymore, but he was certainly a thinly disguised version of the Barrymore family's favorite manager, Charles Frohman. So, all in all, the denials about the Barrymores didn't really convince too many people.

At the beginning of the new collaboration, Miss Ferber was only able to work part-time with Kaufman; she was also putting in long hours daily on the developing musical version of *Show Boat*. Officially, she was not really required to render assistance, since she was only, in that trade phrase, the author of the underlying material and not an actual participant on the project itself. But Kern, Hammerstein, and Ziegfeld were all conscientious workers who were genuinely interested in preserving the author's intentions along with her plot and characters, so they asked her to sit in with them and consulted her constantly on everything from dialogue to songs and production numbers.

After a while, however, *Show Boat* was sufficiently set so that all that was needed was further refining and smoothing out, in which she was not really involved at all, and she was able to work full time on what she and Kaufman had already begun to call *The Royal Family*. The time was needed. The writing of *The Royal Family* did not come at all as easily as the writing of *Minick*. Unlike the earlier play, which had given the collaborators the advantage of being able to lean on and build on the structure of the existing story, they had to start from scratch, from Line One of plot and dialogue, on the new project. They struggled with the writing for more than seven months, typing the final lines on an unseasonably hot day in June 1927. They worked at first mostly in Miss Ferber's apartment on Central Park West, and then, when the telephone interruptions again became too numerous, in a midtown hotel suite rented for the purpose by Miss Ferber.

They worked very long hours, starting at around noon and often working until well after midnight, ending only when one or both of them were drained of ideas and energy. They once worked so late

hat a desk clerk, noting Kaufman's noon arrival and aware that he
was still up there after more than a dozen hours, decided that he had
to face the situation squarely and rang the suite. "I've got to ask you
this, Miss Ferber," he said. "Is there a gentleman in your suite?"
"Wait a minute," Miss Ferber said. "I'll ask him." A moment later
she reported, "He says he certainly *is* a gentleman," and hung up.

The work was back-breaking, but the care they took paid off in
due course. When they finally finished, they had far more than the
mere first-draft manuscript which most new plays turn out to be,
subject to countless revisions before being ready for staging. The
play was so tight in all respects that, except for the later addition of
one brief stretch of offstage dialogue, they never had to change a
line or word; the play went on exactly as written.

They now began to think about the choice of the right producer
for the play, and also began to give a little thought to casting. In
the latter area, they had some pretty firm ideas; they thought, in
their innocence, that the Barrymores themselves ought to be approached to play the parts. The play, they reasoned, didn't really
derogate the theatrical family it portrayed; the characters were all
drawn sympathetically, and, even in the scenes where the audience
might be impelled to laugh at some of their actions, it seemed to
Kaufman and Miss Ferber that the laughter would be affectionate
and even admiring rather than derisive. And then there was the fact,
they insisted, that the play wasn't *really* about the Barrymores, even
though the Barrymores could obviously play the parts so well.

The first hint of how wrong they were came shortly after Kaufman
went to Ruth Gordon's apartment one Sunday evening to read the
play to her and get an outside opinion of its merits. The actress
thought the play was marvelous and was eager to say so when, a
day or two later, Ethel Barrymore phoned her, having heard on the
theatrical grapevine of Kaufman's visit. Miss Barrymore asked without
preliminaries, "Has George read you his new play?" "Yes," Ruth
Gordon said. "It's great." The angry voice cut her short: "Is it about
the Barrymores?" "Yes," Ruth Gordon said again. "You'll love it."
She got no further because the phone clicked suddenly and loudly in
her ear. And a few days later, Ethel Barrymore phoned her again
to tell her that an eminent lawyer, Max Steuer, had been engaged to

bring suit against Kaufman and Edna Ferber. (The Marx Brothers immediately announced that, if the Barrymores sued, so would they.)

The suit never came to fruition because a successful libel or slander action can generally result only when the libeled or slandered person is able to prove that he has been injured to the degree where his earning capacity is affected adversely. And the only member of the clan who had even a slight fighting chance of proving anything like that was John, since some producers might conceivably become uncertain about hiring an actor as unreliable and as trouble-prone as the one depicted in the play. But John was too fun-loving a type to become involved willingly in a matter as serious as a lawsuit. He refused to come to the phone whenever Steuer tried to call him and discuss the matter, and Steuer finally bowed out in indignation and the action was dropped.

Ethel Barrymore, however, never wavered in her own feelings about the play. She would not talk to the authors at all for nearly five years, and her manner was exceedingly cold when she deigned to speak to them after that. She still felt the same way sixteen years after the play's initial appearance when, in 1943, Kaufman approached her and asked her to appear in a show he was putting on for the benefit of the Red Cross at Madison Square Garden. He had, he said, a funny idea: he wanted to present a vaudeville act to be called *The Three Ethels* and to be made up of Miss Barrymore, Ethel Merman, and Ethel Waters. "When is the benefit?" Miss Barrymore asked. "April fifth," Kaufman said, unaware that he was being led into giving the cue for a line originally spoken by the Ethel Barrymore character, Julie Cavendish, in his own play. "I'm sorry," Miss Barrymore said. "I plan to have laryngitis that day."

The authors did no more thinking about casting after their wrong guess about the Barrymores' attitude toward the play; casting was really the producer's headache, anyway. The producer they chose was a brash and unpredictable young man named Jed Harris.

There are two legends which have clung to the name of Jed Harris right up to the present day. The first is that he was, during his period of greatest activity, which ran from 1925 to 1957, an authentic genius of the theatre, capable of turning any play into a hit merely by associating himself with it as producer and/or director. The legend is exaggerated; a considerable number of voices have cried out to the contrary through the years, and there is substantial evidence to support the dissenters. The other legend is that Harris was an absolute monster during his years in the theatre, which also appears to be an exaggeration, but much less so. He was certainly no living doll during those years, or in his years of semi-retirement since that time.

One famous and, some say, typical Jed Harris incident occurred in 1930, when Moss Hart was introduced to Harris and gave the producer a copy of the first draft of *Once in a Lifetime*, which Hart had just completed. Shortly thereafter, Hart found himself with an opportunity to work on a collaborative revision of the play with Kaufman, the collaboration which was destined to grow into the long and glitteringly successful Kaufman-Hart partnership. All this was provided he could separate himself from Jed Harris and give the play to Kaufman's own producer at the time, Sam H. Harris, a sweet-natured man unrelated to Jed in either family or outlook. Hart phoned Jed Harris with great nervousness. "I was aware," he said later, "that his reception of the news that I was withdrawing the play might range anywhere from magnanimity to cold fury, with a likelihood of something fairly bloodcurdling in between. I called the hotel at the unlikely hour of nine o'clock in the morning in the hope that he could not be disturbed and I could leave a message, but to my horror the call was put through immediately."

The horror was followed by relief; Harris was absolutely charming. "I think you're doing exactly the right thing," he said. Then he told Hart pleasantly that he preferred to do Chekhov's *Uncle Vanya* as his first production of the season, anyway, asking Hart if he didn't agree that Chekhov had never been done really well in the United States. He followed up with a few idle questions which told him that Kaufman and Hart had not yet actually met, and ended with an apparent sudden thought which seemed to be an act of great courtesy. "Listen," he said, "this is George Kaufman's home telephone number. Put it down. You call him right away and tell him that Jed Harris says this is just the kind of play he ought to do."

The thing Harris did not mention was that the shaky relationship which he had had with Kaufman since 1927 had finally shaken apart, and he and the playwright had not even been talking for the past year. Hart knew nothing of this, of course; he rushed eagerly to call Kaufman and introduced himself as the author of *Once in a Lifetime*. Kaufman said nothing, waiting for Hart to get to the purpose of the call, and Hart took a deep breath. "Well," he said, "Jed Harris has read the play and he asked me to give you a message. He said to tell you that this was just the kind of play you ought to do." Hart reported afterward: "Even as I spoke the words I was dimly conscious of their peculiar ring"—but he was not really prepared for what happened next. "I would not be interested," Kaufman said, "in anything that Jed Harris is interested in," and hung up.

Fortunately for both men, Kaufman soon realized that Hart was only Harris's innocent dupe, and read the play and liked it. Hart later evolved a possible explanation for what he called "this ill-natured and wayward bit of wickedness": it was Harris's way of punishing him for withdrawing his play. A long-time associate of Harris's, however, had a much simpler explanation. "Jed," he said, "just enjoys being a sadistic son-of-a-bitch."

Not all of Harris's acts of cruelty, of course, were as complex and Machiavellian; frequently, the things he said and did were just garden-variety ugliness and nastiness. Like Kaufman, he had no great love for actors and actresses, but, unlike the playwright, he did not keep his feelings to himself. He never stopped insulting the performers who worked for him, calling them every name which came to his mind, sneering at their abilities, and shouting obscenities at them. He insulted them in person and in print, once stating in an article that intelligence was a handicap to an actor, and that one actor he knew was so dumb that he never understood a line he spoke, which made him one of the best actors around because he took direction without resisting it. Sometimes his mode of operation backfired, as when he began to shout imprecations at Ina Claire, an actress as tough as she was talented. He addressed her repeatedly by her real name, Fagan, a curious type of slur from a man who had himself been born Jacob Horowitz, and finally screamed, "Fagan, you *stink!*" As he did so, the actress moved forward and hit him on the chest, catching him off balance and knocking him to the floor. And as he lay there for a moment, she followed up by kicking him in the stomach. At that

[238]

ime, the actress was out of favor with the Round Table group
because they hated pretense and felt she was always posturing and
showing off, but the story of Harris's downfall, however temporary,
cheered them so much that they promptly readmitted her to the circle.

Harris worked hard to discomfit the men and women with whom
he came in contact. He is a small man, but he perfected an unsmiling,
cold, hard-eyed manner which made a lot of people somewhat afraid
of him. One of these people was Hart, and his edginess toward
Harris lasted a lifetime. After the incident of the call to Kaufman,
Hart's next contact with Harris was three years later, when he ran
into the producer one evening at a party. He was now as important a
personage in the theatre as Harris himself, and ached to ask Harris
why he'd done what he'd done. But, though he kept throwing furtive
glances at Harris all evening long, he never succeeded in working up
the nerve to ask the question.

Sometimes Harris disconcerted his associates with actions far more
bizarre than a simple hard stare. Kaufman worked with him on two
plays in all during their relationship, as co-author on *The Royal
Family* and, the following year, as director on *The Front Page*. It
was during tryouts on the latter production that Kaufman and the
play's two authors, Charlie MacArthur and Ben Hecht, were summoned to Harris's hotel suite for a conference. This was standard
operating procedure, but Harris's appearance, upon their arrival, was
less standard. When the three men entered his suite, he was reclining
stark naked in an easy chair.

This was behavior calculated to distress a man as fastidious as
Kaufman, but he was determined not to show the expected reaction.
He took a comfortable chair himself and began to discuss *The Front
Page* as matter-of-factly as if the producer were fully dressed in the
height of fashion. The authors followed suit, although MacArthur
later complained with a certain amount of disgust about the way
Harris's "hairy and coleopterous nudity stuck in our eye for an
hour." But not a word was said in the suite about Harris's nakedness
until the three men got up to leave, and Kaufman passed Harris on
the way out. "By the way, Jed," he said calmly, "your fly's open."

One other famous story about Harris is told by Frederic Wakeman,
the author of *Shore Leave*, *The Hucksters*, and other best-selling

novels. (Wakeman now lives in Greece, but knew Harris well while living in New York; *The Hucksters*, in fact, is dedicated to Harris. Wakeman later became somewhat disillusioned, however, and his novel following *The Hucksters*, *The Saxon Charm*, is the story of an unpleasant and ugly-tempered Broadway producer who manipulates people's lives just for the fun of it. *The Saxon Charm* is dedicated to Wakeman's father, and Harris had a brief comment after he read the book. "Now," he said, "I want to read the novel he writes about his father.") Wakeman was in Nunnally Johnson's office one day when a call came in from Harris. "Shall I say you're in?" Johnson's secretary asked. Johnson considered the matter for a long time before responding. "Well," he said, finally, "if I take the call, he'll invite himself to dinner. At dinner he'll insult Alice, and I'll order him out of the house. But he'll go into the kitchen where Alice is crying and turn her against me. So the real problem is, 'Do I want to divorce Alice?'" He paused for another moment. "Tell him I'm out of town," he said.

Kaufman and Edna Ferber knew nothing about Harris's eccentricities, however, when they decided to offer him their new play: the first Harris legend was already growing rapidly, but the second was still only a faint whisper. As far as they could see, he was the ideal choice. *The Royal Family* was tough, fast-moving, earthy, and sometimes even raucous, and clearly not right for someone like the gentle and elegant Winthrop Ames. But Harris's background and general approach seemed perfect for the play in every way.

Born in Vienna on February 25, 1900, and brought to the United States by his parents at an early age, Harris earned his first money as a sidewalk photographer and seller of picture frames in partnership with his boyhood friend Herman Shumlin. Both young men were stage-struck, and they broke into theatrical circles together in 1921 by getting jobs as cub reporters on the New York *Clipper*, a theatrical periodical. Shumlin's career eventually became the more distinguished of the two, but Harris got off to a faster start. Shumlin remained on the *Clipper* until 1924 and then worked another year on another theatrical publication, *Billboard*, before becoming a press agent and finally, in 1927, a producer. But Harris left the *Clipper* after a single year to become a press agent, and turned producer in 1925, bringing out *Weak Sisters*, which was a failure, and, the following year, *Love 'Em and Leave 'Em*, which also failed on Broadway but made money by selling to the movies.

Harris's big breakthrough came right after *Love 'Em and Leave 'Em*, with a play called *Broadway*. The author of the play, Philip Dunning, showed him a copy, and Harris liked it and optioned it immediately, tying it up by giving Dunning his share of the movie money from *Love 'Em and Leave 'Em*. He then began to look around for someone to bankroll his new acquisition, and asked another young press agent named S. N. Behrman, later to become a major playwright himself, to introduce him to a producer who was far more strongly established than Harris was at the time, Crosby Gaige.

Gaige (destined, like Harris, to have a business association with Kaufman) was an entirely different type than Harris, an erudite, urbane gourmet and wine expert who had a collection of over 5000 books and a wine collection almost as large, and whose hobby was the printing and manufacturing of small, beautiful editions of classic works of literature. His first production, put on back in 1912 in association with Arch and Edgar Selwyn, had been *Within the Law*, which had earned more than a million dollars, and he and the Selwyns had had many hits after that. He didn't really want or need an association with Jed Harris, but he was amused by the brash young man with the smooth black hair, the almost emaciated face, and the rather thin lips, who came to him via Sam Behrman's introduction and started to pitch at him like a sidewalk huckster. He also, when he read it, rather liked *Broadway*, even though he felt its slant was almost entirely wrong. Dunning had written the play as a rather broad comedy mixed with some melodramatic elements, and it was Gaige's opinion that the play's comedy elements should be toned down and the melodrama emphasized.

Harris was asking for half the money needed for production, saying he would put up the other half himself. Gaige agreed, provided the play was rewritten in accordance with his suggestions. He explained his views to Dunning, and Dunning felt he was right and began work, after which Gaige put up his share of the money. It was at this point that Harris again came to him and told him, very casually, that he'd also have to put up the other half as well. Harris admitted that he really didn't have a cent; his only tangible asset, he said, was a big motorboat he had once bought, and he offered the boat as collateral for the "loan" of his share. Gaige, still amused, told him to keep his motorboat and put up the rest of the money. He was rewarded for his generosity by watching Harris claim credit for turning *Broadway* into more of a meller, and, later on, quietly drop Gaige's name from the credits as co-producer. Gaige was a man of limitless tolerance. He just shrugged, continued to smile, and dismissed the actions, saying mildly that Harris cared more about that sort of thing than he did.

Broadway was a smash hit, and Harris followed up with *Spread Eagle*, which was a critical success if not a moneymaker, and *Coquette*, which starred Helen Hayes and was successful both critically and financially. It was while he was getting *Coquette* ready that he was approached by Kaufman and Edna Ferber, who said that they wanted him to produce *The Royal Family* because he was tough, like their play, and because he had always produced a successful play which, like theirs, was a combination comedy and drama. They did not add specifically, though it was obvious, that they had also selected him because he had become, in less than two years, the hottest young producer in town.

Later, a great many people made it their business to debunk the Harris legend of invulnerability and sun-like brilliance. George Jean Nathan did a particularly thorough job, pointing out that Harris's record did not match up to his reputation. "There is no denying the fact," he said, "that Mr. Harris is an exceptionally shrewd and very skillful theatrical personage. But cast your eye over the *Wunderkind*'s lesser record and look upon the other side of his successful picture. *The Wiser They Are* got absolutely nowhere, nor did *The Fatal Alibi. Mr. Gilhooley* was a failure, and *The Lake* was a sorry botch. *Wonder Boy* fell far short of success, as did the production of *The Inspector General. Serena Blandish* was a box-office disappointment, as was *Spread Eagle*. As for some of Mr. Harris's greatest successes, they were not staged by himself if we are to believe the playbills, but by other hands. *The Royal Family* bore the staging name of Mr. David Burton; *The Front Page* gave credit to Mr. George S. Kaufman; *Coquette* gave credit to Mr. George Abbott; and *Broadway* gave credit to the same Mr. Abbott, plus Philip Dunning. As with all of us mortals, there would seem to be two sides to the eminent Mr. Harris's oil painting." But most of the failures were still ahead of Harris in 1927, and the authors of *The Royal Family* wanted him as their producer and got him.

They were shown the seamy side of Jed Harris almost from the start of the relationship, but decided they could live with it. As it turned out, they had to live with plenty. He was sometimes viciously nasty to them, particularly when a line didn't play as well as he thought it should. They made an early resolution to ignore his outbursts completely, and they held to the pledge throughout the remainder of their relationship with him. It was less easy to ignore another of his practices, his habit of phoning them the moment he had an idea or anything else to discuss with them, whether it was two o'clock in the afternoon or four o'clock in the morning. His insistence on phoning people at any hour of the day or night convenient to himself—and it usually turned out to be the middle of the night because he suffered from insomnia—eventually became a Jed Harris trademark. His habit became so well-known that, when Harris tried to enter television in the '50s, and optioned the *Jeeves* stories written by P. G. Wodehouse for use as a television series, Wodehouse's agent secured as a condition of the deal Harris's promise that he would never phone the author after nine o'clock at night. (Even with the limitation, Harris so unnerved Wodehouse with his daytime calls that, when the option ended, he named one of his dogs Jed. Wodehouse is an animal lover who has donated substantial amounts of money to animal shelters, but the connotation was not complimentary.)

Kaufman and Edna Ferber also had to watch helplessly as Harris behaved with typical thoughtlessness toward the members of the cast. He often overcame his insomnia only as dawn approached, and then slept all day long, coming down to the rehearsal theatre toward evening, unshaven and, as Miss Ferber later described him, "fresh as poison ivy." The moment he arrived, he insisted that the actors do their entire run-through all over again for him, even though they'd been rehearsing all day long, since early morning, and were ready to drop. Miss Ferber found this particularly painful to watch because it was in such strong contrast with Ziegfeld's approach. Both *Show Boat* and *The Royal Family* went into rehearsal at about the same time, and she often attended rehearsals for both of her plays on the same days, running from *The Royal Family*'s rehearsals at the Plymouth on West 45th Street to those for *Show Boat* at the New Amsterdam on West 42nd Street and back again. She became strongly conscious of the differences in mood and attitude at the two theatres.

Ziegfeld was no timid soul. Once, when he felt the cast was sagging, Edna Ferber heard him shout, "What the hell *is* this? You're dragging around like a lot of corpses. This is a rehearsal. You're supposed to play as if you were giving a performance. If you let down in rehearsal you'll do the same thing a week after we've opened. Any of you boys and girls too tired to go on, please get out. Go home and stay there." But there was a direct, engaging quality about him which made people like him even when he was yelling at them. The cast realized that he was bawling them out for the good of the show, and that a successful show meant long-term jobs. It was different with Harris. With Harris, the actors never knew if he meant what he said or was merely indulging in the pleasures of cruelty, so they obeyed him the way the tigers in a circus act obey the trainer, out of hatred and fear.

There could, however, be no denying the fact that Harris worked hard. There were plenty of headaches to make this necessary. Otto Kruger had been cast as Tony Cavendish, the John Barrymore part, and he was clearly going to be great, but the main role, Julie Cavendish, the Ethel Barrymore part, turned out to be a nightmare to cast. No major actress wanted to play it. Kaufman and Miss Ferber, still dreaming their impossible dream at that time, sent Ethel Barrymore the first two acts of the play, but she sent the material right back. Ina Claire refused the role, saying she had no intention of serving as a living ad for the Barrymores. Laurette Taylor wasn't interested. Neither were dozens of other actresses, either because they felt the role made them a Barrymore stand-in or because they just wouldn't dream of playing a woman with a grown daughter—and a daughter, at that, who has a baby at the end of the play and turns her mother into a grandmother. Rehearsals were started twice with the part still not cast, and twice the play was actually abandoned because it looked as though the role would never be filled. The play finally went on with an actress named Ann Andrews in the role, but she was a compromise candidate. She tried hard, but she wasn't truly right, mostly because she was rather brittle and brusque in her acting style and the authors had really envisioned a more "velvety, glamorous type."

There were other troubles. The original director proved to be a bust, and Harris had to replace him with a new man, David Burton. Haidée Wright, the old lady who played the matriarch, Fanny Cavendish, developed bronchitis from all the rehearsing at the Plymouth, which was unheated during rehearsals, and it looked for a while as though she'd be out of the play—though she finally rallied and did a magnificent job throughout the entire run. Harris, dissatisfied with the pacing of the show, put it into a Newark, New Jersey, theatre for a run of tryouts before the Broadway opening, and Richard Watts, then the *Tribune*'s movie critic, whispered to the show's publicity man, Richard Maney, that the *Tribune*'s theatre critic, Percy Hammond, had sneaked over to see one of the tryouts and was going to review that performance. This was painfully below the belt, since such run-throughs were performed solely to shake a play down and detect and correct its weaknesses. New York critics rarely viewed these showings and never, never reviewed them. Harris appealed to Kaufman, Kaufman appealed to Hammond as a colleague, and Hammond grudgingly killed his review, refusing to tell Kaufman if the canceled review had been good or bad.

If things had gone right, the play would have opened on Broadway in September. With all the problems, plus the fact that Harris was still worried even after the Newark showings and sent the show on to Atlantic City for a while, it didn't open at its scheduled theatre, the Selwyn, until Wednesday, December 28. A few hours later, however, Kaufman and Edna Ferber were able to breathe easier. Every review was an unqualified rave.

Edna Ferber was in a state of near-euphoria. *Show Boat* had opened the night before at the brand-new Ziegfeld Theatre and had received equally enthusiastic reviews. She had attended neither opening. She'd been absolutely unable to judge what was going to happen to the plays from the tryout performances, feeling that some performances had seemed great and some had seemed awful, and she was just too nervous on the two opening nights to show up and find out. Kaufman attended both performances, wandering around the Ziegfeld and the Selwyn looking like a dematerializing ghost, suffering at the first theatre for Edna Ferber and at the second for Edna Ferber and himself. Predictably, he told friends before the openings that he felt *Show Boat* had a real chance because there were a lot of good people connected with it, but *The Royal Family* was very probably doomed, presumably because *he* was connected with that one.

He could no longer think or say that after the reviews of *The Royal Family* had been read. Hammond, still smoldering, refused to review the play, and, in an ironic twist, the assignment was given to Watts. He called it "charmingly done and delightful." Woollcott, now writing in the *World*, reported that the audience was often weak with laughter, and Atkinson echoed Watts, saying, "*The Royal Family* is quite delightful."

A few days later, Kaufman and Edna Ferber met and solemnly congratulated each other. Miss Ferber had two hits, Kaufman had one, and they had even managed to survive Jed Harris. But the biggest problem with Harris was still to come. That night, Harris phoned Kaufman and talked to him chattily about a dozen different things, everything from the state of the weather to the state of the nation, every subject except the play. Then, almost as an afterthought, Harris said, "George, I'm going to close the play."

Kaufman thought, at first, that he had heard wrong, and then that Harris must be joking. But when he asked Harris to repeat what he'd just said, Harris repeated it, and it was clear that he was completely serious. "But why, for God's sake?" Kaufman asked. "The reviews were just fine."

"That's exactly the reason," Harris said. "The reviews were great but we're not selling out. And a play which gets reviews like that and doesn't sell out ought to be closed."

Kaufman pointed out patiently that the show had opened during Christmas week, and that a lot of people probably weren't buying tickets because they'd already made plans for the week or were away. He also mentioned that an unusually large number of good

ays had opened that month. But Harris remained adamant, and
e argument grew hotter and hotter. Kaufman finally ended it by
ying quietly, "Jed, listen to me. If you close *The Royal Family*
ithout giving it a chance to build, I promise you one thing. The
ght the show closes, I'm going to come over to your apartment
d murder you."

The play stayed open, and became one of the great hits of the
riod, running 345 performances and being selected for *The Best
ays of 1927–28.*

It also eventually had a long run in London. The possibilities of
ccess in England seemed doubtful at first. Before the play opened,
lot of people protested its impending arrival because they felt the
le would be offensive to Britain's royal family. And after it opened,
the Lyric theatre, a few of the critics panned it on the grounds that
e Barrymores were almost unknown in Britain and it was essential to
cognize the real people on whom the characters were based in order
enjoy the play. One of these critics was an eminent British writer,
harles Morgan, who compared Kaufman and Edna Ferber in his re-
ew to "certain people who have the tedious habit of talking family
ssip in the presence of strangers, of making little, intimate jokes to
hich the casual onlooker has not the key, even of mimicry at the
pense of unknown originals," and complained, "It produced upon
e the uncomfortable impression of being shut out of some secret
ke." But the first of these objections was met by changing the play's
le to *Theatre Royal*, and the second was simply specious; the play
d been written to appeal just as much to people who would assume
was pure fiction as to those who'd heard it was based on cer-
in members of the Barrymore family. *Theatre Royal* was brilliantly
rected by Noël Coward, two fine actresses named Marie Tempest
d Madge Titheradge played Fanny and Julie Cavendish, and a new
oung actor destined for bigger things, Laurence Olivier, did a
arvelous job as Tony. Before many days had passed, there were
ng lines of people waiting to buy tickets at the box office.

The Royal Family also sold to the movies. Here, too, the title
as changed, but for different reasons. The producers, Paramount-
ublix, feared, with typical chauvinistic narrowness, that American

audiences might also think it concerned the family at Buckingham
Palace and shun a picture about those boring British, and changed the
title to *The Royal Family of Broadway*. Fortunately, they limit
their changes principally to this one item. The film, released on Christmas Day, 1930, was co-directed by two able people, George Cukor
and Cyril Gardner, adapted for the screen by two other talented
people, Herman Mankiewicz and Gertrude Purcell, and featured
Henrietta Crosman as Fanny. Even more important, Ina Claire was
finally talked into playing Julie, and, as with the British version
the play, the part of Tony was given to a new but quite brilliant
actor, Fredric March. The result was that the picture was as successful as the play.

Since its original run, *The Royal Family* has been revived an
almost uncountable number of times. Most of the revivals have been
rather mundane, moderately successful or moderately unsuccessful
depending upon the actors and directors involved, but one is still
remembered and discussed in theatrical circles for a reason other than
the play itself. This was a one-week run of the play commencing on
August 13, 1940, at the Maplewood Theatre in Maplewood, New
Jersey, a playhouse managed by Cheryl Crawford, and is still remembered because of the actress who played Fanny Cavendish.
was Edna Ferber herself, finally fulfilling her girlhood ambitions and
trying her luck as an actress. Everybody, to Miss Ferber's consternation, made a big thing of her acting debut. George and Beatrice
Kaufman and all of her other friends journeyed into New Jersey for
opening night, and made her nervous by visiting her *before* the
performance. Presumably they hoped she would not recognize the
motives, but she did. A pre-performance visit is a kindly gesture
which people of the theatre are given when they fear a play or
performance will be a disaster. It spares the star the agony of watching
her friends come in after the catastrophe and try to pretend everything was just great.

Edna Ferber was made even more nervous by the fact that all
the New York papers also took note of her debut and sent their top
critics to cover her opening in tongue-in-cheek fashion. Atkinson's
review was typical. "As an amateur actress, in the tradition of Charles
Dickens, who also wrote novels," he said in his story, "Miss Ferber

ranks halfway between Sinclair Lewis and Alexander Woollcott. She is more perceptive than the one, but she lacks the exuberance of the other . . . After a case of first-night jitters, which were probably mutual on both sides of the footlights, Miss Ferber settled down into a workmanlike performance that did not disturb the drama very much. She acts Fanny Cavendish pretty well for an amateur. After she gets this whim out of her system she can settle down to the writing of a novel we can all enjoy without reservations." To make up a little for these nose-pulling comments, the *Times* put Miss Ferber's name in capital letters in the cast-listing which preceded the review, the only name printed that way even though the cast also included such better-known players as Louis Calhern as Tony and Irene Purcell as Julie. But, unfortunately, even this ended up adding insult to injury. The typesetter set her name, and the *Times* printed it, as ENDA FERBER.

Miss Ferber found that even more humiliating than one other incident which had occurred on opening night. She had gained a lot of weight in 1940, and when Calhern, who was supposed to pick her up and carry her offstage in one scene, attempted this, he dropped her thumpingly to the floor. That time, at least, the error was instantly solved when Calhern picked her up and managed to stagger to the wings. But the typo remains in the *Times*'s files forever.

But the thing which upset Edna most of all was the fact that, to her surprise, she found the whole experience tedious. "I was bored," she reported later, "by the routine of coming down to the theatre nightly and twice on matinee days; making up, putting on and taking off those clothes; going on stage to say those same lines, night after night. I thought of actors who play two years, three years, in the long run of a successful play. The monotony of it, I thought. Petrifaction must set in." She was delighted and relieved when Sunday finally arrived, and she never acted again.

The important thing about *The Royal Family* to Kaufman and Edna Ferber, of course, was that they had succeeded in a major way as a team; they had proved that they could collaborate and produce a very successful play. The realization, as the total of performances grew higher and higher, was so pleasant that Miss Ferber even became more relaxed about Harris, whom she had originally resolved to assassinate in her autobiography, if she ever got around to writing one. She eventually wrote two autobiographies and dealt with Harris in the first of these, but summarized him in just a few lines which were not at all as harsh as originally intended. "Of Jed Harris," she said, "it is almost impossible to write. He is a five-foot shelf or a single paragraph. It would be useless to try to sketch in this strange, gifted and paradoxical creature fated to destroy everything he loves, including himself." Even Kaufman grew more tolerant of Harris for a while. "Jed Harris thinks he's Napoleon," he said. "And you know," he added thoughtfully, "I think he is, too."

15.   THE SOLO

"WHEN A MAN is sensationally successful as a popular writer," Brooks Atkinson commented in an article in the *Times* in 1939, "there is a disposition to urge him on to nobler things." He was noting an age-old truth: the fact that people tend to believe that a writer whose work appeals to the popular taste cannot be as important, or as valuable a contributor to the world of literature or the theatre, as a writer for smaller, ultra-intellectual audiences. This was particularly true, Atkinson said, if the material was light rather than serious. There was even, he pointed out, "a disposition in many quarters to regard the writing of successful and popular comedies as a mean and unworthy achievement."

Atkinson's article was a defense of George S. Kaufman, who had just been attacked by another critic, Joseph Wood Krutch, in a long study which first appeared in *The Nation* and then as part of Krutch's book, *The American Drama Since 1918*. Krutch analyzed Kaufman for thousands of words and then dismissed him, saying he was capable of writing more important things than mere comedies, but instead wrote down and dealt with unimportant subjects in order to pander to low, popular tastes. "Mr. Kaufman's most conspicuous, most persistent, and apparently most cherished weakness," Krutch wrote, "is his willingness to subdue himself to the stuff he works on, to write plays of Broadway as well as about Broadway, to let the least worthy of the drama's patrons establish its laws."

Krutch was one of the country's most distinguished critics; he was the regular theatre reviewer for *The Nation* and served simultaneously as a professor of English at Columbia University, specializing in drama subjects. Atkinson, therefore, was not disrespectful in his response. But he felt that Krutch was dead wrong, and he said so, pointing out such obvious truths as the fact that Kaufman did not write down, but wrote comedies because comedies were the kind of writing Kaufman liked most and did best, that comedies were just as important and significant in their way as serious dramas, and that many of Kaufman's plays were far more than mere comedies, anyway.

"It would be reckless," Atkinson said, "to underestimate the importance of his accomplishments. He has been largely influential in establishing the brand of mordant satire that has sharpened thinking in the theatre. In *Of Thee I Sing* he was co-author and stage director of the most versatile and biting political lampoon of his time. He is the foremost stage craftsman, both as writer and director. He is the master of the wisecrack, which has become a fundamental part of the American vernacular. For twenty years he has also worked in the theatre honestly. Not the least of his virtues is that he has stuck to his last. If his 'references are always exclusively to the local and the temporary,' as Mr. Krutch sagaciously points out, that is the way his mind works and that is the material he understands. The fact of chief importance is that it has helped produce some of the most hilarious and caustic plays of our century and his long-enduring success should not start to count against him now."

As always, Atkinson said it clearly and said it beautifully. The Krutch criticism was not an unfamiliar one to Kaufman; he had heard it before, and he continued to hear it throughout his lifetime. It is, in fact, still being said occasionally today—just recently, for example, by William Saroyan. "In 1934," Saroyan said in a discussion about Kaufman, "when I was beginning to be published at last, my question was the same as it is today, forty years later: if there is somebody who can write, can he get his writing published? Well, I did, of course—and without compromise, ever. And that's the thing I am concerned about still, and always will be. Mr. Kaufman is at the other end of the world—he needed some kind of instant success so he could live with his peculiar despair. One of his collaborators, Moss Hart, virtually went mad at the moment of first success—apparently rejecting his truth in favor of the far more convenient and attractive fantasy, which certainly didn't sustain him well, for he never really was impelled to try for authenticity in any dimension excepting surface Broadway cleverness, at which he was, along with Mr. Kaufman, pretty good. But the stuff just can't hold up—the awful smirk of it grows larger and clearer as the years go by."

But the fact that popular writers are always being shrugged off as unworthy of attention, as Atkinson pointed out, doesn't necessarily mean they're unworthy. Dickens was waved aside by many of his contemporaries as an insignificant hack; it was a later generation which really recognized him as a major social commentator, and, sadly, made him required reading in schools and therefore almost unread today outside of schools. Shakespeare was undoubtedly regarded by many people of his period as a facile writer of plays and sonnets which were mere entertainments and would be forgotten quickly. In Kaufman's case, it is still decades too early even to attempt an assessment for the ages, but one thing is clear: the older anti-Kaufman commentaries lie in archives thick with dust, but the Kaufman comedies, contrary to Saroyan's comment, continue to be played around the world, and seem, most of them, to be as funny and fresh as the day they were written.

Kaufman gave certain critics three reasons for writing about him, on occasion, somewhat less than worshipfully. The first was that he wrote funny stuff, rather than the serious or experimental dramas they preferred to admire. The second was that he was immensely successful, and some critics automatically equate monetary success with worthlessness. (This may seem incredible, but knowledgeable people in the entertainment and publishing industries know that it has been a fact of life for a long time. It may be born partly out of envy, and partly from the fact that some critics can regard themselves as superior only if they spurn things adored by the masses. Whatever the reasons, at least twenty important writers can be named who have pacts with their publishers and agents forbidding release of information about the amounts they've received as advances or for movie rights. They insist on this because they know that reports of large payments will result automatically in some bad reviews, usually beginning, "It is reported that John Smith has received $500,000 for the movie rights to his new opus, but—") The third was that Kaufman appeared to be a weakling who could not operate on his own, but apparently had to lean on collaborators.

These misdemeanors received frequent attention from various segments of the press and writers of books about the theatre. John Gassner, author of a great many books on stage subjects, nearly always discussed Kaufman and nearly always ended up writing him off with faint praise. "George Kaufman, with his numerous collaborators," he said once, in a commentary typical of all his statements about Kaufman, "achieved a veritable compendium of American trends. Since 1921 he has responded to nearly everything in American life, from its pleasant private vagaries to political mismanagement and the serious threat of fascism. His basic outlook has been, however, casually comedic. His work has been long cycle from comedy to comedy. Since it provides, in the main, a very superficial comèdie humaine, the temptation to dismiss it has been strong. Nevertheless, he has a right to some small niche." George Jean Nathan summarized him as merely "a gag man, a slick contriver of stage comedies." Even members of the Round Table reached this surface conclusion, Peggy Leech Pulitzer calling him "only a superior play doctor" and Dorothy Parker describing him as "a worker in mosaics."

Fortunately for Kaufman in his lifetime, and the memory of him since, a lot of people have come to realize, with Atkinson, that he was a great deal more than a minor writer deserving "some small niche." "When I first began my career as a playwright in 1936," Irwin Shaw said recently, "he represented to me much that was wrong with the commercial theatre at that time, frivolity, catering to the tired businessman, etcetera. As I became more professional in the theatre I grew to admire him because of his great skills and I became mature enough to appreciate the brilliance of his comedies, which exist far above the level of mere frivolity." And Roger Bower, the radio and television commentator, said a while ago, "Had he been ponderously intellectual, he would have fared better with biographical compilers. But being brilliantly intellectual, those bio compilers were not up to judging his work properly. Much of his work reflected the times as well as *The Grapes of Wrath*. That it was comedy in the main does not detract from his contribution. Think back; reread those plays. They had a message, though he did not belabor it."

James Thurber summarized the Kaufman contribution in an appreciation of the playwright he once wrote. "The wit for which he was justly famous," Thurber said, "often tended to obscure rather than illuminate the man and his achievements. He was a born newspaperman, more at home and happier at his typewriter at the *Times* than anywhere else. Yet the span of George Kaufman's active years in the theatre was, in large part, the very measure of the rise of Broadway comedy, which seemed to decline as he withdrew from it . . . The legend of George Kaufman will grow; time will brighten the light he brought to American humor, comedy and wit. If the theatre is to have a renascence of comedy, it will need another Kaufman, and the need is extremely great in the present period of decadence, in which we do not seem to be able to tell the difference between *avant-garde* and *fin de siècle*, talent and sickness, the giving up of taboos and the breaking down of morals, the experimental and the expiring theatre."

Many people feel that Neil Simon is today's successor to the Kaufman mantle. If so, the fact carries a measure of irony with it, since Simon has been experiencing some of the same kind of derision which Kaufman endured during his lifetime, being called a "gagster" and a "jokesmith" and possibly even a "worker in mosaics." It is only recently that some of the critics have begun to perceive that there is more to the Simon plays than a simple procession of gags, and even now the discovery is made with surprise and even bewilderment.

How is it possible, the critics seem to be wondering, for the plays to
be important when they're only comedies?

The third accusation so often hurled at Kaufman—that he was
incapable of writing a good play on his own—was considerably
more difficult to refute than the other two. It had, at first glance, the
appearance of truth.

It was being whispered about Kaufman as early as 1924: he was
not really a playwright at all. He was only, at best, half a playwright.
He had, it was true, written *Going Up* on his own—but *Going Up*,
it had to be remembered, remained unproduced. And after that
everything in which he'd been involved had been a collaboration. He'd
been the most uncreative type of collaborator of all on his first two
produced plays, *Someone in the House* and *Jacques Duval;* he'd merely
done additional work on plays conceived and structured by other
minds. His first hit, *Dulcy,* had been written in collaboration with
Marc Connelly, as had the eight productions which followed. And
when his partnership with Connelly had begun to wind down, he
rushed right out and found himself another collaborator, Edna Ferber.

Kaufman's response, on the very rare occasions when he bothered
to respond at all, was simple. His practice of collaboration, he said,
was a matter of preference, not necessity. He *liked* to collaborate.
He *liked* having a partner working with him on a play. He liked it
whether the method of operation was, as it started out with Connelly, the mutual development of the play's basic structure in long
conversations followed by the divvying up of scenes, each man taking and writing first drafts of the scenes which interested him most
or, as it later evolved, with Kaufman's partner sitting at the typewriter while Kaufman paced back and forth, back and forth, and
proposed line after line and plot twist after plot twist. If Kaufman
was, as Charles Martin recently said, "a master of improvisation
with lines simply leaping out of his brain," he was also the world's
most ruthless editor, often suggesting and immediately rejecting
twenty lines before coming forth with a twenty-first line which was
right. But if he was going to work that way, he wanted someone
around whose reactions he could watch to see if the lines he invented

were right or wrong; he wanted collaborators around to spark him and set him off as he sparked them and set them off; he wanted someone waiting there at the infrequent times when the lines and the ideas did not come and, as was his habit at those times, he would stretch out prone on the floor and lie there until his mind started clicking again. But the whole point was that it was what he wanted, not necessarily what he required in order to function and succeed.

That was not to say that Kaufman's collaborators were listening posts and transcribers and nothing more. Nearly all of them—and certainly his three best collaborators, Connelly, Edna Ferber, and Hart—contributed their full share of plot, structure, originality, and wit. But Kaufman was always the dominant and superior writer in his collaborations, better than the good writers with whom he collaborated, more excellent than the excellent ones. Through the years, nearly all of his collaborators said this, and unmistakably meant what they said. Connelly said it all the time to anyone who would listen, and is still saying it. Hart, in writing his autobiography, called Kaufman the real hero of the book and made it clear over and over again that he considered Kaufman the principal reason for the success of most of the plays they wrote together. Edna Ferber paid Kaufman the supreme compliment by falling in love with him. And Howard Teichmann said of himself and Kaufman's other collaborators, "As playwrights, not one of us could hold a candle to Kaufman. Of the eighteen of us who wrote with Kaufman, only three or possibly four were able to write successful plays without him. He, of course, wrote more successful plays than anyone else in the history of the American theatre." (The figure, incidentally, is wrong. Kaufman actually collaborated with twenty-two other writers in his lifetime. It's no wonder that Robert Benchley once said, "Every playwright has to collaborate on at least one play with George S. Kaufman or lose his license.")

But, once again, it took James Thurber, who never collaborated with Kaufman but admired him all of his life, to summarize it all succinctly. "He was, as everybody has emphasized, eminently a collaborator," Thurber said. "It reminds me of Alfred Coullet, the greatest six-day bike rider that ever lived. In six-day racing you have to have a collaborator, and Coullet rode with most of them. Teamed with him, they almost never lost."

In late 1924 and early 1925, Kaufman proved in the best possible way that he could survive alone if he chose to do so: he wrote a play all by himself. The play, *The Butter and Egg Man*, became one of his greatest successes. It played 243 performances in New York and followed up with a long, equally successful road tour. It had a solid run at the Garrick Theatre in London. It was the first American play ever to be published in book form in France. It was picked by Mantle for *The Best Plays of 1925–26*. It sold to the movies and was made into four different films under four different titles: *The Butter and Egg Man* in 1928, *The Tenderfoot* in 1932, *Dance, Charlie, Dance* in 1937, and *An Angel from Texas* in 1940. It is still being shown around the country, and was revived in New York as recently as 1966, where it was staged by Burt Shevelove, who also staged, not long ago, another successful revival called *No, No, Nanette*.

Kaufman did not write *The Butter and Egg Man* on his own to prove anything to anybody, or even to himself. He thought of the idea for the play, in fact, before the decision to end the partnership with Connelly became firm, and suggested it to Connelly as the team's next project. But the truth of the matter was that the two men were no longer thinking alike, and Connelly had an entirely different play idea in mind.

Connelly wanted the team to write a play which he had tentatively titled *The Wisdom Tooth*, a comedy about a young man's struggle to hang onto his individuality in spite of what Connelly called "the stereotyping pressures of New York's business world." Connelly even had an idea for the man to play the lead, a young actor named Thomas Mitchell who'd impressed him tremendously when Mitchell had appeared in an off-Broadway production of *Playboy of the Western World*. But Kaufman felt the idea was too similar in some ways to *Beggar on Horseback*; he just wasn't ready to get involved so soon in another play about the corrupting influences of business. And he was much more inclined toward his own idea. He had been thinking about the team's experiences with *Helen of Troy, New York*, and wanted to do a play about the fly-by-night side of the theatre world, making the lead an innocent young man who comes to New York, invests his inheritance in a terrible new play and almost loses it, but wins out in the end when the play becomes an accidental hit. But Connelly felt that *that* idea was too close to *Merton of the Movies*, with its depiction of a lovable fool who triumphs almost despite himself.

The result was that the collaborators finally faced the fact that it was time to go off separately and write their own plays. Kaufman started by settling on the title for the play, and it proved to be the perfect one. The phrase has pretty much vanished from the language in recent years, but it was well-known slang in the '20s and for a long time afterward; it meant a man, generally from out of town, who showed up in town with his pockets loaded and proceeded to empty them, usually by lavish spending or by making an investment in a patently unsafe scheme. The phrase is supposed to have had its derivation from the time a stranger showed up at a New York nightclub and began throwing money around wildly, buying drinks for everybody and picking up every tab in sight. He was finally asked by an awed observer, another out-of-towner, if he was a New York millionaire. "Not me," the man is supposed to have replied. "I'm a big butter and egg man from the Midwest." The phrase eventually came to mean any kind of big spender, and especially people who angeled Broadway shows.

Kaufman went to work in the same way in which he had worked with Connelly, and in which he later worked with all his other collaborators: he set a finish deadline for himself and tried to stay with it. This was a practice stemming from the newspaper side of his life. He kept up his production by reminding himself that no newspaperman left his paper with blank spaces by failing to turn in his story, and by reminding himself that he should not function any differently merely because the time was before or after his office hours at the *Times*, and he was writing a play instead of a piece for the drama page. It wasn't the same thing, of course; no reporter or rewrite man ever spent hours polishing a single line, as Kaufman sometimes did, but the discipline of a deadline usually worked for Kaufman. He later even refined it and increased the pressure on himself by getting his producers to rent a theatre, the rental to take effect on an agreed date, the moment he began a new play, so that he knew he had to get his script finished in time for the play to open on that date. He also set a quota for himself, and a tough one: four acceptable pages every work day.

Kaufman had a special ritual as he began each day's work on one of his plays: he went into the bathroom and washed his hands as vigorously as a surgeon scrubbing up for an operation. It gave him a sort of subconscious feeling, as he dried his hands, that he was all cleansed and ready to go to work, a response probably not too dissimilar to that felt by pagan virgins given thorough ablutions and anointments before being sent to perform a somewhat different kind of creation. The morning Kaufman first scrubbed up for *The Butter and Egg Man*, he outdid himself at the sink; he stalled there for nearly a half hour, washing his hands over and over again to delay the trip to his study and the commencement of work. He was terrified because, in the course of the restless night preceding that morning, he had managed to convince himself that the whisperers, the people who said that he was incapable of working on his own, were probably right.

To his surprise, however, when he finally entered his study, the work began to move even faster than it had moved on many of the days of collaboration with Connelly. His first job was plotting, the translation of his general idea for the play into specific incidents, and he was startled to find that he had relatively little trouble with this. He gave his hero a name, Peter Jones, and developed his hero's motivation for wanting to succeed as a theatrical producer: Peter had become interested in the theatre because he'd produced plays back home in Ohio and earned a hundred dollars for the Hospital Fund, and he now wanted to enlarge his inheritance, the $22,000 he'd received from his grandfather, so he could be capable of supporting his mother in reasonable style for the rest of her life. In the next few days, Kaufman moved onward from there, creating a crooked and incompetent producer for Peter to meet and give his money, the producer's secretary with whom Peter would fall in love, some additional characters like the producer's outspoken and honest wife, and the events which brought the producer's awful play to a tryout in Schenectady and failure there. Now Kaufman needed a development which would remove the producer from the scene and leave Peter saddled completely with the bad play, and Kaufman accomplished this by having the producer, enraged and disappointed at the poor response in Schenectady, seize on Peter as a convenient target and start to insult him, the secretary defend Peter, the producer fire the secretary, and Peter offer impulsively to buy the entire production so that the secretary could retain her job by working for him.

That would complete the action for the first two acts, but the third act would, of course, be the hardest, since Kaufman had to tie everything up there and make sure there were no loose ends. In particular, he had to arrange some way for Peter to find the money necessary to buy out the producer's share of the play, since Peter would have already given the producer his full $22,000 as his original investment—and, even more important, he had to invent some funny but believable way for the play to succeed on Broadway after bombing out so badly in its tryout. This would be the real test for Kaufman, who was especially nervous about the more complicated aspects of plot construction, and once told an interviewer, "In playwriting, the dovetailing of incident is the tough job for me . . . the employing of all the characters in such a manner as to turn out an integrated, composite thing." He began to do a lot of pacing back and forth, but it just didn't come, and he finally decided to postpone the misery of constructing the rest of the third act by writing the first two.

To his further surprise, since he now had no one on whom to bounce off lines except himself, the writing also went extremely well. He worked very slowly, spending even more time than usual polishing lines and sharpening characterizations because now there was no collaborator to groan and talk about lack of progress, and the writing of the first two acts took three months. But he had to admit, as he finished each day's or night's work, that he'd occasionally listened to worse lines or watched worse scenes in other people's plays.

He spent another disturbed night before finally tackling the third act; this time he'd convinced himself that the writing of the first two acts had been a total waste of a lot of backbreaking labor because the third act would surely never work out. But he also knew that he had no choice other than to do the job, and right then and there. The first two acts lay there finished and staring up at him, so there was no possibility of further stalling in that area. And there was the little matter of casting and rehearsals coming up. This was one of the plays on which he'd managed to impose a deadline on himself by making a deal with a producer which included a theatre-rental date, and the date wasn't far off.

The producer he'd chosen this time was Crosby Gaige, the man who later bankrolled Jed Harris's emergence into the big time. Kaufman knew Gaige fairly well because Gaige's office was one of his regular stops on his tours around town to pick up items for the *Times*, and he selected Gaige as the man to tell about *The Butter and Egg Man* because the producer had a reputation for conservatism and sound judgment. It seemed to Kaufman that Gaige's response to the idea of a solo Kaufman project would serve as a kind of test; the way he reacted to it, whether he welcomed the notion or shied away from it, would tell a lot. Kaufman should have been heartened by the way Gaige responded the moment he heard the general plan for the new play: Gaige began to offer generous terms in a manner which was unmistakably eager. And he was made no less eager when Kaufman went on to state that the rental of a theatre for a specific future date would have to be a condition of the deal, even though that was the sort of thing which usually horrified producers because of the other, associated commitments they'd have to make and then buy off if the playwright failed to deliver on schedule. Kaufman was not heartened, of course. He looked at the quick deal with Gaige as something else to worry about: he would now also be sinking a nice man into a dreadful mess if he failed to come through with a good play. But it was a fact of life; he had to face it; and he began to struggle with the third act.

He solved Peter's financial problems by weaving in a new character, a clerk at the hotel in Syracuse at which everybody stays during the tryouts, and gave the man producing ambitions similar to Peter's and the savings to back this up. And he turned Peter's play into a success with a device which enabled him, at the same time, to poke some fun at bluenoses and censorship. He simply characterized Peter's production as so daring that, when it opens on Broadway, the New York police threaten to close it up—and that, of course, brings audiences flocking in great numbers. The third act wasn't easy to write because it required a lot of short scenes to move things forward, each scene tying tightly into the last one, and a lot of characters dashing on and off. But the act seemed to work when Kaufman finished it, and he surprised Beatrice, as he handed the script to her to read, by saying that he thought *The Butter and Egg Man* had a slim chance. A statement like that, from Kaufman, was approximately equivalent to another playwright's boast that his new script was better than Aristophanes.

Gaige, given the script after Beatrice reacted with strong enthusiasm, thought the whole play worked beautifully, and he asked Kaufman if he had any ideas about casting the all-important lead role. As it happened, Kaufman did, very definitely; he had, he said, written the part with a specific actor in mind. This was a practice which Kaufman followed whenever possible, and he once explained why. "In my early plays," he said, "all my characters talked like me. You could take a line of dialogue and give it to anybody in the cast. I had ancient grandmothers making wisecracks and children of three uttering observations on theatrical conditions—it made no difference. That's why I'm very strong on writing with definite actors in mind. Even when you don't secure their services it's a good thing. It makes you write a part that's specific and distinct and not a lot of meaningless lines."

The man Kaufman proposed was Gregory Kelly, the gentle, soft-spoken, very likable young actor who had played Lynn Fontanne's brother in *Dulcy*, and who seemed to be the personification of the kind of man Kaufman wanted Peter Jones to be. Kelly was married to Ruth Gordon, and Kaufman was so sold on him for the part that he had visited the couple in their suite on the tenth floor of the Algonquin even before he began the writing of the play. He told Kelly he was writing a play specifically for him, a tremendous compliment to a young actor from a playwright as successful as Kaufman, and urged him to keep himself available if at all possible. The Kellys were overwhelmed at the news, and became even more so when Gaige seconded Kaufman's suggestion for the lead role. Their happiness faded, however, when Kaufman returned and began to read the play to them.

It wasn't that they didn't like the play; the play, they thought, was marvelous. But there was one terrible thing wrong. Kaufman read all the other lines in his usual flat, funny style, but his manner changed every time he came to the lines which Kelly would be called upon to speak. He said those in a mincing, simpering, effeminate voice. When Kaufman left, the Kellys stared numbly at each other. "What the hell was *that?*" Kelly asked. "What does he think I am—a fairy?" His wife tried to shrug it off, but she was unconvincing because she secretly agreed with Kelly's impression. "He thinks I'm a fairy!" Kelly said. The Kellys went for a long walk to talk it over, even considering refusing the offer, but the chance to play the lead in a Kaufman show was too important to pass up.

Kelly said, however, that he was damned if he'd play the part in the absurd style Kaufman apparently expected of him. At rehearsals, he spoke in his usual manner: soft, quiet, but definitely masculine. He was relieved to note that Kaufman seemed completely pleased with the delivery, and he finally worked up the nerve to ask the playwright why he'd spoken the lines the way he had that day at the hotel. "Oh, I can't do *you*," Kaufman said. "You've got a style all your own." Kelly was suddenly belligerent again. "What's that supposed to mean?" he asked. "Gentle, unique, kind of persuasive," Kaufman said with obvious sincerity and admiration, and Kelly realized that Kaufman had not meant to indicate effeminacy at all; he was simply not as good an actor as he was a playwright. "In that case," Kelly said, "thanks."

Kaufman was present at the first few rehearsals in a double-barrelled capacity. In addition to being on call as author of the play, he also served for a brief time as its director, having been urged to try his hand at it by Gaige. It was an example of Gaige's extraordinary theatrical savvy and perspicacity; he was the first man in the business to recognize Kaufman's *other* stage talent, an area in which, in time, Kaufman became as successful and authoritative as he had become as a playwright. But it didn't work on *The Butter*

and Egg Man: Kaufman just didn't have as much faith in himself
as Gaige had in him. He was so diffident and shy about giving orders
to the actors in the play that, after a few days, he went to Gaige
and asked to be relieved of the assignment. And Jimmy Gleason,
the actor who had appeared in the touring company of *Dulcy,*
was brought in to finish the job.

The *Butter and Egg Man* opened at the Longacre Theatre on
Wednesday, September 23, 1925. Kaufman, even more than usual,
was nearly overcome with gloom as the final curtain fell; his shoulders
drooped, he seemed close to tears, and he told Gaige sadly, "Well,
we did our best." Gaige, who thought the play had gone beautifully,
looked at him with astonishment, and was soon able to confirm his
own reaction with the reviews. The reviews, Gaige later remarked,
could not have been better if he had written them all himself.
"It is the wittiest and liveliest jamboree ever distilled from the atmosphere of Broadway," Gilbert W. Gabriel said in the *Sun.* "If you
like smart, funny, satirical comedies, here is a chance to enjoy
yourself," Percy Hammond told his readers in the *Herald Tribune.*
"Two hours and a half of constant amusement," Bernard Simon
said in the *Morning Telegraph.* And paying playgoers felt the same
way. "The audience nearly laughed itself to death," John Anderson
reported in the *Post,* and Walter Winchell, starting his career on
the *Graphic,* echoed, "First-nighters roared at the dialogue." There
was also similar enthusiasm for Kaufman's choice for Peter Jones.
Stark Young's comment in *The New Republic* was typical: "If the
character of Mr. Kaufman's play is so lovable, hilarious, and wise,
Mr. Gregory Kelly's performance is not less so."

Charlie Chaplin was present in the first-night audience, laughing so
loudly and piercingly that Woollcott, who had brought him to the
opening, looked away in embarrassment. Connelly was present, too,
and he was one of the first to tell Kaufman, as the final curtain
fell, that he had absolutely nothing to worry about. Connelly had
been having trouble with his own solo effort, *The Wisdom Tooth.*
He had made a production deal early in the year with Martin
Beck, a distinguished producer who later had a theatre named
after him. Beck, anxious to cash in on the strong business being
done at New Jersey resorts like Atlantic City and Asbury Park,

had started the play on a pre-Broadway summer tour in those towns and others, even though Connelly himself had felt that the play wasn't really ready and needed rewriting. The performances had flopped, and the play might have been retired permanently, except for the fact that George M. Cohan was present at one of the performances and told Beck and Connelly afterward that their play, basically, was a good one. "All you have to do," he said, "is think the story out more clearly." The play's sets had then been stored until Connelly could rework his script, and it was a bad time for him, but his congratulations to Kaufman were given freely and happily; he was not a jealous man. Fortunately, Kaufman was able to return the congratulations the following February, when *The Wisdom Tooth*, heavily revised, opened on Broadway and became a hit, too.

Kaufman, as always, wasn't quite ready to accept the praise for his play. He couldn't deny, he said, that things had started off well, but there was always the chance that it wouldn't last. Meanwhile, however, he was content to enjoy it while it lasted. The night after the opening, he covered a play called *Merry Merry* for the *Times*, and walked down Broadway afterward with a friend. "That show seemed awfully good," he said. "But I suppose any show would be all right with me tonight. *The Butter and Egg Man* sold out again tonight at the Longacre." The friend, amused by the typically cautious Kaufmanism, didn't bother to point out that the play was also sold out for the next nine weeks.

Unexpectedly, Kaufman's lifelong pessimism almost proved accurate: in the tenth week, box-office totals suddenly dropped. But the phenomenon was as brief as it was unexplainable. Receipts picked up almost immediately, and continued strong for the rest of the Broadway run and for the tour after that. And the play itself, like most of the Kaufman comedies, remains similarly strong even today. For the 1966 revival in New York, for example, it was necessary to make only one small change. There was a character in the original play called Mary Martin, and, since there is now, of course, a well-known performer with that name, the character in the play was changed to Mary Marvin.

There were two postscripts to the opening and success of *The*

Butter and Egg Man in 1925, one of them extremely sad. Gregory Kelly was an immediate star after the reviews appeared, and people rushed to see him in the play in New York and on tour. He seemed certain for many long years of stardom, but that was not destined. While he was on tour, he had a sudden heart attack, and his slim, frail body did not respond to treatment. He was dead a few hours later, aged only thirty-six.

The other event was not sad at all. Kaufman soon grew tired of the apologies from people who'd said he couldn't make it without a collaborator, and he became even more uncomfortable as the congratulations increased when the play also became a hit in London and a book version was published in France. When the French edition arrived, he studied it with interest. He was no expert in the French language, but he managed to work his way through the book, and he soon discovered a self-deprecating fact which he was able to report happily to the people who came to express admiration. The publisher, it seemed, had written an introduction in which he'd made an interesting admission. He said that he had published *Le Gentleman d'Ohio*, as the play had been retitled in France, only because he'd been unable to clear the rights to *La Rose Irlandaise de Monsieur Abie*.

Around the time Kaufman was putting the finishing touches on the third act of *The Butter and Egg Man*, he received a call from a producer he had known casually for a number of years. The producer, Sam H. Harris, had a proposition. He asked Kaufman, "How'd you like to write a show for the Marx Brothers?"

Kaufman respected and admired Harris, as everybody in the theatre did, but he was appalled by the proposal. "I'd as soon," he said, "write a show for the Barbary apes."

He knew, of course, he told Harris, that Groucho, Chico, Harpo, and Zeppo Marx had recently become the hottest act in show business. But he was also aware, both because it was common knowledge in the field and from personal observation of Harpo and other of the Marxes at poker games and Round Table luncheons, that they were lovable but uncontrollable lunatics who could turn a writer's life into a nightmare. It was true, he admitted, that he'd heard that, during the run of *I'll Say She Is*, the musical in which the brothers had just closed, there had been performances in which the comedians had stayed fairly close to the script. Far more often however, they ignored the script almost completely and devoted th evening to saying or doing whatever popped into their heads, an engaging in repartee with each other or with members of th audience—all of which created great hilarity in theatregoers bu undoubtedly created only thoughts of suicide or homicide in th writers of the play. He was further prepared to admit, he said, tha the script for *I'll Say She Is* was a very bad one, and probabl needed the Marxian ministrations it had received, but it was hi strong feeling that the Marx Brothers would assassinate any scrip good or bad, given to them. All this considered, he conclude pleasantly but firmly, he wanted no part whatever of Harris' proposition.

Less than two years before, the Marx Brothers had been onl a moderately successful vaudeville team. They were receiving $110 a week, which was not sensational even in its entirety since it had to b divided four ways, and was made much worse by the fact that the were also required to dip into that and pay their own transportation commissions, and the salaries of several girls they were then using i their act. The big break came for them when, in 1924, after severa producers had told them that their brand of comedy was simply no for the legitimate stage, a little-known Philadelphia entrepreneu named James P. Beury decided to take a chance and bring the quarte to Broadway in *I'll Say She Is*. The play was poor, so much so tha the generally kindly Brooks Atkinson later called it "ramshackle an awful." But Atkinson, as Woollcott did shortly afterward, fell i love with the Marx Brothers themselves, and so in time did the res of New York. *I'll Say She Is* ran for a year, mostly to jamme houses. And when it ended, the Marx Brothers had offers to do anothe Broadway play from such top managers as the Shuberts, Charle Dillingham, Florenz Ziegfeld, and others.

Harris understood at once, however, why Kaufman might b reluctant to work with the team; he had had much the same re action himself when the idea had first been proposed to him. Harri was fifty-three years old when he called Kaufman that day i

1925, but he had already been in show business for thirty-six years, the last twenty-one of these as one of the most successful producers in the country. His initial response, therefore, to the suggestion that he produce a play starring the mad Marxes had been, like Kaufman's: Who needs it?

Harris had been born, the son of a poverty-stricken tailor, on New York's Lower East Side on February 3, 1872. He went to work at the age of fifteen, running errands, selling boxes of cough drops which contained small prize packages, and making pick-ups and deliveries for a towel-supply company. He entered show business two years later by hiring unemployed actors at Christmastime and putting on little neighborhood holiday shows, and eventually made a lot of money starring Terry McGovern, the featherweight champion of the world, in a melodrama called *The Bowery After Dark*. Harris's own big break came in 1904, in connection with a vaudeville quartet very different from the Marxes, the Four Cohans. He saw the act one evening, decided that the youngest member of the family, George M. Cohan, could become a big star on his own, and offered to put up his total savings of $25,000 and star the young song-and-dance man in a Broadway musical. Cohan accepted enthusiastically, provided Harris would be willing to wait six months while the Four Cohans finished some commitments. This almost ended the relationship before it began. Harris agreed, but then backed some unsuccessful enterprises during the six-month period and lost every cent he owned.

The young producer rushed to Philadelphia to see a gambler who occasionally loaned him money, but he was so shy that he spent three days there without making his request. Finally, as the gambler was taking him to the train station, he blurted out his plea for the money he needed. The gambler simply asked him how he wanted it, and, when Harris said, in confusion, that fives and tens would be fine, the gambler nodded, and, a few hours later, filled his pockets with $25,000 in small denominations. The play which Harris and Cohan put on was *Little Johnny Jones*, which made Cohan a star, and in which he introduced his most famous song, "Give My Regards to Broadway." The musical was such a great hit that Harris and Cohan formed their own permanent production company, and in the next fifteen years produced fifty plays together, among them such great successes as *Forty-five Minutes to Broadway*, *The Talk of New York*, *Seven Keys to Baldpate*, and *Get-Rich-Quick Wallingford*.

Harris's touch remained sure and accurate after he and Cohan dissolved their partnership in 1919. He continued to produce hit after hit, and he became so rich that he was even able to fulfill a lifelong ambition and buy himself some race horses. He was not as accurate at picking horses as at picking plays. A horse he named after his one-time pugilist-star, Terry McGovern, once won a race in six furlongs, but this was the exception to the rule. Far more typical was the race when, discouraged because he had been without a winner for what seemed like forever, he entered all four of his horses in a seven-horse contest, and then watched gloomily as his horses came in fourth, fifth, sixth, and seventh.

Harris was one of the few major producers who did not chase after the Marx Brothers following their scintillating success in *I'll Say She Is*. But, perhaps partly for this reason, the Marx Brothers decided that he was the one producer they really wanted to do their next show. Harpo asked one of the team's most fervent admirers, Irving Berlin, to talk to Harris on their behalf. Harris and Berlin were close friends and business associates; they had built the Music Box Theatre together in 1921, a theatre which was so fortunate right from the start in the plays it housed that it is still known as "the home of hits" and a lucky playhouse. It took Berlin several days to talk the producer out of his initial reluctance, and Harris finally agreed to consider the comedians only if they would come around and show him their stuff right in his own office. The comics hurried over and soon turned the Harris office into a madhouse, leaving Harris and his associates weak with laughter. But even after that, Harris said only that he would let the team know, and he spent a few additional days in deep thought before calling them in Syracuse, where they'd gone to put on a brief run of *I'll Say She Is*, and stating that he'd decided to produce their next show.

The producer described his own doubts to Kaufman, saying, "I wanted to be sure myself that I was willing to rent a room in the lunatic asylum." He went on to explain that he had decided to do the

DOROTHY PARKER

She thought Kaufman was a mess.

OSCAR LEVANT

How to clean up on real estate.

ALEXANDER WOOLLCOTT

A big paunch and a gross insult.

CHARLES MacARTHUR AND HELEN HAYES
The peanuts became emeralds.

JED HARRIS
Casual cruelty.

KAUFMAN AT A FAVORITE CHORE

*Artist Tom Creem's study of Kaufman checking up on a show
from the back of the theatre.*

RING LARDNER (IN HIS NEWSPAPER DAYS)

Kaufman knew there'd be no second collaboration.

MOSS HART

Hiyo, platinum.

show for both artistic and commercial reasons: artistic because the Marx Brothers were clearly the freshest and brightest comedy talents to emerge on the American scene in decades, and it was as important to present them as it had been for him to present *Icebound*, a Harris production which had won a Pulitzer Prize two years before, and commercial because the Marx Brothers in a really good play would bring in a fortune. He then pressed his point home, saying he felt Kaufman should accept the assignment for the same reasons.

Kaufman became slightly less determined, but he was still not convinced. "How can you write for Harpo?" he asked. "What do you put down on paper? All you can say is 'Harpo enters,' and then he's on his own." He went on to state similar problems about the other brothers, whose styles were so different from one another, the difficulties involved in switching gears from line to line and writing Italian dialect for Chico, straight-man lines for Zeppo, and God knows what for Groucho. Harris brushed it all aside, airily. "You just write good stuff," he said. "They'll twist and turn it and fit it to their own styles." "That's what I'm worried about," Kaufman said. But he continued to listen to Harris's persuasive arguments, and, when the conversation ended a half-hour later, he had agreed to write the play.

The one thing Harris did not tell Kaufman was that he was not the first writer called in on the project. When Harris had phoned the comedians to say that he would produce their show, he told them at the same time that he was sending a blackout writer right up to do some new sketches for them. A blackout writer was the last thing in the world the Marxes wanted. They had plenty of comedy sketches and bits of their own, and, furthermore, the employment of a blackout writer sounded as though Harris was contemplating a revue, whereas they wanted a genuine, plotted play and a real playwright to write it. They decided to deal with the blackout writer in their own way.

When the man arrived, they insisted that he remove his coat, and Zeppo, who was a bodybuilding enthusiast at that time and had bulging, rippling muscles, stepped up close to him. "I'll wrestle you to a fall," Zeppo said threateningly. "You write two shows for us or none." The writer, a small man, retrieved his coat and disappeared into the night, and it was after Harris heard of this that he called Kaufman.

Kaufman might have been made nervous if he had heard the story because, though much taller than the blackout writer, he was not much of a wrestler himself. But he really had nothing to worry about. He was exactly the kind of writer the Marx Brothers wanted. The comedians promised Harris sincerely that they would behave— at least within their own interpretation of the word.

The Cocoanuts, the play Kaufman subsequently wrote for the comedy team, is often listed in theatrical histories as Kaufman's second solo flight. This is an error, though an understandable one because Kaufman received sole credit as author of the book in the show's programs and advertisements, and in all other listings. The fact is, however, that he worked with a sort of assistant in writing the play, a man who was not a collaborator in the ordinary sense of the word because he contributed very little actual wordage to the play, but who helped with ideas for comedy situations and plot construction, and also served to fulfill Kaufman's need for someone to whom he could talk and on whom he could try out lines. The assistant was a way-station for Kaufman on his trip back to full collaboration. He had written a play by himself and had found it lonely work, and he never again, after *The Butter and Egg Man* and *The Cocoanuts*, wrote another play without a partner. (Some people regard *Hollywood Pinafore*, a pastiche of the Gilbert and Sullivan operetta which Kaufman put together in 1945, as a solo effort, since Kaufman wrote his own book and his own lyrics for the play. But in the strictest sense, he was collaborating with Sir Arthur Sullivan on that one.)

Kaufman's assistant on *The Cocoanuts* was Morrie Ryskind, who eventually became a full-fledged collaborator—Kaufman's co-author on *Animal Crackers*, *Of Thee I Sing*, and others. Kaufman and Ryskind knew each other because Ryskind, like Kaufman himself and so many others, was also a protégé and discovery of Frank Adams. Ryskind was born in New York on October 20, 1895, was six years younger than Kaufman, and had begun contributing material to Adams's columns while still in high school, eventually achieving enough popularity among readers so that Adams once even accepted and ran a Ryskind contribution which occupied a full column. As a regular contributor, Ryskind was invited to one of Adams's famous annual dinners, and it was there that Adams introduced him to

Kaufman. Thereafter, Kaufman allowed Ryskind to visit him at the *Times* every now and then, making Ryskind feel very professional by permitting him to rewrite some of the material slated for the Sunday drama page. The two men became increasingly friendly, and Ryskind was a very obvious choice when Kaufman decided he wanted someone to assist him on *The Cocoanuts*. He was young, unattached, and eager; he was, and is, a very funny man; and he had not yet succumbed to the fervor of ultra-conservatism which eventually caused some of his friends either to begin to avoid him or make sport of him, as Ira Gershwin did by showing up at Ryskind's poker games with a copy of the *Daily Worker* protruding ostentatiously from his pocket. And when Kaufman phoned and said, "I've signed to do a show for the Marx Brothers. You want to help out?," Ryskind's acceptance was instant and joyful.

The script which Kaufman began to concoct was no masterpiece of ingenuity and complexity; it had to be kept simple and straightforward to allow room for and give full rein to the stars' special brand of madness. But he worked as hard on the show as he had worked on more prestigious projects like *Beggar on Horseback*. As was always the case when he was deeply involved in a play, he ate very little on some days and nothing at all on others. He was never, of course, tremendously concerned about food, a fact which Beatrice once bewailed in print when she was on the staff of *PM* and wrote a guest column for the vacationing food editor, Charlotte Adams. "As a gourmand, and I hope a gourmet," Beatrice wrote, "I find the attitudes of most men toward food irritating. Their reaction to eating goes to extremes, indifference or passion, but this is, one hears, characteristic of them in other important phases of life. Into this first classification, indifference, go those men who eat only because to eat is to live, and they go through the processes of tasting, chewing and swallowing not knowing or caring what they are eating. I cannot go through the pain of discussing them any further. Unfortunately my husband has this attitude toward food. Eating is really a nuisance to him and he wishes he could take a little capsule three times a day and call the whole thing quits." But it was even worse when Kaufman was working on a play: if eating was an annoying interruption to him during leisure times, if often became an unbearable burden to be completely avoided during work periods. He much preferred to spend the time pacing the floors, lying prone on the carpets, picking up hundreds of pieces of lint, tying innumerable and permanent knots in window-curtain cords, and in general struggling over and perfecting every line and plot situation in the agonized way which once caused Woollcott to say about him, "In the throes of composition, he seems to crawl up the walls of the apartment in the manner of the late Count Dracula."

Another critic, Russell W. Lembke, once commented on another aspect of the Kaufman *oeuvre*, saying, "This is the amazing achievement of the Kaufman plays: that we laugh heartily at what amounts to severe criticism of ourselves." Kaufman even managed to get some of this into *The Cocoanuts*. The mid-'20s were the years of the Florida land boom, a bubble of frantic buying and selling which suddenly burst and left a lot of people owning land under water and broke. Kaufman set his musical in that strange milieu, making Groucho a rapacious Florida hotel-owner and real estate developer, and the other brothers deadbeat guests trying to outsmart him. The result was that, simple or not, *The Cocoanuts* was—as the comedians had wanted it—a real play with a real storyline and even some social commentary.

The play was marred by some ethnic gaucheries characteristic of the period, causing even as intelligent a critic as Atkinson to lapse into gauchery himself in describing it. "Groucho," he said in his review, "reduces everything to the mercantile formula: he benevolently frees his employees from the stigma of 'wage slave' by cutting off their wages, and quite properly regards nonpaying guests as 'idle roomers.' To see him auctioning off Florida house lots, or measuring a detective for a suit, or arranging a dinner for one of the guests, spattering the target with puns, insults and vulgarities indiscriminately, is to marvel at the resourcefulness of the invention . . . He is the racial tradesman," meaning Jewish. Chico's role was even more baldly characterized; his name in the play, as no character would be named today, was Willie the Wop. But the musical offered far more than just ethnic bad taste. It presented, in instance after instance for the first time, many of the comedy devices which soon made the brothers world-famous. It was no wonder that Groucho later described Kaufman as "the best writer for me of them all," and also said about him,

"He was great, wonderful, nobody better. I think he was the wittiest man I ever met. I was crazy about him." *The Cocoanuts* was clearly the real making of the team.

The play was loaded with examples of the terrible, wonderful puns for which the characters played by Groucho will always be remembered. "You want ice water in Room 202?" Groucho says on the phone. "I'll send up an onion. That'll make your ice water." It was filled with typical and crazy comedy bits, such as when Harpo seizes Groucho's fountain pen and throws it at a wall plaque, causing a bell to ring and Groucho to hand him a cigar, or when Groucho asks Harpo to take dictation and Harpo takes it on a cash register instead of a typewriter. It introduced one of the most famous characters in the Marx Brothers saga, the statuesque and imperturbable society woman who is constantly assaulted and victimized by the Marxes but is never upset about it. The role gave the lady who played it, Margaret Dumont, a lifelong career; she played the part in virtually every Marx Brothers show and film, and rarely had to work anywhere else.

The musical even introduced the running gag which is probably the most celebrated of all Marxian activities, Harpo's constant pursuit of frightened, though not too frightened, young women. This one, however, was Harpo's own invention rather than Kaufman's. Harpo had a particular problem in the plays and movies in which he appeared: since he always played a mute role and no lines were written for him, he had to invent constant bits of business to make sure he was always visible and not overshadowed by his brothers. Partly for this reason, and partly because he hoped to throw Groucho off balance, he paid one of the show's chorus girls to run suddenly across the stage one day, right in the middle of one of Groucho's scenes, while he ran right behind her, leering and honking his horn. Groucho, of course, was not confused for an instant; he merely looked up, said, "The nine-twenty's right on time," and continued with his scene. As it turned out, Harpo was the one who was thrown off balance, because he learned right after the performance that the chorus girl he'd picked at random was the special friend of Legs Diamond, the gangster, and Diamond had a reputation for quick irritation whenever anyone even looked at one of his women. But the onstage interruption drew such a big laugh that it was left in, with a different girl substituted to do the running.

Like the author of the book, the writer of the show's music and lyrics was equally eminent. He was Irving Berlin himself, lured into the show by Harris, who pointed out to the composer that if he really felt, as he said he did, that it would be a great opportunity and almost an honor to produce a Marx Brothers show, then he must also agree that it would be a similar opportunity and honor to write the songs for the show. As things developed, the songs which Berlin wrote were not among his most memorable, though it appeared to Kaufman for a few brief moments that the show would include one classic, anyway. In the early stages of the production, Kaufman and Berlin took a hotel suite together in Atlantic City to work on the show. Berlin often continued working long after Kaufman went to bed, and he awoke the playwright at around five o'clock one morning and sang to him, in his gravelly voice, a new song he had just completed. The song was "Always," which Kaufman, despite his constant protestations about his inability to judge the quality of any song he was hearing for the first time, recognized at once as a certain hit and eventual standard.

Kaufman, who rarely missed an opportunity, didn't make things easy for Berlin immediately. He told the composer, deadpan, that the song's first line, "I'll be loving you, always," seemed to him to be unrealistic in view of the almost daily newspaper stories about middle-aged husbands who bricked up their wives in cellar walls and left for Toledo with the maid. And he suggested that the line be changed to "I'll be loving you Thursday." But the truth was that Kaufman thought the new song was absolutely great. Before much more time had passed, he and Berlin were leaning out of the window and singing the song to the Atlantic Ocean—"The first performance of the song," Kaufman said later, "in any hotel." He went back to bed content and feeling that the play now had a certain show-stopper, only to learn, some days later, that Berlin did not intend the song for *The Cocoanuts* at all, but had written it strictly for his music-publishing company, and had tried it out on Kaufman only because he was the nearest available audience. The song which Berlin wrote next and gave to *The Cocoanuts* was something called "A Little Bungalow," a tune, Kaufman commented, with lyrics so forgettable that they did not reprise it in the second act because the actors could never remember it that long. But then, of course, even third-rate Berlin was better than most other songwriters' best.

Despite all the good signs, and all the good stuff in the play, *The Cocoanuts* did poorly when it went into tryouts in Boston and Philadelphia. Most of the fault lay with the Marxes themselves, who, as Kaufman had feared from the start, and despite their promise to Harris, threw in every line and stunt which occurred to them, including many which were untested or had fallen flat when they'd tried them in *I'll Say She Is* or in vaudeville. Kaufman had had some warning about this, over and above his instinctive fears, soon after completing his script. When he began to read the script aloud at the very first rehearsal, both Harpo and Chico fell asleep immediately. They both assured Kaufman, upon awakening, that it had happened because they were so confident and relaxed, but certain doubts remained in Kaufman's heart. And now, his doubts were confirmed.

The first performance in Boston ran forty minutes too long, and all of the critics, and a substantial segment of the audience, walked out before the final curtain came down. Harris, Kaufman, Ryskind, Berlin, and the play's two directors, Oscar Eagle, who staged the book, and Sammy Lee, who staged the dances, worked all night, cutting lines and specialties and songs to bring down the play's length. The brothers then rehearsed the new version the entire day. When they went on again that night, the second performance was even longer than the first.

Kaufman and the others went to work again, cutting material so ruthlessly that Berlin protested that they'd soon have a musical without music. "I'll tell you what," Kaufman said. "You waive the songs and I'll waive the story." But even these strong efforts did no good. The show continued so long that a union official finally came to Harris and told him that, if he couldn't find some way to get the stagehands out of the theatre by eleven o'clock each night, he was going to pull them off the show.

Harris was beginning to suffer from deafness, an ailment which plagued him the rest of his life, and he was developing the high, thin voice found in some deaf people. He was also occasionally guilty of non sequiturs or absent-minded statements which didn't make a great deal of sense, as when, in connection with a much later show, he apologized to Franklin Heller, who was stage manager on the show but was taking over a part because of an emergency situation, by saying, "I hear you're going on tonight. I'd send you a telegram of congratulations, but I've got to go to Philadelphia." But despite the voice and the occasional incoherence, Harris's statements and opinions were always considered with great respect because he was so completely honest and reliable; it was said on Broadway that, if Harris promised to pay you some money next month, you could go to a bank and borrow against it today. Now, facing the crisis, Harris met Kaufman and Berlin by arrangement in the Marx Brothers' dressing room, but suddenly changed his mind and asked the writers to wait outside. "Let me talk to the boys by myself," he said. "I think I can settle this problem once and for all."

Kaufman and Berlin stepped into the corridor, and Harris closed the door behind them. A few minutes later, the door swung open, and Harris's clothing came flying out into the corridor. The brothers had seized him as he entered and stripped every article of clothing from his body. Harris walked out, stark naked, immediately afterward. He was still calm, but he said only, as he picked up his clothing and dressed, "I guess you two better handle it." Then he walked quickly around a turn in the corridor and was gone.

Kaufman said afterward, "*The Cocoanuts* introduced me to the Marx Brothers. *The Cocoanuts* was a comedy. The Marx Brothers are comics. But meeting them was a tragedy." He wasn't really at all as bitter as he tried to sound. When he and Berlin took a crack at holding the brothers down, a few minutes after Harris's failure, he found that the comedians, having had their fun, were ready to listen, and their performance that night was shorter and tighter. He found, further, that the brothers were always willing to drop a line or routine at once if he convinced them that the material was wrong and didn't work—that, in fact, as the time grew nearer and nearer to the Broadway opening, they were sometimes even more acute than he was about detecting bad stuff and even stronger in their insistence that it be killed at once. He spoke somewhat differently about the comedians when he mentioned them in the speech he made at Yale in 1939. "Morrie Ryskind and I once learned a great lesson in the writing of stage comedy," he said. "We learned it from the Marx Brothers. We wrote two shows for them, which, by the way, is two more than anybody should be asked to write. Looking back, it seems incredible that this was something we had not known before, but we hadn't. We learned that when an audience does not laugh at a line at which they're supposed to laugh, then the thing to do was to take out that line and get a funnier line. So help me, we didn't know that before. I always thought it was the audience's fault, or when the show got to New York they'd laugh."

Incredibly, when the *Cocoanuts* opened at the Lyric Theatre in New York, on Tuesday, December 8, 1925, a complete transformation had taken place. The play was no longer overlong. It was no longer choked with unfunny lines or with bits of business which didn't click. It was fast-paced and hilarious, and drew worshipful reviews from the critics and erudite essays on the art of the Marx Brothers from many magazines.

The comedians did not, of course, discontinue their improvisations and ad libbing completely. It would have been a mistake to do that, anyway, since audiences expected it from them and looked forward to it; the problem during the tryouts had only been that the quartet had overdone it. During one performance, Groucho suddenly stopped the show and turned an anxious face toward the audience. "Is there a doctor in the house?" he asked. A physician in a front row heard the grim question and jumped to his feet. "I'm a doctor," he said. "How do you like the show so far, Doc?" Groucho asked. Another time, Groucho learned that the President of the United States, Calvin Coolidge, was in the audience. He immediately stopped the show, announced the fact, and looked at Coolidge. "Isn't it a little past your bedtime, Cal?" he asked. He did the same thing when he learned one Election Night that New York's Mayor, Jimmy Walker, was present. "What are *you* doing here?" he asked Walker. "Why aren't you out stuffing ballot boxes?"

It was absolutely impossible to predict what the wild quartet might say or do at any given performance, but Kaufman's injured feelings about his injured script were soothed to a great extent by the size of his royalty checks. The show, beautifully mounted and costumed, had cost $75,000 to bring in, a large amount in those days, even though it is around one-tenth the sum required to bring a musical in today. But the advance sale was so strong that the production moved into the black almost immediately. Opening night tickets had been put on sale at an unprecedented $11 each and had sold out in minutes, and tickets had continued to sell with heartwarming rapidity ever since. A number of the trade journals like *Variety* had criticized the choice of the Lyric for the show, saying Harris would never fill a big theatre like that one with a show starring "an intimate act which had to be watched closely," but there was no trouble at all selling out.

It was also easy for Kaufman to forgive the Marx Brothers' assaults on his original script because their impromptu lunacies helped ticket sales in another way. A whole cult of people quickly sprang up after the show had run a while, people who came to see the play again and again because they knew it probably would be different every time. Heywood Broun was one of these people. He saw *The Cocoanuts* twenty-one times in all, turning up so often to watch the show from a seat or from backstage that he told a friend he could picture his own epitaph. "It'll read," he said, "'Here lies Heywood Broun, killed by getting in the way of some scene shifters.'" Bobby Jones, the golfer, was another untiring enthusiast, though he admitted apologetically that he had only seen the musical twelve times. Between the Brouns and the Joneses and the ordinary citizens who saw the play only once or twice, the musical ran easily into the following summer, and then picked up even more speed when, on June 11, 1926, Harris announced that the show would hereafter be a new "summer edition" with four new songs by Berlin, "new twists and dialogue" by Kaufman and with several new specialty acts added. The critics who reviewed the freshened-up version were as ecstatic as ever. "Thus refurbished," the *Times* said, "*The Cocoanuts* maintains its prestige among the best musical shows of the season. For Harpo Marx has not improved his manners in the least, nor has the garrulous Groucho lost his instinct for trade at any price, upon any terms that offer—honorable, dishonorable, or blatantly fraudulent."

The Cocoanuts ran on Broadway for 218 performances, and then went on the road for a record additional two years, playing in one tour town alone, Chicago, for six months. The play also enabled the

Marx Brothers to break into pictures; their first feature film was the screen version of *The Cocoanuts*, produced by Paramount-Famous-Lasky. It was all so successful, Kaufman remarked to Harris one day, that it almost made a man think about writing another show for the lunatics. "But not," he added hastily, as Harris stared at him with sharp interest, "right away."

16. THE MAGAZINE

THE FIRST TIME Kaufman laid eyes on Harold W. Ross, the future editor-in-chief of *The New Yorker* was kneeling on a blanket in Kaufman's apartment and engaging in a loud and enthusiastic game of dice. This was in 1919, and Ross, not long out of the service and not long off *Stars and Stripes*, had been brought to a party at the Kaufman apartment by Jane Grant, who knew Beatrice. Ross had immediately organized the crap game, pulling a blanket off one of the beds because he'd grown used to shooting craps on blankets at various Army barracks. He was anything but impressive-looking as Kaufman entered the apartment after a long day at the *Times* and peered unenthusiastically over his glasses at him. Ross was tall, awkward, wild-haired, shabbily and carelessly dressed, and slightly drunk. He also had the dirtiest fingernails Kaufman had ever seen in his

ife. He looked, in fact, exactly like what he was: a young man who
had quit high school after two years to tramp around the country and
Panama, supporting himself by working as a reporter on the Salt Lake
City *Tribune*, the Marysville, California, *Appeal*, the Sacramento,
California, *Union*, the Panama *Star and Herald*, the New Orleans
Item, the Atlanta *Journal*, and the San Francisco *Call* before enter-
ng the service.

Ross had been born on November 6, 1892, in Aspen, Colorado, when
that town was not yet a thriving ski resort but only the site of a
played-out silver mine, a place where everybody, including Ross's
father, was flat broke. After his military service, Ross had tried to
start a peacetime version of *Stars and Stripes* called *The Home Sector*,
but it flopped. He was now working unhappily for *American Legion
Weekly*, discontented because the magazine was veering more and
more into right-wing politics and also seemed to have more editors
than readers. Ross became a more or less regular member of the
Algonquin group after the Kaufman party, but his appearance did
not improve perceptibly with the passage of time and association with
some of the well-dressed members of the group. When Edna Ferber
met him some time later—also, coincidentally, while he was deep in
a crap game, this time at Frank Adams's place—he struck her as so
uncouth and ungainly that she was sure he was a bum that Adams
and Woollcott had picked up somewhere and brought around as a
gag.

In 1922, Ross began to assault his friends' ears as well as their
eyes. He had developed a plan for a new magazine focused on the
New York scene, a magazine to be slanted toward sophisticates and
to carry the legend *Not for the little old lady from Dubuque*. He
talked about the idea so unceasingly, holding people tightly by the
arm to keep them from escaping, that he soon came to be regarded
as even more tedious than untidy, which was saying a lot. His friends
also thought the magazine didn't have a chance in the world, particularly with Ross as its founder and editor. "If I had any thoughts
about him then," Kaufman told James Thurber long afterward, "they
were to the effect that he didn't belong in the Army or in civilian life
either. I would have said that he had a good chance of starving to
death, and when he came along with the *New Yorker* idea, it didn't

improve him. On type he was completely miscast as an editor—nobody, not Broun or Woollcott or any of us, thought it would ge started. He carried a dummy of the magazine for two years, every where, and I'm afraid he was rather a bore with it."

Kaufman and the others were almost right; the magazine woul probably never have gotten started if the playwright had not himsel1 though unintentionally, done something which brought it about. H invited Ross to a poker game at his apartment one evening and seate him next to Raoul Fleischmann, a very pleasant and very rich youn, man who was heir to a baking and yeast fortune. Kaufman was no especially fond of Fleischmann's wife, Ruth, telling her once, "You'r a birdbrain, and I mean that as an insult to birds." But he like Fleischmann, and he was distressed to observe that Ross had seize upon the young millionaire, in Ancient Mariner fashion, and was, a usual, pouring out his ideas and dreams for his projected magazine. A it turned out, however, Fleischmann did not share Kaufman's dis may; he was fascinated by the odd-looking man seated next to hin and by the things he was saying. When the card game was over, h invited Ross to meet him again and discuss the matter further. An after a number of additional meetings and discussions, he agreed t bankroll the new enterprise.

The first issue of *The New Yorker* was dated February 21, 1925 and appeared on the newsstands on the 19th. It was terrible. It stories and articles were dull, and its cartoons and humor piece were unfunny. The early issues were also as sloppy as the magazine' editor. Carolyn Wells's first name was misspelled Caroline, Georg Eliot's last name was misspelled Elliot, and a building which wa located at Sixth Avenue and 54th Street was described in *The Nev Yorker* as at Sixth and 55th. A poem was run in one issue and thei accidentally run again a few issues later. By August, the magazine which had started with a press run of 15,000 copies, was selling only 2700 copies per issue, and Frank Crowninshield, editor of the fat ani successful *Vanity Fair*, looked over an early *New Yorker* and saii complacently, "Well, I don't think we have much to worry abou with *this* thing."

The magazine almost ceased to struggle months before it reache its August low. It was doing so badly three months after it startec that Fleischmann, watching his money pour away at a rate fast enough to alarm even a man of his resources, called a luncheon meeting on May 19 and told the glum group facing him that he was pulling out. Ross tried to convince him to hang on, but Fleischmann was adamant, and the lunch broke up with the magazine under death notice. It was saved in the same way in which it had been born, by a chance encounter at a friend's festivities. Frank Adams's first marriage had terminated and he was being remarried that night, and, at the wedding party, Ross seized hold of Fleischmann and began to plead with him again to support the magazine a while longer. In what Thurber later described as "that atmosphere of hope, beginning, and champagne," Fleischmann finally agreed, and this time held on until the magazine became so successful that it began to bring him more money than his family's yeast and baking.

Kaufman's own association with the new magazine was tenuous at best, and remained so for a very long time. He started out as one of nine people listed on the masthead as the magazine's "advisory editors." The other eight were Woollcott, Connelly, Edna Ferber, Alice Duer Miller, Dorothy Parker, Laurence Stallings, an artist named Rea Irvin, and an editor and artist named Ralph Barton. Ross had also approached Adams, Broun, Sherwood, and Benchley, but Adams and Broun were prohibited from joining the group by their newspaper contracts, and Sherwood and Benchley were still working for *Life* and couldn't support a potential rival. The idea for the list was Fleischmann's and was strictly for name value. Ross himself hated the idea and went to his friends with great reluctance; he later said, "It's the only dishonest thing I ever did." The well-known people who were asked to grace the masthead weren't really expected to do much, if anything, for the magazine, and that, for the most part, was the way it worked out at first.

Thurber later summarized the attitude of the advisory editors by saying, "There is little doubt that Ross's famous and busy writer friends of the Algonquin Round Table and its fringes took his fond enterprise lightly, as a kind of joke on him and Fleischmann." Stallings moved to Hollywood and dropped out immediately. Edna Ferber, who had come to like Ross as she grew to know him better, agreed to allow the use of her name but made it clear that she would not write for the magazine, telling Ross frankly that she simply did not feel it could succeed under his editorship. Dorothy Parker wrote only one short piece and two poems for the magazine in 1925, and when Ross met her on the street one day and said, complainingly, "I thought you were coming in to the office to write a piece last week," she turned him aside with a short jab at the firm's fragility. "I did," she said, "but somebody was using the pencil." Kaufman had a slightly better excuse. He had become so busy with his plays that he hadn't written a magazine piece since 1922, and he didn't write for any magazine again until 1929.

It didn't really matter. *The New Yorker's* rates of payment were so low in the early days that Ross could only have run his high-priced friends' stuff infrequently, anyway, even if he did persuade them to write for him. And, as Herman Mankiewicz once remarked in that connection, "The part-time help of wits is no better than the full-time help of half-wits." (Ross was philosophical when Thurber reminded him of that comment years later. "God knows I had both kinds," he said.) Ross's salvation resulted from a hitherto unsuspected strength—his almost uncanny ability to pick up newcomers and unknowns and help them develop, as staffers on *The New Yorker*, into the most literate, most entertaining, and, in some cases, the most intellectual writers in the country. He did this so often, making *The New Yorker* more and more the place in which subscribers could expect to find the best in modern writing—particularly in the areas of humor, the in-depth type of biography which the magazine called "profiles," and certain types of fiction—that in time people in publishing began to use the term *"New Yorker* writing" as a synonym for excellence.

E. B. White was one of the first, and one of the most important, people to be hired by Ross. White—christened Elwyn Brooks, but called Andy since college days because he had gone to Cornell, where every student named White was given that nickname in deference to the university's first president, Andrew White—was hired to work part-time at $30 a week, plus $5 for each first-page commentary he wrote. The short pieces became the world-famous *Talk of the Town* leads, and the clarity and grace of White's language soon set the target and the tone for the entire magazine. Thurber, who had sold the magazine a few free-lance pieces while working on the New York *Post*, came a little later; he was hired at $70 a week in March 1927, but was raised to $90, and then $100, even before he started work, because Ross's conscience had been bothering him, and he phoned Thurber twice at home with amended deals. Wolcott Gibbs, who was Alice Duer Miller's cousin but was introduced to everybody by Ross as Mrs. Miller's nephew with such unbending insistence that Gibbs finally stopped correcting him, joined the magazine right after Thurber. Peter Arno started with a spot drawing in June 1925, and with a captioned cartoon in September, and Helen Hokinson showed up with her first cartoon two months later.

Nearly everybody Ross hired, or who contributed prose or art on a free-lance basis, turned out to be first-rate. White and Thurber and Gibbs were joined in due course by editors like Ralph Ingersoll, eventually the founder of *PM*, James M. Cain, who later wrote *The Postman Always Rings Twice*, Thorne Smith, later the author of *Topper*, William Shawn, who became the magazine's editor-in-chief after Ross's death, Gus Lobrano, another Cornell graduate and one-time roommate of White's, and Bernard Bergman, later book editor of the Philadelphia *Bulletin*. Ross's instincts rarely failed him, although he was nervous about every choice and given to loud complaints. The day he hired Russell Maloney, Maloney left Ross's office in ecstasy, only to have his joy slightly dampened as he waited at the elevator and heard Ross say dolefully, apparently to himself, "I hire every goddam nut who shows his face in here." Ross also hired Thurber strictly as an editor, and tried to discourage Thurber's writing ambitions. "Writers are a dime a dozen," he told Thurber. "What I want is an editor. I can't find editors. Nobody grows up." Fortunately, most of the men he hired were capable of doubling in brass, editing superbly and writing superbly at the same time.

Ross also developed many *idées fixes* about members of his staff, none of them important but nearly all of them maddening because he remained married to the ideas even after it was pointed out to him repeatedly that he was wrong. One of these was his constant insistence on the wrong family relationship between Gibbs and Alice Duer Miller. Another was his notion that Lobrano had worked for *Harper's Bazaar* before joining *The New Yorker*, when in fact Lobrano had

worked for *Town and Country*. "I suppose you learned that on
Harper's Bazaar," he said to Lobrano, long after Lobrano had told
him again and again that his alma mater had actually been the other
magazine, and Lobrano finally sighed and gave up. "Yes," he said,
"and it wasn't easy." Ross also became convinced that Thurber was
an absent-minded dreamer responsible for the loss of every manuscript which disappeared from the premises. He formed the habit
of saying, "Thurber lost it," every time something was missing, even
when Thurber was not in the office or even in the country. Once a
missing manuscript he had blamed on Thurber turned up in his own
briefcase, but that did not stop him. "If it hadn't been there," he said,
"Thurber would have lost it." He also could not be shaken from his
conviction that Morris Markey, the magazine's first reporter-at-
large, had failed when Markey had had to postpone turning in an
assigned piece on Grand Central Station, despite the fact that the
postponement was made necessary because the stationmaster was ill.
He was always a little worried about Markey's assignments after
that, saying, "He couldn't get in to Grand Central." All this didn't
deter his colleagues, however, from admiring his brilliance in important
things and serving him brilliantly themselves.

In time, the big names joined the parade. Benchley, out of *Life*,
first appeared in *The New Yorker* in December 1925, began to write
more regularly for the magazine after that, and became the magazine's
theatrical reviewer in 1929. That same year, Woollcott began his
famous feature, *Shouts and Murmurs*. Dorothy Parker began to write
her stinging book reviews, under her pseudonym of Constant Reader,
in October 1927. Frank Sullivan wrote three pieces for the magazine
in 1925, and many dozens more in the years after that; he still
writes the memorable *Greetings Friends* poem for each Christmas
issue. And when, in the late '20s and early '30s, Sally Benson came
along with her *Junior Miss* stories, Ogden Nash with his unique
style of poetry, S. J. Perelman with his special brand of humor, and
Clarence Day with his *Life with Father* series, and were followed by
people like Leo Rosten, writing his Hyman Kaplan stories under the
pseudonym of Leonard Q. Ross, Ruth McKenney, writing her reminiscences of her sister Eileen, John McNulty, St. Clair McKelway,
S. N. Behrman, John O'Hara, J. D. Salinger, Robert Lewis Taylor,

Richard Rovere, Peter De Vries, and so many others, the magazine had earned a permanent place in the history books. In ten years, it had put Frank Crowninshield and his *Vanity Fair* out of business.

Ross grew with his magazine himself. In 1927, he was still clinging to a raincoat so foul that, when he asked his secretary to bring it one day, she told him calmly that she had thrown it away. But he eventually became a relatively well-dressed man. And his hair, once so high and wild and untended that Kaufman was able to tell people that the jungle scenes in a movie called *Chang* had been shot in Ross's pompadour, became in time much shorter, and so carefully combed and groomed that Connelly finally complained, "Ross thinks too damn much about his hair." But then, of course, Connelly was quick to notice that particular area of interest. Most important, Ross became the toughest and most meticulous of magazine proprietors, watching every line in the magazine so closely that his once-careless brainchild became probably the best-edited publication in the world. He developed so careful a system of double-checking every statement and fact in every piece that a researcher once grumbled to Thurber, "If you mention the Empire State Building, Ross isn't satisfied it's still there until we call up and verify it." Ross was also wise enough to trust the judgment of his associates in areas where he did not feel comfortable personally. *The New Yorker* school of fiction was so formless, and occasionally appeared so unplotted, that a great many people objected to it and made jokes about it. Ross himself didn't like the stuff, saying again and again, "I'll never print another story I don't understand." He also complained from time to time, as the magazine began to publish a great many grim stories by John O'Hara and others of the same school, "If a man in these goddam stories doesn't shoot his wife, he shoots himself." But he continued to allow the people in his office who were concerned mostly with fiction, Lobrano and John Mosher and others, to have their own way, and dozens and then hundreds of *New Yorker* stories appeared in best-fiction collections.

Ross also had blind spots about many cartoons, particularly those with sex connotations; Ross genuinely missed the sexual point on many of these. One of the most famous cartoons ever published by the magazine was a Peter Arno drawing showing a couple entering a police station, dragging an auto seat and saying, "We want to report a stolen car." The idea was invented by a girl friend of Connelly's; Connelly told the idea to Ross, who promptly accepted it, paid the girl an honorarium, and gave the idea to Arno for execution. But Ross missed the sexual aspect of the joke completely. And when somebody explained to him, long afterward, what the couple had obviously been doing on that seat while it was out of the car and presumably on the ground or grass somewhere, he was stunned and complained bitterly, "Why in hell didn't somebody tell me that at the time?" There was later some further trouble about the cartoon idea, when a movie company paid a $200 fee to use the gag in a film, and Arno kept the money instead of passing it on to Connelly's girl friend. But neither the sexual revelation nor the subsequent fiscal flare-up really reduced Ross's faith in the people who conceived, drew, or selected the cartoon humor for the magazine. The moving force behind *The New Yorker*'s art selection was Rea Irvin, the only person on the original list of advisers who really deserved the title and more, because he joined the magazine at the start as a full-time staff member and remained there until his retirement. He designed, among many other things, the typeface for the publication's title and the famous figure of a Regency dandy staring through a quizzing-glass at a butterfly, which appeared on *The New Yorker*'s first issue and which has been rerun on every anniversary issue since then. (Beatrice's cousin, Elmer Adler, suggested another cover idea which was almost run, a stage curtain opening on a panoramic view of New York's skyscrapers, but at the last minute this was abandoned in favor of the Irvin sketch.) Irvin was assisted, through the years, by such talented people as Philip Wylie, Daise E. Terry, and even, for a brief period, Truman Capote. Ross recognized the quality of his art staff, and, though he always tried to attend the Tuesday afternoon art meetings, and grumbled continually about some of the cartoons in the magazine, he generally allowed Irvin and the others to have their way. And as the years passed, the words, *The New Yorker*, on a cartoon became the hallmark for the best graphic humor published anywhere.

Capote, incidentally, went to work for *The New Yorker* at the age of seventeen and remained there for two years. He lost his job because Robert Frost visited the magazine's offices one day, and Capote, who regarded the poet as a stuffed shirt, behaved with something less than abject reverence. As Capote later described the incident, Frost "didn't consider me a sufficiently humble worshiper at the altar of his ego," and he sent an offended letter to Ross. Capote was fired immediately. It was the magazine's loss and literature's gain; Capote went off and wrote *Other Voices, Other Rooms.*

Kaufman's own relationship with *The New Yorker* was the slowest-starting of all of the original advisory board, with the possible exception of Edna Ferber, who never really got started at all because she just didn't write the magazine's kind of stuff. When Kaufman resumed writing for magazines again, in 1929, his first two pieces were not for *The New Yorker* but for *Theatre: Notes on an Infamous Collaboration,* published in the December 1929 issue, a piece on his work with Woollcott on *The Channel Road,* and *How I Became a Great Actor,* published in the December 1930 issue, a piece on the fact that, to his own surprise, he was undertaking an acting assignment and playing the type-cast role of a sardonic playwright in *Once in a Lifetime.* Nor were his next four scripts for Ross; they were *Jimmy the Well-Dressed Man,* a satire about Mayor Walker published in *The Nation* on June 15, 1932, *With Gun and Camera in London,* a lighthearted survey of the British theatrical scene published in the *Times* on January 22, 1933, *Socratic Dialogue,* a satire written with Morrie Ryskind and published in *The Nation* on April 2, 1933, and *The Green, White and Blue,* a look at hysterical anti-Communism published—to the surprise of Kaufman's friends, who didn't think he even knew about magazines like that—in *New Masses* on May 11, 1935. Kaufman finally showed up in *The New Yorker* in the issue dated May 25, 1935, with what the magazine called a "casual," generally a short piece of humor or reminiscence. Kaufman's casual was humor and was called *All We Need Is Horse Sense.* It dealt with the day in the future when the American people, anxious to get horse sense into government, elect a horse to the presidency.

In all, Kaufman appeared in *The New Yorker* only thirteen times, as compared to hundreds of times by other people who were also busy writing plays. After the piece about the equine statesman, he appeared in the May 1, 1937, issue with a poem, *Lines Upon Looking Through a Pile of Old Checks;* in the August 11, 1945, issue with *Notes for a*

Film Biography, a summary of some dramatic moments in his own life, written in the event somebody wanted to make a picture about him one day; a letter about the overused critical and editorial phrase, "judicious pruning," which *The New Yorker* ran as a *Department of Amplification* item on June 29, 1946; *School for Waiters*, published on August 2, 1947, which later also became a sketch in the hit revue, *Inside U.S.A.*; *The Great Kibitzers' Strike of 1926*, published in the November 26, 1949 issue, a piece about the terrible time that onlookers at bridge games stopped looking on; *My Book and I*, a confession about Kaufman's laggard reading habits, published on May 26, 1951; *Does Newark Have to Be Where It Is?*, a gentle complaint about the fact that the scenery often becomes second-rate when one travels from New York City to Bucks County, Pennsylvania, published on September 19, 1953; two more poems, *Lines Written After Four Weeks in a Hospital* and *New York: A Prayer*, published in the issues of May 1, 1954, and September 3, 1955; a complaint about minor harassments, *Annoy Kaufman, Inc.*, which appeared in the December 21, 1957 issue; another complaint, this one about the stickiness of honey, which was called *When Your Honey's on the Telephone* and published on February 22, 1958; and the last piece Kaufman ever wrote for a magazine, *Memoir*, which was mostly about Kaufman's experience with Irving Berlin and "Always" in Atlantic City and appeared in the June 11, 1960, issue.

But though Kaufman's business association with *The New Yorker* never grew very close, he became closer and closer to the magazine's founder as both men grew older. "As the years passed," Kaufman later told Thurber, "I can only say that I got to love him, if the word may be used between men." Ross's private life was a tempestuous one; his first marriage, to Jane Grant, failed, and his second marriage, to Marie Françoise Elie, failed, too, and then he was married, a third and final time, to Ariane Allen. Ross found that Kaufman, despite the playwright's horror of emotional matters, was a good man to see when there were really important personal matters to be discussed and intelligent advice needed.

Ironieally, just as Kaufman was an accidental participant in the birth of Ross's great magazine, he was also a participant, equally accidentally, in the editor's last day of life. Kaufman was in Boston with *The Small Hours* in December 1951, when Ross went to that city to be operated on for what was described as "a minimal bronchial malignancy." At one o'clock on the afternoon of December 6, Ross suddenly and unexpectedly phoned Kaufman at his hotel. "I'm here to end this thing, and it may end me, too," he told Kaufman. "But that's better than going on this way. God bless you. I'm half under the anesthetic now." He hung up almost before Kaufman could respond, and Kaufman was unable to phone and find out how the operation had turned out until after the show was over that night. Kaufman phoned Hawley Truax, a friend of Ross's from the *Stars and Stripes* days who had been with *The New Yorker* from the start, and who eventually became the firm's board chairman. Truax told Kaufman, very quietly, "He died at a quarter to six."

Kaufman was not the type of man to do much thinking about posterity. If the subject ever even occurred to him, which is unlikely, he undoubtedly concluded, in typical fashion, that posterity would forget his name ten minutes after he was gone. He never made any effort to save his finished scripts or their myriad early drafts; once a play was put on or a magazine piece was published, he just picked up his pile of manuscripts and threw them away. For this reason, the tiny collection of memorabilia which Anne Schneider put together after Kaufman's death and presented to the University of Wisconsin, a school whose library specializes in theatrical reference material, contains only a few scraps of manuscript—things which, clearly, Kaufman hadn't so much kept as simply failed to throw away. One of the fragments in the collection, however, is a first draft of *Annoy Kaufman, Inc.*, and it is interesting because it reveals how hard and how carefully Kaufman worked on everything he wrote. Even on a short humor piece like that one, a type of script for which *The New Yorker* paid anywhere from a couple of hundred dollars to a top of a thousand or so, Kaufman gave his script exactly the same kind of word-by-word attention he gave to a play which might bring in hundreds of thousands of dollars.

The beginning of the article, in which Kaufman reveals his suspicion that a vast and complex organization has been established to accomplish nothing more than find new and better ways to annoy him—doing things like sending squads of payroll clerks to stand in front of him on bank lines and make complicated withdrawals, and inventing pneumatic asphalt-rippers only because they've learned where and when he sleeps—obviously satisfied him. It remained unchanged from first draft to published piece, possibly because Kaufman, as he often did, worked it over and worded and reworded it a hundred times in his mind before setting it down on paper. The final paragraph in which Kaufman sets up a punch-line rather like one of his third-act curtain lines, remains the same in first and last draft, too. "With all that," Kaufman writes, "you wouldn't think they'd have time for congressional lobbying, would you? This ultimate move came to light during a visit of mine to Washington a few weeks ago. Having been made suspicious, over the years, by my dealings with the Internal Revenue people, I went to the trouble of looking up the text of the income-tax law, as filed in the Library of Congress. Sure enough, there it was—Paragraph D, Clause 18—just as I had suspected: 'The taxpayer, in computing the amount of tax due the Government, may deduct from his taxable income all legitimate expenses incurred in the course of conducting his business or profession—except,' it added, 'in the case of George S. Kaufman.' "

It's easy to see why he left the paragraph alone; he probably worked forever on its wording, too, before finally typing it. But aside from the first section and the last, there is scarcely a sentence in the piece which has not been retouched and reworded and, fortunately, as Kaufman's great editorial gifts always guaranteed, improved. Charles Martin once commented that Kaufman was a compulsive editor and changer, rewriting his material and making it better and better right up to the last possible minute. That trait in his character is certainly visible in the *New Yorker* piece. The manuscript is only four typed pages in length, but the draft shows more than a hundred penciled changes in Kaufman's handwriting, ranging from the substitution of a single word to the addition or elimination of a paragraph. None of the changes are monumental. A phrase like "It must have great suites of offices" is changed to "It has—it must have—great suites of offices," more effective because it illustrates that Kaufman is reasoning out his suspicions as he goes along, arriving step by step at his conclusion that there is a deliberate campaign against him. A sentence

ike "Next, it is arranged that all of these people should get to the
eller's window just ahead of me" has its final words changed to "just
few seconds ahead of me" to emphasize the efficiency and precision-
iming of his oppressors. And a reasonably funny bit about another
calculated annoyance, the placement of men who are six feet eight
nches tall in front of Kaufman at theatres, is killed because it doesn't
quite work, not 100 per cent, anyway. All small matters, but Kaufman,
with his reluctant admiration for clichés, might well have been remembering the old adage to the effect that success is compounded of
ittle things.

There was also the fact that Kaufman could never resist trying to
mprove the language and effectiveness of the things he wrote just
because he was totally hung up on words—as were, for that matter,
nearly all of the people in the Algonquin group. Unlike other in-
ellectuals of the period, who held the making of puns and similar
pursuits in contempt, they all derived considerable pleasure from try-
ng to top each other with various kinds of play on words, and the
more terrible the pun or joke the better. "I'd like to give you a sentence
with the word 'punctilious,'" Kaufman once told Frank Case, stopping
him in the lobby of the Algonquin for that purpose. "I know a farmer
who has two daughters, Lizzie and Tillie. Lizzie is all right, but you
have no idea how punctilious." "If you're so smart," Frank Adams said,
hearing about this, "give me a sentence with the word 'paraphernalia'
n it." Kaufman thought for a while. "Well," he said, "I know a man
who ate the wax cover off a jar of jelly. Can you guess what people
asked him? No? They asked him, 'Does that paraphenalia?'" And
Case returned in due course with a rejoinder of his own, telling Kaufman that he knew two sisters, too, two poor girls who were in a
terrible quandary. "Their names are Bettina and Anna," Case said.
"And I'm afraid they're Bettina devil Anna deep blue sea."

Alexander Clark, an actor and occasional visitor to the Round
Table, joined the name game by pointing out a girl named Iris
and then saying, "Iris I was in Dixie." Dorothy Parker disposed of
"horticulture" with, "You can lead a horticulture but you can't make
her think." The group also used words to create fictitious law firms,
among them Bold, Resolute, Gay & Berkowitz, Bright & Early, and
Fast and Growthin, formerly Fast & Furious. The gags grew more and

more awful, with one member of the group using the word "burlesque" by saying "I had two soft burlesque for breakfast," Adams wishing people a "meretricious and a happy New Year," and Kaufman remarking that he'd had an experience similar to Sir Isaac Newton's encounter with an apple, which had led to the theory of gravity—except that Kaufman had been hit on the head by a fig and had thereby invented the Fig Newton. It was Kaufman, too, who came up with the perfect title for a play about Swope and his richer and richer, if not always more and more admirable, group of friends: *The Upper Depths*. Kaufman also posed an unexpected question when Charlie Chaplin remarked one day that his blood pressure was down to 108. "Common," Kaufman asked, "or preferred?" It was occasionally simple-minded stuff, but it honed the word-sense of Kaufman and his friends to a fine edge, and sometimes gave magazines like *The New Yorker* more than they were paying for.

"People are always stopping me on the street," Frank Adams said in one of his columns, "and telling me how great it was of me to give George S. Kaufman his start. The shoe, of course, is really very much on the other foot. It was great of *him* to lift the level of my columns with his contributions, and great of him to improve my personal life with his inimitable presence." The truth of the matter was that the members of the Round Table were equally valuable to each other, not only because of their sometimes very successful professional and business associations, and valuable by-products like the meeting of Ross and Fleischmann, but also because they gave each other so much pleasure. They looked forward to their lunches and dinners and their poker and croquet and bridge and word games, and truly enjoyed themselves. But this could also prove dangerous when it became too incestuous, as when one man selected another as a business partner on the sole and shaky grounds that he was so interesting and entertaining in social gatherings that he was bound to be an equally strong contributor in a business relationship. The assumption often proved to be gravely wrong, and that was certainly the case as far as Kaufman was concerned. His two biggest failures in the '20s were scripts he wrote with friends whose credentials in the playwriting area were obviously not examined as carefully as they should have been.

The first of these two plays was *The Good Fellow*, which Kaufman wrote with Herman Mankiewicz, whom he first met when Mankiewicz came to work on the *Times* in 1923. The collaboration was a terrible mistake, as Kaufman was soon forced to admit as he watched the play open and close with sickening speed. Mankiewicz was gifted, witty, engaging, and a marvelously amusing companion at lunch or dinner. But he was also an alcoholic, a compulsive gambler who always preferred playing cards or making wild bets to working, and, in general, a man so determinedly self-destructive that he spent his entire life dissipating his considerable talents, tossing away every opportunity which came to him, and kicking apart everything good he had begun to build for himself. He was not, as people associated with him through the years came to realize, a man to choose as a business partner.

Mankiewicz was born in New York on November 7, 1897, the son of a professor at Columbia University and a graduate of Columbia himself, receiving a B.A. with honors in 1916. He worked for a while as an editor on *The American Jewish Chronicle*, enlisted as a flying cadet in the Army in 1917 and transferred to the Marine Corps to serve with the Fifth Marines in France, and then remained overseas after the war to work first for the American Red Cross News Service and as a foreign correspondent for the New York *World*. When he returned home and switched to the *Times*, he was put to work as Kaufman's assistant in the drama department, and his behavior had already become so erratic by 1923 that he was almost fired a half dozen times. One of his actions also resulted in the only time in Kaufman's thirteen-year career on the paper that he ever lost his temper openly and totally on the job.

The incident occurred when Mankiewicz was assigned to review a revival of *School for Scandal*, an event highlighted by the fact that the part of the teen-aged Lady Teazle was being played by Gladys Wallis, the fifty-six-year-old wife of a multi-millionaire utilities czar, Samuel Insull. The actress was resuming her career after more than twenty-five years of retirement, and the out-of-town reviews had been generally kind. But after the opening, Mankiewicz returned to the office dead drunk, and, apparently infuriated by Mrs. Insull's temerity in essaying a youthful part, proceeded to write a brutal, blistering review, a review which failed to achieve full heights of savagery only because he fell asleep with his head on the typewriter before finishing it. Kaufman entered the office shortly afterward, read the review over Mankiewicz's shoulder, and turned white with rage. It was rage compounded in equal parts of the fact that he felt the review was too vicious and cruel for any performance, however bad, and the fact that his assistant had failed in the primary newpaperman's requirement of getting a story in and finished. Mankiewicz had been married in 1920 to a beautiful girl named Sara Aaronson, and Kaufman phoned her and told her tersely to collect her husband and take him home. He then ordered the Mankiewicz review killed rather than finished by someone else, and, with considerable bitterness, admitted the *Times*'s failure in coverage by running the following notice: "The *School for Scandal*, with Mrs. Insull as Lady Teazle, was produced at the Little Theatre last night. It will be reviewed in tomorrow's *Times*." And when the review appeared, it was unsigned and noncommittal, confining itself to generalities and avoiding evaluations of the actress' talents. "As Lady Teazle," it said, "Mrs. Insull is as pretty as she is diminutive. There is a charming grace in her bearing."

Mankiewicz, hung-over and facing reality the next morning, was certain he had gotten himself fired for sure this time. He showed up for work anyway, exuding desperate charm and carrying a bottle of Scotch to present to Frederick T. Birchall, The *Times*'s assistant managing editor. Birchall was a man with a red beard, and he kept pulling at his beard and shaking his head, but he finally accepted the bottle and forgave his errant employee. That was, perhaps, the trouble; people always forgave Mankiewicz, up to the time when he had done the same things over and over again so often that it became impossible to forgive him any longer. It was a pattern which continued to repeat itself until he died of uremic poisoning at the age of fifty-six. And it manifested itself even more visibly when Mankiewicz left the *Times* after two years, worked briefly as drama critic for *The New Yorker*, and then embarked on his main career—writing for the movies.

Mankiewicz's first screenwriting job was at Paramount, which hired him in 1926 at $400 per week plus $5000 for each accepted story, with an option for a second year at $500 per week and $7500 per accepted story, and a guarantee of accepting at least four stories per year. He thus moved from his drama critic's wages of about $5000 per year to minimum salaries of $40,000 for his first year as a screenwriter and $56,000 for his second, and he actually earned more than that. In his first three years in the movie business, he worked on more than twenty-five pictures. Despite this, because he was drinking and gambling more and more heavily all the time, he was always broke and nearly always in trouble. Among his duties was the recruiting of other talented writers, and one of the people he brought in was Ben Hecht, whom he lured to Hollywood with a seductive telegram: WILL YOU ACCEPT THREE HUNDRED PER WEEK TO WORK FOR PARAMOUNT PICTURES? ALL EXPENSES PAID. THE THREE HUNDRED IS PEANUTS. MILLIONS ARE TO BE GRABBED OUT HERE AND YOUR ONLY COMPETITION IS IDIOTS. DON'T LET THIS GET AROUND. Not long afterward, Hecht wrote a script, *Underworld*, in one week, which was directed by Josef von Sternberg and became an enormous hit, bringing Hecht an Academy Award and a $10,000 bonus from the studio. Mankiewicz was right on hand, as Hecht cashed his check, to seize the $10,000, telling Hecht he needed it desperately but would return it in a few days. He never returned the money. He lost it all by tossing coins and calling heads or tails with Eddie Cantor at $1000 a call.

His gambling became even more feverish; he had reached the point where a wager carried excitement only if the prospect of loss was too terrible to contemplate. "It's no fun gambling if I lose two thousand and just write a check for it," he once confided to a friend. "What's thrilling is to make out a check for fifteen thousand knowing there's not a penny in the bank." So did his drinking, which had always been very heavy. Even while he was still on the *Times*, he had spent a vacation in Woodstock, New York, with the Hechts, and had brought two suitcases, the largest of which proved to contain no clothing—only sixteen bottles of Scotch. He never knew when to stop drinking, either, sometimes continuing until he became violently sick in public. "It's all right," he once said, after he threw up at an elegant dinner given by Arthur Hornblow, Jr., the film producer. "The white wine came up with the fish." Sara Mankiewicz became so long-suffering that Mankiewicz once looked puzzled when a friend asked him how Sara was. "Who?" he asked. "Sara," the friend said. "Your wife." "Oh," said Mankiewicz. "You mean Poor Sara."

By the middle and late '30s, Mankiewicz was moving from studio to studio, constantly being fired by producers he'd failed once too often, or whom he'd offended for other reasons. At M-G-M, Louis B. Mayer, whose daughter Irene was a friend of Sara's, decided to pull Mankiewicz out of his difficulties once and for all by advancing him the full amount he owed in gambling debts, provided he agreed faithfully that he would never gamble again. Mankiewicz warned Mayer that he owed quite a lot of money, $30,000, but the film mogul did not back away; he gave Mankiewicz the money and secured his solemn guarantee that his gambling days were over. The following day, Mayer, walking around the M-G-M lot, suddenly saw Mankiewicz, deep in a poker game in which he had just raised the stakes to $10,000. Mankiewicz saw Mayer, too. When the $30,000 was gone, he left the studio and never returned. Mankiewicz also worked for a short time for Columbia, hired by Harry Cohn, who loved a bargain, because he'd already been fired by all the other major studios and his price was down to $750 a week, a considerable drop from a salary which had risen in the early '30s to $5000 a week and more. He was hired, however, since his indiscretions were well-known, on the strict understanding that he would stay out of the executive dining room and away from Cohn. For a while, Mankiewicz kept his promise, but his office was located close to the dining room, and the luncheon sounds of laughter and gaiety finally proved too much for him. He hurried into the dining room one afternoon and sat down at the long table which Cohn headed. Everything went well until Cohn began to explain his magic formula for determining the quality of each new Columbia picture. "I have a foolproof device for judging whether a picture is good or bad," Cohn said. "If my fanny squirms, it's bad. If my fanny doesn't squirm, it's good. It's as simple as that." The silence which followed was broken by Mankiewicz's slightly slurred voice. "Imagine!" he said. "The whole world wired to Harry Cohn's ass!" And another job was gone.

Mankiewicz's troubles seem to have been uniquely his own and not typical of the Mankiewicz family. His father's lifetime career as an educator was distinguished and unmarred by scandal or eccentric behavior. His brother Joe, born ten years after Herman, also entered the movie field, and has had an impressive career in pictures: he has served as writer, director, or producer, and sometimes all three, on such films as *If I Had a Million, Fury, The Philadelphia Story, Keys of the Kingdom, All About Eve, Five Fingers,* and the more recent *Sleuth.* (Mankiewicz, incidentally, envied his brother's success, referring to Joe more and more often as "my idiot brother" as Joe became more and more successful.) Mankiewicz and Sara also had three children who turned out well. Their oldest son, Don, born in 1922, is the author of such well-known novels as *Trial* and *See How They Run,* many highly regarded teleplays and screenplays, and the pilot scripts for such hit television series as *Ironside* and *Marcus Welby, M.D.;* their other son, Frank, born in 1924, was George McGovern's principal assistant during the McGovern campaign for the presidency in 1972, and before that a prominent attorney in Beverly Hills, an important executive in the Peace Corps, and Robert Kennedy's press assistant; and their daughter Johanna, named after Mankiewicz's mother and born in 1937, was one of the best writers on the Staff of *Time* until her sad and sudden death when she was struck by an automobile not long ago. The only one with even a touch of unreliability is Frank, who is notorious for showing up late for appointments and for failing to return phone calls, but there's no comparison, of course. Mankiewicz's pressures came from within himself; he was as much driven by a suicidal urge as a man who puts a gun to his temple and presses the trigger. The main difference was that Mankiewicz took longer to die, finally achieving it on March 6, 1953.

Kaufman, who made such a fetish of avoiding displays of sentiment, was so stunned by Mankiewicz's death that he sent Sara Mankiewicz one of the few emotional letters he ever wrote. He mentioned how shocked he had been even though Joe Mankiewicz had told him the end was coming. "Subconsciously," he continued, "I flatter myself by implying that I was one of the rare spirits that appreciated him to the full, but damn it! I *was*. Memories of our working together—a play, a movie, the *Times*—glorious memories, some of them, and a few exasperating ones, too. But always shot through with his fantastic and brilliant humor. That's all and little enough. But I just want you to know that I will think of him for a long, long time, and that I hope you'll find a peaceful and happy life."

There is no question about Mankiewicz's great talent and his great contribution to the movie industry. He wrote many of the best pictures to come out of Hollywood, the most important of which is *Citizen Kane*, on which he shared an Academy Award for best original screenplay with Orson Welles. Like nearly everything Mankiewicz did, however, even this special triumph was touched with sadness and a measure of ugliness. Mankiewicz took on the job early in 1940, at a time when he had begun to find it almost impossible to get other movie work; his only income, at that point, came from an assignment to write five scripts at low prices for Welles's radio show, *Campbell Playhouse*. He was offered only $500 a week for the *Citizen Kane* assignment, the lowest amount he'd been paid in years, but he grabbed it eagerly. His drinking problem was now so severe that he was sent away from Los Angeles to work; he was put up at a remote resort called Mrs. Campbell's Guest Ranch in Victorville, California, sixty-five miles from the movie capital, and guarded by a nurse, a secretary, and one of Welles's assistants, all of whom were charged with seeing to it that he never got his hands on anything alcoholic. He even agreed to do the script as a ghost job, because Welles was then the Wonder Boy of the industry and had signed a contract to do all directing, producing, and writing of his pictures personally.

Welles and Mankiewicz had originally met back in New York, and had come away from their first lunch together at 21 full of respect and admiration for each other. The feeling didn't last, at least on Mankiewicz's part; Welles's driving, overbearing style and massive ego soon began to make Mankiewicz feel smothered. By the time he had become one of Welles's employees, he was describing his boss in bitter terms, saying, as Welles walked by one day, "There, but for the grace of God, goes God." He used his new attitude toward Welles as his rationale for breaking his agreement on the deal; he was paid a small bonus, as the job neared completion, to insure his promise to waive his byline, but instead followed the advice given him on the matter by Hecht, who said, "Take the money, and then double-cross him." When the script was finished and it became obvious to Mankiewicz that it was good and the picture was going to be a major production, he went to the Screen Writers Guild and protested his anonymous role. The Guild ruled in his favor and insisted that he receive first creenplay credit and Welles second. Aside from the lack of ethics nvolved, the fact that a deal is a deal and that he had known about he no-credit aspect of the assignment from the start and had agreed o it, Mankiewicz's trip to the Guild was not exactly unjustified. Welles eally had nothing to do with the script. He had told Mankiewicz hat he wanted to do a film biography, but he had no specific person n mind. It was Mankiewicz who first came up with John Dillinger, hen Aimee Semple McPherson, and finally, when Welles did not ike the first two suggestions, with a picture based more or less on the ife of William Randolph Hearst. (It was a cold-blooded suggestion, ince Mankiewicz was friendly with the Hearsts and an occasional ;uest at San Simeon, but Mankiewicz was rarely concerned with the iiceties of life.) Mankiewicz also wrote the full screenplay strictly m his own, and the reason Welles managed to end up with a share »f the screenplay credit is that he insisted he had conferred frequently vith Mankiewicz and suggested many changes and additions in the cript. There is considerable evidence that Welles did not even do hat, because he was extremely busy with other projects and with a omance with Dolores del Rio, the Mexican actress. And even if he lid what he says he did, he would probably not have received :redit if the events had occurred recently; the Guild has become :xtremely tough about producers who try to cut in on screenplay :redit merely because they've made some script suggestions. The :creenplay of *Citizen Kane* is unquestionably the sole product of Vlankiewicz's brain and talents, and many current reference sources imply list the script as "by Herman J. Mankiewicz" and omit Velles's name entirely.

Even so, sadly, most people think of the film only as "Orson Velles's *Citizen Kane*," and Mankiewicz is almost forgotten today by he general public. Pauline Kael, for example, who did a long study of Vlankiewicz and *Citizen Kane* for *The New Yorker*, comments that, vith the rise of Joe Mankiewicz, Herman became simply "a paren- hesis in the listings for Joe."

But most of Mankiewicz's life and career was still ahead of him n 1926, and it seemed like a workable idea when he began to urge Kaufman to collaborate with him on a play. For one thing, he was risibly eager to succeed as a playwright, a trait which commended itself to Kaufman because it suggested that Mankiewicz might match his own compulsive dedication toward his work, and might give playwriting the effort and enthusiasm he'd never given to the *Times*. For another, he was an extremely funny man even then, with a swiftness of comedic invention and repartee not too dissimilar to Kaufman's, and might be counted on to lift from Kaufman's shoulders some of the burden of being responsible for the greatest percentage of the gags and funny lines in his plays. There was also no question of Mankiewicz's intelligence. Everyone who met him became aware almost at once of the quick, superior intellect which later caused Nunnally Johnson, Kaufman's collaborator on *Park Avenue*, to remark that the two most brilliant men he'd ever met were George S. Kaufman and Herman Mankiewicz, and that, all things considered, Mankiewicz was the more brilliant of the two. Mankiewicz, too, was no longer an unproven author; he was now writing scripts for Paramount and doing extremely well. And most important of all, he had an idea which Kaufman really liked: a play which would satirize fraternal organizations.

Kaufman's most famous line is the one which derogates satire. But the truth of the matter was that, despite his uncomfortable suspicion that satire is often uncommercial, he was always at his happiest when working in that area. Every one of his plays makes some effort, at least in some peripheral way when it wasn't possible to be direct about it, to attack the wicked, expose the foolish, and deflate the pompous. And the fraternal orders, growing highly popular as more and more men joined the Elks and the Moose and the Lions and all the other organizations named after animals and various kinds of knights, seemed like an irresistible target in the light of their child-like secret rituals and backslapping Babbittry. So though Kaufman knew, all too well, his former assistant's faults and general unreliability, he agreed to collaborate with him.

The collaboration, as all of their mutual friends predicted the moment word got around, was a disaster right from the start. Mankiewicz remained eager to achieve success as a playwright; he was just, as things turned out, not very eager to work for it. He created agony in his tightly controlled and schedule-bound collaborator by showing up late for work sessions or not showing up at all, went out for lunch or dinner instead of settling for sandwiches and stayed away for hours or just didn't return, and in general conducted himself with the casual disinterest in his projects which became and remained the despair of all of his business associates. It wasn't a manifestation of disrespect toward Kaufman, whom Mankiewicz genuinely admired more than almost anyone else in the world; it was just the way Mankiewicz was. He behaved in exactly the same way during his next theatrical collaboration, which was with his other idol, Marc Connelly. He talked Connelly into working with him on a play to be based on a short skit which Connelly had originally written for Beatrice Lillie, and to be called *The Wild Man of Borneo*, and then became so elusive that Connelly later said sadly, "Mank was always ready to discuss the development of a play, but getting him to share the writing took great effort. Perhaps if he had given George and me more of his time, our resultant plays might have been better than they were." Mankiewicz, in short, made life difficult for all of his collaborators, but for the meticulous and hard-working Kaufman it was pure hell.

And the thing that made it even worse was that the play itself wasn't working very well, either. The authors' idea was to make their hero, whom they named Jim Helton, an enthusiastic and leading lodge member—the Grand Napoleon, in fact, of his organization, the Ancient Order of Corsicans—and then get him into trouble by having him decide that he wants to get the next Corsican convention for his home town, Wilkes-Barre, Pennsylvania, an effort which costs him $10,000 and forces him to take a loan on his life insurance and also borrow money from his daughter's rich fiancé. The trick was to make Helton both a sort of bragging fool and an essentially sympathetic and likable man—and, as the critics subsequently concluded, it just wasn't possible. Another problem was that one of the main attractions for the authors in the play-idea was that it presented a great opportunity to burlesque some of the fraternal-order rituals. This, too, proved more effective in conception than in fact. As things turned out, people who weren't really familiar with real-life secret society rituals were bored with the long scenes which satirized them, and the substantial percentage of men in the audience who were fraternal-order members themselves, and had taken part in similar rituals, were offended.

Between the Mankiewicz disappearances and the plot and character-ization dilemmas, it would have surprised no one if Kaufman had finally decided to abandon the project, and he often said afterward that he wished he'd done so. But he continued instead to struggle along page by page. He plunged his hero deeper and deeper into trouble with costly public relations campaigns to bring the Corsicans to Wilkes-Barre instead of the organization's alternate choice of Little Rock, Arkansas, finally saved him from financial disaster by having his future son-in-law give him a well-paying job in the family mining company, and had Helton exit with happy thoughts about spending some of his spare time starting a local chapter of the Sons of Isaac.

It was a weak effort, but Crosby Gaige agreed to produce it. Howard Lindsay was signed as director, and Kaufman, again at Gaige's farsighted insistence, accepted, very reluctantly, the assign-ment of assisting in the direction, hanging on long enough this time to earn his first directorial credit, if only a shared one. The programs and ads read, "Staged by Howard Lindsay and George S. Kaufman," and an additional career was starting.

The Good Fellow continued on its star-crossed path even as far as the acting was concerned. The actors were terrible at first re-hearsal and remained terrible at the opening despite Lindsay's and Kaufman's efforts, and Woollcott, one of the few critics whose review was partly favorable, said it was "an excellent play but atrociously acted." The comedy is almost unique among Kauf-man plays in not having a single actor in the cast who subsequently became famous enough to be remembered today. The lead was played by John E. Hazzard, an actor from Great Neck, Long Island, about whom *Variety* could only say that "Jack Hazzard's Great Neck friends greeted him with acclaim," and about whom *Theatre* could only say that he played his part "industriously." His wife was played by Jennet Adair, his daughter was played by Ethel Taylor, and his daughter's fiancé was played by Walter Baldwin, Jr.

Aside from Woollcott, nearly all of the other critics were uni-formly negative when the Kaufman-Mankiewicz collaboration opened at the Playhouse Theatre on Tuesday, October 5, 1926.

It was a strong setback for Kaufman, because it made many critics forget all about their earlier encomiums for the deeper intentions of his earlier play, *Beggar on Horseback*. *Theatre*, for example, said in reviewing *The Good Fellow*, "He has talent as a sketch-writer, but as a maker of dramas he has still much to learn." The play closed after seven performances, going down in the books as Kaufman's biggest failure among his plays actually reaching Broadway. Even a later disaster written with Leueen MacGrath, *Fancy Meeting You Again*, managed eight performances. (By way of comparison, the two plays which are "remembered" by some critics as the great failures among those Kaufman wrote with Moss Hart are *Merrily We Roll Along* and *George Washington Slept Here*. The latter has even been described in some theatrical histories as *George Kaufman Slipped Here*. But *Merrily We Roll Along* ran a respectable 155 performances and *George Washington Slept Here* ran 173.) And even the Connelly-Mankiewicz collaboration, *The Wild Man of Borneo*, fared a little better: the curtain went up fifteen times before it folded.

There was a small financial salvage for the play when Paramount bought movie rights. But it took four years after the close of the play for Kaufman to be able to bring himself to regard the matter lightly. On October 27, 1930, finally recovered, and following the appearance of an article on Mankiewicz in the *Times*, he wrote a brief letter to the newspaper. "You say," he wrote, "that he once collaborated with me on a 'half-forgotten' play. The reference, of course, is to *The Good Fellow*, produced about four years ago. I feel I must protest your use of 'half-forgotten.' I have been conducting some inquiries, and am pleased to say that I find no one who remembers it at all. I think you should be a little surer of your facts before rushing into print." Certainly the play was more than half-forgotten by Paramount. Though they acquired film rights in 1926, they didn't make a film based on the play until seventeen years later, releasing it under the title of *Good Fellows* in 1943.

Despite the traumatic experience with Mankiewicz, Kaufman never managed to toughen himself to the point where he was able to look away resolutely when an eagerly would-be but clearly unsuitable collaborator beckoned. Sixteen years after *The Good Fellow*, Kaufman repeated his identical mistake, astonishing observers and himself in 1942 by allowing Mankiewicz to talk him into a second collaboration. This time the joint venture was a screenplay about the world of the theatre, *Sleeper Jump*, a term referring to the tours many plays make after closing on Broadway, and given that name because the participants jump from town to town in quick Pullman-sleeper trips. The outcome was predictable: with Mankiewicz even more deeply imbedded in alcoholism and irresponsibility at the age of forty-five than he had been at twenty-nine, the end product was a weak script which never sold. And again Kaufman had a failure because he was simply unable to say No to the blandishments of his more determined friends and acquaintances.

But far earlier than this recidivistic return, Kaufman found himself agreeing to collaborate with another partner as unlikely as the hard-drinking Mankiewicz. In 1929, just three years after he should have learned a lesson from the quick demise of *The Good Fellow*, Kaufman's new collaborator, incredibly, was Alexander Woollcott.

Woollcott and Kaufman never became really close, despite the fact that they saw each other constantly from the time they first began to work together on the *Times* in 1917 to the time of Woollcott's death in 1943. They were simply too different in habits and outlook for that. The almost totally opposite personalities of the two men were accurately reflected in their physical appearance. Woollcott, paunchy and round and looking a little like a short and overweight Santa Claus, was unashamedly a man of uncontrolled appetites and enthusiasms. He was a total extrovert, ate hugely and happily, attempted to dominate his friends by making most of the social decisions and by including everyone in sight in his plans without asking if they had any conflicting commitments of their own, and grew constantly and publicly emotional about new causes and new books and new plays and performers. He also showed the same lack of restraint in his work, often turning in his reviews and magazine pieces overlength and floridly overwritten. Kaufman, lean and ascetic, was shy and retiring, often ate only because there was no longer any way of getting out of it, never dreamed of dictating other people's social activities, grew more and more reluctant to show emotion, and spent a lot of his time cutting and tightening his material and making one word do where there had previously been three.

None of these differences, however, prevented Kaufman and Woollcott from admiring each other. Woollcott was overcome with delight at some of Kaufman's reviews, going around for years telling people about two in particular—the time Kaufman had written, "I saw the play under bad conditions. The curtain was up," and the time he had written, "There was laughter in the back of the theatre, leading to the belief that somebody was telling jokes back there." The two men sometimes went to the theatre together, Woollcott resplendent in things like Dracula-style capes and Kaufman trying to approach invisibility in very quiet suits. Woollcott beamed with pleasure when, at a very bad play, Kaufman leaned forward to the woman in front of him, who had courteously removed her hat, and asked her to please put it on again. Woollcott also watched with respect when, on another visit to the theatre, they were seated close to a woman who talked unceasingly throughout the first act, Kaufman finally put an end to her chatter by asking quietly, "Madame, have you no *unexpressed* thoughts?" And he quoted with similar admiration Kaufman's epitaph for a departed waiter, "God finally caught his eye."

But most of all, Woollcott admired Kaufman's growing talent and expertise as a playwright, and constantly suggested that they work together on a play which he wanted to call *The Channel Road*. And Kaufman, who in turn admired Woollcott's great energy, Woollcott's loyalty to his favorite people and causes and works, and the sharp wit which always showed up alongside the purple phrases in Woollcott's writings, finally agreed.

It was a decision which was even more ill-advised than the agreement to work with Mankiewicz. There was no problem this time about starting work at the precise minute and hour they'd set for their sessions to begin, or about making each work period very long, or about reworking and rewriting many of the lines in the play dozens of times. Woollcott was completely willing to work as hard as his partner. But the real problem—and it was one about which neither man could do a thing—was that the basic styles and literary tastes of the two men were so diametrically opposed and so inherently incompatible that there was just no possibility at all of their separate contributions meshing together as a cohesive collaborative work.

This was reflected even in the choice of subject for their play, which was to be based on Guy de Maupassant's first published short story, *Boule de Suif*. The story, a sentimental and fairly simple episode, is about a French prostitute named Madeline who, while fleeing from a Prussian-occupied zone during the Franco-Prussian War, is first scorned by a group of French aristocrats fleeing at the same time, and then courted by them when a Prussian lieutenant admires her and it seems possible that the well-being of the entire party may be dependent on Madeline's acquiescence. The lady, of course, shows herself as more courageous and patriotic than the aristocrats by spurning the officer at first, despite the personal danger involved. She finally gives herself to the lieutenant for the common good of the group—and the members of the group repay her, once they're safely away, by resuming their attitudes of contempt and proceeding on their journey without her. *Boule de Suif* was unmistakably Woollcott's choice even to people who were unaware that he'd been urging it on Kaufman for years. He often inclined toward the near-maudlin in literature, and also had a special enthusiasm for stories about hookers with hearts of gold, presumably because, since he had no sex needs, he had probably never met a real member of that tough and cold-blooded sorority. The incredible thing was that he was able to persuade Kaufman, who had such a horror of the sentimental and the obvious, to go along with the choice.

The destructive element in the collaboration, the basic incompatibility of their writing styles, worried them throughout their work together. Every line Kaufman wrote was as lean and as terse as he was himself, and he then went to work to make it even leaner and more terse; every line Woollcott wrote reflected his own image and was soft, wordy, and flamboyant. The two men, noting this at nearly every joint session, worked hard to keep the two styles from combating each other, but they never really succeeded. Since *The Channel Road* was planned as a comedy, they changed de

Maupassant's bitter and ironic ending: the contented officer allows only Madeline and two Sisters of Mercy in the group to escape and sends the aristocrats back to their occupied home area. They also threw in every comedy line Kaufman could conjure up. But there was no way to avoid the inevitable surrounding of the spruced-up plot with many of Woollcott's overwritten and sometimes pompous contributions. And, in due course, nearly every critic noted and hated this.

The collaboration began in July 1929, and Woollcott spent the first month writing the first act all by himself. Then he and Kaufman took a couple of rooms in a small hotel in Westchester County, just above the city line, and devoted a week there to rewriting it. They wrote the second act together in Woollcott's apartment overlooking the East River, working very quickly despite the fact that there was construction going on nearby and the sounds of riveting were deafening and almost continuous. They then took the two acts to Arthur Hopkins, a producer-director they both knew and liked. Hopkins, an ordinarily astute and perceptive man who said afterward that he'd been mesmerized by the two potent bylines on the script, read the material that night, and, without even waiting for the final act, agreed the next day to produce and stage the comedy. And the collaborators, armed now with a deal, moved to the St. Regis Hotel to evade the noise, and wrote the third act there.

The Channel Road was brought to Broadway on Thursday, October 17, 1929, opening at the Plymouth Theatre. With only a few exceptions, the critics promptly tore it to pieces.

Ironically, the one critic who really liked the play was Joseph Wood Krutch, the man who was so rarely kind to Kaufman's projects. This time, writing as always in *The Nation*, he called *The Channel Road* "an entertaining play which will doubtless never be as famous as the original, but which might reasonably be called a good deal more sensible." Krutch explained, "Though Maupassant could tell stories superbly well, he was violently patriotic, violently misanthropic, and (as this combination implies) distinctly deficient in humor. One could hardly propose the stubborn prostitute as a modern Joan of Arc to a modern audience whose sense of proportion does not happen to be, as Maupassant's was, considerably disturbed by the fevers of a wartime hatred. The more seriously one attempts to tell the story, the more comic it becomes, and to discover that is to discover that the situation actually belongs to the realm of comedy. That is exactly what Messrs. Woollcott and Kaufman have done. They have very skillfully transposed the whole thing into the key of comedy, and the fact that their play will stand analysis far better than the original story is proof that they were right in so doing." Atkinson was also fairly favorable, saying, "Although the two authors of *The Channel Road* have taken the situation for their comedy of 1870 from one of Maupassant's short stories, they have given it greater scope and significance."

But the other critics didn't like the play at all, and many of them were vehement in deploring the floridity and verbosity of some parts of it. John Mason Brown, writing in the *Post*, bemoaned the "reams of high-faluting dialogue." Francis R. Bellamy in *Outlook* said, "The faces as they converse may be the faces of de Maupassant's people, but the voice is the voice of Mr. Woollcott, talking brightly to himself." And even Atkinson had to admit that the language of the play had bothered him, saying, "What tempers my enjoyment of *The Channel Road* is the fulsome literary style in which it is written, or rather overwritten."

There was one strong plus factor in the play in addition to the comedy lines, though not quite a saving one: a brilliant performance by a young actor named Siegfried Rumann in the role of the Prussian lieutenant. Most of the other performers—among them Anne Forrest as the prostitute and Selden Bennett, Edith Van Cleve, and Peggy Conway as three of the aristocrats—were mediocre at best, causing Atkinson to refer to the cast in general as "incompetent actors who merely speak their lines" and *Theatre Arts Monthly* to describe the acting as "only tenacious." Every critic in New York, however, made admiring reference to Rumann's performance. Rumann eventually shortened his first name to Sig and drifted to Hollywood, becoming so bogged down in stock German roles that a film critic later referred to him wearily as "the routine Mr. Rumann playing his usual komic Kraut." But his notices were scintillating following the opening of *The Channel Road*.

Rumann's virtuoso performance was not enough, however, to keep the play alive, particularly in the light of another thing which might have killed the comedy all by itself, even if it had been a masterpiece and not so loaded with flaws and problems. This was the unfortunate date of its arrival on Broadway, just twelve days before the stock market crash. The air was soon filled with the flying bodies of suicide-bent brokers and customers, and with worried conversations to the effect that it might be best to avoid buying expensive theatre tickets and keep every cent in the bank as a hedge against oncoming hard times. *The Channel Road* limped along for sixty performances, and then closed.

The play did not sell to the movies, and has rarely been revived. One of the few important revivals set for it was at the Bucks County Playhouse in New Hope, Pennsylvania, in 1940. There, too, it ran into bad timing. The Playhouse's proprietors, Theron Bamberger and Kenyon Nicholson, had run into problems with a previous Kaufman revival, *The Royal Family*, because of the war, and had had to change Tony Cavendish's European trip in the play to a South American jaunt and make many other geographical alterations, but they anticipated no similar problems with *The Channel Road*. The French-German conflict described in that play was, after all, an earlier and much different one, taking place seventy years before. Bamberger and Nicholson borrowed a copy of the manuscript from Arthur Hopkins's files and had additional copies typed up, and they signed Lenore Ulric to play the role of the prostitute. But then an ugly event occurred in Europe: the Germans cracked the Maginot Line and began to invade France, and suddenly there was nothing funny about any French-German war. Bamberger later put it succinctly: "We decided to abandon the project and charge the $12 for typing to Hitler."

The Channel Road was not the end of the business relationship between Kaufman and Woollcott; as had been the case with Mankie-wicz, it took two tries before the partnership was abandoned permanently. Kaufman undertook the second collaboration even less willingly than he had entered the first. It was not the sort of thing he would ever discuss openly, but a friend who happened to see him arrive for the first day's work, most of which took place this time in Woollcott's apartment, said he looked as though he was trudging the last half mile.

The trouble, in the case of both plays, was that Kaufman found himself in no real position to refuse when, after long periods of hinting, Woollcott finally made it clear that he was really serious now about wanting to collaborate. Except for the occasional displays of pettiness and even cruelty which all of Woollcott's friends and acquaintances came in time to expect as part of the natural order of things, Woollcott had in general been extremely kind to Kaufman. He gave Kaufman's plays strongly favorable reviews most of the time and also talked them up so enthusiastically that he unquestionably helped business—and that included the plays which needed that kind of help. He was also, like Mankiewicz, so clever and so amusing at the dinner table that Kaufman was able to seize again on the hope that perhaps this time he would be just as quick and inventive as a co-author. And in addition, Woollcott had become a closer and closer friend of Beatrice's through the years, including her in just about every one of his social activities from his rentals of summer houses to the "breakfast salons" he started at his apartment in the winter of 1928, and which soon became famous and popular.

Woollcott, in fact, had begun to spend so much time with Beatrice that, as mentioned, people around him came to realize that he had actually fallen deeply in love with her. Her principal biographer, Samuel Hopkins Adams, calls it "one of his chaste passions belonging in the category of anomalous attachments peculiar to his type" and points out that it was "so wholly frank and aboveboard that it became a household cliché, a subject of standard banter among the three friends." But, Adams goes on to say, "Some of Aleck's friends believe that, back of all the fun, there was on his side a genuine, if covert, sentiment; Beatrice appealed to more than impersonal feelings and, had she been free, his attentions might well have taken a serious turn." Adams is being very discreet; the main reason Woollcott never attempted to do anything about his infatuation with Beatrice, of course, was that he was impotent and there was nothing he could do. But the fact that he was so close to Beatrice, and at the same time, for all practical purposes, a sort of eunuch-friend toward whom Kaufman did not even have to feel pangs of jealousy, added one more

trong reason that made it difficult and even impossible for Kaufman
o refuse when Woollcott again suggested that they write a play
ogether.

Furthermore, Woollcott did not approach Kaufman until more
han three years after *The Channel Road* had closed. By this time,
he pain of the demise had subsided pretty completely, and there
had been a number of extremely successful collaborations with other
people in between. Woollcott came to see Kaufman in the spring of
1933, and his new project was an even more unlikely one than the
ast time: he wanted to collaborate on a mystery melodrama. The
prospect undoubtedly filled Kaufman with horror, but, just as he had
done in 1929, he ended up agreeing.

The play was one which Woollcott wanted to call *Snake in the
Grass*, and, when Kaufman threw him a sardonic look and Woollcott
made it clear that he was serious, the collaboration nearly ended
right there. The title was then changed to *The Dark Tower*, which
was retained to the end. The play was to be an original this time,
not based on previously published material, and was to deal with a
young actress, Jessica Wells, who has suffered a mental collapse as
the result of an unhappy marriage with a villainous man named
Stanley Vance, now believed dead. As the play opens, Jessica is
under the care and guardianship of her brother, Damon Wells, a
highly regarded character actor, and is almost recovered and about
to appear in a new play. Suddenly and without warning, Vance
reappears; it develops that he was not dead but in prison under an
assumed name. In very little time, Jessica is again under Vance's
almost hypnotic spell, and Vance is hinting to Damon that he might
just possibly be bought off and sent away. But then a foreign producer named Max Sarnoff, a mysterious and fairly sinister figure
himself, arrives at the Waldorf, and expresses interest in acquiring
both Jessica's play and her services. Vance goes to the Waldorf to talk
about a deal, but suddenly Sarnoff produces a knife and stabs him
to death, and then disappears forever. The police investigate the
murder and fail to solve it. The audience, of course, knows the
answer: Max Sarnoff is really Damon Wells, disguised. And Jessica
recovers from Vance's influence and lives on happily.

Work began on *The Dark Tower* early in May, and, though Kaufman was involved simultaneously in several other projects, the script was finished early in September. Sam H. Harris agreed to produce the play, Jo Mielziner was signed to design the sets, and Woollcott and Kaufman decided to direct it themselves. They assembled a generally excellent cast, the one unfortunate exception being the actor who played the villainous Stanley Vance, a thespian of the old school named Ernest Milton who was later described by *Vanity Fair* as "the greatest over-actor in today's English-speaking theatre. Give him," the magazine went on to explain, "a simple single line to the effect, say, that it is raining outdoors and he not only goes promptly into an *aria di bravura* but so comports himself physically that the audience isn't certain whether it is in a theatre or at the Olympic games." But the other performers were excellent, with Margalo Gillmore playing Jessica Wells, Basil Sydney as her brother, William Harrigan as the man who loves Jessica and gets her after Vance is gone, Margaret Hamilton who later became famous as the Wicked Witch in *The Wizard of Oz* as the family maid. Porter Hall, later also a mainstay in many movies, was particularly good, playing a quiet and pragmatic little detective who says frankly, "Well, we aren't much worried about this case. We don't care if one crook murders another crook—especially if they're out-of-town crooks," and tells Jessica she can get him at police headquarters if she needs him, adding, "It's in the phone book."

The Dark Tower opened at the Morosco Theatre on Saturday November 25, 1933. The play brought two interesting innovations to the theatre world, the first of which was Harris's decision to sell opening-night tickets to people other than the usual first-nighters. This was a move which was so much a deviation from the norm that it was regarded almost as heresy. First-night tickets were ordinarily offered only to people on lists as proscribed, rigid, unchanging, and as carefully scrutinized as the list made up by that early arbiter of society, Ward McAllister, when he decided to confine his catalogue of American elite to four hundred names. The theatre list was made up of the most celebrated and publicized people in the New York area, and it was so difficult to get on it that a fairly well-known syndicated gossip columnist, whose principal sin was that the more than one hundred papers in which his column appeared did not in-

clude one published in New York, once complained that it had taken
him ten years to make the list, and even then the best he had been
able to do was a pair of tickets in the first balcony and on the side
near the wall. The trouble with the regular first-nighters was that
they knew they were famous and important and behaved in keeping
with the role, showing up late, too full of food and often too full
of rye or Scotch, and moved noisily down the aisles, calling attention
to themselves and to their equally famous friends by greeting each
other in loud voices and killing the actors' opening lines and the
opening impact of the plays.

Harris had been irritated for years by the bad manners of the
opening-night group, and he finally decided to do something about it
as *The Dark Tower* approached Broadway. He threw out the
standard list entirely, and put together an entirely new list made up
of the names of friends and of prominent people who were not part
of the regular rialto set. He sent out a letter explaining, "The
management of *The Dark Tower* has promised the distinguished
players assembled for its cast the unusual luxury of giving a first-
night performance before an audience not predominantly composed
of Broadwayites. To this end, a list of 500 citizens of this city has
been drawn up, and the first call on the opening-night seats will
be reserved for them. Your name is on this list." And in an even
more startling decision, he put the seats not reserved for the reviewers and the special list on open sale at the box office on a first-
come, first-served basis.

Surprisingly, the move, which Harris had assumed would be applauded by the freedom-loving press, instead created both fury and a
furor, and was widely attacked. One newspaper described Harris's
letter in angry terms as a peremptory summons rather like Tap Day,
and *Vanity Fair*, assuming that the decision had really been Kaufman's
on the basis of no better evidence than the fact that it sounded like
typical Kaufman irascibility, called the revised list "Kaufman's ruthless Broadway Nazism." Kaufman, as both a Jew and a strong
liberal, was bitterly anti-Nazi, and had just made the requirement of
his deals that none of his plays would ever be shown in Germany. He
was also already spending a substantial part of his income rescuing
relatives and possible relatives from Germany (the latter group were

people who had the same last name and had written him that they were distant relatives, even though they couldn't prove it). The description offended him deeply, and the worst part of it was that Harris's experiment really didn't work, and apparently did more harm than good. As *Vanity Fair* said in its article, "The result, as might have been anticipated, was an audience whose excessive and self-conscious friendliness for Mr. Kaufman and his collaborator not only caused it to lean so far backward that the play, whether it deserved it or not, didn't get half the applause it would ordinarily have got from the usual indiscriminately exuberant and strange bums, but in addition, vouchsafed to it the familiar privilege—always so avidly seized upon by close friends and acquaintances—of apprising one another, in somewhat audible lobby and sidewalk confidence, that the play was all right, of course, but. It remained for the theoretically unfriendly reviewers to persuade Mr. Kaufman's hand-picked audience of friends to feel the following day that they had seen a more entertaining play than they had the night before allowed to themselves." And they were just as noisy and ill-mannered as the regular set.

One of the chief offenders, in fact, was Edna Ferber, though it was really not her fault. Miss Ferber came to the opening as a guest of Stanton Griffis, an industrialist who later turned diplomat and became Ambassador to Poland, and Griffis had also set up an elaborate pretheatre dinner on his yacht. The dinner ran longer than anticipated. In addition, Gary Cooper was also in the group and was surrounded by a screaming circle of girls when the party arrived at the Morosco, an incident which created a disturbance and got them to their seats even later than they'd feared. Woollcott had been extremely enthusiastic about Harris's plan, and later said about criticism like *Vanity Fair*'s, "Bloody nonsense. We merely hoped to keep out the bad-mannered element," but he was livid at what he considered the defection of special friends like Edna Ferber. Miss Ferber realized this, and sent Woollcott a letter of apology the next day, even though she had had no way of controlling what had happened. But this was not enough for Woollcott, who cut her dead the next time they met. And this, in turn, infuriated Miss Ferber, who tended

oward impatience as far as Woollcott's fits of petulance were con-
erned, anyway. Not long before, there had been a party at the
'erber apartment which had included a game requiring all the lights
o be turned out. When the lights were turned on again, it was dis-
overed that Woollcott, offended by some unintended slight, had
eft under cover of darkness. That incident caused Miss Ferber to
ay, in disgust, "I'm growing weary of that New Jersey Nero who
hinks his pinafore is a toga." This one capped it, and she made a vow
ever to talk to him again.

Woollcott, as was typical of him, became concerned about the
ift once his own irritation had worn off, particularly when months
nd then years passed and Miss Ferber continued to keep her vow.
And in 1939, when Miss Ferber's first autobiography, *A Peculiar
Treasure*, came out and she was still not talking to him, he decided
o try to make amends by reviewing her book and plugging it
eavily on his radio shows and in some of his magazine pieces. But
hough Woollcott's enthusiasms or hatreds were often ill-advised,
nd occasionally motivated by affection or spite rather than reason
or intelligence, he was never intentionally dishonest. And it turned
ut, when he read Edna Ferber's book, that he just didn't like it.
Dorothy Parker once admitted blandly to Kaufman that she some-
imes reviewed a book without reading it, simply looking at the
acket blurb and forming her opinion that way, a statement which
aused Kaufman to stare at her in stunned disbelief for a moment or
wo and then walk away from her. Woollcott, too, was totally
opposed to the idea of casual immorality about items up for review.
He decided that the best thing to do was not review the book at
ll, and the two old friends were still not talking at the time of
Woollcott's death.

The play's other innovation was a bit more subtle. Kaufman and
Woollcott were concerned about the realization that some perceptive
heatregoers might notice, in thumbing through the program book-
ets during the play, that there were no credits listed for the actor
playing the producer-murderer, Max Sarnoff, and thus guess too soon
hat Sarnoff was really Damon Wells in disguise. They decided to plug
up this hole by stating, in the appropriate order-of-appearance

position in the Cast of Characters, that Sarnoff was played by some one called Anton Stengel. And in the back of the program booklet they gave Sarnoff a complete biography of about the same length as the biographies of the real actors, including the fact that he had been a member of Max Reinhardt's companies in both Berlin and Vienna and was making his first Broadway appearance in *The Dark Tower*. People attending the play were, of course, urged at the end not to tell their friends about the stunt. It was perhaps the first time in theatrical history that an attempt was made to fool the audience in the Playbill as well as on the stage, but few theatre historians today give Kaufman and Woollcott credit for the invention because their play was so short-lived that it was all soon forgotten. When, nearly forty years later, a more successful melodrama, *Sleuth*, came along winning the Tony Award for the 1970–71 season, and used the same trick, running long biographies of two non-existent actors in the playbill to keep audiences from guessing that there were only two characters in the play (two men who showed up in different disguise in attempts to fool each other), several eminent critics who should have known better applauded the stunt as a brand-new theatrical device.

In the end, the innovations and the good actors didn't help *The Dark Tower* very much. The big problem was exactly the same as last time, the fact that Kaufman's lean terseness and Woollcott's fat flabbiness simply didn't mix. Contrary to *Vanity Fair*'s impression the critics were not kind to the play, and expressed their dislike of Woollcott's dramatic techniques in even more emphatic terms than they had back in 1929. "There is little in this witty, amusing but bungled melodrama," Allene Talmey said in *Stage*, "to show the incisive brilliance of George Kaufman, his theatrical bravura, his icy mind. It is, on the other hand, distinctly Mr. Woollcott's play with all his rambles into pleasant byways, his intricate weavings which even in the syntax of his sentences are so devious that they seem like the tattings of another generation." "In *The Dark Tower*," Krutch said in *The Nation*, "the Messrs. George Kaufman and Alexander Woollcott have pooled without exactly combining their talents. The result is a portentous drama of sinister influence and dark crimes upon the troubled surface of which Mr. Kaufman's springly witticisms bob up and down with a gay irrelevance. The ponderous and creaking machinery of the melodrama does not help to render any more impressive the tall tale." The play ended up falling short of even *The Channel Road*'s sad record, closing after fifty-seven performances.

After it was all over, Woollcott decided to treat the two failures as lightly as possible. On the one hand, he began to pretend that he had almost never been in the playwriting business at all, and when Burns Mantle included him in a study of contemporary playwrights, he wrote Mantle, "What's all this nonsense of classifying as a playwright one who (on the most liberal of interpretations) is no more than five-sixths of a playwright? I wrote half of one play (with G.S.K.) and (with G.S.K. and G. de M.) a third of another." And in preparing his biography for *Who's Who in America*, he never mentioned the two plays at all; he included just about everything he had done from birth onwards, but omitted *The Channel Road* and *The Dark Tower* entirely. On the other hand, he indicated to friends that at least one of the two plays, the later one, hadn't been such a dreadful failure at that. "It was a tremendous success," he wrote to a friend about *The Dark Tower*, "except for the minor detail that people wouldn't come to see it. Yet it really was a kind of success at that. I mean that we enjoyed it enormously and it seemed to be attended with great relish by all of the people (without exception) whose good opinion I would respect." He also grew fond of pointing out that the play had made quite a lot of money for its authors—a claim which, because of a series of show business ironies, happened to be the truth. Despite the failure in New York, the melodrama was put on at the Shaftesbury Theatre in London and had a respectable run there, Random House published it in book form, and it was also produced in Vienna, several Scandinavian cities, and in Prague, where the Park Avenue apartment of the American version was changed to a shabby room with a circular table covered by a shawl and with an oil lamp, and where the ladies in the play all wore babushkas.

The play was also bought for the movies by Warner Brothers,

which released it in July 1934, with an all-star cast: Mary Astor, later to become Kaufman's most publicized girl friend, played Jessica Wells, Edward G. Robinson was her brother Damon, Louis Calhern was Stanley Vance, and Ricardo Cortez was the lady's admirer. The brothers Warner blew the surprise right at the start by changing the title to *The Man with Two Faces*. But this may have been because, in their pragmatic way, they realized that there wasn't much chance of fooling movie audiences with the Max Sarnoff trick, not with the glaring eye of the camera picking up every blemish on the skin and not with Edward G. Robinson playing the dual role. A lot of movie critics obviously felt the same way, and revealed the secret in their reviews. "I am not supposed to give away the identity of the mysterious murderer," *Variety* said in a typical review, "but I don't see how any character which is played by Edward G. Robinson—no matter how thick the disguise—can remain a secret. They can doll him up all they want to with a fake goatee and a foreign accent, but they can't disguise that wide and unmistakable Robinson mouth and that broad Romanian face of his. Take off those whiskers, Robinson, I knew you all the time."

It didn't really matter; the picture was a success, and the studio felt it had gotten its money's worth and more, despite the fact that they had paid $35,000 for the rights, a very good price for the early '30s. The amount was, in fact, one of the two biggest paid by Warner Brothers for a play during that period. They also paid $35,000 for another play, *Big-Hearted Herbert*, but only $20,000 for a play called *Heat Lightning*, and they got a play called *Dr. Monica* for only $10,000. Other studios were also paying lower prices for many plays: RKO, for example, paid $22,000 for *By Your Leave* and $17,000 for *A Hat, A Coat, A Glove*, Paramount paid $32,000 for *The Pursuit of Happiness*, and M-G-M paid $18,000 for *All Good Americans* and only $15,000 for *The Wind and the Rain*. Nor was the $35,000 figure substantially below the prices being paid for smash hits. M-G-M got *Men in White* for $47,500, RKO got a bigger hit, *Roberta*, for $65,000, and Metro's payment for an even bigger hit, *Ah Wilderness!*, was $75,000. "If all this befalls one who writes a flop," Woollcott wrote with wonder and pleasure in a letter to another friend, "what happens when one writes a success?"

Kaufman, of course, knew the answer to that question: one did a hundred times better over-all. He viewed the failures with Mankiewicz and Woollcott with his usual mixture of pain and a kind of perverse pleasure at the fact that what he had always predicted was coming true. But he was quick to go on to other and, fortunately, better things.

17. THE QUIET MAN

THE ONE THING Kaufman knew positively, when he teamed up with a new collaborator shortly after the demise of *The Good Fellow*, was that his new partner, unlike Mankiewicz, would never prefer to talk about their projected play rather than write it. Kaufman's new collaborator was Ring Lardner, also known to the Algonquin group as Silent Sam, and the truth of the matter was that he hardly ever talked at all.

Of all the strange birds who flocked to the hotel on West 44th Street, the tall, cadaverous, inarticulate man who became Kaufman's co-author on a play called *June Moon* was probably the strangest and in many ways the saddest, of them all. He was a man who said early in life that he had three great ambitions: to see a lot of baseball, to sell stories to magazines, and to write a successful play. He ended up achieving all three of these ambitions plus many others. But he was so beset with self-loathing and deep black fits of depression that, when he died at the early age of forty-eight on September 25, 1933, many of his friends felt that he had closed his eyes almost with a feeling of relief.

Born Ringgold Wilmer Lardner in Niles, Michigan, on March 6, 1885, Kaufman's new partner originally planned to attend the University of Michigan and become "either a football player or a dentist," but shifted gears at the last minute and enrolled instead at Armour Institute in Chicago to study mechanical engineering. He quit Armour after one semester and returned to Niles, got a job as a freight agent but lost it when he missent a shipment of cream cheese to the wrong city, and then went to work for the local gas company, at $6 a week, in a curious job in which he spent half of his time doing bookkeeping and the other half as a handyman. His switch to a writing career came about because his older brother, Henry, had been doing some free-lance sports reporting for a paper in the neighboring state of Indiana, the South Bend *Times*, and had been turning in such good stuff that the paper sent a representative to Niles to offer him a staff job. The representative stopped at the gas office to get directions to the Lardner house, and Ring, who knew that his brother would not be interested in moving to South Bend, told the man that Henry was not available but that he was. He was given the job and remained with the South Bend *Times* for two years as sports editor, achieving his first ambition by covering baseball for the paper and, to fulfill a corollary requirement of his job, serving as official scorekeeper for the local team.

In 1907, he took a busman's holiday and spent his vacation watching the World Series in Chicago. A mutual friend introduced him to a well-known Chicago sports-writer, Hugh Fullerton, and, when Lardner confided shyly that he was extremely interested in moving into the bigger-time Chicago writing world, Fullerton got him a job on the *Inter-Ocean*. Not long afterward, Lardner switched to the Chicago *Examiner*, where he saw still more baseball by traveling with and covering the White Sox, worked for two years as editor of *Sporting News* in St. Louis, and then moved East to work for the Boston *American*. In 1911, he married a girl named Ellis Abbott, and the Lardners were just beginning to pay for the furniture in their new apartment when the Boston paper folded. Lardner borrowed some money from the owners of the Boston Braves and Red Sox (and later, he said in an autobiographical piece, astonished them by actually repaying his debts,) moved back to the Midwest and got a job on the Chicago *American,* and then returned to the *Examiner,* now combined with another paper and called the *Herald Examiner.* He said afterward that he began, around this time, to hunt seriously for a real breakthrough of some kind, and in 1913 he found it. A very popular sportswriter named Hugh E. Keogh had been writing a column called *By Hek* for the *Tribune* for years. When Keogh died suddenly, Lardner applied for the column spot and got it.

He soon began to regret his burst of ambition; his column, which he called *In the Wake of the News,* was so unpopular at first that the *Tribune*'s proprietors received a minimum of twenty letters a day urging them to get rid of their new columnist. But this was really more a reflection of the fact that readers missed Keogh than that the Lardner columns were inferior. In time, Lardner won everybody over and ended up staying on the *Tribune* staff for six years. The only reason he left even then was that his columns had become so much-admired that the Bell Syndicate took over and began to sell the columns to newspapers all over the country.

His columns were also the indirect path to the fulfillment of his second ambition: his desire to write for magazines. Because he was required to write seven columns a week, he began to fill space by running monologues allegedly spoken by assorted lowbrow types— mostly ballplayers. The monologues, a very funny mixture of atrocious grammar and innate shrewdness, were Lardner's first revelation of his extraordinary gift for reproducing the spoken language of the millions of Americans without too much education or too many of the social graces, and they were instantly applauded. One particular admirer was a man named Charles E. Van Loan, who wrote fiction for a lot of magazines. Van Loan suggested to Lardner that he write some new first-person, mangled-English pieces and try them out on *The Saturday Evening Post.* Lardner followed up immediately by sending a story about a fictitious White Sox pitcher named Jack Keefe to the *Post*, and the *Post* bought the story a few days later and asked for more. Before long, Lardner had sold enough magazine stories to turn them into a collection which became one of his most famous books, *You Know Me, Al*, and was soon also the author of *Gullible's Travels, Treat 'Em Rough, The Love Nest*, and many other books.

In 1919, when his column was being syndicated and he could live and work anywhere he chose, Lardner and Ellis and their family—they now had four sons, John Abbott, Ring W., Jr., James Phillips, and David Ellis—moved to Great Neck, Long Island. Lardner told friends frankly that he was making the move strictly to be near the "headquarters of the theatre" and attempt to achieve his remaining ambition: successful playwriting. The third area of success was one which had already begun to elude him, and, as things developed, would continue to do so for another decade. Some time before, Morris Gest, making a trip West, had stopped in Chicago and offered him a five-year playwriting contract, but the contract was canceled by mutual consent when Gest began to reject everything Lardner wrote for him. Lardner then tried other producers, but had no luck with the other people, either; everything he submitted to them was also turned down. Things became only slightly better after the Lardners had settled in the New York area. Lardner managed to get a baseball sketch into *The Ziegfeld Follies of 1922*, with the very popular Will Rogers as his ballplayer, and also contributed a funny sketch about three fishermen to *The 49ers*, but that wasn't really what he was seeking; he wanted to write a successful full-length play. The ambition continued to be elusive. On December 22, 1927, a play based on a Lardner story, *The Love Nest*, was finally produced, but it was written by Robert E. Sherwood rather than Lardner, and it wasn't very successful; it remained alive for only twenty-three performances. It wasn't until September 24, 1928, that one of Lardner's own plays, *Elmer the Great*, reached Broadway, and that, too, was a failure, closing after forty performances despite the fact that it was given a very skillful production by George M. Cohan and starred Walter Huston in the title role.

It took the collaboration with Kaufman to give Lardner the fulfillment of the last of the three dreams. The irony of his life was that this added success, when it finally came, did not bring him happiness any more than his earlier successes in other areas had done. It was almost as though there was something lacking in his emotional structure, some missing ingredient which kept him from feeling pleasure and pride in himself at times when other men would have been swaggering and grinning at themselves in the shaving mirror. The realization was bewildering to his friends and family, but it was also inescapable as the years passed: the things which satisfied most other men, and allowed them to live in relative peace with themselves, did nothing to halt or diminish Ring Lardner's lifelong hatred for Ring Lardner.

By all the rules of logic, he should have been one of the happiest men alive. He had a beautiful wife whom he loved and who loved him. He had four bright, healthy sons. He had become one of the best-known writers in the country. His house in Great Neck was a showplace. He had become an accepted and well-liked member of the Round Table soon after his arrival in New York, forgiven for his long silences because, when he finally opened his mouth and spoke, he generally said something worth hearing. "It's the children's night out," he said once, making his departure, "and I have to stay home with the nurse." He commented obliquely on Calvin Coolidge's lack of humor by describing the time he had met Coolidge and told him a joke. "He laughed," Lardner said, "until you could hear a pin drop." He called his children "his four grandsons" because they all went to expensive schools and cost him four grand a year. And he was also, of course, admired by the other members of the Round Table for the funny lines in his writings, among them the classic, "'Shut up,' he explained," his equally celebrated, "He gave her a look that you could have poured on a waffle," and his famous tongue-in-cheek response to a questionnaire about the way his wife had helped him and furthered his career. "In 1914 or 1915, I think it was July," he wrote, "she cleaned my white shoes. She dusted my typewriter in 1922. Late one night in 1924 we got home from somewhere and I said I was hungry and she gave me a verbal picture of the location of the pantry. Another time I quit cigarettes and she felt sorry for me."

He should indeed have been a happy man; the only flaw in the logic was that he wasn't. He grew more and more silent, so much so that Corey Ford, then a young writer who idolized Lardner and was introduced to him by Sherwood, described the meeting as a "brief wordless encounter . . . our conversation consisted of a couple of grave nods," and continued, "He was the most completely silent man I have ever met, solemn and unsmiling and yet curiously appealing. His face was gaunt, with high cheekbones and shadowy hollows—someone compared his vaulted features to a cathedral—and reminded me in an odd way of Buster Keaton. Like Keaton, the mournful expression gave his comedy an incongruous and eerie value. The dark melancholy eyes were extraordinarily sensitive." He began to drink heavily, sometimes going off on benders which lasted for weeks and longer. He began to suffer from insomnia, often wandering in aimless exhaustion through the Great Neck streets and dropping in on friends in the middle of the night. Once he awoke Clarence Buddington Kelland, another successful author who lived in the same town, at three o'clock in the morning, and then sat so silently in Kelland's living room that Kelland fell asleep across from him. At dawn, Kelland was awakened by Lardner's hand on his shoulder. "I don't want to seem rude," Lardner said, "but aren't you ever going home?" He also ate so little and grew so thin that, in the last year of his life, his chairs had to be padded to keep them from giving him pain.

After Lardner became famous, a great many writers, both those who knew him intimately and those who had never even met him but noted the increasing cynicism of many of his short stories and heard about the sadness of his personal outlook, commented on his attitudes in print and occasionally tried to analyze them. F. Scott Fitzgerald, who was probably Lardner's closest friend, and was similarly fated to experience deep fits of depression, constant drinking problems, and an early death, said simply that Lardner had become bitter about his writing soon after achieving success at it, and stopped finding any fun in his work from about 1923 on. Fitzgerald felt that even Lardner's habit of silence was the result of the fact that he had come to despise his accomplishments in life and therefore himself, and represented a kind of living suicide, a deliberate self-repression, a way of "getting off." Don Elder, Lardner's biographer, tended to agree, calling Lardner's increasing despondency "the penalty of having been precocious." Lardner, Elder said, "had come early to the enjoyment of his pleasures and his talents and his social life; they had palled on him too soon. He was, like so many other puritanical idealists, a perfectionist. He had been praised and applauded for achievements which he himself did not think good enough, and so he was skeptical of his success. Since his work was never good enough to suit him, he found less and less satisfaction in it, and he had less and less respect for those who thought that his second-best was first-rate."

Other men probed even more deeply. William Bolitho summarized the reasons for Lardner's despair in a single sentence, calling him "the greatest and sincerest pessimist America has produced." Pat O'Brien, the actor, who occasionally spent time with Lardner because both were members of the Lambs Club after Lardner moved to New York, called Lardner "a strange and sad genius who saw only the darkest side of life" and a man who died young because he was "worn out by a bitter view of the world." O'Brien added: "He was one of those forlorn, gifted God's creatures who could not submit to any faith or a hope in mankind." And Clifton Fadiman was most specific, and probably the most accurate of all of Lardner's observers, in a piece which appeared in *The Nation* shortly before Lardner's death.

"He just doesn't like people," Fadiman said. "I believe he hates himself; most certainly he hates his characters; and most clearly of all, his characters hate each other. There is no mitigating soft streak in him as there is in the half-affectionate portraiture of Sinclair Lewis, and none of the amused complacency of H. L. Mencken. He has found nothing whatever in American life to which to cling; he is cursed with intuitive knowledge of the great American swine. Everything he meets or touches drives him into a cold frenzy, leaving him without faith, hope or charity. Even in his simplest magazine stories, he is interested in getting at the core of egotism from which even our most impeccable virtues spring." Fadiman concluded: "Somewhere Lardner has a remark about 'this special police dog' which 'was like most of them and hated everybody.' Lardner himself is the police dog of American fiction, except that his hatred is not the result of mere crabbedness but of an eye that sees too deep for comfort."

Despite his growing sadness and disillusionment, Lardner was still capable of a certain amount of hope and ambition when, early in

1929, he approached Kaufman and suggested that Kaufman collaborate with him on a comedy to be based on a well-known Lardner short story, *Some Like Them Cold*. He was still trying, Lardner said, to get a play on Broadway which represented his own viewpoint and style, and explained that he didn't really feel that *Elmer the Great* fit that description, even though he'd written it all by himself, because he'd given Cohan carte blanche after turning in his script, and Cohan had changed the play very substantially. It had ended up in tone, language, and general outlook far more a standard Cohan product than a Lardner play, even containing moments of flag-waving and super-patriotism—a kind of chauvinism which would never have entered Lardner's cynical mind.

Kaufman was interested: he liked and admired Lardner, respected his strong determination to succeed in the theatre, and felt that the theme of the short story, a satire on Tin Pan Alley and the songwriting business, might well serve as the basis for a Broadway play. He asked for a day or two to reread *Some Like Them Cold*, enjoyed the story when he reread it, and phoned to say that the collaboration was okay with him. He also, with typical respect for his collaborator's needs, proposed a plan of operation entirely different from the working methods he had usually followed in the past. It would be a mistake, he said, to meet on a daily basis and compose the play together line by line; he feared that, if that were done, he might find himself unconsciously dominating the meetings because of his greater experience in the play field, with the result that the new comedy might end up more a Kaufman than a Lardner play in the same way that *Elmer the Great* had ended up more Cohan than Lardner. The way to insure the preservation of the special Lardner touch, Kaufman suggested, would be for Kaufman to block out the basic, technical structure of the play and then turn the project over to Lardner to write the entire first draft on his own.

Lardner was agreeable; he even, Kaufman later reported, "indicated a measure of solemn elation." Kaufman went to work, mapping out a schematic of the comedy, scene by scene through its projected three acts. He decided to add no plot complications and leave the plan of the play as simple and straightforward as the short story. It would deal with a young songwriter from Schenectady, New

York, Fred Stevens, who is first seen on a train enroute to New York City to make his fortune and meet Paul Sears, a famous composer whom Fred admires. (In the original story, Stevens came from Chicago, but Kaufman decided to change the town because he felt that a place like Schenectady would give Stevens a more instant image of small-town innocence than the more sophisticated Midwestern city.) On the train, Fred meets Edna Baker, a nice girl who is coming to New York on a visit, and falls in love with her, but soon forgets her when he meets Sears and Mrs. Sears's attractive young sister, Eileen. The thing Fred doesn't realize is that he is being used by Sears and his sister-in-law. Sears offers to work with Fred only because he has had a long dry spell and is desperate for a hit, and Eileen, who is really the recently discarded mistress of a song publisher, and a tough dame underneath the beautiful exterior, allows herself to become engaged to Fred only because he helps Sears write a hit song called *June Moon* and begins to earn a lot of money. In the end, however, a cynical but kind-hearted piano player named Maxie manages to make Fred see the light and helps him back into Edna's arms.

But the plot, of course, wasn't the important element. As in the short story, the valuable thing would be the endless opportunities to satirize the songwriting industry and have fun with it. The Sears-Stevens collaborative song, *June Moon*, for example, would become successful not because of originality, but because it is so ordinary and so similar to a lot of other songs. There would be a reference to the practice of songwriters to compose tunes about various states: "If songwriters always wrote about their home state," Maxie would say, "what a big Jewish population Tennessee must have!" There would be a reference to a songwriter who was using up his ideas too rapidly; he had recently completed a composition called *Montana Moon*, and thereby committed the unpardonable sin of using up a state and a moon in the same song. There would also be a discussion about a song telling the sad story of a girl who had an illegitimate child; the song would not only make a moral point but "you can also dance to it." And, most important of all, Fred Stevens would be a typical Lardner hero—or, more accurately, principal character—sincere and goodhearted and dumb and English-fracturing as he expresses things like his vow to desecrate himself to the piano.

Kaufman had one further suggestion: that the name of the play be the same as the hit song which Sears and Fred write, *June Moon*, rather than *Some Like Them Cold*. Lardner resisted the suggestion a bit at first, feeling that, since his story was so well-known, the retention of the original title might give the play some added commercial value. But Kaufman persisted in his low-key convincing way, pointing out that whereas *Some Like Them Cold* didn't really conjure up any special pictures, *June Moon* was evocative immediately of the theme of the play, the essential corniness of much of the current Tin Pan Alley product and the comment that that fact made on public taste. Lardner finally agreed, and never regretted his agreement. The title became famous from the day it was first announced; people even seemed to enjoy just saying it.

Lardner worked on the first draft of the play throughout the spring of 1929, putting himself on a seven-days-a-week schedule and working every day from early morning until late each night. He followed Kaufman's detailed blueprint but discovered with relief that the structural plan did not impede him in any way when he set out to employ some of his special little tricks of characterization or insert some of his wild and unique humor lines. When he delivered his draft to Kaufman, however, to see if his more experienced partner had any rewrite suggestions, he found that Kaufman had plenty: literally hundreds, in fact. Many of the lines, Kaufman said, just wouldn't play: they looked all right on the printed page, but, Kaufman was certain, wouldn't emerge as believable spoken speech on the stage. Some of the little bits of business designed to characterize people in the play wouldn't work: they would either be too unclear or too slow. And you couldn't be as leisurely in your characterizations as you could sometimes be in a story or a novel: you had to label and identify the people on the stage almost at first look and first speech. There were other problems, too—small twists in the plot which were turning out, at least for the play version, to be wrong and unnecessary, lines and speeches which weren't true to the characters who said them, and many other things.

Now Kaufman called for a series of daily meetings, and, at these work sessions, explained all of the problems in detail, slowly, reasonably, and never overbearingly, making every point strictly as a suggestion and explaining why he was suggesting it. He also discussed at length why and how he thought the changes could be made without altering or doing damage to Lardner's original intentions in the story and in the play, with Lardner listening in silence and nodding solemnly and making note after note until the piles of notes grew higher than his original manuscript.

When Kaufman had discussed Lardner's script from the first page to the last, he began to make many of the changes himself, adding dozens of his own sparkling and hilarious lines, but never in the egocentric, overriding way in which Cohan had worked on *Elmer the Great*. Every alteration or addition Kaufman made, even those he'd already outlined pretty much word for word when he'd first described the existing problems to Lardner, was weighed again to see if it would fit into the over-all tone and point of view of the play, and then discussed once more with Lardner before actually being inserted.

All the rest of the changes, the ones Lardner could handle best, were left for him, and he picked up his pile of notes and his manuscript with all the new hand-written interlineations and returned to his typewriter. He did not, as another writer might have done, work only on the remaining lines and scenes which still needed changes. He put fresh paper into his typewriter and began to type the entire play from beginning to end, rewriting and repairing as he went along. When he was finished, he delivered his new script to Kaufman, and again Kaufman read the script and told him that a lot of changes were necessary. More daily work sessions were set up in which Kaufman made some of the changes and advised Lardner on how to make the rest.

The process was repeated a half dozen times in the next several months, and each time Lardner refused to take short-cuts and concentrate only on the sections requiring repairs; he broke out fresh reams of paper and ran the play through his typewriter again from Page One to the final curtain. It was backbreaking work, and it required immense discipline on his part. There were several times when, in retyping a long scene, he decided that it was the entire scene which wasn't right and not just some of its lines, and he ended up throwing out more than sixty pages each time and starting again from scratch. But it was the way he preferred to work, and the way he had always worked. He wasn't, he once told a friend, a carpenter who could build a part of a house and leave the rest to the bricklayer and the plasterer and the glazier and all the others; he just couldn't pick up an isolated section of a story in a casual, detached way and work on it. In order to tell a story right, he had to feel it by living along with his characters from beginning to end. The method worked for him. In its final version, *June Moon* is a smooth, flowing, beautifully integrated work.

By early summer, Kaufman felt that the play was ready for a try-out. Sam H. Harris had agreed to produce it, and arranged to give the play a trial run in Atlantic City. "Do you think we're okay?" Lardner asked Kaufman. "That," Kaufman said grimly, "is what we'll find out in Atlantic City."

The performances, beginning in Atlantic City on July 29, were disasters; it was clear from the first showing that Kaufman and Lardner weren't okay at all. The first act worked beautifully, but the second and third acts fell apart. Sadly, Lardner went for a solitary walk on the boardwalk, and the gloomy realization was confirmed as he was stopped three times by people who had been in the audience. "Your first act is great," the first man said, "but the last two acts need a lot of bolstering." "I'd say that you have a good first act," the second man told him, "but your second and third acts really need a lot of work." "Great first act," the third man said, "but you'd better do some surgery on the last two." When he was stopped a fourth time, Lardner began to bristle, but the fourth man turned out to be an acquaintance he hadn't seen in years, a baseball umpire who didn't even know he'd written a play. "Why, hello, Ring!" the umpire said in surprise. "What are *you* doing in Atlantic City?" "What could I say?" Lardner subsequently reported. "I told him, 'I'm down here with an act.'"

Kaufman and Lardner returned to New York for more work sessions, and then Lardner rented a suite at the Pennsylvania, a hotel he liked, and began another of his stem to stern revisions. He took the suite so that he could work in complete isolation and without interruptions, but couldn't resist causing an occasional interruption of his own by inviting a few friends over now and then for small drinking parties. This turned out to be fortunate, because one of the parties helped him over one of his most serious hurdles. A big problem in Atlantic City had been the fact that the second act had ended limply, and neither Kaufman nor Lardner had been able to come up with a better finish since that time. But Lardner got an idea when, right in the middle of one of the parties at the Pennsylvania, a hotel employee entered his suite and began to wash the windows. Lardner phoned Kaufman and told him the idea; Kaufman liked it and told him to use it; and, as both men had sensed, the new second act finish rocked audiences with laughter when the play opened again.

The setting is a music publisher's office, and it is empty for a moment as the end of the second act approaches. Suddenly, the window washer spots a piano in the room and eyes it for a moment, then finally places his sponge on the window sill and starts to pick out a tune on the piano, tentatively at first and then more and more loudly. (Lardner and Kaufman had decided to write and insert a few awful and extremely unoriginal songs into the play, and the song is one of these, *Hello Tokio*.) Soon, the window washer is playing and singing the song enthusiastically.

The stage directions for the rest of the act tell the funny finish: "The window washer is plunging recklessly into it, oblivious of his surroundings, when Maxie the piano-player comes in behind him. Maxie stands perfectly still for a second, taking in the situation. Then he makes up his mind. Turn about, he decides, is fair play. He picks up the sponge and starts washing the window."

Kaufman also had a touch of his own to add to the play, based on a story Oscar Levant had once told him. Levant had gone to visit Irving Berlin at Berlin's music-publishing company, and, in passing the tiny office of one of Berlin's orchestrators, had noticed that the orchestrator had a picture of Beethoven on his wall. This in itself was unusual in an office of a firm devoted to popular music, but the orchestrator had further improved the scenery by writing an inscription on the picture. The inscription read:

To a swell little arranger
Ludwig

This, too, was used with hilarious results.

The authors finished their revisions at the end of the summer, and the play went into rehearsal immediately afterward. Norman Foster, a popular young actor then married to Claudette Colbert, and who later became an important film director and producer, played Fred Stevens; a pretty actress named Linda Watkins played Edna Baker; Lee Patrick, later the wife or the other woman in a hundred movies, appeared as Eileen; and Florence Rice, daughter of Grantland Rice, the sportswriter, made her first stage appearance in a small role. The part of Maxie was played by a man named Harry Rosenthal, an inspired casting choice credited solely to Lardner because nearly everybody thought he was crazy when he first suggested it. Rosenthal was not an actor at all; he was a real piano player who appeared mostly at one of Lardner's favorite restaurants, Joe Smallwood's, in Garden City, Long Island, not too far from Great Neck, and often accompanied his playing with precisely the kind of funny, cynical commentary spoken by Maxie throughout the play. Lardner's suggestion met with strong opposition when it became clear that he was serious about it, but he persisted, finally prevailed, and was proven right. Rosenthal outshone the professional actors and became, at least temporarily, a celebrity.

It was obvious from the very first rehearsal that this time the play was right on the nose; this time everything worked. Jubilantly, Lardner wrote a funny introduction for the play's program, calling it *Let George Do It* and pointing out that he always worked with people named George—first Cohan, now Kaufman, and next, presumably, George Bernard Shaw. He went on to hint, however, that he had had to hold Kaufman down, because Kaufman had noted that a play called *Journey's End* had no women characters and a play called *One Beautiful Evening* had no men characters, and had wanted to emulate both of them by writing a play which had no characters at all. In regard to *One Beautiful Evening*, he added, Kaufman had commented that *he* would never dream of giving a play a title like that, because it might turn out to be prophetic of the play's total run. Lardner also wrote gag biographies of the actors for the playbill, calling Norman Foster ideally suited to play the songwriter because "he is the stepfather of Stephen Foster, who turned out such smash hits as *Swanee River* and *Old Black Jolson*," saying that Linda Watkins "won instant recognition from the critics for her portrayal of Ibsen in the play of that name," and confiding that "Florence Rice's parents have no idea that she is on the stage, and every time she leaves the house she tells them she has to run down to buy a stamp."

The play opened at the Broadhurst Theatre on Wednesday, October 9, 1929, and it was a smash hit. "The theatre that aims at amusement alone," George Jean Nathan said in *The American Mercury*, "which isn't such a bad aim after all, is represented in Ring Lardner's and George S. Kaufman's *June Moon*, as funny a spiel as has come this way in some time." "From the first curtain to the last," *Vogue* reported, "audiences laugh almost without interruption. Yet there are very few lines in the entire comedy that, if quoted out of their context, would seem funny. *June Moon* should assist greatly in putting the quietus on the mere phrasemakers, the wise-crackers, the apostles of the New Wit. Every word belongs to the situation, the milieu, the character who speaks it; there is no striving for cleverness, no straining for a guffaw—every one of the thousand laughs is indigenous and spontaneous. The authors have treated their fable with a fine, indulgent sympathy and a gay irresponsibility that is irresistible." And *Variety* loved it, too, though Kaufman and Lardner, remembering all the work and all the revisions and all the agony, winced in unison when they read the review's opening line. "This one," *Variety* said, "wrote itself."

June Moon ran on Broadway for 273 performances, and a touring company was equally successful, playing in Chicago for ten weeks, in Philadelphia for four weeks, and with additional runs in Cleveland, Cincinnati, Milwaukee, St. Louis, Kansas City, Boston, Los Angeles, and elsewhere. Mantle picked it for *The Best Plays of 1929–30*, and Scribner's published the play in book form with a deadpan introduction by Lardner which began, "In the year 1898 there were 201 fatal street accidents in the city of New York," and went on to give a page and a half of other statistics without ever mentioning *June Moon* at all. The play was also bought for filming by Paramount-Publix and released in March 1931 with an adaptation and screenplay by Mankiewicz in collaboration with a writer named Keene

Thompson, and with Jack Oakie playing Fred and Frances Dee playing Edna, and was remade in 1937 under the title of *Blonde Trouble*. A music publisher even bought the rights to two of the terrible songs Kaufman and Lardner had written for the play, *June Moon* and *Montana Moon*, bringing them out, because they were so derivative, with the byline, "Eavesdropped by Ring Lardner and George S. Kaufman." The songs confirmed the play's comments on Tin Pan Alley and public taste by achieving strong sheet-music sales.

It should have been a time of high triumph for Lardner, and, for a very brief period, it was. He finally had his hit Broadway play, and his hard work on *June Moon* also seemed to spark his productivity in other areas. 1929 became and remained his most successful year in the publishing field, with eight of his stories and nineteen of his articles appearing in magazines. He enjoyed the play's success immensely, passing the Broadhurst again and again to look at his name on the marquee, wandering around backstage, and listening with particular pleasure whenever anyone mentioned that he had seen the play more than once. Lardner also talked to Kaufman about a second collaboration and secured Kaufman's agreement; the new play was to be a serious one on a subject very important to Lardner, alcoholism. But then, very suddenly, his deep unhappiness returned. He went off on one of the worst binges of his life, a bender which lasted three months, and he phoned Kaufman in the middle of it to ask if Kaufman thought box-office business would be affected if he committed suicide. The question was not humor, not even sick humor; Lardner had never managed to save much money, and the play income was essential to his family, and would become even more so if he were gone.

Kaufman managed to talk Lardner out of the idea, and he also helped sustain him through the few remaining years of his life by meeting with him regularly and talking over ideas and scenes for the new collaboration, even after it became obvious that Lardner was never really going to complete another play. But in those last years, Lardner remained almost constantly depressed, and, some years after he died, a few of his more mystical friends formed a new theory for his great unhappiness: the theory that he had lived with an accurate premonition of ultimate disaster for himself and his family. In retro spect, the theory becomes almost believable.

It really all began three years before *June Moon*, in the summer o 1926, when Lardner went for a routine physical examination an was stunned to learn that he was suffering from tuberculosis. Th ailment was in its earliest stages, but even early tuberculosis wa extremely serious in the '20s. The ailment was also particularl abhorrent to Lardner because he hated causing problems for othe people and was horrified at the thought that he might be spreadin an infectious disease. He insisted on going into the hospital eve though his case was mild enough to be treated at home; he hid th reason for his hospital stay even from close friends like Fitzgeralc and he would no longer embrace or even shake hands with his son The disease was soon arrested, but there were occasional recurrence and he was never again in totally good health throughout the remain ing seven years of his life.

His heavy drinking did not, of course, help matters, and after *Jun Moon* he occasionally told people that the only thing that kept hir alive was his hopes of another success with Kaufman. But he neve really got the play going, and, though he continued to write othe things, his output grew smaller and smaller. In 1930, he had only tw stories in magazines, and a substantial part of his writing productio after that was confined to brief reviews of radio programs for *Th New Yorker*. He was also invited to try a screen treatment fo Harold Lloyd, and he took a stab at it, but the attempt was half hearted and his material was rejected. More and more, he continue to pin his hopes on the play about alcoholism, and he expressed thi one day in a letter he wrote to a friend. "I am fortunate, I guess, he wrote, "to be one of those chosen to work with George. Ther are flocks of more experienced playwrights seeking his partnership an the only thing that wins consideration for me is the fact that he keep promises and as soon as we had finished *June Moon* we agreed to d another one on a subject I had in mind—as soon as I got around to it which has been a long, long time. I only hope I can stay well enoug to work. If I can, I promise you and the rest of the world on thing: that never again will I take a vacation when I am through wit a job. I think it is the biggest mistake a person can make—not to kee on going. I never felt better in my life than when I was working twenty hours a day, trying to get *June Moon* into shape, and never felt worse than afterward, when it was in shape and I treated myself to a layoff."

Other things kept *June Moon* on Lardner's mind and reminded him of how pleasant its success had felt at first. In 1932, the social season at Newport opened with a special showing of *June Moon* at the town's plush Casino Theatre, with many members of the original cast hired for the showing, and with Vanderbilts, Auchinclosses, Woodwards and other leading citizens rolling in the aisles. Around the same time, during a brief period in which Lardner was feeling better, he and his wife went to the track and saw that there was a horse named *June Moon* in one of the races; they bet on him and won across the board. And a year later, a producer named Thomas Kilpatrick brought the play back to Broadway, opening it at the Ambassador Theatre on Monday, May 15, 1933, with Harry Rosenthal given top billing this time, and it was a hit all over again.

But, sadly, there was to be no repetition of the experience for Lardner. On the morning of September 25, 1933, he suffered a heart attack, and shortly afterward lapsed into a coma. He never came out of it, and he was gone by evening. In going through his papers and files, later on, his family discovered that, though he had worked intermittently on the play about alcoholism since early in 1930, he had completed only the first act, one scene for the second act, and a few notes for the third act. All of it was awkwardly written, talky, undramatic, and simply not useable.

And as the mystics later noted, all four of his sons were pursued by a similarly dark Fate. His son James fought with the Lincoln Battalion in the Spanish Civil War and died during the Ebro offensive, lynched by Moors. David was killed during World War II. John died of a sudden heart attack, and was even younger than his father when he died; Ring had lived forty-eight years and six months, but John was two months short of his forty-eighth birthday. Ring, Jr., is still alive, but his career was nearly destroyed, and in some ways that is worse. He was one of the Hollywood writers victimized by McCarthyism, and he remained penniless and without work for years.

18. THE DIRECTOR

EARLY ONE MORNING in 1928, Kaufman received a telephone call which sent a cold chill through his heart. The call was from Jed Harris, who had been watching *The Royal Family* settle into a comfortable routine as a big hit and was now ready to begin work on a new project. "It's time," Harris said with his customary elegance, "that you stopped crapping yourself up that you're no director. I've got a new play I want you to direct for me."

The prospect terrified Kaufman. It was true, he had to admit, that he had some strong convictions about the right and wrong ways to direct a play, and it was also true that he had occasionally felt twinges of dissatisfaction at some of the things other directors had done with some of his own plays. But, on the other hand, his two personal forays into the directing profession had hardly been distinguished: he had

ended up labeling himself unqualified on *The Butter and Egg Man*
and had turned the reins over to Jimmy Gleason, and he had assisted
Howard Lindsay in shaping *The Good Fellow* into a play which had
lasted seven performances. Kaufman started to remind Harris of these
facts, but Harris wasn't listening; he rarely listened to anybody or
anything once he had made up his mind about something. "It's a play
by those nuts Hecht and MacArthur," Harris said, as he started to
hang up. "I'll send a copy over for you to read."

Kaufman knew both Ben Hecht and Charles MacArthur, and had
even heard about their play, though only the fact that it was called
The Front Page and that its principal character was a Chicago newspaperman. But that in itself indicated that the play might be good,
because Hecht and MacArthur had themselves both been newspapermen in Chicago and knew the milieu intimately. They were, in fact,
loaded with tough, authentic, and sometimes grimly funny stories
about Chicago newspaper life—stories like the time MacArthur had
covered the public execution of a convicted murderer and seen the
man pause as he mounted the rickety steps of the scaffold leading up
to the noose and ask in complete seriousness, "Is this thing safe?" and
the time Hecht had stolen a photo of another murderer from a shelf
in the man's apartment, right under the noses of the man's family,
and had almost been thrown in jail himself for the theft.

The fact, however, that Harris was producing the play was mildly
surprising to Kaufman, because Harris was being offered a lot of
plays, and obviously had liked this one a lot to select it over all the
competition. And it was difficult to envision a play all *that* good from
Hecht and MacArthur, because they were such an unlikely team. The
only similarity in their background was their Chicago newspaper work.

Hecht was born on New York's Lower East Side, the son of Rus-
sian-Jewish immigrants, and, when his family moved to the Midwest,
brought up in Racine, Wisconsin, and Chicago. He was short, fast-
talking, and flashy; he wore loud clothes, bow ties, and a mustache.
He had been a child prodigy on the violin good enough to give
concerts at the age of ten; he had spent his high school vacations
working as an acrobat in a circus in which his mother's brother was
the strongman; and he entered newspaper work at the age of
seventeen by getting a job on the Chicago *Journal* as a "picture

[343]

snatcher," a man who had to provide illustrations for current news stories by any means necessary. He was brash, abrasive, and tough; and in later life, as an extremely successful screenwriter, earning as much as $400,000 a year, he achieved fame when, asked to spend a train trip from Los Angeles to New York working on another writer's bad script, and at a price he considered inadequate, he took on the deal but stipulated that he'd work only as far as Kansas City. He also, in a town where most screenwriters trembled at the sight of important studio executives, once told off a studio head who tried to advise him on how to develop a screenplay. "Look, imbecile," Hecht said. "I'm here at your request to do a script for your goddam movie. I'm a writer and you're not, and what's more, I'm a writer who knows his business. So I don't want any of your goddam horning in." And the studio head, bewildered by the unprecedented treatment, agreed meekly and left him alone.

MacArthur, born in Scranton, Pennsylvania, on November 5, 1895, was, on the other hand, the son of a minister and educated at the posh Wilson Memorial Academy in Nyack, New York. He was tall, quietly dressed, obliging, extremely handsome, and so charming that Dorothy Parker fell hopelessly in love with him when they first met at an Algonquin luncheon in 1922, a passion so strong that another occasional visitor to the Round Table, Donald Ogden Stewart, later commented, "Charlie was something else. Charlie was marvelous . . . and she was so in love it was really a serious, desperate thing . . . it was really the works. She fell in love so deeply: she was wide open to Charlie." Nearly everyone else liked MacArthur tremendously, too; Woollcott once said about him, "Everybody who knows him always lights up and starts talking about him as if he was a marvelous circus." Even the cynical and suspicious Hecht had liked him immediately when they first met in Chicago, later saying, "Charlie seemed never interested in attracting anyone, yet people scampered toward him as if pulled by a magnet."

MacArthur was no stuffed shirt; the reference to a circus in Woollcott's comment stemmed from the fact that MacArthur's sense of humor was sometimes as wild and unfettered as the more flamboyant people with whom he associated, particularly when, as occasionally happened, he drank too long and too deeply. Early in his newspaper career, he got into trouble when, waiting to interview Otto H. Kahn, the banker, he passed the time in a manner similar to Irving Berlin's arranger; he was caught pulling Greek volumes from the shelves of Kahn's library and inscribing them:

> To my friend Otto,
>   without whose help this could not have been written
>   Socrates

He also once, on a voyage to Europe with Woollcott, emerged from his cabin and told Woollcott uneasily, "I can't get over the feeling that I'm on a boat." And once, when he, like Hecht, moved to Hollywood, he hired a plane and bombed the homes of several producers with empty whiskey bottles.

Despite the difference in their personalities and approach, Hecht and MacArthur became friends in Chicago, and even closer friends when they happened to meet again after both had moved to New York. The *Front Page*, however, was their first collaboration. Hecht had begun writing when, just after the First World War, he found himself $3000 in debt and earning only $40 a week on the Chicago *News*, to which he had moved from the *Journal* in 1914. He dashed off a quick short story called *The Unlovely Sin* and sent it to H. L. Mencken at *Smart Set*, a magazine edited by Mencken and George Jean Nathan, in the innocent hope that Mencken would pay at least $1000 for it if he bought it. Mencken bought the story, but paid his usual price, $45. The shock stopped Hecht only for about an hour. He soon accepted the fact that he would have to write twenty-three stories to earn that thousand dollars, and in the next few months wrote and sold twenty-five stories to *Smart Set*, sometimes having as many as eight stories under various names in a single issue. He also wrote several books, but their sale was modest, and when he broke into the play field with two productions, *The Egotist*, an original play, produced on Broadway in 1922, and *The Stork*, a French play by Laszlo Fodor which Hecht adapted in 1925, they fared rather poorly, too. MacArthur's situation was pretty much the same: after turning from newspaper work to playwriting, he collaborated with Edward Sheldon on a hit, *Lulu Belle*, produced in 1926, but then slipped backward two years later with *Salvation*, a quick failure written with Sidney

Howard. As Kaufman discovered when he received the script of *The Front Page* and began to read it, it took the merging of the two talents to cause real fireworks.

In the present period of relative freedom from censorship, with bedroom and nudity scenes a commonplace in films and on the stage, and with even repeated use of the popular Anglo-Saxon verb which used to mean "to plant" no longer automatically earning an X rating in pictures, a play like *The Front Page* would not raise a single eyebrow, not even the hairy parentheses of a Sunday school superintendent. But to Kaufman, reading the manuscript nearly five decades ago, the play was a revelation and a revolution. In 1928, even plays labeled as realistic weren't truly realistic; they censored themselves by avoiding impolite language, nearly always portrayed their male leads as heroic, or at least gentlemanly, and used the name of the Deity in strictly respectful ways. *The Front Page* did none of these things. The play's principal character was callous, vulgar, drunken, and unprincipled; the play blasphemed God at every turn; and it was loaded with words which were not—in those days, anyway—found in dictionaries.

There had been a minor breakthrough four years before that with *What Price Glory?*, which used a few mild four-letter words and created quite a sensation, a furor which died down only when newspaper commentators, feeling very liberal about it, told people that that, after all, was probably the way men really talked "in the passion of battle." As any ex-serviceman can testify, remembering the constant check he had to keep on his tongue when he first returned to civilian life and his family, the words in *What Price Glory?* aren't really the language of men at war at all; they're the merest hint, the most cautious and careful suggestion, of real wartime talk. But *The Front Page* moved a thousand miles in the direction of reality. The reporters in the play were tough and casually cold-blooded and habitual users of four-letter words because Hecht and MacArthur knew from personal experience that that is the way men became when they covered a police beat for some of the more rough-and-tumble Chicago newspapers. They were not gentlemanly and scholarly reporters for the New York *Times*, which one of the characters in the play, an ex-*Times* man, describes disparagingly as "like working in a bank." They were members of a yellower and more vigorous journalism, grown casual about violence and venality and vulgarity not necessarily because they were amoral but because they came across so much of it in their daily work, in the same way that medical students grow faint or nauseated at their first sight of a cadaver or an operation but eventually eat sandwiches while a corpse or an excised organ lies three feet away from them. There is eventual total acceptance of the milieu, police reporters will tell you, and eventual development of a special and unique brand of profane humor. Detectives will talk about baseball and their families while a captured rapist hangs suspended in a detention cell across the room, his arms above his head and handcuffed to a restraint bar, and say things like, "That bastard is so dumb he spells shit with two t's," and police reporters begin to think and talk in the same way. That atmosphere, Kaufman discovered as he read, was portrayed brilliantly in the Hecht-MacArthur play.

The play's plot has become familiar to nearly everyone in the years since 1928; it is about a reporter named Hildy Johnson who has grown disillusioned with his job and the way it has taken over and colored his entire life, and is completing his final assignment before leaving for New York to be married and start a job in an entirely different field. The assignment is the coverage of the execution of a convicted murderer named Earl Williams; there is some question about whether or not Williams is really guilty, but it no longer matters because an ambitious and unscrupulous mayor and sheriff have railroaded him into a conviction and he will soon be dead. Suddenly, however, sirens begin to scream all over the building, and it develops that Williams has escaped. All the reporters except Hildy rush out to get details, but Hildy is too bored to do even that, and so he is alone in the room when Williams climbs in through the window. Hildy talks to him and finds him a tired and defeated man who is already regretting his escape attempt and has nearly decided to give up and allow himself to be executed.

One of the reasons Hildy is quitting his job is his editor, Walter Burns, a vitriolic, sarcastic, driving man who will do anything to get a story or a picture to illustrate it. The character, Hecht and MacArthur later admitted, was based on a real-life editor they had both known back in Chicago; they had even used his real first name. He was

Walter C. Howey, born in Fort Dodge, Iowa, on January 16, 1882, who had first become well-known in Chicago as the city editor of the *Tribune,* but quit the paper after a dispute with Joseph M. Patterson, then the *Tribune*'s co-publisher. Howey immediately walked six blocks across town to the offices of a Hearst paper, the *Herald and Examiner,* and got a job there. He remained a Hearst man for the rest of his life, helping Hearst set up the New York *Mirror,* serving as supervising editor of *The American Weekly,* Hearst's Sunday supplement magazine, and working at the time of his death at the age of seventy-two as editor-in-chief of Hearst's Boston papers, the *Record,* the *American,* and the *Sunday Advertiser.* Howey admitted frankly throughout his career that he would lie, cheat, employ trickery, cajole, plead, bribe, and tongue-lash his employees to get a story or a picture, but his papers were often the ones to get exclusive stories. He was also well-connected politically. In 1919, the *Herald and Examiner* was the only Chicago paper to back a mayoralty candidate named Big Bill Thompson, who ran on an anti-British ticket connected with an impending visit to Chicago by the British monarch, and whose slogan, "Keep King George out of Chicago," appealed to the town's many Irish voters. When Thompson won, he gave the paper "on permanent loan" two patrolmen and a sergeant, who arrested and delivered people Howey wanted to see, and interrogated people from whom Howey wanted specific areas of information.

Hecht and MacArthur had made Walter Burns exactly the same type of man. But, as Hildy continues to talk to Williams, he forgets his dislike of Burns and just about everything else, including the fact that his bride-to-be and her mother are waiting. He begins to think only of the prospect of a scoop. He phones Burns for instructions, and then persuades Williams to hide inside a rolltop desk until his paper can run his story and the exclusive details he's gotten from Williams.

In the final act, the police discover Williams inside the desk, but by then it's all right: Williams's innocence has become unquestionable, and a stay of execution has come in for him. Hildy prepares to leave for New York with his future wife and her mother, deaf to Burns's insistence that he is a born newspaperman and too good to desert Chicago and his job. Burns finally capitulates and bids him goodbye, giving Hildy, as a farewell present, his most valued possession, a watch he himself had earned and which carries the inscription, *To the best newspaperman I know*. But at the very end of the play, Burns reveals that it's all a trick to keep Hildy in Chicago. Right after Hildy leaves, Burns phones the police and tells them he wants the reporter arrested. "The son of a bitch," he says, "stole my watch."

The plot was interesting and amusing enough, but the real quality of the play stemmed from its toughness, authenticity, and irreverence. "H. Sebastian God!" a reporter shouts, in a line never before used in a play for fear of offense to the clergy. "I'm trying to concentrate!" The pressroom is as filthy and litter-strewn as police pressrooms usually are, and a single esthete among the newspapermen who goes around squirting antiseptic is treated with contempt and scorn. The politicians in the play are, without exception, portrayed as venal, and the message is clear: Aren't they all? Another character, Williams's girl friend, is a type of woman extremely rare at that time on the American stage: an out-and-out hooker. And the reporters behave throughout the play the way reporters of that type really behaved, covering the impending execution and the escape, but also dealing simultaneously by telephone with other items under their purview—things like talking to the victim of a Peeping Tom and getting details about a baby born in a police car to a young mother being rushed to a hospital.

Kaufman, phoning Harris to give his opinion of the play, did not have to hesitate at all; he phoned the moment he put down the script. The play, he said, needed a little work here and there, but, these relatively minor things aside, he thought it was great.

The question of whether or not he felt equipped to direct it, however, was another matter again, and for that, he told Harris, he wanted considerably more time. That evening, as he often did when he was troubled and uncertain about his own abilities, a condition which was practically constant, he turned to Beatrice for advice. Beatrice's response was instant and emphatic. She had felt for a long time, she said, that he should become involved in directing, and then more and more involved, so that he could eventually direct all of his own plays and keep some of the idiots who functioned as directors around town from getting their dumb hands on his work. She concluded by saying that she thought he would become the best director in the business once he understood the job the way he had come to understand playwriting. Her statement, Kaufman later admitted to friends, was exactly the kind of encouraging and comforting advice he had wanted to hear, but he studied it warily nevertheless, his mind moving around and around it like a dog circling a dinosaur bone, wondering if it was really genuine.

In the end, he decided that it was: Beatrice was simply not capable of dispensing what was then called soothing syrup. As always, she was stating what she truly felt and thought, and Kaufman also knew, after eleven years of marriage, that what Beatrice truly felt and thought was nearly always right. There was still considerable doubt in his own mind about his talents as a director, but since Beatrice had been so strong in her reply, and since Harris also seemed extremely confident, calling him five times in two days and urging an affirmative response, he finally gave it. "Well," he told Harris, his voice pitched very low so that the producer would not hear the tremor in the tones, "if you really want me to take a shot at it, I'll take a shot at it."

Unfortunately, Beatrice didn't remain in town for very long to continue to encourage him. On Saturday, May 19, she sailed for Europe on the S.S. *Roma* with Woollcott, Harpo Marx, and Alice Duer Miller. Woollcott had rented a villa in France for the summer, a lovely old house on a cliff overlooking the Mediterranean not far from Cap d'Antibes, and had persuaded the other three people to join him there for the hot months.

The summer trip to Europe was a switch for Woollcott, who had begun to spend nearly all of his non-working time at a stone house he had built for himself on Neshobe Island, an eight-acre strip of wooded land, seven miles long and a mile and a half wide, located in the middle of Lake Bomoseen, Vermont, near the western border of the state. The little island had originally been owned by a young New York lawyer named Enos Booth and his wife, and Woollcott had first seen the place when a sculptor named Sally Farnham, who was a friend of his and of the Booths, took him, Neysa McMein, Janet Flanner, who now writes the *Letter from Paris* articles for *The New Yorker* under the pseudonym of "Genêt," and Raymond C. Ives, a prominent insurance executive, up to spend a weekend with the Booths. The Booths' summer home on the island was pretty primitive; it was illuminated by kerosene lamps, heated on cool evenings by a wood stove, and had only outdoor plumbing. But Woollcott fell in love almost immediately with the wild, solitary beauty of the place, which wasn't difficult to do. Even Harpo Marx grew serious about Neshobe Island in his memoirs, describing the island lyrically as containing "a wonderful variety of terrain and vegetation—miniature meadows, hills and cliffs, quarries and beaches, wild flowers, flowering vines and bushes, maples and evergreens. The water surrounding the island was forever changing. It could be as smooth as glass one minute, then suddenly churning with whitecaps, from updrafts and downdrafts of mountain winds."

Woollcott soon persuaded the Booths to sell the island to him and his friends, envisioning it as a kind of communal retreat rather like the colony in which he had grown up in Phalanx, New Jersey. Fees were set at $1000 for initiation and $100 for yearly dues, and, in addition to Woollcott, charter members of the ownership group included Beatrice, Alice Duer Miller, Ruth Gordon, Neysa McMein, Raoul Fleischmann, and Harold Guinzburg. But Woollcott found himself chafed by some of the more inelegant aspects of the place, objecting mostly to the fact that the household help consisted solely of a general handyman named Bathless Bill and his common-law wife, an equally aromatic lady who cooked meals which were anything but gourmet. A controversy developed with some of the other owners who insisted that the simple life was, after all, the reason they had first been attracted to the place. Woollcott, of course, won the argument. He bought up controlling interest in the island and built a modern stone house not far from the small Booth residence, which had been serving as a clubhouse for the members. And since all of his friends continued to come up to the island exactly as before, even though some of them were no longer shareholders, and brought along with them entertaining guests like Dorothy Parker, Harpo Marx, S. N. Behrman, Ethel Barrymore, Noël Coward, Irene Castle, and Alfred Lunt and Lynn Fontanne, Neshobe Island became for the rest of Woollcott's life a blissful residence and hideaway. He was so happy there that he was able to ignore the fact that native Vermonters frequently rowed close to the island to observe the celebrities, and he was even able to smile at the time a woman in a rowboat pointed to a figure floating sleepily in the water and shrieked to her friend, "Look —there's Marie Dressler!" The figure was actually Woollcott himself, his belly mistaken for Miss Dressler's massive bosom.

But for the summer of 1928, Woollcott decided that he and his friends needed some of that old-style European culture, and, as Kaufman began to struggle with *The Front Page*, Beatrice went to Antibes and began to have herself a ball. Most of this was due to Harpo Marx, who continued to behave in even more lunatic fashion offstage than on. He even saved the quartet from spending the first week of their vacation in total boredom.

The group had to stay that first week at a tiny hotel, the Antibes, because the villa wasn't quite ready for them. Woollcott made the mistake of insisting on the Antibes because it was off the tourist path and occupied mostly by elderly and dignified Frenchmen and French-women, forgetting—or refusing to accept—the fact that they would be considered tourists, too, and snubbed. Harpo discovered that the lone object provided, grudgingly, for the entertainment of the guests, a one-franc slot machine in the lobby, made a terrible, grinding sound when played, and upset all the elderly guests sitting around the place. He took his revenge by gathering together a lot of one-franc coins and dropping one or more into the machine every time he passed it. His decision to infuriate the local residents, however, ended up achieving precisely the opposite effect. When he dropped a coin in one time and started to walk away, he was stopped in his tracks by the totally unexpected sound of hundreds of coins gushing forth. This changed everything. Every Frenchman in the hotel shook Harpo's hand, people began to buy the group drinks, and, when the party left for the house Woollcott had rented, the Villa Galanon, it was Harpo whom the desk clerk hurried forward to bid goodbye, and not Woollcott. The reason was simple. Literary celebrities were a franc a dozen on the Riviera, but Harpo was the first person to hit a jackpot on the Antibes Hotel's slot machine in nearly four years.

Harpo continued to keep things informal and relaxed after the group moved into the villa, preventing Woollcott from sopping up all of the culture he was seeking but making things a lot more fun. The Villa

Galanon was presided over by an imperious combination chef-chauffeur named Guy. Guy was upset at first because Harpo made exaggerated gagging sounds at some of his more exotic concoctions and refused to eat them, but ended up finding Harpo as lovable as the rest of the world and cooking simple dishes for him, even though he remained puzzled to the end about why a man would have a name which was either Harpon, which meant harpoon, or Appeau, which meant birdcall. Harpo also enlivened the quartet's stay by gaining entry to the Monte Carlo Casino along with the others, after he had been barred for appearing tieless at the front door, by fashioning a makeshift bow tie out of one of his black socks. He then mourned a loss of a thousand francs at roulette by standing on his head in a corner of the casino until officials made him get on his feet again, went around after that asking people for a suitable and quiet place where he could commit suicide, and was finally given his thousand francs back and escorted out of the casino and begged never to return. And when Alice Duer Miller left for Egypt because her friend Pearl White, the movie serial queen, was there and had invited her to come, writing mysteriously and intriguingly, "I think you ought to know I'm living with an Egyptian prince," and was replaced in the villa by Ruth Gordon, Harpo immediately took the actress to several local bistros and got both of them drunk. It took only a couple of drinks apiece because neither of them was a drinker. But it was enough to send the pair scrambling around the countryside, where Harpo succeeded in bewildering a substantial percentage of the citizenry by pleading for the most direct route to Cincinnati.

Harpo was equally unawed by the more intellectual types he met on the Riviera, some of whom were held in considerable reverence by Woollcott and even by Beatrice. Woollcott took Harpo one day to W. Somerset Maugham's villa, one of the most beautiful houses on the Riviera, a cool and lovely place built around a swimming pool fed by four springs, with the walls covered by tropical flowers and major Impressionist and Post-Impressionist paintings. Harpo listened in silence when Maugham showed them around the house. But then, when Maugham lifted the window of his own bedroom to point to the pool below, Harpo stripped naked immediately and dived into the pool. Woollcott was horrified, but Maugham was delighted; he took off his own clothes and followed Harpo through the window. (Harpo, incidentally, continued to try to shock Maugham for years after that, but never succeeded. Years later, Harpo spotted Maugham in the dignified company of S. N. Behrman and others at a New York theatre, and scrambled, apelike, over to him across the seats. Maugham eyed him affectionately, and then said, "Sorry I haven't got a banana for you, Harpo.")

Nudity was also involved in Harpo's first encounter with George Bernard Shaw. Shaw and his wife were also staying at Antibes that summer, and Woollcott was nearly overcome with happiness when the couple accepted his invitation to come over to lunch one afternoon. Shaw was considered the prize catch of the social season but had been turning down most invitations, explaining with his usual calm acceptance of his own desirability that there simply weren't enough afternoons and evenings in the season. Woollcott went around in an ecstasy of anxiety for days before the arrival of the Shaws, conferring with Guy again and again to make sure the luncheon menu was outstanding without doing violence to the bearded playwright's celebrated vegetarianism. He spent hours selecting exactly the right wines, and constantly reminded all the members of the household to remain on their best behavior. The only person who was not impressed was Harpo, who asked disdainfully if Shaw had once been known as Bernie Schwartz, and then, an hour or so before the arrival of the playwright and his wife, wrapped a towel around his middle and went off for a solitary swim in the Mediterranean and a sunbath. Inevitably, it was Harpo who met the Shaws first, crossing the path of the arriving couple as he started to return to the house. Shaw's opening salute to Harpo was worthy of Harpo's own approach to celebrities. Shaw had been walking a little ahead of Mrs. Shaw, and he summoned her forward to meet Harpo. As she arrived, he suddenly seized Harpo's towel and threw it to the ground, telling his wife blandly that she was now gazing at the real Harpo Marx.

To Woollcott's great surprise and disgust, Harpo became Shaw's closest friend on the Riviera, presumably because he was the only one there who was not in awe of the playwright—a coupling which Woollcott described as "corned beef and roses." At the luncheon, Shaw grinned at Harpo's wink when a mention of Ellen Terry was cut short by Mrs. Shaw's pointed hammering with her spoon on the table. He also roared with laughter when Harpo lifted his beard, noted that he wore no tie underneath, and told him he could never get into the orchestra of the Loew's Delancey because that theatre, which then catered mostly to orthodox Jews, had a policy of making the same kind of examination and sending patrons sans ties up to the balcony. Shaw was not even offended when Harpo brought up a forbidden topic, the fact that Shaw's last play had been *The Apple Cart* and he hadn't written anything new for years, urging him to get busy on a new script. "Got any ideas?" Shaw asked pleasantly. And for the rest of the season, Harpo became the Shaws' unofficial chauffeur, borrowing Guy's car and spending long hours with them almost daily driving them up and down the Riviera.

It was a delightful time for the men and women at the Villa Galanon. They were invited to so many parties that even Harpo had to buy a tuxedo, selecting one of a bilious hue which made him famous in the area as "the American with the green tuxedo." They buzzed with amusement about other Riviera visitors like King Alfonso of Spain, who was so tone deaf that he included an Anthem Man in his entourage, an employee whose sole duty was to tell the monarch to stand up whenever the Spanish national anthem was played. They spent time with a lot of other friends passing through or staying nearby, going up to Paris once to meet Noël Coward at the railroad station and attempting to irritate Coward into losing his temper by having Harpo disguise himself as a ragged street musician and press for a tip. Coward, however, noticed that Harpo had selected a miniature harp for his instrument, calmly dropped a sixpence in his hat, and asked him where Woollcott was hiding. And they went on frequent side trips to places like Naples, where Beatrice spent hours at a local aquarium watching a weird variety of shellfish called a "sensitivo," a creature which popped immediately into its shell at the approach of any strange object and popped immediately out again when the object was gone, and Amalfi, where Harpo reversed the natural order of things by making a deal with a local citizen, whose job was to place prospective diners in chairs and carry them two hundred steps to a restaurant located at the top of a cliff, and carried the *bearer* up to the restaurant.

After the visit to the aquarium, Beatrice talked frequently about the strange shellfish she had watched in such fascination, saying she knew some people who were sensitivos but refusing to name names. Not long afterward, however, Woollcott was about to comment, in his usual tart fashion, that he thought he knew at least one of the people she had in mind. One sunny afternoon, Beatrice was summoned to the telephone, took a transatlantic call from Kaufman, and returned to tell the others that she was leaving immediately for the United States. Kaufman, it developed, had phoned to plead with her to return home, saying frankly, if shamefacedly, that he could not continue working as director on *The Front Page* if she were not around to hold his hand.

As a director, Kaufman was totally unlike anyone that Harris, the authors, and the actors in the play had ever encountered in the past. Most directors tended to bully the people with whom they worked, shouting if they were masculine types and shrieking if they weren't, and never giving a second thought to the fact that the people who were being bawled out might be embarrassed by the presence of other people onstage or in the auditorium. If a line didn't work and it was clearly the fault of the script, the director told this to the author right then and there, sometimes in terms so scathing and insulting that the playwright's face turned purple with rage or embarrassment. And if a line or a scene didn't play right and the director felt that an actor was at fault, he often stopped the rehearsal in mid-sentence and asked the man what it was that led him to believe he had any ability as an actor.

Kaufman didn't work that way at all. He sat quietly in a seat in the third or fourth row of the theatre, his eyes closed or half closed and his chin cradled in the palm of his hand, and sometimes he lifted his other hand to his mouth and chewed so gently on a well-manicured fingernail that he never really bit into it. Sometimes, very quietly, he pulled the paper off one of the candy bars he often carried with him, usually milk chocolate or fudge, and ate the candy, but he virtually never spoke or interrupted while a scene was in progress. It was only after a scene was finished that he uncurled his long legs, stood up, and summoned Hecht and MacArthur or one of the actors over to a quiet corner. And there, out of earshot of everyone else, he explained why a scene or a line was not right and asked that it be rewritten or played differently.

He was unique among directors in other ways as well. Most directors felt about directing the way Lardner felt about writing: they could work properly on a play only by becoming emotionally involved in it. For this reason, each day's rehearsal was generally called "from the top," with the actors starting from the first scene and moving through to the last, interrupted only by the director's frequent bursts of temper or hysteria, angry comments, and shouts that a line or scene be tried again differently. Kaufman did not feel at all the need to keep seeing and working on the play in its entirety. He was completely able to judge the validity and effectiveness of a scene played out of context and all by itself, and his technique was almost exactly the opposite of the usual. Because he felt that a good, strong ending was all-important, causing audiences to leave the theatre in the right frame of mind and tell their friends to go see the play, he generally started rehearsals with the very last scene, asking that the scene be played over and over, his requests made in a voice so soft that he sounded more apologetic than demanding, until the timing grew perfect. Then he worked his way backward through the play, skipping scenes and even whole series of scenes which had played well in previous rehearsals, and concentrating solely on those scenes in which there were things wrong. He rarely, as many other directors did, kept a copy of the script clutched in his hands for frequent consultation. Most of the time, when he called for a new scene to be played and sent the actors scurrying frantically to reread their "sides," the pages showing their individual parts, his own script copy lay unused on the seat next to him while he cued the scene in by quoting the first few lines word for word.

He also, observers at the rehearsals were quick to note, had as sharp an ear for a word or a line while directing as he had as a writer. Sometimes, when a scene had just been played, and was obviously very bad, he asked Hecht's and MacArthur's permission to kill a single line, and the scene was perfect when tried again. Sometimes even the excision of a single word would accomplish miracles, and a line over which an actor had stumbled, or which had fallen flat, was marvelously effective when tried again with its rhythm changed by the removal of the word. His instinct was unfailing, and he backed it up, he explained years later, with ordinary commonsense. Once, as he sat slumped in his seat with his eyes almost shut, his lips moved silently, and one actor asked another, loudly and nervously, "What do you suppose he's doing? He looks like he's counting, for God's sake!" That, in fact, was precisely what Kaufman was doing. He had discovered that an actor's exit was ineffective because his exit speech was taking longer to say than his legs were taking to get him offstage, and he was rushing the line. So Kaufman counted the words in the actor's exit line, got the authors to write a line with fewer words, and the exit worked beautifully.

Despite his appearance of quiet relaxation, Kaufman was generally exhausted by the rehearsals. But he was not too tired to pour out a long litany of woes when, finally, Beatrice reached New York and he went to the pier to pick her up. First of all, he said, Hecht and MacArthur were total madmen. They took absolutely nothing seriously, and, when he sent them off to rewrite some lines or some pages, he sometimes went to look for them and found that they hadn't written a thing, but had instead broken out a deck of cards and were busily playing rummy. "What do you do then?" Beatrice asked. "Well," Kaufman said, "I take the cards out of their hands and point them toward their typewriters." "And does that work?" Beatrice asked. "Well," Kaufman admitted, "sooner or later, they do get the right words written." "So what are you complaining about?" Beatrice asked. "We can't all be compulsive workers like you."

Kaufman moved to other complaints. He was becoming convinced that the actors, most of whom he had hired himself, were terrible; they forgot sections of the play a day or two after playing them perfectly, and he was certain that opening night would be a disaster. He was beginning to wonder if he was doing Hecht and MacArthur possible permanent damage, talking them into rewriting lines and scenes which he now suspected were better as written originally. He was experiencing grave doubts about his sense of timing, wondering if certain speeches he had slowed up should be faster and if other speeches he had sped up should be slower. He had even begun questioning the sanity of Jed Harris, who, after all, did behave rather eccentrically at times.

When Beatrice asked if there was any special reason which made him question Harris's sanity at this particular time, Kaufman explained that it was clearly extraordinary behavior for a man to risk backers' money by entrusting a play to a totally inexperienced director. It all came down to a plaint that Beatrice had often heard before from her self-doubting husband. Since George S. Kaufman was involved with the play, how could it possibly turn out good?

Nevertheless, even though Beatrice had heard it all before and had usually gone on to discover that her husband's fears were totally unfounded, she went to a rehearsal of *The Front Page* with a certain amount of trepidation—because this time Kaufman was even more vehement and convincing than usual. To her relief and amusement, the rehearsal was one of the smoothest she had ever attended. She had read the original script, so she could see that Hecht and MacArthur had already made a lot of good changes which clearly improved the play. The authors were also very amiable about making some further changes that Kaufman suggested at the rehearsal, and would undoubtedly actually make the changes once he took their cards away; and the actors were stumbling fewer times than was usual at rehearsals and would unquestionably stumble not at all once the play opened. "You'll be all right," Beatrice told Kaufman reassuringly, each time he came to her for sympathy after that.

The Front Page opened at the Times Square Theatre on Tuesday, August 14, 1928, with a company of actors who delivered their lines with perfect timing and never fumbled an entrance, exit, or speech. Lee Tracy played Hildy Johnson and achieved immense popularity which lasted most of his lifetime; he nearly always played tough, brash, fast-talking characters after that. Osgood Perkins was excellent as Walter Burns. Allen Jenkins was outstanding as a reporter and went on to become a fixture in pictures; Joseph Calleia, then called Joseph Spurin-Calleia, played another reporter and also went on to substantial success in films; Eduardo Cianelli, a sinister-looking actor who was really a gentle, cultured man who had been a physician back in Italy, played a gangster and proceeded to appear as a gangster a hundred times more in Hollywood productions; and Dorothy Stick-ney and George Barbier were exceptionally strong as the condemned man's girl friend and as the mayor. *The Front Page* ran 276 perform ances on Broadway and was followed by an equally successful tour it was picked by Mantle for *The Best Plays of 1928–29;* and it ha been revived repeatedly ever since.

As a film, *The Front Page* also began a long and successful caree for another actor, Pat O'Brien, Lardner's friend. The depressio had New York City in a tight grip when the movie rights to *Th Front Page* were bought by RKO in early 1930. Nearly 25,00 actors were out of work, and it was estimated that theatrical peopl owed landlords and landladies more than a half million dollars i back rents. O'Brien was one of the luckier ones. He had recentl finished working in a play for which he had received a salary o $275 a week, and was set to open in two weeks in another play *Tomorrow and Tomorrow*, produced by Gilbert Miller, at an im proved salary of $350 per week. For this reason, he was intereste but not overwhelmed when he was called to the phone at th Lambs Club and found himself talking to a representative fo Howard Hughes, then a mere multi-millionaire rather than a bil lionaire, and the man who would be producing the film version o the newspaper play for RKO.

The representative told O'Brien that Hughes wanted to sig him for the picture. When O'Brien remained silent, thinking hard the representative asked, "You played in the stage production, didn' you?" O'Brien had not been in the New York cast at all, but h answered calmly, "I did." "Good," the representative said. "Good Then Mr. Hughes wants you." O'Brien explained that it might no be possible, that he was about to open in a new play and woul have to see if he could get a release from Gilbert Miller. Ther was an instant's pause. Then the representative said, "Well, we'l talk again tomorrow," and hung up.

The next day, the actor learned that Hughes's representative ha phoned Miller and offered him $10,000 for O'Brien's release. Mille told O'Brien that he was willing in principle to release him if h wanted to be released, but only provided another actor that Mille had in mind agreed to talk over O'Brien's part. "Who's the actor?" O'Brien asked. "A man who should *really* be hired to appear in th film version of *The Front Page*," Miller told him. The man he ha in mind was Osgood Perkins, who had scored so strongly as Walter Burns in the original cast.

But Hollywood, in typical fashion, had passed over both Perkins and Lee Tracy for the film. Shortly afterward Perkins, who had told Miller he had to see a run-through of *Tomorrow and Tomorrow* in order to determine whether or not he wanted the part, watched a rehearsal and said he was willing to sign if O'Brien decided to leave. O'Brien was still uncertain, and went to talk to a more experienced actor in the play, Herbert Marshall, later to become an important film star himself. Marshall listened patiently, and then said, "Look, you say you've never been to California, and it could be the start of a whole new career for you. If I were in your place, I'd take the gamble." Then he added convincingly, "Anyway, is it much of a gamble to go to work for a man as rich and successful as Howard Hughes?" The next day, O'Brien signed with Hughes to play Hildy Johnson in the picture, under a five-year contract which started at $750 a week and brought him raises of $250 every six months.

O'Brien's casual duplicity didn't get found out until he had arrived in Hollywood and was attending a reading of the script on the set. A question arose concerning a scene in the New York production, the scene in which the frightened and half-collapsing accused murderer, Earl Williams, first appeared at the window of the pressroom. The question was whether Hildy had carried him over to hide him in the rolltop desk or merely led him there. The film's director, Lewis Milestone, turned to O'Brien and asked him which way he had done it. "Neither way," O'Brien said. "I've never played the Hildy Johnson role at all." As the silence grew louder and louder around him, he explained that, like Osgood Perkins, he had played the Walter Burns role—the one difference being that *he* had played it in a stock company in Cleveland. "I also," O'Brien added, "now have an unbreakable contract."

The silence, O'Brien later remembered, continued while everyone on the set stared at him in open-mouthed astonishment. Then Milestone sighed, put an arm around him, and said, "Let's go, Hildy. I think we've got a good picture going."

O'Brien received excellent notices, and the picture was a great financial success. It was also later remade, in 1940, as *His Girl Friday*, with a superb screenplay by Charles Lederer and with some significant alterations. The second time around, the producer realized that the principal character had a rather feminine-sounding first name and recast Hildy Johnson as a girl reporter, with Rosalind Russell playing the part. Cary Grant was both her editor and her ex-husband, determined to keep her around not only because of her prowess as a newspaperwoman but also because he was still in love with her. The new picture was loaded with fresh new gags, and, despite the complaints from some traditionalists who resented the changes in what had become a classic play and film, the second picture became even more successful and admired than the first. Two of the gags in the picture, in fact, achieved a sort of classic status of their own, and are mentioned respectfully to this day in articles about the art of the cinema. One is a throwaway line spoken by Grant, a reference to the time a man named Archie Leach was hung for doing something terrible. Archibald Leach, as most movie fans know, is Grant's real name. The other gag is a bit more physical: Grant, pleading that he and the girl reporter really musn't part because too much has gone on between them, emphasizes his argument by waving his hand back and forth, the hand hanging low beneath his waist. The censors missed the significance of the movement completely, apparently forgetting what goes on down there, but movie audiences roared with laughter.

The Front Page will soon be appearing in still another film version; it has just been penciled into the schedules at Universal with Jack Lemmon as Hildy Johnson and Walter Matthau as Walter Burns, and with a screenplay by Billy Wilder and I. A. L. Diamond, with Wilder as director, and with Paul Monash as producer. The newspaper drama has been lucky for everyone connected with it. Hecht, MacArthur, Hughes, Harris, Tracy, Perkins, O'Brien, Milestone, Grant, Rosalind Russell, and Kaufman all prospered following their association with the play or its film versions. Tracy, Perkins, O'Brien, Grant, and Rosalind Russell became important, or more important, stars; Milestone became an increasingly successful director; Harris became a more and more successful producer, at least for a time; and Hughes became richer and richer. And

Hecht and MacArthur made *The Front Page* their stairway to life-long fame and success.

The period of the launching and the run of the play had been a happy one for the team; Hecht later remembered it wistfully as "a glorious time when a mot by Kaufman took precedence over an utterance by the President." And Hecht and MacArthur maintained their friendship through the rest of their lives. They wrote two more expert plays together, *Twentieth Century* and *Ladies and Gentlemen*, and a great many superior screenplays, among them *Gunga Din* and *Wuthering Heights*. They were not always as lucky apart; a play by Hecht called *Lily of the Valley* lasted eight performances, and a play by MacArthur called *Johnny on a Spot* lasted only four. But most of the things they did were successful, and their lives were good.

They also, for a time, conducted their own motion picture producing organization in Astoria, Long Island, a company founded in the belief that they could make better pictures than the factory-like studios for which they worked. Like many of their activities, their projects were pretty wild and unruly, but turned out all right. They decorated their offices with life-size photos of beautiful nude models and with huge signs reading, "If it's good enough for Metro-Goldwyn-Mayer, it isn't good enough for us," dispensed with such little luxuries as directors and film editors and did nearly everything on their pictures themselves, including playing some of the minor roles, and satirized Hollywood pomp and ceremony by giving their few employees exalted titles. Their janitor, for example, was called Supervisor in Charge of Sanitation. Hecht, to avoid losing touch with the violin, also hired Oscar Levant, then temporarily unemployed, to play duets with him between periods of shooting, and soon, feeling that Levant's salary of $15 a week was too much for just that, gave him the title of Assistant President of the Music Department and put him to work writing some of the music for the firm's current picture. (The only other person in the Music Department was a man named Frank Tours, the musical director of the picture.) Levant soon found that his cabfare alone to the studio was costing him more than $15 a week, and protested that he should be receiving more money for his dual job. Hecht

handled the problem by sending Levant memos raising his salary t
$350 and then $500 and finally $1200 a week, but still paid hir
only $15.

And they made some pretty good pictures. For their first, *Crim*
Without Passion, they hired a young dancer named Margo and mad
her a popular star; the picture was assumed to be a failure becaus
it grossed only a half million dollars, low by industry standards, bɩ
it actually earned quite a bit of money because it had cost onl
$172,000 to make. Their second film, *The Scoundrel*, starring Noë
Coward, also did all right, as did several others. They might hav
gone on from there to uncharted heights if they had not grow
bored with the whole thing and returned to working for other peopl

Later in life, Hecht and MacArthur were also involved in mor
serious things. Hecht was a strong supporter of the birth and growt
of Israel, and MacArthur was Assistant to the Chief of the Chemicа
Warfare Service during World War II, making his travels then aɴ
afterward simpler by filling in the "Person to Notify" space in hɩ
passport with, "Harry S. Truman, The White House, Washingtoɴ
D.C.," a ploy which brought him instant courtesy from immigratio
and customs officials. MacArthur died at the age of sixty on April 2ı
1962, and Hecht at the age of seventy on April 18, 1964. The tw
partners are buried near each other in Oak Hills Cemetery in Nyacl
New York.

But the real beneficiary of the success of *The Front Page* wа
Kaufman. Just as Beatrice had expected, and in total contradictio
to Kaufman's gloomy forebodings, he was hailed as an extraordinaɾ
new director, perhaps even destined to become the greatest o
them all, and as everything from the brilliant midwife to the reа
father of the play. "George S. Kaufman," Atkinson said, "has se
the play spinning across the stage in a perfectly timed and space
performance"; Robert Littell, writing in *Theatre Arts Monthl*
called the direction "uncanny"; and *Theatre*'s anonymous criti
commented, "Into Hecht and MacArthur's lustily-written scrip
Mr. Kaufman has breathed the breath of verity and made the piec
scorch, sizzle, and scintillate until the most sophisticated among it
customers forgets himself." Kaufman's virtuoso debut as a directo
was viewed with such wide-eyed admiration that even eighteen yeaɾ

[364]

later, in 1946, when the play was revived at the Royale Theatre in New York with Lew Parker and Arnold Moss playing Hildy Johnson and Walter Burns, and with MacArthur trying his own hand at directing his play this time, many of the critics who had been around in 1928 wondered wistfully in print, as Atkinson did, if the impression that "the original performance, staged by George S. Kaufman, was a bit more vibrant" was sentimental or merely the plain truth.

This was not to say that the original production, when it first burst upon the theatrical scene, was completely headache-free. Many prominent publishing executives and newspapermen, particularly those on the more dignified papers, considered the play "a libel on the Fourth Estate." A few even tried to suppress it. The chief advocate for suppression, surprisingly, was Adolph Ochs, the ordinarily liberal publisher of the *Times*, who ignored the fact that one of his employees was the director of the play and another, Atkinson, was perhaps its greatest admirer. Atkinson, in fact, had greeted the play's arrival with an extraordinarily enthusiastic commentary beginning, "Ever since last Spring, when it was tried on the road, ecstatic reports have been heralding the popular wares of *The Front Page*. They do not estimate it too highly." Ochs considered for a time refusing all advertising for the play, but finally settled for having the *Times*'s house counsel, George Gordon Battle, write a long signed editorial in which Battle adjured *The Front Page* for failing to discriminate between "worthy and unworthy newspapers," and summarized the play's dialogue as "of unprecedented vulgarity" and its general effect as "unworthy and meretricious."

Various official bodies also became interested in the question of whether or not the play was immoral to the point of illegality. There were dozens of stories in the newspapers about investigations by the District Attorney and his assistants before it was decided to leave the play alone. The police, too, became interested in the play, attempting to view it anonymously and measure its depravity and possible deleterious effect on the innocent, and there was at least one occasion when there was so much fuzz in the audience that Harris decided to run what Richard Maney, the principal press agent for the play, later described as a "perfumed version." And on another occasion, it became so essential to defuse two particularly antagonistic detectives that Tracy invited them to his dressing room after the first act and got them so drunk on bootleg liquor that they were unable to watch and report on the remainder of the play.

But the play survived and flourished despite the bluenoses, and only what might be termed a typically Jed Harris act prevented the increasingly important producer and the hot new director from moving on together to new triumphs. Instead, as mentioned earlier, an incident occurred which brought their relationship to an end. In 1929, Harris produced an S. N. Behrman play, *Serena Blandish*, and tried it out at the Broad Street Theatre in Philadelphia. It was the *Times*'s practice during that period to run one out-of-town review of each play headed for Broadway, and the only one which had appeared at presstime was the *Inquirer*'s coverage, a strongly unfavorable review which later turned out to be one of the few bad ones. Kaufman didn't okay the use of the *Inquirer* review; he didn't even see it, since it happened to be clipped and run in the *Times* on his day off. When Harris descended on him, and began to scream about what he described as "the deliberate use of the play's only bad review just to destroy me," Kaufman didn't explain the circumstances or the fact that he hadn't even been aware of the review. Nor did he explain that Behrman was a close friend of his and one of the last people in the world he'd injure just to do an equal injury to Harris—if indeed he'd use anybody for that purpose, which he would not. (Behrman was, in fact, one of the relatively few people close enough to Kaufman to become the occasional subject of his unmalicious jibes. Once, in Hollywood, Kaufman attended a farewell party for Behrman, who had just finished a picture. Shortly before leaving, however, Behrman was asked to stay on to write some material for retakes, and Kaufman ran into him a few days later. "I see," Kaufman said. "Forgotten but not gone.")

But it was Kaufman's simple philosophy and belief that, as head of the dramatic department, the dramatic section of the paper was his personal responsibility whether or not he had okayed every item in it. He took full blame for the incident, adding calmly, however, that the *Times* would continue to run whatever it decided to run. His statement infuriated Harris, who went home and wrote Kaufman a letter in which he sneered at the fact that Kaufman was deeply in love with Beatrice but couldn't get her to go to bed with him, a situation which nobody had ever before been tasteless enough to mention directly to Kaufman. Kaufman never worked with or talked to Harris again, and he continued to despise Harris for the rest of his life. Many years later, when he was working with the producing team of Cy Feuer and Ernie Martin on *Guys and Dolls*, and found them as unlovable in some ways as the producer of *The Front Page*, he still felt strongly enough about the ancient hurt to describe them to Irwin Shaw as "Jed Harris rolled into one." And it was about Harris that Kaufman first spoke the line which has since been credited to a hundred other people. "Jed is his own worst enemy," a mutual acquaintance said one day. "Not while I'm alive," Kaufman said.

As the years moved along, the critical estimation of Kaufman as a director grew adoring to the point of reverence. It was not undeserved. His path as director after *The Front Page* was sometimes strewn with stones the size of boulders, but, once he had really learned his trade, it was exactly as Beatrice had said things would be. His credit as director appeared on success after success, including all of his own plays and such blockbuster hits under other bylines as *Of Mice and Men, My Sister Eileen, The Doughgirls,* and *Over 21.* And in the cases where the plays were not his own, the hint was strong that Kaufman had done far more than merely tell the actors where to stand and how and when to move and speak, a statement which Kaufman invariably denied and which his associates invariably confirmed, adding that Kaufman just couldn't help becoming more collaborator than director.

Kaufman continued to insist that it was all nonsense, and the expressions of adoration embarrassed and even horrified him. He told everyone who would listen that his contribution to all of the hit plays he directed was negligible, even when evidence to the contrary was overwhelming. He described his directorial chores in a *Time* interview as "a lot of over-rated goings-on," and—contrary to standard procedure in the theatre—refused throughout his lifetime ever to accept the usual in-front fee which most directors demand as an advance against the customary director's-share of a play's weekly box-office receipts. Instead Kaufman waited to be compensated strictly by the weekly percentage, feeling there was justification for accepting payment only if the play got past its opening night reviews and achieved a run. And when his favorite collaborator, Moss Hart, also began to direct now and then, and then more and more, Kaufman urged and convinced him to adopt the same policy: no money in advance.

Max Gordon, the producer with whom Kaufman eventually had his longest and most successful association, once talked admiringly about Kaufman's modesty as a director, an attitude totally opposite to most directors' insistence that the director was twice as important to a production and its success as all of its actors combined. "George's theorem," Gordon said, "was that the best-directed play was the one in which there did not seem to have been a director at all, in which what truly counted was the over-all effect, not the highlights of showy pyrotechnics. His approach as a director was simple and straightforward. Just as he had little use for idle talk about art in the theatre, so he refrained from the hocus-pocus common to many contemporary directors. He did not regard himself as a combined psychoanalyst, father confessor, and high priest. Nor did he conduct extensive excursions into the motivations of each character in a play, his or her psychological background, or the deep hidden intentions of the playwright. In contrast to some of the present lot of directors, George never considered himself the stage's all-around actor—a genius who could portray every role better than any member of his company. He had the old-fashioned notion that the actors he had chosen possessed intelligence, taste, and talent— otherwise they would not have been selected. And given a chance and some guidance, he believed they could work out their roles and problems in their own way."

The truth, actually, was that Gordon was even understating it a little. Kaufman was more vehement than that in his feelings that a director should butt out as much as possible, and he emphasized this when he contributed a brief piece to a book by John Gassner called *Producing the Play*.

Kaufman wrote the article at Gassner's request because Gassner, a drama professor at Yale and author of many books about the theatre, had sometimes been kind to him in reviews and essays. But the short script that Kaufman delivered wasn't precisely the how-to piece that Gassner was expecting. Kaufman truly felt that there was no how-to to it, and that anyone with a little intelligence and a certain amount of experience in the theatre could direct, and he labeled his piece, deprecatingly, *What Is Direction, Anyhow?*

"Some years ago," he wrote, "a young friend of mine, after a considerable apprenticeship in the theatre, finally directed his first New York production. The play was a failure, and that was that. A few months later he directed another play. Again it was a failure, and again nothing was said about direction. Then came a success. It was a good, resounding success, with two popular stars in it, and the reviewers were unanimous about the direction. They said it was wonderful. Then followed three more failures—not a word, of course, about direction. Then came another success, and this time the critics went to town. It was absolutely the best direction of the season.

"Now I am not aiming my shafts at the critics—that is not my point. I simply feel that there is a natural tendency to confuse the direction and the script. Good plays have a way of being well directed. I am not sure that there are three people in the land who can sit in front of a play and tell you definitely just what is direction and what is the performance. But everybody tries. My own opinion—and I hope it will go no further or I shall certainly lose out on some jobs—is that the whole business of direction is overrated. I am not so fatheaded as to claim that it doesn't matter at all, mind you. Certainly if you put a theatrical ignoramus in charge of a fine play he will probably make a mess of it. But if a director has a competent sense of theatre and a bit of an ear he will turn out a success when a play is good and a failure when it isn't, year in and year out. Personally I am always a little bit suspicious when the director is too highly praised. A play is supposed to simulate life, and the best direction is that which is so effortless and natural that it simply isn't noticed at all. Once it begins to call attention to itself, something is wrong."

Kaufman later stated the same viewpoint in even blunter and briefer terms. "The word," he told a colleague who had a tendency to force his own views on all the other people associated with the plays he directed, "is director. Not dictator." And when Abe Burrows once got the notion of adding a scene on an escalator into a play he was directing, and asked Kaufman if he thought that a director could make an escalator scene funny, Kaufman looked at him sadly. "Abe," he said, "it's time you realized that the director has nothing to do with it, and neither has the escalator. It's what the actors say on that escalator that counts."

No one would argue these days with Kaufman's insistence that the directorial touch be kept in the background and invisible. He was simply expounding the theory of the naturalistic play, the play which seems like life and not like a play at all, which has become the absolute and accepted standard in present-day theatre all around the world. The only thing surprising about it at all today is that this standard, so closely associated with "serious theatre," was apparently first put into operation, or at least first vigorously urged and endorsed, by a man who worked mostly with comedies. But Kaufman was hugely wrong, of course, about the importance of the contribution by a really good director to the structure and success of a play, and it's fortunate for the balance-sheet of the twentieth-century theatre, and the over-all score card on which credit is given where it's due in the world, that knowledgeable theatre people took his self-deprecation as a director no more seriously than they took his insistence that every new play he wrote would be a dreadful failure. Despite his increasingly urgent efforts to convince people that the substantial percentage of success among the plays he directed really had little or nothing to do with the direction, the respect which his associates in the theatre felt for him as a director became stronger and stronger as the years moved along.

John Gassner, for example, contradicted Kaufman's long disclaimer in a brief note which appeared directly below the article; the note didn't even mention the article, but made its point clearly enough. "Direction," Gassner said simply, "is important. It is of extreme importance since it translates dramatic literature into living theatre." Max Gordon was equally unwilling to accept Kaufman's statements of his own unimportance. "There was something about the plays that George directed," he said once in refutation, "that had his special touch no matter how much in the background he kept himself. There was a neat, unified pace to those plays. The comedy always seemed sharper and wittier under his guidance. The lines and situations seemed always to have been heightened by his unerring eye and ear."

Gordon went on to speak more specifically. "There was a modesty about his general demeanor," he said, "a reticence that sometimes left the viewer wondering whether the play would ever be ready. Holding a script in his hand, George could be seen on the stage at the beginning of a sequence talking in hushed tones to an actor, as if he were himself asking advice. At the end of the conversation, in which plans for the playing of the scene had been discussed, George would return to his seat, slouch down, and peer intently at the stage. When the scene was over, he would again haul his lanky frame to the stage. There would be more conversations with individual members of the cast. He may have detected a flaw that needed correcting; he may have detected a piece of business he wished retained for the future. Gradually, the actors seemed to find the pattern they were seeking. Nothing had been imposed on them. What they accomplished came from their own inner consciousness. As the rehearsals progressed, they gained in poise and in naturalness, achieving more in a week than others do in twice the time. And the reason for it all was that George's easy manner, seemingly so laissez-faire, concealed a firm determination to get what was needed, a devotion to detail, a dedication to discipline."

The compliments, the recognition that Kaufman's talents as a director matched his enormous talents as a writer, continued to pour in. James Forbes, author of many successful plays of the period, among them *The Commuters, The Traveling Salesman,* and *The Famous Mrs. Fair,* wrote him shortly after seeing *Of Mice and Men,* "I always say that since Henry Miller you are the only director that knows a goddam thing about bringing out the playwright's intentions, but in *Of Mice and Men* you have surpassed yourself. It is great work." George Oppenheimer, whose comedy, *Here Today*, was directed by Kaufman, later said, "As a writer of occasional plays, I have mixed feelings about directors. As a critic of other people's plays, I have a definite sense of bewilderment. I once worked on a musical with a director who had had his name on several hits and held an unshakeable sense of what was and what was not commercial. He treated me as a rank novice, overrode me again and again, broke my spirit (a dry twig after so many months of work) and was largely responsible for one of the worst and most costly disasters of all time. Although he withdrew as director before the foundering ship reached New York (I had been dropped as excess cargo several weeks before) the scuttling had already been done by him and the producers who, had they had the ability to know where he was going, lacked the spine to tell him.

"On the other hand," Oppenheimer continued, "my initial encounter with a director was with George S. Kaufman, twenty years before that, who treated me not as a novice but as a senior collaborator, helping me to shape my faulty construction, prodding me into sharper and wittier dialogue (and at times not only prodding but providing) and making the casting and conferences and rehearsals smooth, efficient, and fun."

But the supreme paean of praise for Kaufman as a director, summarizing it all, came from a critic who had occasionally attacked Kaufman in earlier days. This was John Mason Brown, and his comments on Kaufman in his review of *My Sister Eileen* in the *Post* were applause to a director of a degree probably never seen before or since in a critical essay. "Although, with the chilliest of my critical brethren," Brown wrote, "I insist on keeping the word 'genius' on ice, the Kelvinator must be robbed to describe Mr. Kaufman at his best. Genius is the only accurate term to apply to him when it comes to suggesting the consummate skill of his showmanship, his joyous mastery of the wisecrack, his fleet professionalism, his sharp sense of pace, and his magnificent invention when he has embarked upon one of his inspired excursions into the blissful realms of madness . . . The pleasures Mr. Kaufman can provide may be of the moment. They may evaporate with the falling of the final curtain. They may be beyond the accounting of future historians and present theorists, both of whom are destined to write when those moments are past. This evanescence, however, is only a proof of the high virtues these pleasures can claim not as drama but as theatre. For the moments he fills with gaiety—the Kaufman moments—when nonsense is so supreme that things come to a temporary halt and the ridiculous and the sublime seem near to being one, are experiences to be treasured. In a theatre they must be counted among the most enjoyable moments the stage has yielded in our time.

"When he directed *Of Mice and Men*, Mr. Kaufman showed how unsuspected and genuine was his range. But it is with comedy—his kind of comedy—that he is chiefly associated. There he is without a peer. And there, in his topnotch form, he is to be found as a director who is really a collaborator in *My Sister Eileen*. In its materials, *My Sister Eileen* is like all the Greenwich Village comedies you may recall. In its basic fable it is much the same as last year's *Night Music, Two on an Island, Young Couple Wanted*. Yet it is like none of them. It is in part Ruth McKenney and her lovely sister; in part the excellent cast Max Gordon has assembled; in part the work of Mr. Fields and Mr. Chodorov, who adapted Miss McKenney's book as a play. But mainly, and triumphantly, it is George S. Kaufman."

Kaufman's response to Brown's comments was not unpredictable. He told Beatrice, his long face showing anguish, that he felt that the comments were extremely kind but truly undeserved. And for weeks afterward, he went out of his way to avoid people who, he suspected, were the type to stop him and congratulate him at length on the review.

19. THE PUBLIC SPIRIT

ONE EVENING IN 1928, Kaufman was having dinner at a midtown restaurant when Oscar Levant stopped at his table and asked him if he'd heard anything lately from Harpo Marx. "How?" Kaufman asked. "How can you hear from Harpo? He can't talk and he can't write, so how can you hear from Harpo?"

This wasn't entirely exaggerated. Offstage, of course, Harpo was not always wordless; he sometimes became so loquacious, in fact, that Woollcott and other friends complained about it. But Harpo's lack of formal education revealed itself most visibly whenever he put pen to paper, with the result that he very rarely put pen to paper. His practice whenever he was out of town, as he was the evening Levant stopped to talk to Kaufman, was to remain as silent as the character he played, and Kaufman once commented on this in a letter he wrote to Ruth Friedlich. "I had a letter from your son at school," he wrote. "It seems the boys talked about Harpo, and he told them I knew Harpo, and they offered him various graft for autographed pictures. I doubt if I can get them; Harpo can hardly write, as you know." Harpo's journeys into prose, for this reason, were so infrequent and so treasured that one of the few letters Kaufman kept until the end of his life was a short note Harpo had once left for him, a note characteristic of Harpo's unique writing style despite its brevity. "I was hear," the note says, "but where were you ha ha you thought I couldnt right didnt you." Levant also eventually received and saved a communication from Harpo; it mentioned Kaufman's response in the restaurant, which by that time had become famous. "Some years ago," Harpo wrote, "you were in N. Y. and you met George Kaufman you asked him if he ever heres from Harpo and he answered how its true I seldom write in fact this is the first leter in about ten years the last one was to George B. Shaw he never answerd me so i figured whats the use of writing he gave me a first addition of St. Joan."

A few days after the encounter with Levant, however, Kaufman was surprised to receive a letter written in Harpo's unmistakable scrawl. "Whats this I here," Harpo wrote, and then proceeded to answer his own rhetorical question. "I here," he continued, "that your righting another play for us well thats good see you soon." This was news to Kaufman, but he had an uneasy feeling that it would not be news for long. He was correct. Shortly afterward, he received another interminable but persuasive phone call from Sam H. Harris, a call he kept trying to bring to a close with protestations that he was simply too busy with his directing assignment on *The Front Page*. It ended only when he had agreed to hunt up Morrie Ryskind and work with him on another musical comedy for the Marx Brothers.

This time, however, Kaufman told Ryskind, the play would carry a joint byline instead of Kaufman's name alone. Any man willing to work for months with the Marx Brothers and help spring them on an unsuspecting world again, he said, ought to share in the credit as well as in the money. "Or," he added gloomily, "would 'blame' be the better word?" Whichever it was, Ryskind was delighted with the new opportunity, and work proceeded on the play every time Kaufman could snatch a few hours away from *The Front Page.*

As with *The Cocoanuts,* Kaufman and Ryskind realized, it would not be essential for them to work too hard on their story, because who cared about the story, anyway, in a Marx Brothers epic? The plot could be kept absolutely simple and unsurprising, because the brothers would add their own surprises onstage no matter how earnestly they agreed in advance to stick strictly to the script. The important thing would be to try to conceive and contribute a fair share of the kind of wild gags and inspired nonsense which seemed to pour forth from the comedians spontaneously, and it wasn't going to be easy. The complaint was one which was echoed by every writer who ever worked with the Marx Brothers throughout their careers: How could any writer possibly invent anything as funny as the things the brothers seemed to do and say naturally every day of their lives offstage and on?

How, for instance, could any writer match the lunatic ribaldry which seemed to come so easily to the Marxes in real life? A typical example occurred the time Groucho searched for an excuse to get out of taking his wife to see a picture he didn't want to see, Victor Mature and Hedy Lamarr in De Mille's *Samson and Delilah.* "I've made it a rule," he said finally, "never to see a movie in which the man's tits are bigger than the woman's." How could any writer match Harpo's inventiveness the time he decided to fill a dull afternoon by shaking things up at Tiffany's, a store whose stodgy respectability irritated him? He went to the store, asked to see a tray of diamonds, and pretended to tip over the tray accidently when it was handed to him—at the same time surreptitiously and loudly emptying onto the floor a pocketful of fake jewels he'd bought earlier in the day at Woolworth's. Chaos erupted: bells and buzzers sounded, store detectives raced to the scene from every corner of the building, and other customers were hustled away and the store was shut tight. When the jewels on the floor were examined, Harpo was escorted grimly to the street, but he walked with dignity. He also had a final touch waiting. As he reached the street, he turned and tipped the doorman a giant artificial ruby.

And how could any writer match the time Chico and Harpo decided to enliven another quiet afternoon by walking up Broadway and selling money at discount prices, dollar bills for ninety cents and $5 bills for $4.50, waving away a suspicious police officer's questions by pointing out that the money was real and they weren't breaking any laws? "We just like to sell money, that's all," Chico said blandly, and the policeman finally shrugged and walked away. Or Harpo's two famous verbal put-downs: his dismissal of *Abie's Irish Rose* as "no worse than a bad cold," a comment which was eventually entered in a contest in *The New Yorker* for the best brief description of the play and won first prize, and the time he took care of a no-talent movie producer. The incident took place at a party given by Harpo at which Mischa Elman, the violinist, was present, and some raconteurs have credited Elman with the line because it was in his style of quiet humor. But most witnesses insist that it was Harpo who finally spoke up after the producer had droned on endlessly about the problems and headaches with which he was confronted every business day. "If it's so hard to make bad pictures," Harpo asked gently, "why don't you make good ones?"

Kaufman himself was the recipient of some of Harpo's attentions through the years. Harpo once learned that the playwright was tremendously embarrassed by the struggle which sometimes ensued when he and another man shared a cab and then tried to outrace each other to pay the fare. The horror at watching the other man get there first now and then wasn't quite a phobia with Kaufman, as so many other things were, but it bothered him sufficiently so that he never left home without putting strategically placed bills and coins in his pockets which he could whip out and hand cabdrivers before arguments even started. Harpo therefore went Kaufman one better; he stuffed a pile of bills into his undershorts, and contrived to share a cab with Kaufman. When the cab arrived at its destination, he leaped into the street, and, before Kaufman's horrified gaze and the stares of a dozen fascinated onlookers, zipped open his fly, pulled out a $5 bill, and paid the fare. On another occasion, he had dinner with Kaufman at a restaurant, promising to behave and keeping his promise almost to the end of the meal. But then a woman nearby was handed her check, and Harpo seized it, quickly shook salt and pepper over it, and ate it.

On still another occasion, a popular female impersonator named Bert Savoy was drowned off the coast of Coney Island. A great many homosexuals in the New York area went into public and noisy mourning, among them a columnist who wrote a memorial to Savoy in his column in the form of an open letter. The letter was so sticky and sentimental that Harpo later described it as one of the most revolting and mawkish things he'd ever read in his life. That night, at dinner with Kaufman and several other people, a substantial part of the evening was devoted to composing fictitious telegrams from Savoy to the columnist, among them WHERE WERE YOU WITH THE WATER WINGS?, LETTER RECEIVED: NO CHECK, and I'M FOREVER BLOWING BUBBLES. As far as Kaufman was concerned, it was just cynical fun between friends. He was absolutely horrified when, at the conclusion of the evening, Harpo told him that he actually intended sending the telegrams. Harpo was no more serious about doing so than he was about the rest of it, but he made his statement sound completely convincing, and then listened with great pleasure as Kaufman went into an agitated speech to try to prevent him from doing such a tasteless and terrible thing. Afterward, describing the incident, Harpo said with real satisfaction, "For all his flair for the theatre and his biting, irreverent wit, George was a very conservative guy and something of a timid soul in public. I never saw a man so easy to embarrass." He allowed Kaufman to plead on for a long time before admitting that he was only kidding.

Another time, the Kaufmans were suddenly descended upon at home by a couple of dull visitors, and seemed doomed to have to invite the people to dinner. Harpo put on an old apron, covered it with ketchup, and entered the Kaufmans' living room. "I've killed one of the cats, ma'am," he told Beatrice, "but I haven't been able to catch the other one. Do you think one will be enough for dinner?" The visitors fled soon afterward, leaving Beatrice limp with laughter and Kaufman devastated with embarrassment.

Harpo had a lovable nature and everybody liked him. Kaufman was included, but he never felt at ease around the funny little man. The first meal they had together, Harpo accidentally stabbed a chicken pot pie the wrong way, and it skidded across the table and into Kaufman's lap. From that time on, though he accepted Harpo's statement that it was an accident, he was always a shade apprehensive when the comedian was around him.

Harpo's idea of humor took some peculiar, and expensive, turns. Once he had four full-length portraits of his brothers and himself painted in the styles of great masters, depicting the Marxes in medieval court costumes and costing five thousand dollars each. He also placed engraved plates under the paintings crediting them to Tintoretto, Botticelli, Leonardo da Vinci, and Michelangelo. His library was a bit less impressive. It contained only two books, which Harpo was fond of showing to his guests. They were George Bernard Shaw's *Saint Joan* and W. Somerset Maugham's *Of Human Bondage*, both affectionately inscribed by the authors. For years Harpo assured everyone that someday he was going to find time to read them.

Remembering some of these things, Kaufman told Ryskind about them, and they both laughed loud and long. It was laughter, however, not untinged with nervousness. No, they agreed, it wasn't going to be easy to match the comedians' own wild creativity.

They began working at night because the weather was so hot. Ryskind would begin to type while Kaufman paced, but Kaufman soon stopped him each time. He couldn't stand Ryskind's careless typing and poor spacing, so he'd eventually sit at the typewriter himself and let Ryskind do the walking and talking.

The play which eventually began to emerge became one of the best and most famous of the Marx Brothers' vehicles: *Animal Crackers*. The story, more an excuse to get the brothers onstage and keep them there than a genuine plot with a problem and complications and a resolution, is about a house party at the palatial Rittenhouse mansion on Long Island, scene of many celebrity-loaded parties because Mrs. Rittenhouse is a sort of early-day Perle Mesta—she has, in fact, invited the characters played by the Marx Brothers in the mistaken impression that *they* are all celebrities—and about what happens when a valuable painting disappears. Margaret Dumont, of course, played Mrs. Rittenhouse, impressively stately but tolerant at the same time, and never seeming to notice the obvious fraudulence of her guests; it was in *Animal Crackers* that the role achieved full dimension and became the character she played in nearly all of the Marx Brothers' subsequent adventures. And the brothers brought their own characterizations to full flower in the play.

Groucho played the part of Captain Spaulding, an intrepid big-game hunter, by his own description, but clearly nothing of the kind, a suspicion he later confirms when he faints at the sight of a caterpillar. Even more than in *The Cocoanuts*, his speeches were loaded with atrocious puns and other liberties with the language, among them the now classic lines, "One day I shot an elephant in my pyjamas. How he got into my pyjamas I'll never know." Chico was Ravelli, owner of the world's heaviest Italian accent but with a remarkably light touch at the piano. Harpo was The Professor, loping around wildly in a costume capacious enough to hide everything stolen by the brothers, however huge, and equally able to contain and deliver anything needed by anyone in the cast, including even a good copy of the missing painting. And Zeppo, not funny but an expert straight man, was there to provide the love interest.

But the most important presence in the play was the humor, as fantastic as *Alice in Wonderland* and as fresh and original. Harpo, rushing over courteously to help a butler set up a bridge table, instead starts to close a leg each time the butler puts up the opposing leg, the action becoming faster and faster until the table is spinning between them like a wheel. Groucho scoffs at Harpo for failing to steal anything important, an accusation Harpo quickly disproves by lifting his sleeve and revealing that he has just stolen Chico's birthmark. Groucho and Chico decide that if the missing painting is not in the Rittenhouse mansion, it must be in the house next door. And when someone points out that there *is* no house next door, the two immediately start designing one, ending up arguing bitterly about which bedrooms each will occupy. It was crazy stuff, thrown at audiences so fast that people were left breathless.

The play was also helped substantially by good music and a good score written by Bert Kalmar and Harry Ruby, who had worked with Kaufman five years before on *Helen of Troy, New York*, and by exceptionally innovative dance numbers choreographed by Russell Markert. Markert, a youngster who had been a chorus boy in the *Vanities* only a few years before, had had a meteoric rise and clearly deserved it. The distinguished critic for *The New Republic*, Gilbert Seldes, was so impressed with the young dance director's work in *Animal Crackers* that he gave him top billing in his review, titling it *Markert and the Marxes,* and he also talked about Markert in a second review of the play which appeared in *The Dial*. "A few years ago, three or four," he wrote, "Mr. Markert was in the chorus of the first *Vanities;* later he did some stage-managing; last year he directed the dancing in *Rain or Shine*. This is a brief record for one who, in the present show, arrives at the very top of a difficult profession. In *Rain or Shine*, a group of dancers came on, exceedingly well trained in the usual peppy manner of American dancers, doing everything well and stepping out of the average by a single number in which the girls sat perfectly still and did what is called a hand drill. Their hands, gloved in green, moved to the music. I am told this is a revival of an old musical show trick, but in fifteen years of fairly faithful attendance I haven't seen it done elsewhere. It was, old or new, beautifully done, with rhythmic perfection and a good sense of the design a number of hands can create. In *Animal Crackers*, the dancing is all individual, and has the special imprint of a director who knows the traditions and the business of stage dancing and adds to it something of his own. The high spot is again a hand drill elaborated from the same type in *Rain or Shine* and suffused with beauty. It is at once the perfection of mechanical training and the perfection of created lines and masses. It has nothing to do with either gesture or interpretative dancing, since it is pure movement to music. It is one of the few things of the season I am most happy not to have missed."

The play opened at the 44th Street Theatre on Tuesday, October 23, 1928, and ran a solid 191 performances, closing on Saturday, April 6, 1929. It was staged by Oscar Eagle, Kaufman having refused absolutely to become involved in another directing job without at least a pause for breath after *The Front Page*. And, not unexpectedly, another of the things which kept the play on a Standing Room Only basis throughout its run was the fact that the Marx Brothers could be depended upon, just about every performance, to do things not in the script.

Once, for example, Chico began a piano solo which was only supposed to last about three minutes, but he kept playing on and on until his brothers finally pulled him away from the piano. Chico's explanation to the audience was simple and even logical: he'd forgotten how the piece ended, so how could he possibly stop? Another time Harpo arrived late at the theatre and hurried into the cape he wore in the first scene, a scene in which the Rittenhouse butler announces Harpo at the head of a marble staircase and then removes his cape, revealing that Harpo is wearing nothing underneath but a pair of swim trunks. This time, however, Harpo had forgotten, in his haste, to put on the trunks, and was wearing only a special and unusual type of underwear he favored—briefs the size of a G-string. Harpo, not easily shocked, fled the stage in panic, but Groucho turned and leered at the audience. "Tomorrow night he's not going to wear *anything*," he said. "Get your tickets early!" Harpo soon recovered his composure, and was himself again when, a few days later, he was told that Woollcott had come to visit him and walk him home. Woollcott, waiting in Harpo's dressing room, was wearing an article of clothing as eccentric in its way as Harpo's underwear—a big, black, broad-brimmed impresario's hat. The headpiece, Harpo discovered when he returned to his dressing room, was exactly the same size as a ten-gallon sombrero he wore in the show, a wild-looking object covered with gold and silver spangles, so he seized Woollcott in an enthusiastic bear-hug and quietly and imperceptibly switched hats. Then he walked home with Woollcott by way of Times Square, watching gleefully as Woollcott, delighted at what seemed to be recognition by a vast horde of people, smiled and waved at the people grinning at him.

The incident, like most of the others, received considerable publicity, helping *Animal Crackers* sail blithely along through its successful run, go on a long and equally successful tour after that, follow up with another good run at the Carlton Theatre in London, and finally emerge in late 1930 as a highly profitable Paramount-Publix picture for which Ryskind wrote the screenplay. (Kaufman, asked to assist in the transition of the play from the stage to the cinema, declined with thanks. It had been tough enough, he said, to be associated with the Marx Brothers for the run of the play without having to do it all over again. And, he added, with a group of additional and less

[382]

pleasant lunatics, the people who make pictures, added to the torture chamber as well.)

Kaufman's occasional statements about the horrors of involvement with the freewheeling comedians, as everybody realized, were strictly in jest right from the start, characteristic of his saturnine style of humor, and became even more so as he grew to know them better and better. A little to his own surprise, in fact, he became very fond of the brothers, and would probably have become especially close to Groucho if geography had not separated them. The two men were dissimilar in most ways: Kaufman had an almost puritanical distaste for four-letter words, whereas Groucho used them constantly and joyfully; Groucho reveled in public displays of lechery while Kaufman always shied away from the subject of sex; and Groucho, in contrast to Kaufman's love of poker and bridge, was and remains a rather careful man with money who, as his son, Arthur, once put it, "never indulged in cards, or *any* game of chance, if he could help it." But the incredible ability of both men to summon up brilliant and sophisticated wit at a moment's notice and seemingly without effort continually increased the admiration each felt for the other. Things finally reached the point where Kaufman even went with only token protest to a dinner party at Groucho's house, despite the fact that it was located all the way out near Lardner's place, in the wilds of Great Neck.

The party was a disaster, as it turned out. The Marxes had invited ten people to the dinner, a tight squeeze in the house's small dining room. Included in the group were a pair of neighbors of whom the comedian and his wife were a little in awe: a rich manufacturer and his wife, Mr. and Mrs. Parks, who lived across the street in a huge house which, according to Arthur Marx, "made ours look like a shanty," and who had impressed the Marxes a few weeks before by inviting *them* to dinner and having four in help to serve the four people. Mrs. Marx managed to get ten chairs around the dining-room table. But then Kaufman phoned and asked if it would be okay if he brought Ryskind along, for which Groucho gave casual permission despite Mrs. Marx's expression of stunned horror, and Ryskind showed up with two guests of his own, Mr. and Mrs. Harry Ruby. This was handled by the quick setting-up of an auxiliary bridge table. The peace which then descended was shattered a few moments later when a serving-girl, hired for the occasion, became mysteriously drunk and dropped a plateful of hot hors d'oeuvres in Mrs. Parks's lap. "She had to drop them on one of the invited guests," Groucho commented audibly, not helping the situation. "She couldn't have dropped them on Ryskind." Even this was smoothed over—until Ryskind noticed that the butler, in elegant fashion, was bringing in the coffee one cup at a time. Ryskind insisted that thirteen separate trips be avoided by the service of coffee on one large tray, and then a few minutes later managed to collide accidentally with the butler as the man tottered in under the weight of a tray containing thirteen coffee cups filled to the brim. It was a tribute to Groucho's charm, or perhaps to the admiration everybody felt for him, that, despite everything, the Parkses remained friendly with the Marxes, and Kaufman commented without satire on the way home that it had been quite a pleasant party.

Kaufman also became very fond of the comedians' mother, Minnie Marx, a dynamic little woman who had first urged the brothers to go into show business and had helped and encouraged them in many ways since then. He was deeply saddened when, just as the company was preparing to take *Animal Crackers* on tour following its close in New York, she suddenly died. The family, the four brothers who were in show business and two others who were not, had arranged a reunion, all of them getting together, for the first time in four years, in Zeppo's apartment. Minnie Marx, aged sixty-five and suffering from heart trouble, though she'd kept this fact from her sons, was bubbling with happiness and resplendent in a new blond wig she'd bought for the occasion. She joined her sons in a merry, conversation-filled dinner, and then, still hungry and exuberant, had another complete dinner and challenged the boys to several games of Ping-pong. But on the way home in a limousine, she suddenly suffered a stroke and lapsed into a coma, and a few hours later, brought back to Zeppo's apartment, she was gone. Harpo later talked about her last moments in an eloquent and moving description. "Minnie's eyes were open when I came into the bedroom," he said. "She did the hardest thing she had ever done in sixty-five years of doing the impossible: she smiled. Her lips trembled. Her eyes were glazed with fear. But two tiny stars twinkled through the glaze, and she smiled . . . The smile went quickly out. Her fingertips fluttered against the bedcover. She was trying to say something. I knew what she was trying to say. I reached over and straightened her wig, the new wig she had bought for that night. The smile came back for a second. Then it faded, and all the life in Minnie faded with it."

Many years later, there was another death more or less related to *Animal Crackers*. Groucho was booked to do a song from the play, *Hooray for Captain Spaulding*, on a television show, *The Hollywood Palace*, and he also did a brief scene from the comedy with Margaret Dumont. It was the actress' last appearance, and two days later she was dead. But in spite of these sad events associated with the play, the Marx Brothers always remembered *Animal Crackers* with warmth because it was their real breakthrough to the biggest time, the play which established them unmistakably and permanently as major talents. Groucho in particular always talked about *Animal Crackers* with special enthusiasm. And once, when he accepted a one-line "cameo appearance" on *The Hollywood Palace* because his career had moved into a temporary decline and he felt that even a brief exposure was important, and he learned later that that single line had been cut and he would only be appearing silently on the screen for that instant, he reminisced wistfully in a letter to another comedian, Fred Allen, about the time he had had "about ninety sides of dialogue" in the Kaufman-Ryskind play.

Groucho was always quick to express his gratitude to Kaufman, once saying that Kaufman had been largely responsible for his success in show business. Since Kaufman frequently spoke with similar warmth about Groucho, there is no telling how far their friendship might have developed if the Marx Brothers hadn't begun to make pictures in California and if Groucho hadn't fallen in love with the area and settled there. The friendship had, by then, already reached the point where Kaufman felt free to throw insults at Groucho, an affectionate act he saved strictly for his closest friends. Once, when other friends gave a party for Groucho in Hollywood and wired Kaufman to express their regret that he couldn't be with them, he wired back promptly, COULDN'T THINK OF A WORSE PLACE TO BE. But Groucho's move to the West Coast put a mortal crimp in the relationship, since, of course, Kaufman visited California, and every other place away from New York City, as infrequently and as briefly as possible. He said once, "I never want to be anyplace where I can't be back in Times Square in thirty minutes," and he continued to prove throughout his lifetime that he really meant it.

For Kaufman, his work on *Animal Crackers* brought a special dividend, in many ways the most important one in his life thus far. The dividend was the strengthening and the cementing of his relationship with Morrie Ryskind. The fact that, with *Animal Crackers*, the association stopped being a casual one, a sort of unplanned calling-in of an assistant when and as needed, and became a true collaboration such as Kaufman had previously had with Marc Connelly and Edna Ferber, was crucial to Kaufman's career because it helped him move off in an entirely different direction and helped change him. This was, in a word, because Ryskind was so political that in time Kaufman became political, too.

It was not because the two men were close or even thought similarly. They were never especially fond of each other, and, as Kaufman remained liberal and Ryskind moved inexorably from liberal to ultraconservative, they eventually reached the point when they were totally unable even to spend time together. But before that happened, Ryskind performed a service for Kaufman for which it would have been impossible ever to repay him adequately. Ryskind was so steeped in politics, so much a partisan on every issue, so much an exuder of political thoughts and political opinions every waking moment, that he finally influenced Kaufman into abandoning *his* normal posture of neutrality in most things and turning his attention and massive satiric talents toward politics. And this, ultimately, brought the team of Kaufman and Ryskind one of the great rewards of the twentieth century, the Pulitzer Prize.

In many ways, of course, Kaufman had always been rather interested in politics himself. Like most Jewish families of their period, nearly all of the Kaufmans and the Bakrows were strongly liberal people who were enthusiastically pro-union, felt that most bosses had more than a touch of evil even though many of the Kaufmans and the Bakrows were bosses themselves, and spent a lot of their time and money assisting charities and otherwise working for organizations pledged to alleviate the plight of the poor. Kaufman's father, in particular, held especially fervent liberal and even socialistic views on many subjects, and, more than most people, practiced what he preached; few employers, after all, even the most dedicated believers in share-the-wealth, end up, as Joseph Kaufman did, giving away their businesses without compensation to their employees. All of this had its natural effect on George Kaufman and he, too, was a liberal all his life, and, unlike some other highly paid people in the '20s and '30s, a strong supporter and admirer of the various social-welfare programs put into motion by Franklin Delano Roosevelt and other legislators.

But in the pre-Ryskind days, Kaufman's political and public-spirited inclinations were essentially passive, and, as mentioned, usually anonymous to the point of stealthiness. From just about the first day he began to earn large amounts of money in the theatre, he was almost painfully aware of the differences between his own luxurious way of life and that of out-of-work actors and other people not too many steps away from starvation, and his regular handouts were estimated by some observers of the scene as going to as many as forty or fifty different people. The contributions became so much a daily affair that he even developed a technique which he thought might keep the public at large from learning about his activities, from discovering, as Moss Hart later said, "that underneath that stern exterior there beat a heart of pure marshmallow." He told every one of the scores of people he gave money, in amounts which were sometimes as low as $5 or $10 but sometimes as high as $500 or even $1000, that the recipient was the only person in the world for whom he was doing this, and his price for the money was total secrecy, because otherwise he'd become the target for so many requests that he'd soon be penniless himself. His scheme didn't work, but it was typical of his constant efforts to keep people from learning that he wasn't really a total curmudgeon. And even the statements of his beliefs which crept, inevitably, into his writings were rather muted. Plays like *To the Ladies* and *Helen of Troy, New York* poked fun at big business and the Babbitts of the world, and *Beggar on Horseback* pictured the millionaire businessman as venal and vulgar and the poor artist, the struggling composer, as a creature of sensitivity and even nobility, but the emphasis was very much more on the humor of it all than on the social considerations.

The first real indication that Kaufman was getting ready to break loose came in 1925, at just about the time he began his association with Ryskind on *The Cocoanuts*. The event was Kaufman's decision to become involved with the Dramatists' Guild, the organization of playwrights which eventually became the most effective bargaining and negotiating body for writers in the world. Kaufman's membership in the group was not surprising in itself because the need for a playwrights' protective association was so obvious that nearly all American dramatists joined up quickly. Most people, however, would have predicted only his usual self-effacing behavior in the organization: prompt payment of dues but otherwise a lot of silent sitting in the back of the room at meetings. Instead, Kaufman became extremely active in the group, and in time was even elected its board chairman.

Before the development of the Dramatists' Guild and its arrival at a position of genuine bargaining power, decisions on payments for plays were almost totally in the hands of the producers. Except for a very few writers whose past plays had been so popular and successful that they were able to set fair terms for their new work, receiving a substantial advance against anticipated earnings and a royalty payment per performance, most playwrights had to be content with whatever the producer chose to pay them. And it was the average producer's attitude that he was doing the playwright a favor by putting on his play, so he was therefore perfectly in order when, after setting a payment figure by whim or by careful calculation of the smallest possible sum with which he could get away, he tossed the writer a tiny bag of gold, or sometimes a bag of pennies, and told him to get lost.

Back in Shakespeare's day, the average complete payment for the rights to a play was £4 to £6, with the producer keeping all profits and paying not a cent more to the author of the production. Even Shakespeare himself managed to keep his head above water only by buying an interest in the local theatre and becoming a producer, too. (It was for this reason that some of the Shakespearian authorship is so confused. Shakespeare rewrote a lot of other people's plays because he wanted them to be successful in his theatre.) Things were not much better three centuries later, and sometimes were worse.

When Harriet Beecher Stowe's *Uncle Tom's Cabin* was turned into
a play, the man who did the dramatization was paid off with a gold
watch, and Mrs. Stowe's sole compensation for the dramatic rights
to her novel was a free box at the theatre on opening night. Im-
provement was still slight by the end of the nineteenth century and
the beginning of the twentieth: many playwrights were still churning
out scripts for flat fees or for salaries as low as $15 a week. And
when royalties were paid, they were often tiny and frequently stopped
at specified totals instead of continuing as long as the play continued
to be shown. When, for example, Richard Mansfield, one of the
richest and most successful actor-producers of his day, hired Clyde
Fitch in 1889 to write a play for him, the deal Fitch accepted was $30
a week salary during the writing of the play plus $7.50 per per-
formance until a total of $1500 was achieved, after which Mansfield
would own all rights forever afterward. The play was *Beau Brummell,* one of the most successful dramas of all time. Fitch soon earned
$1500 and was out in the cold, but Mansfield continued to appear in the
play for the rest of his life.

There was such a clear need for an organization to help playwrights
improve their lot that attempts along these lines were being made as
early as 1878, when two writers, Steele MacKaye and Clay M. Greene,
formed an organization called the American Dramatic Authors' Society. But it didn't last, and neither did another group formed by thirty-
three writers in 1896, the Society of American Dramatists and Composers. In 1913, a more effective organization of writers of all types,
the Authors' League of America, was formed, and soon had 350
members, including about a dozen playwrights. But when a sub-
group of dramatists got together and tried to do something to al-
eviate their special problems, they proved similarly ineffective. Most
producers were by now agreeing to pay advances and royalties rather
than trying to get authors to write plays for them on salary or for a
flat fee, but remained pretty casual or forgetful about living up to
their contracts with playwrights. In a typical occurrence, Owen Davis,
addressing a group of producers invited to an Authors' League meeting, cried out accusingly, "There's a producer here right now who
owes me over a thousand dollars in royalties." In the next few days,
he received checks and letters apologizing for the oversight from

four different producers. And when, in 1917, the playwrights within
the League suggested a conference with all New York producers fo
the purpose of working out a standard contract form which would
include a guaranteed minimum advance and royalty scale, the Man
agers' Protective Association, the most powerful producers' organi
zation of the period, sent a release to the press expressing shock a
"the writers' gall," and the producers' group's vice-president, Le
Shubert, said he would sooner close down all the Shubert theatre
than accept and sign the playwrights' proposed basic contract. Week
and then months passed with the producers standing firm and th
writers giving in one by one, sneaking shamefacedly into producers
offices to sign the same old unfair contracts because they needed th
advance money. In due course, the playwrights' protest movemen
was dead of malnutrition.

By the time Kaufman joined the organization, the playwright
in the Authors' League had formed a separate and more cohesiv
sub-section called the Dramatists' Guild, and the nation's economy
was surging upward so rapidly that conditions for playwrights ha
improved substantially, in the same way that conditions in genera
had improved for most people in the country. But there were stil
plenty of abuses. Major playwrights were receiving higher and highe
advances and better and better royalty percentages, but new and less
established authors were still being offered pittances and told they
could take it or leave it; producers were still, just as they had alway
done, rewriting lines or scenes or even whole acts of plays withou
bothering to secure the consent of the plays' authors. And there wa
one particularly virulent abuse of playwrights' rights: the producer
favoring division of motion picture money. The first movie based on
a play had been made back in 1905, a 1000-foot film version of
Raffles. Nobody got any money out of that except the film's pro
ducer; there was as yet no definition under law of a form of property
called "motion picture rights," and the filmmaker simply lifted and
used the play's name and plot without permission or payment. Before
long, however, the courts, watching the flourishing movie industry
ruled that authors should be paid for the use of their material in th
new medium. But jubilant writers soon realized that they were also
being given a partner, because the courts ruled at the same time that

since film versions of plays might compete with the stage versions and diminish attendance at stage performances, the producers of the stage version should receive a "fair share" of the motion picture monies (no specific percentage was named) as their compensation for possible loss. It was a valid point: a moviegoer, seeing a film version of a play, might not be especially interested in seeing it again on the Broadway stage or when it turned up on tour in his home town, and so most writers suggested a straight 50-50 split between themselves and their stage producers. The trouble was that a lot of producers, recognizing the strength of their power of veto because they knew that movie companies, already super-cautious in matters concerning the law, would never make a deal with an author of a play without also getting his producer's signature on the dotted line, grew greedy and insisted that a mere half would never repay them adequately. And in 1925, there were a number of producers who were demanding, and receiving, as much as 90 per cent of the movie money as their price for okaying film deals.

The president of the Dramatists' Guild at the time Kaufman joined was a bright, tough man named Arthur Richman, author of such hits as *Ambush* and *The Awful Truth*. On December 7, 1925, he anticipated Pearl Harbor Day by launching a surprise attack of his own. He borrowed a large room at Actors' Equity headquarters and asked every important playwright in the New York area to attend a secret meeting for the purpose of beginning to set up a new minimum-standards contract for dramatists which, this time, would be made to stick. This new contract, Richman told the writers at the meeting, would be accepted by producers because two things would be done to give the playwrights' drive a degree of strength and power that prior efforts had not had. In the past, all proposed basic contracts had been put forth timidly as "only suggestions." The one constructed in 1917, for example, had been sent around with the added footnote that it was strictly for "educational effect." It also carried a second footnote which pulled the rest of its teeth, an admission that it was "subject to changes to meet special conditions," the effect of which was that any writer who decided he had to knuckle under to a producer and accept a sub-standard contract in order to eat could do so. This time, however, Richman said, the minimum terms set forth in the new basic contract would be made absolutely binding on every member of the Guild, and any playwright thereafter discovered to have signed any contract other than the Guild's own form would be fined a thousand dollars. Richman's second suggestion was strategic: that the group's recruitment campaign be designed specifically to sign up the one most successful and profitable playwright associated with each producing office, so that each producer would either accept the Guild contract or stand in danger of losing his most valuable meal ticket.

About thirty playwrights, including Kaufman, signed the document put together at the meeting, a single sheet of paper which was essentially a promise to be bound by the basic contract and its $1000 penalty clause, provided its terms, when completed and studied, were found acceptable by a majority of the members. A month later, a second meeting was held with many more men and women attending. A lot of other dramatists signed up, bringing the total of signatories to 121. And then the membership went to work.

A committee was formed to list and discuss all existing abuses and then write the final basic contract. Kaufman was asked to become a committee member—more, a few people later admitted, out of politeness and recognition of his increasing eminence in the profession than from any real expectation that he would become directly and visibly involved to this extent. To everyone's surprise, he accepted at once, and became one of the committee's most active participants.

Kaufman's work on the committee proved invaluable; he was one of the few people in the organization whose experience was not limited to his own deals, but who could talk knowledgeably about practices and events in every producer's office because of his coverage of the whole Broadway beat for the *Times*. He was able to talk about the size of advances and royalty percentages being paid around town, the fact that some young playwrights had told him that they had had to accept advances so small they were nearly invisible, and other onerous conditions like waiving their shares of money from motion picture sales and foreign productions, in order to be produced in New York. He also told a few horror stories about instances where producers retitled plays and then rewrote them so completely that their authors almost failed to recognize them when they finally opened.

Kaufman was particularly strong about the latter problem, insisting on a clause in the new contract which would give the author complete control over the work which carried his byline. "Nobody can change a single word in one of my plays without my permission," he said, "and every writer ought to have that protection."

The committee met every day for three weeks in the apartment of Rachel Crothers, author of *Susan and God* and others, having first secured the promise of all members that any play completed while the committee was at work would be held and not submitted to producers until the new contract had been formulated and approved and could be used for deals on the plays. A contract draft was delivered at the end of the series of meetings and was approved at once by the full membership. It gave the authors all the protection they'd ever wanted.

The contract set minimum acceptable advance and royalty terms; members could, of course, accept terms higher than the established minimums if they could get them, but never lower. Royalties and all other income were required to be paid when due, never "forgotten" and delayed by producers who wanted to use the money for their own purposes for a while. Plays could no longer be kept out of circulation; either the producer opened a play within a reasonable period of time or returned the rights. Corporate entities were strictly controlled; a producer could no longer fail to meet his obligations by going bankrupt under one corporate name and then reappear, still controlling a play, under another corporate name. Disputes would be settled by mandatory arbitration; playwrights would no longer have to spend thousands of dollars in the courts to protect themselves if they felt or knew they were being cheated, or simply have to forget about their rights if they didn't have the money to sue. The "Kaufman clause" was present in unmistakable language: a producer could not change a word of a script without its author's permission. And the Basic Agreement, as it was titled, carried two other clauses which really made its terms binding forever afterward: all Guild members agreed never to give any further scripts to any producer discovered and proved to have violated a Guild contract, and, conversely, all producers signing Guild contracts agreed never again to produce the work of any author discovered and proved to have violated a Guild contract.

As expected, most producers complained bitterly once the terms of the new contracts were announced. A few producers, noted for their fairness, accepted the new standards immediately; one of these men, Henry Miller, said simply, "I know you fellows. Anything you want is all right with me." But the great majority of producers took the opposite stance. Earl Carroll, who put together the yearly *Vanities*, said sourly, "Concerted effort like this sounds incongruous to me, coming from a profession predisposed toward brains and individuality," and others were quick to brand the agreement unfair, inequitable, and unworkable. A group of producers, looking undignified but determined, met in bathing suits at Miami Beach and sat in a circle on the sand and put together a list of the clauses they found unacceptable, which ended up including most of them. And the most virulent of the opposition, the Shubert brothers, sent out a news release stating that they were "starting a war on the dramatists." They promptly went to court with the matter, charging the Guild with "secondary boycott."

But this time, it was clear that the producers were going to be the ones on the losing side. For one thing, the producers had now had a taste of what it was like not to receive any material from established playwrights—the period in which all scripts had gone into storage while the Basic Agreement was being written. Despite the brevity of the period, they hadn't liked the feeling very much. For another thing, the Guild had a piece of evidence of producer treachery, possibly typical, right in its possession. This was an indiscreet memo a major producer had written to his lawyer instructing him to "write the contract so I can get out of it," and which the lawyer had absent-mindedly attached to the contract when sending it on to the playwright, a Guild member, for signing. For a third, too many important writers were involved; eventually, in fact, every professional playwright became part of the pact. George Kelly, author of *Craig's Wife* and *The Show-Off* and a long list of other hits (and, incidentally, the man who, years later, helped his young niece, Grace Kelly, get her first acting job) was one of the few who had demurred at first from becoming involved in the Guild action, saying he'd never had any trouble getting the terms he wanted from his own producers. But he quickly became one of the Guild's most enthusiastic members when Kaufman and others described some of the deals being imposed on newer playwrights. Eugene O'Neill, asked to lend his prestigious byline to the proceedings, signed his name at the bottom of a sheet of blank paper and told the Guild to use it in any way necessary. And when another very active Guild member, George Middleton, went to England to sign up some British dramatists, he added to the roster such legendary names as George Bernard Shaw, John Drinkwater, Clemence Dane, W. Somerset Maugham, John Galsworthy, A. A. Milne, and Arnold Bennett.

The fourth and most important thing was that every producer, even those who fought hardest against the new contract, actually realized, underneath it all, that the Basic Agreement was really not one bit unfair but was simply a clear statement of the minimum terms and protections which playwrights had deserved all along. It was awareness of this fact which enabled the Guild's lawyer, Arthur Garfield Hays, to accept the Shuberts' lawsuit without nervousness, saying imperturbably that the Guild "welcomed the action because it was time the whole matter was brought out into the open," and caused George Middleton to comment with scorn that it was the first time in history that "any group of American writers had ever been hauled into court on the issue of trying to protect themselves." The Shuberts soon dropped their suit, every producer in America in time accepted the Guild's minimum standards, and in due course American playwrights became and have remained the best-protected and most fairly paid writers in the world. As just one example of the benefits of the new agreement, the requirement that playwrights receive no less than 50 per cent of movie monies brought members, in the twenty years following the acceptance of the contract form, a total of $12,240,033 in film income, which was probably about $6,000,000 more than they'd otherwise have received. And in later years, a further negotiation changed that clause to 60–40 in the authors' favor, putting added millions into playwrights' pockets.

For Kaufman, his activity in helping to prepare the new contract, and in soliciting other playwrights to support it, was the beginning of the turning over of a new leaf for him, the beginning of more active and open participation in what must be termed, though he would have hated the phrase and considered it pretentious, matters related to the public good. He remained so active in the Dramatists' Guild that, in 1927, he was elected the group's Chairman of the Board, and he was also selected by the Guild in 1933 to represent the organization on the committee formed to administer the NRA for the legitimate theatre. And he became involved in many other public activities.

Also in 1933, for example, Kaufman was in the forefront of a fight to keep the Senate from passing a restrictive and ugly law which had already been approved by the House of Representatives. The bill, pushed through the House by a group of isolationist legislators, prohibited producers from "importing alien actors unless of distinguished merit and ability." It was ostensibly set up to preserve most acting jobs for Americans, in the dwindling employment market caused by the depression, while still allowing theatrical employers a few really major foreign stars whose talents were so unique that their work could not be duplicated by American performers. But Kaufman recognized the bill as one more anti-foreigner effort by an amalgamation of men who were always trying to reduce immigration quotas and otherwise keep the United States separated from the rest of the world, and the acceptance of the major stars a mere token bow at the few men and women who were so famous and important that they had to be tolerated even if they *were* foreigners. And he hated the whole idea, in general because he always despised racial, religious, and national prejudices, and specifically at that point in time because he was all too aware of the fact that Hitlerism was on the rise in the country from which his grandparents had emigrated, and realized that he might well himself have been one of the Jewish intellectuals hauled off to prison or dragged into an alley and beaten to death if it had not been for the United States' traditional hospitality toward immigrants and foreign visitors.

He made it his business to appear before the Senate Immigration Subcommittee in the company of two other distinguished theatre people, William A. Brady, the producer, and Austin Strong, the grandson of Robert Louis Stevenson and the author of *Seventh Heaven*. All three men spoke eloquently against the new bill, Strong saying that producers needed the right to bring in the best possible actors from everywhere in the world in order to present plays strong enough to pull in customers despite shortage of cash, Brady pointing out that most American actors and actresses just couldn't give accurate representations of Germans, Frenchmen, and the like, and Kaufman becoming even more specific. He talked about Lynn Fontanne, describing her as a "timid, frightened girl who had not yet reached stardom when she came to this country from England," and emphasizing the fact that she would probably never have developed into one of the greatest attractions of the American stage if the proposed law had been in existence at that time, because she would have been prohibited from working here. He was joined in his argument by a liberal member of the House, Representative Emanuel Celler of New York, who was also against the bill. Celler pointed out that Charlie Chaplin and George Arliss would also have been barred from working in the United States because nobody would have been aware of their "distinguished merit and ability" when they first arrived here, and the bill was thrown out.

As the Nazis grew stronger and stronger, Kaufman also became deeply involved in nearly every campaign to get refugees out of Germany and into the United States. He was particularly quick to come up with his own money when a refugee claimed to be related to him, even if the relationship was clearly distant at best, or based on nothing more tangible than the fact that the refugee also had the very common name of Kaufman, or even when the evidence was overwhelmingly against the refugee's claim. Kaufman's lawyers argued strongly against these contributions, telling him that he might be letting himself in for more than he intended because some of the refugees might come to regard themselves as his responsibility, fasten themselves to him, and expect him to support them even after they arrived in the country. The lawyers were right; a few of the people Kaufman rescued got into the habit of coming to him for handouts as regularly as some of the actors who waited for him in Shubert Alley or on Broadway. But he never stopped bringing people out of Europe as long as it was possible to do so, and he almost never refused a request for money even when the man or woman making the request admitted unashamedly that it was for a luxury rather than for ne-

cessities, or even when the person was someone Kaufman had become almost certain was not really a relative at all. "How can I turn
him down?" he said about one man to Beatrice one night. "What if
he really *is* a relative? I can't take the chance." The truth was that it
really didn't matter. Relatives or not, the people qualified for his
contributions, anyway, since they were less fortunate in life than he
was. In the years until the war started and cut off the exodus of
Jews and other refugees, he was partly responsible for the escape of
about three hundred men and women, and solely responsible for the
welfare of about thirty of these people, bringing them to the United
States and supporting them until they were settled or longer, entirely
with his own funds.

By the early '40s when the country was getting ready for and entering the war, Kaufman was so active in public matters that he was
spending more time with these things than at playwriting and directing. He began to accept most assignments offered to him, provided
they were associated with the war effort or benefited people hurt or
displaced by the war. He was no super-patriot or war lover, not in
any sense one of those people, surprisingly large in number, who
revealed themselves, with the arrival of World War II, as essentially
delighted with the glory and adventure of it all. On the contrary, he
had always been, like most of his friends and associates, bitterly anti-
war and a constant pleader for world peace, a fact that Frank Adams
once noted in one of his columns written in the Pepys manner. "So
home, and thence to Mistress Alice Miller's for dinner," Adams wrote
"and all did play a game of answering questions, such as What were
the names of Columbus' ships? and Who wrote 'The child is father
of the man' and such like queries. And How many words beginning
with a given letter can you say in one minute? And I did well enough
at that game, though I could name no more than two of the wives
of Henry VIII. But I knew who said, 'Let us have peace.' Yet G.
Kaufman and I could not see why General Grant, who said it but
once, should gain fame for such an utterance, when George and I,
who say it every day, get no fame whatsoever." But Kaufman had
begun to feel a little guilty about his non-participation in the country's
military efforts. He had, after all, been a reject in World War I and
seen no service then, and there was no chance whatever that he was

going to be called up and accepted this time, since he was fifty-two years of age and even more nervous now. So he took on a lot of jobs —all of them minor and some of them silly, but, still, *something*.

The jobs he undertook were pretty varied, too. He and Beatrice were the organizers and sponsors, along with Sam H. Harris, Max Gordon, Herman Shumlin, and Irving Berlin, of *It Happened in Vienna*, a show starring and for the benefit of twenty-five refugee Austrian actors put on at the Music Box Theatre. He joined Vinton Freedley, the producer, in setting up a show for the benefit of British air-raid victims, *A Carnival for Britain*, which was presented at Radio City Music Mall on February 22, 1941: it began at midnight to allow performers from various Broadway shows to complete their chores and appear, and featured such diverse performers as Gertrude Lawrence, Bill Robinson, Boris Karloff, Danny Kaye, Victor Moore, William Gaxton, Olsen and Johnson, Arthur Treacher, Fred Allen, and Vera Zorina. He became Vice-Chairman of the Advisory Committee on Entertainment to the War Department, planning shows around the world for the services. He and Moss Hart wrote and appeared in a one-act play, *Dream on, Soldier*, a little sketch about a private who dreams that the war is over and a lot of marvelous things are happening to him, including marrying his boss's daughter, having his high school and home town named after him, and, best of all, giving a handout to a bum and discovering that the bum is his former commanding officer. The sketch was part of a benefit show for the Red Cross presented at Madison Square Garden on April 5, 1943, and, according to the reviewers, the two authors outshone such other participants as Ethel Merman, Helen Hayes, Tallulah Bankhead, Clifton Webb, Paul Muni, Gypsy Rose Lee, Ray Bolger, Fredric March, and Milton Berle. Kaufman also agreed to write a sketch for a revue titled *Fun to Be Free*, being put together for an organization called *Fight for Freedom*, and he also promised to assist in staging the show and talked Edna Ferber, Russel Crouse, Jerome Chodorov, and others into contributing sketches, too. The show was subsequently scrapped because some quarrels developed among other people involved in the project, but Kaufman shrugged and instead donated some money to the organization.

He also answered an urgent summons from Ben Hecht one day,

and learned that Hecht had been given an assignment to recruit distinguished writers to do a series of training shorts on subjects like what to do in case of an air attack. Hecht told him he wanted him, Clifford Odets, Maxwell Anderson, Lillian Hellman, George Oppenheimer and some other people to write scripts for the program, and that the scripts were needed within a week. Kaufman and Oppenheimer collaborated on two assignments and delivered the scripts right on schedule. He became Chairman of the National Community Theatre War Bond Advisory Committee, and tens of thousands of copies of letters bearing his signature and printed on Treasury Department stationery were sent out urging people to buy bonds. He even wrote a poem to help the bond drive, a rollicking little number called *In Nineteen Fifty-four* which appeared in theatre programs. The poem reminded people that, when they redeemed their bonds a decade later for the money they'd paid plus interest, there'd be a lot of delightful things they could buy, some of them strictly unobtainable when the poem was written: "Paper clips, buggy whips, marshmallow candy, Napoleon brandy, dynamos and rubbers and twenty-course meals, butter and nylons and automobiles, high heels, flywheels, Hershey bars, Kiddie Kars, perfumes with a rare aroma, down front seats for *Oklahoma!*, railroad seats for distant places, solid platinum shoelaces, gorgeous coats of countless sables, Coca-Cola and racing stables, and e'er we leave the festive scene, *gasoline and gasoline!*"

Sometimes, of course, the requests made of him were too absurd or too offensive to be borne, such as the time he was summoned before a group of senior officers. The military men told him pompously that they had come to realize that some soldiers would seek loose women no matter how many films were shown to them warning of the dangers of venereal disease, and that the only solution would be for Kaufman to write a show so entertaining and wholesome that it would distract the men permanently from their pursuit. "Gentlemen," Kaufman said, "that would have to be one hell of a show," and he turned on his heel and left. He also turned and departed when, after he, Robert E. Sherwood, and Leonard Sillman, later the producer of the *New Faces* shows, had conceived and begun a campaign of recruiting performers to entertain servicemen which was eventually formalized into the USO program, the three men were called to the office of a banker. The banker told them patronizingly that they'd come up with a pretty fair idea, but, since a lot of money would have to be collected and used to keep the program going, it was time to turn things over to businessmen used to handling substantial sums. Sherwood responded first. "My friend," he said, "I don't know how good a businessman you are. But I've been in the theatre for twenty-five years, and I have a million dollars in securities, stocks, cash, and real estate." And he left. Kaufman spoke next. "My friend," he said, "I've been in the theatre for twenty years, and I have considerably *over* a million dollars," and he left, too. That left Sillman alone, and with many of his most profitable productions still ahead of him. But he was nevertheless also equal to the situation. "My friend," he said, "I've been in the theatre for fifteen years." And then he also left.

In addition to all this, Kaufman was also able to continue to work at the same time for the Dramatists' Guild, and for the general good of his field in other ways. When the Dramatic Workshop of the New School for Social Research, now a solid institution but just an interesting notion thirty-plus years ago, was being considered at the end of 1939 and the beginning of 1940, Kaufman was one of the first people to warm up to the idea of a place where young actors and writers could try out their talents. He became one of the Workshop's initial sponsors, helping persuade Sherwood, Levant, Eddie Dowling, and Clifton Fadiman to join him in financing the project and get it running. And when the Dramatists' Guild and the Authors' League suddenly found themselves temporarily overspent and in need of funds, it was Kaufman who went out to persuade writers to loan the organizations money, suggesting $500 at 4 per cent interest per man. He wasn't successful in all his approaches. One predictable failure was with William Saroyan, then as now a rebel, and never a man to hang onto his money and remain in funds himself for very long. Saroyan wrote Kaufman a letter which Kaufman filed and kept because he found it interesting and amusing, if disappointing. "I would like to join you and the others," Saroyan wrote, "in lending $500 at 4 per cent to the Authors' League and the Dramatists' Guild, each of which is probably beneficial to me even though I am opposed to each on general principles, but I haven't got the money. You will forgive me for wondering how and why the League and Guild got in the desperate spot. It appears to be imperative for all of us to be in sympathy with a good many things these days, but I am afraid the tendency is running away with everybody and doing a good deal more harm than good. I am in favor of wholesale material bankruptcy all around, with a consequent more modest living scale and a more generous national creative activity. All of which is boring, and beside the point." Fortunately, however, few other writers were as probing and argumentative as Saroyan, and the organizations got the money they needed.

Most of these matters, of course, were comparatively simple and limited, since they took Kaufman into tame and familiar battlegrounds associated with his own field. But by the mid-20s, Kaufman was also getting ready to involve himself in more significant concerns by expressing some of his strong views on national and global problems in his plays, and it is here that Morrie Ryskind's influence is most clearly traceable. Ryskind, in those days, was an even stronger pacifist than Kaufman, talking more often about his hatred of war and all things connected with war than about any other political subject. And Kaufman's first genuinely outspoken, unguarded, and totally honest play in every sense was an anti-war musical called *Strike Up the Band*.

Ryskind had been an extremely vocal pacifist ever since his college days at the Columbia School of Journalism, which he attended during the First World War. His views on the subject, as he later said wryly, had gotten him girls and gotten him expelled. His comments were popular with a few feminine fellow students, who considered them humane and admirable, but not with too many other people in the period of the War to End All Wars, a time of wild-eyed patriotism when other women rushed up to young men in civilian clothes and handed them white feathers or painted yellow streaks on their suits, failing in their fervor to notice that some of the men were blind or limping along on artificial legs. One of the people who deplored Ryskind's statements was the president of Columbia, Nicholas Murray Butler. And when Ryskind responded to a reprimand from Butler by writing a poem which was not only savagely anti-war but also anti-Butler, and getting it published in the school paper, he was expelled even though it was just six weeks before his graduation. The unjust act of retaliation didn't stop Ryskind. He had started life thinking it would be fun to be a baseball player, and later changed his mind and pointed his ambitions in the direction of a writing career, and he told himself philosophically that a college degree wasn't really a requirement for either career. Columbia eventually relented and gave him his B. Litt., but this didn't change his attitude: he continued to deliver bitterly anti-war speeches for many years afterward to anyone who would listen. He did this so often in Kaufman's presence that, one day in 1927, Kaufman went to his desk and began to construct a play which would heap scorn on warmongers, war profiteers, and the militaristically inclined.

The viewpoint was still not a totally popular one even in 1927. A certain amount of disillusionment had set in after the Armistice, but there were still a lot of people around who were quick to point out that the Americans had walked in and whipped the enemy in just a year and a half, and that a period of strong prosperity had followed the war, and express the opinion that war was still a far more sensible and honorable method of settling international controversies than cowardly arbitration. Kaufman set out to demonstrate that this was total nonsense. Despite the controversial aspects of the subject, his track record was too strong for him to have any trouble getting his play produced. A good, solid producer, Edgar Selwyn, snapped it up the minute he heard about it.

Selwyn, a colorful and flamboyant man who had started in the theatre as an actor, written many plays himself, and eventually became an ambidextrous and immensely successful producer of both plays and motion pictures, had been born Edgar Simon in Cincinnati, Ohio, on October 20, 1875. He went to Chicago at the age of seventeen to try to make his way in the world, but nearly, according to a story which seems pretty apocryphal but which Selwyn swore all of his life was absolute truth, and which he later used as an incident in a play he wrote called *Rolling Stones*, put an end to things when he was unable to get a job and found himself penniless and hungry and totally discouraged in mid-winter. As Selwyn told the story, he went to a high location and jumped into the Chicago River, but all that got him was sore feet because the river had frozen over and he landed on solid ice. And then, the minute he stepped onto the shore, he was met by a man who pulled a gun on him and made the traditional demand for his money or his life. "My life," Selwyn answered, explaining that he was trying to kill himself, anyway. Instead of shooting him, Selwyn said in telling the story, the stick-up man became interested, and the two men talked together for a long time. The upshot was that the thief pawned his gun and divided the receipts between them, and the grubstake kept Selwyn going until he finally managed to get a job.

In time, Selwyn came to New York and worked for a while as a necktie salesman at $9 a week, but abandoned this when he became fascinated with the theatre and took a job paying only fifty cents a night as an usher at the Herald Square Theatre. He lost the job when he did a pretty good, but not too complimentary, imitation of Richard Mansfield one night for the amusement of the other ushers. Mansfield, who was starring in the theatre at the time, overheard him doing it and got him fired. In 1896, Selwyn decided to try for an acting job in a new William Gillette play, *Secret Service*, and then learned that all the roles had been filled, but he persisted by learning the hotel at which Gillette was living and sending up a card marked only *Edgar Selwyn —Important*. Gillette was irritated to learn that his mysterious visitor was only a job-seeker, and referred Selwyn coldly to his stage manager. Selwyn pleaded for a letter of introduction, and Gillette, who could find no stationery, finally wrote the word, "Introducing," above Selwyn's message and signed his name below it. The stage manager took the total message as a direct order from his boss, let somebody else go, and hired Selwyn for the part of a Confederate soldier. The job paid only $8 a week, a dollar less than Selwyn's employment in the necktie business, but it was work in the theatre.

By 1912, Selwyn had appeared in scores of important roles, written a number of successful plays, and was becoming increasingly active as a producer both in the theatre and in films. That year, in association with his brother Arch, who had come to New York to join him and was also developing into a busy producer, and with Crosby Gaige, he brought out *Within the Law*, the play which made a million dollars for the three men and put them all in the bigger time. Selwyn had first met Kaufman through Gaige, and his path crossed Kaufman's frequently after that for the rest of his life. In 1940, for example, four years before his death on February 14, 1944, Selwyn was involved in a multi-picture producing deal with M-G-M, and one of the pictures he produced for them was the third film version of *Dulcy*. He had admired Kaufman ever since he'd attended *Dulcy*'s opening night back in 1921. And so, when he heard one day in 1927 that Kaufman was working on *Strike Up the Band*, he was quick to request and receive the producing assignment.

But Selwyn expressed relief privately to friends when he learned more about the project and discovered that Kaufman envisioned his play as a musical rather than as a drama or comedy. He, too, shared Kaufman's pacifist emotions, but he wondered a little about how audiences would go for an unadulterated dose of straight truth.

The musical form would, at least, allow him to tone down Kaufman's obviously strong and bitter intentions with softening factors like songs and dances and pretty girls. He also made it his business to sign the hottest and most reliable songwriting team in the business, George and Ira Gershwin. Selwyn had asked the Gershwins to meet him at one of his favorite vacation resorts, Atlantic City, New Jersey, on September 4, 1926, shortly after he made his deal with Kaufman. The brothers accepted the assignment immediately upon learning that the book would be by the man, they told Selwyn, they considered the funniest and most intelligent playwright in America.

Unlike Mozart and other composers who first showed signs of their musical genius and love for music at the age of four or five, George Gershwin, born on September 26, 1898, had no interest whatever in music during his early boyhood. The generic wellspring of his brilliant talents as a composer is a mystery because neither his parents nor his grandparents were especially musical, and he was never urged to take music lessons of any kind. The great passion of his youth, like a great many other boys, was baseball, and he tended to regard other youngsters who did take lessons as "little maggies," a contemptuous term of the period suggesting effeminacy. But when he was twelve, he was strongarmed into attending a violin recital at school given by a neighborhood boy named Max Rosenzweig, who later shortened his last name to Rosen and became a successful concert violinist, and was tremendously moved by the performance. Shortly afterward, Gershwin came upon a piano at another friend's house and started to spend long hours there, picking out popular tunes on the keys. His parents, learning about the sudden interest, arranged for him to take piano lessons, first from a young woman who gave music lessons in the neighborhood and then from a better-known teacher named Charles Hambitzer, and he was on his way.

He wasn't always encouraged; young Max Rosenzweig, to whom he took the first fragments of songs he'd written, listened courteously but then shook his head and said, "You haven't got any talent for writing music. You'd better forget about it." But Hambitzer was impressed both by Gershwin's ability and by his developing and extraordinary devotion to music, even though he regretted the fact that his young pupil had begun to show more and more interest in current rather than classical music, and had begun to argue that popular music could achieve importance and significance. "I have a new pupil who will make a mark in music if anybody will," Hambitzer wrote to his sister one day. "The boy is a genius, without a doubt; he's just crazy about music and can't wait until it's time to take his lesson. He wants to go in for this modern stuff, jazz and what not. But I'm not going to let him for a while. I'll see that he gets a firm foundation in standard music first." He continued to stress the values of a knowledge of classical music, but urged his student to devote his life to music regardless of which branch of it he finally chose.

Gershwin made his move in this direction in a way which pleased neither his parents nor Hambitzer. He had been attending the High School of Commerce, but quit when he was sixteen and took a job at $15 a week as a song-plugger at Remick's, a big music-publishing company. Then he went to work as rehearsal pianist for a Broadway show written by Victor Herbert and Jerome Kern, *Miss 1917*, and went on from there to become tour accompanist for Nora Bayes, Louise Dresser, and other singers. He sold his first song, *When You Want 'Em You Can't Get 'Em*, when he was eighteen, wrote his first score for a musical show, *La, La, Lucille*, when he was twenty-one, and shortly afterward had his first hit, *Swanee*, which was recorded and promoted by Al Jolson and sold millions of copies. Before long, he was writing songs for *George White's Scandals*, one of the best-paying and most sought after assignments in town, and a job he kept for five years, and was also contributing songs to many other Broadway and London musicals.

In 1921, Gershwin's brother, Ira, began to write lyrics for his music. Ira, born on December 6, 1896, was a shy, soft-spoken young man whose gentle, whimsical sense of humor had brought him the nickname of Pixie, and who had made his first tentative and embarrassed attempts at writing lyrics while earning a living as a desk clerk at a couple of enterprises started by their father, Morris Gershwin. These were the Lafayette Baths in downtown Manhattan and the St. Nicholas Baths in Harlem, two public-ablution centers which eventually managed to fail even in that period, when places of that type were very popular because many apartments had no bathing facilities at all. Ira quickly revealed a gift for writing fresh and inventive rhymes almost as impressive as his younger brother's ability as a writer of music. (Ira may have inherited his way with words from his father, a man with a special way of expressing himself. All his life, Morris Gershwin could never remember the name of one of the most famous of all the Gershwin songs, *Fascinating Rhythm;* he always referred to it as *Fashion on the River.* The elder Gershwin also composed a pointed reminder when George promised him a dog one time and then forgot about it. Morris Gershwin sent his son a telegram: THANKS FOR THE PRESENT SO FAR.)

Three years later, George further enhanced the Gershwin name and family fortunes by releasing his most ambitious and important work to date, *Rhapsody in Blue.* It became extremely popular almost immediately after the most famous orchestra leader of his day, Paul Whiteman, introduced it at Aeolian Hall on February 12, 1924, in the first "serious" jazz concert ever given in the United States, and with the young composer himself playing the piano solo. Gershwin's next triumph came with his *Concerto in F,* for piano and orchestra, which was commissioned by Walter Damrosch and performed by the New York Symphony Society, with Damrosch conducting and Gershwin at the piano, in 1925. And by the time the brothers joined Kaufman on *Strike Up the Band,* they had collaborated on such hits as *Lady Be Good!, Tip Toes, Promise,* and *Oh, Kay.* Selwyn was considered to have gotten quite a plum when he signed up the team.

There were even greater things to come for George Gershwin; it was not until 1928 that Gershwin wrote *An American in Paris*, not until 1932 that Serge Koussevitzky and the Boston Symphony Orchestra introduced Gershwin's *Second Rhapsody*, with the composer again appearing as soloist, and not until September 30, 1935, that *Porgy and Bess* had its world premiere.

He worked all the time. Once André Kostelanetz, the orchestra conductor, asked Gershwin how many songs he wrote each week while he was involved in a show or a film. "I write fifteen songs a day," Gershwin said. "That's the way I get the bad ones out of my system." He was never willing to pause and rest, even when he just finished bringing a major project to fruition. The day after the premiere of *Porgy and Bess*, at the Colonial Theatre in Boston, Gershwin went for a walk with a friend of his, a girl named Lois Jacoby. Gershwin walked faster and faster, and Miss Jacoby, who was wearing high heels and had to struggle to keep up with him, was certain that he was thinking about the premiere and was showing his inner excitement in that way. Suddenly, however, Gershwin stopped and looked at her. "But what will I do next, Lois?" he asked.

Miss Jacoby thought at first that he was joking. Nobody, she thought, could brush off the long period of work and the immense achievement that way. She pointed out that there was still the New York opening to come, and probably a London opening. And then perhaps Paris and Vienna and a lot of other places.

"A symphony, maybe," Gershwin said thoughtfully. "I wonder if I can do it. I'll have to learn all about the form. Perhaps if I work hard for a couple of years . . ."

Miss Jacoby still couldn't believe he was serious. She continued to pursue the subject of the new opera. "What fun it would be," she said, "for you to go around the world with *Porgy and Bess!* What a kick you'd get out of it!"

Gershwin shook his head. "If it's that good," he said, "it'll go without me. In the meantime, I've got to think about the future." And he began to talk again about the idea of a symphony.

By 1927, Gershwin was already a world-famous figure and a constant guest at society and celebrity parties in New York. Most of his invitations resulted from the real admiration, and even awe, people had begun to feel for him as a composer. His desirability as a guest was also enhanced by the fact that he had become his own best ambassador; unlike most other writers, who went to parties to relax and forget their work, and who were often resentful if asked to perform their compositions, it was almost impossible to keep Gershwin away from the piano—provided it was understood that he would play only his own stuff. If he was invited to perform, he accepted with such alacrity that Kaufman once commented that Gershwin should have been a runner instead of a writer. "I'd bet on him any time in a hundred-yard dash to the piano," he added. And if Gershwin was not invited to play, he wandered over to the piano, anyway, and started to finger the keys softly until the rest of the people at the party had gathered around him.

His eagerness to perform his own work became so well known that a whole file case of jokes sprang up about the fact and about Gershwin's ego in general. Most of the gags were invented by his own friends, and they remained friends because Gershwin was aware of the truth of it all and never resented the jokes, laughing as happily as everyone else when he heard them. Nearly everyone in town had a go at him at one time or another. "George," Oscar Levant once asked him, "if you had it to do all over again, would you still fall in love with yourself?" And when someone asked Levant if he thought Gershwin's music would still be played fifty years in the future, he replied, "It will be if Gershwin's still alive." "An evening with Gershwin," another friend said, "is a Gershwin evening," and Kaufman once commented glumly on the business hazards involved in Gershwin's habit of showing off his new songs at parties immediately after writing them. "George's songs," he said, "get around so much before an opening that the first-night audience thinks the show's a revival." But it wasn't just ego of the ordinary variety; Gershwin had genuinely come to enjoy nothing more in life than music, and particularly his own music. He was a tall, dark-eyed, intense and handsome man who attracted women and had a lot of girl friends, but he never became serious enough about any of them to get married. He often talked wistfully about Ira's happy marriage to a gentle and beautiful girl named Leonore Strunsky, but he was simply too preoccupied to do the same sort of thing himself. Once he learned that a girl friend, a lady about whom he was rather serious, had grown tired of waiting for him and had married another man. For a minute or two, Gershwin considered the news in silence. Then, finally, he spoke. "If I wasn't so busy," he said with absolute seriousness, "I'd feel terrible about this."

Gershwin never gambled, rarely drank, and smoked cigars only in moderation; he often had to be reminded, as Kaufman did, to stop and eat. (This kept him in good condition. Years after his death, Ira Gershwin, who has a tendency to gain too much weight, looked admiringly at a picture of his brother. "George kept himself like a boxer," he said. "He didn't have an ounce of fat.") The money the composer earned meant relatively little to him, except for its usefulness in enabling him, as he did throughout his life, to support a great many relatives, contribute to a lot of causes, and subsidize scores of promising young composers. He did have a hobby which he pursued with intense concentration many afternoons and evenings, painting in oils. He painted portraits of Jerome Kern and Arnold Schoenberg and others which critics considered so good that it was generally agreed that he'd have become an equally brilliant painter if he'd concentrated on art instead of music. But even here, his subjects were nearly always people from the world of music, and he always regarded his painting as a necessary pause so that he could return refreshed and relaxed to the piano.

Gershwin's almost childlike recognition of his own talent and his own value was clearly illustrated when, one day, Harry Ruby came to meet him at a little place Gershwin had rented in the country. It was a lovely summer day, and the two men wandered outdoors and began to toss a baseball back and forth. Inevitably, the throws grew harder and harder, and then, suddenly, Gershwin called a halt to the game.

"It's too risky," he told Ruby. "My hands are too valuable for me to risk them this way."

Ruby dropped the baseball with a thud. "What about *my* hands?" he asked.

Gershwin shrugged. "It's not the same thing," he said.

Ruby was offended, but he said nothing more about the matter. He left Gershwin's country place shortly afterward, and the paths of the two men didn't cross for two years. They met unexpectedly on the boardwalk at Atlantic City, and Gershwin greeted Ruby with warmth and affection. Why, he asked, hadn't he seen Ruby in all that time? Why hadn't Ruby ever telephoned him? Then a disconcerting thought entered Gershwin's mind. Could he possibly, he asked, have done something to offend Ruby?

Ruby decided to be frank about the matter. He reminded Gershwin about that day in the country and outlined the incident in minute detail. "And then," he said, "you said, 'It's not the same thing.' "

Gershwin nodded agreeably. "Well," he said, "it isn't."

He rarely listened to anyone else's music, and once Kaufman expressed surprise when he was told that Gershwin had asked a friend to play another composer's new song for him. "If Gershwin wanted to hear someone else's song," Kaufman said, after thinking it over, "it's because he suspected the song was stolen from him." Mostly, the composer concentrated on his own music, on the pursuit of his great ambition: "to interpret in music," he once said, "the soul of the American people," and he was at his sunniest when he was at the piano doing it. "I've never seen a man happier, more bursting with the sheer joy of living than George was when he was playing his songs," Bennett Cerf said one day. "He would improvise and introduce subtle variations and laugh with delight when his audience exclaimed over them." There was, of course, a lot to enjoy and admire. Even other composers, lured to the piano, sometimes found themselves giving Gershwin evenings rather than performances of their own work, as Richard Rodgers once did. "Hell," he said, suddenly realizing that he had played nothing but Gershwin music for over an hour, "I'll never earn a nickel *that* way." Then he turned to one of his own lovely compositions. But he'd already made it clear that he felt as nearly everyone did about the genius of the young composer from Brooklyn.

Alexander Woollcott once described his own attitude toward Gershwin. He told about the time that Gershwin had moved into an impressive penthouse on East 72nd Street, a fourteen-room apartment with a huge, paneled reception hall, three pianos, the largest bar that Woollcott had ever seen in his life, and a special telephone which was actually a direct line from George Gershwin's workroom to Ira's apartment across the street. Woollcott, invited to inspect and admire the place, felt an overwhelming urge to deflate the composer. "I found myself," he said afterward, "struggling with a mischievous impulse to say, 'If, instead of dying of starvation in a garret, Franz Schubert had had a place like this to work in, he might have amounted to something."

"I suppressed the impulse," Woollcott said. "But on my way home I fell to wondering what there was about Gershwin that incited me to such teasing—what, indeed, there was to make faintly derisive, in intention at least, all the characteristic anecdotes people tell about him. And it dawned on me that if we're all moved at times to a little pebble-shying in his direction, it might be because of our knowledge—our uncomfortable, disquieting knowledge—that he is a genius." Woollcott added that the term was one he didn't use very often. "And perhaps," he concluded, "the rest of us instinctively snatch at, and magnify, any little failing of his—so we can console ourselves with the reflection that he's just like the rest of us after all."

Kaufman felt the same way about Gershwin, and, as a worker with words himself, he also felt special admiration for Ira. He set out with real determination, therefore, to make *Strike Up the Band* the best play he'd ever written. For this reason, though Morrie Ryskind had in a sense started it all, and though, as things turned out, Ryskind would eventually have to be called in to save the play, Kaufman didn't for a minute consider collaborating with the young firebrand from Columbia—or with anyone else, for that matter—when he began work on his book. He felt that he had some extremely strong things to say about wars and about the people who caused and glorified wars, and he wanted no help, and no interference, from anybody in saying it.

He worked for many months on his script: sweating, he later said ruefully to a friend, not only over every line and every word in the play, but over every letter in every word as well. He was typically worried about his script when he finally delivered it to Selwyn early in the summer of 1927. But Selwyn, reading the material once very quickly and then twice more very slowly and carefully, was totally delighted with it. Selwyn felt that the script was fresh, startling, biting, and original, and that Kaufman had achieved singlehandedly an absolute revolution in the Broadway musical field, proving that the

musical did not *have* to be a brainless mélange of legs and low
comedy, but could have a real story, a measure of almost operatic
seriousness, and a genuine social point to make. Selwyn phoned and
told all this to Kaufman in grateful language. He admitted that he
was still glad that the play would have songs and girls to soften the
message a bit for the tired-businessman type of playgoer, but genuinely appreciated the opportunity to be associated with what he called
"a landmark play, a real work of art." He never suspected, he said
many years later, that he would be adding in just a few months, "I
still say your play is all those things, George. And I guess that's why
we're in trouble."

The play made its first point by reminding people that many wars
are begun to further special interests rather than for the good of
the general public. Kaufman pitted the United States against, of
all unlikely countries, Switzerland, and had the war start at the insistence of a cheese manufacturer named Horace J. Fletcher, Fletcher's
reason being that the Swiss need a lesson because they're protesting
against and trying to strike down a 50 per cent tariff on the importation of Swiss cheese. Kaufman's next point dealt with the curious
practice of some American Presidents of leaning on personal friends,
some of them of questionable competence, for advice on matters of
the gravest importance. Fletcher persuades a presidential adviser
named Colonel Holmes, obviously modeled on Woodrow Wilson's
Colonel House, to force Switzerland into the war, convincing him
by offering to finance the entire war, provided only that the country
show its gratitude by giving the conflict the official name of the
Horace J. Fletcher Memorial War. And then Kaufman went on from
there. He satirized war hysteria, things like the changing of the name
of sauerkraut to Liberty Cabbage during World War I, by showing
patriots removing *Swiss Family Robinson* and *William Tell* from
libraries, and by having his hero, a reporter named Jim Townsend,
get into trouble when it's learned that he's wearing a Swiss watch. He
talked about the fact that wars bring soldiers death and mutilation
far more often than glory, and about the difficulty that ex-soldiers
meet in finding jobs once the cheering has died down. He even concluded the play on a sour note instead of the traditional happy ending
expected in musicals: when the war with Switzerland winds down,

the United States sets an oppressive tariff on caviar, and finds itself at war with a far more formidable and realistic enemy, the Soviet Union.

The Gershwins worked simultaneously to achieve the same tone and mood in their songs. They did most of their writing at first in a country house that the brothers and Leonore Gershwin had rented in Ossining, New York, in early April, and then, when the play went into rehearsal in July and they were needed for daily changes and additions, at George Gershwin's apartment. Kaufman had given them one guideline as unusual in 1927 as the book with which he himself emerged. The usual practice in that period was to instruct the composer and lyricists merely to deliver a specified number of songs—a certain number of love songs, a certain number of dance songs—and then just fit them into the play at planned intervals whether or not the lyrics had anything much to do with the plot, such as it was. The only real requirement was that the music and lyrics be "good." Kaufman wanted the Gershwin lyrics and music to be good, too, but he also wanted more than that; he wanted the music and lyrics to be integral to the play and its social point, either by furthering the plot development in the lyrics or by heightening and underlining the mood of the play. The requirement seems ordinary in the present period of the theme musical, in the period since the story-telling musical play became the norm with *Oklahoma!* and *South Pacific*, but it was extraordinary and innovative when Kaufman broached the plan. The brothers reacted with enthusiasm. They too, worked harder than they had ever worked before, and every song they wrote, even the love songs, attempted to serve as emphasis for the savage and bitter attitudes of the play.

Typical of the special effort put into the songs for the play was the enormous amount of work which went into developing precisely the right title song. Kaufman and the Gershwins envisioned the song as a march with a double purpose, serving first as a strong patriotic number, and then later, played more slowly, almost as a dirge to underscore the uglier aspects of war. Gershwin wrote four complete and different marches. But each time, as Ira approved the music and asked if he could start writing the lyrics for it, Gershwin changed his mind and decided the new composition was not quite good enough. Ironically, the four rejected marches were all composed at the keyboard, where Gershwin worked best, but the fifth and final version came to him while he was lying in bed. The brothers had gone to Atlantic City to have a conference with Selwyn and to do some uninterrupted work, and Ira, returning from a walk one Saturday night, assumed his brother was asleep because the lights in his room were out. A few minutes later, the lights went on, and George, dressed in pajamas, appeared. "I think I've finally got it," he said. "Are you sure you won't change your mind again?" Ira asked. "Yes, I'm pretty sure this time," George said. The march remained acceptable to its creator, lyrics were added to it, and the song became famous and popular.

Selwyn, as impressed with the music and lyrics as he had been with the book, set the musical for a week's tryout, beginning on August 29, 1927, and with Jimmy Savo and Vivian Hart starring, at the Broadway Theatre in Long Branch, New Jersey. The mood of every participant in the project except Kaufman—who remained, as always, downcast and despondent—was more than optimistic; the general attitude, based on certainty that they really had something good here, was confident almost to the point of arrogance. But a few nights later, every face in the place showed a look of dejection which matched Kaufman's. As the playwright had begun to state with increasing emphasis, but which everybody else had ignored because that was what he *always* said, it was becoming apparent that they didn't have a hit at all. They had, instead, an absolute disaster.

The local critics, and the critics who had come down from New York to cover the production, were kind enough, one of the critics even calling the play the most intelligent musical of all time. And some of the young people in the audience, as strong in their anti-war sentiments as Kaufman, liked it. Typical was a girl of about twenty, sitting with her father just behind Ira Gershwin, who made Ira breathe easier by saying enthusiastically, "Father, I think it's just wonderful!" But her father's verdict was somewhat different. "Awful!" he said, and, unfortunately, most of the people in the audience agreed with him. The play was just not entertainment; it was too savage, too raw, too thought-provoking, too frightening. As a Gershwin biographer, Lawrence D. Stewart, later put it, "It was 1927, the height of Coolidge well-being, and aficionados of musical comedy didn't want to study about war." It was just too early for a musical with as much underlying seriousness as this one, a musical which even had a bitterly satiric lyric stating, "Oh, this is such a charming war." It wasn't until thirty-seven years later, in 1964, that the American public was ready to embrace a musical with a very similar title, *Oh, What a Lovely War*, and make it a moderate hit—in part, ironically, because it seemed to be so original. Business at *Strike Up the Band* dropped off day after day, and when the production moved on to the Shubert Theatre in Philadelphia, where it was booked for a six-week tryout, and where the real test would come, things were even worse.

The first week's cost, including hanging the sets and all the rest, was $39,000; the play took in $17,000. The second week, the take was down to $9000. *Variety* later reported, "Although the critics raved, there wasn't a chance. Attendance dwindled gradually every performance, until the last few days there wasn't a handful of people in the big theatre." At the end of the second week, Selwyn threw in the towel.

It was, everyone agreed, a shame, but there it was, and there was no choice other than to try to be philosophical and even lighthearted about it. The tone for the appropriate attitude had been set by Ira just before the play closed in Philadelphia. The lyricist was standing outside the theatre with his brother and with Kaufman as darkness closed in, noting glumly the small number of people arriving to attend the evening's performance. Suddenly, a cab stopped in front of the theatre, and two men emerged—two very old men who were wearing bowler hats and long, old-fashioned overcoats redolent of the turn of the century. "Thank God!" Ira said. "Gilbert and Sullivan have arrived to fix up the play!"

Kaufman later took the same approach when he was in the lobby of another theatre one evening, attending someone else's play, and was hailed by a man he recognized at once as the principal backer of *Strike Up the Band*. Many producers in the '20s financed their plays strictly with their own funds. Selwyn was not one of this courageous number, and the tycoon he had brought in to put up the bulk of the money for the Kaufman play was this man, whom he had introduced around, by way of protecting his total identity so that no other producer could steal him away, only as Mr. Levy of Kentucky. Levy was now leading a small, plump woman who was obviously his wife. Kaufman watched warily, expecting recriminations over all the lost money. Instead, however, the backer smiled with pleasure as he approached, urged his wife forward, and said warmly, "My dear, here's the man you've been wanting to meet all these years. George Gershwin!" Kaufman tried to correct him, but the backer kept talking without giving him a chance. "Tell me, Mr. Gershwin," he said, "tell me one thing. With all the magnificent music you've written, with all the money your shows have made, why is it that *I* had to invest in the only one that was a failure? Why wasn't *Strike Up the Band* a big success?"

"I've always flattered myself," Kaufman later reported, "that I made the only possible answer. I said, 'Kaufman gave me a lousy book.'"

But it was still a shame, and Selwyn continued to brood about it for many months. Finally, in April 1928, he wrote to George Gershwin, who had gone to France to "soak up Parisian atmosphere" and begin the composition which would eventually become *An American in Paris*. He asked Gershwin if he and Ira would be willing to revise the musical and make it gentler and more commercial for another shot at Broadway—provided, of course, he could also get Kaufman to agree to the even more important requirement of softening the book. Gershwin was willing, and was sure his brother would be, too, though he pointed out that he and Ira had other commitments and wouldn't be able to start work on the revisions for about a year. That was all right with Selwyn, who was in no hurry, and rather liked the idea of putting more time between the two versions of the musical. He then approached Kaufman. But Kaufman, it turned out, was not willing at all.

One of the reasons was that Kaufman had also become involved in other things, and his mind was now totally elsewhere. He had written *The Still Alarm*, a sketch about two insouciant young men who find themselves caught in a hotel fire and discuss the whole business with great calmness, considering at length such matters as the correct way to dress when escaping from a fire, and inserted it in a revue called

The Little Show which opened at the Music Box Theatre on Tuesday, April 30, 1929. (His brief contribution became a strong factor
in the play's success. The revue also had the sterling services of
Clifton Webb, Libby Holman, Fred Allen, and Portland Hoffa, but
every critic pointed to Kaufman's sketch—which *Theatre* called
"delightful," the *Times* called "immaculate," and *The New Republic*
described as "capital"—as the high point of the evening.) He had
undertaken the direction of *The Front Page*, and joined with Edna
Ferber on *The Royal Family*, Lardner on *June Moon*, and Woollcott
on *The Channel Road*. And there were private things happening,
such as H. H. Frazee's death on June 6, 1929, which was deeply
saddening to Kaufman both because of the personal loss and because
the event represented the end of an era in his own life, the closing of
a door on one of the starting points in his own career.

But these were subsidiary factors. The main reason was what a
critic named Isaac Goldberg later described as his "obstinate integrity"; he had conceived *Strike Up the Band* as a crying-out
against war, and he just couldn't bring himself to return to the play
for the purpose of removing its essential message. He couldn't help
feeling the way he did, he told Selwyn, and he continued to resist
Selwyn's blandishments even after the middle of 1929 had arrived
and the Gershwins announced themselves ready to begin their part
of the job. By now, Selwyn was nearly frantic. He began to phone
Kaufman almost every day, and finally, on one of these days, Kaufman told him flatly and finally that he was simply unable to do the
revision, and would never be able to do it. Then he added, as Selwyn
began to protest in anguish, that he was perfectly willing to permit
Morrie Ryskind to revise the book in any way necessary, assuming,
of course, that Ryskind was acceptable to Selwyn and assuming
Ryskind was interested.

Selwyn accepted the substitute proposal, after some hesitation, and
talked to Ryskind, who was more than merely interested; he was
enthusiastic, eager, and excited. This, too, was an irony in itself,
since Ryskind was, of course, even more fervently anti-war than
Kaufman. But he told Selwyn candidly, in leaping to accept the
assignment, that his career had to come first at this stage in his life.
He went to work to remove, mercilessly, every element which had

made the musical something special, but which had also made it unpalatable to most of the public.

The play which Ryskind and the Gershwins delivered late in 1929 had been toned down in every way. Even the tariff-heavy product which started the war had been changed; it was altered from Swiss cheese to Swiss chocolate because chocolate presents a "sweeter image." "What's the difference?" Ira, who suggested the change, said with a shrug. "They're both made with milk." The war was no longer a real war; it was just something that Horace Fletcher dreamt when he became ill and his doctor gave him a sedative. And even a quite beautiful song, *The Man I Love*, was dropped from the new *Strike Up the Band* because it was feared that some people might consider it a shade too sad.

The song had a curious history. The Gershwins had originally written it for *Lady Be Good!*, but it had been dropped from that musical, too, for being "out of tone" with the play, and kept on the shelf until it was resurrected for the first version of *Strike Up the Band*. When it was evicted from the new version, it was put into a third show, a Ziegfeld production called *Rosalie*, but it was soon also cut out of that one. In disgust, the Gershwins gave up the idea of the song as a show tune and turned it over to their publisher to be brought out as a single piece of sheet music. They even accepted his proviso that, since he was truly doubtful about the success of the song in any form, he be permitted to pay a reduced royalty. Almost immediately afterward, the song was picked up by Helen Morgan and other singers and became a hit, and, eventually, a classic. But the song did do some earlier good during its brief stay in *Lady Be Good!*, at least for a few people: the play's producers and Otto H. Kahn, the financier. The producers went to Kahn to ask him to invest in the show, and were turned down because Kahn was really only interested in giving support of a philanthropic nature to experimental and non-commercial productions. He changed his mind and put in $10,000 when he was told that *The Man I Love*, a song he'd heard around and had admired, was going to be in the show. So the producers got their money, and Kahn, since the show became a hit even with the song removed, enjoyed the unique experience of getting his donation back plus a profit.

The Man I Love was not the only song cut out of the new version of *Strike Up the Band;* more than half the songs in the original version were eventually dropped or replaced, and one, *Soon,* was changed totally. It had only been an eight-bar strain in the original Act One finale, but it was expanded for the new version and used as a full song, and became popular at once. There were also many other consequential changes, a particularly important one being the hiring of the team of Bobby Clark and Paul McCullough for leading roles. Clark and McCullough were very funny, but pretty broad and slapstick in their comedy style, and Ryskind had to write a lot of new material for them, humor which was far less subtle than the Kaufman brand. Ira, too, had to change his own style a little, and even had to allow a few lyrics written by Clark to be used in the show. Fortunately, they weren't too bad; they included such Gershwin-like rhymes as "decorum" and "floor-um," and Ira was later able to report, though perhaps with more generosity than truth, that the Clark lyrics had drawn as many chuckles as his own. One thing was certain, anyway, when all the work was done: the new play was very different from the first one.

But if it was, as many critics said when *Strike Up the Band* was shown again, an infinitely less courageous show, it was also infinitely better box office. It opened in Boston for a tryout at the Shubert Theatre on Wednesday, December 25, 1929, and moved to New York for its official opening at the Times Square Theatre on Tuesday, January 14, 1930, and this time audiences applauded. Many critics applauded, too, feeling that even a watered-down anti-war play was a long step in the right direction. *Theatre* called the play "delightful satire, freshly, amusingly done," *The Nation* said the play was "not only boldly original in plot but even flirts with social satire," and one critic, William Bolitho of the *World,* felt that the play was quite strong even in its expurgated version, saying a while after the opening, "Of all things in the world, here is a bitter, rather good satirical attack on war, genuine propaganda at times, sung and danced on Broadway to standing room only." All the other critics liked it well enough, too, and people formed long lines at the box office.

There was an extra added attraction at the Boston premiere: George Gershwin appeared in the pit and conducted the orchestra personally the first night. He also repeated his performance at intervals after the play had begun its New York run. He proved to be an extremely able conductor, despite a tendency to sing his own songs, as he waved his baton, in a voice sufficiently audible to distract the musicians and the actors. He admitted, when chided about it, that "my voice is what is known as small but disagreeable," and grinned sheepishly when Kaufman told him pointedly that he ought to put his name in the program as a member of the cast. But he never stopped doing it; his music always managed to get to him, and he always forgot himself and started singing again. Since the play also brought him one of his closest friendships—a play called *Ripples*, with music by Oscar Levant, was appearing right across the street at the New Amsterdam Theatre, and it was during the concurrent runs that the two music-lovers kept running into each other and really got to know each other—Gershwin's appearances at the theatre and in the orchestra pit became more and more frequent. Nobody, of course, minded; quite the contrary. The possibility of picking a night in which the conductor might be George Gershwin, even a singing George Gershwin, instead of some unknown wielder of the baton, became an added sales point. The play ran a solid 191 performances plus a good road tour.

It was all living proof that, though virtue may sometimes be its own reward, there are times in our history when compromise is rewarded quicker. The horrible flop of 1927 had become, in 1930, a big hit and a big moneymaker for its participants. And there was also another, and far more important, reward to come. As it turned out, the watered-down *Strike Up the Band*, successful as it was, was destined to go down in the books of judgment as a mere dress rehearsal for a more significant play. This was a play which would, furthermore, be presented when it was no longer necessary to do any watering-down: the prize-winner, the really really big one, *Of Thee I Sing*.

20. THE PRIZE

ALL HIS LIFE, Kaufman lived, as described, with the feeling of absolute certainty that, though his present play seemed to be doing all right, his next one was sure to be a failure. The theatre, he knew, offered no safe haven for its participants because there was really no such thing as a genuinely faithful following for any author, actor, or producer. There were endless examples around of men and women who were almost beatified while involved in a hit, and then scourged as enthusiastically when the next play failed to catch the public fancy. And, since Kaufman was also certain that even his longest-running plays had become successful mostly because a lot of critics and theatregoers were not too bright and had greeted the plays with more enthusiasm than they deserved, he never swerved from his suspicion that each new script which emerged from his typewriter would be the one which would finally reveal to the world his lack of talent.

In 1966, five years after Kaufman's death, a man named Abe Raufe wrote a book called *Anatomy of a Hit*, in which he gave convincing proof that playwrights rarely pull in audiences by their byline alone, describing a lot of times that impressive ups had been followed by thudding downs. Among the examples given by Raufe were Jack Kirkland, who adapted Erskine Caldwell's novel, *Tobacco Road*, into a play which ran an astonishing 3000 performances, and next developed another famous novel, John Steinbeck's *Tortilla Flat*, into a play which closed after five performances; Mary Chase, who wrote *Harvey*, which ran 1775 performances, and followed it with *The Next Half Hour*, which Kaufman directed but which ran only eight; Ketti Frings, whose *Look Homeward, Angel* achieved 564 performances, and whose subsequent *The Long Dream* closed after five; Dore Schary, with *Sunrise at Campobello* at 556 and *The Highest Tree* at 21; Noël Coward, author of *Blithe Spirit* (657 performances) and *Look After Lulu* (39); John Van Druten, who wrote *The Voice of the Turtle*, which had 1557 performances, and *I've Got Sixpence*, which barely managed 23; and John Patrick, who followed *The Teahouse of the August Moon*'s 1027 showings with *Good as Gold*, which racked up four. If Kaufman had been alive to read the book, he would have done so with total sympathy and understanding, but also with a certain amount of *déjà vu* because statistics of that sort were old stuff to him, the sort of thing he thought about all the time.

The constant fear that his success would not last proved to be a very fortunate thing for Kaufman when, on October 12, 1929, stock market prices suddenly stopped streaking upward and started plummeting down, and the country plunged into its long depression. Unlike other playwrights, who developed such euphoria over their current hits that they spent every cent they earned in the comfortable assurance that their next plays would bring the same kind of income, Kaufman banked and retained a substantial part of the money he earned (in banks, fortunately, which were not among those which folded when the depression arrived) because he was always so sure that the golden flow would soon stop. And because he was such a prodigious worker, his own failures, though he had his share of these along with everyone else, were never especially painful, or even particularly noticeable in the same way they were with other playwrights who showed up on Broadway less frequently. Of Kaufman's first thirty-four plays, eleven lost money, and five others would have done so and were saved only by movie sales. But by the time a Kaufman flop reached Broadway and closed, he was already involved in another play which became a hit, and sometimes two or even three hit plays at once, quickly dimming memory of the failure and replenishing his exchequer.

He was also one of the very few people in show business not hurt too badly by the market crash; he distrusted the market, and generally reacted to all stock offers the way he did when a high-pressure salesman tried to sell him some stock in a gold mine. The salesman said the mine was so rich that gold was just lying around on the ground for the taking. "On the ground?" Kaufman said. "You mean I'd have to stoop for it? Not interested." As a result, he owned only one stock, and so lost only a comparatively small amount in the crash, $10,000. The stock was one that Groucho and Harpo Marx had talked him into buying, and he took the loss philosophically, telling a friend, "Anyone who buys a stock because the Marx Brothers recommend it *deserves* to lose $10,000." It was not difficult to treat the loss fairly casually because his income was becoming as prodigious as his literary output. In addition to his royalties from his plays and their constant revivals and their professional, semi-professional, and amateur showings around the world, and his share of the money from movie sales, he had also begun to invest in his own plays, sometimes putting up part of the money needed and sometimes putting up all of it. Since the usual practice in the theatre is for the producer to receive 50 per cent of the profits (the money remaining after paying out authors' royalties, actors' salaries, theatre rentals, and other costs) and the collective backers to share the other 50 per cent, this helped considerably, particularly on those hits where Kaufman had put up all the money and thus received a weekly share of profits equal to the producer's *plus* his substantial royalties.

He was also, as a silent partner in a production as well as author, able to bargain especially hard on the movie rights to his plays. This was a position strengthened by the fact that, though he might perhaps *want* a sum of money proffered to him, he was never in desperate need of it like some other writers, and could spurn or appear to spurn an offer he considered inadequate. He did this once when Adolph Zukor, the head of Paramount, offered him $30,000 for the movie rights to one of his plays. "I guess not," he said cordially. "But I'll tell you what I'll do. I'll give you $40,000 for Paramount." Zukor got the message, and continued to revise his offer upward until Kaufman accepted. Kaufman gradually became as businesslike about his business affairs as he had always been at the typewriter. He watched all income sources carefully and went after people who tried to give performances of his plays without paying a royalty. One such man was a summer stock producer who said he hadn't thought about paying a royalty because his place of business was such a small, insignificant theatre. "Fine," Kaufman said. "So you'll go to a small, insignificant jail." The man paid up.

By 1930, *Variety* reported that Kaufman was earning $7000 a week, in a period in which the figure held the buying power of about $50,000 a week now, and the trend continued upward after that. In June 1927 an observer of the theatrical scene named Katharine Roberts, writing in *Stage*, estimated that Shakespeare would have earned $527,416 in stage royalties and shares of movie money in the years from 1934 to 1937 if he had been around to collect, and then went on to estimate that Kaufman had earned more in that period. By 1939, twenty of Kaufman's plays had sold to the movies for a total of $1,500,000, probably equivalent to at least $10,000,000 in present times. And, despite his gloomy prognostications, money continued to pour in for the rest of his life. It is still coming in. In a typical season, for example—1969–70—only three other authors received more productions of their plays in the United States, and they were all "classic" playwrights: Shakespeare, Shaw, and Chekhov. Kaufman tied with Molière for fourth place. By way of comparison, there were eight separate productions of Kaufman plays that year, whereas Tennessee Williams had seven productions, O'Neill five, Noël Coward four, and Beckett and Brecht three apiece.

The result of Kaufman's increasing prosperity was that, in 1930, in a period in which other playwrights were moving out of large homes or expensive apartments or hotel suites and moving into board-inghouses and furnished rooms, Kaufman and Beatrice began to live more and more luxuriously, exchanging their large apartment at 200 West 58th Street for an even larger town house at 158 East 63rd Street, between Lexington and Third Avenues, and adding several more maids. The town house had been the former residence of Peggy Hopkins Joyce, a very rich and much-publicized playgirl of the period who was so casual about her possessions that, when the Kaufmans moved in, they found that she had left behind, along with a lot of other expensive things, a solid gold police whistle presumably kept for summoning help in the event of intruders. The Kaufmans also added to their social status by buying a limousine and hiring a chauffeur to drive them around town, hiring the first of the series of aristocratic and high-salaried mademoiselles to keep an eye on Anne and help out with the cultural side of her education, and renting a series of beautiful homes for the summers, first in Sands Point, Long Island, next in Manhasset, Long Island, and then in Katonah, New York, a small and rustically attractive town in Westchester County.

All the new and added luxuries made Kaufman feel a bit guilty and defensive, with so many people around him struggling just to eat and pay the rent. He began to pretend that he, too, was working as hard as he did, and sometimes on so many different projects at once, out of necessity rather than choice. "All I know," he once told a reporter, "is that I've earned a great deal of money and I haven't got any of it. If I don't get a hit each year, I'm in a damned bad way." He said that sort of thing so often that he even convinced Ruth Fried-lich's son Bruce that he was just like Joseph Kaufman and other members of the Kaufman family, a family which Ruth summed up in general as "legendary for its financial ineptitude." "I'm the black sheep of the family," Bruce, who now runs a large advertising agency, told Ruth in a determined voice one day. "I'm going to make and keep a nickel." Kaufman alternated that pose with an equally distorted one of himself as a man interested strictly in the buck, and never missed an opportunity to keep that image alive. Near the end of his life, when he was appearing on the television show, *This Is Show Business*, and had enough money on hand and coming in to keep him in luxury if he lived five times as long as he did, he was asked by a fellow panelist on the show, Martha Wright, the singer, if he could supply her with a formula for happiness. "Well," Kaufman said, "we all know that money doesn't bring happiness—so just give your money away. Give it to me." But friends and observers knew better, watching his charities and loans increase as more and more people around him showed need.

One of the neediest was Max Gordon, not yet his producer and partner, who had taken advice from the Marx Brothers and others on a lot of stocks, and who was completely wiped out by the collapse of the market. Gordon's real name was Max Salpeter, though he had changed it years before, and he got the news of the crash in a call from Groucho Marx. "Salpeter?" Groucho said in a conspiratorial whisper. "The jig's up!" Gordon did not take the news quite as lightly; he had struggled for years to amass the money which was now gone, and he suffered a nervous collapse, even beginning to think seriously about suicide. He never forgot Kaufman's generous response when, finally, he pulled himself together and went to the playwright and asked him, in high embarrassment, for a loan. Kaufman totaled up his resources and told Gordon quietly that he could draw on up to two-thirds of it.

The other thing which tipped people off to the spuriousness of Kaufman's claims of money hunger was the fact that he never once in his life took on a project merely because it looked as though there might be a lot of money in it. There was no question about the fact that he had a sharp eye for the commercial aspects of his field, even to the extent, according to one of his associates, of being able to size up the social pattern on an audience. This was a knack which was apparently unique with Kaufman: he could look over an audience for a moment or two, gauge the financial and social status of the majority of people looking up at the stage, think a minute or two about whether or not people of that type were regular theatregoers, and estimate with startling accuracy the probable remaining run of the play. But though, obviously, he wrote and directed his plays to make money, the money motive was never enough by itself. The idea or theme of the project also had to interest or amuse him tremendously, or, as in the instances when he entered the wild world of the Marx Brothers, he had to be talked into it by someone as persuasive as Sam H. Harris. And even on those projects, there was the widespread suspicion that, underneath all the grumbling, Kaufman was secretly pleased to be mixing with the mad, entertaining Marxes.

It was finances, both his own and the rest of the country's, which made Kaufman decide to undertake the project which became *Of Thee I Sing*. His own financial situation, examined carefully before he began work, entered into it because he had to be sure he could afford the luxury of writing another controversial musical which might suffer the same fate as the first version of *Strike Up the Band* and close out of town. It was a play which, furthermore, might turn out to be even more controversial than the earlier play, and which, in the depressed times, would probably not be given a second chance if it flopped on tryout. The financial condition of the country, however, was far more the determining factor in his decision. This was no longer 1927, with people enjoying a booming economy and lulling themselves into believing it would go on forever, and therefore unwilling to face and think about the grimmer realities of life. It was now 1930, with the stock market destroyed, the country plunging deeper and deeper into hard times which looked, frighteningly, as though *they* might go on forever, and with more and more people jobless and hungry every day. It seemed to Kaufman that, with people growing increasingly disgusted at the prosperity-is-just-around-the-corner platitudes and ineptitude of Herbert Hoover and others of his type, there was a good chance that the theatregoing public had now become serious-minded enough, matured enough by the problems which faced the country, to accept a musical which dealt with the foibles and fatuousness of government and government officials.

That was the theme which Kaufman had in mind this time: a play which would take on and satirize American politics, and particularly the special absurdities of presidential campaigns, covering every aspect of American political foolishment so thoroughly that, as the critic for *Commonweal* later reported in admiration and astonishment, "Nothing is left unscathed: the torchlight processions, the informal hotel room meeting-ground of the national committee, a political rally at Madison Square Garden, the pageant of the inauguration, the hectic life of the White House, the inconsequential ramblings of the Senate, and, last but not least, the gullibility of the whole American public. All are raised up to a shattering ridicule which would make W. S. Gilbert's treatment of his First Lord of the Admiralty seem like a compliment." And this time, having had further proof of Morrie Ryskind's substantial talents and abilities in the job he'd done to save *Strike Up the Band*, regrettable though the necessity to tone it down had been, Kaufman again invited Ryskind to join him as collaborator right from the start.

Once more, Ryskind was willing, but rather doubtful this time about the play's prospects even in the present climate, particularly after he had had three meetings with Kaufman and learned more about how mercilessly Kaufman wanted to treat his subject. "Well," he said finally, "before we go into this thing seriously, we might as well make up our minds that no one will produce it. But we'll have a lot of fun writing it." Kaufman told him that he was wrong, that he already had a producer in mind who *would* produce it: Sam Harris. "Harris," he reminded Ryskind, "is a producer who believes in his authors." Then he added, "Furthermore, we won't have any trouble about backers. I've talked to Harris about this a little already, and he tells me the show will probably cost around eighty to eighty-five thousand to bring in. I've decided to put up all the money myself."

Actually, Kaufman's decision to finance the play personally was based strictly on his recent decision to do this whenever possible, and keep all the profits for the producer and himself. It was not because of concern about being unable to attract backers; it had been quite a few years since there had been any trouble finding backers for a Kaufman play. And it would be many, many more years before skyrocketing production costs would bring the price tags on musicals into the hundreds of thousands of dollars, and destined to go over a million dollars on some productions, and make it virtually impossible for any single individual to finance a play. (When that state of affairs arrived, Kaufman complained one day to Harold Ross, "Now the backer wants to *read* the script!" Kaufman's complaint was later recalled by James Thurber in a discussion of the sad state of the theatre, in the years after Kaufman's death, brought on by increased costs and decreased attendance. "Kaufman's years on Broadway,"

Thurber added, "started with the era in which any backer would risk his money in a Kaufman collaboration sight unseen, and ended in the present desperate financial condition of the theatre." Then Thurber summarized the state of the theatre by quoting from a letter he had received from a friend while he was on a trip to London. "For God's sake," the friend had written Thurber, "get back here and prevent me from putting any money into any play at all.")

But there was no such problem back in the Thirties, even with investment money in general growing tighter. There were, of course, occasional complaints about receipts as opposed to costs, such as the statement made in 1934 by Rowland Stebbins, the producer of *The Green Pastures*, about the state of affairs while the play was on tour. "I have some figures," Stebbins said, "which will show that, even with a successful play, the picture that you could give a capitalist to put money into it is not a particularly attractive one. Speaking of my season this year with *Green Pastures*, I paid our stage crew about $19,000, which did not include the crews at the local theatres. I paid the house crew about $15,700; taking in and taking out, about $7000; extra stagehands and extra time, about $6000; car loaders, $2836—a total of $51,000. Baggage and scenery transfer, $8900. I paid to union labor, about $61,000. I paid the actors $76,000. A total of about $138,000. I grossed $312,000. After the costs of production, my profit was $9740, or three percent." But *The Green Pastures*, needless to say, was very profitable over-all for everybody concerned, and so were enough of the Kaufman plays so that backers kept flocking in and asking to be allowed to invest.

Kaufman and Ryskind started out by planning to call their play *Tweedle-Dee*, stressing the disturbing similarity of the two principal parties by focusing the plot around a rivalry between the parties to develop a new national anthem, and having the parties race to produce separate songs but end up with anthems which are almost identical. And since the project was one which depended so strongly on a musical angle—and a project which, furthermore, was, in a sense, an effort to disprove the conviction in theatrical circles that bitterly satirical musicals could never succeed because of the failure of the first version of *Strike Up the Band*—there was really, in logic and justice, only one team to invite in to write the music and lyrics: the Gershwin brothers.

The Gershwins were interested immediately, and George was especially enthusiastic about the idea of the twin anthems. "We'll sing each anthem against the other for a first act finale," he said. "We'll handle it contrapuntally."

Kaufman wasn't entirely sure that he understood what the word meant, but he nodded. "I'll take your word for it," he said.

But when he locked in with Ryskind and began to put together the actual plot of the musical, he came slowly and unhappily to the conclusion that the idea of rivalry for a new national anthem just wasn't going to work. The trouble with the idea, he discovered as he began to get into specific plot details and developments, was that a competition of that sort was just too impersonal, too uninvolving. The result was that he and Ryskind were ending up with a play in which the only protagonists, the only opponents, were the political parties. And even a play with satiric intent needed something more than that: like nearly all forms of fiction, it needed a lead character with whom the audience could identify, an individual with a personal problem to overcome or a personal goal to reach. "And come to think of it," Kaufman pointed out to Ryskind, "we can also use a heroine."

They started all over again, this time beginning with a political party so devoid of genuine issues as they sit around their smoke-filled hotel room that they finally turn in desperation to a chambermaid and ask her what interests her most in life. "Money," the chambermaid says unhesitatingly, but the political pundits reject that because the subject of money can sometimes be too controversial, and instead concentrate on the chambermaid's second all-consuming interest: love. Since the party's political candidate, John P. Wintergreen (the P., Kaufman later confided to Ira Gershwin, stood for Peppermint), is a bachelor, his strategists arrange a beauty contest at Atlantic City at which the winner will become not merely Miss America but also Miss White House because Wintergreen will marry her. He will thereby gain for himself not only the respectability of the married state but, surely, political victory because all the world, and America most of all, loves a lover. The plan backfires when Wintergreen is elected but spurns the beauty queen, a Southern type named Diana Devereaux, nearly precipitating a war with France because the lady is of French descent, and instead marries his secretary. Things grow worse and worse until Wintergreen is up for impeachment. But he's saved at the end when his wife presents him with twins—since, as everyone knows, parenthood and motherhood are even more appealing to the sentimental American public than love.

That was the basic plot, and it would have been mindless enough to qualify as a stock, standard musical of the period if it had been left at that. But it was not left at that; with total determination, Kaufman and Ryskind, and then George and Ira Gershwin, used the simple story as a framework around which they built satiric comment of the frankest variety and fiercest intensity. Their intentions were clear the instant the curtain lifted: the opening lines dealt with a formerly forbidden subject, something which everybody knew but nobody ever discussed, the shameless pandering of politicians to racial, religious, and other special-interest groups. "He's the man the people choose," sing a procession of torchlight campaigners for Wintergreen. "Loves the Irish and the Jews." Nor was any other opportunity for eyebrow-lifted observation overlooked. The cynicism of political promises is displayed via posters and signs with slogans like *Vote for Prosperity and See What You Get*. The casual enthusiasm of American voters is shown by flashing election returns in which a number of votes go to Mickey Mouse, Mae West, and the Wall Street firm of Goldman Sachs, and the occasional confusion of the voting process is emphasized when two New York districts are lost and then turn up with their votes credited to Nebraska. The foolishness of some political bills is shown as a Senator from Nebraska argues for a pension for Paul Revere's horse, and almost gets it until somebody points out that the horse is probably dead by now. The minuscule role of the Vice-President is noted by depicting Wintergreen's second in command, Alexander Throttlebottom, as a timid little man whose name nobody can remember, who is constantly refused admission to meetings and caucuses because nobody recognizes him, and who gets into the White House after his election only by joining a guided tour and sneaking away from the group. It was all there—"heavenly funny," a critic later said, "but also serious as hell."

By mid-March 1931, Kaufman and Ryskind had the play worked

out in sufficient detail so that they could write and mail a 5000-word synopsis to Harris, who was vacationing and avoiding the New York winter in Palm Beach, Florida. A similar synopsis, accompanied by an explanation of why the double-anthem plan had been abandoned, plus a carefully worded statement of why the Gershwins were needed even more urgently now to strengthen the new concept with their music and lyrics, was sent to the songwriting team in Hollywood, where they were working on a picture. Harris's response came the next morning via telegram. WELL, the wire said, IT'S CERTAINLY DIFFERENT. The telegram dipped Ryskind into dejection. "Didn't I warn you?" he told Kaufman. "Didn't I tell you it was no use?" He was surprised to see Kaufman respond with one of the rare smiles which lit up his long, sad face. "Listen," Kaufman said, "you don't know Harris. He's a low-pressure type. That's the equivalent of wild enthusiasm from another producer. You know what it means? It means Great—try and have it ready for rehearsal in August."

A few days later, a letter arrived from the Gershwins expressing their approval, too. The letter said the long sales pitch had been unnecessary because they had no intention whatever of dropping out of the project, and added that they really liked the new title that Kaufman had cooked up now that *Tweedle-Dee* was no longer applicable: *Of Thee I Sing*. It was decided to begin work on the book, music, and lyrics in July, by which time Kaufman would be rid of some of his other chores and the Gershwins would be back in New York. Shortly afterward, however, Kaufman was stopped on the street by one of his friends. "I love the music for your new show," the friend said. "What music?" Kaufman asked, genuinely bewildered. "The title song particularly," the friend said. "*Of Thee I Sing*, I mean. I also liked the other new one for the show—*Who Cares?* Gershwin played them at a party when I was in California last week."

"I'm going to patent an invention," Kaufman said grimly, "which will keep composers away from pianos at parties. It might be expensive, though; eight strong men would probably be needed to make it work. Maybe I'd better come up with something which'll keep pianos away from composers."

But his nervousness at the composer's early revelation of his songs was nothing compared to the way he felt when the friend went on to describe the way the Gershwins had handled the title song. Kaufman had already received some adverse criticism of the new title for the play from people he knew, people who felt it was unpatriotic and in bad taste to use the revered words in a musical comedy in any manner whatsoever. The Gershwins, however, he now learned, had gone considerably further than mere use of the words as a title. The team had developed the title song as a love melody and had employed an ironic juxtaposition of the phrase with a slang term of endearment, making their opening line "Of thee I sing, baby."

Kaufman had not envisioned the title song as a love song, but that didn't bother him in itself; the Gershwins' ability to surprise listeners in this way was something he always found interesting, amusing, and effective. Years later, listening to the Gershwins sing and play *They All Laughed* soon after they'd written it, he heard the lyrics starting, "They all laughed at Christopher Columbus when he said the world was round, they all laughed when Edison recorded sound, they all laughed at Wilbur and his brother when they said that man could fly . . ." and cut in disbelievingly, "Don't tell me this is going to be a love song!" It was only when the Gershwins arrived, late in the song, at, "They laughed at me wanting you," that his doubts disappeared, and he later commented to Beatrice that that was the sort of thing that made Ira such an impressive lyricist. But here, of course, he was afraid that, if the simple use of the four words as a musical comedy title was regarded by some people as heresy, then the Gershwins' use might be declared entirely beyond the pale. "Well," Kaufman said, reporting it all to Ryskind, "we *did* decide to pull out the stops, didn't we?" "Sure," Ryskind said hollowly. "And they say a firing squad just hurts for a split second."

Despite their trepidation, they began work on the book in July as planned, working on weekends at Kaufman's summer place in Sands Point. They were pleasantly surprised to find themselves moving ahead so fast that they completed the entire book in a total of only seventeen days. The Gershwins, back in the East and working equally fast, soon had the rest of their songs ready. And Kaufman, convinced that he ought to do his own staging on this one, began to think about casting.

He showed, very quickly, the sure touch in this area which remained with him all his life. For Wintergreen, he looked around for a comedian who was fast-talking and smooth enough so that he would be convincing in the role of a successful politician, but could still remain essentially likable. He had heard that William Gaxton, a song-and-dance man appearing at the Palace, was very good, so he asked Ryskind's wife to catch Gaxton's act and give him an estimate of the performer's appeal to women. Mrs. Ryskind returned with a glowing report, and Kaufman interviewed Gaxton and hired him. And then, for total contrast, Kaufman hired Victor Moore, a specialist in hesitant, bumbling roles, to play Throttlebottom. It was the first time the two men had ever appeared together in a play, but they were so hilarious and worked so well together that they formed a team and were inseparable after that. A fine character actor named Florenz Ames was signed to play the French Ambassador, a lovely young actress named Lois Moran was hired as Wintergreen's secretary and wife, Grace Brinkley played Diana Devereaux, and the principal dancing role was given to a man who eventually became a movie actor and then a real-life politico: George Murphy, ex-Senator from California.

The play opened for tryout on Tuesday, December 8, 1931, at the Majestic Theatre in Boston, and first signs were favorable. The title song, far from offending, became a catch-phrase among members of the audience, with people addressing each other all over the place with, "Of thee I sing, baby!" The Governor of Massachusetts was not present at the opening, but his surrogate, the Lieutenant-Governor, was there. He did not rush, as some people expected, to summon the local police and close the show, but, instead, remained in his seat and turned red-faced and short-breathed with almost constant laughter. And Boston's toughest and most-respected critic, H. T. Parker of the *Transcript*, was almost equally breathless in his admiration for the play, giving it perhaps the best review he had ever given a play throughout his career. "From half-past eight to a quarter to twelve," he said, "the first audience rejoiced unflaggingly in what was set before it. We who are fond and foolish, and so ambitious for the

American theatre, went home with the warming sense that the new play had enlarged it. Hitherto our theatre has produced nothing like Mr. Kaufman's and Mr. Gershwin's musical play. It is a long, brave step upward in the progress of such pieces from characterless, threadbare convention to lively reflection of our life and comment upon it. For once, in its modest way, Boston is the seat of a theatre event."

Despite all this, Kaufman remained unconvinced, even when the other local critics echoed Parker's hosannas and the cast and play began to receive standing ovations at every performance. He began to say over and over again that Boston was not New York, and had managed to depress himself so deeply by the time the trial run ended that, on the train trip home, he turned to the Gershwins and asked, with embarrassment, if they were interested in taking over any part of his 50 per cent ownership. The Gershwins took him up on his offer almost before he'd finished making it, writing out checks at once which bought them 15 per cent of the pot. Ryskind, however, also given the opportunity, responded more along the lines that Kaufman expected. He smiled in a manner that Kaufman later described to Beatrice, who had returned to New York a few days before, as "weakly and unconvincingly," and said in a hesitant voice that he really didn't know a thing about the managerial side of the business and rather thought he'd content himself with his share of the royalties, which he was sure would be both substantial and prolonged. The reason he rejected Kaufman's offer, Ryskind later admitted to Sam Harris, was that his career, after all, was still in relative infancy, and he simply didn't have the money to buy a share of ownership, however much he had ached to do so. But either Kaufman never thought of this reason, or it occurred to him and he discarded it as not the real reason, since Ryskind could presumably have borrowed money—even from *him*—to buy a share if he'd really wanted it. Ryskind's refusal convinced Kaufman that sophisticated New York critics would tear the play to pieces and New York audiences would ignore it, or that he and Ryskind would be arrested and tried for some form of treason, or both. He spent the rest of the train ride with his chin sunk on his chest—trying to steel himself, he told Beatrice when he arrived home, for the oncoming debacle.

His mood diminished a little in intensity once he was actually back on home turf and had Beatrice around to assure him that he had a hit. And when Marc Connelly phoned him the next morning and asked if he wanted to sell off some more of his ownership, he thought about it a moment or two and decided to keep what he had. But he remained anything but confident about the success of the new play.

Nor was he alone in his fears. Wandering around the Broadway area that afternoon, he soon learned that the word was out that a lot of smart theatre people were betting, and even giving odds, that, despite the tryout raves, the play would never achieve a solid run on Broadway. It was just, the smart money said, "too intelligent and too lacking in pep" for that legendary and vitally necessary member of the audience, the tired businessman, and furthermore women were not really interested in politics and wouldn't go for it. Kaufman also learned that a number of actors in the play were considering the possibility of official vengeance as seriously as he was, a few even going so far as to work out arrangements for the sustenance and support of their families in the event they were arrested and stopped receiving salaries. None of these things did much to lighten his gloom.

By the time the play opened at the Music Box on Saturday, December 26, Kaufman was so nervous that he was unable to devote himself even to his usual practice of prowling around backstage until the final curtain had fallen. He showed up at the theatre as always, but left almost immediately to go for a long and solitary walk. Harris had also lost some of his customary cool, admitting that he had an upset stomach and deciding to spend the evening in his office above the theatre instead of coming downstairs. The actors were also exceptionally jittery, standing around in small groups and talking about censorship or bursting into dressing rooms for worried confabs. This is what Gaxton did, showing up in Moore's room a few minutes before first curtain and asking abruptly, "You don't really suppose we'll be arrested, do you, Vic?" He got little comfort from Moore. "I don't know," Moore said, his tremulous voice even shakier than usual. "I hear Hoover and a lot of other people are pretty sensitive about the dignity of the presidency and vice-presidency."

The only participants who were calm about it all were the Gershwins. George had conducted the opening night music in Boston and was doing the same thing in New York, telling the musicians in an undertone to "play it hot—not Harlem hot, Park Avenue hot," and was too busy to worry about anything except what he was doing. Ira who was absolutely confident that everything would work out fine stood at the back of the theatre casually greeting friends, calming Ryskind down, and watching with interest as celebrity after celebrity showed up. The strong Boston notices had brought requests for first-night tickets from what seemed to be every notable on the East Coast, and among the people who showed up that night after Christmas were Al Smith, the unsuccessful candidate for the presidency in 1928, Mayor Jimmy Walker, Lillian Gish, Beatrice Lillie, Ethel Barrymore, Florenz Ziegfeld, George White, Otto Kahn, Owen Davis, Irving Berlin, Ina Claire, Martin Beck, Gilbert Miller, Judith Anderson Condé Nast, Harold Ross, Morton Downey, and Samuel Goldwyn.

Ira attended the opening with his wife and with a writer for The New Yorker. The writer had phoned Ira and said he wanted to do a short piece about him, and Ira replied that his time was limited, but suggested that the writer come to the opening and ask questions during the intermission. When the intermission arrived, the writer soon saw that the lyricist was clearly one of the most honest men on earth.

The first proof of this occurred when a man called to the lyricist from the other side of the lobby. "Ira!" he said. "It's wonderful!" "That's my brother-in-law," Gershwin told the writer. A moment later, a woman appeared suddenly at Gershwin's side. "It's marvelous Ira," the woman said. "I love it." "My sister," Gershwin whispered to the writer. In the next few minutes, a man and woman told Gershwin that they thought the play was excellent, and the lyricist identified them as his brother, Arthur, and his sister-in-law. Just before the intermission ended, another woman walked over to Gershwin and told him she thought the show was wonderful. The writer looked inquiringly at the lyricist. "My mother-in-law," Ira said.

Kaufman returned to the theatre just as the second act was beginning, and was met with more gloom: an acquaintance confided to him that he'd overheard Bob Benchley, covering the show for The New Yorker, tell his companion that he didn't like the show very much. That seemed like the last straw to Kaufman. If a poker playing buddy and friendly critic like Benchley was going to rap

KAUFMAN AND HART

The relationship became too close.

To My Favorite
Collaborator (No Comma)
Named Moss Hart —

George

KAUFMAN GAVE THIS PICTURE TO HART

But couldn't resist a play on words.

A SCENE FROM THE FILM VERSION OF
ONCE IN A LIFETIME
Aline MacMahon gives lessons and Jack Oakie stares in awe.

GEORGE GERSHWIN

A race to the piano.

IRA GERSHWIN

He used a pen name.

Copyright 1931 by New World Publishing Company. Reprinted by permission.

THE FIRST DRAFT OF A TITLE SONG

Brilliant juxtaposition or bad taste?

MORRIE RYSKIND

The gulf grew wider.

ROBERT E. SHERWOOD
But Eddie Cantor interfered, anyway.

the show, the other critics were sure to slaughter it. Kaufman rushed off into the night again, and did not rejoin his associates until the reviews were beginning to appear.

As it turned out, the information on Benchley was accurate; his review was almost totally unfavorable. "I was definitely disappointed," he wrote. "*Of Thee I Sing* struck me as dull musically, and not particularly fresh satirically. The whole thing, during great stretches, was reminiscent of an old Hasty Pudding 'spoop' in which *lèse-majesté* was considered funny enough in itself without straining for any more mature elements of comedy." But since he was a magazine critic, his review didn't appear until many days later, and by that time it no longer mattered because he was absolutely alone in the world. Walker and Smith laughed as hard as the Massachusetts politician had laughed in Boston, and Smith later used the play to explain why he would not be interested in the second spot on the 1932 Democratic ticket, for which Franklin Delano Roosevelt seemed the certain choice for the top position. "Have you boys," he asked a group of reporters who questioned him about it, "seen the Vice-President in *Of Thee I Sing?*" And every New York critic except Benchley joined their Boston colleagues in describing the play as a landmark work and the best musical in American theatrical history.

The two men in bowler hats and long overcoats who had shown up at the Philadelphia tryout of *Strike Up the Band* were not needed this time, not even if they had really been who Ira Gershwin had said they were. Many of the critics commented that the United States now had its own Gilbert and Sullivan, and one or two even felt that Kaufman, Ryskind, and the Gershwins had surpassed them. One of these critics was Montrose J. Moses of *The North American Review*, who pointed out that *Of Thee I Sing* was doing to Congress and the Supreme Court what *Iolanthe* had done to Parliament, but doing it better, handling the material so delicately and wittily that no really intelligent politician or patriot could be offended in the way that *Iolanthe* had shocked Londoners when it first opened. "I can imagine," Moses wrote, "a party of the authors of our Constitution cracking a smile at the well-aimed satire." John Mason Brown, writing in the *Post*, also compared the play to the work of the British satirists, saying, "There is a new sun in a new sky: *Of Thee I*

Sing. From the first note of Mr. Gershwin's overture to the re-grettable dropping of the final curtain, it succeeds in cramming as much gaiety into an evening of giddy spoofing as any evening has the right to hold. By the very nature of that spoofing, and by virtue of the high order of Mr. Gershwin's music, the gay lyrics with which his brother Ira has accompanied it, and the intelligent lunacy of Mr. Kaufman's and Mr. Ryskind's book, it represents not only a new and welcome departure in the world of entertainment, but also in the field of American musical comedy. Here at last is a musical comedy which dodges nearly all the clichés of its kind, which has wit and intelligence behind it, which brings Gilbert and Sullivan to mind without being derived from them." The other critics said the same kind of thing.

Even Kaufman had to admit that the play had gotten some pretty fair reviews, though he soon found one thing in them to worry and embarrass him: the casual assumption of some critics that all of the inventiveness and sharp humor in the play was strictly his and never Ryskind's, or, even worse, that all of the good things in the book were his and the few bad things were Ryskind's. A typical offender was *The Christian Science Monitor*, which praised *Of Thee I Sing* enthusiastically but which also found "various coarsenesses which are quite gratuitous and which belong to a lower order of musical comedy." The newspaper's critic then added bluntly, "Here, we think, we discern the hand of the assistant librettist. So long as there is the unmistakable Kaufman touch, all is well." Other critics made the same point less directly by mentioning only Kaufman's name when praising the book, or by omitting Ryskind's name from the credit listings. This caused Kaufman to go around trying to make it clear to people, including some people who hadn't even raised the question, that all four collaborators had contributed equally to the project. Each collaborator, Kaufman said, provided equal talents and material of equal value—united, Kaufman added, by two hopes, "to make money and to write something to which we might listen for ten minutes without being ashamed." The minor slurs, however, didn't seem to irritate or offend Ryskind at all. He grinned at Kaufman the next time they saw each other and said, quietly but happily, "Well, it looks like we're in." This caused Kaufman to abandon that worry immediately and leap at once to another one. "Not quite yet," he said. "Let's wait and see if the general public takes to the play after the dedicated theatregoers are used up."

But that concern, too, was soon gone. Business was phenomenal from the start, and remained phenomenal throughout the long run of the play. The Music Box was one of the larger legitimate theatres in New York in 1932, capable of bringing in a maximum of a little over $30,000 a week, a huge total for the period and rarely achieved. But *Of Thee I Sing* brought in the top figure every week without exception for the first twenty-eight weeks of the show, selling every seat and every inch of standing room at every performance. Even when summer came along, a season in which, traditionally, many theatregoers leave town on vacation and grosses sometimes drop to half their normal level or less, the weekly totals at the Music Box never fell below an extremely healthy $24,000, and often did better than that. Right in the middle of the summer, Harris was able to report that a Thursday matinee performance, the show given on August 4, 1932, had broken all records for the ten-year period since the theatre had been erected. The box office had sold every seat and then sold an unprecedented additional seventy-two tickets to standees, bringing in over $2700 for the matinee. And when, on October 8, the musical left the Music Box to make room for another play—as it happened, it was another project of Kaufman's, *Dinner at Eight*, which he had written a few months before with Edna Ferber—and moved to the 46th Street Theatre, the play began immediately to earn that theatre's absolute capacity of $27,000, and continued to earn it.

Kaufman viewed the phenomenon with pride, but also with some remaining vestiges of astonishment. One night, standing inside the theatre with George Gershwin and watching the reactions of a typical audience, he was amazed to see that some of the people had tears glistening in their eyes during one of the love scenes. "What's the matter with them?" Kaufman whispered. "Don't they know we're kidding love?" "You're doing nothing of the kind, " Gershwin whispered back. "You may *think* you're kidding love—but when Wintergreen faces impeachment to stand by the girl he married, that's *championing* love. And the audience realizes it even if you don't."

Ira Gershwin had once chided a friend who asked him if he ever grew bored with writing lyrics about love. "Don't knock love, my boy," he said. "I'd be out of business without it." This recognition of love interest as a prime commodity with audiences was, of course, especially evident in the evolution of *Of Thee I Sing*, since the entire original plan for the play had been discarded at the realization that the conception failed to provide for natural inclusion of a strong hero and heroine and an important relationship between them. But though the final version of the play had made love a central theme, Kaufman, uncomfortable as always about displays of emotion, and especially so when the emotion was love, had clearly assumed that he and Ryskind were being as satirical about the love angle as they were about all the other elements in the play, and that audiences would never take the romance material seriously. The composer's comment, however, obviously made it suddenly evident to Kaufman that he and Ryskind had accomplished far more with the love material than they'd supposed, and that the love scenes were not merely leavening for the bitter political stuff but had emerged as genuinely touching. Gershwin was startled to see a look of almost unbearable sadness appear on Kaufman's face, quite different from the surface look of worry and gloom the playwright showed about things like the possible failure of a project. It was gone an instant later, so quickly that it could almost have been imagined. But Gershwin, very sensitive to other people's emotions and responses, and aware of Kaufman's situation at home of deep love without consummation, knew he had not imagined it, and later confided to a mutual friend that he'd been horrified to realize that he'd touched a chord that he hadn't intended to touch at all. He turned the conversation at once into purely professional channels, starting to complain that the music in the next scene was being played too fast.

In essence, the fact that the love scenes worked so well was a key to the enthusiasm with which the play was being greeted by both critics and audiences. The happy truth of the matter was that *everything* worked. Gaxton had proved to be an absolutely perfect John P. Wintergreen, and Moore's endearing portrait of Alexander Throttlebottom was so appealing to people who saw the show that John Chapman, then a member of the drama department of the *News* and later its chief reviewer, summed it all up one day by paraphrasing Lovelace's famous poem in a letter to his wife, writing her, "I could not love thee, dear, so much, loved I not Victor Moore." Ira Gershwin's lyrics blended so smoothly with his brother's music that Oscar Hammerstein later named one of the songs from the play, *Wintergreen for President,* as the perfect example of "words wedded to music," pointing out that you think of the music the moment you hear the words and the words the moment you hear the music. The songs blended with similar smoothness with the book. The Gershwins had also attempted many innovations with their songs, some of these trying for effect that had never before been attempted. A typical experiment was their use of *Who Cares?,* which they hoped would serve the show in two ways. In its first rendition in the play, the team marked the song to be sung "brightly, even glibly," so that its love lyrics would appear merely amusing and lighthearted. In a later scene, however, when Wintergreen is told to give up his wife, but refuses and embraces her, he sings the song again. This time, however, he sings very gently and on a darkened stage, and the Gershwins' hope was that the song would now be moving rather than devil-may-care. It worked beautifully, accounting for some of the moistness of the eyes that Kaufman had observed.

Even the effects of the political statements were stronger than Kaufman had anticipated. Here, of course, the emotional responses were planned and not as surprising to him as the reactions to the love material, but they surpassed his greatest hopes for them. He was becoming more and more interested in politics all the time, even reaching the point of active participation some years later, in 1940, when he joined Hendrik Willem Van Loon, Edna Ferber, John Gunther, S. N. Behrman, Moss Hart, Hervey Allen, Russel Crouse and others in forming a group to write speeches and make personal and radio appearances in support of Roosevelt's campaign for a third term. It was an interest which remained with him the rest of his life, so that, in his last years, he was still thinking hard about politics and writing glumly to Ruth Friedlich on June 8, 1960, "I would like Mr. Stevenson, but there's little chance, so I'm reconciled to Nixon and Kennedy." But he always thought of himself strictly as a concerned person and never as a pundit, and he was genuinely surprised and pleased when the serious thought and intent underlying the political humor in *Of Thee I Sing* was indeed taken seriously and discussed at length in newspaper editorials and in magazine articles.

By the time the play had been running a year, it had been seen by 450,000 people, had grossed over $1,400,000, and was bringing Kaufman a check for $2000 each week. This was considerably less than he would have been receiving if he had not, in his period of gloom, sold part of his ownership to the Gershwins, but eminently satisfactory even as reduced. The first anniversary also meant an added achievement to him; in those days of relatively small cost in putting on shows, a play could be a financial success and run only a matter of months, and no earlier Kaufman play had ever completed a full year. The success of the play also brought special satisfaction, for a similar reason, to the Gershwins: despite *their* record of successes, *they* had never had a play which had merited a second company. This time, it was obvious that their play was receiving so much publicity all around the country that it would do strong business outside of New York, and Kaufman and Harris began to talk about a second company before the play had been running on Broadway for a month.

They were in no hurry, and vetoed a suggestion from several of the people in Harris's office that a touring company be put together quickly so that it could open in Chicago in time for the 1932 conventions. For one thing, Kaufman felt that it was essential that actors be found who were as good, or nearly as good, as Gaxton and Moore and Lois Moran and all the other people in the Broadway company, and that would take time; and for another, both men agreed that political conventions and similar events tended to be bad for theatre business rather than good. Harris, discussing the matter with the press, pointed to the 1924 Democratic Convention as the perfect example of what he and Kaufman meant. The convention had been held at Madison Square Garden, and it had been assumed that the influx of thousands of additional visitors would bring substantial added business to theatres and similar enterprises, but instead business fell off sharply while the Democrats were in town. There were too many free shows, too many side shows, too many special entertainments like private drinking parties and co-operative ladies to compete for the attention of the delegates and others involved in the convention. For these reasons, Kaufman and Harris decided to proceed in a manner totally counter to the advice given to them. Instead of hurrying a second company through for the conventions, they deliberately held up the second production until the conventions were over, and then opened in Detroit, not Chicago, on September 12, 1932. The part of Wintergreen went to a good song-and-dance-man named Oscar Shaw, the role of Throttlebottom went to Donald Meek, a skillful stage and screen actor who specialized in playing characters matching his last name, and Lois Moran's role went to a young actress named Harriette Lake, who later became a popular screen and television comedienne under the name of Ann Sothern. The company did record business in Detroit, moved to Chicago for eleven weeks of excellent business there, and then did similarly well in St. Louis, Kansas City, Los Angeles, San Francisco, and elsewhere, touring for a total of eight months and making *Of Thee I Sing* a double success.

Life wasn't all work for Kaufman, of course. He never learned to love big, formal parties, but he always enjoyed evenings of talk and quiet fun with his friends. There were a lot of those evenings; Kaufman and his friends flitted in and out of each other's apartments and houses like neighbors in a development of tract homes. Frank Adams remained one of Kaufman's most frequent visitors. The two men saw a lot of each other because they had genuine mutual affection and admiration, and because Kaufman realized that Adams was one of the few people he knew who were truly happy about his ever-growing success as a playwright and director. Adams and Kaufman, in fact, developed a sort of ritual each time Kaufman had a new hit—a symbol of recognition that Kaufman's work was essentially over but the money would continue to pour in week after week. "I heard about the new one," Adams would say. "You sure you don't want me to find you a job as a columnist somewhere?" Kaufman's reply was always the same. "What?" he'd say. "And have to think up new things every day the way you do? Not a chance. It's much better getting paid for the same jokes over and over."

For years, nearly every one of Adams's diary-style columns carried accounts of the various types of get-togethers in which Kaufman,

Adams, and their friends were involved. One of the columns described Adams as having dinner at the Kaufman apartment, sitting next to Dorothy Parker, and playing hearts and losing $18. Another mentioned going for a long walk, ending up at the Kaufman apartment, and being given a sumptuous breakfast because the day turned out to be March 15 and therefore the Kaufmans' wedding anniversary. Another mentioned going over to Raoul Fleischmann's apartment and playing cards there, and still another mentioned a dinner at Alice Duer Miller's house in which both Kaufman and Adams excelled at the games which were played after dinner. There were countless other small social events: the Kaufmans and the Adamses going out to celebrate birthdays and other events; Kaufman going over to spend a pleasant day with George, Ira, and Leonore Gershwin; and Adams staying so late talking with the Kaufmans that he finally accepted an invitation to remain overnight. All unsensational, but all relaxing, and, in their way, rather special.

But work continued, too, and, inevitably, there were a few problems to mar the idyll of *Of Thee I Sing*. The first of these was a problem nearly everyone had anticipated from the start: governmental objections and an attempt at governmental interference. But it came from an unexpected quarter. It was not, as it developed, the United States which tried to bring pressure on the participants in the production, but, surprisingly, the government of France.

The French, it seemed, had three objections to the play as written. The first was that they felt that the character of the French envoy, the man who threatens war over Wintergreen's rejection of Diana Devereaux, was burlesqued too broadly and should be toned down "out of respect for the person and great office of the Ambassador." The second objection was to a reference to the war debt, which the French regarded as insulting. "You will pardon the intrusion, Monsieur," the French Ambassador tells Wintergreen, "but I have another note from my country." "That's all right," Wintergreen says. "We've got a lot of notes from your country, and some of them were due ten years ago." "But this is not a promise to pay," the Ambassador says. "This is serious!" (Kaufman admitted privately that the inference *was* insulting, when he was told about this one. But, he pointed out, it was also accurate.) And the third complaint was about the genealogy of Miss Devereaux, as described in a song called *The Illegitimate Daughter*.

The character had originally been called Joan Devereaux, and her first name had been changed early in the game to the more euphonious Diana, but the decisions about her specific family history proved considerably more difficult to make. "It turns out," Kaufman and Ryskind had said briefly in the synopsis they sent the Gershwins, "that she had a French father, so the French government is up in arms about the slight inflicted on her." And that was all they said, so it was up to Ira to invent specific details. He thought briefly of making the beauty contest winner the daughter either of a baker in Lyons or a prefect of police in Dijon, but then realized that the father's social or economic or political importance had to be major in order to justify the French government's threats in the play. He later reported, "Not wishing to use the names of any contemporary personages, I went historical. And, illegitimacy being not too socially disadvantageous among many broad-minded Europeans, I scribbled this possible genealogy for her on a page of the outline: 'She was an illegitimate daughter of an illegitimate nephew of Louis-Philippe (or Napoleon) so you can't inflict this indignity.'" The illustrious ancestor was eventually firmed up as Napoleon, and the real French government was furious at the reference to its hero.

The French government did not approach the theatrical management directly. The complaint came from a prestigious organization called the France-America Society, which passed a resolution condemning the offending lines and sent the resolution to Kaufman via one of its most important members, the Right Reverend Bishop William T. Manning. Kaufman, however, felt amused rather than threatened by the incident. It seemed to him that this was *really* Gilbert and Sullivan history repeating itself, an event similar to the time British authorities had, in panic, halted all performances of a new London sensation, *The Mikado*, for a few days because some Japanese dignitaries were coming to visit the country. Furthermore, there was support for his impression that not all Frenchmen felt the same way. A distinguished French journalist, Stephane Lausanne, editor of *Paris Matin*, had just visited New York and had been asked about the

[447]

French references after he'd been quoted as saying that the evening he'd spent seeing *Of Thee I Sing* had been his most enjoyable evening in America. "It would be foolish and unbecoming for a Frenchman to object to a few witticisms directed at France," Lausanne said, "when the whole piece pokes unmerciful fun at the President and Vice-President of the United States itself." Kaufman considered his own response carefully, and then released a brief statement to the press. "I'll be glad to drop the lines," he said, "if Bishop Manning will write a couple for me which will get the same big laughs." No new lines were forthcoming from the theologian, and the French furor soon evaporated.

Another problem, a recurring one, was the extreme topicality of the play. Kaufman and Ryskind had none of Ira Gershwin's sense of delicacy about referring to contemporary personages, and the play was loaded with references to real-life people and events which were constantly being altered by new occurrences, and had to be rewritten again and again. A typical occurrence of this sort was the sudden death of Calvin Coolidge on January 5, 1933. There were two references to Coolidge in *Of Thee I Sing*, and his death dated them instantly. In one scene as originally written, Wintergreen's campaign managers decide to phone Coolidge and ask him to write a thousand-word press release for them on the subject of love, a funny line because love would probably have been the last subject in the world to interest the former chief executive. And in another scene, Wintergreen comments that an ex-President has no career problems because he can go right into the insurance business, which is what Coolidge had done after leaving office. By coincidence, Ryskind was in Harris's office when the news of Coolidge's death was announced. He wrote some quick, new lines which were handed to the actors in New York and then wired to the members of the second company, appearing that week in Milwaukee. Kaufman and Ryskind continued to provide revisions each time the need arose, and, in that way, managed to keep a half-step ahead of a play which seemed to date every time they turned their backs.

There was one other problem which was far more serious: the sudden arrival of one of the things that Kaufman hated most in life, a lawsuit. Despite his fatalistic acceptance of legal problems as a part of life for a successful playwright, Kaufman was totally unprepared for this one because it was so well-known and so clear that *Of Thee I Sing* was entirely the product and result of his own political attitudes and convictions. But a man named Walter Lowenfels claimed otherwise. Lowenfels was a poet and playwright who had shared the Richard Aldington Poetry Award for 1931 with e. e. cummings, but he had never made any real money as a writer, and he was now an expatriate living in poverty in Paris. Lowenfels had written a play called *U.S.A. with Music,* the score for which had been contributed by a friend of his who later became a well-known composer of avant-garde music, George Antheil, and Lowenfels claimed that his play had been inspired by antics and foolishness he'd observed at the 1924 Democratic Convention and that *Of Thee I Sing* was a direct imitation and plagiarism of his play. He had, he said, written *U.S.A. with Music* in bits and pieces between 1924 and 1929 and had had it copyrighted on February 17, 1930, though it had never been produced. He brought suit in August 1932 against the four authors of *Of Thee I Sing,* as well as against Sam Harris, Irving Berlin, because of his ownership of the Music Box, the Alfred A. Knopf Company, which had published the play in book form, the New World Music Company, publishers of George and Ira Gershwin's songs, and George Jean Nathan, who had written an introduction to the Knopf book. Lowenfels' summons and complaint contained forty pages of alleged similarities between his play and the Kaufman-Ryskind-Gershwin play, and he asked for an injunction to halt the production, sale, and distribution of *Of Thee I Sing* in all its forms, immediate confiscation of all plates, manuscripts, and copies of published books, and an accounting of the profits of the play, which he estimated as between $750,000 and $1,000,000.

Kaufman could have stopped the action in its tracks; the lawyer selected by his group, Wolfgang S. Schwabacher, was quick to point out that Lowenfels was broke and would have to drop the matter if the defendants demanded that he post a bond to cover the costs of the action, which would be levied against him in the event that he lost. But Kaufman didn't want it that way at all. He wanted the action dismissed, not on a technicality, but on its total lack of merit, so that no lingering doubts whatever would remain in people's minds. He insisted that the matter go forward, and the case was placed before Federal Judge John M. Woolsey in United States District Court.

Woolsey threw out Lowenfels' action four months later, on December 29, and assessed full attorneys' fees of $3500 against him. Lowenfels' play, Woolsey said, was built around a real-life event in which a man had been entombed in a Kentucky cave by a landslide, and a carnival atmosphere, with everything from food-vendors to entertainment, had sprung up during rescue operations. The play then flashed back and shifted to scenes based on other ugly real-life events. In short, he went on, the play bore no resemblance to *Of Thee I Sing* at all. "The plaintiff's play," Woolsey said, "was obviously written in a white heat of resentment against the social injustice displayed in some aspects of life in the United States. It is described by its author as an operatic tragedy. Reading the plaintiff's play, however, does not leave me with any real sense of tragedy, but rather with the feeling that I have been looking into a kaleidoscope of headlines clipped from sensational papers, or reading an anthology of exhibitions of bad taste. The defendants' play belongs to an entirely different species of dramatic composition. It may be called a musical satire burlesquing operatives in the United States." He concluded with a satiric comment of his own. "I am faced," he said, "with page after page of alleged parallelisms of phraseology. Obviously, however, the plaintiff cannot claim a copyright on the words in the dictionary or the names of the seasons."

It was all worth it, of course, headaches or not. *Of Thee I Sing* had 441 performances on Broadway, and then the company spent the winter of 1932 on a successful tour of its own and returned to New York on May 15, 1933, for 32 more performances at another theatre, the Imperial. The published version of the play was equally successful, selling out seven large printings in a very short time. The play's four creators became even more sought after socially than before, and were overwhelmed with invitations to dinners and parties, most of these from hosts and hostesses with the frank intention of cornering their guests and telling them how much they loved their play. A typical invitation came to Kaufman from Langdon Mitchell, author of *The New York Idea* and other popular plays of the period, who urged Kaufman to come to a dinner party "so that I may say to you all sorts of glorious things about *Of Thee I Sing.*" Equally typically,

Kaufman was horrified and refused the invitation, but saved Mitchell's letter all his life.

And in the middle of the play's long run, on May 2, 1932, there was one other thing: the best plaudit of all, even more impressive and satisfying than the show's financial success. The musical, suddenly and unexpectedly, was awarded the Pulitzer Prize.

There had been rumors that the play was being considered for the award almost from the day it opened, but no one associated with the production gave the gossip more than token attention. It was just too unlikely, and Kaufman was quickest of all to dismiss the possibility when Beatrice mentioned it to him. The Pulitzer Prize play committee, he reminded her, didn't even include musicals in its voting, and considered only "straight" plays. And furthermore, he added, "Look at the competition"—pointing out that the season had brought in such major dramas as Eugene O'Neill's *Mourning Becomes Electra*, Philip Barry's *The Animal Kingdom*, Robert E. Sherwood's *Reunion in Vienna*, and Elmer Rice's *Counsellor-at-Law*. But the one thing that Kaufman didn't take into consideration was the fact that the play committee had been in a rebellious mood for a number of years, chafing at the narrowness of the Pulitzer Prize rules and the limitations imposed upon the judges in the part of Pulitzer's will which established the prizes. The committee had shown its spirit of rebellion several years earlier by giving its prize to O'Neill's *Strange Interlude*, a frank drama about incest which hardly fit the pious requirement that the selection be the play which contributed most to "raising the standards of good morals, good taste, and good manners" on the stage. The judges now took another step outside the rigid limits, and ignored the prior interpretation of the rules which confined consideration to spoken plays. They announced matter-of-factly that musicals were plays, too, and that the 1932 award was going to *Of Thee I Sing*. The move wasn't quite as courageous as it might have been; the judges couldn't also bring themselves to face the fact that the music was an integral part of the play they were honoring, playing an inseparable role in making *Of Thee I Sing* worthy of the prize. Just before announcing the award, they decided that the rules of the game were simply too specific in that area, too definite in making it clear that the Pulitzer Prizes were strictly for writers of words. They passed over George Gershwin as though he didn't exist, awarding the prize only to Kaufman, Ryskind, and Ira Gershwin.

It was thrilling stuff, despite this foolishness, and for one man in the group, Ryskind, it also carried its special irony. The certificate which gave Ryskind his Pulitzer Prize was signed by Dr. Nicholas Murray Butler, since Columbia University administered the awards. The last time Ryskind had seen that signature had been on the letter throwing him out of the school. (Ryskind later heard that the two men most directly responsible for his dismissal, Butler and a professor named Odell, had paid their own money to see the show a short time before the awards were announced. Butler sat in a center orchestra seat and liked the show. Odell sat in the balcony and, not necessarily for that reason, thought it was lousy.)

The award, despite the rumors, took the country by surprise. The *Times* was so startled that it headlined its long front-page story *Musical Play Gets the Pulitzer Award,* confining mention of the other important choices—Pearl S. Buck's *The Good Earth* as best novel, General John J. Pershing's *My Experiences in the World War* as best book dealing with the history of the United States, and Walter Duranty's *Times* articles on Russia as best journalism—to a sub-head. The departure from the norm was also resented in some quarters—with, surprisingly, such ordinarily forward-looking critics as Atkinson and Mantle among the opposition. "When the Pulitzer committee selects a musical comedy in preference to *Mourning Becomes Electra, Reunion in Vienna,* or *The Animal Kingdom,*" Atkinson wrote irritably a few days after the announcement, "its judgment, I think, is skittish. Mr. O'Neill has had the prize three times. But Mr. Barry, who has written a great many intelligent plays and two or three fine ones, has had no encouragement from the prize committee, although the current *Animal Kingdom* is one of his best. This year's award is a popular one. It takes official note of a long step forward in musical comedy writing. But when the committee turns its back on the drama in a season that has yielded several excellent plays and starts equivocating about the book of a musical comedy, the Pulitzer Prize loses a great deal of its value. There is more whim than judgment in this year's award." Mantle was even more a narrow traditionalist in his complaint. "*Of Thee I Sing,*" he said in the *News,* "is the most intelligent, the most consistent, the most timely satire of American politics the native theatre has entertained. But by no conceivable stretch can it be classed as a play in the accepted sense of that term. Strip it of its lyrics and its music and there will be little left of the prize winner but a half-hour of farcical and satirical sketches."

This was something like saying that Renoir wouldn't be much good without his composition and sense of color; most of the other critics felt that a play was a play whether it was put together with words and music or words alone, and that it was the total impact of the play, the effect of all its combined ingredients, that really counted. They deplored the omission of George Gershwin but applauded the choice, and the critic in *Commonweal* summarized the majority voice. "*Of Thee I Sing* is a distinctly brilliant choice," he wrote. "If satire is to be recognized at all as a form of effective propaganda, I cannot see but that this arraignment of national politics meets to a nicety the definition of the award as going to the play that demonstrates the power of the stage in 'raising the standards of good morals, good taste, and good manners.' What presidential party can possibly thunder out its platform without keeping a chastened eye toward *Of Thee I Sing?* Messrs. Kaufman, Ryskind, and Gershwin deserve a nation's thanks, and, if the Pulitzer award can be considered as such, they have now received it. *Of Thee I Sing* offers something fresh and spontaneous in the American theatre, something richly of the times and pointedly of all time as well. It is much closer to Aristophanes than O'Neill ever came to Euripides."

The money wasn't much, of course: the prize of $1000 divided down into pretty small portions, as Atkinson pointed out in a preamble to his article, before growing more serious and disputing the selection. "If George S. Kaufman and Morrie Ryskind, authors, and Ira Gershwin, poet, divide the reward honestly," he wrote, "they will receive $333.33⅓ each. If they privately include in their accounts George Gershwin, who performed the slight service of composing the music, they will drop to $250 each. If in a spirit of good fellowship they include Sam Harris, who had the courage to try something new in a hazardous field, they will sink further to $200 each. If they include Victor Moore, who is their funny man, they go to $166.66⅔ each. When questions of honor are at stake one should not talk figures.

But it is difficult to ignore the fact that the omnibus award of the prize this year will scarcely pay for the parties the recipients owe their friends."

Kaufman, in fact, did not even keep his share of the prize money. He slipped it to a fund for indigent theatre people, Affiliated Theatrical Charities, and was appalled when someone in the organization tipped the *Mirror*, and the newspaper ran an item which was headed *A Noble Deed* and gave all the details in badly written tabloidese. The account concluded embarrassingly, "Mr. Kaufman's commendable action, we feel, should be made public, despite his laudable reticence. The prize went to a grand guy for a swell show. Well done, judges." The money, in any case, wasn't really the point. The important thing about the award was that it emphasized the value of the play in making people take a clear-eyed look at the sordidness and silliness of much of American politics. The award also, a lot of people felt, finally took note, in an official sort of way, of the contributions of a man who had become a major force in the theatre. Even Atkinson conceded this in his article, if somewhat grudgingly. "On his own terms," he said, "Mr. Kaufman is the most brilliant man of the theatre in this country, both as a writer and a director, and he, more than anyone else, has developed the sort of swift, brittle satire that *Of Thee I Sing* represents. His genius is for wit. In his hands the common wisecrack becomes an instrument for a point of view. Hating buncombe, it reveals the buncombe in every person or subject it attacks." Then Atkinson went on to pursue his attack on the prize committee's choice, but it isn't difficult to see why he didn't have too much company.

It would have been too much to hope that a play as deeply founded in topicality as *Of Thee I Sing* would hold up through the years. It didn't. The play was constantly available for revival because, despite its great success on Broadway and elsewhere, it did not draw a single movie offer. (Film people admitted frankly that, even though the large audiences in New York and on tour seemed to prove that the musical had strong appeal for general entertainment-seekers and wasn't just for sophisticates, they were still convinced that the play was too special and too elevated for the really huge audiences required to make a motion picture profitable.) For this reason, there was constant talk about bringing the play back to Broadway, discussions made plausible by the fact that amateur and semi-professional productions were always being presented around the country and always selling out. But Kaufman was so busy with other projects that it was nearly a decade and a half later, in 1947, before he was able to find the time to grow serious about the notion. And then, as stated earlier, he was stopped by a factor he couldn't have anticipated when he first called in Morrie Ryskind to serve as assistant and then collaborator. This was the political distance which had developed between the two men in the intervening years. The playwrights, once so similar in their thinking, now, it turned out, held views which were almost completely opposite. Kaufman was still as liberal as ever, if not more so, but Ryskind had grown more and more conservative as he grew older, becoming as suspicious of "radical elements" as he had once been about members of the right wing during his own period of youthful radicalism. By 1947, Ryskind had completed a 100 per cent turnabout in his political thinking, veering so sharply from the left to the right that he became a key figure in many of the arch-conservative organizations which eventually brought on the era of McCarthyism and blacklisting in Hollywood and the rest of the entertainment industry. Among many other things, he was a spokesman for the most powerful of these organizations, the Motion Picture Alliance for the Preservation of American Ideals, and a close friend and supporter of Lela Rogers, Ginger Rogers' mother, who made frequent speeches about the menace of Communism on radio shows like *Town Meeting*, some of the speeches written by Ryskind. Kaufman knew all this when he phoned Ryskind one day to talk to him about the idea of reviving *Of Thee I Sing*, and did not expect or want any help from his one-time collaborator in writing new material to replace the lines and scenes which had become dated or no longer relevant. He hoped, however, that, since the basic play was so strongly liberal in tone, Ryskind would recognize his own inability to work on the new production and simply give Kaufman carte blanche to proceed by himself. Kaufman's hopes went out of the window the moment he finished broaching the idea. Ryskind launched at once into a bitter tirade accusing him of planning to insert a lot of new liberal stuff, which was quite true, and said he would never consent to the revival unless he was given an equal opportunity to add some of his own anti-Communist views. Kaufman hung up the phone, shrugged hopelessly, and abandoned the plan.

He did not try again until five years later, when, early in 1952, he was approached by a man named Chandler Cowles, who told Kaufman that he had a strong urge to bring *Of Thee I Sing* back to Broadway, and the money to accomplish it. There was no reason whatever to doubt Cowles's financial assurances: in addition to being a successful producer, he was also a member of the very wealthy publishing family which owned *Look* and a great many newspapers and radio and television stations. Once again, Kaufman picked up the telephone, and this time, to his surprise, Ryskind agreed at once. Ryskind gave no explanation, but the answer clearly did not lie in still another change in political ideology. He was still on the right politically, and has remained there to the present day, devoting his current energies to writing a column espousing conservative politics for the Los Angeles *Times*. The theory which developed later on was that Ryskind simply needed the money which would come to him if the revival was successful. He had done some extremely good work on his own in the late '30s and early '40s, such as the screenplays for *My Man Godfrey, Claudia, Penny Serenade,* and the film version of a Kaufman-Ferber play, *Stage Door,* but the calls for his services had grown less and less frequent after that, and he had written almost nothing for either Hollywood or Broadway since 1945. Whatever the reason, Kaufman didn't stop to analyze it. He thanked Ryskind, arranged with Ira Gershwin, who had also remained liberal politically, to update the show's lyrics while he did the same with the book, and told Cowles that he was ready to proceed. He also agreed, when Cowles proposed it, to direct the new production personally.

Cowles, in association with a partner named Ben Segal, went to work on his part of the job at the same time, determined to make his own contribution toward presenting a fresh and different version of the play with fresh and offbeat casting. He conceived the notion of trying to sign Van Johnson, then at the height of his popularity, for the role of Wintergreen, an interesting idea because Johnson's freckled boyishness would give the role a tone entirely different from Gaxton's slick, smooth-talking, sophisticated rendition. The idea received Kaufman's blessing, and Cowles hunted Johnson all over the world and finally located him at the Grand Hotel in Rome, only to have the red-haired actor turn down the telegraphed offer because of a conflicting film commitment. But the general angle was right. Cowles continued to search, eventually assigning the role to another movie actor, Jack Carson, a performer whose fast-talking characterizations were closer to Gaxton's than Johnson's would have been, but who could still be counted upon to have more box-office appeal than a conventional stage star because he was seen so rarely on Broadway. The Throttlebottom assignment also went to an unexpected choice: Paul Hartman. Hartman was a man who had developed a very popular ballroom-dancing act in conjunction with his wife, Grace, headlining the best supper clubs in the country, but who had done relatively little acting up to that point. The roles of Mary Wintergreen and Diana Devereaux went to Betty Oakes and Lenore Lonergan, two strong young actresses; a touch of nostalgia was added by giving the part of the French ambassador once again to the man who had played the role in the original version two decades before, Florenz Ames; and the play tried out in New Haven and Philadelphia and then opened in New York on Monday, May 5, 1952, at the Ziegfeld Theatre.

The reviews were nearly all good. Carson was applauded as an excellent John P. Wintergreen, the two girls received similarly approving notices, and Hartman's characterization of Alexander Throttlebottom, played in a hesitant and diffident manner similar to Victor Moore's, launched a whole new career for him. It also enabled him to start a small acting dynasty of his own: his son, David, also, years later, became a successful actor, and was very popular in a starring role as a doctor in a television series, *The Bold Ones*. The revisions and modernizations were also reviewed favorably despite last-minute doubts on the part of the revisers. Kaufman had begun to suffer from his usual certainty that his work was no good, and Gershwin had come down with a severe virus while the production was being put together and had had to do most of his work in a sickbed, even phoning in his changes, causing the natural fear that this might affect his creative quality. The critics assured the authors and the public that the opposite was the case—but, unfortunately, it developed that all the good notices just didn't matter. People just didn't turn up in large enough numbers at the box office, and the earnings which Ryskind and the others were anticipating never materialized. The new production, in fact, achieved a negative financial result because, ironically, it blocked a motion picture deal. After all those years, Paramount suddenly decided that the play might make a good film after all, as a vehicle for Bob Hope, and made an offer contingent on being allowed to proceed at once, because Hope had just finished another film and had nothing else to do. But Kaufman had already signed with Cowles and Segal, and the producers would not, of course, allow a film to be made and perhaps released in competition with their stage production. So the offer could not be accepted.

There were varying explanations for the failure of the new version of *Of Thee I Sing*, the most popular of which was that, for all their good qualities, Carson was no Gaxton and Hartman was no Moore. But that wasn't really the answer: a whole new generation of theatre-goers had grown up who hadn't seen the 1932 production, and couldn't have been staying away because of unfavorable comparisons with the original cast. Nor was another theory really accurate: that the original play had had weaknesses which were hidden by strong performances, and that the new version also required bolstering which was not supplied by the present, somewhat weaker actors. The real answer was much simpler. The major problem of the 1952 version stemmed from the fact that all the line changes and scene changes and lyrics changes couldn't give meaning and significance to a play which had been written for another time, another world. The play no longer mesmerized people with its innovativeness and its daring because there had been many other innovations, some of them even more daring, since that time, and the play's story about the threat of war over the jilting of a girl could no longer interest and amuse audiences which had recently lived through a real and horrible war in which millions had died. So there was just no impetus to go to the box office at the Ziegfeld, and people did not go. There was a final effort to save the play; every member of the cast and creative side took a voluntary pay cut, and the theatre reduced its percentage of the take. But even that didn't help, and the play limped to a close.

That was pretty much the end of *Of Thee I Sing*, though there have been other revivals, some of them moderately successful, through the years. A one-week run with little-known performers at a huge amphitheater on an island just off the island of Manhattan, New York City's Municipal Stadium on Randall's Island, drew near-capacity crowds and seemed to several critics to be an even more enjoyable presentation than the original. But that was mostly, one critic decided in a follow-up piece, because it was summertime and pleasant to sit outdoors, and "in the Broadway production, you couldn't smoke a pipe or cigar or eat an ice cream cone as the show went on." A revival at the Kalita Humphreys Theatre in Dallas, Texas, in 1965, also did all right; the producers there presented the play frankly as an interesting piece of nostalgia and sold most of their tickets for the musical's scheduled twenty-four performances. And a 1968 revival at the Equity Library Theatre in New York City was a smash, turning away lines of people at every performance. But the Equity Theatre is a tiny showcase playhouse for young actors and actresses, with a sharp eye for budding talent and a history of having given first or early roles to many people who subsequently became stars—among them Jason Robards, Jr., Charlton Heston, Anne Jackson, Eli Wallach, and Rod Steiger—and it did not charge admission to its shows in 1968. The manager merely suggested a donation of $1.50, and didn't even insist on that from people who didn't have it. So the little theatre was often the scene of smashes.

The only big-time revival of the musical since the Cowles-Segal presentation has been a television special: a much-touted hour-and-a-half production which appeared on CBS on October 24, 1972. It looked good when first announced. It was obviously going to be an expensive and well-mounted show, and the Wintergreen role was being undertaken by a very talented and likable actor, Carroll O'Connor, who had become immensely popular because of his portrayal of Archie Bunker in the most successful comedy series in television history, *All in the Family*. But, as television critics reported sadly the following day, it took only a few minutes of viewing to realize that the writers who had adapted the play for television had obviously become aware, as they started their adaptation, that nearly every one of the acerbic political comments of the play, the elements which had given the musical its special strength and quality back in the '30s, no longer worked or applied or mattered. The writers had clearly dealt with their dilemma—or, more accurately, had gone down in defeat to it

—by simply tossing out nearly every topical and political reference until there was nothing left but the love story, looking absurd and childish by itself. And O'Connor, who gained fame playing an ignoramus and bigot in his series but is actually an intelligent and intensely liberal man, and perhaps even assumed he was becoming involved in something of political significance when he signed for the special, played his role almost with embarrassment. He then hurried back to *All in the Family*.

In retrospect, it's easy to dismiss the executives who set up the television production as fools who should have realized that a play so closely wedded to the politics and viewpoints of another time would be bound to fail in a presentation nearly forty years later. But the truth of the matter is that the error is one which every expert in the entertainment business has made at least once in the course of his career, and which future experts will continue to make until the end of time. It's just too tempting to assume that something which has been a hit once is likely to be a hit again, and forget that the extraordinary circumstances which made the project a hit in the first place, the miraculous and unique fusion of talent and timing, nearly always can't be duplicated. Kaufman and Ryskind, in fact, made precisely the same kind of error themselves after *Of Thee I Sing*— and not once, but twice.

The first error began with a brief announcement which appeared on the theatrical pages of most New York newspapers on April 7, 1933: a statement that the four authors of *Of Thee I Sing* would begin work at the end of that month on a sequel to their prize-winning play, and that the sequel, to be called *Let 'Em Eat Cake*, would probably open on Broadway in October. (It was actually Beatrice's error, to begin with, because it was she who first suggested the idea of a sequel to *Of Thee I Sing*—one of the rare instances in which she gave her husband bad advice.) There were no details given, and Kaufman, interviewed the following morning by the press, said frankly that he and Ryskind already had their whole plot worked out from beginning to end, but didn't want to reveal anything further and perhaps tempt somebody to start another plagiarism suit. "If there's somebody like that lurking in the bushes," he said, "we'd like him to emerge after we've had a chance to recover a bit more from the Lowenfels experience." It wasn't possible, however, to keep things quiet for long. Kaufman and Ryskind finished the first act in New York in May, and then moved to Altantic City to write the second and final act there. There was only one rough spot in their work; they needed a single strong line to finish up one of the scenes, and the line eluded them for two full days before they finally came up with it. But everything else went well, and they completed the second act in June; the entire script had taken just four-and-a-half weeks from beginning to end. Details soon began to leak out. The new musical would again star Gaxton, Moore, and Lois Moran in their original roles—but this time Wintergreen and Throttlebottom would be defeated in their bid for re-election, and would have to cope with their own problems rather than the nation's.

Let 'Em Eat Cake went into rehearsal on August 15, and, at first, no other play in history had ever seemed to have so much going for it. Wasn't it, after all, a continuation of the best thing to dance across a New York stage in the past decade? Everyone from producer, backers, and cast to prospective members of the audience felt that here was another Of Thee I Sing for sure. The list of enthusiasts, however, did not include the senior author. He was as glum as ever as he sat in the third row watching his characters come to life on the rehearsal stage. He smiled occasionally, but he never laughed. He would sometimes laugh uproariously at a particularly good line during the writing of a play; all of his collaborators testified to that. But at rehearsals, as Sam Harris once put it, "he watched the actors like a hawk—or perhaps even like a vulture," and he seemed even more funereal than ever this time.

He never sat upright, but slouched in the theatre seat, often squirming restlessly. He was never still. Sometimes he dragged out a little black leather notebook and jotted down notes about the performance, or lack of performance, he was watching. As always, he waited until a scene was played out before getting an offender off in the wings to sharpen a bit of business or the delivery of a line. But this time, he seemed to be doing it more often, and spending longer periods in the wings with each performer—"in an unsuccessful effort," he admitted afterward to Beatrice, "to make the actors stronger than the play."

He was also less cordial than ever toward comments from outsiders. Once a British director arrived uninvited and made a long and involved suggestion. Kaufman peered at him over his glasses for a moment, and then brushed the suggestion aside. "Possibly," the visitor snapped, "you don't know who I am." "That's only half of it," Kaufman said.

He was also, he admitted when Ryskind asked him about it, not too enthusiastic about the music for the play. During the rehearsals of *Of Thee I Sing*, Kaufman had occasionally been heard humming tunes from the play under his breath, and had even been observed, once or twice, tapping the metal end of a pencil against his teeth in time to a song being played in the pit. But this time, Ryskind noted unhappily, there was not too much of the teeth-tapping or the humming of the *Let 'Em Eat Cake* score. The reason, Kaufman said, was that Gershwin's insistence on constant counterpoint was not always pleasing to his admittedly traditional ear, and he feared that audiences might feel the same way. He liked the contrapuntal device in the beginning of the play, which started with *Wintergreen for President* from the earlier play while *Tweedledee for President* welled up in the background to set the stage for what was coming in the new one, but felt that the steady use of counterpoint thereafter was too much.

Gershwin told a reporter his theory for using counterpoint in the new score. "I've written most of the music for this show contrapuntally," he said, "because it's that very insistence on the sharpness of a form that gives my music the acid touch it has—and which points the words of the lyrics, and is in keeping with the satire of the piece. At least, I feel that it's counterpoint which helps me to do what I'm trying to do." Kaufman shook his head over the interview. "It's giving me acid indigestion," he said.

As rehearsals progressed, Kaufman's normally morose outlook turned to total gloom. His attitude had no effect whatever on the ebullient spirits of his co-workers. Kaufman had, they remembered confidently, been nearly as gloomy at the rehearsals of *Of Thee I Sing*. But the difference this time was that Kaufman had a solid foundation for his distrust. *Of Thee I Sing* was solidly rooted in the political realities of its day, and its witty barbs had said something pertinent and current to the audience. *Let 'Em Eat Cake*, however, flew off into fantasy with a basically unpopular idea: a revolution in the United States.

The book for *Let 'Em Eat Cake* opens with Wintergreen locked in a tight re-election race with John P. Tweedledee, played by a good character actor named Richard Temple. Despite such attractive slogans as *He Kept Us Out of Work, Wintergreen Wants Wintergreen*, and *Mrs. Wintergreen Wants Wintergreen*, Wintergreen and Throttlebottom are defeated. Wintergreen, to keep from starving in the depression, starts a blue-shirt factory in association with his wife, Throttlebottom, and some former members of his cabinet, but business is so bad that he's forced to plot a Blue Shirt revolution to stimulate sales of his product. The revolt catches fire when the plotters promise to collect the foreign war debt and use it to pay their revolutionary army. The revolution is successful, but Wintergreen is unable to persuade the debtor nations to pay up. Finally, since there are nine debtor nations, an agreement is reached that representatives of the nine nations will play a baseball game with the nine members of the United States Supreme Court, with the winner taking all.

Things look good until Wintergreen makes the mistake of appointing bumbling Alexander Throttlebottom as umpire. And Throttlebottom rules in favor of the League of Nations. The infuriated revolutionists seize the government and condemn Throttlebottom and Wintergreen to the guillotine, a recent gift from the French government. Throttlebottom has his head under the knife when Mary Wintergreen rushes in a style show that diverts people from the execution. Wintergreen then restores the republic, but finds he prefers the shirt business to being President, and Throttlebottom becomes President of the United States.

Anticipation was still high when *Let 'Em Eat Cake* opened for tryouts at the Shubert Theatre in Boston on August 15. Ticket scalpers were getting $17.50 a pair for orchestra seats—and this was 1933, when the depression was at its worst. And in addition to the local audience, two hundred people came up from New York for the tryout opening. The New York *Times* reported that "the first night audience entertained as well as the players. It ranged from emissaries of New York brokers, through scores of celebrities, through local politicians and their considerable families, to the topmost layers of Boston society." Heading the political crowd was Boston's famed Mayor James Curley. When the curtain dropped on the last act, sometime around midnight, Curley climbed onstage to join the authors in taking bows and made an extremely complimentary speech, but one Boston newspaper reported accurately that "Curley seemed to enjoy it all more than the modest four standing beside him." Kaufman, Ryskind, and the two Gershwins all looked sad and deflated because the applause given their efforts was extremely sparse, and later Kaufman admitted that he could not recall a single word Curley had said. He was already hacking away in his mind at the deadwood in the play, seeking some way to turn failure into success.

The local critics were not kind, and the New York press was even less so when the musical opened at the Imperial Theatre on Saturday, October 21. Kaufman and Ryskind had worked frantically to breathe fresh life into the play, but critical opinion was against them. Nor did Harris's belief, that the critics had been influenced by an unfriendly opening-night audience in New York, really convince anyone. Several publications reported his statement briefly, *Variety* writing, "Sam Harris says he'll never again have a Broadway mob on hand for one of his openings, as a result of newspaper treatment handed out to *Let 'Em Eat Cake*. According to Harris, the audience was mostly Broadwayites and had come into the theatre with ready-made hatchets." But most people felt that the play was bad, and the critics would have reacted exactly the same way even if they'd been surrounded by fervent rooters.

In *The Nation*, Joseph Wood Krutch thought "the further adventures of Wintergreen and Throttlebottom occasionally dull and the trifling conclusion almost an evasion of the issues the authors themselves have raised." *Time*'s critic reported that "critics and spectators went out grumbling that the nation's great musicomedy quadrivirate had lain down on their job, had served up a poorly warmed-over dish." *Stage* put it most pointedly of all. "Sequels," the magazine said, "are not equals." An acquaintance reported this line to Kaufman, adding, "That's pretty clever. I bet you wish you'd said it." Kaufman replied sadly, "I wish that nobody had said it."

Now Kaufman had a genuine reason for unhappiness, and he began to show occasional signs of being afraid of the future. He revealed this once in an offhand remark he made to Harris, shortly after *Let 'Em Eat Cake*'s opening. He had found the producer deep in thought, and Harris said he was thinking of the reaction to the play. Kaufman replied quietly that he had been thinking of Owen Davis. Harris did not immediately grasp the significance of Kaufman's statement. Then he understood. Owen Davis had won a Pulitzer Prize in 1923 for his play, *Icebound*, and had never been able to do anything successful since. The idea remained rooted in Kaufman's mind, and he began to tell friends frequently that he did not want to become another Owen Davis. He said it often as *Let 'Em Eat Cake* limped toward its unhappy finale, and he continued to say it the rest of his life, even when he had just completed a play which was destined to become a huge success.

Crowds were fair the first few weeks despite the lukewarm reviews, but there were only two sellouts. Both of these were benefit performances. One was for the benefit of the Travelers' Aid Society, and the second was for the Boys Club of New York. Regular showings drew smaller and smaller audiences, and *Let 'Em Eat Cake* closed after ninety performances. The road company was also a failure. This was due in part to high overhead, since the total cast numbered 125 people. Dr. Henry Moskowitz of the League of New York Theatres later furnished some typical figures on the play's experience in a typical city, Baltimore. The week's receipts, after cast salaries and royalties, was $3318. From this, the management had to pay $1166 to musicians and $1738 to stagehands, leaving a profit of $414, out of which taxes and operating expenses had to be paid.

There was only one bright spot in the firmament. Irving Berlin had come to watch a rehearsal of the play, and, more impressed than Kaufman by the new musical's potential, offered to trade 5 per cent of his own new musical, *As Thousands Cheer*, for a matching share of *Let 'Em Eat Cake*. Kaufman accepted. *As Thousands Cheer*, which introduced one of Berlin's most popular songs, *Easter Parade*, was a smash success, and Kaufman's income from his 5 per cent more than made up for the income which never came from *Let 'Em Eat Cake*.

Let 'Em Eat Cake was also destined to be the last collaboration between Kaufman and the Gershwins. Neither side intended it to be that way, and, four years later, the three men agreed to write another musical together, planning to begin work on it just as soon as the Gershwins completed a commitment to write the score for a new film called *The Goldwyn Follies*. But George Gershwin had been suffering for years from dreadful headaches, some of them so severe that he sometimes had to stop right in the street and sit down on the curb, rocking back and forth in agony and clutching his head. A long series of doctors dismissed the headaches as merely psychosomatic, the imaginings of an artistic type of man. But on July 10, 1937, he collapsed and was rushed to Cedars of Lebanon Hospital in Hollywood, where his condition was finally diagnosed correctly as a brain tumor. A five-hour operation followed. It was too late, and at 10:35 on the morning of July 11, with his brother at his bedside, he died. He was thirty-nine years old.

It was also nearly the end of the road for the team of Kaufman and Ryskind. Shortly after *Let 'Em Eat Cake* closed, the two men made their second mistake and wrote still another political satire.

This time, to keep production costs low, they decided to write a straight comedy rather than a musical, but got off immediately on the wrong foot by calling their play *Bring on the Girls*, a title which led playgoers to expect a show full of songs and chorus girls. Instead, they got a rather labored satire on the Reconstruction Finance Corporation, an agency begun by Herbert Hoover to provide loans for businesses in trouble, and the project was doomed from the start.

The plot revolved around two ex-convict bankers, fresh out of Atlanta, who decide to acquire a railroad—the two-mile-long Black Creek Line, running from Black Creek to East Black Creek—so they can get an RFC loan and keep most of the money for themselves. They get the loan, but then can't get the railroad because it has already been seized for back taxes. In order to avoid being arrested for fraud and sent to Atlanta again, they turn their penthouse apartment into a farm by stocking it with chickens, turkeys, and a cow—because the RFC also gives loans to farmers. And the play ends happily when RFC investigators arrive and fall in love with the farmerettes the con men have also scattered around the place.

Harris, hopeful all over again, gave the play a lavish production, hiring Jack Benny, then a young radio comedian who had just zoomed to the top of the ratings, for his first stage role, Porter Hall, a clever actor who underplayed all his parts beautifully and later became a popular character actor in films, as his sidekick, and two beautiful actresses named Muriel Campbell and Claire Carleton as their girl friends. Harris also brought real fowl and animals on to the penthouse set, including a cow which ate its meals off the top of the piano. But the plot and gags were just too wild and absurd for a straight play, unbolstered by a lot of music and dancing, and the play rolled over and died in its tryout on Monday, October 22, 1934, at the National Theatre in Washington, D.C.

E. DeS. Melcher of the Washington *Star* summed up his opinion of the play by saying, "In the battle waged between the RFC and Messrs. Kaufman and Ryskind at the National, the RFC probably won out." The Washington *Post* stated what came to be the general opinion of the play: "What George S. Kaufman and Morrie Ryskind have written here is a perfect libretto for the tuneful inconsistencies, dramatic extravagances, and hollow humors of a great girls-and-music show. With a snappy score and a thick sprinkling of chorus people, line girls and specialists, *Bring on the Girls* would be one of the banner hits of Sam H. Harris's star-studded career. As presented, it's awful." And the Washington *News* said, "The first act is fair, the second act is worse, and the third is terrible."

For the next two weeks, the authors struggled at the typewriter to bring some life into the sagging script. The play reopened on November 22 at the Shubert Theatre in New Haven, Connecticut. *Variety* sent a reviewer to cover the revised version. The reviewer echoed the Washington critics: "It should have been a musical. Kaufman himself states that there never was a musical tangent in mind, and he thinks it isn't particularly adaptable as such, but a load of first nighters as well as local crix disagree with that opinion. Play's title is misleading, with everybody looking for a musical."

Harris tried twice more. After the authors struggled through a third rewrite and then a fourth, he opened again in Springfield,

Massachusetts, and then moved to Hartford, Connecticut, finally closing in Hartford on December 15 when reactions were still bad. There was some talk afterward that Harris would reopen in the spring after still another rewrite, but this was just hopeful speculation. *Bring on the Girls* was gone for good.

That was it for Kaufman and Ryskind on Broadway, although they would get together one more time in Hollywood to write a Marx Brothers film, *A Night at the Opera*, for Irving Thalberg. In all, they had collaborated on six plays, and they also wrote one short prose piece together, *Socratic Dialogue*, which appeared in *The Nation* on April 12, 1933. *Socratic Dialogue* is eighty-nine lines long and consists of exchanges between a Mr. K and a Mr. R, in which they poke fun at everything from 3.2 beer to bankers, the Supreme Court to Eleanor Roosevelt. Reread today, *Socratic Dialogue* remains one of the funniest scripts ever written by the team, loaded with little gems like the exchange in which Mr. R asks Mr. K if Franklin Delano Roosevelt is married:

Mr. K: Sure he's married. Been married for years.

Mr. R: Funny. You never read anything about his wife.

21. THE BEST COLLABORATOR

IT MIGHT HAVE seemed unlikely, to those who knew Kaufman, that his most successful collaborator would also be the first one young enough to regard him as an idol, an ideal, and even a father figure. It would have seemed at least doubly unlikely, if not laughable, that the young man would also bring to his hero-worship a shyness and a sense of self-doubt and worry even greater than that of his hero. By the obvious standards, these were not the elements of a good match, but, as happened often in Kaufman's life, the obvious standards did not apply in the case of Moss Hart.

Moss Hart was born on October 24, 1904. His father, Barnett Hart, worked as a cigar maker, sitting all day at a table heaped with tobacco leaves and rolling cigars, an occupation which seemed as secure as any other until the invention of the tobacco-rolling machine threw the elder Hart out of business. He was frail and unable to take the common heavy-laboring jobs open to most men, so the family subsisted by taking in boarders and running a small newsstand. "Poverty," Hart said later in life, "was always a living and evil thing to me," and it was partly the desire to leave poverty completely and irrevocably behind which eventually fueled his determination to become a success as a playwright. And as a child, the strongest and perhaps the only antidote he had for the hardships of his family's life was the occasional magic evening when he would be taken by his Aunt Kate to the theatre.

By the time he was going to school, in Brooklyn, his temperament reflected the harshness of his physical surroundings in terms of sensitive retreat, and he was a shy, lonely, unhappy boy. From the age of thirteen he was forced to work after school, and took a job as clerk in a music store and spent two-and-a-half gray years, an eternity, as a storage-vault clerk for a fur company. At seventeen, however, he obtained a more or less similar job, office boy, but the difference was that it was as office boy for Augustus Pitou, a producer of touring shows. And here—after a year—Hart was assigned to read plays as a precious extra duty. Hart read plays for six months and decided that he could do at least as well as the formula-ridden scripts he'd been reading, and he wrote a composite of melodramatic conventions titled *The Hold-up Man or The Beloved Bandit*. Pitou accepted it for production, since, after all, it had all the ingredients of his former successes. But, unfortunately, the ingredients were not as well arranged, and Pitou lost $45,000.

When the producer decided that he could do with a less expensive office boy, Hart began a series of odd jobs that eventually led to a position as social director of a popular Catskills hotel in the summer and director of Little Theatre groups in the winter. For six years during this period he wrote a play a year, choosing very serious themes, but his attempts at high drama failed consistently to make an impression on the producers to whom he sent his scripts. Finally, an agent, Richard J. Madden of the American Play Company, shocked him by suggesting that he try writing a comedy, and shocked him still further by saying that the light moments in Hart's sober dramas were just about the only good things in them. For the most part, Hart hated comedy, and, as far as he could tell, always would. But after thinking over Madden's incredible suggestion, he decided to go ahead and try just one comedy, since he certainly was going nowhere with his dramas. As Hart later told it, "I grumpily removed the mantle of Shaw and O'Neill from my shoulders and regarded the yellow pad of paper in my lap." Since the only kind of humor with which Hart felt comfortable was the satirical style of Kaufman and Connelly, he knew his comedy would necessarily be written in the same vein as theirs. And when he wrote the title of his first comedic effort across the top of his yellow pad, *Once in a Lifetime*, it was the title for an idea Hart had conceived while sitting in a balcony and watching a performance of *Dulcy*.

Before seeing *Dulcy*, Hart had been reading in *Variety* about the panic in Hollywood over the advent of sound in film, a development which was wreaking havoc in the star rosters of the big studios since some of the greatest stars either spoke with atrocious accents or spoke in a manner completely alien to the public's conception of their heroes and heroines. To an aspiring playwright whose stock-in-trade was talk, the Hollywood panic was pricelessly funny. Hart's idea involved three unemployed actors—two men and a young woman—who go to Hollywood to open a school of elocution for movie stars. Until this time, Hart had always taken from six months to a year to write a play, but he surprised himself by finishing *Once in a Lifetime* in three weeks. Then began the tough task of looking for a producer. Once he thought he had made it when a friend named Dore Schary, who later headed M-G-M and also wrote the hit play *Sunrise at Campobello*, arranged through another friend for Hart to get the play to Jed Harris. Harris was mildly interested but kept procrastinating until Hart sent a second copy of his script to Sam Harris.

Sam Harris later described the beginnings of his association with the team of Kaufman and Hart. "Back in 1930," he said, "Moss Hart was a name that was familiar to a small circle of his relatives. Certainly I hadn't ever heard it till Max Siegel, who was my general manager in those days, came into my office one day with a script in his hand and a rather excited look." Harris took the script home and decided it had been written by someone who had lived and worked in Hollywood "and developed a disgust for the mad things that used to go on there." He was as impressed as Siegel had been. "It was authentic satire," he decided, "but I felt it needed work. It needed pointing up and a general reconstruction which would give it polish and a finish. There was one answer to that. George S. Kaufman. If he'd consent to work on it, I'd tie it up in a minute."

Harris sent the script to Kaufman, who read it immediately, as he did with all manuscripts sent to him, and said in a note to Harris: *I'd love to be mixed up with it.* Harris then summoned Hart; it was only two days after the script had been submitted. When Harris told Hart that he needed a collaborator, the young playwright asked cautiously, "And who would you suggest?"

"I never saw a face change so suddenly as when I said George Kaufman," Harris later recalled. "First a look of incredulity came over it, then this melted into a thin smile which spread until he was beaming like a little child who had just been presented with a toy he never fancied he could own. Later he told me that he felt that I had passed a miracle for him, that Kaufman had been his ideal since boyhood, and that he had never dreamed that his play would enable him to sit down at the same typewriter with Kaufman."

"There's one point that should be mentioned," Harris said next. "Kaufman has never been to Hollywood and hasn't your background and experience there. You'll have to provide the source material."

"That's no drawback," Hart said. "You see, I've never been to Hollywood either. I picked up my dope from the fan magazines and Hollywood columns."

It was after that that Hart nearly became the victim of Jed Harris's casual cruelty, and it took the combined efforts of Sam Harris and Max Siegel to convince Kaufman that the young playwright had been hoaxed and should be forgiven. Hart was finally told to appear at Kaufman's town house at 158 East 63rd Street at eleven o'clock the following morning.

At precisely five minutes before the hour, Hart started climbing the stairs, somewhat disappointed by the modest appearance of the brownstone building to which the Kaufmans had recently moved. He had expected a man of Kaufman's stature to live in a penthouse, an expectation which owed a great deal to the difficult circumstances of Hart's early life. Once inside the house, however, he was impressed by the pretty maid and by the elegance with which Beatrice had furnished the place. But his disappointment returned and increased when he went upstairs, since the studio in which Kaufman worked was small, dark, and dreary, furnished only with a studio couch, one easy chair, and a particularly ugly typewriter desk. "I'm not sure what I expected the atelier of Kaufman and Connelly to be like," Hart said later, "but this certainly wasn't it." He was especially disappointed to find nothing theatrical in the room. He had expected to see signed pictures of stars, theatre programs, lobby posters, and the like, but the only picture on the wall was the framed etching of Kaufman's idol, Mark Twain.

Hart was already at a fever pitch of insecurity after the Jed Harris incident, and the barren room just made things worse, along with Kaufman's casual greeting, which consisted, as always, of nothing more than a raised finger and a languid "Hi." In case this was not sufficient initiation, Kaufman then ignored his new partner and suddenly became absorbed in the view from his window, after which, having failed to invite Hart to be seated, he strolled casually about the room, picked lint from the rug, scratched his right ear by slipping his left hand behind his neck, sharpened some pencils, straightened some typing paper, and only then seemed to notice Hart huddled in the arm chair. He announced, without any preliminaries, "The trouble begins in the third scene of the first act." He had begun to "stab"—in Hart's words—at the offending sections with a pencil. Hart sat stricken as line after line was altered or cut by the ruthless pencil. But the days that followed were a revelation to Hart, as Kaufman began to teach him the elements of playwriting.

Hart's play concerned a cheap vaudeville team, one of whose members happens to see Al Jolson in *The Jazz Singer*, the first successful sound picture, and who decides that a fortune waits anyone who can conduct a school of elocution for the silent stars. Without consulting the others, he sells their act for $500 to get them all to Hollywood, and the first person the team meets is a Hollywood columnist patterned after Louella Parsons. At last the team is fronted and affronted by a Mr. Glogauer, the archetype of the boorish, tasteless Hollywood producer. George Lewis, the hero, insults Glogauer, is immediately taken to be a genius for this reason alone, and goes on to make a masterpiece of the cinema by producing a film based on a script he was supposed to reject.

As the writing of *Once in a Lifetime* continued, Hart went on learning and also went on chain-smoking cigars, the odor of which Kaufman despised. Kaufman said nothing about it, however, and for some time remained completely unaware that the cigar-smoking was simply the counterpoint of Hart's near-starvation. In fact, Kaufman, with his limited interest in food, never realized that Hart was continually famished and had only occasional cookies and small slices of cake brought up, until one day, while Kaufman was washing his hands before the snack, Hart ate all the cookies and slices of cake which the maid had brought up for both of them. The two started having lunch together. But when Hart dawdled lovingly over the food of their first lunch, Kaufman said, "If you'd take bigger bites, we could finish the third act in a week." As the writing neared conclusion, Kaufman, in his first return to the early acting ambitions of his youth, decided that the part of Lawrence Vail, a bilious Broadway playwright who has been brought to Hollywood to do nothing, was just right for him. Hart agreed enthusiastically, and the prospect of appearing in the play made Kaufman even more eager to finish it.

The play was rushed into rehearsal and set for a tryout at the Apollo Theatre in Atlantic City on May 26, 1930. On opening night, with Kaufman in the back of the theatre, nervously pacing, Hart matched him pace for pace and finally surpassed him by rushing to the men's room to throw up. He got back as the first act curtain was dropping to applause so sweet that he burst out laughing—only to hear Kaufman's voice say savagely in his ear, "But there were a lot of places where they didn't laugh." At this point, when the play looked like it might be a hit, Kaufman went backstage to take the role of Lawrence Vail, who had a second-act entrance. His appearance had been well-heralded, and when the curtain went up he received the best applause of the evening. For his first professional role, Kaufman was superb. *Commonweal* said, for example, "The gifted Mr. Kaufman, not content merely to collaborate in the writing of *Once in a Lifetime,* and to stage it, manages to act in it as well. His impersonation of the world-weary playwright is whimsically delightful." (Woollcott did not agree and observed privately that it was hardly *acting* for Kaufman to behave like a playwright soured on Hollywood, but the truth is that it takes more than being a playwright to act like one. Later, Moss Hart also took on the role in a West Coast production of the play, and his friends said he underplayed to the point where his lines sounded like mumbled Chinese.)

But most of the critics gave Kaufman better notices than they had given the play, since Kaufman's excellent acting debut and the well-received first act were not enough to carry the whole performance. Laughs dwindled in the second act, and the third act was a disaster. Back at their hotel afterward, Hart got his first look at Kaufman in a tough situation. Now Kaufman cut his own lines as ruthlessly as he had once cut Hart's. "Cut it to the bone," he told Hart. "Then we can see the good stuff left and build from there." But the surgery didn't work, and the second night was worse than the first. The team rushed back to the hotel each night during the week's run to cut and rewrite the play.

They opened a second tryout at Brighton Beach, a small community in Brooklyn not far from Coney Island, but it was a repeat of the Atlantic City failure: the second and third acts simply would not play. At the end of the week's run, Kaufman talked before the final performance with Sam Harris, who agreed with him that the play could not be salvaged. Kaufman passed the decision on to Hart as he wiped cold cream from his face after the show, and broke the news as gently as possible, trying to ease the sting. "You'll get it done again," he said. "There's a lot of good stuff there. Someday you'll be able to lick that second and third act." He said that he was giving the play back to Hart, and added that, if it could be repaired, he would ask no part in any proceeds. Then, by way of parting, he said gently, "I'm sorry it had to turn out this way, but I'm no use to you any more."

"I see," Hart said. Then, after an awkward pause, knowing that Kaufman did not want any speech or even any thanks, Hart just said, "Goodbye," closed the door quietly behind him, dragged himself home, and fell exhausted into bed. But by morning his determination had reasserted itself. He grabbed his yellow pad, some pencils, a sandwich, and a bottle of soda and went to his writing spot on the beach, where he scribbled all day. By evening he thought he had it. He went to sleep and then rewrote the material carefully the next morning. Laying the material aside, he headed for Kaufman's apartment.

Kaufman, munching toast at the breakfast table, looked up in surprise when his ex-collaborator burst in unannounced. The maid, not knowing that the collaboration had ended, had admitted him without question. Kaufman was now thoroughly sick of the words *Once in a Lifetime*, but he was struck by Hart's urgent intensity and agreed to listen to new suggestions for the second and third acts.

Hart said he would need no more than fifteen minutes, and launched into his desperate, life-or-death recitation while Kaufman continued to eat. As the fifteen minutes came and went, Kaufman finished eating, got up and paced, then sprawled out on the rug and looked balefully through his horn-rimmed glasses at Hart, who kept talking. Finally, when Hart had finished, Kaufman got to his feet and walked over to the window, staring out exactly as he had at their first meeting. It seemed an eternity to Hart before Kaufman turned and said quietly, "Bea is going to Europe this summer with Aleck Woollcott and Harpo Marx. Can you move in here so we can work?"

They worked all summer, while the wastebasket piled high with crumpled yellow sheets and wadded typescripts day after day. As things began to fall in line at last, Kaufman's manner lightened and, in the privacy of the studio, he occasionally laughed uproariously at particularly good lines. But, typically, at rehearsals he did not even smile.

The new version tried out in Philadelphia and then finally opened on Broadway at the Music Box Theatre on Wednesday, September 24, 1930. It was a smash hit, running 305 performances, with Kaufman once again taking the Lawrence Vail role. He wrote a satirical account of his acting debut under the title, *How I Became a Great Actor*, which appeared in *Theatre*'s issue of December 1930. He told of sitting alone into the late hours of the night, gulping coffee and struggling to learn his lines. "But I kept on," he wrote, "and

[476]

when the opening night arrived walked onto the stage at the Music Box and spoke every 'if,' 'and,' and 'but.' And if it had not been for a certain pardonable nervousness, I would have spoken some of the other words, too." He wasn't really exaggerating about the nervousness; on several occasions, he told friends that he never got over stage fright, right up the end of his series of performances. Nor was this confined to the stage, since he had the same kind of butterflies at every public gathering, and this was one of the reasons he sometimes had to be dragged to parties. His well-known reluctance to appear in public was what made his decision to play the Vail role so surprising, and his friends were even more surprised when, on opening night, Kaufman appeared onstage for a curtain call. But he had a special reason, as mentioned earlier. "I would like the audience to know," he said quietly, "that 80 per cent of this play is Moss Hart." Then he turned and signaled the stage manager to drop the curtain.

Reviewers, however, did not seem to pay attention to Kaufman's statement, and many completely ignored Hart or mentioned him only in passing. Kaufman's fame as a wit was so well established that both critics and audience assumed that anything funny in the play was Kaufman's contribution. But Kaufman knew better, and was truly grateful to every one of his collaborators. He expressed his views in a letter to Howard Teichmann, in which he wrote:

"A thought on collaboration. It is marriage without sex, and subject to many vexations. But pay no attention to them, because in one respect at least it is wonderful. The total result is frequently far more than the combined abilities of two people might give you— one person feeds the other, and in some way something absolutely great comes out of it—much better than the two talents added together . . . The two people fly far above their talents, and if I don't know about collaboration who the hell does?"

Still, nearly all the credit was given to Kaufman, and nearly every letter he received concerning *Once in a Lifetime* never even mentioned Hart. Otto H. Kahn wrote, "You must be weary of being assailed with expressions of admiration and congratulations anent your gorgeous satire, *Once in a Lifetime*, not to mention your excellent acting. But having seen and enjoyed hugely the play last Friday, I cannot refrain from letting my shouts of joy come to your ears." William Allen White, the famous newspaper editor, also sent a letter which made it sound as though Kaufman had done it alone: "It was a swell show," he wrote. "Edna and I went to see *Lysistrata* this evening and old Aristophanes had no more on the ball—if you know what I mean—than you!" His old friend, Neysa McMein, said simply, "I have always been economical with the word great. I think it applies to you." And a well-known playwright of the period, A. E. Thomas, wrote, "Since I am obviously the model for Lawrence Vail, it seems to me it would be a grateful act to let me play the fellow when you step out or, at least, understudy the part. Nothing, I assure you, happens to him that didn't happen to me." Thomas then added that he paid $12.50 for his ticket, but had a great time in spite of the cost, concluding, "I'm sure that this is no slight praise."

Aside from his curtain speech, Kaufman had shown his appreciation of Hart in the play's financial arrangements, giving his collaborator 60 per cent of the author's share, and top billing, so that the by-line read: *By Moss Hart and George S. Kaufman.* Kaufman was acutely embarrassed by all the praise for himself and the omission of Hart, and was quick to agree when a few people said that the final play was close to Hart's original and that he'd only been a kind of lapidary. But Hart, in turn, was quick to insist on the truth: that the play had been stripped bare and that the final script had been a true collaboration.

The Dramatists Guild finally put matters straight by awarding both men jointly the Roi Cooper Megrue Award, made from a fund donated by playwright Roi Cooper Megrue and his mother, Stella Cooper Megrue, "to be given to a member (of the Guild) whose play, produced in New York, makes an audience a little brighter and a little more cheered up when it leaves the theater than when it came in." The citation was a legitimate summing up of the impact of *Once in a Lifetime*. The play was chosen for *The Best Plays of 1930–31*, and also had an extremely successful run at the Queen's Theatre in London. It has been revived many times since, once, in an off-Broadway production, by Peter Bogdanovich, before he became a top film director.

When the play's smash opening insured its success, Hart fulfilled a long-standing ambition. He went home to his family's Brooklyn apartment, told his family to leave everything in place just as it stood and walk away from it, abandoning the furniture and everything else, and moved the family into a swank tower apartment at the Edison Hotel. He also, in his boyish delight with his success, had an interior decorator make four different layers of curtains for his own bedroom at the new apartment: net, chiffon, satin, and velvet. He also had tailored dinner clothes made for himself and used them for the first time by taking Beatrice out.

Hart's success came as no surprise to his father, a peppery and proud little man whom everybody called the Commodore. He told a family friend, "I had it in me. Why shouldn't he have it in him?" Hart himself, however, was overwhelmed with joy at his new status as a celebrity, continuing for years to use his success as a wonderful new toy. Eventually, he rented a beautiful new town house on East 57th Street, and there, and later at his Bucks County estate near Kaufman's, he threw many lavish parties. At one of these, a July Fourth party, he even worked up the nerve to chide his collaborator for standing around, as Kaufman usually did at big parties, merely observing the proceedings without joining them. "Come on, George," Hart told Kaufman. "Get into the spirit of the thing." Kaufman shrugged. "Okay," he said. He began to talk to himself, audibly. *"Those damn British!"* he said. *"Those damn British!"* At another party, there was a guest present who was even more impressive than Kaufman: Greta Garbo. Miss Garbo, furthermore, startled Hart by making an open and visible play for him. Hart was flattered, but just didn't know how to deal with the situation, so nothing came of it.

Hart also learned, unfortunately, that fame sometimes brought frustrations along with the rewards. He found himself unexpectedly, one day, in the vicinity of a school he'd attended many years before. Visions of a triumphant reappearance rushed into his mind, and, before he even took the time to think things through, he was entering the big double doors of the school building. Was it possible, he wondered, that the same principal, Mr. Cartwright, might still be there? It was. Hart entered the principal's office, and there was Cartwright looking almost exactly as Hart remembered him: a fussy little man seated behind a big desk, rummaging through a mountain of papers. "What do you want?" Cartwright asked.

"My name is Moss Hart," the playwright said. But Cartwright's face remained blank, and Hart added, "I used to go to school here." "Well, what do you want?" Cartwright asked. Hart said lamely, "I—I thought I'd like to look around." "All right," Cartwright said. "Here's a pass." Hart left the principal's office and walked down the hall, stopped in front of his old classroom, Room 5, and opened the door. There was a teacher seated at the front desk, a woman he'd never seen before. "I'm Moss Hart," Hart said. The teacher nodded politely, but without interest, and Hart said, "I used to go to this school." "I see," the teacher said. "Well, sit down behind one of the empty desks, Mr.—Hart, was it?"

For two hours, Hart sat there in stultifying boredom, a captive observer of the New York school system, squeezed into a small seat. As he finally made his escape, the teacher asked, "What is it you do, Mr. Hart?" "I write plays," Hart said. "Isn't that interesting!" the teacher said. "I happen to write plays myself." On his way out of the building, Hart suddenly paused. Surely Cartwright must have made the connection by now—recognized the famous name. Hart turned and re-entered the principal's office. "What do you want?" Cartwright asked.

Kaufman had hardly expected Hollywood to join in praise of *Once in a Lifetime.* Even though the film version of *Merton of the Movies* had done well, the humor of that play had been sympathetic to Hollywood, while *Once in a Lifetime* was biting. Interestingly, however, with the vocal exception of Louella Parsons, Hollywood didn't mind being satirized. Miss Parsons, the formidable Hearst columnist, realized that Kaufman and Hart had her in mind when they created their gossip columnist, and included several savage attacks on the play in her columns. Hollywood's generally warm attitude toward the play, however, was reflected by an actress who had previously earned Miss Parsons's wrath and couldn't understand why Miss Parsons thought the role was patterned after her. "The one in the play," she said, "was *likable.*"

Another sign of Hollywood's reaction came in a letter from a man

Kaufman had never met, but had often seen in films, Adolphe Menjou. Menjou, who had been in Hollywood since 1913, had played every kind of role from seducer to, finally, the city editor in the first movie version of *The Front Page*. Menjou wrote Kaufman, "Sincerest congratulations on your enormous success. You have written the great tragedy of Hollywood. I hope its message will have the necessary effect. To me, who has spent as many years in pictures as Mr. Glogauer, it was tremendously moving, as it was the truth."

Then a more important response came from Sid Grauman, who wanted West Coast production rights. Harris was glad to make a deal with Grauman, a pixyish little man who resembled Harpo Marx and who was one of the shrewdest showmen in the world. Grauman and his father had opened one of the first movie houses in San Francisco, only to be wiped out in the 1906 earthquake and fire, but rebuilt and prospered so much that Grauman moved to Los Angeles, where he built the Million Dollar Theatre, the Mayan Theatre, which resembled a Mayan temple, the Egyptian Theatre, where King Tutankhamen might have felt at home, and Grauman's Chinese Theatre, site of the concrete footprints. Kaufman turned down Grauman's offer to stage the West Coast production, preferring to stay in New York and play his pet Vail role. In Kaufman's place, Harris sent Hart and a young director named Robert B. Sinclair. In time, Sinclair, truly a product of the Kaufman "academy," would become a phenomenally successful director, staging such hits as *Dodsworth*, *The Postman Always Rings Twice*, *The Women*, *The Philadelphia Story*, and others. In 1931 he was simply an ambitious and talented young man who had been lucky enough to get a job as assistant stage manager to Kaufman.

Sinclair had taken a degree in Industrial Management from the University of Pennsylvania in 1926, but the sum of his education was the knowledge that he wanted no part of business. A professor, agreeing that he would not make a good businessman, gave him an introduction to Kaufman, whom the professor knew slightly. This sort of thing was not new to Kaufman, who, ever since he had hit with *Dulcy*, had been bombarded with letters asking him to do something for some young man or woman. One even came from Al Smith. Smith had written, "This will introduce to you Miss Dorothy Graves, who will explain her mission to you. Because of her family connections, both Mr. John H. McCooey of Brooklyn and I are interested in her and anything you can do for her will be a personal favor to both Mr. McCooey and myself."

Unfortunately, most of those who came bearing such notes had little or no talent. And even when they did, there just weren't enough jobs. In Sinclair's case, Kaufman received the young man, apologized for having nothing for him at the moment, and promised to call if and when he did. Sinclair left with Kaufman's advice to look for a job as an assistant stage manager somewhere so that he could learn theatrical science at the source. A few days later, Sinclair secured just such a position, but it folded after ten days. Sinclair then went to Cleveland, where he gained considerable experience in stock before returning to New York. Then a series of sad experiences so disgusted him that he blasted theatrical commercialism in an article which he sold to *Theatre* for $75 and which he titled *Why I Am Leaving the Theatre*.

He kept his vow to stay away from the theatre for two years, but then ran into Kaufman on the street one day. Kaufman, feeling guilty about his unfulfilled promise to call Sinclair in case of an opening, offered him the job of assistant stage manager on *Once in a Lifetime*. Sinclair's ambitions came to life all over again because he recognized Kaufman as the perfect theatre figure on whom he could model himself. While Kaufman watched his actors, Sinclair watched Kaufman, soaking up enough stagecraft to launch himself into a long career.

Grauman, the man Hart and Sinclair were traveling to meet, might himself have stepped out of the play, since he was at least as colorful as any of its characters. He met the two Easterners in a rented armored car, claiming it was necessary in order to protect them from Hollywood's wrath; then he got two women friends to attack him with their purses on opening night on the grounds that he had betrayed Hollywood by putting on such a malicious play. The stunts got the play a lot of publicity, but Hart was so unnerved that he was unable to appear as Vail on opening night, taking to his bed instead. When he did take on the role several days later he was still shaky in it, finally contracting influenza and dropping out of the cast. But the play itself drew SRO audiences throughout its run.

Carl Laemmle and Universal Pictures bought the screen rights and the story was filmed in 1932 with Jack Oakie, Gregory Ratoff, Aline McMahon, and Louise Fazenda in the cast.

Everyone assumed that Kaufman's flyer at acting was only a sort of gag and wouldn't last long, but he seemed reluctant to give up the role even though Sam Harris and several would-be collaborators were trying to entice him with new scripts. The truth was that despite his satirical self-portrait in his article, Kaufman was rather proud of his acting. In a letter to his sister Ruth he declared his intention to continue the role, beginning his letter in a light vein:

"Kaufman is my name—cloaks and suits. Or, in these times, one cloak and one suit. Anyhow, one pair of pants . . .

"I have been doing no work for several weeks. I'm just an actor —it's a good deal like going to the office, and I find I don't mind it a bit. I shall stay on for a few months longer—I'm a little reluctant about breaking up a winning combination, and then there *was* that one woman who came to the box office and bought tickets on condition that I would appear . . ."

In addition to his role, Kaufman indulged his love of acting by giving more than a little care to dressing up for the occasional costume party he attended. He came to one party as Abraham Lincoln and created quite a stir—so much so that *Theatre* ran a full page cut of Kaufman in his outfit. He looked so much like the sixteenth President that John Drinkwater, who was then casting his Lincoln play, approached Kaufman about taking the leading role. Kaufman considered it seriously but decided that he had better stay with writing and directing. When he finally left the Vail role after three months, the part was taken by Sinclair. Sinclair eventually became famous for directing plays Kaufman had declined, then became a Hollywood director, and, when Hollywood began to sag under the impact of television, shifted to the new medium to direct several plays for *ALCOA Playhouse*, some of the *Maverick* segments, and many others. He died January 2, 1970, in Montecito, California, when a deranged man entered his home at random and stabbed him.

After *Once in a Lifetime*, Kaufman and Hart went on to separate projects and it was not until 1934 that they worked together again, on *Merrily We Roll Along*. In the interim Hart joined Irving

Berlin to write the book for *Face the Music*, which opened at the New Amsterdam Theatre in February 1932, and followed this with another successful collaboration with Berlin, *As Thousands Cheer*, in 1933. The next year he wrote the light operetta, *The Great Waltz*, set to the music of the Strausses, and embarked on a round-the-world cruise with Cole Porter which resulted in their musical, *Jubilee*. It was reported that the cruise with Porter was one long party until it was more than half over, at which point the writer and the composer went to work and dashed off book, music, and lyrics in record speed. In addition to these Broadway hits, Hart found time to write the scenario for two movies, *Flesh* (1932) for M-G-M and *The Masquerader* (1933) for United Artists.

The weeks Kaufman spent in the Vail role constituted his longest vacation from writing since the beginning of his career. He eventually grew restless and was happy to step out in favor of Sinclair. But a week or so later he insisted on resuming the role for one performance, since Ruth was in town and Kaufman wanted her to see him perform. Kaufman's friends noted, incidentally, that while Ruth's children were allowed to call Beatrice by her first name, they were careful to refer to Kaufman in a more dignified and respectful manner, calling him "Uncle George."

At about the time that he began his collaboration with Hart, Kaufman finally severed the umbilical cord which had bound him to the New York *Times*, leaving the paper on August 16, 1930. Why Kaufman, with so many hits behind him, persisted in his $80-a-week job as drama editor, was a mystery that confounded almost all who knew him. Kaufman explained it away by saying that he needed the money, but this was clearly a joke. He was making thousands of dollars a week in royalties from *Dulcy*, *Merton of the Movies*, *Beggar on Horseback*, *The Butter and Egg Man*, and *The Royal Family*. Brooks Atkinson had his own theory. "Those of us who were associated with him in the drama office," he wrote, "suspected that he had more confidence in newspapers than he had in the theatre." Another *Times* story adduced another explanation which fits well with Kaufman's character. "It took years of soul-searching," the story said, "before he would commit his future to anything as transient as the theatre. The *Times* was real. It came out late each night. It had presses and

[484]

newsprint and friends and a check each week." The same story explained why Kaufman finally decided to leave. "In the end it was the depression which forced him to leave the *Times*. There they were, so many editors and reporters out of work, and there he was keeping one of them from a salary while his royalty checks piled up week after week. So, being a fair man, he left to make room for someone else."

Still another reason for his long stay at the paper was given by an associate who speculated that Kaufman liked the job in part because it gave him an excuse to slip away from social gatherings he found annoying. He could always say, "Got to get back to the *Times*." His attitude toward some social events was expressed in a comment he once made about a party for Arthur Krock, the *Times* columnist, and Raoul Fleischmann, a joint party since the two had birthdays reasonably close to each other. "It was," Kaufman said, "a party which brought together, by the arbitrary accident of birth, people who would not normally go within ten miles of one another."

Kaufman was well known, of course, for the scrupulous care he took to keep his own involvement with the theatre completely separate from his position with the paper, and producers who worked with him had continued to find that this made it extremely difficult for them to secure coverage in the paper. Atkinson speculated that the rigors of maintaining this strict objectivity may have been another reason for Kaufman's resignation. "He thought his increasing involvement with the theatre made his news objectivity vulnerable to criticism," Atkinson said. "It was a characteristic decision of conscience."

Beatrice also was careful not to use her own and her husband's influence for personal gain, and the single exception to this is interesting for the way in which it highlights this rule of her character. Albert Hirschfeld, the caricaturist, had done a drawing for the *Times* drama page depicting the celebrities in attendance at the opening of the Bucks County Playhouse in Pennsylvania, and Beatrice was included along with Kaufman, Harpo Marx, Woollcott, and many others. He had made her look old and fat, and she was hurt. She complained to Arthur Hayes Sulzberger, the *Times*'s publisher, and Hirschfeld was banished from the paper for a while. But Kaufman was deeply embarrassed by Beatrice's complaint, and she never did anything of that kind again, having done it only once under what was, to her, an extreme provocation.

The departure from the cast of *Once in a Lifetime* robbed Kaufman of a major excuse for staying away from social events, and he went with Bea to a party celebrating the end of Prohibition, as well as to a considerably more meaningful party celebrating his and Bea's fifteenth wedding anniversary on March 15, 1931. Descriptions of Kaufman at parties never vary. One portrays him as always alone in a crowd, "tall, gaunt, his hair brushed up in a high pompadour, a pair of tortoise-shell glasses riding well down on his nose, his eyes fixed on some invisible object on the ceiling." He spoke very little. Once a friend claimed to have monitored him and reported that he only spoke three lines all evening, each a comic blockbuster.

As always, Kaufman, during this period, received piles of scripts from producers, would-be playwrights and even actors and actresses, properties it was hoped he would direct. He turned down some colossal hits, including *Grand Hotel, The Postman Always Rings Twice*, and *Dodsworth*, feeling that these were not of sufficient interest to him personally to bring forth a first-rate job. Another script he turned down was a translation from a Russian author, submitted to him by Eugenie Leontovich, the actress, who was than a refugee fresh from Russia. The innocently broken English of her letter replying to his rejection conveyed, perhaps more eloquently than usual, the hopes which Kaufman knew were pinned to each script submitted to him. "It was not rude of you," she wrote, "not to answer me at once. The bad news better get later. Let me assure you only that the author of this unfortunate play is one of the best we had in Russia—I mean in the time when Stalin was a mere child. I put all the blame on us—2 translators, we've killed it. May it rest in peace. After all the whole thing is not so bad. I've met you. Please don't turn me away for ever from your memory and if you think I can act—give me to play one of your wunderful play. (Cen you write a play wher one of the caracter speks very bad English?) . . . Now forgive me for taking your time and permits me to remain your admareres—or what ever is the English word for what I am about you."

A little later, Kaufman also turned down Walter Damrosch, the celebrated orchestra conductor, who wanted to collaborate on a play. Another request of this period, and a difficult one, involved Theodore Dreiser's battle with Paramount Pictures over Paramount's interpretation of *An American Tragedy*, his famous novel. Dreiser was furious with Paramount's changes, contending that the social and artistic meaning of his book had been erased in the film, and asked Kaufman to sit on a panel of well-known writers to view the film and pass judgment on Paramount's interpretation. Kaufman declined, saying modestly that he didn't feel qualified to make the judgment.

On January 17, 1934, there was, as mentioned, a fiftieth wedding anniversary party for Joseph and Nettie, with 125 guests, at the Savoy-Plaza ballroom. Kaufman's special gift to his parents was a film record of their lives, showing this by projecting old photos on a screen. He also asked his parents to appear with him in a special dramatic short subject which he arranged to be shot at a studio in Fort Lee, New Jersey. Kaufman wrote the script, which presented Nettie in the act of deciding, after fifty years of domesticity, to seek a career, with Joseph asking Kaufman's help in dissuading her. "What is it you want to do?" Kaufman asked Nettie in the film. "Review plays," Nettie responded, adding that she'd then be able to give her son better notices than Brooks Atkinson.

The evening also included music and dances from his parents' youth. Kaufman hired an old-time dancing master by the name of Duryea to call the old dances. The happy event was soon followed by a sad one, when Walter C. Percival died on January 28. It had been seventeen years since George Tyler had asked Kaufman to spruce up Percival's and Larry Evans's *Among Those Present*.

The seminal idea for what proved to be the next Kaufman-Hart collaboration had first occurred to Hart while he was in Hollywood to stage *Once in a Lifetime* for Sid Grauman. He plunged immediately into the writing, only to read in the newspapers that his idea—to trace a family from New Year's Eve 1899 to New Year's Eve 1929—was exactly like that of *Cavalcade*, a new play by Noël Coward. He shelved the idea during the period of his work with Irving Berlin, but returned to it later and revised the conception completely so that the play would obviously owe nothing to Coward's hit. On a cruise through the West Indies, Hart reached the decision to keep his original idea of a play which compared different periods of a family's life, but with a reversal of the sequence of acts so that the first act would cover the most recent action, the second act a period prior to that, and the third act would reveal the genesis of what the audience had seen in the first two.

Hart rushed the idea to Kaufman as soon as the cruise ship docked at New York. "It's good," Kaufman said. "Let's bat it around for a few weeks." For the remainder of Hart's stay in New York, the team held non-writing work sessions in which they worked out a comprehensive plot, including individual scenes and key dialogue. Then Hart had to leave for Hollywood again, and, once there, found that his commitments prevented him from returning to New York for the collaboration with Kaufman. He asked Kaufman if he could come out to the Coast. Kaufman agreed, paused only to reminisce with Marc Connelly on the WEAF radio show, *Hall of Fame*, and left for Hollywood by train on February 12. Although plane travel was becoming more widely accepted, Kaufman continued to refuse to travel by air, saying once at a party that the only way he would be killed in a plane crash was to have a plane fall on him as he walked down Broadway.

Hart and Kaufman retired to Palm Springs, where they wrote the new play in five weeks, a speed which was possible only because of the earlier discussions in New York. They called it *All Our Yesterdays* at first, then changed this to *Career*, and finally settled on *Merrily We Roll Along*. The family idea had been discarded early in the sessions. The protagonist was now a famous playwright whose career has ground to a barren and miserable halt, and the first act opens at a drunken party in his home. The playwright, it seems, has sold out his youthful ideals in order to achieve popular success. The play then shows, in nine scenes and in reverse, how his personal integrity deteriorated through the years. The final scene, and the final monologue as the curtain falls, is the playwright's valedictory address, in which he begs his fellow students not to compromise their lives.

There was a lot of comedy in the play, but reviewers complained that it was not the Kaufman and Hart they remembered and enjoyed. They were not comfortable with the reverse order, and some referred to it as *Merrily We Roll Backward*. Critics and audience had a field day trying to match the characters with real people. Everyone was sure that Sam Frankel, a brash composer, was supposed to be George Gershwin, and a Broadway columnist wrote, "Gershwin saw the play from second row center on Thursday night last week and seemed, according to an eager observer, to be slightly embarrassed now and then." Kaufman, the columnist said, "contented himself with a broad grin when asked if Sam Frankel was intended as a playful portrait of George Gershwin." Kaufman was also non-committal when everyone assumed that the character of Julia Glenn, a sharp-tongued writer who worked only to keep herself in whiskey, was Dorothy Parker. He issued a tongue-in-cheek statement saying, "It is downright outrageous for anyone to dare say we were attempting to draw an authentic portrait of Mrs. Parker. We do not deny that there are certain Parkeresque traces. Since when have authors been denied the privilege of taking certain facets of the characters of persons whom they know and embodying them in fictional presentations? However, we deny categorically, specifically, and in minute detail, that we ever intended Julia Glenn to be Mrs. Parker. And if we, the authors, say this, who is there to say us nay? We know best what we intended."

Mrs. Parker never commented on the matter. She never went to see the play, and she had a stock response for people who wondered aloud why she hadn't done something they'd expected her to do. "I've been too fucking busy and vice versa," she always said, and the line seems appropriate enough here.

The lead character of the play, Richard Niles, the playwright who sacrifices ideals for gold, was played by a man named Kenneth MacKenna, a former silent star whose real last name was Mielziner. His brother was Jo Mielziner, the scenic designer who created the play's sets and who is still one of the top designers in the business. MacKenna was Jewish, but had taken the Scottish name because it had a romantic sound to his ear. He later left acting and became an M-G-M executive. He is now dead. Also in the cast in a small role was Walter Abel, later a popular film star.

Merrily We Roll Along opened at the Music Box Theatre on Saturday, September 29, 1934, and, while it did not do as well as *Once in a Lifetime*, it had a healthy enough run at 155 performances, which, since production costs were only $60,000, produced a good profit. There was so much interest in the play that scalpers were able to sell opening night tickets for $300 a pair. The play was also a contender for the Pulitzer Prize, though the award finally went to Zoë Akins for *The Old Maid*. After closing in New York, the play toured the country, starting in Philadelphia.

Merrily We Roll Along was the subject of a lot of ink in the press, and brought forth a typically cutting comment from Herman Mankiewicz.

"Here's this playwright," he said, "who writes a play and it's a big success. Then he writes another play and it's a big hit, too. All his plays are big successes. All the actresses in them are in love with him, and he has a yacht and a beautiful home in the country. He has a beautiful wife and two beautiful children, and he makes a million dollars. Now the problem the play propounds is this: How did the poor son of a bitch ever get in this jam?"

22. THE FERBER REPRISE

DESPITE THEIR DIFFERING temperaments, Kaufman and Edna Ferber were very much alike in their insistence on personal honesty and directness, and their contempt for any form of false sophistication, hypocrisy, or cant. They both, accordingly, detested the artificiality of fashionable social functions. Kaufman's feelings were well known, while Miss Ferber publicized hers by reading aloud to friends from the society page and adding her own caustic commentary.

This shared dislike caught fire in 1929 when Miss Ferber approached Kaufman about a play to follow *The Royal Family*. After they had discarded various ideas, Miss Ferber suggested writing a play about the sordid truth behind the façades of an elegant dinner party. The theme had huge appeal for Kaufman. But as he and Edna Ferber met at lunch, dinner, and various other places to develop their ideas, he began to see the enormous technical problems the script would present. The basic concept was to present a party given by a social schemer and then reveal the grasping, calculating motives each guest had for attending, and this involved much more than a conventionally structured play. It meant that each character had to be developed singly to show motivation, requiring, in effect, a group of playlets strung together on the line formed by the culminating event, the dinner party. The problem of sustaining interest and continuity as the play jumped back and forth was appalling to Kaufman, and he told Miss Ferber that it simply couldn't be done. When she tried to argue, he just walked away.

Undaunted, Edna Ferber—who was as stubborn and persistent as she was small—presented the idea to Winthrop Ames while she was his weekend guest in October 1929. He agreed that the idea was a good one, but his professional judgment confirmed Kaufman's.

"It can't be written," he said. "The technical difficulties are insurmountable. And I mean both construction and production. No matter what you do, you'll end bogged down."

Miss Ferber had intended to poll Sam Harris and others she knew in theatrical production, since she needed expert opinion to break down Kaufman's refusal. But after talking to Ames, she realized that she would get the same answer from the rest. They would see the project from a practical standpoint, while she viewed it with the eye of faith. As she admitted later, she solicited no further opinions for fear that she would be persuaded to abandon her own idea. But if she did not approach any other producers, she never failed, in her conversations with Kaufman, to smuggle in the subject of *Dinner at Eight*, as she and Kaufman had titled the idea in their first discussions.

She kept chipping away at him each time they talked, while he went on to other projects and she wrote her best-seller, *Cimarron*, a novel based on the Oklahoma land rush. Then she had dinner with the Kaufmans on New Year's Eve, 1931. After dinner, Beatrice, Franklin P. Adams, Alexander Woollcott, and the other guests left for another party, leaving Kaufman and Miss Ferber to enjoy and endure each other alone. She promptly brought up still another proposal for the handling of *Dinner at Eight*—the sixth fully developed treatment she had tried to sell him since his refusal. They discussed the new idea for hours before Miss Ferber was willing to concede that it was no better than the five previous ones.

Years later, Miss Ferber described how three years of frustrations suddenly were swept away as their ideas finally began to chime together: "'Well,' I said, with that grace and charm which so endears me to a collaborator, 'I still think you're wrong and Winthrop Ames is wrong and everybody's wrong who says we can't make a fine play of *Dinner at Eight*. It has stuck in my mind all these years. It can't be so bad.'"

"All right, all right," Kaufman replied. "If you're still so stuck on it, let's dig it up and have a look."

He reminded her, however, that the basic format was similar to that of *Grand Hotel*, the recent hit which had brought a group of ill-assorted people together in a Berlin hotel to work out their intertwining destinies. Edna Ferber, seeing him again trying to talk himself out of the project, pointed out that they had had their idea years before *Grand Hotel*. "But we didn't write our play," Kaufman said. "So who'll believe it?"

However, he had agreed to talk about it, and for the next hour they considered new approaches. After all, *Grand Hotel* had shown that character playlets could be made into a cohesive whole, and this undercut Kaufman's major objection.

"Suddenly," Miss Ferber recalled, "the difficulties that always before had beset the plan of the play seemed to melt away. We warmed to the idea, we sparked, we became excited about this scene, this character, we began to interrupt each other, to argue, we were both talking together and walking up and down the room, gesticulating in each other's faces, acting out a bit as it came to one or the other of us. It was fine, it was exhilarating, it was glorious fun."

It was also hard work. The legend that Kaufman told Edna Ferber they would start *Dinner* the next day at eleven is not true, since he had other commitments. They did not get to the writing until March, when, after weeks of argument over the basic outline, they went to Atlantic City to write the first act. The team then returned to Manhasset, Long Island, where they now had summer homes near each other.

The play took exactly nine weeks to write, and the work schedule was unvarying. Promptly at eleven each morning, Kaufman was at her door ready for work. Although his other collaborators usually came to his place, Kaufman elected to go to Miss Ferber's, and it was not entirely chivalry. It simply was easier, when he was fed up with her arguments and interruptions, for him to leave her house than to throw her out of his. Despite her admiration for Kaufman, Miss Ferber had her own opinions and she fought for them with ferocity. Love and playwriting were two quite different and separate concerns.

Miss Ferber once described the mechanics of collaborating with Kaufman. She did the typing, while Kaufman wandered "hither, thither and yon or draped himself over and under or around such pieces of defenseless furniture as happened to be in the room." The two authors discussed each scene and each speech in detail before committing it to paper. Miss Ferber would jump up at the slightest provocation to launch into a portrayal of what she had in mind or to test the dramatic qualities of one of Kaufman's ideas. Often Kaufman would join her. Then, she said, "We'd wander all over the place, deciding on positioning, and we'd experiment with the spoken lines. I might add that we didn't spare our voices in the dramatic scenes. One of my maids and the man who cared for my lawn are still, I think, a little suspicious of our sanity."

On another occasion, Edna Ferber amplified this a bit, describing how Kaufman stalked around the room as they worked. "George jiggles the curtain cord; plays tunes with a pencil on his cheek which he maddeningly stretches taut into a drum by poking it out with his tongue; he does a few eccentric dance steps; wanders into the next room; ties and unties his shoestrings." Others have commented on this shoe tying, and sought to find some Freudian symbolism in it. The actual answer seems to be that Kaufman simply liked his shoelaces to be tied tightly.

Another of Kaufman's traits which annoyed Edna Ferber was his unwillingness to compliment her on her work. Nor was Miss Ferber the only one to be frustrated by Kaufman's refusal or inability to bestow praise. When Ruth Gordon became angry at Kaufman for this reason while he was directing her hit play, *Over 21*, she finally said, "Don't you *ever* pass a compliment?" "Certainly not," Kaufman said. "You're supposed to be good. I'm supposed to tell you when you're not."

The final script of *Dinner at Eight* opens with the fashionable Mrs. Jordan, played by Ann Andrews, planning a dinner party for visiting British nobility, and shifts to show the people she has invited to the party to meet the British visitors. They include Dr. and Mrs. Talbot, played by Austin Fairman and Olive Wyndham, an aging movie star named Larry Renault, played by Conway Tearle, Mr. and Mrs. Packard, played by Paul Harvey and Judith Wood, and an agent named Max Kane, played by Sam Levene. Also to be present are Mr. Jordan, played by Malcolm Duncan, and the Jordans' young daughter, Paula, who was first played by Marguerite Churchill, for a while a popular film star. Miss Churchill was succeeded in the role by Margaret Sullavan in March 1933, who was succeeded in turn by Jane Wyatt the following May. Cesar Romero also had a small role.

As the characters are developed, we learn that Jordan is dying and that Packard is trying to swindle his way into ownership of the Jordan factory. The Jordan girl has been seduced by the aging actor. Mrs. Packard, who quarrels constantly with her husband, is having an affair with Dr. Talbot, to the anguish of his forgiving wife. All their lives are gradually shown to intersect, and the authors reveal the double-dealing and hostility behind the small talk and polite smiles. They even show that the maids, the chauffeur, and other servants are as devious as their employers and the guests. When Mrs. Jordan finally announces that the guests of honor cannot attend, after all, everyone goes in to dinner and the curtain falls.

The script was delivered to Sam Harris on July 3, 1932, and casting began in August. Rehearsals for *Dinner at Eight* proceeded smoothly, except that Kaufman and Miss Ferber, extremely cautious about the casting of the play on which they'd worked so hard, could not find an actress they liked for one other important part: the role of Carlotta Vance, a once-famous actress who has retired to "nurse her double chins in private." They considered every possible candidate, even including Mary Garden, the ex-opera diva, but wanted Constance Collier, who had played Lady Macbeth to Herbert Beerbohm Tree's Macbeth before World War I, and whose regal dignity, spiced with a comic flair, was exactly suited to the role. Kaufman had dispatched a copy of the script to her in London, and she wanted the part, but she was tied to a commitment to a British producer named Charles B. Cochran.

Sam Harris was increasingly afraid that the play would open with a stage hand reading the part, as sometimes happened during rehearsals when no one else was available. He called Cochran by transatlantic phone to beg him to release Constance Collier. Cochran agreed but said that the favor put Harris in his debt—a debt which could be repaid only by allowing Cochran to make a deal for the play in London if it proved to be a hit on Broadway.

Miss Ferber later recalled that when Miss Collier walked into the Music Box Theatre for her first rehearsal, she swept across the stage, offered her hand to Kaufman, presumably to be kissed, and said in pear-shaped tones, "Georgie, darling! How ducky!" Kaufman reacted by saying that there was no need for her to rehearse—she was born for the part and simply had to learn her lines. Another indication of her suitability for the part was the fact that, with the advent of talking pictures, it was Constance Collier whom Louis B. Mayer and Irving Thalberg imported to coach M-G-M's stars in speech. It was even said that it was the story about this in *Variety* which had provoked Hart's idea for *Once in a Lifetime*.

Harris skipped the out-of-town tryouts and instead presented a week of invitational performances before the official first night. The production problem that had stymied Kaufman and Miss Ferber in the beginning—the rapid shift of scenes from one character and his home to another character and another home—was neatly eliminated by the revolving stage which Hassard Short had recently employed and introduced in *The Band Wagon*. Very few changes were made during the invitational performances, despite Kaufman's habit of rewriting until the last minute.

The new play opened at the Music Box Theatre on Saturday, October 22, 1932. Its competition was the final performances of *Show Boat*, a play called *I Loved You Wednesday*, starring Humphrey Bogart, then known primarily as the son of Maud Humphrey, a well-known artist of the period, and *Earl Carroll's Vanities* with Milton Berle and 155 chorus girls. There was also a certain amount of competition from a hit movie called *A Bill of Divorcement* with John Barrymore, and also starring Katharine Hepburn in her first film. (Miss Hepburn had recently rocked Broadway with her performance in *The Warrior's Husband*.) Edna Ferber was as nervous as Kaufman, but both had to vary their customary opening-night routines this time. Miss Ferber, who had never before been able to sit through an entire opening-night performance of one of her plays, took a seat high in the top balcony to watch her second concern of the night —her niece, Janet Fox, who was the daughter of Fannie Fox, Miss Ferber's sister, and who was playing the role of a predatory maid. Family ties were always strong with Miss Ferber, and she was nearly as worried about her niece as she was about the play.

As for Kaufman, his usual pacing around the theatre was halted when he learned that one of the actors had not yet appeared at the theatre. He wasn't due on stage until an hour-and-a-half after opening curtain, but he had always, during the five-day invitational run, shown up at eight sharp. Kaufman called the man's apartment, but there was no answer. He called the police and put someone on the phone to the emergency wards of all the hospitals. When this brought no word of the missing actor, Kaufman, nearly frantic, grabbed the utility understudy. The major characters had their individual understudies, but since this was prohibitively expensive for the minor parts, two actors, a man and a woman, were designated to assume any of the smaller roles which might become open. This meant that the utility understudy often knew no more about the role than what he had observed. Kaufman enlisted another actor to read the cues, and started to rehearse the man. As he worked, Kaufman could hear laughter from out front. The play seemed to be going well, but he couldn't hear and concentrate well enough, under the circumstances, to associate the laughs and the silences with particular parts of the script. Normally on first nights, despite his extreme agitation, he always listened intently, cataloguing lines that worked and marking those that would have to be revised or removed. Then revisions would follow for the rest of the night and the next morning. Now he was losing the opportunity to catch flaws, and that could mean the difference between a hit and a failure.

He could always ask the opinions of others, and he was sure to get a lot of this in any case, unsolicited. But he never really trusted any report or opinion but his own when repairing a play. Hart once described the time that Harris sent Kaufman several pages of written opinion after the opening of *Let 'Em Eat Cake*. After Kaufman had worked all night correcting flaws and was about to quit, he noticed Harris's suggestions still lying untouched on the table, and brushed aside an associate's questioning glance. "I'll get to those later," he said. If he read them, nobody ever knew it. As for asking Edna Ferber's opinion, Kaufman felt that she reacted too emotionally at times and that this clouded her artistic judgment.

In any case, the first order of business was to prevent complete disruption of the play by the minor but essential role. Kaufman had been working for about a half hour when a breathless stage manager rushed up to say that the missing actor was in his dressing room, having merely stepped out into the alley for a few minutes for a breath of air when he was first being sought. No one had thought to look for him outside the stage door.

Dinner at Eight was a solid hit. Since the play opened on a Saturday night, too late for the Sunday papers, Kaufman and Miss Ferber had to wait until Monday for the reviews, which proved worth the waiting. The *Sun* said, "A play to thank the theatre for," and the *Herald Tribune* said that "*Dinner at Eight* is one of the best of the shrewdly literate Broadway dramas." The *Times* called it "an extraordinarily engrossing piece of work," and the *Daily News* said the play was "the theatre at its current peak." Janet Fox was also a success in her role, which pleased her aunt immensely.

The play went on to record 232 performances on Broadway, and has had many revivals; as late as 1966, when Tyrone Guthrie brought it back, it played an additional 127 performances. It was also picked for *The Best Plays of 1932–33*, had a hit run in Vienna, and was also a hit in Paris under the title of *Lundi Huit Heures*.

The morning after the verdict on the play was in, Sam Harris got on the phone to London, as promised, to close a deal with Charles B. Cochran for the production there. Cochran thanked Harris for remembering that he was owed this for releasing Constance Collier, but added that he also wanted a bit more.

"What kind of cigars do you smoke?" Harris asked.

"Never mind cigars," Cochran said. "I want Kaufman to direct the London company."

Kaufman agreed to take on the job. In November, he went to London, taking along Robert B. Sinclair as his assistant. Edna Ferber followed two weeks later. Kaufman and the play were great successes in London, but Kaufman was lonely in the strange new city on his first trip abroad. He couldn't complain that Cochran was interfering, since the British producer was away in Birmingham, bringing out a new musical there. Cochran had departed with all of his staff except one man, leaving Kaufman by himself and adding to his loneliness.

Cochran made up for his neglect in a note to Kaufman. "Before the curtain goes up tomorrow," he wrote, "I want to tell you that I think your play is a great bit of theatre construction and writing. Moreover, I believe it will be a hit in this town. I am more than grateful for your work on the production and I think I'm inclined to give you a dead heat with the only three great stage directors I have come in contact with during my fairly easy and amusing career. I am very proud and happy I have been associated with you."

It was Kaufman's habit to pass any praise along to his collaborators, but, though Cochran's letter was among those he kept the rest of his life, he did not show it to Miss Ferber. It embarrassed him, as always, that his collaborator's name had not even been mentioned, and that Cochran had called it Kaufman's play. The withholding of the note was also an act of special thoughtfulness, since Miss Ferber was in bed with a high temperature, due to a London epidemic of influenza. She was already annoyed with Cochran on account of his absence, and his casual dismissal of her efforts might have blown the mercury out of her fever thermometer. But it was, as usual, a tribute to Kaufman's reputation that those who knew show business automatically assumed that every good line was his.

Opening night in London, January 6, 1933, was a triumph. This time Kaufman's opening-night routine had to be varied for a different reason. In between stalking, listening, and fretting, he had to call Edna Ferber at the end of each act and report on the audience reaction, since she was still too ill to attend.

The New York *Herald Tribune*'s London correspondent cabled the good news back to New York. *"Dinner at Eight* by George S. Kaufman and Edna Ferber," he wrote, "was well received by a brilliant first-night audience which packed the Palace Theatre here tonight. Most of the excellent cast did not attempt to simulate American accents and mannerisms, but this did not appear to detract from the play's realism for the audience." Another London reviewer felt that one playgoer would find it excruciatingly funny while another would find it equally painful. "The fact is," he wrote, *"Dinner at Eight* is both; it is extremely amusing *and* thoroughly remorseless. Which of these aspects will predominate in your retrospect depends upon whether you happen to be tender or tough, but while you are in the theatre, in either case, you will be swept along by its vivacious velocity."

One other thing that pleased and surprised London was Kaufman's diplomacy as the director. The top performers in the stage capital were given to determined battling in order to upstage or outshine the rest of the cast. Alan Parsons, noted critic of The London *Daily Mail*, marveled at "Mr. Kaufman's ability to persuade a cast of London stars to forget all their possible inhibitions and work cheerfully together as a team for the general good."

Kaufman mooned around his hotel room for a few nights, and then resolved to overcome his gnawing feeling of loneliness. He attempted to accomplish this by behaving in a totally uncharacteristic way: he solicited and secured a whole string of social engagements. His letters to Beatrice were suddenly filled with references to visits, parties, bridge games and other social affairs. He dined with Mr. and Mrs. Raymond Massey, lunched with Jack L. Warner of Warner Brothers, met a couple of other Hollywood visitors, Douglas Fairbanks and Harold Lloyd, attended a party with Herbert Marshall, ran into Alexander Woollcott, who had just returned from a visit to the Soviet Union, and went to lunch with a Hollywood director-writer, Edmund Goulding. He wrote of winning £30 at bridge, of meeting Robert Benchley at dinner with a British playwright, Frederick Lonsdale, author of *The Last of Mrs. Cheney*, mentioned shopping for a present for Anne and picking up an antique mirror for Beatrice. He also found time to write *With Gun and Camera in London*, his survey for the *Times* of plays currently showing in London. None of it really worked; all through his stay, he ached to return home. (Eventually, he visited London often enough in connection with his plays so that he grew fond of the city, even though it wasn't New York, and he finally rented a house at 39 Blomfield Road for his occasional use and Beatrice's. But the Old World was a strange new world to him that first trip.)

He found it necessary to curb his rapid-fire wit, since the British just didn't understand the Broadway style of humor and repartee. He wrote Beatrice, "I gradually have discovered that they are never kidding, no matter what they do or say. No remark is too absurd to be taken literally by them, and I have finally got myself to the point of not saying anything except what I mean." This entailed the stifling of strong natural instincts, as when, back in the United States, an acquaintance arose to go to the toilet and asked if Kaufman would excuse him. "I prefer that," Kaufman had said, "to the alternative." He could not, however, resist every opportunity. After attending a play starring a famous British actor noted for underplaying to the point of near emotionlessness, Kaufman said, "I have a slight cold caught while watching Sir Gerald du Maurier make love."

Kaufman stayed on in London for a week after the play opened, so that he could help smooth any late problems, and then sailed home on the *Europa*. Soon after he returned a West Coast company was formed to present *Dinner at Eight*, but he refused to leave New York again, and Sinclair directed the company in his place.

Kaufman then declined to write the script for the film version which David O. Selznick was producing for M-G-M. Sam Harris had originally sold the rights to Joseph Schenck at United Artists, but Schenck turned sour on the purchase when his associates advised him that the film would not attract audiences outside the larger cities. Selznick, with the success of *Grand Hotel* fresh in his mind, did not agree, and proposed to change the basically unsympathetic story by rewriting the ending so that everyone, in true cinematic fashion, would be happy, and by using an all-star cast. Frances Marion and Herman Mankiewicz collaborated on the screenplay, with additional dialogue by Donald Ogden Stewart, and neither Kaufman nor Miss Ferber objected to the results, even though their play had been altered fundamentally. George Cukor, later Garbo's favorite director and director of *My Fair Lady* and many other films, handled the megaphone, and the cast included John and Lionel Barrymore, Marie Dressler, Wallace Beery, Jean Harlow, and Billie Burke. The picture premiered on August 24, 1933, and was a hit. The best notices were given to Wallace Beery and Jean Harlow, with Marie Dressler also receiving considerable praise. So much attention was paid by the press to the stellar cast, at the expense of any mention of the script or the underlying play, that Miss Ferber commented, "Very good. I wonder who wrote it?"

Miss Ferber and Kaufman had had a big argument before Kaufman left London, and he wrote to Beatrice, "I know that Edna does not want to work with me again. She is so sure that she is right in everything she says—it must be wonderful to be like that. There is never the possibility in her mind that anything she thinks or says could be less than gospel." It is characteristic that he said, "Edna does not want to work with me," and not, "I don't want to work with Edna," despite the fact that she had continually irritated him. She smoked, which he hated, annoyed him with her interruptions, challenged his theatrical decisions, and infuriated him with her tolerance of outside intrusions into their work. Once when she had kept answering the telephone during a work session in London, he said, "My God. Everybody called today except Queen Mary."

He later told a friend that it took ten years to write a play with Edna Ferber. "We only get ten minutes a day with each other. She works from 9 A.M. to 3:10 P.M., and I work from 3 P.M. to 9." Miss Ferber also confirmed that they fought often. Once when Kaufman interrupted their work on *Dinner at Eight* for a conference with Sam Harris, the playwright called to apologize. "No matter," Miss Ferber said. "We would only have spent the time quarreling as usual."

But each writer had enormous respect for the other's ability, so that the frictions of *Dinner at Eight* subsided. Exactly four years to the day after *Dinner at Eight*'s opening, they opened another hit, *Stage Door*. Later Edna Ferber talked about the origins of *Stage Door*, and it was very similar to what she had said about the genesis of *Dinner at Eight*. She said that she and Kaufman had stayed behind at Kaufman's home on New Year's Eve, 1935, after Beatrice left to go partying. They first talked about and abandoned several old notions, and then Miss Ferber resurrected an idea they had discussed years before about a girls' boarding house. Miss Ferber's account even included the same statement as that in her description of the discussions on *Dinner at Eight,* that she and Kaufman were startled by the noise of celebrants welcoming the New Year at midnight.

Miss Ferber's original notion had been simply that she and Kaufman write a play with an all-female cast. Kaufman was interested and they toyed for a while with the idea of writing about a girls' boarding house, but discarded the plan when they learned that Crosby Gaige was bringing out an all-female cast in a play called *Blind Mice.* *Blind Mice,* however, was a failure and soon forgotten, so they returned to the idea in the New Year's Eve discussion. In the years since their first talk, Miss Ferber had been taken to the Rehearsal Club, the hotel for young actresses. It had inspired her in much the same way that Winthrop Ames's mention of a show boat had sparked her into writing her very successful book. She contributed this element for the possible setting of the play, but suggested that the all-female cast be revised in favor of enough men to provide romantic interest. The landlady, of course, would be a retired character actress.

The completed script disguises the Rehearsal Club as the Footlights Club, and revolves around Terry Randall, played by Margaret Sullavan, and Jean Maitland, played by Phyllis Brooks. Terry spurns a Hollywood offer in order to stay true to theatrical ideals, while Jean accepts and becomes a famous film star. But when Jean returns to star on Broadway, she flops as a legitimate actress, and the curtain falls on the assumption that Terry will get her more satisfying reward in the role her former friend couldn't manage.

Kaufman and Miss Ferber delivered the script to Harris in late April, and *Stage Door* tried out in Philadelphia on September 28, 1936, at the Forrest Theatre, to a good reception for both play and cast. When the play opened in New York on Thursday, October 22, the critics echoed the earlier opinion, and in spite of a slow start—advance sale was only $12,000, and by November 12 only $26,000 was in hand—the show became a hit. The play was selected for *The Best Plays of 1936–37,* and Burns Mantle found it amusing that Kaufman and Edna Ferber had brought Margaret Sullavan from Hollywood to play a girl who refuses to compromise with the cinema. But amusing as it might have been, the audiences loved Miss Sullavan in the role, and the chief reason for the play's relatively short run of 169 performances was her withdrawal from the cast. Miss Sullavan, who was married to Leland Hayward, became pregnant, and she was so identified with the role that Harris and Kaufman did not think the play would draw without her, and closed it. Joan Bennett was brought in from Hollywood and paid $2000 a week to play the role on tour, but it was impossible to consider having any actress try to succeed Miss Sullavan in the role on Broadway.

It was during the preparations for *Stage Door* that Kaufman's private secretary, assistant, and general factotum, Myra Hampton Streger, also assumed the duties of casting director. Miss Streger was a slim, tiny woman who had worked for Kaufman since 1932, and who was pretty enough to be described in a theatrical paper as "a hundred per cent winner in most any pulchritude contest" after her New York acting role in *The Bad Man*. She had also been in the cast of *Cradle Snatchers* while married to Raymond Hackett, the actor, whom she divorced. She later married Paul Streger, also an actor. She was a favorite with the poker-playing members of the Thanatopsis Literary and Inside Straight Club, and when her son was born, they chipped in to buy the baby a gift of one share of U. S. Steel, then worth $200. At the time of the Crash, Frank Adams said, "I hear Myra's kid got clipped in the market." It was during the rockiest times of the depression, when she was having difficulty finding acting jobs, that Kaufman hired her. After her work as casting director on *Stage Door*, she also earned credit as casting director on John P. Marquand's and Kaufman's *The Late George Apley*. She became very ill, suffering from tuberculosis, in 1944, and died in a New York sanitarium on July 19, 1945.

Movie rights to *Stage Door* were bought by RKO for $130,000, but whereas Universal had filmed *Once in a Lifetime* virtually as written, with its satire of Hollywood intact, Pandro S. Berman, the producer, hired Morrie Ryskind and Anthony Veiller, son of Bayard Veiller, the playwright, to revamp the script. Ryskind and Veiller retained the title and the Footlights Club, but rewrote the rest so that heartless Broadway producers were the villains and Hollywood was the shining ideal. Ginger Rogers and Katharine Hepburn were the stars, and the film was a hit despite the changes.

At about this time, Kaufman noticed that there was a playwright named George S. Kaufmann. This happened to be the author's real name and he never claimed to be the Kaufman of Broadway, even though the coincidence was made stronger by the fact that Kaufmann had also been born in Pittsburgh. Recently, Kaufmann recalled a letter that the more famous playwright wrote him in the mid-1930s. "He wrote to me saying he knew I was entitled to the name," Kaufmann said, "but suggested that, since he had prior claim, I adopt another. Concluding, he said he knew neither of us would want credit for anything the other wrote. I was rather sensitive in those days and thought I detected a note of horror in his last sentence, so I told him I would dispense with George on anything I wrote. Thereafter, to this day, I use G. S. Kaufmann on anything for publication." Kaufman finally dismissed the matter with a brief comment. "Kaufman," he said, "is a very popular name. In fact, Lee is Kaufman in Chinese."

Kaufman and Edna Ferber worked together several times after *Stage Door*. In 1939, they discussed a possible play about a Jewish family but nothing came of it. Then, in December 1940, Miss Ferber fell in love with the idea of a play to be set in the resort town of Saratoga, New York, in the late nineteenth century, and involving a Texas adventurer and an equally adventurous European beauty in the chicanery of railroad-empire building. She managed to drag Kaufman up to Saratoga that winter but the hotels were closed, Kaufman froze, and left after one day of the planned two-day visit. Miss Ferber stayed with her notion, and finally used her idea in her best-selling novel, *Saratoga Trunk*. Nineteen years later, on December 7, 1959, her concept finally reached Broadway as a musical called *Saratoga*. Neither Kaufman nor Miss Ferber was involved with it. Morton DaCosta wrote the book with music by Harold Arlen and lyrics by Johnny Mercer. The show played the Winter Garden for eighty performances and quietly died.

Miss Ferber's next idea did develop into a play, *The Land Is Bright*, on which Kaufman collaborated. It jarred critics who didn't quite know how to handle a straight drama from two authors so strongly associated with satire and comedy. The story concerns three generations of a family whose fortune was founded by an industrial bucca-neer. The second generation is corrupted, but the third, sobered by international developments leading to World War II, turns to social and moral reform. Kaufman wrote a piece to promote the play, *Notes of a Co-Author*, which appeared in the New York *Times* on No-vember 2, 1941, and the play went into rehearsal August 22, 1941. Max Gordon owned 20 per cent of the show and Miss Ferber and Kaufman the other 80 per cent. It tried out at the National Theatre in Washington, and opened at the Music Box Theatre on Tuesday, October 28. It closed January 3, 1942, after seventy-nine perform-ances. In contrast, *Let's Face It*, Cole Porter's lighthearted musical, opened one day later and ran 263 performances.

Edna Ferber and Kaufman tried again in 1948 with *Bravo!*, which opened at the Lyceum Theatre, Thursday, November 11, but closed on December 18 after forty-four performances. Kaufman and Gordon were to split the proceeds evenly between them, but there were no proceeds to split. *Bravo!* is the story of a refugee European playwright, said to be patterned after Ferenc Molnar, and his mistress, a faded European star, who live in a shabby house with assorted refugees like themselves. They manage a bare subsistence working in a restaurant and doing other odd jobs. (Kaufman once described a waitress' job as "serving soup to nuts.") When the play-wright is accused of having falsified his entry papers and is about to be deported, the authors save him with a *deus ex machina*. They have him meet Bernard Baruch, the eminent financier and presidential ad-viser, on a park bench; Baruch, hearing his story, makes a telephone call to the proper authorities, and the hero is saved. Baruch was well-known for granting interviews while sitting on a park bench, and for wielding considerable influence when needed, so the plot twist had a certain amount of logic.

Gordon wasn't really wild about the play, having taken it on largely because Kaufman had faith in it. The tryout audience in Boston agreed with Gordon, but despite this, Gordon risked the Broadway opening at the Lyceum. It was a sentimental occasion for Miss Ferber whose first play, *Our Mrs. McChesney*, with Ethel Barry-more in the role of the corset saleswoman, had played the Lyceum in 1915. Oscar Homolka was superb as the playwright, and Lili Darvas was also well received as the mistress, but the reviewers were unenthusiastic.

Among the critics, Robert Garland of the *Journal-American* offered the most logical explanation for the play's failure. "Miss Ferber, a romantic sentimentalist, and Mr. Kaufman, Broadway's brightest wise guy," he wrote, "are continually at odds where the ideology of *Bravo!* is concerned. She dearly loves to play with unhomed, therefore unhappy paper dolls of two dimensions. He, on the other hand, dearly loves to knock them down."

Bravo! was Edna Ferber's last play, although her career as a novelist continued and prospered. She died April 15, 1968, at her home at 730 Park Avenue, in New York City.

23. THE OTHER COLLABORATORS

IT'S OFTEN FORGOTTEN that, in addition to those writing partners with whom Kaufman worked for substantial periods of time, there's a long list of others who collaborated with him only once or twice. Some of these writers, like Woollcott and Lardner, were very well established on their own, and the fact that they wanted to write plays with Kaufman is an added testimonial to his prowess. After the first decade of Kaufman's career, his long list of collaborators continued to grow, and the roster is sprinkled with more well-known names, including Howard Dietz, Laurence Stallings, John P. Marquand, Abe Burrows, Alan Campbell, and a very special collaborator, Leueen MacGrath.

The collaboration with Howard Dietz was *The Band Wagon*, a hit revue which opened at the New Amsterdam Theatre on Wednesday, June 3, 1931. Dietz had written a hit the year before with an attorney-turned-songwriter, Arthur Schwartz, a revue called *Three's a Crowd* which featured a stellar cast—Fred Allen and Portland Hoffa, Clifton Webb, Libby Holman, Tamara Geva, Fred Mac-Murray, and Allan Jones. It ran for 272 performances, and Max Gordon, its producer, yearned for a successor. Dietz agreed to try to provide him with one, but only on the condition that Gordon could get Kaufman to work with him. Kaufman agreed readily.

Howard Dietz, son of a dealer in diamonds, is a remarkable man who juggled two highly volatile careers side by side for more than a quarter century. During the period that he wrote the lyrics to such hit songs as *Louisiana Hayride*, *Moanin' Low*, *Dancing in the Dark*, and *Give Me Something to Remember You By*, Dietz was also director of advertising and public relations for Metro-Goldwyn-Mayer, a post which he held from 1924 to 1957.

After graduation from Columbia's School of Journalism in 1917, Dietz served in the Navy during World War I. While still in college, he had begun contributing bits to Frank Adams's *Conning Tower*, and also won an advertising contest for students sponsored by Liggett and Myers, the tobacco company. After the war he went to work for an advertising agency which had among its clients the newly formed Goldwyn Producing Company. The president of the firm, Samuel Goldwyn, had been partner with Adolph Zukor and Jesse L. Lasky in Famous Players-Lasky, under his real name, Samuel Goldfish, until one day Zukor told Lasky that the company was too small for either him or the highly opinionated Goldfish. Goldfish then joined forces with Edgar Selwyn, choosing Goldwyn as the name for their new firm and as a new, less eccentric last name for himself. Howard Dietz was assigned to design a trademark, and came up with Leo the roaring lion encircled by the Latin motto, *Ars Gratia Artis*, Art for Art's Sake. The trademark is still used, of course, to identify M-G-M films. Goldwyn was sufficiently impressed by Dietz to offer him the job of publicity director, and when the Goldwyn company merged with Metro, Dietz went along as head of advertising and public relations.

He began his song-writing career in the same year, 1923, when he furnished lyrics, without credit, for one song used in *Poppy*, the show which is remembered mainly for the classic performance by W. C. Fields. He teamed with Jerome Kern on a flop, *Dear Sir*, in 1924, and joined Morrie Ryskind and Jay Gorney on *Merry-Go-Round*, another flop, in 1927, but finally hit when he teamed with Arthur Schwartz on *The Little Show*, which ran 321 performances. *The Second Little Show* was a failure, running sixty-three performances, but then came *Three's a Crowd*. Although Dietz continued to be very successful on Broadway, he always insisted that his real career was press agentry, and that his song-writing was just a hobby. "Some people crochet," he said. "I write songs."

The Band Wagon was a hit and boosted the careers of all associated with it, but its greatest long-range importance to Kaufman was that it marked his first association with Max Gordon, who eventually superseded Sam Harris as Kaufman's producer. Max Gordon was born Mechel Salpeter on June 28, 1892, but later changed his name in imitation of his brother, who was becoming known as a comedian under the name of Cliff Gordon. In later years, friends could always tell when Max Gordon was rattled by calamity. Normally when he telephoned them, he would not identify himself—they were supposed to know who he was. But when things were really bad—as they decidedly were when he was wiped out in the stock market—he opened conversations with "This is Salpeter." As he once explained, he wanted the name Gordon associated only with success.

His early life contained some parallels to that of the younger Dietz. He attended the same high school as Dietz, Townsend Harris, but did not go to college, choosing instead to work as a press agent and then as a booking agent. After returning from service in World War I, he and his former booking agent partner, Al Lewis, joined Sam Harris in production, and their hits included *Welcome Stranger, Six-Cylinder Love, Rain, Secrets, The Nervous Wreck, The Family Upstairs*, and *Easy Come, Easy Go*. Gordon tried his first independent venture, *Three's a Crowd*, in 1930, and then brought Kaufman in for *The Band Wagon*.

Gordon has always been controversial with those who know him. Some picture him as always seeking something for nothing, and like to tell the story of a party where he was introduced to a doctor. He immediately began asking about the possible cause of a pain in his shoulder. "But I'm a doctor of economics," his new acquaintance said. "Oh," Gordon said. "Then tell me, will Kennecott Copper go up or down?" On the other hand, Gordon's word was so good that he and Kaufman never had a written contract. Each relied on the other's word, and it was never broken.

Outside his family, Gordon never became personally close to anyone. George Jessel once said that Gordon was the only man he knew who, by 9 A.M., had already been lonesome for two hours. Stories are told about his lack of refinement and culture, such as the time he heard Andrés Segovia, the classical guitarist, tell Groucho Marx about his concert tour of Europe and America. "My God, Marx," Gordon said later. "It's just one-night stands with a banjo." On another occasion, Gordon was asked what he thought of nepotism in Hollywood. He asked, "What's that?" And when told that it meant hiring one's relatives, he exclaimed, "You mean they have a *word* for that?" Gordon was also pretty casual about using the telephone at offbeat hours, and Kaufman once asked Ruth Gordon, "Does your phone ever ring when you're in the bathtub?" "It does," she replied. Kaufman asked, "Is it always Max Gordon?" (Miss Gordon has told this story about various people. When Kaufman actually said the line, however, he said it about Max Gordon.) A noted director, asked about Gordon recently, said, "No taste. No talent. The only good thing you can say about him is that he loved his wife." But the fact remains that Gordon produced many distinguished hits, and in a business with an overabundance of sharpies, he was scrupulously honest and always kept his word.

Though Gordon was strict in his business ethics, his associates weren't always pleased with his business sense. Fred Allen once, for example, wrote Groucho Marx in his usual uncapitalized manner, complaining that "mr. saltpeter recently tapped me into investing in one of his ventures with the usual results. if you have any money i suggest you leave it home. i believe mr. s. is planning another venture." But Gordon, for his part, never complained when his authors' works failed and he lost money. Kaufman said that Gordon never reproached him for a failure—not even *Bravo!*, which Gordon had opposed and which lost him considerable money. Those who complained about the often low return on their money from Gordon's shows undoubtedly failed to consider that musicals, Gordon's forte, are the most expensive type of show to produce, and a hit does not always make a producer and his backers rich. Even *The Band Wagon*, for all its success, earned no more than $100,000 profit.

Expenses were also often increased by some of Kaufman's secret generosity. When he later co-produced with Gordon, he would tell the stage manager to slip $100 cash gifts to various retired and down-and-out actors who came to the theatre. Once he wrote to Gordon from London and asked him to provide free first-row tickets for an acquaintance, adding, "He's ninety-five years old and entitled to anything."

Kaufman's policy with his collaborators on the matter of author's credit was to alternate in taking first billing. His generosity in this area was proverbial. In the same spirit that he had told *Once in a Lifetime*'s first-night audience that the play was "80 per cent Moss Hart," he insisted, as stated earlier, on the added credit in *The Band Wagon*'s program reading, *Entire Production Supervised by Howard Dietz*. Dietz expresses his gratitude for the gesture to this day.

Work on *The Band Wagon* went smoothly as the authors wrote short skits to make up the revue. Dietz would suggest a sketch idea and Kaufman would write the first draft, which Dietz rewrote before Kaufman did the final draft. Dietz said later that Kaufman did the bulk of the work and never questioned his half share of authors' earnings.

The Band Wagon tried out in Philadelphia to such critical acclaim that Kaufman told Dietz and Gordon that it might be a good idea to leave the play in Philadelphia and bring the notices to Broadway. As often happened, he was worrying needlessly. From the moment Frank Morgan opened the revue by telling the Broadway audience frankly that the show's purpose was to make money, *The Band Wagon* was a hit. It ran for 260 performances, closing January 16, 1932, and then began a long and successful road tour with Boston's Colonial Theatre as the first stop. In addition to Morgan, later a popular film comedian and the Wizard in *The Wizard of Oz*, the cast included Helen Broderick, also destined to become a successful screen performer (and whose son, Broderick Crawford, later became a well-known actor), Tilly Losch, and Fred and Adele Astaire. The show's stage manager, Hassard Short, also stirred a lot of excitement with his imaginative use of revolving stages, which as mentioned, he introduced for the first time in this play. Instead of using them for quick changes of scene, as Kaufman and Edna Ferber would later have him do in *Dinner at Eight*, Short incorporated the stages into the scenes themselves, using one of the stages, for example, to carry a carousel, while on another the Astaires did a show-stopping dance. Sime Silverman of *Variety* summed the opening up by saying that the laughter made it seem as though 75 per cent of the audience were backers of the show.

Eighteen years later, George Jessel produced *Dancing in the Dark*, a film for Twentieth Century-Fox, which was billed as having been based on *The Band Wagon*. All the film had in common with the original, however, was the Dietz-Schwartz score, since the show had been a plotless revue and a story line had to be supplied. The screenplay was written by Mary C. McCall from an adaptation by Marion Turk.

After *The Band Wagon*, Kaufman's next new collaborator was Laurence Stallings. It was an association on which neither would later care to dwell, but the fiasco that resulted was not the fault of either writer. They were simply guilty of letting Sam Harris lead them into an impossible situation. It began in 1928 when a stage-struck dress manufacturer from the Bronx, Isadore Polisuk, saw a bad play at a Greenwich Village little theatre, and it ended nine years later with Kaufman explaining to a judge how a play is written.

When Polisuk saw the play, *Hot Pan* by Edward Eustace, he decided it was just what he needed to fulfill his ambitions to become a producer and make a fortune. He bought the play, a comedy about the 1849 gold rush, for $100, and spent the next three years trying to find a producer who would do it. Finally, Sam Harris, in a rare instance of bad judgment, agreed to produce the show provided it was rewritten totally and provided Polisuk agreed to put up $10,000 to pay half the costs, with Harris providing the other half. Harris then talked Kaufman into doing the rewrite and Kaufman in turn suggested that, since the play dealt with a rough and tough setting like a Western mining camp, a collaborator ought to be brought in, a man who could help write about raw, perhaps violent situations. Harris suggested Laurence Stallings.

Stallings seemed to be the ideal choice. In 1924 he had collaborated with Maxwell Anderson on *What Price Glory?*, the play which was considered ultra-realistic in its day and which stripped much of the glamour away from war. Stallings had followed *What Price Glory?* with the screenplay for *The Big Parade*, the movie classic with John Gilbert.

Stallings was born in Macon, Georgia, on November 25, 1894, attended Wake Forest College, and served in the U. S. Marine Corps in World War I, suffering the loss of one of his legs. He returned to school, took his master's degree from Georgetown University, and went to work as a book reviewer for the New York *World* until he and Anderson, who was working as an editorial writer for the same paper, wrote their great success. After *What Price Glory?*, Stallings and Anderson wrote two other plays, *First Flight* and *The Buccaneer*, both produced in 1925, but when these failed, the team separated. Stallings followed his script for *The Big Parade* with an equally successful adaptation of *What Price Glory?*, and in 1930 added screenplays for *Song of the West, Billy the Kid*, and *Way for a Sailor*. In the meantime, he kept trying to repeat his initial stage success, writing book and lyrics for *Deep River* in 1926, teaming with Oscar Hammerstein II in 1928 to do *Rainbow*, and also writing a stage version of Hemingway's *A Farewell to Arms* in 1930. None of these productions worked out.

It was Kaufman's hope that, with Stallings supplying the realism of the gold rush, and with his own brand of humor, they might be able to make something out of *Eldorado*, their name for *Hot Pan*. But nothing the two men did could make the play work. They rewrote it three times only to see it die after playing a split week in New Haven and Hartford, Connecticut.

Polisuk, brooding over his $10,000 loss, soon decided that it had occurred because Kaufman had been too busy with *Of Thee I Sing*, which had been written and rehearsed at the same time as *Eldorado*. It was a short step from there to the conclusion that Kaufman had contributed directly to *Eldorado*'s failure through neglect. Polisuk decided to sue for repayment of his money, so intent on Kaufman as his target that neither Harris nor Stallings were made parties to the suit. The trial was held in January 1937. Kaufman's defense was that he and Stallings had finally come to the conclusion that the play really didn't have a viable idea, and had simply been unable to come up with a good idea for it themselves. "You can't coax ideas," Kaufman said. "They have to come to you. You can't say you'll think ten hours instead of two. You reach an impasse. Stallings and I worked over the play again and again, even after it appeared to be such a flop. We worked at bedroom conferences—they last all night—and in hotels and in speakeasies." Polisuk's lawyer then asked him where he had sat down with Stallings for their writing sessions. "I don't sit down," Kaufman said. "I'm the man who paces."

Kaufman went on to say that he did not give up on *Eldorado* for four months after it folded, and that he and Stallings kept hoping that lightning would strike with an angle that would revive the play's chances. He denied emphatically that he lacked interest in the play just because he had two successes, *The Band Wagon* and *Of Thee I Sing*, running on Broadway at that time. "I would have been very happy," he said, "to have had three successes running." Polisuk took the stand right after that, but became so excited that the judge told his lawyer, "I'll pay for his lunch if you can calm him down during it." A short time later, the judge directed a verdict for Kaufman without giving the case to a jury.

Kaufman never worked with Stallings again, even though he continued to admire him. Stallings tried two more plays with other collaborators, both unsuccessful, and then worked primarily on screenplays for the rest of his life. He wrote, among others, *Too Hot to Handle, Northwest Passage, Three Godfathers*, and *She Wore a Yellow Ribbon*, the last three directed by John Ford. He also edited and wrote the captions for a best-selling book of photographs, *The First World War: A Pictorial History*, published in 1933. Stallings died on February 28, 1968, at the age of seventy-two.

Kaufman's next new collaborator was a girl named Katharine Dayton, and their play was *First Lady*. Katharine Dayton was the daughter of a former publisher of Hearst's New York *Journal-American*. She had originally wanted to be an actress and had studied with Yvette Guilbert, but later gave up the stage in favor of a writing career, selling her first story to *Vanity Fair* in 1920. Later, she became a Washington correspondent, and wrote a group of witty stories for *The Saturday Evening Post*, giving her series the title of *Mrs. Democrat and Mrs. Republican*. Around the same time, she mentioned to her literary agent an idea for a play about the in-fighting among leaders of Washington society. The agent discussed her idea with Kaufman, who liked it enough to agree to meet with Miss Dayton. Miss Dayton later expressed her feelings about her collaborator in an article titled, *'It Must Be Such Fun to Work with Kaufman.'*

"I'm going to explode that Kaufman myth," she wrote. "I mean the one in the title. It is not fun to work with George Kaufman—but it is work being funny with him." She said that, when they had their first meeting, he was extremely polite, but told her that he really didn't want new collaborators, since the old ones were still warm. As they talked, however, he became more interested in the concept of the play, and they finally agreed to hold meetings to develop the plot. Then suddenly one day, after several meetings, he told her he was leaving for Hollywood to write *Merrily We Roll Along* with Moss Hart, and he said, "I'll see you in May."

He returned in May and they worked for three more weeks, while Kaufman grew gloomier each day. Finally, he told her he wasn't sure they had a play. She was stricken, since she didn't yet know that Kaufman always felt that perhaps he and his collaborator didn't have a play. But they continued to work together, Miss Dayton mostly at the typewriter and her collaborator mostly pacing back and forth, though she sometimes felt compelled to walk with him and wore the heels and soles off her shoes. It took two years, with frequent interruptions, to complete the play. Every time they gathered momentum, Kaufman had to leave for other projects, leading his co-author to the conclusion that Kaufman was the "travelingest collaborator" possible. All she could do, she said, was to put a light in the window to guide him back. Eventually, he showed one act of the play to Moss Hart, and Hart liked it tremendously, but this proved to be of little comfort to Miss Dayton. "Kaufman's first reaction to any-thing complimentary," she discovered and reported, "is to feel that the person uttering it must be crazy."

Most of the work, in Miss Dayton's phrase, was "written, re-written, and walked" at Kaufman's town house on East 63rd Street, a place she quickly named "All Work and No Play." The experience, her article states, revealed to her Kaufman's great gifts as a play-wright, and his intellectual honesty, but she adds that she would not for anything in the world ever collaborate with him again. "Not, that is," the article concludes, "unless he asks me."

First Lady centers on Mrs. Lucy Chase Wayne, whose grandfather had been President of the United States. Mrs. Wayne is married to the present Secretary of State and is ambitious for him to move into the White House. She is opposed by Irene Hibbard, whose husband is a doddering Supreme Court Justice, but who is pushing her lover, young Senator Keane, as a presidential hopeful. To stop Senator Keane, Mrs. Wayne convinces a conglomeration of women's clubs with five million members to support the candidacy of old Justice Hibbard, a move planned to spoil Mrs. Hibbard's plans to divorce her husband and also designed to humiliate her when Hibbard loses the nomination. A major newspaper chain, however, takes up the cry for Hibbard, and he almost wins before Mrs. Wayne is able, in the final act, to halt his campaign.

Jane Cowl took the role of Mrs. Wayne, and Lily Cahill played Mrs. Hibbard. Many reviewers, Burns Mantle among them, thought they saw the unmistakable portrait of Alice Roosevelt Longworth in the character of Mrs. Wayne. "Princess Alice" was the daughter of Theo-dore Roosevelt, had married Speaker of the House Nicholas Long-worth, and was a leader of Washington society for many years. The actress playing Mrs. Wayne was a great lady of the stage whose background included such hits as *The Garden of Lies* and *Smilin' Thru*, and whose temperament included a kind of imperious insistence on being allowed certain idiosyncrasies during rehearsal. Kaufman did not object until the rehearsal of one scene in which, after delivering a long speech, Miss Cowl paused, held attention to herself during a long and dull silence, while she slowly put her gloves, purse, and other props into her bag, and finally made her exit. Kaufman took her aside and suggested that it might be better if she picked up the props during the speech, since he considered the pause nothing but dead time. The actress glared at him. "That's impossible!" she said, and when Kaufman asked why, she told him, "It can't be done!" Again he asked why, his quiet voice contrasting with hers. "Are you suggesting that I do *this?*" she asked, speaking her lines and picking up her props at the same time. She ended the speech in embarrassment, realizing that she had just done the bit she had characterized as impossible. She played the scene Kaufman's way for the run of the play.

Eventually her respect for Kaufman became so strong that she sent him a long and glowing letter. "I know how you hate sentiment brazenly expressed," she said, "but I have to tell you that I have never worked with anyone so close to my affection, or who commanded in my funny mind such respect and admiration—and a not inconsiderable devotion. You're a grand guy and I would obey you blindly, even if you were wrong, which you are so seldom, if ever, that it's practically disgusting."

First Lady opened for tryout at the Playhouse Theatre in Wilmington, Delaware, on November 9, 1935, and moved to Broadway on Tuesday, November 26, opening at the Music Box. It was a solid hit, running for 238 performances, and was included in *The Best Plays of 1935–36*. Reviewing the play for the *Journal-American*, Gilbert Gabriel wrote, "Be grateful for *First Lady*. All first nighters were." And Richard Lockridge said in the *Sun*, "With the utmost good humor and the sharpest of claws, the authors dab, cat-like, at things and people, providing entertainment for man and sadist. It's cheerfully merciless comedy and crinkles the mind in smiles."

Despite *First Lady*'s success, Miss Dayton and Kaufman did not collaborate again, although he was called in to try to salvage her 1938 flop, *Save Me the Waltz*, a comedy set in a mythical kingdom, which Sam Harris and Max Gordon were co-producing. The combined efforts of Gordon, Harris, Miss Dayton, Kaufman, and Robert B. Sinclair, who directed the play, could not prolong the play's life for more than eight performances.

The movie version of *First Lady*, which was produced for Warner Brothers by Stanley Logan with a screenplay by Rowland Leigh, was released in September 1937, but was not successful. Kay Francis played Mrs. Wayne in the film, and one reviewer commented that the difference between the film and the hit play was the difference between Kay Francis and Jane Cowl.

Miss Dayton continued writing, but she did not attempt another play after *Save Me the Waltz*. She died in New York on March 4, 1945, aged fifty-five.

Kaufman was called in as play doctor on at least two other shows which could not be saved. One was *Spring Song* by Bella and Samuel Spewack, which Max Gordon produced at the Morosco in 1934. *Spring Song* told the story of Flossie Solomon, who steals her sister's boyfriend and then dies in childbirth, and was described by Gordon as a show about the kind of people he knew when he was growing up. But Broadway wanted people who were more interesting than those from Gordon's past, and *Spring Song* closed after forty performances.

Another play which Kaufman's first aid could not cure was *Franklin Street*, written by Ruth and Augustus Goetz, and produced in 1943. Kaufman also directed the play, and felt very badly for his friends as well as himself when it failed to go farther than its tryout in Wilmington, Delaware. To cheer the Goetzes, he later wrote them a funny letter in which he reported that he had sold the movie rights to *Franklin Street*. "This," he wrote, "was in a dream induced by two sleeping pills. It took place in a large store which seemed to handle a good many other things besides movie rights—shirts, nails, custard, everything. I sold the play an act at a time, which is a new idea that I rather like. The first act went for $30,000, and the second act for $60,000, which I thought was doing pretty well. The girl who was waiting on me knew all about these two acts, but the third act was all new to her. However, she took my word for it. I said there were two very nice situations in it, and that it should bring $35,000. I remember her saying. 'Well, as long as we've got the other two. . .'"

24. THE SILVER SCREEN

KAUFMAN WAS FOURTEEN when Edwin S. Porter made *The Great Train Robbery*, the first movie to tell a story, but he was no more impressed by the new rival of the theatre than all the other people who considered films merely an interesting novelty. He was already writing plays, for this was the year that he and Irving Pichel wrote *The Failure*. Then, when he moved into dramatic criticism, he continued to show contempt for the loosely conceived, crudely melodramatic films. He once said, "Who wants to look at shadows when he can see the real thing?"

But if Kaufman was slow to develop an interest in Hollywood, Hollywood showed its enthusiasm for him through purchase of the screen rights to most of his plays. Just about each time a play was sold, he also received a screenwriting offer. He turned them all down until

1929, when Groucho Marx persuaded him to join Morrie Ryskind in writing the film version of *The Cocoanuts*, and a major reason he accepted that one was that it was being filmed in New York and did not require him to go to Hollywood.

In 1933, Kaufman finally relented again and signed with Samuel Goldwyn to collaborate with Robert E. Sherwood on the screenplay for Eddie Cantor's *Roman Scandals*. It was, of course, on this project that Kaufman and Sherwood ran into their $25,000 misunderstanding with Goldwyn. But despite their troubles with the producer, the collaborators were happy with each other. Sherwood was a great admirer of Kaufman's wit and once wrote in his diary, "Kaufman steadily comical," and Kaufman had been a fan of Sherwood's movie reviews in the old *Life*. Sherwood began writing about films in *Life* when few other magazines took films seriously enough to do this. Many authorities have stated that Sherwood's feature was the *first* regular column of film criticism, and years later, when Sherwood and Kaufman were at a dinner together, Kaufman paid him a special tribute. "Do you know," he said, "that there sits at this table the founder of a new form of journalism?"

Kaufman was also responsible for getting Sherwood interested in Franklin Delano Roosevelt. Sherwood had originally been a Republican, but had switched to the Democratic Party largely out of admiration for Al Smith, and resented the way Roosevelt edged Smith out of the 1932 presidential nomination. Sherwood was at Kaufman's apartment when Roosevelt was scheduled to make a radio speech. Kaufman, who already admired Roosevelt tremendously, insisted that Sherwood sit with him and listen. Sherwood was impressed by the speech, which included the memorable phrase, "We have nothing to fear but fear itself," soon joined Kaufman in his admiration for Roosevelt, and later became the President's close associate and speechwriter.

Sherwood's dedication to Roosevelt grew so great that he was willing to make extraordinary personal sacrifices to advance FDR's cause. He was once embezzled out of a considerable sum by a broker, but refused to testify at the man's trial because Thomas E. Dewey, then the District Attorney of New York, was a political enemy of Roosevelt. Sherwood did not want to help, even indirectly, to enlarge

Dewey's reputation. He was subsequently asked why he never checked on the broker. Sherwood, who always spoke very slowly and deliberately, said, "He was so bo-ring that I a-voi-ded him."

When Goldwyn first asked Kaufman to collaborate with Sherwood on *Roman Scandals,* and told him that Eddie Cantor would be the star, Kaufman said no, having received plenty of warning from others who had worked with Cantor that the comedian continually interfered with his writers. Kaufman agreed only when it was written into his contract that he wouldn't have to listen to Cantor, and that the writing would be done in New York. The contract also divided their chores into three parts, original story treatment, screenplay, and final polish, and gave the collaborators the right to quit after any of the three phases.

The screenplay tells the story of a bumbling young man in West Rome, New York (later changed to Oklahoma), who runs afoul of a corrupt local politician. Later the young man is overtaken by sleep and awakes to find himself in ancient Rome, where he is captured, sold as a slave, and made food taster to the emperor, whom enemies are trying to poison. Eventually he is brought back to the twentieth century, armed with a document from the Romans which will enable him to overpower the politician.

Kaufman had assumed that, by working in New York, he and Sherwood would avoid interminable story conferences in which everyone connected with the film tried to tell the writers what to write. But he and Sherwood found that if they didn't go to Hollywood, Hollywood would come to New York. After one particularly exasperating session where Eddie Cantor suddenly appeared and made a great many suggestions, the writers informed Goldwyn that they were quitting. Although the basic story was completed, the script had not had gags added, and Goldwyn seized on this as grounds for withholding the writers' pay, which amounted to $25,000. The authors sued for the money, saying that they had performed according to the terms of the contract, and that Goldwyn's minions had interfered with their work in violation of the contract. Goldwyn also claimed that Kaufman's and Sherwood's departure had left him in difficulties, but the playwrights were able to refute this, too. Before leaving, they had arranged for George Oppenheimer to take over the job.

The case never made it to court. On August 26, 1936, almost two years after the suit was filed, Kaufman and Sherwood settled for $20,000, and when the film was released they shared writing credit with Oppenheimer, William Anthony McGuire, Arthur Sheekman, and Nat Perrin. The New York *Times* said in its review of the film that "any one of them might have written a more effective story alone," but Cantor and the Goldwyn Girls cavorting in Busby Berkeley's extravagant kaleidoscopes of dance were more than sufficient to attract moviegoers.

Goldwyn did not continue to feel ill will toward Kaufman, and Kaufman even became reasonably amiable toward Goldwyn again. The producer was best summarized in the words of George Oppenheimer. "How shall I describe Samuel Goldwyn?" he said. "The answer is 'with difficulty,' for he was a mass of contradictions." This ambivalence in Goldwyn's nature became visible in the relationship with Kaufman. Before the settlement, he talked bitterly about Kaufman; not long afterward, he asked Kaufman to work with him as co-producer, adding jovially, "I need a genius to do my work for me." "I need the same thing," Kaufman replied.

Kaufman's next involvement with Hollywood was with Irving Thalberg, a man who was fully as powerful—and as tyrannical—as Samuel Goldwyn or Louis B. Mayer, but who administered his despotism in a much more elegant and disarming way. Thalberg was born in Brooklyn on May 30, 1899, the son of an importer of lace. There was nothing in the family background to point Thalberg toward an entertainment career, but one summer, while still in his teens, he met Carl Laemmle, head of Universal, who hired him as an assistant. By the time he was twenty, Thalberg was studio manager, and his remarkable story sense immediately became apparent in the rising quality of Universal's products. Then, in 1923, Thalberg left Universal to join Louis B. Mayer in a partnership that lasted the rest of Thalberg's short life.

Groucho Marx was responsible for bringing Kaufman and Thalberg together. The Marx Brothers had had sensational successes in movie versions of *The Cocoanuts* and *Animal Crackers*, and in *Monkey Business*, *Horse Feathers*, and *Duck Soup*. Thalberg admired the zany brothers and loved their movies, but felt that they needed fresh material to keep them on top. He noted that their more recent films had lacked story, and, hilarious as they were, amounted to patchworks of gags with nothing to hold interest between laughs. He suggested that their next film have a stronger storyline and that the gags themselves be field-tested in vaudeville before being committed to film. His idea for their new film was to put the brothers in the most ridiculous place possible for them, and he decided that this should be that strongest bastion of pomp and propriety, the opera house. This, then, was the idea for *A Night at the Opera*.

The original story had been written by James K. McGuinness, but Groucho—remembering very well who had been responsible for the brothers' original Broadway successes—urged Thalberg to try to get Kaufman and Ryskind to do the screenplay. But he added that he felt sure that Kaufman would never be induced to leave New York. "I think that can be arranged," Thalberg said, and proceeded to arrange it by offering the collaborators $100,000.

The deal, however, was not made between Kaufman and Thalberg. Although Kaufman had never used an agent in any of his Broadway deals, he did not feel qualified to negotiate with the Hollywood producers. His first agent had been Leland Hayward, but when Hayward became a producer himself, Kaufman turned to Irving Lazar. Lazar was a good agent, meaning, among other things, that he could hold up his end of any conversation, even with Kaufman. It was Lazar's habit to visit New York about twice a month, and he never failed to time his visits to Kaufman for meal times. When Kaufman pointed this out one day, Lazar replied that he only got 10 per cent of his deals for Kaufman, while Kaufman got 90 per cent. "And you still begrudge me a meal!" he said. Kaufman told Nunnally Johnson that he saw more of Lazar, a Hollywood resident, than he saw any of his friends in New York.

Aside from the influence of Lazar and the rich Thalberg offer, Kaufman told a reporter that there had been an added reason for his acceptance of the deal. It had started when the Marx Brothers had sent him a telegram inviting him to do the screenplay. He ignored it. A few days later, he received in the mail a train ticket to Hollywood. He disregarded that. Then came a wire which said: COMING TO GET YOU.

"I took the next train to Hollywood," Kaufman said. "I knew, if I didn't, that they'd be after me. I can control Groucho, Chico, and Harpo when they're concentrating on a show or a picture, but not when they're concentrating on me, as they have on several occasions. Shall I show you my scars?"

Kaufman made the trip in early 1935. Once he was established at the Garden of Allah, then a lavish Hollywood hotel, he immediately joined the "Waiting for Irving" Club, the popular name for all those who had spent hours sitting outside Thalberg's office. S. J. Perelman, the humorist, once said that he had seen sitting there, all at one time, such literary lights as Sidney Howard, Robert E. Sherwood, Marc Connelly, S. N. Behrman, Donald Ogden Stewart, and Kaufman. He could also have listed everyone else connected with M-G-M except Louis B. Mayer, Norma Shearer, who was Mrs. Thalberg, and Greta Garbo, who never waited for anybody. The earnings of those who waited for Irving had caused the settee in his anteroom to be named the Million Dollar Bench. "On a clear day," Kaufman once said, "you can see Thalberg."

Despite his elusiveness and inaccessibility, however, there was no question about Thalberg's artistic intuition and innate taste. He brought quality and distinction to M-G-M's products, and he was one of the few Hollywood producers whose films Kaufman admired. And though Thalberg infuriated people with his casual disregard for appointments, he was unfailingly charming once his visitors got inside his office. At his first meeting with Kaufman, Thalberg began by asking Kaufman if he had read the original story by McGuinness. Kaufman said that he had. Thalberg then began to question him about a number of points in the story, and Kaufman interrupted and said, "Did you bring me out here to write or to play 'Twenty Questions'?" Thalberg did not take offense at Kaufman's remark. Nor did he do more than smile at Kaufman's response, which has become famous, when he asked if Kaufman could give him a treatment of the story quickly. "Do you want it Wednesday," Kaufman asked, "or do you want it good?"

The screenplay was written rapidly, despite Kaufman's unwillingness to promise this, and Sam Wood was signed as director. Kaufman now had little to do except be available for script changes, and he now began to spend time with Marc Connelly, who had bought a house in the nearby community of Bel Air in 1932. But he remained lonely and ached to return to New York. Until this time, he had been so busy that, when Leonard Lyons, the columnist, asked him what he had been reading, Kaufman pointed upward to where a skywriting plane had puffed *DRINK PEPSI-COLA* across the blue. "That's the only thing I've read since I've been here," he said.

Whenever he heard that someone from New York was on the lot, he looked happier and sought out the visitor. Once he met Rosalie Stewart, a Broadway producer turned author's agent, in the M-G-M commissary, and she mentioned that her brother, Stewart Stewart, whom Kaufman knew, was also in town from New York. She added that Stewart was a professional name for both of them, and that the family name was Muckenfus. "You mean," Kaufman said, "that Stewart Stewart is really Muckenfus Muckenfus?"

He was able to make a brief visit back to New York in March and resumed his work with Katharine Dayton, interrupting their schedule only to attend a party welcoming Ralph and Margaret Leech Pulitzer back from a hunting trip in India, and to attend the opening of a play directed by Robert B. Sinclair. The play closed after seven performances. He had told Sinclair, "The audience paid a good price—at least give them one good joke," but Sinclair didn't listen. He and Miss Dayton finished their work during the trip, but production of *First Lady* had to be delayed when he was called back to Hollywood in May to stand by during the filming of *A Night at the Opera*. He did not return to New York until September 23, and even then he left before Thalberg was really ready to see him go.

A Night at the Opera did not do well at its sneak preview. Thalberg was so disappointed with the audience's reaction that he took the film to another theatre the same night and asked the manager to show it. The second audience did not find the film funny, either. So Thalberg decided to carry out the suggestion he had made to Groucho Marx, working up a vaudeville act using some of the clips and gags from the film for presentation by the brothers on stage. Thalberg wanted the writers to go along on the tour to monitor audience reactions and make corresponding changes, but Kaufman refused. Ryskind and a studio gagman, Al Boasberg, went without him.

During his stay in Hollywood, Kaufman was also fascinated by the head of the studio, the Napoleonic Louis B. Mayer. He enjoyed listening to stories of Mayer's tearful dramatics when his stars disagreed with him, and to reports that Mayer was still complaining, six years later, because King Vidor, who had made *The Big Parade*, had shown a toilet in one scene. Mayer was still so disturbed by what he considered a terrible lapse of good taste that he checked the rushes of *A Night at the Opera* repeatedly to see that no such crudity slipped into that film. Like many men of casual personal morality, Mayer was also tremendously impressed by religious leaders and other public figures he considered truly moral, and talked all the time of his admiration for Cardinal Spellman, leading to the inevitable whispers at M-G-M that Mayer was considering converting to Catholicism. If it happened, Kaufman said, the Catholics' loss would be the Jews' gain. "When the conversion takes place," Kaufman added, referring to a romance between the studio head and a young singer which was noted for the inventiveness of its methods of fulfillment, "I can imagine Cardinal Spellman saying, 'What about this Ginny Simms thing, Mayer?'" Kaufman also worked up a little song he was fond of mentioning. He called it *I'd Rather Have TB than L.B.*

A Night at the Opera was released in November 1935 and was a tremendous hit. Groucho said years later that it was the only one of the Marx Brothers pictures he could still view with pleasure. The story concerns Otis P. Driftwood, played by Groucho, who has the task of introducing a rich widow, played by Margaret Dumont, into society. He chooses to have her back an opera company. The company's pompous tenor, Walter Woolf King, hopes to marry the leading lady, Kitty Carlisle, but she loves an undiscovered singer, played by Allan Jones. Harpo is dresser to the tenor and Chico is self-appointed agent for Jones. Eventually, Miss Dumont fires Groucho and Miss Carlisle is also fired for refusing King's advances. The Brothers set out to avenge the injured parties by disrupting the opening of the opera, mixing up the music so that the overture is replaced by *Take Me Out to the Ball Game*, played while Harpo and Chico do a lunatic baseball routine and Groucho goes through the audience selling peanuts. In the ensuing shambles, the police arrive, and Groucho comments, "Either there are cops in *Il Trovatore* or the jig is up." But then the scheduled stars leave, and Jones and Miss Carlisle take over and shine.

Kaufman's touch can be observed in such lines as Groucho's speech to a waiter. "Do you have any stewed prunes?" he asks. The waiter nods. "Well, give them hot coffee," Groucho says. "That'll sober them up." Later Groucho asks the waiter if he has change for $10. "Yes, sir," the waiter says quickly. "In that case," Groucho says, "you won't need the dime I was going to give you."

The film was Kaufman's first association with Kitty Carlisle, who became Mrs. Moss Hart ten years later. The young actress, whose real name was Catherine Conn, was born in New Orleans on September 3, 1915, the daughter of a prominent physician and surgeon. Her education began at two swank schools in New Orleans, the Newman School and Miss McGhee's School. But when she was eight years old, her father died suddenly, and her mother decided to leave the scene of sadness and take up residence in Europe.

The actress later described her mother, Hortense Conn, as a "determined, decisive woman who was rather larger than life." Mrs. Conn continued her daughter's education at the best schools and with the best teachers in Europe, among these Chateau Mont-Choisi in Lausanne, Switzerland, and Princesse Mestchersky's select academy in Paris. When Miss Carlisle was sixteen years old, her mother took her aside and delivered a blunt appraisal of her future. "It's obvious you're not going to make a good marriage here," Mrs. Conn said. "You can either be a model at Hattie Carnegie, or you can go on the stage. You're not the prettiest girl, or the best singer, or the best actress, but if you put them all together, you'll do well in musical comedy." Miss Carlisle chose the stage, and her mother promptly enrolled her for study at the Royal Academy of Dramatic Arts in London. Two years later, the study completed, the pair left for the United States.

Theatrical work came quickly. The young actress' first job was at the Capitol Theatre in New York City, appearing in the title role in a "tabloid," or condensed, version of *Rio Rita*. She toured with the capsulized version of *Rio Rita* for a number of months after it closed at the Capitol, and then returned to New York to open in a Broadway play, *Champagne Sec*. Then she was signed for films, and appeared in rapid succession in three forgettable Paramount pictures: *Murder at the Vanities, She Loves Me Not,* and *Here Is My Heart. A Night at the Opera* followed not long after that, plus a great many stage appearances. And eventually, as she was fond of saying in later years, "Along came Moss."

Up to the moment of their meeting, Hart was a man who worked hard and constantly to maintain his blissful state of bachelorhood. He was pursued by so many friends and acquaintances with a familiar have-I-got-a-girl-for-*you* look in their eyes that he developed a convincing defense, telling people that he would never marry because he was still mourning his first and only love, a schoolteacher who had died. He delivered this explanation so emotionally that nearly everybody accepted it—including Beatrice, who finally began to plead with him one day to try to forget his schoolteacher and lead a more normal life. Hart stared at her in astonishment. "My God!" he said. "You didn't *believe* that stuff, did you?" But he continued to use the story with everyone else, and Kaufman summed things up when he saw Hart and Hart's newest girl friend enter a restaurant one evening. "Take note," he said. "Here comes Moss Hart and the future Miss Smith."

Things changed drastically when Hart met Kitty Carlisle. The actress fell in love with the playwright almost at once, a fact she confirmed years later when, blissfully married, the couple had dinner at the Colony Restaurant in New York. They began to play a little conversational game, asking each other what they'd say if they were seeing each other for the first time. "I'd say, 'That's a very attractive girl,'" Hart told his wife. "'Wonder who she is?'" The actress told Hart, very quietly, what *she* would say. "I'd say," she told him, "'There goes Moss Hart. Why doesn't he marry me?'" The playwright's defenses took a little longer to disappear, but only a little, and the couple were married on August 10, 1946.

The marriage was intensely happy for the fifteen years it lasted before it was brought to an end by Hart's death. Before the marriage, the actress's clothes were selected by her mother; then Hart took over the job. "I never bought a dress he didn't pass on," Kitty Carlisle Hart recalled after his death. "Moss dressed me and he liked fantasies. I used to wear headdresses and veils and a marvelous gold djhellaba he bought me in Tangiers. I'm more sedate now. You have to be when you don't have a husband to back you up." Her conversation is still tinged with sadness when she talks about the playwright. She selects her own clothes now, but she still finds herself "remembering what Moss would have liked"; she has worn the same perfume, Piguet's Visa, for more than twenty years because Hart liked it. The Harts had two children, a son and daughter named Chris and Cathy, now aged twenty-six and twenty-three, and she still misses her husband's sure touch in dealing with them. "Nobody who hasn't brought up children without a husband can know how difficult it is," she said a few years after Hart's death. "You're constantly dancing on the wrong foot. You find yourself being mother when you should be father." One of the few areas of disagreement during the marriage was in connection with the children, since Hart believed in discussing misconduct while Mrs. Hart sometimes preferred a more direct response. But, even there, she has come to accept Hart's attitude. "My threshold of tolerance for impertinence was a quarter of an inch," she said a while ago, "and I was not above the clobber system. He was given to reason. I've sort of gone over to his side."

After Hart's death, Kitty Carlisle Hart returned to work, appearing in a number of new plays and revivals, and she is still very active in the theatre and as a panelist on television shows. But she has never remarried, and close friends say she never will.

A by-product of Kaufman's stay in California was a piece in *The Nation* of August 6, 1938, titled *Einstein in Hollywood*. He opens the piece by quoting from a news item which states that Warner Brothers have cabled Sigmund Freud an offer for his help in preparing a new Bette Davis picture, *Dark Victory*, a film concerned to some extent with psychoanalysis. From this, he speculates about what might happen if Warner Brothers should next decide to hire Einstein for a screen treatment on the theory of relativity.

Thalberg later asked Kaufman's advice on a writer for the next Marx Brothers picture, *A Day at the Races*, after Thalberg had determined that Kaufman himself was not available. Kaufman, who was always helping his friends, again suggested George Oppenheimer, as he had done with Goldwyn. It was 1947 before Kaufman personally accepted another Hollywood job, and the offer came from Nunnally Johnson, with whom Kaufman had collaborated on *Park Avenue* the previous year. Johnson had gotten a job as producer at Universal and was assigned a property called *The Senator Was Indiscreet*, based on a magazine story by Edwin Lanham. After the successes of *Of Thee I Sing*, *First Lady*, and another play which followed those, *I'd Rather Be Right*, any political comedy naturally made producers think of Kaufman. Another former Kaufman associate, Charles MacArthur, had already been hired to write the screenplay, so Johnson asked Kaufman to direct.

The story concerns a senator with presidential aspirations, who, after being snubbed by a party chief, reveals that he has been keeping a diary of all indiscretions committed by party members for the last twenty years. The party's attitude toward him undergoes an immediate and drastic reversal; he becomes *persona grata* and will remain so as long as he keeps the diary to himself. And then the diary is stolen, with many complications resulting. William Powell had the starring role of Senator Ashton, and Ella Raines was his girl friend. Allen Jenkins, Arlene Whelan, and Peter Lind Hayes were also in the cast. The film was released on March 8, 1948, and was enthusiastically received. Bosley Crowther said in a typical review in the *Times*, "Unless this country lacks humor (which has been a moot question of late), it should get a great deal of amusement from *The Senator Was Indiscreet*."

The film marked a brief reunion with Marc Connelly, who was brought in for three weeks to work with Kaufman in improving some of the dialogue. A certain amount of assistance was also needed with the direction, since Kaufman knew nothing about the camera or the technical aspects of filming. He was a stage director and grouped his cast accordingly, which would have given the film a static feeling. He was also accustomed to playing a scene straight through, and now had to adjust to shooting in tiny segments with the camera shifting attention from person to person. Johnson therefore hired Gene Fowler, Jr., son of the writer, to handle technical aspects, leaving Kaufman free to handle the actors. The arrangement worked beautifully, since Kaufman never tried to change any of Fowler's technical decisions and Fowler respected Kaufman's ability to bring out the best in his actors.

At the end of his assignment, Kaufman left Hollywood forever. It was not anything about his work on the film that kept him away, but the peculiarly virulent Hollywood version of the McCarthy hysteria, was then in full flower, or full weed. Because *The Senator Was*

Indiscreet poked fun at the Senate and at American politics, some McCarthyites, including Westbrook Pegler, the columnist, denounced the picture as subversive, centering their anger on Johnson as producer and MacArthur as writer. Another columnist, Robert C. Ruark, defended the film, saying in one of his columns that Senator Ashton was silly, "but not a great deal sillier than some we've had. And I would say that both Nunnally and Charlie are too rich and fun-loving to be included in any plot to downthrow the country." Kaufman was never attacked personally, but he was horrified and disgusted anyway by the absurdity and ugliness of the furor, and the fact that he had not been one of the victims made no difference.

After this, Kaufman confined his involvement with the movies to the sale of film rights to his plays, occasionally quoting George Bernard Shaw's famous advice to playwrights. "Go on writing plays," Shaw had said, "and don't be diverted by brummagem side offers. If you write one good play, it will help support you in your old age."

25. THE BEST PLAYS

LIKE SO MANY successes, the most sensational Kaufman-Hart hit grew out of discussions of an idea which proved unworkable. In 1936, Kaufman and Moss Hart began consideration of Hart's notion, enthusiastically presented, for a play to be based on a Dalton Trumbo novel, *Washington Jitters*. The novel concerns a sign painter who delivers a sign marked "co-ordinator" to a Washington office. A columnist strolls in, mistakes the painter for the new co-ordinator, and questions him about the state of the nation. When the interview is published, the painter is universally taken to be the real head of the department. And since government leaders are too embarrassed to fire him and admit their error, they decide to kick him all the way upstairs by getting him elected President.

Hart was convinced that there was another *Of Thee I Sing* in the

[533]

book, and Kaufman was intrigued enough to agree to travel to Hollywood to talk about it, since Hart was tied to a contract there. Hart had rented Frances Marion's Hollywood home while she was in Europe. Miss Marion, a major screenwriter and widow of Fred Thompson, once a popular cowboy star, was then at the peak of her career, and her palatial mansion reflected her position. Kaufman took one long look around the place and told Hart, "We're suckers, Moss, to let Sam Harris have this play. We can produce it right here and get a $5.50 top."

But the idea of the play didn't pan out. After batting it around with Hart for two days, Kaufman decided that it presented the same problems as *Bring on the Girls;* it was excessively fantastic and wouldn't dramatize convincingly. (Kaufman's judgment was confirmed when two years later, in 1938, *Washington Jitters* was produced by the Actors Repertory Company in association with the Theatre Guild. The two-act play by John Boruff and Walter Hart lasted twenty-four performances.)

Hart had been very much taken with the *Washington Jitters* idea, and seemed crushed when Kaufman told him it would never play. To cheer him up, Kaufman started talking about other ideas. Finally, he said, "What about that idea of yours about a mad family?" Hart gave him a blank look. For a moment, he couldn't recall ever having had such an idea. Then he remembered that he and Kaufman had discussed it two years before, although only in the most tentative way. Hart had suggested that there might be something in a play about a family in which everyone does precisely what he wants to do, without interference from the rest. Suddenly Kaufman started throwing out ideas about what a wild and funny household it would be if every member indulged in a different and highly individual pastime. Hart joined him in suggesting ideas, and in three days the framework was complete for what would eventually be titled *You Can't Take It with You.* The two men had done just what Kaufman once said should be done in developing a play. "Get a terrific idea," he said. "Work it all out in your mind and put paper in the typewriter, and sketch it out. Then throw the sketch out the window and begin with a new idea, one which will work."

Kaufman was anxious to return to New York, and set a tough

MAX GORDON IN HIS PRE-PRODUCING DAYS

The inscription reads, "Don't hang this. Just look at me before the trouble started."

NETTIE KAUFMAN AT SEVENTY-THREE

"My son collaborates with a lot of people."

JOSEPH KAUFMAN AT SEVENTY-FIVE

A forty-hour week.

**MARIE DRESSLER AND LIONEL BARRYMORE IN THE FILM
VERSION OF *DINNER AT EIGHT***

"I wonder who wrote it?"

MARY ASTOR

She made the mistake of keeping a diary.

KITTY CARLISLE AND HARPO MARX IN
A NIGHT AT THE OPERA

$100,000 arranged it.

JOHN STEINBECK

"You've got to tie this one up."

THE KAUFMANS IN BUCKS COUNTY

A chauffeur was necessary.

schedule: a finished act per week. The schedule was not met, but the job was still done in record time—five weeks to complete the draft and two weeks to polish the lines. That left only the title to be selected, but it turned out to be a chore which took even longer than the writing of the play. Kaufman's and Hart's original choice was *Grandpa's Other Snake*, but Beatrice talked them out of it on the grounds that snakes had an unpleasant connotation. Then the authors came up with *Money in the Bank*, *Foxy Grandpa*, and *The King Is Naked*, all of which were eventually discarded. It was only after months of discussion that *You Can't Take It with You*, obvious and natural as it seems today, was selected.

The play presents the Sycamore family, who live in the home of Grandfather Martin Vanderhof. The authors describe the single set, the Sycamore living room, and thereby the theme of the play, as "the every-man-for-himself room. For here," they continue, "meals are eaten, plays are written, snakes collected, ballet steps practiced, xylophones played, printing presses operated—if there were room enough there would probably be ice skating. In short, the brood presided over by Martin Vanderhof goes on about the business of living in the fullest sense of the word. This is the house where you do as you like, and no questions asked." The play, in short, to everyone who knew the Kaufman family, was Kaufman's private tribute to his father and to Joseph Kaufman's philosophy.

Vanderhof refuses to pay income tax. His son-in-law invents fireworks. His daughter, Penny, writes plays simply because someone once delivered a typewriter to the house by mistake. The granddaughter, Essie, practices ballet to the xylophone music of her husband and under the tutelage of a mad Russian. Another granddaughter, the only non-eccentric member of the family, is in love with the son of her Wall Street boss. Eventually, Henry Travers was cast as Grandpa, Josephine Hull as Penny, Paula Trueman as Essie, and George Tobias as the Russian ballet instructor. Jess Barker, later a film star and husband of Susan Hayward, played Tony Kirby, the boss's son.

The authors' greatest difficulty was with the role of the unmarried granddaughter. Kaufman was ill at ease, as usual, with writing love scenes, and Hart, always quick to take on the coloration of his idol, proved to be equally uncomfortable at the job this time, too. The part was a weak one, and neither author felt that the actress finally chosen for the role helped matters much, either. Kaufman, in fact, always believed that the actress' performance was the weakest in the play. In *Of Mice and Men*, there is a scene in which George and Lenny shoot a dog. Asked how the dog was doing, Kaufman replied, "He's already better than that girl was in *You Can't Take It with You*."

During rehearsals for the play, Kaufman was disappointed with the sound effects for a scene in which the son-in-law's fireworks factory suddenly explodes. The sounds were created by rattling beans in an old bladder and amplifying the noise through a microphone. Otto Diehl, the electrician, suggested that they get another bladder. "Good," Kaufman said, choosing a popular target in the theatre, "how about Lee Shubert's?"

A couple of incidents occurred offstage, during the play's run, that seemed in keeping with the spirit of the show. In the play's final scene, the company is seated at dinner, and Grandpa Vanderhof gives grace, which ends, "We want to say thanks for all You have done for us . . . We've all got our health and as far as everything else is concerned, we'll leave it to You." The Booth Theatre, where the play was running, is back-to-back with the Shubert Theatre, which was presenting Sherwood's *Idiot's Delight* with Alfred Lunt and Lynn Fontanne. The final scene in the Sherwood play, a war story, calls for air raid sirens, gunfire, and the sounds of cannon. Kaufman had timed his play to finish just ahead of the other, but one night the play ran long. The crazy tumult from next door burst in on the middle of Grandpa's prayer, giving the startled audience the feeling that perhaps heaven was not as happy with the family as the spectators.

On another occasion, Kaufman dropped in to check on performances, and found workmen laying new carpet in the balcony and making vast amounts of noise. The job, it seemed, could not be delayed and done after hours. Kaufman walked up to the workmen. "Matinees Wednesdays and Fridays," he said bitterly.

The play was chosen for *The Best Plays of 1936–37*, and the reviews were exceptionally enthusiastic, even for a Kaufman hit. Atkinson said in the *Times* that "Kaufman and Hart have written their most ingratiating comedy," and Richard Watts, Jr., wrote in the *Herald Tribune* that the play was "a merry and engaging vaudeville that assuredly belongs among first-rank hits." John Anderson, writing in the *Journal*, said, "Sam H. Harris opened not so much a play as a madhouse last night, and set his audience down at 11 o'clock still laughing at the delirious doings." And to supplement the massive amounts of publicity the show received from the day it opened, Harris sent out 5000 brochures containing the reviews to all newspapers with a circulation of over 10,000, to theatre managers, mayors, chambers of commerce and others, suggesting that everyone see the play when visiting New York.

The play which had taken so little time from conception to completion, and which had emerged from discussion of a bad idea, created a tidal wave of success and enduring enjoyment for audiences throughout the nation. It tried out at the Chestnut Street Opera House in Philadelphia for two weeks beginning November 30, 1936, opened at the Booth Theatre on Monday, December 14, and had a sensational run of 837 performances. And on May 4, 1937, it was announced that the play had won Kaufman his second Pulitzer Prize.

By that time, tickets were selling five months in advance, with every seat in the house sold plus about thirty standees for each performance. *You Can't Take It with You* finally became so popular that when the film version was released on September 6, 1938, and opened with great fanfare at Radio City Music Hall, and the play had already run for 750 performances, the house continued to sell out and the play ran for eleven more weeks. And even after that, the play continued to compete successfully against the film, with performances by three separate road companies.

The revival record of *You Can't Take It with You* is as phenomenal as the play's original success. The Association of Producing Artists Repertory Company revived the play at the Lyceum Theatre on November 23, 1965, and it ran for 217 performances, enough of a run to make it a major Broadway success all over again. The same company had already presented the play in Ann Arbor, Michigan, for 300 performances, and their success on Broadway sparked others. The Cleveland Playhouse, which had staged the play in 1940, revived it in 1966. The Alley Theatre in Houston, Texas, staged it on February 16, 1966, for twenty-two performances; the Kalita Humphreys Theatre in Dallas presented it on February 17 for twenty performances; the Studio Arena Theatre in Buffalo followed on April 14 for twenty-six performances; and the Baxter Theatre in Abingdon, Virginia, began a run of ten performances on April 28. The play had also been revived briefly at the City Center, New York, on March 26, 1945, for seventeen performances. By 1966, when a tally was made, amateur rights had earned $427,000, and stock rights earned an additional $40,000.

Like Kaufman's Pulitzer for *Of Thee I Sing*, the decision for *You Can't Take It with You* was not a unanimous one, and it was not a popular decision with the critics, despite the popularity of the play. Many critics wanted the prize to go to Maxwell Anderson's drama, *High Tor*, winner of the Critics' Circle Award. Just prior to the announcement of the prize-winners, John Anderson wrote on the subject in the *Journal*. "If the Pulitzer judges are wise," he wrote, "they will give the prize to *Johnny Johnson;* if they are bold they will give it to *High Tor;* and if they are cowards they will give it to *You Can't Take It with You.*" The critics agreed that the show was the most entertaining play in years, but most of them felt that "seriousness" was essential when it came to the Pulitzer Prize. "Comedy had become like castor oil," Kaufman said, when this was mentioned to him. "People fight it."

It had been a year of general disagreement among the critics, anyway. Even the Critics' Circle Award, frequently determined very quickly, required eleven ballots for settlement that year. Eighteen critics voted in 1937, with fourteen identical votes required to register a decision. On the first ballot, *High Tor* secured nine votes, *Johnny Johnson*, a play by Paul Green, received five votes, *You Can't Take It with You* received two votes, and two votes also went to another play, *Daughters of Atreus* by Robert Turney. By the third ballot, *High Tor* was still at nine, *Johnny Johnson* had gone up to six, *Daughters of Atreus* had gone down to one, and two new contenders, Arthur Kober's *Having Wonderful Time* and Mark Reed's *Yes, My Darling Daughter* had gone on the list with one vote apiece. *You Can't Take It with You* was off entirely. It returned on some of the later ballots, but the concluding vote listed *High Tor* with fourteen, *Johnny Johnson* with three, and *Daughters of Atreus* with one.

The Pulitzer committee felt differently and gave its award to *You Can't Take It with You.* The storm of protest was immediate. John Mason Brown said in the *Post*, "Mr. Hart's and Mr. Kaufman's play is a comedy which is unusually entertaining and immensely lovable. Yet vastly as I enjoyed it, I still think the judges showed a disregard of standard. I may be wrong, but my own belief is that a prize play should stand for more than a box-office success. To my way of thinking *You Can't Take It with You* is a box-office play, pure and simple minded, and admirable as such. But to crown it as the season's most distinguished drama is quite another matter." The *News*'s editorial page liked the choice, saying, "*You Can't Take It with You* is a perfectly swell hit show, humorous, human, beautifully acted. We feel the reason why the professional critics snoot this play is that from long theatre-going they have become somewhat sombre minded; contract the feeling that if a play is not built on a heavy theme, it does not deserve a dignified prize award. We can't concur." But Burns Mantle, the *News*'s own critic, and usually an admirer of Kaufman and Hart, disagreed. "If the Kaufman-Hart comedy in any way suggests such a prize play as Joseph Pulitzer himself would endorse," he said, "then my editor is right and I'm a Chinaman." *The Saturday Review of Literature* went along with the choice, but very grudgingly. "*You Can't Take It with You*," the magazine said in an editorial, "is the most diverting piece of the year in the New York theatre, and this is a year when, by common consent, the New York theatre has been below par, whatever modest valuation may be assigned to par. Mr. Maxwell Anderson cannot be designated every year and his *High Tor* had, besides, already received the Critics' Award for 1937. In the absence of any really distinguished play, it is probably best to give the prize, as the committee did, to expert entertainment."

It took the *Times*'s editorial page to bring its usual cool logic to the situation. "The acknowledged connoisseurs, the dramatic critics," the *Times* said, "picked out their favorite in advance of the Morningside judgment. These cognoscenti selected Mr. Maxwell Anderson's *High Tor*. The official bench chose the madcap rollicking comedy of Mr. Kaufman and Mr. Hart. So you have a popular opinion and an élite opinion. If the court had adopted the latter, it would have been accused of being hopelessly highbrow. It is pleasant to see the prize-givers follow the public, as has been the habit or hope of most dramatists. It is also pleasant to see the dramatic critics seeking to lead the public to nobler things. Most of us, confessing ourselves permanent members of the primary and incapable of reaching the high school of the theatre, are grateful to Mr. Kaufman, who with divers collaborators has often charmed away our doleful dumps."

And there was one other fact which could not be ignored. Interestingly, the Pulitzer committee did not regard *You Can't Take It with You* as merely the best choice in a year of mediocrity. It regarded the play as not heavy but a heavyweight in a year of heavyweights, and the other selections were heavyweights indeed. Among the other Pulitzer Prize winners were Margaret Mitchell for *Gone With the Wind*, Van Wyck Brooks for his history, *The Flowering of New England*, Allan Nevins for his biography, *Hamilton Fish: The Inner History of the Grant Administration*, and Robert Frost for his book of poetry, *A Further Range*.

Despite the great success on Broadway, *You Can't Take It with You* did not fare well in London; the British simply could not relate to the screwball American characters and their typically American desire for total personal freedom. "The blighter," one British critic said in horror and astonishment, "won't even pay his rates!" The play was a total failure, opening at the St. James Theatre on December 22, 1937, and closing on December 29. As it turned out, it was a week of double disaster in Kaufman's life. The day before that, on December 28, a sad event of more consequence occurred in his life, when Julius S. Bakrow, Beatrice's father, died.

The price which Sam Harris had set for the movie rights to *You Can't Take It with You*, $200,000, was higher than any amount ever paid for a story property up to that time. Louis B. Mayer was in New York and told Harris that if he liked the play, M-G-M would meet his price. In Hollywood, D. A. Doran, who scouted properties for Harry Cohn of Columbia Pictures, heard of Mayer's

interest, traced Cohn and his top director, Frank Capra, to Santa
Anita Racetrack, and told Cohn about it. Cohn, a very competitive
man, relished the idea of beating Mayer to something Mayer wanted.
He sent Doran to place a bet for him, which lost, and then told
Doran to get a copy of the script to Capra. If Capra saw any
possibilities in the play, he said, he'd pay the price Harris was
asking. Doran had a copy of the script waiting for Capra when the
director returned home that evening. When Cohn phoned later that
evening, he found that Capra was in his bedroom, laughing helplessly as he read the script. After a long series of calls in which
Cohn awakened almost everyone he knew in New York in an
effort to get Sam Harris's unlisted home number, he got Harris
out of bed at 2 A.M. and closed the deal.

Robert Riskin wrote the screenplay, and Capra selected a fine
cast with Lionel Barrymore in the role of Grandpa, Spring Byington as Penny, Ann Miller as the ballet-dancing granddaughter, Mischa
Auer as her Russian coach, Jean Arthur as the granddaughter who
wants to marry the Wall Street scion, played by James Stewart, and
Edward Arnold as the banker. Others in the cast were H. B. Warner,
the actor who had once said that Kaufman had no future as a playwright, Samuel S. Hinds, Eddie Anderson, the black actor who played
"Rochester" on *The Jack Benny Show*, Harry Davenport, and
Donald Meek in the role of Mr. Poppins, a character who had not
appeared in the stage play. Later, when Kaufman and Capra met,
Kaufman asked, "Who's this guy Poppins?" Capra just waved his
hands vaguely and said, "Oh, you know." In this way he dismissed
his invention of a new character. Capra liked Meek, and simply
wanted to make a place for him in the film.

The picture won Academy Awards for Best Picture and Best
Direction. The honors came as a total surprise to Capra, who had
expected to be barred from serious contention as a result of the
events of the previous year. He had been elected negotiator for the
Screen Directors Guild, which was trying to work out a union
contract with the Motion Picture Producers' Association, but all
he got at first was a runaround. Joe Schenck, the producers' president, replied to Capra's accusation that they were stalling by saying,
"Not stalling, Frank, we're procrastinating." Capra, who was also pres-

ident of the Academy of Motion Picture Arts and Sciences and slated to be master of ceremonies at the forthcoming Academy Awards banquet, immediately threatened to resign from the Academy and called, successfully, for a strike vote by the 250 directors in the Guild, who also agreed to boycott the banquet. The producers gave in and signed the Guild contract, but after his tooth-and-nail fight with the Hollywood money men, Capra expected to be ignored when the prizes were awarded. He was stunned when Fred Niblo, director of the silent *Ben-Hur*, opened the envelope for Best Director and read his name. He was even more shocked when James Roosevelt, FDR's son, who had agreed to open the most important envelope of the evening, announced that *You Can't Take It with You* had also won the award for Best Picture.

Capra later credited the movie's success to a special recording. He had found that the people who were hired to monitor preview audiences' reactions were too often influenced by their own opinions about the film and didn't give an objective report of the audience response. Capra had the audience reaction recorded, and then had his record played along with the film while he matched the laughs and the silences with the action. "And so," he recalled years later, "like tailors tearing apart and rebuilding a coat to their chalk marks, we re-edited our film to the record." He had shot 329,460 feet of film, and eventually cut it to 11,530 feet.

In 1937, having moved on February 17 into a town house at 14 East 94th Street, Kaufman began to discuss new projects with Moss Hart. (He told a mutual friend that he was always ready to start a new project with Hart. "It's a case," he said, "of gelt by association.") One of these, a revue about the writing of a revue, to be titled *Curtain Going Up*, fell through when Groucho Marx told Kaufman that he could not serve as emcee, and when George and Ira Gershwin had to rule themselves out because of their work on *The Goldwyn Follies*. Groucho's note, dated "Thursday evening, wrinkled and gray," read, "I don't say I would object to appearing, perhaps in a sketch, if there was a reason for it, but to appear in a revue for a whole evening in the old traditional outfit would put me back precisely where I was fifteen years ago. Secondly, the length of time you would expect me to remain in the show: I would not want to stay in New York indefinitely. If the show was a hit, for example, I would not want to be locked up in it for a couple of years—and I definitely would not want to m.c. the show . . . I hope you are not too aggravated by these many conditions that spring from a combination of fear, inertia, impudence, greed and a dame I just met in Culver City."

This was the period just before George Gershwin's brain tumor overpowered and killed him, and the fact that Gershwin did not seem his old self left Kaufman feeling depressed. When Hart suggested that they try to develop a play dealing with psychoanalysis, he was unable to work up any enthusiasm for the subject; he was simply incapable of dealing casually and objectively with anything related to health. He finally convinced Hart to throw away what they had written, and the team then conceived an entirely new idea, a musical which they first called *Hold Your Hats, Boys,* and then *I'd Rather Be Right.* It was to be a hard-hitting spoof of the New Deal with President Franklin D. Roosevelt portrayed as a character on stage.

Hart wondered whether they could get away with portraying a living President, but Kaufman thought that they could if they were able to get George M. Cohan to play the role. Cohan, the greatest flag-waver of his day, would never be accused of anything other than harmless fun. Cohan's professional standing on Broadway had been tarnished when he had refused, after World War I, to support Equity, the actors' union—he had been in a difficult position, as both actor and producer—but to the public he was still Mr. Fourth-of-July.

The plot of the musical revolves around a boy and girl who can't get married until the national budget is balanced, since his boss will give him a raise only when that happens. The boy falls asleep in the park and dreams that FDR comes along and promises to put the government on a sound financial basis so that the wedding can be held. This was the basic idea, but it was just a thread around which Kaufman and Hart wove sketches satirizing all aspects of government. They finished the play on the West Coast in June, and on June 21, Kaufman returned to New York, traveling by train, and gave the script to Sam Harris. Harris, Cohan's longtime friend and former partner, loved the script and didn't think he would have a problem persuading the dean of song and dance to come out of semi-retirement. Harris was proved right when he sent the script to Cohan in Europe, where the actor was vacationing. Cohan liked the script and wanted the part. Trouble began almost at once, however, when Cohan returned to New York. Rodgers and Hart had been hired to write the score for the play, and Cohan hated it the moment he heard it. He began to refer to the team, sneeringly, as "Gilbert and Sullivan," and threatened to quit. Harris, Kaufman, and Moss Hart went to Cohan's apartment to change his mind, feeling that the fate of the play would hang on this talk. Cohan finally agreed to remain with the play, but he did so reluctantly, and he never wavered in his dislike of the score and its composers.

The team of composer Richard Rodgers and lyricist Lorenz Hart had been active since the two met in 1919. Rodgers, seven years younger than Hart, was just about to enter college, and Hart (unrelated to Moss Hart) had a job putting on shows at a boys' camp and also worked as a translator of German operettas. Hart, born in New York in 1895, had been raised in a well-to-do atmosphere and educated in private schools before entering Columbia's School of Journalism in 1913. His interests centered around the school's annual Varsity Show, for which he wrote and performed material, but he left the school before he could earn his degree. Rodgers was also born in New York, in 1902, and grew up in a family with strong musical interests. His talent for music was manifested and developed early—he could play the piano at the age of six—and he had already been writing songs, although not professionally, for two years before he and Hart met.

Their introduction to each other was a kind of collaboration at first sight. When Rodgers entered Columbia that year, Hart collaborated with him in writing the score for the Varsity Show, even though Hart was no longer a student. The team also wrote and placed a song in a Broadway show the same year, and they were asked to write a few more for another show. But despite their early start and their strong efforts to establish themselves on Broadway, they became stalled, remaining virtually unemployed for the next five years. They were close to quitting, with Rodgers considering taking a job selling children's underwear, when, in 1926, they were hired to write the score for *The Garrick Gaieties*. It became a hit, and they followed with eight more shows in the next five years, including *A Connecticut Yankee*, produced in 1927, and *America's Sweetheart*, produced in 1931. The team then spent a few years in Hollywood. Their work there included such songs as *Isn't It Romantic* and *You Are Too Beautiful*, but working for films didn't suit them ideally, and they returned to Broadway to start a new string of hits, beginning with *Jumbo* in 1935, *On Your Toes* in 1936, *Babes in Arms* in 1937, and then *I'd Rather Be Right*.

Although Cohan had agreed to live with the Rodgers and Hart score, he started a small battle at the opening in Boston on October 11, when he deliberately omitted some lines in a song spoofing Al Smith, and added some lines of his own. Hart, who was highstrung even when he was not being provoked, was so furious that he threatened to withdraw his lyrics from the show. Kaufman ordered Cohan never to tamper with the lines again. Cohan obeyed, confiding afterward to a friend that he would never have taken such an order from anyone other than Kaufman. "There was just a little argument," Cohan told the press. "It was just something about Al Smith and the Liberty League. Al's been an awful good friend of mine. It's all straightened out now, as far as I'm concerned. I've reached the point in life where I refuse to fight any more."

Cohan was tough and temperamental, but he was also capable of special kindness. Spencer Tracy once told about the time that he, as a young actor, appeared in a Cohan play. When the play opened in Milwaukee, Tracy's home town, Cohan changed the billing, putting Tracy's name above his own to impress Tracy's family and friends. "That," Tracy said, "was the real Cohan."

After a Boston tryout, *I'd Rather Be Right* opened on Broadway at the Alvin Theatre on Friday, April 2, 1937, backed by an advance sale of $247,000. Rodgers conducted the overture personally, pausing first for a little ritual of kissing his wife, Dorothy, for good luck. The play, in any event, owed more to Mrs. Rodgers than just her lucky presence; it was she who suggested the musical's final title, taking it from Henry Clay's famous line, "I'd rather be right than President." There were several minor disasters at the opening; Cohan had to play in a rubber ankle brace because he had tripped over a cable a few days before, and Beatrice had her fur coat stolen during intermission. But the play received a thunderously enthusiastic response from the audience, and Cohan scored a great personal success.

Among the critics, John Mason Brown said it was too unpleasant a question to ask what the play would be like without Cohan. George Jean Nathan said that *I'd Rather Be Right* had had the biggest opening since the Grand Canyon, and added that he couldn't understand why calling George M. Cohan Franklin D. Roosevelt should engender such controversy, unless it was because FDR had been called everything but George M. Cohan. Lucius Beebe wrote in *Stage*, "New York seemed completely overwhelmed by the return of Mr. Cohan, and popular rejoicing and dancing in Longacre Square complemented the most insufferable crush, confusion, and amiable uproar Fifty-second Street has ever known." After the performance, Kaufman and Rodgers hosted a party for the cast, which Beebe described as the season's most illustrious gathering of professional celebrities. In addition to Cohan, participants included Gertrude Lawrence, Constance Collier, Paul Muni, Samuel Goldwyn, Fredric March and his wife Florence Eldridge, Libby Holman, Mitzi Green, Heywood Broun, Clifton Webb, and many others. The show went on to become a hit, running for 266 performances.

Because of *I'd Rather Be Right*'s excellent reception, Cohan mellowed to the point of giving several expansive interviews to the press. He denied that the play would have political influence, as one editorial had complained. "It won't change my vote," he said, "so why should it change anyone else's?" He also pretended to agree with an apocryphal story which said that he had taken the part blindly, without knowing that he would play Roosevelt. The truth, as everyone in the theatre knew, was that he always weighed a script carefully before taking any part, and he never left anything in his professional life to impulse or chance.

Rodgers and Hart continued to achieve success after success after *I'd Rather Be Right*, including *I Married an Angel* and *The Boys from Syracuse* in the following year, *Too Many Girls* in 1939, *Pal*

Joey in 1940, and *By Jupiter* in 1942. But on November 19, 1943, the volatile Hart, who was increasingly prone to severe depression, disappeared from the opening of a revival of *A Connecticut Yankee* and was finally found, after a long search, in a hotel room, suffering from acute pneumonia. He died three days later, with Rodgers at his bedside, on November 22, 1943. He was forty-eight years old.

Richard Rodgers went on, of course, to become a giant in his field, teaming with Oscar Hammerstein II on a string of impressive and enduring hits: *Oklahoma!* in 1943, *Carousel* in 1945, *South Pacific* in 1949, *The King and I* in 1951, and *The Sound of Music* in 1960. Like Kaufman, Rodgers has won two Pulitzer Prizes, for *Oklahoma!* and *South Pacific*. After the death of his second great collaborator, Rodgers has continued to excel, writing his own lyrics for *No Strings*, and working with new collaborators.

The next Kaufman-Hart collaboration was already taking shape before *I'd Rather Be Right* had had its tryout in Boston. Moss Hart, always a worrier, couldn't sleep one night after attending a bad rehearsal of the political play and, for the lack of anything better to do, started browsing through some old bound copies of *Theatre* magazine. The magazine, which was started in 1900 and published for about twenty years, was beautifully printed on coated stock and lavishly illustrated. Hart had recently bought an entire set of issues from a friend who needed money, and he became more and more excited as he looked through the old volumes, seeing the pageantry and excitement of the theatre in the century's early decades spread out before him. He told Kaufman about it the next day and suggested that they do a play which would offer a panorama of recent stage history.

Kaufman was equally fascinated, and work began in the spring of 1938, when Kaufman went to California by train to discuss the projected play with Hart. Hart then talked Kaufman into returning with him to New York by boat, a slow trip via the Panama Canal, and the two began writing on board the ship. They discarded their first draft when they reached the canal, and evolved a new plan as the ship steamed through the Caribbean. As their play, which they called *The Fabulous Invalid*, finally worked out, the first act presents the opening night of a new playhouse called the Alexandria Theatre, and is made up of a montage of scenes from hit plays, ranging from Charles Klein's turn-of-the-century *The Lion and the Mouse* to *What Price Glory?*, showing the passing of the years. Kaufman and Hart read 165 old plays to make their selections, and finally used excerpts from twenty-six of these. The second act shows the effect upon the theatre of the coming of motion pictures and the passage of time, and the Alexandria becomes moldy and decrepit, finally being converted into a burlesque house. But at the end, in the third act, it is taken over by a young acting group, symbolizing renewed hope for the theatre, and modeled after Orson Welles and his Mercury Theatre Group, and the enthusiasm and fresh ideas of the group portend a theatrical renaissance in the old Alexandria. Continuity is achieved by having the ghosts of an actor and actress present throughout the play. Doris Dalton and Stephen Courtleigh played the two spirits, who don't have to be locked up in heaven as long as theatre exists.

The Fabulous Invalid opened Saturday, October 8, 1938, at the Broadhurst Theatre, but managed to rack up only 65 performances. Critics liked the basic idea, but complained that the short scenes from old plays just weren't substantial enough to hold interest from excerpt to excerpt. The play was revived by the Century Theatre Group in Los Angeles in January 1950, but the result was no more successful.

It was during this period that Hart encountered a typical example of Kaufman's horror of showing sentiment, an attitude which was subject to unfortunate misinterpretation because people sometimes assumed that he just wasn't interested. Hart had dinner one night with Kaufman before going off on a long, difficult, and extremely important business trip, and was deeply hurt when Kaufman said absolutely nothing about it during the evening, not even wishing Hart well when he left. But when Hart arrived home, there was a long letter waiting for him which Kaufman had sent over by messenger, and it contained all the advice and good wishes Hart wanted and needed. Kaufman's fear of emotional involvements was similarly reflected in his standard parting line to Ruth and other members of his family: "Call me if you need money." They sometimes read into it the implied, "But don't bother me about anything else." When Ruth worked for a while as a television writer, collaborating with another writer named Edward Mabley on a series called *The O'Neills*, which ran for thirty-nine weeks, Kaufman refused to watch it. He explained it away with a gag—telling Ruth, since he was between shows, "Hell of a note. You've got a show and I haven't." But he confessed to Beatrice that he avoided watching because he wouldn't know how to tell Ruth he didn't like it if he didn't.

The next Kaufman-Hart collaboration, *The American Way*, was a patriotic American cavalcade, telling the story of a German immigrant and his family. The immigrant—a character suggested by the first Kaufman to arrive in America, George Kaufman's grandfather, a passionate patriot—rises to wealth, loses his son in World War I, and becomes bankrupt when he tries to save a friend's bank during the depression. He is finally killed at a bund meeting while trying to prevent a grandson from joining, but the family and their American ideals endure. Neither author had much confidence in the idea, and Beatrice was alone in predicting success, but all those involved—Kaufman, Hart, and co-producers Max Gordon and Sam Harris—wanted to do it to show the dangers of Nazism and to demonstrate their love for America. Fredric March and Florence Eldridge came from Hollywood to take the roles of Martin Gunther and his wife Irma—demanding roles that required them to age forty years in the course of two hours. Oscar Levant conducted the orchestra, stationed with his musicians in a studio seven stories above the stage, his music broadcast downward via amplifiers. The stage had had to be extended to make room for the large number of actors, and the regular orchestra pit was covered up.

The American Way opened on Saturday, January 21, 1939, at the Center Theatre, and ran for 244 performances, which would ordinarily have meant it was a substantial success. The problem was that the play had a huge cast of 250. The play also required a total of 2200 costume changes, and a strike by 150 extras to have their weekly pay raised from $15 to $18 also increased costs. In addition, the Center was a white elephant, a gigantic theatre of 4000 seats built as part of Rockefeller Center. The management hoped to fill the theatre with crowds attending the World's Fair, but even though large audiences attended, almost filling the place, costs outran profits.

Many reviewers found the show more spectacular than engrossing. "*The American Way* has nostalgic, exciting, touching moments," the *Times* said, in a typical comment. "But in its sheer emotionalism, it parallels a cinema spectacle, vintage 1924." And Dorothy Parker said coldly, "It's a wonderful picture of Graustark." Current stage historians tend to feel that the show was much more than that. The Marches won many awards for their work in the show, among them the Drama Study Club's plaque for "the foremost achievement of the season in the theatre," and the Badge of Tolerance from the Unity of American Protestants, Catholics, and Jews.

Descriptions of the 250 actors and actresses milling around backstage just prior to curtain time make it seem like a minor miracle that the show could be held together for its substantial run. The cast included thirty-eight children, and at curtain time backstage a seven-year-old-boy could be seen bouncing a ball off the ceiling, a girl playing jacks, three older boys blowing imaginary trumpets in a simulated jam session, other boys wrestling in real and impromptu matches, and stage mothers bustling about, trying to get their children into costumes.

Kaufman's shyness asserted itself during rehearsals, since he felt too many eyes on him during the mass scenes. He withdrew from these scenes and asked Franklin Heller, the assistant stage director who had been with him on *You Can't Take It with You* and would work with him later on *My Sister Eileen* and *The Naked Genius,* to handle the job of staging the mobs. The great number of actors was needed since the play was designed to be a sweeping panorama of American history from the arrival of immigrants in McKinley's time to the time of the play. When the play closed for a month in the summer because of the slow theatre season, Kaufman was upset because many of the actors in it had long been unemployed and were working happily just for eating money, and now they wouldn't even have that. The play closed permanently on September 23, 1939. It was bought for the movies by Columbia, but Hollywood's enthusiasm for patriotic themes was dampened when

Max Gordon was hired to produce Robert E. Sherwood's *Abe Lincoln in Illinois*, starring Raymond Massey, and the film made no money, so *The American Way* was never produced.

If *The American Way* was a disappointment, it was more than compensated for by the next Kaufman-Hart play, *The Man Who Came to Dinner*. The authors had occasionally used thinly disguised portraits of other real people in their earlier plays, but there was no disguise whatever this time: Sheridan Whiteside, the leading character, *was* Alexander Woollcott. The play, in fact, originated when Hart was telling Kaufman about the trials he had recently had with Woollcott as his house guest. Woollcott had written in Hart's guest book, upon departing, "This is to certify that I had one of the most unpleasant times I ever spent." After telling this to Kaufman, Hart said, "Wouldn't it have been awful if he had broken a leg and been on my hands for the rest of the summer!"—and the two men suddenly stared at each other in discovery. They began to put together a play about a nationally known broadcaster who slips on the ice during a Midwestern tour and is confined as a troublesome and unwelcome guest in a reluctant household. He sticks his nose into everyone's business, even attempting to thwart his secretary's romance so she can remain in his employ.

In theory, Kaufman and Hart were writing the play as a role for Woollcott to perform, since Hart had once promised Woollcott that they would do a play for him. But the authors became progressively uneasy as they worked, and stopped to show the first act and half of the second to him. Woollcott said he thought that Sheridan Whiteside was a caricature rather than an accurate characterization, but Kaufman and Hart were so enthusiastic about the project that he gave his permission for them to proceed. He said, however, that he really couldn't see himself playing the role, and suggested Robert Morley, the British star of the hit *Oscar Wilde*. When the play was finished, Woollcott showed the script to Edward Sheldon, an old friend, who was aghast. "Do you really think you're like that?" he asked indignantly. Woollcott didn't answer, but he was touched by Sheldon's regard, saying later that he never knew he had a friend who cared that much for him.

Morley was not available, and Kaufman and Hart began to look elsewhere for an actor to play Whiteside. They finally decided on Monty Woolley, a bearded ex-Yale professor who was playing small roles in Hollywood. In manner and in temperament, if not in appearance, he was a lot like Woollcott. They phoned him. Woolley refused to believe that the offer was on the level and snarled into the phone, "What's the idea of waking me up in the middle of the night with your lousy jokes?" Then he hung up. Kaufman and Hart called in an agent to see Woolley and arrange the deal, and later found considerable pleasure in reminding Woolley that his tantrum had cost him 10 per cent of his salary for the play's run.

The New York run of *The Man Who Came to Dinner* was phenomenal, lasting 739 performances after opening at the Music Box Theatre on Monday, October 16, 1939. The play was also selected for *The Best Plays of 1939-40*.

When the play had become a tremendous hit, Woollcott decided that he wanted to play the role, after all. He asked for the Chicago company, but that went to Clifton Webb. He finally got the role in the Pacific Coast company, and in his curtain speech on opening night told the audience, "It's not true that the obnoxious Sheridan Whiteside was patterned after me. Whiteside is merely a composite of the better qualities of the play's two authors." He was more objective, however, about his abilities as an actor. "I don't know what you were told about my performance in this play in Santa Barbara and Los Angeles," he wrote to a friend, "but I am a far better judge in such matters than anyone who could have reported to you. You may take it from me that I was pretty lousy. It was at Fresno that I began to be comparatively good, and by San Francisco I am giving a performance I wouldn't mind your seeing." Woollcott showed openly his childlike pride and delight in being the center of attention, but his enjoyment was cut short suddenly and ominously by a heart attack which forced him to leave the cast. It was Woollcott's first serious illness of any kind in thirty years.

Kaufman went to the Coast after Woollcott's heart attack and took over the role for a few days, playing the part with such perfect timing that the curtain rang down eleven minutes early—startling stagehands who were used to Woollcott's more leisurely characterization. He also played the role at the Bucks County Playhouse with Moss Hart in the role of Beverley Carleton, a character similar to Noël Coward, and with Harpo Marx, speaking lines for the first time in twenty-five years, playing Banjo, a character based on himself. Woollcott returned to play Whiteside at the Erlanger Theatre in Chicago for the 1940–41 season, but became ill again after two weeks.

The Man Who Came to Dinner was an obvious choice for the movies, but Woollcott suddenly and unexpectedly balked, refusing to sign the routine waiver sent to him by Warner Brothers, who had bought the film rights. Woollcott gave as his reason the fear that screenwriters might change the lead character in a way that might damage or embarrass him. "I should suffer considerable damage," he wrote to Kaufman, "if Mr. Whiteside in the picture turned out to be a pansy." He then proceeded to reveal the real reason for his obstructive attitude; he had begun to feel angry at the realization that a lot of money was being made out of a play based on *him*—without even, as he saw it, an adequate display of gratitude on the part of either Kaufman or Hart. He brushed aside the fact that the film company was offering him a substantial amount of money, $12,375, for his signature on the waiver. "I thought and still think of the sum," he told Kaufman, "as a token payment acknowledging the considerable indebtedness to me in the matter of the whole venture, which neither you nor Moss had ever recognized or at least admitted."

Woollcott's example of possible injury, in his letter to Kaufman, was a curious one in the light of all the speculation about his masculinity, as mentioned earlier. Anita Loos, author of *Gentlemen Prefer Blondes*, recently recalled an unsettling incident that took place in the course of a visit with Woollcott. During a conversation in his apartment, he suddenly showed her a picture of himself wearing women's clothing in a college play, then burst out, "All my life I've wanted to be a girl. All my life I've wanted to be a mother." In the stunned silence that followed, he said, "Now that you understand me, do you think we can be friends?" Miss Loos managed to gasp, "Why not?" but she left soon afterward. It would have been difficult to convince her after that that Woollcott did not, at the very least, have homosexual tendencies.

Kaufman finally managed to make Woollcott realize that the Warners payment was a generous one. Woollcott signed the waiver, and the picture was released in late 1942 with Monty Woolley again excelling in the Whiteside role, and with Bette Davis as his secretary. Also in the cast were Jimmy Durante, Billie Burke, Reginald Gardiner, and George Barbier.

Woollcott died suddenly on January 23, 1943, stricken in the middle of a radio broadcast. It was another heart attack, and he was dead before an ambulance arrived. Despite his eccentricities, Kaufman missed him constantly after he was gone. He told Hart one day, "Life without Aleck is like a play with a crucial scene dropped. It still plays, but something good has gone out of it."

The Man Who Came to Dinner was done much later as a musical called *Sherry*. Produced by Lee Guber, Frank Ford, and Shelly Gross, with book and lyrics by James Lipton and music by Laurence Rosenthal, *Sherry* opened at the Alvin Theatre on Monday, March 27, 1967. It was a dud, and closed May 27, after seventy-two performances.

You Can't Take It with You, I'd Rather Be Right, and *The Man Who Came to Dinner* brought Kaufman and Hart another manifestation of success: they became so well known that they began to appear in a number of ads. One of these, an ad for New England Life Insurance, shows Kaufman leaning back and blowing smoke rings, despite the fact that he rarely smoked, the picture of ease and contentment. Both men were also featured in an ad for Schrafft's, which ran a picture of the team with the legend, *From Schrafft's Album of Distinguished Guests.* The ad also provided employment and revenue for another writer, S. J. Perelman. Perelman was amused at the idea of prominent guests at the modest-priced restaurant, and wrote a hilarious satire on the subject, calling his piece *A Pox on You, Mine Goodly Host.*

Despite the increasing success of the team, however, Hart's continued dependence on Kaufman began to pose a threat to the relationship. Hart had come to regard Kaufman almost as a surrogate father and, ironically in view of Kaufman's own insecurity, saw him as a pillar of strength. Hart was also becoming more and more dependent on Beatrice, still consulting her about girls and business moves. But eventually, with every new collaboration with Kaufman, and with every new bit of help and advice from Beatrice, Hart became more and more worried about his dependence on them. The worry was aggravated by the statements of friends, who told him that he soon wouldn't be capable of functioning professionally without Kaufman to help him. This was nonsense, since Hart had undertaken many projects on his own, and handled them very successfully, but he continued to worry. In time, Kaufman became aware of his fears and felt they were completely unjustified, but he always encouraged Hart, anyway, to take on projects which interested Hart but not him, and he began to help and advise only when asked.

Nevertheless, their next collaboration was destined to be their last, and they ended their long run of hits with a near miss. The team's last play together was *George Washington Slept Here*, a satire on people who leave the comforts of the city to buy ramshackle country places requiring enormous repairs in order to be made livable. The typical selling point of the realtors involved is, of course, "George Washington slept here." Kaufman and Hart were both living in Bucks County, Pennsylvania, at the time, and Brooks Atkinson commented in the *Times* that "George S. Kaufman and Moss Hart are now putting their country estates to work." Despite a poor critical reception, the play ran 173 performances after opening at the Lyceum Theatre on Friday, October 18, 1940. It closed March 15, 1941. Many theatregoers liked the play far more than the reviewers. Groucho Marx, for example, wrote a friend, "Saw *George Washington Slept Here*. Very amusing, and the critics should be ashamed for the knifing they gave it." Fontaine Fox, the cartoonist who created *The Toonerville Trolley*, also liked the play, and sent Kaufman a suggestion for a gag to be included, illustrating the idea with a cartoon sketch. Warner Brothers produced a movie version of the play, with a screenplay by Everett Freeman. Jack Benny played the lead, which had been played by Ernest Truex on Broadway, and Ann Sheridan appeared as his wife. The film's reception was just lukewarm.

Clare Boothe Luce once described the '30s as the age of psychoanalysis, when, if one didn't need an analyst, one went anyway, in keeping with the fashion. Beatrice had been one of the first people in New York to be psychoanalyzed, and she had urged Hart into psychoanalysis early in their relationship. Kaufman was not enthusiastic about this particular item of advice to Hart; he, personally, disliked psychoanalysis and scoffed at Freud, so much so that some of his friends decided that he was afraid of the subject. Mrs. Luce, for example, speculated that "he just didn't want to be told why he was the way he was," though Kaufman insisted that his attitude stemmed from the simple fact that he was convinced that psychoanalysis was just pseudo-scientific nonsense. Hart, however, felt deeply the need for psychoanalysis, and had been seeing a psychiatrist since 1934. Hart's continued and increasing success should have kept him in a constant state of euphoria. Instead, he found, he was experiencing more and more frequent sieges of deep depression, periods in which he lost all faith in himself, and in which his self-doubt was so strong that he mistrusted his own judgment and often made wrong decisions or failed to follow his own convictions.

He stressed this one day in a conversation with Garson Kanin, who was about to direct a new play. Hart asked Kanin how he really felt about the actress he was considering for the lead, and Kanin admitted that he didn't really care for her, but said that the author of the play liked her. "Don't have her," Hart told Kanin urgently. "Don't say Yes. Listen to what I'm saying to you. All the mistakes I ever made in my life were when I wanted to say No and said Yes."

Most important of all, Hart found in time that even his successes no longer brought him pleasure. "Just a few days after winning the Pulitzer," he told a friend, "I practically had to be carried feet first to my analyst's couch." He once discussed his strange plight. "The great mystery of unhappiness," he said, "is not the story of a failure. A man who is a failure complains about fate, about bad breaks, and you can understand it. But when you're completely successful and you're unhappy, it becomes a mystery. Most of the successful people I know are unhappy. Success is like anesthesia. You can increase the dosage and increase it and finally it doesn't work."

Hart eventually became convinced that he couldn't write plays without Kaufman, and in 1941 his psychiatrist, Dr. Gregory Zilborg, told him that it was essential to his psychological security that he make a permanent professional break with Kaufman. Zilborg was not alone in this opinion. Marc Connelly, too, felt that the relationship was not healthy for Hart. He said, "Moss is in such a state of genuflection toward George all the time that I don't how they ever get a play written. Moss really wants to be George's son." Kaufman didn't agree with the advice; he felt that there was ample evidence that Hart could write plays with or without him, and that the break was unnecessary. He was deeply disappointed, but he accepted the decision without argument, and he and Hart remained friends to the end of their lives.

Hart's first play after the break was *Lady in the Dark*, which was, not surprisingly, about psychoanalysis. He took it to Kaufman and Beatrice when it was finished. Buoyed by their praise, he next took it to Marshall Field, the Chicago multimillionaire and patron of the arts, who agreed to underwrite production. When *Lady in the Dark* went into rehearsal, Kaufman was rehearsing *My Sister Eileen*. Kaufman timed his rehearsals on *My Sister Eileen* so that it corresponded exactly to the hours when Hart was rehearsing *Lady in the Dark*. He knew how important it was to Hart that he stand on his own feet, and he arranged it so that no one could say he was helping his former collaborator.

Hart went on from *Lady in the Dark* to write *Christopher Blake*, *Winged Victory*, *Light Up the Sky*, and *The Climate of Eden*. He also wrote the screenplays for the Academy Award-winning *Gentleman's Agreement*, and the Judy Garland version of *A Star Is Born*, and then returned to the theatre to direct the monumental hit, *My Fair Lady*, following up by directing *Camelot*. Hart suffered a mild heart attack a few months before Kaufman's death in 1961, but when, in December 1961, Hart started to suffer from severe pain in his jaw—frequently a sign of an imminent heart attack—a cardiogram could detect no new heart trouble. The pain persisted, and Hart was on his way to a dentist, on December 20, when he was felled by his second and fatal attack. At fifty-seven, Hart had been fifteen years younger than Kaufman, but he survived his friend and collaborator by only six months.

26. THE DIARY

AN APOCRYPHAL STORY says that Kaufman had a charge account at Polly Adler's. Miss Adler did not refer to Kaufman in her book, *A House Is Not a Home*, but the story nevertheless persists that Kaufman *did* use the services of her establishment, and that he carefully arranged matters so that her place would appear to be neither a house nor a home to him. Allegedly, he insisted that the girl of the evening meet him at a designated spot well removed from Miss Adler's premises, go through the deception of being picked up, be taken out to dinner and perhaps a show, and go with him, finally, to an apartment to be seduced. Miss Adler, the story goes, sent Kaufman a monthly bill. But people who knew Kaufman well say that this is nonsense. They point out that Kaufman never needed to resort to prostitutes, and that furthermore, the elaborate and spurious routine in the story is out of keeping with Kaufman's consistently direct and honest character.

The fact of the matter is that Kaufman achieved such an enormous reputation as a success with women, and seemed to many so unlikely for the role, that the assumption, and then the legend, grew that he used paid partners. He never did, but he always had a young dancer or actress in tow, and some famous ladies as well. He had a huge appetite for work and for sex, and his prowess in both seems to have been about equal, so that often he had simply to be seen with a woman and it would be assumed that he had made another conquest.

One well-known actress cried on the set because a scene in one of her first jobs, a supporting role in a Kaufman play, had been shortened. Ordinarily, Kaufman was indifferent to actors' indignation at his cuts, such as when he had told another actress, "The author giveth and the author taketh away." But this time, since the weeping miss was young and pretty, he was sympathetic. He explained to her gently that the scene had held up the play, and that cutting it was to her advantage. "It won't hurt your role," he said, "because it will point up the rest of what you do." Shortly after that, they were something more than casual acquaintances. Another theatrical lady of even greater renown said that she was appearing in a play one night when Kaufman was in the audience. He liked what he saw, and though they had never been introduced, that made no difference. He came backstage at intermission and asked her, "Where can a Stage Door Johnny get your phone number?" She told him without hesitation. Still another star is supposed to have given a library intimate correspondence from Kaufman which is not to be opened until fifty years after Kaufman's death. Then there was the movie star—the one before the celebrated affair with Mary Astor—with whom he carried on an affair during a cruise and whom he had trouble shaking. He was normally not embarrassed by friends seeing him with new and different girls, but this time his mother had come down to see him arrive, and Nettie just didn't understand. Kaufman also had a long friendship with Natalie Shafer, the blond actress who was a mainstay of *Gilligan's Island* and a million films.

Among Kaufman's male friends, he was considered, as Max Gordon described him, a "male nymphomaniac." While this explained, at least superficially, Kaufman's continuous pursuit of women, it still left some people wondering about what attracted women to Kaufman. Other people who knew Kaufman felt that the reasons for his attractiveness to women were obvious. Irwin Shaw said, for example, that "women were attracted to him, in part, because of his wit, but also because of the quiet sense of strength and authority he gave off." A chorus member in one of his plays described him as "a very romantic person, very warm, very tender." She said that she thought she could not be noticed in the back of the chorus line, but that during an out-of-town tryout, Kaufman stopped her in the alley outside the stage door and asked, "How about a drink?" Over her drink—it's unlikely that he would have done more than taste his—he told her that he found her attractive and wanted to go home with her. "And that's the way it started," she said. She added, "It lasted two years."

In 1936, Kaufman's reputation as a ladies' man grew suddenly from a secret among friends to a scandal in headlines throughout the Western world. It started when a mystery man identified only by the letter "G" was introduced into the testimony at a child custody trial in Hollywood. Mary Astor, then a very popular young screen actress, had been granted a divorce from Dr. Franklyn Thorpe the previous year, and custody of their young daughter, Marilyn, had been granted to Thorpe. But in 1936 Miss Astor filed suit to set aside the custody award and have the child given to her. Dr. Thorpe retaliated with the contention that his former wife was unfit to keep a child, and he tried to introduce as evidence a diary Miss Astor had kept, revealing her involvement with the man identified to the public and the press as G. Judge Goodwin Knight had not permitted the diary to be used as evidence, but material purported to be from the diary was leaked to the press, and G, it was learned, stood for George, and George was a writer or a musician. There was speculation about both George Oppenheimer and George Gershwin, until subsequent leaks indicated that the mystery man was Kaufman. (When the guesses hovered for a while around Oppenheimer, his mother sent him a reassuring telegram: I KNOW YOU HAVEN'T DONE ANY-THING WRONG. "Unfortunately," Oppenheimer said recently, "I hadn't.")

According to Miss Astor's later account, the first materials leaked to the press were a forgery, and many of the other details were simply invented by reporters. It was claimed, for example, that she was having affairs with numerous famous names and had compiled a "charm rating" of Hollywood lovers, with Kaufman second on the list. The charm rating, plus the fact that the diary had been written in purple ink, made the case the hottest story of the day. And although the charm rating and other details were soon proved to be false, the real diary was obtained by the press and the Kaufman-Astor affair continued to make lurid headlines.

Mary Astor was born Lucille Langhanke in Quincy, Illinois, on May 3, 1906. Her father, Otto, was an improvident man who carried from his native Germany the belief that a child's role in life is to provide for its parents. Her mother was a farm girl who simply never understood her daughter. As Lucille entered her teens and blossomed into a superlative, madonna-like beauty, Otto Langhanke decided that his daughter could become a movie star and support him in luxury. He submitted her picture to a talent contest conducted by *Motion Picture Magazine*, and fourteen-year-old Lucille was a winner. But the Langhankes found—as Clara Bow did three years later—that it was all just a promotion gimmick for the magazine, and that the promised "movie contract" consisted of nothing more than an appearance before a camera the magazine had hired. Hollywood was inundated with contest winners and wanted no more. Langhanke, however, kept plugging, and in 1921 interested Jesse L. Lasky in Lucille. Lasky changed her name to Mary Astor, and, after she attracted attention in a two-reeler called *The Beggar Maid*, put her in two undistinguished Paramount pictures.

She was noticed by John Barrymore, who insisted that Warner Brothers give her the lead opposite him in *Beau Brummell*, and who undertook to teach Miss Astor how to act, and a good deal more. She was seventeen, and the Langhankes sat in the parlor watching Barrymore give lessons to their pretty daughter, until one day Barrymore finally pointed out that their presence made Miss Astor self-conscious. The parents retired, and the scope of the lessons expanded. The Barrymore romance ended when he married Dolores Costello, but Miss Astor's career progressed extremely well. In 1928, she married Kenneth Hawks, brother of Howard Hawks, the director. When Hawks died in a plane crash, she married Thorpe.

The false diary details initially released in the press were based on a forged document leaked by a man who was afraid that damaging information about his own sexual adequacy was in the real diary, and who invented the "charm rating" simply to get his own name included in the top ten. Unfortunately for Kaufman, a newspaperwoman named Florabel Muir secured reproductions of the real diary, for $300, and her paper, the Los Angeles *Herald-Express*, spread her scoop across the front page in gigantic type. BARE MARY ASTOR'S DIARY TELLING KAUFMAN AFFAIR, the headline read, with the subheads adding, "Fell Like Ton of Bricks! Lavender Love Secrets Book Revealed!"

"In lavender ink," the story began, "Mary Astor wrote in her diary love secrets of the romantic interludes she experienced with George S. Kaufman . . .

" 'I am still in a daze—a kind of rosy glow. It is beautiful, glorious, and I hope my last love. I can't top it with anything in my experience . . .' "

These and other passages, together with the inclusion of Kaufman near the top of the charm rating, suddenly thrust the embarrassed playwright into the position of most celebrated national lover. Someone had had pages of the diary removed to protect a star in whom a major studio had invested heavily, and, since a mutilated document could not legally be introduced as evidence in court, Thorpe's lawyer could not use the diary. But the lawyer could and did get Judge Knight to issue a subpoena forcing Kaufman to testify in court about his relations with Miss Astor.

Kaufman, who was then living in Hollywood at the Garden of Allah, went into seclusion the moment his name first came into the Thorpe-Astor case. The revelation of his address was sufficient in itself to increase rumors of his sexual activity, since the Garden of Allah, a mansion formerly owned by Alla Nazimova, the bizarre stage and screen star, had quite a local reputation. In 1927, Miss Nazimova had built a group of bungalows around the original home and made the place into a hotel, giving it the name of one of her stage successes. Sheilah Graham wrote a book about the hotel, and the publisher's jacket copy described the establishment as "a prison and a playground, a sanctuary and a glorified whorehouse, where the greats of Hollywood's golden years could carry on their private lives unobserved by the public eye." "In the thirty-two-year span of its life," Miss Graham wrote, "the Garden would witness robbery, murder, drunkenness, despair, divorce, marriage, orgies, pranks, fights, suicides, frustration, and hope. Yet intellectuals and celebrities from all over the world were to find it a convenient haven and a fascinating home."

Although many hotels have witnessed the events in Miss Graham's list, the lavish Garden of Allah seemed almost to specialize in them, and Kaufman had indeed found it a haven to which he could and did bring a different date virtually every night—until reporters and Judge Knight's process servers suddenly descended upon him. He fled to Moss Hart's home, but reporters tracked him there. While Kaufman stood concealed behind the drapes, causing them to flutter suspiciously, Hart was questioned by reporters and denied that Kaufman was there. Judge Knight, angered because Kaufman had ignored the subpoena served on him at the Garden of Allah, issued a bench warrant for his arrest. Along with Kaufman, Hart was now in danger of going to jail for harboring a fugitive. In order to help his friend and partner, Hart got a large laundry basket, covered Kaufman with clothing and linen, and called for a laundry truck whose driver was well paid to keep quiet. Kaufman was taken directly to the railroad station in San Bernardino, but missed his train—and the next would not come for another six hours. Afraid that he would be recognized if he stayed at the station, Kaufman left with Myra Hampton Streger for a nearby movie house where he could sit in the dark. But the house was showing an old Mary Astor film, and Kaufman had to sit through it two-and-a-half times before he could escape and catch his train for New York. Meanwhile, Judge Knight was telling the press, "I'll put this man Kaufman in jail if we ever find him," and he issued a search warrant and had a deputy sheriff scour Hart's home.

Headlines about the affair and the attempted arrest not only popped up in papers all across the country, but the story was also big news abroad. Marc Connelly, on a vacation in London, was startled to see a headline, I LOVE GEORGE, SAYS MARY, but thought the story was so ridiculous that he paid no more attention to it. Beatrice was on the Continent with Ellin Berlin when the story broke, and she went to London, where she was finally cornered by reporters. She decided to grant an interview as the best thing she could do for her husband and herself.

She spoke first, as mentioned, about Kaufman's meeting with Mary Astor in Hollywood, implying that the relationship was a casual one which had developed fairly recently. Then she said, "George is a good husband. I love him very much. He is in love with me, no matter what may happen. When I arrive in New York, George will be at the dock to meet me." She said that Kaufman had sent five telegrams to reassure her. "That's sweet of him, don't you think? No, please don't ask me about Miss Astor. She's a film actress. She kept a diary. Very stupid, that. I'd prefer to stay out of this affair. I'd like to preserve some dignity."

Beatrice's statement about Kaufman's meeting with Mary Astor was incorrect, since Kaufman had squired Miss Astor around New York in 1933. But, true to Beatrice's prediction, Kaufman did show up at the dock—and reporters were also there to wring all they could from the occasion. On August 27, 1936, the Brooklyn *Eagle* ran a story with the heading, "'Come On' Is Kissless Greeting of G. S. Kaufman to Wife at Ship." They had merely nodded to each other and left in a taxi.

Kaufman had granted an interview, earlier, which showed his usual spirit and style. He asked the reporter to tell the American people that he never kept a diary himself. "My leave-taking from California may have been undignified," he said, "but I felt it necessary. I have been in the public eye too long, and I think the public might be glad, and should be glad, to get me out of its eye." Judge Knight, meanwhile, was settling the case by negotiations among the lawyers, ordering the diary impounded and awarding Miss Astor custody of her daughter. But he was slow to forgive Kaufman. "The law is no respecter of persons," he said, "be they prominent, rich, intelligent, or dumb or stupid." He seemed nonplused at least, and perhaps outwitted, and pointed out that ignoring a subpoena in California could mean a sentence of $1000 and ninety days in jail. "Kaufman," he said, "had better have a good excuse for leaving California." Kaufman told friends that he felt Judge Knight was excuse enough. But no one concerned, including many prominent people in the motion picture industry, wanted the case continued, and Knight was persuaded to drop the charges.

Miss Astor, who, just a few months later, would elope to Yuma with Manuel del Campo, a Latin playboy, was sure that the scandal would ruin her career. But Samuel Goldwyn, for whom she was filming *Dodsworth*, declined to invoke the morals clause in her contract. "A mother fighting for her child," he said, "that's good." The actress's career soared, after that, with roles like the female lead in *The Maltese Falcon*, until she began to drink heavily and was eventually hospitalized as an alcoholic. But she proved to be made of sterner stuff than many former stars, and rebuilt her career in films, radio, and television, finally retiring to develop an entirely new career as a writer. Her autobiography, *My Story*, was a best-seller, and a subsequent novel received good notices. She lives quietly today in her beach apartment, almost a recluse, and when she sits in her garden and writes, she wears a hooded robe, which she pulls over her head at the arrival of a stranger. She recently suffered a mild heart attack, and is frequently visited by her children, one daughter and one son.

Kaufman was always touchy afterward about any mention of Mary Astor, and when *Time* was doing a cover story on him, he phoned Louis Kronenberger, who was writing the story, to ask if he was going to mention the affair. Kronenberger told him that the story would deal only with him as a playwright, but Kaufman remained doubtful and asked permission to read the story prior to publication, which was granted. When he arrived at the Time-Life Building at the appointed hour—2 A.M. on a Sunday—he was relieved to find that the writer had kept his word. Franklin Heller had been warned never to mention the Astor case in Kaufman's presence, a gratuitous warning since Kaufman's manner ordinarily barred even the most minor forms of personal probing. One day Heller picked up the first issue of *Life*, and Kaufman noted it with great interest. Where did you get it?" he asked. "Around the corner at the Hotel Ast—" Heller began, and caught himself. Kaufman just smiled.

The ironic thing about the Astor affair was that it was just one of many romantic experiences for Kaufman, and he was no more or less involved with Mary Astor than he was, before and after the scandal, with scores of others. Gene Fowler, Jr., said that during his work with Kaufman on *The Senator Was Indiscreet,* he stopped each morning to pick up Kaufman at his cabana at the Garden of Allah, and always found a different young lady there. Kaufman never introduced him to any of them, and acted as if there was no one in the room but Fowler and himself. The Astor liaison had become famous simply because of the court fight and diary, and was otherwise quite an ordinary occurrence in Kaufman's life.

Other events during this period of Kaufman's life included an offer to direct Clare Boothe Luce's play, *The Women,* which he turned down, and which Robert B. Sinclair directed instead. Max Gordon produced the play, which opened December 26, 1936, at the Ethel Barrymore Theatre, ran for 202 performances, and was picked by Burns Mantle for *The Best Plays of 1936–37.* Mrs. Luce is, of course, a society woman and widow of Time Inc.'s Henry Luce. There were also occasional rumors, since Kaufman sometimes took her out, that she was one of his special friends, and one columnist, O. O. McIntyre, persistently referred to them as "that twosome." Inevitably, Broadway gossip denied her the ability to turn out a hit play and, almost as inevitably, attributed part of the writing—specifically, the rewriting of the third act—to Kaufman and Hart. Ilka Chase, who had a leading role in the play, is certain that this was not true. "Clare wrote the play alone and unaided," she says. "but I suppose that after the Philadelphia opening Kaufman and Hart may have offered a few suggestions as to rewriting and rearrangement of scenes, all of which work she did herself. That kind of doctoring is a common or garden occurrence in the theatre, where, at one stage or another in production, every manager who ever breathed calls in all his friends for their opinions and walks around with lumps of ice at the end of his legs instead of feet."

The most plausible and convincing account is Mrs. Luce's. She said that Gordon had doubts about the third act after the Philadelphia opening, and that since Kaufman and Hart had seen the show that night, she did ask their advice. Before she knew it, they had found a typewriter and were at work. Their working methods astonished her. Hart would write a line and read it to Kaufman, who suggested changes, after which Kaufman would write a line, read it to Hart, and so on. She knew that she could never fit into that system, so she went upstairs and rewrote the third act herself. Kaufman, she added, had made the best comment on the matter when he said, "*The Women* was one of the great hits. If I wrote it, why on earth would I put *her* name on it?" She also said that Kaufman made more from the play than she did, since all she received were author's royalties, and he had a share in the show. Her reason for not investing was that, as a rich woman, she did not want to give the impression that she was subsidizing her own play.

Kaufman did help her a bit, though, when her play *Margin for Error* was in trouble out of town. Having asked his opinion over the phone, she then asked him if he could come see the play, but he said he was too busy to leave town. She asked him if he would look at the play if she brought it to New York for a night. He agreed, reluctantly, and she had sets and cast brought by train and truck for a special Sunday night performance at the Plymouth Theatre. Kaufman watched the entire play in silence, and started to leave without a word. When Mrs. Luce stopped him, Kaufman asked, "Why did you write this play?" Mrs. Luce replied that she had written it because it was time someone did something for the Jews. Kaufman sighed and said, "Clare, we've gotten along several thousand years without your help." But then he went ahead and made many helpful suggestions.

Kaufman also wrote several articles in this period, including *God Gets an Idea*, which appeared in *The Nation*'s issue of February 19, 1938. A piece on the small-mindedness of radio show sponsors, *God Gets an Idea* describes God's frustrations when He tries to line up a radio program on which he can publicize His views. For *Stage*'s issue of August 1938 Kaufman wrote *Music to My Ears*, a humorous review of his experiences working with composers and of his feelings about music. Kaufman's *The Meek Inherit the Earth*, a satire on inheritance fees, red tape, and taxes, appeared in *The Nation* on October 1, 1938. In the piece, the meek, who were supposed to receive the entire earth, wind up with only Yuma, Arizona. In *Interpretation*, which was published in *The Nation* on May 13, 1939, Kaufman makes fun of political columnists who predict future government actions based on scanty evidence. Kaufman weaves an elaborate and brilliant interpretation of President Roosevelt's policy plans on the basis of a report that the chief executive had recently said "Good Morning!" to his staff.

On September 25, 1936, Kaufman and Beatrice signed an escrow agreement for purchase of a fifty-nine-acre estate in Holicong, Bucks County, Pennsylvania, near New Hope. The estate was formerly the property of a socialite and director of the Whitney Museum, Juliana R. Force, who was in England at the time that the Kaufmans decided they wanted the estate. The final details, including the price of $45,000, a considerable sum at that time, were settled in a transatlantic call to her. Mrs. Force had called the place Barley Sheaf, but Kaufman nicknamed it Cherchez La Farm. The estate consisted of a mansion house with twelve rooms, a guest house, swimming pool, and pond, and had been sold to the Kaufmans by a real estate agent in a nearby Pennsylvania town. The agent had in that year alone sold more than three dozen farms and estates to writers, lawyers, actors, and businessmen, all New Yorkers, who were beginning to move out to Bucks County in numbers to live. Other buyers included Mary Urban, widow of Joseph Urban, the artist who designed many of Florenz Ziegfeld's productions, Leroy A. Lincoln, president of the Metropolitan Life Insurance Company, Edwin Justis Mayer, a playwright, Sidney K. Bennett, a magazine publisher, and Jackson Scholz, a former Olympic runner and also a writer of sports fiction for magazines and author of many novels with sports backgrounds.

The Kaufmans moved in on October 1, bringing two servants with them, one of whom doubled as chauffeur and drove the limousine. They left the decoration pretty much alone, with traditional early American furniture and strawberries on the wallpaper. Woollcott, on a visit there, was surprised and even upset at the lack of personal touches. "Why no record of *The Royal Family?*" he asked rhetorically. "Why none of *The Butter and Egg Man? Why no record of Dulcy?* Why do they let a decorator erase their life?" The answer was that no decorator could erase their life, and no records or reminders were needed.

Hart bought his country house right across the road from theirs. He had spent a weekend with them and was riding home when he caught a glimpse of an old stone farmhouse on the top of a hill. A glimpse was all that Hart required. He didn't feel it was necessary to stop and examine the house; he simply bought it by long-distance phone the next day. He proceeded to add wings and ells to the house, converted the tool shed into a library, and refurbished the old beams with oak casings. There was just one well on the entire eighty-seven-acre estate, and this tended to go dry during the summer months, which was a particularly serious problem since Hart was also building a swimming pool and needed water for that. Hart had seventeen wells drilled before he got one that would deliver sufficient water. He also wanted nothing less than a forest on the hilltop, and this is when he had 3500 pine trees imported. He also wanted more and better shade trees, and had 139 elms planted, each at least twenty years old, and also brought in many beeches, larches, and willows, all also over twenty years old. Woollcott had a comment about all this, too. "Well," he said, "it just goes to show what God could do if he had money."

The Kaufmans still needed a residence in the city, and it was for this purpose that they rented the town house at 14 East 94th Street in February 1937. The neighborhood was a very fashionable one, with such neighbors as Howard Lindsay, an ambassador, and several brokerage executives, and the five-story building had previously belonged to a leading Republican politician. Kaufman later used his frequent trips between New York and Cherchez La Farm for his *New Yorker* piece, *Does Newark Have to Be Where It Is?* "I have a farm in Bucks County," Kaufman said in the article, "and to visit it I travel frequently between New York and Trenton on the Pennsylvania Railroad. I like Bucks County, and when I depart for the farm, I am in a gay and emancipated mood, eager for a holiday and the wide countryside." He goes on to complain that the train, upon leaving Pennsylvania Station, plunges immediately into the darkness of a tunnel, but he says that he grows anticipatory again for the sight of rolling hills and fields. However, the first thing he sees upon leaving the tunnel is a rusting auto graveyard—and Newark. "I am not exactly blaming Newark for being there," he continues. "I know that years ago the city founders didn't say, 'Now, let's put Newark where

it will annoy the hell out of Kaufman.' I just say it's all wrong for
it to be there, and I would like to have it moved."

Kaufman had considered the possibility of going into production
himself for some time, and made his first such venture when he joined
Max Gordon and Moss Hart in co-producing *Sing Out the News*
by Harold Rome and Charles Friedman. Gordon and a group of
investors put up $50,000 and owned half the show, and Kaufman and
Hart put up $25,000 each and owned the other half. Rome and Fried-
man had first worked together on *Pins and Needles*, an outstanding
hit produced off-Broadway by the Labor Stage of the International
Ladies Garment Workers Union and then moved uptown, and *Sing
Out the News* was designed as a musical revue similar to the earlier
play. Rome was like Arthur Schwartz: a lawyer who preferred writing songs. He had been given his start when Gypsy Rose Lee liked
one of his compositions. Friedman, who also had been a lawyer before
switching to the theatre, had directed *Pins and Needles*, and was officially credited with having conceived and directed *Sing Out the
News*, although Rome said later that Kaufman and Hart wrote some
of the sketches for the show without asking for credit.

Sing Out the News opened Saturday, September 24, 1938, at the
Music Box Theatre, and ran 105 performances. Reviews were generally warm and appreciative, but critics agreed that the revue lacked
some of the sparkle and excitement of *Pins and Needles*. In criticiz-
ing the score, Brooks Atkinson wrote, "Having a social conscience,
Rome is none too gay." *Variety* said that those who responded to the
social significance of *Pins and Needles*, "due to its amateur auspices,
that of the International Ladies Garment Workers Union, may be
more captious under the de luxe production auspices of Max Gordon,
George Kaufman, and Moss Hart." Of the cast, June Allyson, a member of the chorus and later a Hollywood star, attracted attention, as did
Jimmy Lydon, who had a featured spot in the revue and later went
on to film roles.

Kaufman's next business deal was to join Sam Harris, Max Gordon,
Moss Hart, and Joseph and Mark Hyman in buying the Lyceum
Theatre at 149 West 45th Street. Otto Diehl, a member of Harris's
staff, handled negotiations, and agreed on behalf of the buyers to a

clause stipulating that Daniel Frohman, whose celebrated studio was in the Lyceum building, would continue to occupy his quarters at a rental of $1 per year, as long as he lived. Ownership was split, with Kaufman and Harris owning 25 per cent each, and Hart, Gordon, and the Hymans each owning 12½ per cent. They made the purchase in May 1940 and produced several hits there, including *The Dough-girls*, *Born Yesterday*, and the Kaufman-Marquand collaboration, *The Late George Apley*. The group earned a profit of $250,000 during its ownership and sold the theatre at an additional profit in 1945.

Kaufman ventured out as a producer on his own in 1941 with *Mr. Big*, a comic murder mystery by Arthur Sheekman and Margaret Shane. The show concerned a murder in a theatre, and involved the audience in the show with actors sometimes running up and down the aisles. It opened Tuesday, September 30, 1941, flopped, and closed after seven performances. John Anderson of the *Journal-American* summed up the critics' feelings. "Since the First Nighters at the Lyceum were supposed," he wrote, "for the sake of the play, to be held by the police, they were served refreshments during intermission, and Ray Mayer, in addition to giving an admirable performance, gave me a sandwich. I hate to bite the hand that fed me, but the sandwich, though hammy, was the freshest item of a badly blotched evening."

Mr. Big had been produced on an experimental basis at Columbia University the previous year, and Lee Shubert had assumed that he had sewed up the Broadway performance rights. He sued Kaufman before the Broadway opening and settled out of court for 17½ per cent of the show, which led Kaufman to say, after the play flopped, "It's a pleasure to lose money for Lee." But it was only a joke, since a flop never failed to disturb him.

Like anyone else, Kaufman was never *really* happy to lose money, and in 1937 he wrote the wry poem for *The New Yorker*'s issue of May 1 called *Lines Upon Looking Through a Pile of Old Checks*. The poem complains about poker losses, bridge losses, Mrs. Kaufman's clothes, the cost of books, furniture, gas, telephone, and electric bills. And then, having enumerated almost every kind of bill that can be paid by check, it takes a swipe at "that little sweet, the Income Tax," and pleads that it's time some other "poor schlemiel" foots the bill for the New Deal. Finally, Kaufman observes that he's now writing checks for the same things all over again this year, "only just a trifle bigger."

The pleasantly conventional tone of the poem may seem difficult to reconcile with Kaufman's torrid record as a Don Juan, but the fact is that, aside from all the extramarital sex, Kaufman's attitudes were essentially orthodox. As stated, Kaufman engaged in his many affairs because of physical need, but would have been much happier just having a normal sexual relationship with Beatrice, in line with his rigid standards of morality in other areas.

But, of course, Kaufman's needs did not allow him to stay within the bounds he would have preferred. Jack Paar said that Kaufman once passed along some advice he had been given by his father. Joseph Kaufman had said, "Son, try everything in life except incest and folk-dancing." Kaufman never tried either, but, as far as romance was concerned, he clearly tried everything else.

27. THE GENIUS

IF KAUFMAN HAD never written a play, he would still be remembered as a giant in the history of theatre, simply on the basis of his work as a director. "A man's a good director," he once told Lynn Fontanne, "if he has a good play. He's a bad director if he has a bad play." But this statement was just self-deprecation on Kaufman's part and could not have been said of Kaufman himself, who was a superlative director regardless of the play. His directing career had begun with *The Front Page* in 1928, but he had grown to love the job only with his second effort, on *June Moon* in 1929. This was probably because the play was his own collaboration with Ring Lardner, and he confided later to Morrie Ryskind, "You lose the flavor of what you write if you don't direct it." Afterward he directed all his hit plays.

[573]

But some of the greatest tributes to Kaufman's genius as a director were given for his work on plays which he, officially at least, had not written, but which his direction gave a new dimension, a dimension of theatricality which the author had not thought possible until Kaufman created it. Perhaps Kaufman's most brilliant contribution of this kind was set in motion one morning when Beatrice interrupted his breakfast.

She came downstairs with a book she had just finished reading, and told Kaufman urgently, "You've *got* to tie this one up." The book, *Of Mice and Men* by John Steinbeck, was hardly what Broadway would have considered likely material for a "Kaufman play," but that did not bother Beatrice, nor did it deter Steinbeck later. The novel is a grim story of two wanderers, George and half-witted Lennie, whose ambition is someday to own a farm. Their hopes are extinguished when Lennie accidentally kills the wife of the foreman of a farm where they've stopped to work, and George, rather than let his friend fall into the hands of his pursuers, shoots Lennie himself. Kaufman found the book both brilliant and moving, and had Beatrice send Steinbeck an offer. Although the book had only been published for ten days, Steinbeck already had two offers, but Kaufman's name and reputation decided it for him immediately. "Beatrice has bought the dramatic rights," Alexander Woollcott wrote a short time later to Harpo Marx. "I'm in on it with her. One of the characters is an amiable and gigantic idiot, so tender that he has to fondle everything he likes, and so clumsy that he eventually breaks their necks—mice, puppies, rabbits, tarts—whatever he happens to be petting. I tried to get Broun to take the part, and he was very hurt." The part eventually went to Broderick Crawford, with Wallace Ford in the role of George.

Steinbeck, who had playwriting ambitions, had permitted a group to stage *Of Mice and Men* in San Francisco, but the version presented there consisted of nothing more than dialogue and narrative abstracted directly from the book. "Steinbeck made no pretense," a reviewer said, "that this was a critic-proof, completed play. So it would be unjust to criticize the play, as given in San Francisco, from a structural, technical angle." When Steinbeck set out for New York aboard ship, he wrote a new version on the way, and apparently, in light of what happened later, he did as he had done earlier, abstracting sections of the novel verbatim without much regard for dramatic construction or the limitations of the stage. This was made clear to him when he took the play to Cherchez La Farm for Kaufman's opinion.

There has long been a controversy over how much of the play Kaufman wrote, and one Steinbeck defender even felt compelled to go through the play and the book line by line, and reported that 85 per cent of the dialogue as finally written came from the book. But the fact is that, after the conferences at Cherchez La Farm, which lasted for only a few days since Steinbeck had to return home, Kaufman went to work on the play alone. A few news stories actually appeared referring to "the play by Kaufman," and Steinbeck corroborated this in his earliest interviews about the play. But Kaufman quickly scotched all talk of his authorship, and thereafter it has always been "the play by John Steinbeck and directed by George S. Kaufman." The one overriding reason for Kaufman's policy on the matter was due to the way Steinbeck had written *Of Mice and Men*. Steinbeck had conceived the book as an eventual play or film, and frequently said that he therefore wrote the book with that in mind, writing mostly in dialogue. Kaufman had only, for the most part, to select dialogue, and use it, for the most part, unchanged, and therefore felt that he had functioned primarily as a carpenter only, and shouldn't take credit away from the primary material or its author. It was a modest and generous attitude, because, of course, knowing what to select and constructing it dramatically is everything. In a glowing and heartfelt letter of gratitude written to Kaufman after the successful opening of the play, Steinbeck called it "your play," and described the play throughout the letter as purely Kaufman's. It was another of the few letters Kaufman kept for the rest of his life.

Steinbeck's gratitude for Kaufman's version of his novel was based entirely on reviews he had read and on letters from friends, since he was not in attendance when the play opened at the Music Box on Tuesday, November 23, 1937. He was in Los Gatos, California, well into the research for *The Grapes of Wrath*. Nor was he present when the Drama Critics Circle gave its Best Play of the Year Award to *Of Mice and Men*, since he was then among the migrant workers in Oklahoma doing further research. Eventually, Steinbeck became one of only six Americans to win the Nobel Prize for literature, but Steinbeck said of Kaufman, "I didn't realize that little things in writing made such a difference, and George taught it to me for the first time in my life." The play ran for 207 performances, opened in London at the Gate Theatre in April 1939, and was a big hit there, too, and was bought for films by United Artists. The movie, produced and directed by Lewis Milestone, with a screenplay by Eugene Solow, was released on February 2, 1940, and was also very successful.

Critics at the opening night performance lauded Kaufman's direction as much as the play. "Although Mr. Kaufman is celebrated for his wit and his craftsmanlike facility in stage direction," Brooks Atkinson wrote, "admit *Of Mice and Men* as evidence of the fact that he can also enter into the spirit of a fine play and give it the must humble sort of expression." Edith Isaacs wrote in *Theatre Arts*, "To the author's accomplishment George S. Kaufman has added a perfect piece of direction, with exactly the pace, the movement, the emotional crescendo, and the pauses that enrich the action."

Of the many accolades bestowed upon his work on *Of Mice and Men*, Kaufman was especially gratified with three. Chief among these was Steinbeck's letter. "As the reviews come in," Steinbeck wrote, "it becomes more and more apparent that you have done a great job. I knew you would, of course, but there is a curious gap between the thing in your head and the thing set down and you've jumped that gap . . .

"To say thank you is ridiculous for you can't thank a man for good work any more than you can thank him for being himself. But one can be very glad he is himself and that is what we are—very glad you are George Kaufman.

"It doesn't matter a damn whether this show runs a long time. It came to life for one night anyway, and really to life, and that's more than anyone has a right to hope.

"Sometimes in working, the people in my head become much more real than I am. It seems that for two hours you made your play far more real than its audience so that Mr. Black's loss in the market and Mrs. Klick's hatred of the Vanderbilts disappeared from them and only the play existed. I wish I could transpose into some mathematical equation my feeling, so that it might be a communication unmistakable and unchanging."

The other two letters came from Arthur Hopkins and from James Forbes. "On rare occasions," Hopkins said, "there happens in the theatre a unity of writing, acting and direction which pierces levels of gratitude that are usually immune. To my small gallery of rare experiences has been added last night's play and to all concerned I feel indebted." Forbes wrote, "Always I say that since Henry Miller you are the only director that knows a goddam thing about bringing out the playwright's intent, but in *Of Mice and Men* you have surpassed yourself. It is a great work."

In 1940, Kaufman worked briefly as director on a satirical drawing room comedy by Irwin Shaw. Speaking of Kaufman years later, Shaw said, "George was completely professional in that he never wrote or directed anything merely for his own pleasure or indulgence, but always with a cold eye on its effect on the audience. I worked with him on *Retreat to Pleasure*, which he finally would not do because he could not find a leading man to his taste. Even as we worked together, George would search and search until he found the exact number of words which would get an actor off the stage with a bright or funny exit line, precisely timed out."

Kaufman's next venture in directing, aside from those plays which were explicitly his own, was undertaken primarily in order to help Max Gordon, who had fallen on very evil days. Gordon had had a string of flops on Broadway, after which he had invested and lost large sums of money in some Hollywood productions, taking a particularly disastrous loss on *Abe Lincoln in Illinois*. He was $300,-000 in debt and owed the government another $100,000 in taxes. He had gone to pieces and had made several suicide attempts. At this critical juncture, Moss Hart, knowing that what Gordon needed was something tangible that would give him a new will to live, brought him a copy of a play by Joseph Fields and Jerome Chodorov, based on a series of stories written by Ruth McKenney for *The New Yorker*. It was *My Sister Eileen*, a web of hilarious complications which arise when Ruth and her sister leave the midwest to conquer Greenwich Village and the rest of New York with only $40 in their purses. Their adventures so captivated Gordon that he laughed out loud and began to feel better for the first time since his troubles had begun.

The play needed work, and Gordon asked Kaufman to do the job. Kaufman wanted to do all that he could for Gordon, but was trying to develop a new play with Edna Ferber. The best that he had time for, he said, was to give advice in his spare moments away from the project with Miss Ferber. But when that project fell through, he agreed to direct the play. The failure of the collaboration with Miss Ferber, with the subsequent decision to go ahead with *My Sister Eileen*, marked one of the turning points which steered Kaufman into a period in which he did much more directing than writing.

Gordon had no money, so he gave notes for scenery and costumes and got 15 per cent of the show, and Kaufman got 25 per cent for his services, which included a good bit of play-doctoring. Fields and Chodorov invested $2500 apiece, Beatrice invested $1500, Sam Harris $1000, Hart $750, other friends, including Woollcott, a total of $6000, and outsiders the rest. Joseph Fields was the son of Lew Fields of Weber and Fields, the comedy team, and Jerome Chodorov was a former newspaperman who tended toward the stout side, and who Kaufman liked to needle. "Chodorov," Kaufman said, "thinks that if he refuses food the first time and takes it the second time, he's dieting." Chodorov and Fields had first teamed up as screenwriters at Republic Studios.

Kaufman later gave his own view of the team's working methods. He said that they enticed him into a hotel room, locked the door, and offered him some of the worst candy it had even been his misfortune to eat. "In the ensuing weeks," he said, "they did valiant work with the script; the candy, however, got no better . . . To my certain knowledge, they wrote about six plays, not one. It was a rare day, in the weeks preceding rehearsals, that they did not come along with eight or ten new scenes. I'd leave them at four. Then along about five-thirty, just as I was playing four spades doubled—my partner's fault, incidentally—they would call. 'We just finished those scenes,' they would say. 'And, oh, yes—we've got a new second act.'" Typically, Kaufman never talked about the fact that he had made a lot of contributions to the script, but Franklin Heller tells a story which shows Kaufman's hand in the writing. When Max Gordon sold the film rights to the play to Columbia, Heller was retained as dialogue director, but was told by the director, Alexander Hall, "I don't want any smartass New York types. If you want to stay on the set, keep your mouth shut." So Heller sat and calmly drew his salary until Hall approached him one day, complaining that the script wasn't going right—it just wasn't funny. Heller looked at the script and told Hall that the play's best jokes were missing. A subsequent investigation revealed that Gordon had mistakenly given Columbia the pre-Kaufman script.

In the play, Shirley Booth was cast as Ruth, the girl who wants to be a writer, and Jo Ann Sayers was her sister Eileen, an aspiring actress. Kaufman preferred to use seasoned professionals in his casts, once saying that he was a director and not a schoolteacher, and that he had no great desire to be a discoverer of new acting talent. When casting, he liked to be able to select an experienced and reliable actor who didn't require a director pushing his elbows through a scene. As courteous as Kaufman was in his criticisms and corrections, it always annoyed him to have to tell an actor twice about a shortcoming. But when required to use beginners, he worked hard to help them overcome their lack of experience, and occasionally offered at least a backhanded compliment, something he never did for veterans. After Edna Ferber forced Janet Fox on him in *Dinner at Eight,* and she performed well in her role, Kaufman told the young girl, "You're pretty good for a niece." In *My Sister Eileen,* Kaufman did not give direction to Shirley Booth beyond blocking out each scene in the early stages of rehearsal. Jo Ann Sayers, on the other hand, was a very nervous newcomer and Kaufman knew he would simply aggravate the situation if he called attention to her problems. Instead, he created so much stage business for her that Miss Sayers was too busy doing natural things like picking up clothes, putting them away, and even ironing them, to remain selfconscious, and she did fine. Saint Subber, who was assistant stage manager for Kaufman in a few plays in his early days, and who later produced most of the Neil Simon shows, once described Kaufman at work as a director. "His greatest thing," Subber said, "was timing. He would keep clicking his fingers. Pace and tempo were the important things. Actors adored working with George. He was quick and knew what he wanted. There was a relaxed blue-room quality about his rehearsals. When it was time for work, everybody worked. When it was time for play, there would be laughs, lots of laughs."

For a few hours, it appeared that *My Sister Eileen* might not open. The original McKenney stories had been based partly on fact, and there really was a sister Eileen. Just before the opening she and her husband, Nathanael West, author of *Miss Lonelyhearts*, were killed in an auto accident. Gordon thought that the tragedy would blight audience reception, and he was ready to withdraw, but Kaufman insisted on opening. "Let it be a memorial to her," he said, and Ruth McKenney agreed.

The play opened at the Biltmore Theatre on Thursday, December 26, 1940, without an out-of-town tryout. It was an overwhelming success, running 865 performances on Broadway, and Burns Mantle selected it for *The Best Plays of 1940–41*. Columbia bought film rights for $225,000 and made the film twice. The first version, filmed in 1942 with Janet Blair as Eileen and Rosalind Russell as Ruth, and also starring Brian Aherne and Richard Quine, was a big hit. The second version, filmed in 1955 with Janet Leigh as Eileen and also starring Betty Garrett, Jack Lemmon, and Robert Fosse (now, of course, a top dance director and film director, with an Oscar for *Cabaret*) was a failure. The play was also remade as a stage musical, under the title of *Wonderful Town*, with Rosalind Russell again as Ruth and with Edie Adams as Eileen, and with music by Leonard Bernstein. It was a success all over again.

After *My Sister Eileen*, Fields and Chodorov again turned to *The New Yorker* and fashioned a hit from the sub-deb stories of Sally Benson, *Junior Miss*. The play, which became Moss Hart's first assignment as a director, was warmly received, and ran for 246 performances.

Fields next ventured out on his own and wrote *The Doughgirls*, a satirical comedy about three girls working in wartime Washington. Kaufman, again opting, in this period, for a role as director rather than writer, agreed to stage it and had 25 per cent of the show. Production of the show was enlivened by a running feud between Fields and Max Gordon, who took exception to some of the lines and ordered them removed. One of Fields's expurgated lines, for example, had

had a woman saying, "I had children at the drop of a hat. Then my husband went to Australia and took the hat with him." Kaufman was caught in the middle of the dispute. He continued to be polite to the cast, as usual, but his irritation at the author-producer arguments caused him to bear down harder on Fields. He badgered Fields, particularly about the exits. His words, "You've got to be funnier—you've got to brighten up the exits," kept reverberating in Fields's ears until he was sick of hearing it. One day at rehearsal, an old charwoman crossed the stage to clean up after a spill. Fields watched her leave, then turned to Kaufman, and said, "I know. Don't tell me. I've got to brighten up *her* exit, too."

The Doughgirls' three leading players were Virginia Field, Arleen Whelan, and Doris Nolan, but Arlene Francis attracted the most attention in the role of a Russian guerrilla fighter. The play opened Wednesday, December 30, 1942, at the Lyceum Theatre. The critics found it slight, but pointed to Kaufman's direction as a major redeeming factor. "Mr. Kaufman has paced the show with fury," Louis Kronenberger said in *PM*, "so that there is not much time for thought," which he felt was just as well since, in his view, the play did not offer much about which it was worth thinking. John Anderson expressed a similar opinion. "If Mr. Fields's little story is as flimsy as a piece of tissue paper," he said, "at least Mr. Kaufman blows it around in some gusty patterns and keeps it dancing." The fast-paced tissue-thin play was entertaining, however, and *The Doughgirls* was a big hit in spite of the critics, running for 671 performances. Mantle picked the play for *The Best Plays of 1942–43*, and the show was produced in London by Firth Shepard, a comedy specialist who had previously produced *The Man Who Came to Dinner* and *Arsenic and Old Lace*. It was also a hit there.

Charles Martin recalls an incident connected with the road tour of *The Doughgirls* which illustrates what he calls Kaufman's "Midas touch." Kaufman accepted, on Martin's recommendation, a young actress named Marianne O'Brien to play Arleen Whelan's role in the touring company. But when the company reached Los Angeles, a Warner Brothers scout noticed her and was impressed by her handling of the role, and got her to break her run-of-the-play contract to accept a part in a movie. The part was mediocre. But at the end she attended a publicity party, met and then married Richard Reynolds of the Virginia tobacco family, and was, in Martin's words, "ensconced in a fourteen-room riverhouse apartment in New York, together with a mansion in Florida, plus other fringe benefits. So, indirectly, Kaufman made her one of the richest women in the world."

Kaufman's next venture in directing another writer's play led to a rather bizarre situation, which found Kaufman and the author trying to prevent the opening, but being forced to proceed by the producer. Mike Todd was the producer, Gypsy Rose Lee was the author, and Joan Blondell, who later married Todd, was the star. The play, *The Naked Genius*, concerns a stripper who hires a ghostwriter in order to produce a book that will prove that she's really an intellectual. She maintains the illusion successfully enough to become engaged to her publisher's son, but realizes at the wedding that she's moving with the wrong crowd and marries her manager instead. Miss Lee had once written a book called *The G-String Murders*, and the play was partly autobiographical.

Kaufman was hired as both director and play doctor, and worked hard to put some humor into what Todd himself finally realized and admitted was a turkey. The results were still so bad that Miss Lee and Kaufman implored Todd to forget the whole thing. The play had first tried out in Boston at the Wilbur Theatre, was moved back to New York for rewriting and further rehearsals, then tried out in Baltimore, the traditional bastion of strippers, and then Pittsburgh, where all reviews were bad and the plea was made to Todd. Todd might have agreed, but he had already sold the play to Twentieth Century-Fox. The deal was for $350,000 plus 15 per cent of the film's gross in New York, and 10 per cent of the gross elsewhere, provided the play reached Broadway and ran at least thirty-five performances. Needless to say, Todd had no intention of allowing it to run less than that.

Todd opened at the Plymouth Theatre on Thursday, October 12, 1943, and, for once, Kaufman missed the opening of a play with which he was concerned. Like Miss Lee, he didn't even want to be in the same town with *The Naked Genius*, so he stayed out at Cherchez La Farm. It was a wise decision. Burton Rascoe reported in the *World-Telegram* the next day that he had thought the rumors about Kaufman's and Miss Lee's desire to close out of town had been just a gag. "But they weren't kidding," he said. Howard Barnes said in the *Herald Tribune* that Miss Lee "might better have stuck to bumps." "Mr. Kaufman's direction keeps things moving," Louis Kronenberger said, "but I could only pray that they would stop." Despite the panning, Todd kept the play open just beyond the thirty-five performances he needed for his movie deal. He closed the play after thirty-six performances, and in 1946 the film was released, with Vivian Blaine in the role originated by Joan Blondell. The title had been changed to *Doll Face*, but that didn't help, either. Miss Lee refused to have her stage name connected with it, and the play was credited to Louise Hovick, her real name. Bosley Crowther knew who Miss Hovick was, and wrote, "With all due respect for Miss Hovick, her talents have been better demonstrated otherwise."

Kaufman's next hit, *Over 21*, was written by Ruth Gordon as a vehicle for Ruth Gordon. Based on Miss Gordon's own adventures while following her new husband, Garson Kanin, from Army assignment to Army assignment, the play concerns a lady writer whose thirty-nine-year-old husband has joined the Army out of patriotism, and the ways in which she helps him with his problems and frustrations. Max Gordon read the script in a hospital while recovering from a prostate operation, and said he almost burst his stitches laughing. But Kaufman was unimpressed. "It's not a play," he said. "There's no plot. It's just a bunch of lines." Gordon threatened to go ahead without him, and Kaufman relented to the point of saying that he would leave the decision up to Moss Hart. If Hart liked the play, he'd direct it. Hart loved it. Kaufman had assumed that Hart would agree with him, but he carried out his promise, accepted the directorial assignment, and held 25 per cent of the play.

Over 21 tried out in New Haven, Philadelphia and Washington, D.C., and opened at the Music Box Theatre on Monday, January 3, 1944. Much of the critical praise for the show was focused on Kaufman's direction. Ward Morehouse wrote in the *Sun* of the "delightfully inventive direction of George Kaufman." Burton Rascoe of the *World-Telegram* said, "The farcical first act is as funny as it is only because it was directed by George Kaufman, with all those inventive pieces of 'business' which Mr. Kaufman manages to get into most plays he directs, and with that genius he has of making highly artificial patter seem witty and up-to-date. Two-thirds of the laughs in that first act are got by Miss Gordon without opening her mouth; they are Kaufman tricks of the player in relation to the set and props." Kaufman was right in saying that the story was thin, but his directorial fireworks, the play's lighthearted, war-related theme, and Miss Gordon's skillful performance (Rascoe's comment notwithstanding), helped make it a success. *Over 21* ran for 197 performances.

The play was also selected for *The Best Plays of 1943–44*, and became the first full-length legitimate stage production exported overseas by USO Camp Shows for the entertainment of American forces in the combat zone. Erin O'Brien-Moore appeared in Ruth Gordon's role, and the reception given the play was so good that it was soon followed by others, including *The Barretts of Wimpole Street* with Katharine Cornell.

During these years when Kaufman was busy primarily with directing jobs, he continued to wire articles, including one called *The Great Caviar Riots*, which appeared in *The Nation* of February 10, 1940, and in which Kaufman presents the spectacle of New York's top society figures rioting when they are cut off from their supplies of unsalted Russian caviar. Kaufman then wrote a piece called *Expectant Playwrights Saved*, which the New York *World-Telegram* published on February 15, 1941. In 1942, Kaufman wrote two introductions for books. One was a lighthearted guide to playing bridge for Charles Goren's *Better Bridge for Better Players*, and the other, *Forked Lightning*, was an article in praise of Moss Hart for the Modern Library's *Six Plays by George S. Kaufman and Moss Hart*. Hart in turn wrote a piece on Kaufman for the book, *Men at Work*, and Brooks Atkinson preceded both with an article lauding both members of the team. Kaufman also wrote a funny piece for the *New York Times Magazine*'s issue of September 17, 1944, *A Playwright Tells Almost All*.

The Naked Genius was not the only play among those directed by Kaufman which failed, of course, and there are several others spaced between his hits. In 1930, there was *Joseph*, written by Bertram Bloch, who had been head of the Eastern story department for M-G-M since 1928, and whose previous play, written with Thomas Mitchell, the actor, in 1926, was *Glory Hallelujah*. The play was the biblical story of Joseph, but burlesqued. Joseph, played by George Jessel, is first a slave, then becomes an overseer, but is desired by Potiphar's wife and condemned to death when he spurns her. He is pardoned when he interprets the Pharaoh's dreams, and is made over-seer of Egypt. The part was played broadly by Jessel, with a lot of modern references and anachronisms. Kaufman was called in during tryouts to add a few lines and serve as director, but it just didn't work. The play opened on Wednesday, February 13, 1930, at the Liberty Theatre, and lasted only thirteen performances. Since Kaufman had taken a piece of the show rather than a salary or royalties, he made nothing from his work on *Joseph*.

Bloch continued with his job at M-G-M until 1939, and then held a similar position with Twentieth Century-Fox from 1941 to 1956. His plays after *Joseph* were *Jewel Robbery*, in 1932, adapted from a play by Lazlo Fodor, and, in 1934, *Dark Victory* with George Brewer, Jr., and *Spring Again* with Isabel Leighton. He went on to write several novels, including *Mrs. Hulett* in 1953, *The Little Laundress* and *The Fearful Knight* in 1954, and *The Only Nellie Fayle* in 1960.

Kaufman also missed with *Here Today*, the story of a brittle lady writer whose ex-husband falls in love with an upper-crust Boston girl. The heroine of the comedy invents an impeccable social background for her ex-husband so that the Boston family won't oppose his suit, but then discovers that she still loves him, so she ruins his reputation with the Bostonians and gets him back. It was while rehearsing this show that Kaufman heard one of the players read, from the script, "I've never been to Boston." He added a classic line: "I went through once but it was closed."

Here Today's author, George Oppenheimer, switched to full-time writing after co-founding Viking Press, and has one other play credit, *A Mighty Man Is He*, written with Arthur Kober, in 1960. He has also written thirty screenplays, including *Libeled Lady*, *A Yank at Oxford*, *Two-Faced Woman*, and *The War Against Mrs. Hadley*, and a book of reminiscence, *The View from the Sixties*. Since 1955, he has been drama critic for *Newsday*, the Long Island daily, and he is also the editor of a book titled *The Passionate Play-goer*, a collection of articles about the theatre.

The heroine of *Here Today* was modeled partially after Dorothy Parker, as was the character of the lady writer in *Over 21*. After *Over 21* appeared, Mrs. Parker commented that she would never be able to write her autobiography without being accused of plagiarizing George Oppenheimer and Ruth Gordon.

Here Today opened on Friday, September 16, 1932, at the Ethel Barrymore Theatre, and failed, running thirty-nine performances. It closed on October 8. Fortunately, however, it went on to become a great success in summer stock and similar performances, and has brought in a lot of money through the years.

Inevitably, Kaufman also sometimes found that he had passed up a play only to discover that someone else had taken it and had a hit. One such play was *Dodsworth*, which Sidney Howard had dramatized from the Sinclair Lewis novel, and which Max Gordon asked Kaufman to direct. Like several other top directors, Kaufman turned it down, saying that no audience would sit through a badly written play about a middle-aged man and his nagging wife. But Robert B. Sinclair took the job and turned out a hit that ran for 315 performances after it opened at the Shubert Theatre on February 24, 1934. The play had to close temporarily for two months during its run because its star, Walter Huston, had also had little faith in it, and signed a contract to play *Othello* for the month of July in the restored Central City Opera House in Central City, Colorado. But the success of the play didn't alter Kaufman's opinion of the dramatization. "I still say it was a shabby job," he said. Samuel Goldwyn paid $165,000 for the movie rights, and it was in the role of the "other woman" that Mary Astor was playing when the diary scandal broke. In later years, whenever Max Gordon had occasion to mention Kaufman's error regarding *Dodsworth*, Kaufman could even matters quickly by reminding Gordon that he'd once wired Gordon from London, suggesting that he pick up Agatha Christie's *Witness for the Prosecution*. Gordon replied promptly, "It'll never go in New York." The play then became a great success here, with another management producing.

Another failure in which Kaufman was involved was *Tomorrow's a Holiday*, adapted by Romney Brent, the actor, from a Viennese farce, and produced by John Golden and Joseph Schildkraut. The story concerns a minor bank executive who finds that he's short in his accounts, with bank examiners coming the next day. He persuades a gambling friend to try to win the needed money for him, but the friend loses, and the despairing hero leaves. But the friend gets into another game and wins just in time. Schildkraut persuaded Golden to co-produce the play with him so that he could portray the gambler. The play opened at the Golden Theatre on Monday, December 30, 1935, and lasted only eight performances. Kaufman had been called in to direct, but realized that the play was hopeless and withdrew. The play opened without a director credit in the program listing, Kaufman having insisted that his name be withdrawn. But Kaufman had been repeatedly announced as director prior to this, and Burns Mantle so credited him in the appendix to *The Best Plays of 1935-36*, which includes, as each edition does, a roster of all plays produced during the season.

One other play which Kaufman passed over in favor of Robert B. Sinclair was *The Postman Always Rings Twice*, which James M. Cain had dramatized from his best-selling novel. The story is that of a drifter who takes a job at a refreshment stand, and helps a discontented woman kill her husband, the owner of the stand. They're arrested and acquitted, but, in an ironic twist, they're later in a car accident. The woman is killed, and the man, although innocent this time, is convicted of her murder. Kaufman was called in as "consulting director," which meant play doctor, but he was unable to save it. The play opened at the Lyceum Theatre on Tuesday, February 18, 1936, and ran for seventy-two performances. Jack Curtis produced, and Richard Barthelmess, the former screen star, played the drifter. Jo Mielziner's sets—one of which featured the wrecked car on stage—received more praise from the critics than either the play or the cast.

Kaufman had a hand in almost every aspect of his plays, but he never became involved with the set designs; he felt that this was strictly the province of the designer. Jo Mielziner said recently, "Brilliant as he was as an *oral* director, Kaufman had little or no visual sense and was rather literal in discussions with stage designers." Others, however, say Mielziner has mistaken courtesy for inability. In a contrary story, Donald Oenslager, another major designer, says that Kaufman had a strong theatrical sense of what was needed. Oenslager recalls that, while he was designing the sets for *Of Mice and Men*, Kaufman said, "I know they're just shacks, but can't they be beautiful? We must get a poetic quality into them."

After the beginning of *Over 21*'s successful run in 1944, Kaufman took on the job of director for Max Gordon's production of *While the Sun Shines*, a comedy by the leading British playwright Terence Rattigan. Born June 10, 1911, Rattigan has written many successful plays and films, and his plays include *The Deep Blue Sea*, *The Sleeping Prince*, *Separate Tables*, *The Browning Version*, *Ross* (based on the life of T. E. Lawrence), *French Without Tears*, *The Winslow Boy*, and many others. *While the Sun Shines* concerns a young earl who is about to be married and who asks an American Army officer to take his mistress off his hands. The officer, who has seen neither woman, accidentally takes the fiancée instead, but everything is straightened out in a manner described by one reviewer as half Noël Coward and half P. G. Wodehouse. The play opened at the Lyceum Theatre on Tuesday, September 19, 1944, but could manage only thirty-nine performances. Several reviewers called attention to the fact that Kaufman was doing much more directing than writing in this period. One of them, the *Post*'s Wilella Waldorf, said, "We can't help wishing that Mr. Kaufman would write more of the plays he directs instead of lavishing so much precious energy on other people's labored scripts."

But the fact was that Kaufman never felt that his energy or talent was being wasted, as long as he was helping to improve a play or produce a good evening for the audience, and it was his genius as a director that made all the difference in sustaining some of Broadway's best hits. Kaufman's strongest sense of loyalty was not to himself as a writer, director, or producer, but to the play, its performances, and the enjoyment of those who saw it. He expressed this in his funny, modest way one afternoon when a doorman failed to recognize him as he was entering a theatre where one of his shows was in rehearsal. The doorman asked, "Excuse me, sir, are you with the show?"

"Well," Kaufman replied, "let's just say I'm not against it."

28. THE LOSS

FOR KAUFMAN, WHO had always feared death and who hated the idea of growing old, the first six years of the 1940s brought the facts of death home most forcefully and painfully, and seemed to substantiate his fears with the deaths of a number of people who had been important in his life, including one death with a supremely devastating impact.

The period started when Joseph Kaufman died on June 14, 1940, and Nettie followed on November 1. Although Kaufman had had relatively little in common with his parents except the bond of family, he had treated them with respect and provided for them. Joseph, who lacked a will to work in his later years, was quite proud of his son, and Kaufman in turn, as mentioned, patterned the gentle character of Grandpa Vanderhof in *You Can't Take It with You* partly on his father. Once, after Joseph's death, Kaufman was dining in Lüchow's, the restaurant that had been Joseph's favorite, and the waiter who had always served Joseph apologized because Joseph's preferred table was taken. In the course of the evening, the waiter mentioned that Joseph had always given him and his wife theatre tickets on his birthday, adding that this came to mind because his birthday was approaching. It was just conversation, not a hint, and Kaufman did not reply, but the next day a messenger brought two tickets to *South Pacific* to the restaurant. The popular show had cost Kaufman $28 for the pair, at scalpers' prices, and were accompanied by the note, *In memory of Joseph Kaufman.*

Kaufman had always felt closer to his mother, and once told Ruth that she had inherited Joseph's traits, while he had taken after Nettie. But Nettie was an emotional woman, and Kaufman, caught between his horror of any display of sentiment and his unfailing respect and love for his mother, simply preferred to stay away from her as much as possible. However, Nettie used her telephone to good advantage. From the time of *Dulcy* to the end of her life, Nettie considered it her duty as a mother to give her son advice about his plays and career. She told Kaufman that *Dulcy* had too much talk, and that *Once in a Lifetime* was exaggerated. A tremendous success would not influence her opinion in the least, and she told Kaufman that *You Can't Take It with You* was silly. "People like that," she said, "should be in the crazy house." And when another playwright received especially good notices, Kaufman could usually expect to hear from Nettie on the phone soon after the papers were out. "Did you read what the critics said about the new Eugene O'Neill play?" she would ask. "My, how they plugged it! They never say things like that about *you*." Kaufman could only reply that people like O'Neill were geniuses. But Nettie had an answer for that, too. "They're friends with the critics," she would tell her son. "You should go out more, be more sociable."

Other deaths followed during this period. After Alexander Woollcott's death on January 23, 1943, Kaufman's mother-in-law, Sarah Bakrow, died on April 14, 1943, at the age of seventy-eight. Robert Benchley died on November 21, 1945, and in 1946 the death of George Arliss, the actor, on February 5, was followed on March 13 by the death of George C. Tyler. These deaths alone would have been enough to make Kaufman realize in the most profound way that he was aging. There's a story Garson Kanin tells, appropriate here, about a conversation with David Niven. "Well, David," Kanin had begun, "now that you and I are middle-aged—" and Niven interrupted, saying, "What do you mean, 'middle-aged'?" "Well," Kanin said, "I'll be fifty-five shortly." Niven's reply was, "And how many men do you know who are 110?" Similarly, Kaufman felt that with so many people dying in their seventies and some dying prior to that, thirty-five was really middle age, and he was well into old age. But though all these deaths affected Kaufman, there were others which cut much more deeply.

Sam Harris was not feeling well, and went to Florida in March 1941 to escape the harsh New York weather. But he developed appendicitis there, had to undergo an operation, and had difficulty regaining strength. He was sixty-nine years old. When he returned to New York, he contracted pneumonia, and died on July 2, 1941. Kaufman, Max Gordon, and Moss Hart were all affected deeply by his death. Kaufman's association with Harris had been fabulously rich, and included production of both his Pulitzer Prize plays, *Of Thee I Sing* and *You Can't Take It with You*, and most of the other plays which would stand out as the most famous ones in Kaufman's career, among them *Animal Crackers, Dinner at Eight, Once in a Lifetime, Stage Door,* and *The Man Who Came to Dinner.* Gordon later spoke to Hart and Kaufman about the three of them continuing the producer-writer relationship which the writers had had with Harris, sometimes in association with Gordon. Hart had promised his friend Joseph Hyman that he would go with Hyman, but Kaufman remained with Gordon.

Harris's death and the loss of his sure hand as producer were very difficult for Kaufman. But when Beatrice died suddenly on October 6, 1945, it was a staggering and awful blow that affected Kaufman more than any other event in his life. She was only fifty-one, and her death was a total and grotesque surprise. Kaufman was at the theatre directing Mary Chase's *The Next Half Hour* when Beatrice's doctor phoned him to say that his wife had died suddenly of a cerebral hemorrhage. She had not been feeling well for about a week, but had not been considered in anything remotely approaching a dangerous condition.

Beatrice died on a Saturday night, and her body was cremated, with funeral services held at Campbell's in New York at eight o'clock Monday morning. The chapel was crowded with friends, including many show business greats and such men as Bernard Baruch, former Mayor Jimmy Walker, and Mayor Fiorello H. La Guardia. After the ceremony by Rabbi Jonah Wise, Moss Hart—who had come to Beatrice so often for help and understanding—delivered a eulogy, and he was followed by others. Bennett Cerf's eulogy summed up the feelings of most of Beatrice's friends. "Beatrice Kaufman's love of life and laughter, her abiding interest in the affairs of a myriad of friends, were so great," Cerf said, "that it will be a long time before they realize she is gone. She was the core and the connecting link of scores of people in every walk of life who owe some of their success today to her ever-ready counsel and sympathy when the going was roughest. Part of the fun of doing things was telling Beatrice about them. Her death will leave an unfillable gap in our lives."

"Unfillable gap" was appropriate and literally true for Kaufman. He endured the ceremony white-faced and shaken, repeating over and over, "I'm through. I'll never work again. I'm through." The marriage had not been a sexual union, but Beatrice had been indispensable to him in every other way. She had made an excellent home for him, and was his most prized and trusted guide and critic and friend. For twenty years, she had been a fixture at all his first nights, both plays he had written and those he directed. She had suddenly stopped going, not out of indifference, but because she cared too much about Kaufman's work to stand the pressure. "Openings are unbearable," she said. "The theatre is the cruelest form of creative effort. In a few hours your whole fate is decided."

Not long before Beatrice's death, the Kaufmans had moved to the Park Avenue apartment. "You've at last reached the fifties," Kaufman told Beatrice when they celebrated her fiftieth birthday. "But at least it's the East 50s." Beatrice had nearly always enjoyed good health, but she had been troubled with adolescent acne as a teenager and had taken X-ray treatments, then a popular remedy. More than thirty years later, in the last year of her life, her skin trouble suddenly recurred, perhaps set off by excessive exposure to the sun, and the condition became so bad that she had to have skin grafts and had begun to wear veils to hide her scars. But there had been no expectation whatever of sudden death, and Kaufman was stunned completely. Their problems aside, Beatrice was simply everything to him. His friends, knowing this and then observing the appalling effects of her death upon Kaufman, were certain that he was right when he said that he was through in his work, and they were even more certain that he would never marry again.

Kaufman went through the motions of continuing to direct *The Next Half Hour*, but his heart and mind weren't in it or in anything else. The play opened Wednesday, October 29, 1945, at the Empire Theatre, and closed on Saturday, November 3, after eight performances. Mary Chase had previously written *Harvey*, a comedy, and people expected another comedy, but *The Next Half Hour* was a grim drama. The story concerns a superstitious Irish woman, who believes that the cry of the banshee heralds death. She hears the banshee cry, and fears for her older son, who has been having an affair with a married woman, and she sends her younger son to warn him. But the younger son is killed, and it is the woman's fault for interfering with fate, since "the next half hour belongs to God." The dark, death-filled nature of the play was all too consistent with the events in Kaufman's own life.

The listlessness that gripped Kaufman after Beatrice's death was especially evident because the years prior to her death had been busy ones for Kaufman, and had included a hit, *The Late George Apley*, in 1944. Kaufman had collaborated on the play with John P. Marquand, based on Marquand's Pulitzer Prize-winning novel of the same name. Marquand, one of the most immensely successful writers of his time, was born in Wilmington, Delaware, on November 10, 1893, but grew up and spent most of his life in Newburyport, Massachusetts. He graduated—in three years—from Harvard, where he wrote for *The Lampoon*, and then worked briefly in newspaper reporting and magazine editing before serving as an officer in France in World War I. After the war, and after another period of newspaper work and a brief try at advertising copywriting, Marquand decided to attempt to become a writer of fiction for magazines, and was immediately successful, consistently selling all his work to the best magazines and at the highest rates. His fiction was snapped up by Hollywood and by stage groups, and the income from these and other subsidiary sales helped his earnings soar. Among his better known creations during this period was the Japanese detective, Mr. Moto. But in 1937, Marquand took a more serious, deliberate turn in *The Late George Apley*, bringing his talent to bear on characters coping with deep personal crises and conflicts. Sales of his new, serious work matched those of his lighter books. Between the publication of *The Late George Apley* and the time of his collaboration with Kaufman, Marquand had written three more best-selling novels in the same general style, *Wickford Point*, *H. M. Pulham Esq.*, and *So Little Time*.

The Late George Apley had been published for seven years when Kaufman and Marquand began their collaboration, but neither film nor stage producers had shown strong interest in it until Max Gordon read the book, fell in love with it, insisted that Kaufman work with Marquand, and arranged for the collaboration. Marquand later referred to the fact that his book was set in the social and cultural life of Boston, saying, "I know nothing about writing for the stage and I understand Mr. Kaufman knows nothing about Boston. We should get along famously." And they did, in fact, despite Marquand's socially inbred anti-Semitism, which he dropped completely with regard to Kaufman. However, Beatrice did once bring about Mrs. Marquand's abrupt departure from a stay at Cherchez La Farm. Mrs. Marquand had joined her husband at the estate, and gave her number to her friend, Anne Morrow Lindbergh, the wife of Charles Lindbergh. When Beatrice learned that Mrs. Lindbergh had called for Mrs. Marquand, she questioned Mrs. Marquand's taste, and Mrs. Marquand reacted by bursting into tears and leaving. Lindbergh, of course, had been prominent in the ultra-right "America First" movement, and Beatrice's politics were liberal.

The Late George Apley is a rich and rambling novel, and had to be condensed to a few episodes for the play. The play concerns a Boston Brahmin in the years before World War I, and the consternation and conflict caused by his son's and daughter's decisions to marry outside their circle. The son relents and returns to the fold of the Boston establishment, but the daughter elopes, and the implication is that she will lead a freer, more rewarding life. The play opened at the Lyceum Theatre on Tuesday, November 21, 1944, after a successful tryout tour which included runs in Wilmington, Delaware, Washington, D.C., Baltimore, and Boston, and received very enthusiastic reviews. "*The Late George Apley*," said Robert Garland in the *Journal-American*, "is high comedy with a bite, adroitly dramatized from a fine American novel, staged with every excellence the modern showshop has to offer, acted to perfection. In other and few words, Max Gordon has another good one on his hands." Wilella Waldorf wrote in the *Post* that the play "ought to have little trouble running as long as *Life with Father*," and said that it was "genuinely comic in the best theatrical sense." The critics also were pleased with Leo G. Carroll's performance in the leading role. But they had a field day picking out anachronisms in the play, such as a reference to the Copley-Plaza Hotel in 1912 when it hadn't been built until 1915, a discussion of the appointment of Judge Felix Frankfurter to the faculty of the Harvard Law School two years before it happened, and several other points. Kaufman commented on this in a funny piece called *On Getting 'Mr. Apley' Straight*, which appeared in the New York *Times* on November 26, 1944. Kaufman wrote, "Never write a play that depicts the habits and modes of a certain group of people, for they will arise to confront you with a thousand accusations of inaccuracy. Never write a play laid in any particular period, for the same reason. Never write a play with a room in it, still for the same reason.

"And oh yes—never write a play."

The Late George Apley was a great success, and ran for 357 performances before closing on November 17, 1945, and going on a very profitable tour. Kaufman owned 25 per cent of the play, which was included in *The Best Plays of 1944–45*. The play was bought by Twentieth Century-Fox, and the film, directed by Joseph L. Mankiewicz with a screenplay by Philip Dunne, and with Ronald Colman in the leading role, was released on March 20, 1947. Gordon thought that he had done extremely well to have produced such a hit from a seven-year-old novel, and later mentioned having been nettled by Kaufman's carefully unimpressed attitude. "I remarked to George," Gordon said, "about what a good idea it had been to make him read the book. 'I can't understand,' I said, 'why no one else ever thought of doing this play.' 'Oh,' he said drily, 'someone would have.' "

Marquand, who worked during the Second World War as a Navy correspondent and special consultant to the Secretary of War, went on with his string of best-selling and highly regarded novels, including *Repent in Haste* in 1945, *Point of No Return* in 1949, *Melville Goodwin, U.S.A.* in 1951, and *Women and Thomas Harrow* in 1958. He died on July 16, 1960, at the age of sixty-six.

A month following the opening of *The Late George Apley*, Kaufman was represented by a sketch in Billy Rose's revue, *The Seven Lively Arts*. The sketch, *Local Boy Makes Good*, concerns the lofty independence of stage hands. Kaufman had been slated to direct the show, but withdrew after arguing with the fiery Rose the first time they discussed it. Rose had had a remarkable career. In his teens, he won a shorthand speed contest, setting a world record, and became secretary to Bernard Baruch. He then drifted into song writing, which in turn led him into production. He learned a lot from Baruch and salted away much of his money in blue-chip stocks, so that at his death, Rose was the largest single private owner of stock in American Telephone & Telegraph. Kaufman liked to poke fun at Rose's short stature, and once, during the planning of *The Seven Lively Arts*, was asked, "What's Rose up to?" "Your waist," Kaufman replied.

The Seven Lively Arts included, in addition to Kaufman's sketch, sketches and monologues by Hart, Ben Hecht, "Doc" Rockwell (the comedian whose son, George Lincoln Rockwell, became head of the American Nazi Party and was eventually murdered), and others. The revue, which was backed by an advance sale of $500,000, featured music by Cole Porter, music for a ballet by Stravinsky, for which he was paid $5000, and murals in the lobby by Salvador Dali. Opening night tickets, which officially were $24, were sold at vastly higher prices by scalpers. The revue tried out only in Philadelphia, at the Forrest Theatre, and was rushed to open December 7, 1944, at the Ziegfeld Theatre, as a "commemoration and denial of Pearl Habor." *The Seven*

Lively Arts was a hit and ran for 183 performances, closing May 12, 1945.

Kaufman's next venture—also before Beatrice's death—was *Hollywood Pinafore*, a satirical update of Gilbert and Sullivan's H.M.S. *Pinafore*, using the original score. Kaufman got the idea during a card game when he heard Charles Lederer playing with W. S. Gilbert's lyric about how one becomes "ruler of the Queen's navee." Lederer's verse ran,

"He nodded his head and never said no,
"And now he's the head of the studio."

Kaufman was electrified. He asked where Lederer had got the lyric, and when Lederer said that he'd made it up, Kaufman offered to buy it. Lederer couldn't see the point of selling anything of that kind, but said he'd sign a paper giving Kaufman the lines in return for a present for his wife. Lederer asked what earthly use Kaufman could have for such doggerel, and Kaufman said, "Those two lines will grow into *Hollywood Pinafore*." They did, and the idea delighted Kaufman so much that he enjoyed working on it more than he had enjoyed writing anything in years. Recalling some past troubles with composers, he said, "It's a pleasure to work with a composer who's dead." Meyer Davis, "bandleader for millionaires," joined Max Gordon in producing the show, and also made a large investment. Davis had started his career with one band and expanded until he had thirty bands playing under his name for society functions. He understood music and thought he understood show business, but when he ventured to make a suggestion at rehearsal, Kaufman's cold look cut him short. He learned, as the cast and Gordon already knew, that Kaufman was boss at rehearsals.

Kaufman used the plot of the original *Pinafore*, but, in keeping with Lederer's original notion, changed the Admiral to the head of a studio. Brenda Blossom, the studio's star, is in love with Ralph Rickstraw, a writer, and this, of course, is too far beneath her station for them to marry. But things are resolved in the end, thanks to the efforts of Louhedda Hopsons, celebrated gossip columnist, who takes the place of Gilbert and Sullivan's Little Buttercup. The cast included Victor Moore, William Gaxton, and Shirley Booth, and the show, of which Kaufman had 25 per cent, opened

[597]

at the Alvin Theatre on Thursday, May 31, 1945, after a tryout in Baltimore. The show seemed a likely candidate for a hit, but achieved only fifty-two performances and closed July 14. Robert Garland summed up critical opinion when he said, "Well, *Hollywood Pinafore* is better in theory than in performance." The trouble seemed to be that the original lyrics were so familiar that audiences didn't like having them replaced by something new.

The devastation caused by Beatrice's death was so crippling to Kaufman that he wavered and wandered for months, feeling, in an abstract way, that he should try to resume work, but remaining unable to concentrate on or feel enthusiasm for any new project. He managed a short humor piece for *The New Yorker's Department of Amplification*, which appeared in the June 20, 1946, issue, and, as mentioned, dealt with a phrase popular with critics, "judicious pruning." John McCarten, the magazine's movie critic, had used the phrase, saying that the film version of *Henry V* needed it, and Kaufman speculated on what the phrase really meant. But the short article was not a sign that Kaufman had recovered, and Kaufman had to be talked into returning to work on the stage. When he did return to work, however, he entered several projects without enthusiasm, still missing Beatrice. He agreed to collaborate on a new play, *Park Avenue*, with Nunnally Johnson, the screenwriter and producer whose film credits included *The Grapes of Wrath, Holy Matrimony*, and others. Arthur Schwartz and Ira Gershwin joined them to do the music and lyrics. The story concerns a much-married group of people who constantly shed and wed new mates, and critics called it a "one-joke play," praising the score far more than the book. Kaufman's lack of enthusiasm and confidence plagued him throughout his work on the show, making him apathetic about issues which he normally would have handled crisply and decisively. During the tryout, when Jed Prouty had to be replaced in the part of Mr. Meacham, Max Gordon was so exasperated with Kaufman's delay in hiring David Wayne, the only available replacement, that he said, "George, stop fucking around and hire him," language rarely used by Gordon and virtually never used by or to Kaufman. When the play got a bad reception in Boston, the little strength that Kaufman had been able to pool out of his misery evaporated, and he told Gordon, "You've got to save me."

The show, of which Gordon and Kaufman each had 25 per cent, opened at the Shubert Theatre, despite everyone's misgivings, on Monday, November 4, 1946, and limped through seventy-two performances. Leonora Corbett received best reviews for her handling of the starring role.

Kaufman had been contributing articles to magazines regularly before Beatrice's death, but afterward, with the exception of the "judicious pruning" column, it was two years before he began to resume his old pace. Before Beatrice's death, he had done the poem, *In Nineteen Fifty-four*, for the February 4, 1945, issue of *Playbill*, a funny piece called *By the Way* for *The Saturday Review*'s issue of August 11, 1945, and, for *The New Yorker*'s issue of the same date, he wrote *Notes for a Film Biography*. The latter article was prompted by Kaufman's viewing of the movie version of George Gershwin's life, and is a hilarious satire on the liberties taken and the melodramatic padding added by Hollywood biographers. In the piece, Kaufman describes quite ordinary events in his own life and gives pointers to screenwriters on how they might improve on them whenever they get around to committing his life to film.

It was not until August 2, 1947, in *The New Yorker*, that Kaufman returned with a piece of the usual length, *School for Waiters*. Then he wrote a poem, *That Morning Mail*, which appeared in the *New York Times Magazine* on April 18, 1948. The poem contrasts the things Kaufman would like to receive in his mail with what he actually gets. For *The New Yorker*'s issue of November 26, 1949, Kaufman wrote *The Great Kibitzers Strike of 1926*, the lighthearted fantasy in which he describes the havoc wrought when the bridge-game kibitzers of the nation walked out in protest of their mistreatment at the hands of players.

After *Park Avenue*, Arthur Schwartz turned producer for a revue called *Inside USA*, starring Beatrice Lillie and Jack Haley. It was announced that Kaufman would write sketches for the revue, but when it opened on Friday, April 30, 1948, at the Century Theatre, Kaufman was given credit only for supplying the idea for one sketch, based on his *New Yorker* piece, *School for Waiters*. It was written by Arnold Auerbach.

Kaufman next became involved in directing Gertrude Tonkonogy's *Town House*, based on John Cheever's stories in *The New Yorker*. Miss Tonkonogy had written *Three-Cornered Moon* in 1933, when she had been a $25-a-week secretary in Brooklyn, and the play had been well-received by the critics, with a nine-and-a-half week run which might have been longer in any other year but depressed 1933. That play had also been notable to Miss Tonkonogy because Eric Pinker, her literary agent, misappropriated $10,000 of her royalties, along with $20,000 belonging to E. Phillips Oppenheim, the mystery writer, and went to prison.

Recently, Miss Tonkonogy, now Mrs. Charles Friedberg and the mother of a grown son and daugher, recalled working with Kaufman. "After discussing some of the faults in my play, he said, 'Well, how shall we do this? Do you like to sit at the typewriter or do you pace?' I was too befuddled to realize that he was suggesting collaboration. I didn't know what he was talking about.

"I couldn't have collaborated anyhow. I can't work that way. We set up a series of conferences, after each of which I took the play home to rewrite according to his suggestions, until the script suited him.

"I admired his professional honesty and lack of cant. No emotion, no sentiment shadowed the work. There was no ego to struggle with, no temperament to step carefully around. There was just the job at hand. Nothing else mattered. He was generous, painstaking, brilliantly critical, always constructive."

Town House opened on Thursday, September 23, 1948, at the National Theatre, and failed badly, running only twelve performances.

Kaufman also worked as director in 1949 on *Pretty Penny* by Jerome Chodorov, with music and lyrics by Harold Rome. An actor in the play, David Burns, who has since died, would not take direction and grew quite heated and ugly about it, calling Kaufman obscene names. Kaufman brought him up on charges before Equity, which reprimanded Burns. Burns left the play, which was then in tryout. "We originally intended," Rome recalls, "to try it out on summer circuit, but found after opening in Bucks County that, under Equity rules, we could not rehearse once we opened, so we played the summer tour and closed it. We played Boston after Bucks County, and ended the tour at Westport. All in all, it was a rather disappointing venture which George's sense of humor made bearable."

Failure plagued Kaufman again when he took on William Walden's *Metropole*, which opened on Wednesday, December 6, 1949, at the Lyceum Theatre. Walden is a native New Yorker who, after a variety of jobs and a stretch in the Army, went to work at *The New Yorker* as a secretary to Harold Ross, and eventually became a department head on the magazine. *Metropole* tells the story of the editor of a periodical of that name, who has to fight *Gothamite*, founded by one of his former wives. The editor, who was patterned after Harold Ross, loses his job, but regains it in the end when his readers protest his departure. Lee Tracy did well in the leading role, but the play was universally panned. "The astonishing thing," Whitney Bolton wrote in the *Telegraph*, "is that it is offered under such important and habitually wise auspices. Not only does the sagacious and learned Max Gordon produce it, but no less a monarch of drama than George S. Kaufman has staged it. Alas, the result is disordered, dislocated, and not very funny." Kaufman and Gordon each had 25 per cent of the play, but it ran for only two performances.

During the casting for *Metropole*, an actress who applied was appearing in a Shakespeare play, but said she would leave if she got the part in *Metropole*. Kaufman told her, "From Shakespeare to Walden is quite a sleeper jump, even for Eskimos." Then, during rehearsals, a young actress pronounced "editor" so it sounded like "aiditor." Kaufman asked her, "Are you Southern?" The girl hesitated, then admitted, "I was." "Honey," Kaufman said, "you *is*."

Max Gordon had decided to close *Metropole* without bringing it to New York, but then changed his mind, and Walden had assumed at the time that the decision was Gordon's alone and had been based on his assessment of the play's chances. But three months later, he read an altogether different explanation in *Variety*. "Decision to bring *Metropole* to Broadway," *Variety* reported, "instead of closing during the out-of-town tryout, was at the insistence of stager George S. Kaufman. Arguing that because the author, William Walden, had never had a play produced on Broadway he was entitled to at least a hearing, Kaufman guaranteed to make good any losses involved in bringing the show to Broadway. Kaufman's action is understood to have cost him about $5000. Situation has been a closely held secret. Not even Walden was informed." After reading the item, Walden called Kaufman to thank him. Kaufman replied, in the distant manner he always used when someone tried to thank him, that *Variety* was in error. "Knowing *Variety* and George S. Kaufman," Walden says, "I knew better."

In the wake of Beatrice's death, Kaufman had resigned from the Players Club, a membership he had held for ten years, and his visits to his other club, the Lambs, grew increasingly infrequent. It was at the Lambs Club in that period that someone suggested he read Laura Z. Hobson's *Gentleman's Agreement*, which dealt with anti-Semitism. He replied, "I don't need to spend $2.50 to find out what it means to be a Jew."

There were other reminders that Kaufman was enduring this greatest crisis of his life with his wit fully intact. One of the best of these occurred during the unsuccessful run of *Park Avenue*, just a little more than a year after Beatrice's death. After one performance, Kaufman and Nunnally Johnson came to the stage door late, just as Leonora Corbett, the leading lady, was leaving the stage. "How did it go?" Johnson asked her, although he and Kaufman already knew that the performance had been just another losing battle in the play's dismal run. "Terrific!" Leonora replied. Kaufman gave her a sour look. "Some people live in a fool's paradise," he said, "and you, Leonora, have a duplex."

29. THE SECOND WIFE

WHEN KAUFMAN FIRST saw Leueen MacGrath, at a party given by Ruth Goetz, he didn't try to meet her, despite the fact that she was the party's center of attention. Robert Morley had just brought his hit London play, *Edward, My Son*, to Broadway for an opening on September 30, 1948, and along with the raves for Morley's performances, the critics, as described earlier, were captivated completely by the beauty of Miss MacGrath, pronounced "McGrah," who played Morley's mistress. Kaufman's silence at the party was anything but a sign of indifference to the young actress' beauty and grace. He was fascinated. He stalked discreetly around her part of the room, content, for now, simply to watch. Something about Leueen affected Kaufman as no woman except Beatrice had ever done.

Kaufman had had a great deal of experience in arranging meetings with young ladies, and, since Leueen was especially important, his arrangement of their first encounter was skillful and cautious. He set up a party at his Park Avenue apartment and invited Ruth Gordon and Garson Kanin, knowing that they were having Leueen as a dinner guest that night. When Ruth tried to express regret, saying that she and Kanin were taking a couple of friends to dinner, Kaufman brushed the problem aside. "Bring them along," he said. Leueen, it developed, wanted to meet Kaufman about as much as he wanted to meet her, since she came straight to the party from rehearsal, carrying the bound copy of the play by Philip Barry, with her name, hotel, and phone number inscribed on the flyleaf. When she left the party, as mentioned, she forgot the book. Asked about this later, she said quickly, "I don't think I left it intentionally—" then paused, and added, "Well, maybe—" Kaufman lost no time in responding. He was on the phone to her early the next morning. She didn't answer, and he dashed off a note and sent it to the hotel by messenger. He'd be glad to return the book—at dinner, that evening, at his apartment. Leueen accepted, and the romance flourished.

Leueen, born in London and educated at Sacré-Coeur, in Lausanne, Switzerland, Farnborough Convent College, England, and Les Tourelles, Brussels, was the daughter of a mining engineer who took his family with him in his travels through Europe and Asia. Her mother loved the theatre, and in her last years wrote plays that were never produced. The first play Leueen saw herself was *Peter Pan*, when she was seven. She immediately announced that she was going to be an actress, so that she could fly like Peter, and her ambition never wavered. When she completed her general education, she accepted what she considered a compromise and enrolled in the Royal Academy of Dramatic Arts in London. "There was a row with Father," she later recalled. "I ran away on a Saturday, got a job with a repertory company on Monday, made up with Father on Tuesday, and returned to the Academy on Wednesday." After graduating from the Academy at the age of nineteen, she got her first part, which she described as "a one-liner in a ghastly thing called *Beggars from Hell*." A succession of roles followed until January 1937, when she succeeded

Jessica Tandy as the ingénue lead in Terence Rattigan's *French Without Tears*, for a two-and-a-half year run.

She appeared in a variety of roles during the war years. She said that the British government was conscripting labor for the coal mines, and any actor whose roles amounted to less than a certain minimum was liable for service. "I had a horror," she said, "that they were going to count the minutes in some of mine and send me off." However, she obtained the part of the spirit in Noël Coward's *Blithe Spirit*, which toured the soldiers' camps in Italy and North Africa, and other roles after the war led to her part in *Edward, My Son*, which opened in London in May 1947. Although American movie companies usually wait until an English play is firmly established on Broadway before they will even consider buying film rights, M-G-M moved swiftly to acquire *Edward, My Son* while it was still in London, and even filmed its version of the play in London while the show was still running. Leueen played opposite Spencer Tracy in the film, returned to the play, and moved with it to New York.

Shortly after she met Kaufman, Leueen talked about men in an interview. After discussing Robert Morley, Alexander Woollcott, whom she had met in London, and Emlyn Williams, she said of Kaufman, "I admire George S. Kaufman, as a human being, more than anyone I know. It's rare to find anyone of such staggering honesty." Kaufman felt that she was just as rare, and pursued her ardently. He had plenty of competition, especially from Thomas Heggen, the young ex-sailor who had written *Mister Roberts*, the very popular book which Heggen and Joshua Logan turned into the equally successful play and film.

It was no secret on Broadway that Kaufman was interested in the lovely British actress, but it was assumed, especially in light of Kaufman's continued sadness about Beatrice, that this was a more or less casual affair. It came as a complete shock when Kaufman announced on May 19, 1949 that he and Leueen would be married the following week. They were married on May 26, at Cherchez La Farm, with a local justice of the peace performing the ceremony. He was fifty-nine years old and she was thirty-five. It was her third marriage, her previous ones having been to two young Englishmen, Christopher Burn and Desmond Davis.

"I don't know what George was thinking about when he asked Leueen to marry him," one of his friends said, echoing the feelings of most of Kaufman's friends.

The day after the wedding announcement, Thomas Heggen was found dead in his bathtub, in the apartment he shared with Alan Campbell. Campbell, Dorothy Parker's former husband, was in California at the time. A partially filled bottle of sleeping tablets was found on the washstand near the tub, and the police announced that it was not a homicide. Campbell said that Heggen was under doctor's orders to take a sleeping pill each night for insomnia, and it was his opinion that Heggen had taken just one pill, dozed off in the bathtub, and slipped under fourteen inches of water in his sleep. Campbell rejected emphatically any hypothesis that Heggen was a suicide. "I talked to him yesterday on the phone and he was in wonderful spirits," he said. "He said he was feeling fine and his work was going well. A young man with that much money, such a great success, busy and thanking his stars to be out of the Navy, could never have killed himself." But many people feel that he took his life because of his loss of Leueen to Kaufman.

Anne later said that the first years of Kaufman's marriage to Leueen were the happiest of his life. "I think Daddy found both a wife and a daughter in Leueen," she said. "She seemed to be what neither Mummy nor I could ever be to him." Others commented on Kaufman's desire to please his new wife, and saw his eagerness as being almost sad. Mrs. Richard Rodgers once saw him literally run up the stairs to get a sweater for Leueen when the weather turned chilly, and Moss Hart was another who thought that Kaufman was behaving like a teenager in love for the first time.

Leueen made some remarkable changes in Kaufman. He had always avoided animals, but Leueen wanted a pet. She first talked about getting a dog, but settled for a blue-eyed Siamese kitten. Kaufman tried to ignore the cat, whose name was Adam, "but somehow or other," Leueen said, "the cat worked his way into George's affection. One day I discovered Adam curled up, sleeping on three-quarters of George's typewriter chair. George, perched precariously on the edge of the chair, was typing away." Leueen also felt that they would be happier in a new apartment, one without the memories of Beatrice, so Kaufman took a penthouse apartment at 1035 Park Avenue. It was light, airy, and modern, in contrast to the more sedate, dignified style Beatrice had favored. Kaufman's bedroom in the penthouse was still furnished with his narrow bed and the old writing desk he had used for a quarter century, and he also brought along his old, four-foot-high wastebasket. But the walls were covered with pictures, enough to have made up for the disappointment Moss Hart had felt at the beginning of his first collaboration with Kaufman, when he had found a dark room decorated only by the picture of Mark Twain. Now, among others, there were pictures of Leueen, Beatrice, and Anne, and Alexander Woollcott and Edna Ferber shared wall space with the etching of Mark Twain, a portrait of George M. Cohan, and a picture of Moss Hart inscribed, "To George—without whom—" Kaufman also began to adopt a brighter style of dress, and an interviewer described him in the penthouse as "turned out with some care in a blue, pin-striped suit, shocking red weskit, and black and red argyle socks."

A month after the marriage, it was announced that Kaufman would direct a Broadway presentation of Jean Giraudoux's *The Enchanted*, with Leueen playing the schoolteacher who falls in love with a ghost. The play was set to open in late September, but Leueen suddenly began to suffer loss of appetite and general weakness, and had to spend two weeks in Johns Hopkins Hospital in Baltimore, delaying the opening at the Lyceum Theatre to Wednesday, January 18, 1950. The play, with Wesley Addy, Malcolm Keen, Una O'Connor, and John Baragrey also in the cast, was a flop, running for only forty-five performances and closing on February 25 with a loss of $65,084. William Hawkins in the *World-Telegram* had high praise for Kaufman's work on the play. "George S. Kaufman has done one of his best jobs in years," Hawkins wrote, "directing an extraordinary cast with a dry sort of containment that never lets any of them seem to be 'acting,' and does the play the honor of letting it speak for itself." But other critics felt that the play was just too weak. Howard Barnes of the *Herald Tribune*, for example, said, "All of George S. Kaufman's cunning direction is dimmed by a muddle of aphorisms, metaphors, and odd pronouncements on a wide range of subjects."

A flop always bothered Kaufman, but this one was especially upsetting since he had wanted a hit for Leueen.

With nothing on the theatrical horizon for either of them, Leueen persuaded Kaufman to take her to London. In the meantime, two young producers, Cy Feuer and Ernest Martin, had decided to present a musical, called *Guys and Dolls*, based on a short story by Damon Runyon. Cy Feuer was born in New York on January 15, 1911, son of a theatrical general manager. Feuer attended Juilliard School of Music, headed the music department of Republic Pictures from 1938 to 1942, joined the U. S. Army Air Corps for the war, and returned to Republic from 1945 to 1947. He then joined Ernest Martin to form a play production company. Martin was born in Los Angeles on August 18, 1919, and was also working for Republic when he met Feuer. The two decided to go to New York together and try to scrape up enough money to finance a play. Their first production was *Where's Charley?*, the hit musical update of the venerable *Charley's Aunt,* and a tremendous success for Ray Bolger.

Feuer and Martin gave their new idea to Jo Swerling, the screenwriter and dramatist. Born April 8, 1897, Swerling's credits included *Platinum Blonde* for Jean Harlow. The producers felt that Swerling's adaptation needed more work, and turned to Abe Burrows, then a radio writer with no playwriting experience, but whose radio credits were so impressive that Feuer and Martin felt that he was just the man to breathe the spirit of Damon Runyon's lovable gangsters into the play. Burrows was born in New York on December 18, 1910. His father was a retailer of paints and wallpaper, and sent his son to college to learn to be a businessman. Burrows dutifully went to work as an accountant and on Wall Street, but changed his direction and went into radio, working on the writing staffs of *Texaco Star Theatre, The Rudy Vallee Program,* and *This Is New York*. He was the writer of *Duffy's Tavern, The Dinah Shore Show,* and *The Joan Davis Show,* before getting his own show, *The Abe Burrows Show,* on CBS in 1946. Burrows had met Kaufman in the course of his radio work, and it was Burrows who suggested to Feuer and Martin that Kaufman would be the best director for *Guys and Dolls*.

The producers were delighted with Burrows's idea, and Martin flew to London to talk to Kaufman, taking only the first act, which was all Burrows had completed. Burrows had discarded all that Swerling had written, and had started fresh. Kaufman was unenthusiastic about the assignment during his first conversation with Martin, both because he didn't want to cut short his stay in London with Leueen, who was close to a deal for a play there and would have to stay, and because he had heard that Feuer and Martin had been difficult to work with during the production of *Where's Charley?* But he agreed to read the script while Martin left for a week in Paris. When Martin returned, Kaufman had studied the script until he knew it from memory and had even worked out a lot of stage business. He was still, however, reluctant to leave Leueen, even though he was quite taken with what he had seen of the script, and Martin wired Feuer that he doubted Kaufman could be persuaded to leave.

Feuer was disappointed, but Frank Loesser, the composer, was even more upset. He sensed a big hit—if the direction was right—and he wanted Kaufman badly. Loesser, one of the better popular song writers, had done the score for the films *Sing You Sinners* in 1938, *Priorities on Parade* in 1942 and *The Perils of Pauline* in 1947. His songs, *Praise the Lord and Pass the Ammunition* and *Rodger Young*, had been World War II hits, and his *Baby, It's Cold Outside*, in 1948, from *Neptune's Daughter*, the Esther Williams film, had won an Academy Award. His first Broadway show had been *Where's Charley?* Loesser hit upon the idea of approaching Max Gordon and asking his help in persuading Kaufman to direct the musical. He played and sang the score for Gordon, who then cabled Kaufman to stop resisting. TAKE IT, Gordon cabled, IT'LL BE ONE OF THE PLUMS OF YOUR CAREER. Kaufman took the next boat home.

When Kaufman saw the finished script, he observed, "Abe can get closer to the flavor of Broadway than that," but he did not do any actual writing. He gave his opinions and Burrows executed them. Burrows had a tremendous regard for Kaufman and followed his suggestions fully, except in the love scenes, the traditionally bad area for Kaufman. The two men worked together in a hideaway in New Jersey, and Kaufman's instructions were very explicit. "Write the next scene like this," he'd say, outlining the scene in great detail, and Burrows would go upstairs and write the scene exactly as outlined. Kaufman was constantly impressed by the speed with which

Burrows wrote the scenes, and Burrows was impressed by Kaufman's generosity in giving so much help without demanding payment or even credit. Later, Burrows was equally generous in telling people how much Kaufman had helped him. "All I did was just what Kaufman told me to do," he said. "And it worked."

But while Kaufman continued to prompt Burrows to polish his lines throughout the rehearsals, he was, as always, death on actors who tried their hand at improving the script. When Tom Pedi, who played Harry the Horse in the show, undertook to alter a couple of his lines, Kaufman called him and Burrows over to a corner. "Mr. Burrows," he asked, "would you consider giving Mr. Pedi credit as co-author?"

Guys and Dolls opened for its tryout in Philadelphia and was a hit from the first moment. But because Feuer and Martin wanted it to arrive on Broadway in what they called "perfect" shape, everyone continued to tinker with the show, and it was kept in Philadelphia for five weeks. At one point, Feuer and Martin were so steeped in revisions that they were beginning to lose perspective, and during a taxi ride to the theatre, Kaufman warned the producers not to press the panic button and start pandering to the lowest common denominator. Martin had said that he wanted a show that would appeal not just to the Broadway audiences, but to audiences everywhere. "Don't degrade it," Kaufman said, "by throwing in more girls and stuff. I think we've got something exceptional, almost literary, in a way."

The well-known story concerns a gambler, Skye Masterson, who bets that he can persuade any girl to go with him to the then fashionable resort of Havana after only a brief acquaintance. Nathan Detroit, the gambler betting him, has the right to pick the girl, and chooses a young woman from the Salvation Army, Sarah Brown. Masterson gets her to go to Havana by capitalizing on her concern for her failing mission, which is about to close for lack of business. He promises to deliver plenty of sinners, and fulfills his pledge by supplying the mission with all the gamblers it can handle. Masterson not only wins his bet, but also marries the girl. Robert Alda, who had played George Gershwin in the film about Gershwin's life, played Skye Masterson, Isabel Bigley played Sarah Brown, Sam Levene played Nathan Detroit, and Vivian Blaine was his girl friend, as she was later in the film.

Guys and Dolls opened at the 46th Street Theatre on Friday, November 24, 1950, and was an immediate and sensational hit. The critics were wildly enthusiastic. Brooks Atkinson said, "*Guys and Dolls* is a work of art, gutsy and uproarious," and Robert Coleman said in the *Mirror*, "Cy Feuer and Ernest Martin brought a musical champ to the 46th Street Theatre last night. It had everything, as a top-flight stake runner should." The show had an incredible run of 1200 performances, and at one point a net profit of $1,865,816 *before* movie money was reported. The price for the film rights was the highest ever paid up to that time. Samuel Goldwyn got the movie rights by bidding $1,000,000 plus 10 per cent of the world-wide gross over $10,000,000, outbidding M-G-M's offer of $850,000 and outdoing the highest previous payment for film rights, which was $850,000, paid by Columbia for *Born Yesterday*. The cast of the movie seemed somewhat miscast, with Marlon Brando playing the lead and singing in an indifferent voice, Frank Sinatra as Nathan Detroit, and a British actress, Jean Simmons, as Sarah Brown, but the picture was a hit, anyway. After the close of its Broadway run, the show was taken, cast intact, to London's Coliseum Theatre, where it ran a year and a half.

When the show was being prepared for its London opening, Martin and Kaufman went to see Oliver Messel, the set designer they wanted for the show. Messel was highly placed socially and a friend of the royal family. On the way down to see him, Kaufman kept reminding Martin not to lose his temper and to be as agreeable as possible. But it was Kaufman who objected when Messel wanted to keep a scene which Kaufman had cut, because Messel thought it would make a great set. "You want me to leave in a bad scene," Kaufman asked, "just so you can have an excuse for a set?" In another demonstration of his overriding concern with the quality of the show, he opposed Frank Loesser when Loesser wanted to include a reprise of songs in the second act. "If you reprise the songs," Kaufman said, "we'll reprise the jokes."

Soon after their marriage, Kaufman learned that Leueen had writing aspirations. Leueen, it developed, had written verse, short stories, and dramas since she was eighteen. Beatrice had picked collaborators other than her husband, but Leueen wanted to work with Kaufman. They started with a movie script, *And Baby Makes Two*, which they wrote in the summer of 1950, and which was never sold. It tells the story of a lovely, naive girl who has an affair with an artist whose name she never bothers to ask. After he goes away, she discovers she's pregnant, and she and the baby make two instead of three. The family do all they can to find the artist, but, in the meantime, Grandma becomes famous as a primitive painter à la Grandma Moses. A portrait by her of her granddaughter and fatherless great-granddaughter is seen by the straying artist and brings him back to his former love. Grandma happily retitles her painting, *Family Reunion*, but the screen then enlarges to show that this has been a screening of the film by censors, who proceed to voice complaints that the girl was not punished for her sin. The film's director protests that they should wait for the ending, and when the ending comes it shows the girl ten years later, in a kitchen crammed with dirty dishes and ten screaming kids. She's reading a note from her husband, which says, "I've left for Paris."

When Kaufman and Leueen went to London after the failure of *The Enchanted*, they were already talking about collaborating on a play, but no adequate idea occurred to them. They talked about revising *And Baby Makes Two*, but Kaufman knew that while it had been fun to write, no studio would ever buy it. But before the voyage was over, Kaufman and Leueen had begun speculating about a married couple they had observed among the passengers. It seemed to Leueen that the husband had outgrown the wife intellectually, and they began discussing this as the basis for a play until they had a play outlined by the time they docked. Later they flew to the Riviera to write the play in the sun. This was a shock to all who knew Kaufman, who, traditionally, avoided flying, but he was continuing to change with Leueen. The play, originally titled *The Still Small Hours*, and finally called *The Small Hours*, concerns the mousy wife of a dynamic publisher, and her feeling of being excluded from his circle of intellectual friends. "It was hard work," Leueen said later about the collaboration. "But it was fun. And, if I must say so, George is a driver. He knows writing discipline, and I was thoroughly introduced to that art."

Kaufman enjoyed initiating his wife in the rigors of playwriting, and pursued the project with the same fervor that he displayed in his most serious and professional collaborations, but he was ambivalent about Leueen's writing ambitions, and tolerated rather than welcomed them. Throughout his life, Kaufman knew, he had frequently made the mistake of accepting collaborators whose skills and talents did not really begin to approach his, and he was at his most vulnerable with regard to Leueen. Now, all at once, they had a full play, and he had to try to get it produced.

The deal he eventually made was the usual split of 50 per cent of ownership with Gordon, with investors owning the other 50 per cent. Gordon went in extremely reluctantly, and when he discovered that he'd made a major mistake—he first estimated costs at $75,000, then realized that the play would cost $100,000—he suggested to Kaufman that they scrap the project. But Kaufman talked him into going ahead. Kaufman also boosted the play by doing a piece about the writing of it, *Amazing Anecdotes,* which appeared in the New York *Times* on February 11, 1951. *The Small Hours* opened on Thursday, February 15, 1951, at the National Theatre. Kaufman, who staged the play, was there on opening night, but Leueen was out of town playing in a tryout of *The High Ground,* a British murder mystery set in a nunnery. *The High Ground* came to Broadway on February 21, and Leueen, who played an unfortunate artist who is condemned to death for the murder of her brother but later exonerated through the efforts of a nun, received excellent reviews. But both *The Small Hours* and *The High Ground* failed, *The Small Hours* closing after twenty performances and *The High Ground* after twenty-three.

Kaufman then wrote *My Book and I,* for *The New Yorker,* which appeared in the issue of May 26, 1951. The article concerns the fact that Kaufman always carried a book when he traveled to places like Hollywood, but it's always the same book, because he gets so busy that he never reads.

The Kaufmans' next project was a comedy, *Fancy Meeting You Again,* about a girl who pursues a man, via reincarnation, from the Stone Age to the present. Leueen first had the idea while riding the Super Chief with Kaufman to California, and the couple wrote the draft partly in California and partly at Cherchez La Farm, and completed the play in London. Kaufman had parked most of his other collaborators at the typewriter while he paced, but since Leueen could not type, Kaufman sat while Leueen did the pacing. They would first rough out a situation and then throw dialogue back and forth between them without any deliberation or mental editing, in the hope that something would emerge which could be polished into a usable line or idea.

Fancy Meeting You Again, with Leueen in the lead role and with Walter Matthau as the object of her pursuits, tried out in New Haven, moved to Boston, where it underwent heavy rewriting, and then moved to Philadelphia, where it was rewritten again. Max Gordon had been the first to read the script, and he had stunned everyone by turning it down—not only because he'd been hurt badly by *The Small Hours,* but because he believed that *Fancy Meeting You Again* was simply not good enough to produce. Kaufman had to search for other producers, and got Chandler Cowles and Ben Segal to do the play. When most of the major Boston critics applauded the tryout there, Cowles and Segal felt certain that Gordon had been wrong and that they had a hit. Both Kaufman and Leueen were optimistic as they continued rewriting, but it was in Boston that Kaufman received the call from Harold Ross just a few hours before Ross died in the hospital, and the death of his old friend, accentuated by the poignant call, shook Kaufman severely. Other friends and associates had died recently, and added to the sadness and loss was the fact that each death served as further grim reminders to Kaufman that he was aging. Bert Kalmar had died on September 17, 1947, Crosby Gaige on March 9, 1949, Neysa McMein on May 13, 1949, and Rufus LeMaire on December 3, 1950.

Kaufman's mood was not helped by the fate of *Fancy Meeting You Again,* which opened on Monday, January 14, 1952, at the Royale Theatre, and folded after eight performances. Kaufman began talking to Gordon again about how the last thing he wanted to become was another Owen Davis, writing play after play that nobody wanted. This feeling was confirmed when he and Leueen wrote a television play called *The Hat,* about the quarrels between two catty actresses, and it was never produced.

However, relief came when Kaufman was approached by Feuer and Martin to do the book for *Silk Stockings*. Kaufman accepted the assignment, but only on the condition that he would be allowed to collaborate with Leueen on the project—a proviso which the producers finally, though reluctantly, accepted. *Silk Stockings* is a musical adaptation of *Ninotchka*, the film which had been such a strong comic vehicle for Greta Garbo. The story brings an apparently humorless female Russian commissar to Paris, to keep an eye on a traveling Russian composer. During the commissar's stay in Paris, her serious façade disappears when a romance develops, and she becomes feminine and lovely. In addition to hiring the Kaufmans, Feuer and Martin brought in Cole Porter to do the score, and cast Hildegarde Knef, the German star, whose name was simplified for American audiences to Neff, and Don Ameche in the leading roles. It looked like a natural hit, and would eventually be a success at the box office, but for Kaufman the time spent on *Silk Stockings* was the most miserable and disastrous duty of his career.

This became the case because Feuer and Martin's tendency toward tyranny, only a hint of which had appeared when Kaufman worked with them on *Guys and Dolls*, suddenly emerged full-blown. All at once, the producers insisted on inserting stale gag after stale gag and inserting bad bits of stage business. It was then that Kaufman began calling them "Jed Harris rolled into one," and an even more pointed pair of names: "Mr. Hyde and Mr. Hyde."

Kaufman was extremely unhappy, and was ready to throw up his hands, but kept on largely for Leueen's sake. Reviews for the Philadelphia tryout were good, but no one involved with the show felt that it was ready for Broadway, and the conflicts and changes continued. Miss Knef says that she became so confused by the cuts, and the sudden restorations of lines previously cut, that at one tryout rehearsal someone had to stop her, saying, "That's the part that was cut out yesterday." Feuer and Martin continued to insist that the show needed more "pep," and kept pressing Kaufman for more and broader jokes. In late December 1954, Kaufman walked out for two weeks, and Miss Knef recorded in her diary, "George Kaufman refuses to go on rewriting and adding the crude gags that Cy and Ernie insist on. He is more taciturn than ever. Cole Porter doesn't leave his hotel room."

Leueen stayed on to see if she could cope with the required additional rewriting, but she couldn't, and Martin decided to bring in Abe Burrows to work on the show as it moved to Boston. Burrows wasn't effective, and Miss Knef's diary reads, "The 'play doctor' is slicing through the play like a snow plow, peppering it full of rancid Capitalist-Communist corn, strangling Ninotchka with mouthfuls of partyese." In early January 1955, Kaufman and Leueen finally told the cast that Kaufman couldn't continue his work "for reasons of health." Kaufman, who hated the thought of abandoning any show, told the cast quietly, "Please forgive me." Feuer assumed the title of director.

On January 26, the New York *Post* ran the story under a three column headline, MR. KAUFMAN STEPS OUT OF HIS 'SILK STOCKINGS.' Neither Kaufman nor Feuer and Martin would give any information to the press, beyond the fact that they had disagreed about the book. Miss Knef, meanwhile, grew increasingly unhappy about Burrows's changes, and told the producers that she wanted to quit. "*Ninotchka*," she told them, "has nothing more to do with the part I signed for." In an attempt to soothe her, Feuer assured her that there would be more changes before the show reached New York, but that was precisely what Miss Knef didn't want to hear. "There have been too many changes already," she replied. She stayed on, however, and Feuer and Martin, still afraid to risk New York, moved to Detroit for three weeks. Miss Knef's diary records, "Kaufman's soufflé has become hash."

Amid the show's conflicts and vacillations, backers could take heart in the fact that the score was being done by Cole Porter. Born in Peru, Indiana, on June 9, 1893, Porter, who had excelled in music early in his childhood and had written two songs before he was ten, went to Yale and to Harvard Law School at the insistence of his wealthy grandfather. He defied his grandfather by switching to the School of Music, where, in 1916, he collaborated on his first Broadway show, *See America First*, which failed. He then joined the French Foreign Legion, and entertained fellow legionnaires on a portable piano. Later, after writing the scores for three successful revues and spending part of a million-dollar inheritance, left to him by his grandfather, on a series of world tours and lavish parties, Porter settled down to compose a steady series of hit scores, including *Fifty Million Frenchmen* in 1929, *The Gay Divorce* in 1932, and *Anything Goes* in 1934. In 1937, an accident on horseback crushed both his legs, and, although doctors were certain that amputation would be required, Porter underwent dozens of operations to save his legs, and succeeded until the right leg had to be removed twenty-one years later. The accident did nothing to halt Porter's work or even daunt his pursuit of world travel. His next hits included *Let's Face It* in 1941, *Kiss Me Kate* in 1948, and *Can-Can* in 1953. Many of his songs have become classics. Among them are *Let's Do It, You Do Something to Me, Night and Day, I've Got You Under My Skin, Don't Fence Me In,* and *It's All Right with Me.* Porter died in Santa Monica, California, on October 15, 1964, and *Silk Stockings* was his last hit show.

Eight days before *Silk Stockings* opened in New York, Miss Knef noted that "several scenes from the original version have been reintroduced." In the end, about half of the book came from Kaufman and Leueen, and the rest was Burrows's. When the show finally opened at the Imperial Theatre on Thursday, February 24, 1955, Kaufman did not attend, but instead left town. Critics called the book and direction weak, but the stars' charisma, Porter's music, and the remnants of Kaufman's magic made it good enough to run for 478 performances. John Chapman called the show "handsome, slick, brisk, and intelligent" and said that "whenever the plot shows the merest sign of taking over more than its share, Cole Porter shoulders it aside with some of his best melodies, lyrics, and rhythms." Walter Kerr said, "It opened at the Imperial Theatre the end-product of a fabulous out-of-town sortie in which the authors were changed, the choreographers were changed, and the changes were changed. What has been wrought in all this travail? Well, not a miracle, certainly. But not precisely a clambake, either." Film rights were bought by M-G-M, and the movie was produced by Arthur Freed with Rouben Mamoulian directing. The screenplay was written by Leonard Spigelgass and Leonard Gershe, and the film was released in July, 1957, with Fred Astaire, Cyd Charisse, and Janis Paige in leading roles. It was a hit.

On October 17, 1953, Kaufman sold Cherchez La Farm at public auction for $71,700, with the bulk of the estate—the mansion, the pool, several of the smaller buildings, and 29 acres—going to Dr. Bradford Green of Buckingham, Pennsylvania, for $45,000. Another 22 acres went for $18,000, and the remainder was parceled among small bidders. It was quite a bargain, since, in addition to the $45,000 which Kaufman had originally paid, he had also spent $100,000 for improvements. The reason for the sale of the farm was that Leueen and Kaufman wanted a home in London, and were spending so little time in Bucks County, anyway, that the maintenance of three separate residences just didn't make sense. The couple sailed to England in April 1954, and found a house on a canal leading into the Thames, at 17 Blomfield Road, near the house at 39 Blomfield Road in which Kaufman and Beatrice had once lived. 17 Blomfield Road was a very old building and required the services of an architect to rebuild and strengthen it. Ironically, in view of Kaufman's distaste for psychoanalysis, the architect hired was the grandson of Sigmund Freud. The couple returned to the United States for their tour of duty on *Silk Stockings*, and before they left again for London, Hildegarde Knef came to see them. "I felt dismal and discouraged," she says, referring to the departure of the Kaufmans from the show, "as though I had witnessed the triumph of fatuity over aestheticism and dignity."

In London, Kaufman relaxed while Leueen played the role of Cassandra in an adaptation by Christopher Fry of Jean Giraudoux's *Tiger at the Gate*, sleeping even later than usual and looking around for British plays which he and Gordon might want to produce. He complained in a funny letter to Gordon that Gilbert Miller had asked him to catch a performance of a play Miller was producing, and that he had had to pay for the tickets. He said that he had written to Miller to protest and to demand that Miller's manager return Kaufman's thirty-one shillings, plus six pence for the program. Gordon assured Kaufman that justice would prevail, telling him about the time Dwight Wiman had made Noël Coward pay for seats to one of Wiman's plays, despite the fact that Wiman was Coward's producer, which so infuriated Coward that he gave his next play to Gordon instead of Wiman.

Kaufman's distaste for Feuer and Martin cropped up in his letters. In one to Gordon, he said that Irving Lazar had come to see him and had reported "that Cy and Ernie have nothing to produce and can't get anyone to work with them, and are going to make a movie." He added, "The mills of the gods grind quickly in the theatre, thank God." Then in a letter to Ruth, he wrote, "To hell with Feuer and Martin. Incidentally, if their new show closes prematurely, I am giving a small party to which you will be bidden. Wear your smartest clothes and get stewed."

In another letter to Gordon, Kaufman said, "I read a great many books—do little else except rest." He then told Gordon that life was "easy going, with little or no pressure," but, in a more frank letter to his sister, Ruth, he described the speed and pace of Leueen's life-style. "Last night Peter Brook and his wife came to dinner," Kaufman wrote, "an old date, and I couldn't persuade Leueen to break it. She had been up very late all last week, and then up at 7:30 Sunday morning to fly to Paris, and up until six Sunday night in Paris. Much champagne and brandy. Then the flight back here, no food, more brandy, and a performance Monday night. After she got back home, she had another brandy and more wine. Then, in the middle of supper, she gave out. Claimed that the wallpaper in the dining room was too wavy and moving. I told her this morning that she was right—I *had* seen the wallpaper attack her, and from behind, too. However, one night's sleep puts her right back on top, so she is fine and off for a fitting for an evening dress." Anne visited Kaufman in London, and noticed immediately the beginning of change in the relationship between her father and Leueen. One night, as Anne and Kaufman were riding home in a cold drizzle, Anne said, "Really, Daddy, couldn't you have met a nice Italian actress?" Kaufman said nothing, but looked rather wistful.

Kaufman and Leueen returned to the United States in late summer 1955, as *Tiger at the Gate* moved to Broadway, opening October 3. The play did not do well, but Leueen had a hit when she appeared next in Graham Greene's *The Potting Shed*, a drama about a tormented man who had attempted to hang himself in a potting shed—a garden tool shed—when he was fourteen. The event continues to haunt the man and threatens to destroy him. Robert Flemyng played the lead, and Leueen was excellent as his divorced wife. Carmen Capalbo and Stanley Chase, who had previously produced *The Three-Penny Opera* and Eugene O'Neill's *A Moon for the Misbegotten,* produced the play, with Capalbo also directing. The play opened January 29, 1957, at the Bijou Theatre.

It was during the run of *The Potting Shed* that rumors began to grow concerning Leueen's interest in other men, notably Alan Campbell and Carmen Capalbo, and the problems inherent in Kaufman's marriage with Leueen surfaced. Leueen began increasingly to appear in public without her husband, while Kaufman, now nearing seventy, stayed home, torn between his desire to see his wife enjoy herself and uncharacteristic but inevitable feelings of loneliness and jealousy. As so often happens, the genesis of the marriage contained the germs of the marriage's eventual deterioration. Kaufman had been flattered by the interest of a beautiful young woman; Leueen had been flattered by the attention of one of the world's most famous playwrights and directors. He was still lonely, with Beatrice gone; she married rather casually. And these elements had been enough to cause the marriage, but not hold it together.

In the spring of 1957, Leueen moved out of the penthouse on Park Avenue, and the newspapers picked up the fact that the couple were estranged. A reporter asked Leueen if her association with Capalbo had grown into a romance. Leueen smiled, and said, "I have Adam. He's my Siamese cat." Leueen and Kaufman continued to be friends until the end of Kaufman's life, and continued to collaborate as writers, but the marriage was over, and a divorce was granted in August 1957.

Leueen married Stephen Goodyear, a young physician, on December 16, 1961, six months after Kaufman's death; it was her fourth marriage and Goodyear's third. This also ended in divorce, and Leueen was recently married and then divorced for the fifth time.

30. THE PANEL

TELEVISION WAS FAR from a favorite source of pleasure for
Kaufman as a viewer, but it provided him with a great deal of fun
as a participant. He became a regular feature during the developing
days of television, and enjoyed himself more than he would ever
admit. And since more people saw him and heard his name in a single
night on TV than the combined audiences of all his plays, television
also increased his fame in a way that his work on stage could never
have done.

Kaufman became involved in television through radio. Irving
Mansfield, a brilliant young producer with the CBS network, and
husband of Jacqueline Susann, conceived a show to be called *This
Is Show Business*, which would feature a panel of celebrities emceed
by Clifton Fadiman, who had also emceed the very successful show,

Information Please. Guests would be from the entertainment world, and in addition to presenting their act, they would also reveal a problem they had, so that the panel could offer advice on finding a solution.

Mansfield needed genuine wits for the panel, since the shows were done live and were unrehearsed. The panel and guests were on their own and whatever happened was the "script." In this situation, Mansfield wanted Kaufman, the best of the natural wits. Uncertain about Kaufman's attitude, Mansfield made a circuitous probe, getting his wife to forward the proposal through one of her friends, since she didn't know Kaufman well enough to ask him herself. (Much later, after the program had been established and Kaufman was a regular panelist and Miss Susann was a guest on the show, she told about one of her few personal meetings with Kaufman. She had been an actress before beginning to write books, and Myra Hampton Streger had suggested her to Kaufman for a part in one of his plays. According to the story, Kaufman simply replied, without looking at Miss Susann, "I hardly think so." Kaufman's comment during the program was, "It's a very amusing story, but completely apocryphal," a statement which confused Miss Susann, since she didn't know what apocryphal meant. Years later, she became, of course, a best-selling novelist, and Mansfield now devotes himself to managing her career, a job he does extremely well, and Miss Susann's story about Kaufman's rejection has passed into legend. But the fact is that it never happened that way. Kaufman listened and watched while she read for him, and from that decided that she was not right for the part. His courtesy as a director was proverbial, and the story is simply uncharacteristic of him.)

But the invitation interested Kaufman more than Miss Susann's reading years before, and he came to CBS to talk to Mansfield, telling him that he was quite willing to participate. He had given several radio interviews through the years, had emceed the WOR Defense Department program during the war, and had also been an occasional panelist on *Information Please*. There's a story which Clifton Fadiman tells about one of Kaufman's appearances on that show. Kaufman sat quietly between Frank Adams and John Kieran, the sportswriter, permanent members of the panel. The program had the standard fifteen-minute warmup before going on the air, to loosen up both audience and celebrities, and Kaufman sat through the entire warmup without saying a word. Fadiman inquired, with a smile, "And what have you been doing for the past fifteen minutes, Mr. Kaufman?" Kaufman peered at him over the rims of his glasses—a look which would later become familiar to millions of television viewers—and replied, "Listening to *Information Please.*"

Kaufman did much more than listen on *This Is Show Business*, which began on radio in 1948 and switched to television the following year. He was not a raconteur, but behaved just as he did at the Round Table, at parties, and everywhere else. He listened, and when the time was right, darted out with his devastating comments, retreating into silence until the next opportunity. He was the special delight of all the show business columnists, who found him excellent copy. Irving Hoffman described Kaufman's reaction when he signed for *Information Please* and was told that, although the usual guest fee was $500, celebrity guests usually donated the money to charity. "Good," Kaufman said, "I'll turn my fee over to a very needy family —of which I am the head." Earl Wilson, calling Kaufman "Mr. Unpopularity," said that Kaufman "has become an important man in America's living rooms by not liking anything—not even George S. Kaufman. On one television show recently, the acerbic and angular Mr. Kaufman admitted that his mind had been wandering. 'Why don't you advertise for it?' he was asked. Said Kaufman, 'I don't know whether I want it back.'" Columnists were delighted when Kaufman said during a program that television was a mistake, and that there was entirely too much talking on it. He suddenly realized, while he was saying this, that he was adding to the problem, and announced, "I'm going to do my share by shutting up right now." He was quiet for several seconds. Another columnist told how a non-singing member of the cast of *The King and I* complained on the show because he never got a chance to sing on stage. "Why don't you just break out in song some night?" Kaufman said. "You're stronger than Gertrude Lawrence. Just do it. For good measure, sing an Irving Berlin song and get me a close-up picture of Richard Rodgers's face at the same time."

Kaufman's wit was sometimes directed toward his fellow panelists. After Abe Burrows left the show and was replaced by Sam Levenson, there were often hilarious and merciless exchanges between Levenson and Kaufman, leading to a report that they were feuding, even though it was completely in fun. Levenson once said, "George's motto is, If you can say something nice, don't say it." Levenson was referring to Kaufman's assaults on guests such as Joey Adams, who had just written a book about his adventures in Korea entertaining the troops. Since all guests had to have a "problem" for the panel, Adams's problem was the dilemma, since the book was successful, of whether he should now become a writer or stay in show business. He drew Kaufman out by adding, "Maybe we could form a team, Kaufman and Adams, or maybe it should be Adams and Kaufman." Kaufman replied, "I read as much of your book as it was possible for me to read, and I suggest that you don't have much choice as to whether you should be a comedian or a writer. And having seen your act, I don't know but what you should open a candy store." "Oh, you know my book, huh?" Adams said. "Who read it to you?" "The same person who wrote it for you," Kaufman replied.

No one received much sympathy from Kaufman. When the dance team of Lewis and Van confessed that, after working together for eight years, they were bored with each other, Kaufman advised them to quit and go back to starving, while they hunted for other employment. "Then," he said, "you'll be very glad to meet each other again." He took pot shots at anything, including children who hounded celebrities for autographs. "They should be home," he said, "learning their lessons, eating their oatmeal, or doing whatever they do at night and bothering their parents instead of complete strangers. I'd like to knock their heads together until they ring like a Chinese gong." Nor was his own program sacred; he sometimes called it *This Is Not Show Business.* Once he said that he was considering suing TV because of the way it made him look. Clifton Fadiman, who was capable of dealing in the same currency, replied, "And vice versa, Mr. Kaufman." Once after Kaufman had dispensed his brand of tongue-in-cheek advice to a guest, Fadiman said, "A lot of people have succeeded by *not* listening to Mr. Kaufman."

Despite his slurs on television, Kaufman enjoyed his work on the show, and was dismayed when it suddenly was halted. On December 21, 1952, Kaufman remarked on the air, "Let's make this one program where no one sings *Silent Night*." Before the program was over, the CBS switchboard was jammed with calls protesting Kaufman's "irreligious" remark. Many viewers jumped to the conclusion that Kaufman was deliberately derogating Christianity, and hundreds of complaints also reached the American Tobacco Company, the show's sponsor, and its advertising agency, Batten, Barton, Durstine and Osborn, Inc. Kaufman, however, was not immediately aware of any trouble. He left the studio that evening following the broadcast, and took a train to Boston, where Leueen was due to open with Rex Harrison in a tryout of Peter Ustinov's *The Love of Four Colonels*. He first knew he was in trouble when Mansfield phoned him the next day. Mansfield had just come from a heated conference with officials of the American Tobacco Company, the ad agency, and CBS. The sponsor was canceling its support, even though the season only had three more weeks to run, and CBS demanded Kaufman's removal. Mansfield suggested that Kaufman take a vacation, which Kaufman had asked for, anyway, so that he could be with Leueen during the Boston tryout. Kaufman agreed, and the matter was settled for the moment, quietly and without publicity, or so it was then assumed.

But Franklin Heller was working at CBS at the time, and though he was not associated with the program, he was incensed by the treatment given his old boss. Recalling the incident recently, Heller said, "I felt that letting George fade away was bad for several reasons: the network's fear of any outcry, basic speech freedoms, and the essential harmlessness of George's statement, but most of all because I suspected that George would have had a horror of any public embroglio. Nevertheless, he needed a defender he did not seem to have." Heller tipped off Jack Gould, television editor of the *Times*, who called Kaufman in Boston but got Leueen instead. Kaufman had usually avoided talking to the press ever since the Mary Astor affair, but Leueen had no such inhibitions. She confirmed the report that Kaufman had been fired for his "Christmas remark," but made it clear that he had not intended a slur on the hymn but had only been protesting the overcommercialization of Christmas. Leueen insisted that Kaufman come to the phone, and he verified what she had said. "It wasn't an anti-religious remark," he told Gould. "I was just speaking out against the use and over use of the carol."

The story broke in the *Times* of December 30, and was picked up by papers across the country. Angry columns by radio and TV writers, scathing letters from viewers, and even opinions from both Christian and Jewish religious leaders poured in, supporting Kaufman. Show business figures rallied behind Kaufman, and when CBS asked Fred Allen, John Daly, and then Garry Moore to take Kaufman's place for the remaining three shows, all refused. Allen, who could be as caustic as Kaufman, added that there were only two real wits in television, Groucho Marx and George S. Kaufman. "With Kaufman gone," Allen said, "that leaves TV half-witted." Clifton Fadiman also expressed his dismay at the almost McCarthyist tenor of the objections to Kaufman's remark. Unfortunately, however, Steve Allen was approached next by CBS and readily agreed to take Kaufman's spot.

The action taken by Heller to set in motion Kaufman's defense illustrates a side of Kaufman that is rarely discussed, the loyalty he inspired in those who worked for him. He was always tough on those who worked with or for him, but his associates were selected carefully and then given the benefit of his vast expertise. "He impressed upon us his spirit and style," Heller says. "I wanted to reciprocate in some way for the tremendous experience I had working for George S. Kaufman, and for the confidence he put in me. I never told George —or anyone—that I had done this."

Kaufman's first reaction to the controversy was to say, "The whole thing is just a tempest in a teevee." "It shouldn't surprise anyone," he said soon afterward. "It's a fear-ridden industry, and that's the way it's ruled. When they get some letters, they're afraid not to fire somebody, and then they're afraid to hire him back. I have no complaint. After all, I didn't *have* to get into television. It's bad news for the dramatic critics, though. It means that I have to go back to show business." He added that he had been wanting to quit for some time, saying, "I have said nothing in as many ways as I know how to say nothing."

However, Kaufman was reluctant to quit under fire, so when American Tobacco dropped the program after the final three Kaufman-less programs, he accepted CBS's offer to return to the show when it resumed in January as an unsponsored program. "I suppose this is vindication of a sort," Kaufman told reporters when he re-joined the show. But the controversy had taken the fun out of it for him, and he was now seeking a graceful way to withdraw. *The Love of Four Colonels*, having opened on Broadway on January 15, 1953, closed on May 16, freeing Leueen from her obligations in New York. And when *Guys and Dolls* opened in London twelve days later Kaufman seized the opportunity to take a look at how it was doing. He never returned to television as a regular participant.

In the meantime, Kaufman had begun work with Howard Teich-mann on a play they called *The Solid Gold Cadillac*. Teichmann was born in Chicago on January 22, 1916. He attended the University of Wisconsin, became Orson Welles's stage manager, and then wrote the Welles radio program, *The Mercury Theatre of the Air*, for two years. He shifted to television writing, and in 1952 wrote a play, *Howe and Hummel*, based upon the lives of two flamboyant shyster lawyers who practiced in New York around the turn of the century. He gave the script to Max Gordon. "The play," Gordon said later, "was badly written. But it had something that struck my imagination —a scene, perhaps, a sense of humor, a comic twist. Instinct told me that Teichmann in proper hands might turn out something worth-while." Gordon called Kaufman, and told him that *Howe and Hum-mel* wasn't worth reading, but suggested that Kaufman should see the author. "I think he's got something," Gordon said. The meeting resulted in an agreement to collaborate, and the two men began work-ing on a spoof of the United Nations. But Kaufman soon dropped it when the idea didn't work out well.

Teichmann was stunned by Kaufman's decision, went out for a drive, and began to go faster and faster until he was stopped by a state trooper for doing ninety-five miles per hour on the freeway. Teich-mann says that the trooper remarked, "General Motors doesn't build cars to last long at the speed you were going." Teichmann says, "My body stiffened. My mind began clicking like an IBM machine." Ten days earlier, Kaufman had told him that he'd love to write a play called *Poor General Motors*. Kaufman had heard someone make the consoling remark after GM stock had dropped on the market, and it had struck him as being funny. The story immediately tied in, in Teichmann's mind, with a story once told him by a rich friend who visited a company in which he owned a few shares of stock. He was treated contemptuously during his visit, so he went to a broker and bought enough stock to own 51 per cent of the company, at which point he fired all the people who had insulted him. The story is one which has been told in many contexts and about a variety of people, and its original version involved a Colorado mining king who was snubbed by a clerk at the Brown Palace Hotel in Denver, and who bought the hotel just to fire the clerk. Teichmann went back to relate his new twist on the story to Kaufman.

Kaufman liked the idea that Teichmann sketched for him, a play about a little old man who, with only ten shares of stock in a giant automotive corporation, succeeds in wresting control from selfish directors. Kaufman suggested, however, that the stockholder be an elderly woman—someone like Josephine Hull, he said—and Teichmann agreed readily. Kaufman called Mrs. Hull, whom he had directed in *You Can't Take It with You*, and she said she'd be delighted to try the part. Thereafter, as the project developed, the collaborators always referred to the main character as "Mrs. Hull."

Josephine Hull gave her age as sixty-seven when she appeared in *The Solid Gold Cadillac* in 1953. She admitted, however, having graduated from Radcliffe College in 1899, which would have made her thirteen years old at the time she received her degree. She was probably closer to seventy-five. She first went on the stage in 1902 under her maiden name, Josephine Sherwood, and retired in 1910 when she married Shelley Hull, a rising young actor and brother of Henry Hull. She returned to show business in 1919 after Hull died, and had her first hit role in *Neighbors* in 1924. She had subsequent hits in *Craig's Wife*, *The Wild Man from Borneo*, and others, but achieved her greatest successes in *You Can't Take It with You*, as Penelope, the playwriting wife, in *Arsenic and Old Lace*, as one of the befuddled old ladies who poisoned homeless men with elderberry wine, and in *Harvey*, as the equally befuddled sister of Elmer Dowd.

The writing of the play was slowed by Kaufman's trip to London to check on *Guys and Dolls*, but Teichmann continued work, sending his material to Kaufman. Teichmann's work was not up to the standard that Kaufman wanted, and Kaufman was finding it impossible to correct the problems and make his own contribution through correspondence. "My work with Teichmann is going rather badly," he said, in a letter to Ruth, "and I shall go home much earlier than I had planned, so as to work right with him." Kaufman had been in rather low spirits in the early part of 1953, with a month spent in Mount Sinai Hospital for a hernia operation. This was followed by the death of Herman J. Mankiewicz on March 6, and then the emergency curtailment of his trip to England. But his spirits rose after he returned to the United States and took charge once again of the writing of the play.

The Solid Gold Cadillac opened for tryouts in Hartford, Connecticut and received good reviews, but critics slaughtered the play at the next stop, Washington, D.C. After fast rewriting, reviews at the next town, Philadelphia, were excellent. But the cast and Kaufman realized that Philadelphia wasn't New York.

New York, however, was more optimistic about *The Solid Gold Cadillac* than was the cast. The show was capitalized at $100,000, and it took only three weeks to line up backers, who owned 50 per cent collectively, with Kaufman and Gordon splitting the other 50 per cent. There was a lot of smart money among the investors, including Louis A. Lotito, president of City Playhouses, who invested $1000; Mrs. Marshall Field, $1000; Maurice Sachs, vice-president of RCA, $1000; Mrs. Russel Crouse, $1000; Fred Allen, $2000; Worthington Miner, the television producer, $2000; Mayer D. Mermin, the theatrical attorney, $1000; Morris Schrier, MCA attorney, $1000; Elaine Perry, producer, $1000; Clinton Wilder, producer, $5000; Leonard Goldenson, president of ABC, $4000; William Leibling, talent agent, $1000; Tom Ewell, the actor, $2000; Oscar Hammerstein II, $1000; Moss Hart, $1000, and Howard Cullman, a famous angel, $2000. They were rewarded handsomely. The advance sale was $270,000, and backers immediately got back 25 per cent of their investment three weeks after the opening, with the rest being held temporarily against future costs. "It was the fastest and largest return in show business," Gordon said.

The backers later made a lot more. When the show opened at the

Belasco Theatre on Thursday, November 5, 1953—with Kaufman, who was very nervous, arriving only five minutes before curtain time—it was a very solid hit. It was a smash from Josephine Hull's first joke to her acceptance of a solid gold Cadillac, in the final scene, for her services to the corporation. Critical notices were warm and appreciative, with Walter Kerr recommending the play "for a hatful of chuckles." "It is as bright and shiny and stylish as a new car," John Chapman wrote. "And it has a top-hole cast which is sensitive to director Kaufman's genius for perfect timing. I felt I was back in show business again—and it felt oh, so good."

Praise was particularly lavish for Josephine Hull. Kaufman, knowing that Mrs. Hull *was The Solid Gold Cadillac,* set down rules to guard her health. "1. Rest. 2. Please rest. 3. Save your voice. 4. Don't see anyone." She broke all the rules immediately, and, after talking at great length with an interviewer, said with a smile, "Mr. Kaufman would scream if he knew I had been talking so long!" During the interview, she mentioned the devastating Washington reviews, and quoted one which said, "Mrs. Hull has the shape of a battered coal barge and the face of an amiable bulldog." She had cried when she first read the review, but now, she told the reporter, it only made her laugh. "I hear Washington does that to everybody," she said, "to the Lunts and Cornelia Otis Skinner, too. We can't take it as a personal insult." Max Gordon was also aware that the play's success was rooted firmly in Mrs. Hull's extraordinary performance, and said later, "The play would be running yet if she had lived." The play closed after 526 performances, when Mrs. Hull, who had missed performances during the run due to illness, became too ill to continue. She died on March 12, 1957.

The play did not make *The Best Plays of 1953-54,* edited by Louis Kronenberger, but John Chapman included it in his *Golden Dozen* list in his book, *Theatre '54,* and John Gassner included it in his collection, *Best American Plays.*

Columbia bought the film rights, releasing *The Solid Gold Cadillac,* with a screenplay by Abe Burrows, on October 1, 1956. Mrs. Hull's role was taken in the film by the younger and prettier Judy Holliday, who had appeared in Max Gordon's production of Garson Kanin's *Born Yesterday* in 1946. That was Gordon's last hit before *The*

MONTY WOOLLEY, STAR OF THE STAGE AND SCREEN
VERSIONS OF *THE MAN WHO CAME TO DINNER*

Disbelief cost him ten percent.

KAUFMAN AND HART WITH ADDED HAIR AND HARPO MARX
WIGLESS IN THE BUCKS COUNTY PLAYHOUSE VERSION
OF *THE MAN WHO CAME TO DINNER*

Acting ambitions sometimes surfaced.

ANNE KAUFMAN SCHNEIDER,
AS SEEN BY ARTIST MARTIN KOPP

A shade less than charming.

THE *SING OUT THE NEWS* CREW

*Left to right: Hart, Kaufman, Harold Rome,
Charles Friedman, and Max Gordon.*

JOHN P. MARQUAND
Kaufman knew nothing about Boston.

LEUEEN MacGRATH AND SPENCER TRACY IN THE FILM
VERSION OF *EDWARD, MY SON*

. . . and Kaufman even flew.

FRED ASTAIRE AND JANIS PAIGE IN THE FILM VERSION
OF *SILK STOCKINGS*

The changes were changed.

EDNA FERBER, NEAR THE END OF HER LIFE

Still single, still no regrets.

Solid Gold Cadillac, but it had been such a fantastic success that it kept him going for a long time, running one month short of four years with a total of 1642 performances. Kaufman's part in *Born Yesterday* has often been debated, and there's a story that Kanin moved into Cherchez La Farm for several weeks while he was writing the play. Another source, a friend of Kaufman's, says, "I do know that George was responsible for the hilarious gin rummy scene in *Born Yesterday*, since Garson Kanin wasn't a card player."

After *The Solid Gold Cadillac*, Kaufman set out to work again with Teichmann, and their next project was *Exile*, completed in early 1954. *Exile* is the story of a Czechoslovakian political figure and his wife, who is a concert pianist, and their exile from their country. It was never produced.

It was around this time that Kaufman became much less interested in working with Teichmann than Teichmann was in working with Kaufman. Their last attempt at collaboration was *In the Money*, about a poor man whose relatives, all of whom have married into money, shun him, until he strikes it rich. Then they fawn on him, but in the end turn against him again, when poor investments destroy his fortune. The first draft was completed in early 1954, and Kaufman left with Leueen for London, where he again scouted plays for himself and Gordon. Kaufman and Gordon had to spend a good deal of energy at this time handling Teichmann, since Teichmann was continually approaching them with proposals for other projects besides *In the Money*, and the Kaufman-Gordon correspondence is filled with passages about tactful ways to duck or dodge Teichmann. Kaufman was now interested in the collaboration only to the extent of putting *In the Money* into final shape, and then that project proved unsuccessful. Kaufman finally told Gordon, "Tyke and I are stuck as hell in the middle of our play and may never get out." They never did.

Eventually, Teichmann struck out on his own, and proved he was unable to succeed without Kaufman. He wrote four failures: *Miss Lonelyhearts* in 1957, *The Girls in 509* in 1959, *Julia, Jake and Uncle Joe*, which closed after one performance in 1961, and, in 1963, *A Rainy Day in Newark*. He is presently a professor of English at Barnard.

At this point, it might have seemed that Kaufman was just drifting, appearing now and then on *The Jack Paar Show* and taking on no new projects. The fact is that most of what was being offered was little more than junk, and he knew it, and he also did not find other suitable writing partners. And there was the fact that he was older and wanted to work less. He wasn't as anxious about the quiet periods between hits as he had once been, and simply would not take on a new project unless it truly interested him.

31. THE LAST HIT

DURING THE MIDDLE and late 1950s, Max Gordon's letters to Kaufman were concerned largely with financial details. Gordon reported religiously each week's gross on all the plays they had running, including all revenue from revivals and subsidiary rights sales, and even items like $10 and $15 royalty payments from amateur groups. Gordon also invested small amounts in plays of other producers, and he always got an equal share for Kaufman. The plays sometimes made money, and sometimes lost, but a note to Kaufman recorded every transaction. In the fall of 1954, for example, Gordon wrote to Kaufman, "I have just signed the papers for *Quadrille* and, for the record, you own ½ per cent. I paid $1500 for 1 per cent interest, so you owe me $750." Gordon also invested money for both of them in Sidney Kingsley's *Lunatics and Lovers*, which opened at the Broadhurst Theatre on December 13, 1954, and was profitable. He handled all the details on these investments, and all Kaufman had to do was cash his profit checks—when there was a profit. Gordon forwarded the checks to Kaufman the same day that payment was received. *Lunatics and Lovers*, for which Gordon paid $2000 for ½ per cent shares for himself and Kaufman at $1000 each, played 203 performances, and checks came in for some time. The last one was in December 1956, when Gordon wrote to Kaufman, "Enclosed herewith you will find check in the amount of $7.50, as your half share of the $15.00 I received today from *Lunatics and Lovers*."

Kaufman and Gordon occasionally disagreed in their financial opinions, such as the time Gordon wrote to Kaufman that he was hanging on to a particular stock, despite a piece of advice Kaufman had once given him. "Baron Rothschild," Kaufman had told him, "made his fortune by selling too soon."

But though most of the correspondence was concerned with details of investments and returns, the greatest energy was spent in search of another hit which Kaufman could write or direct, and which Gordon could produce. In the summer of 1954, they pinned their hopes on a novel by Geoffrey Kerr, *Under the Influence*, which Kaufman had sent Gordon from London. Gordon responded enthusiastically. "If you can fashion a play out of *Under the Influence*," he said, "and get Wally Cox to play it, all you'll have to do is bend over and pick up the money." But Kaufman's next letter cautioned that, although he and Kerr had blocked out the play in London, he wasn't certain that Kerr would be able to carry his part of the collaboration, which, due to Kaufman's age, would have to be greater than the contribution made by collaborators in the past. He also demurred at a later suggestion of Gordon's, after Cox proved unavailable, that they might get Tom Ewell for the lead. Ewell had made a big hit in *The Seven Year Itch*, and had suddenly raised his price to unrealistic heights. "Suddenly having to give Tommy Ewell ten per cent of the gross offends my artistic sense," Kaufman wrote.

Gordon's enthusiasm for the project and his anxiety to see it consummated knew no bounds, and once, when a week had gone by with no word from Kaufman, he sent Kaufman a cable to find out what was wrong. Kaufman had to remind him that, with advancing age, things tended to move a bit more slowly. Furthermore, Kaufman said, he was feeling awfully tired, and Kerr might even end up being required to do most or all of the writing. "I have no strength at all these days," he wrote, "and very few plays left in me, I'm afraid." But he added, "That can change—on good days, which I occasionally get, I want to write a bushel of them."

The confidence which Kaufman and Gordon had in Kerr was well-placed, for Kerr had a distinguished background both as a writer and as an actor. Kerr was born on January 26, 1895. He made his acting debut in London in 1913 in *A Cardinal's Romance*, at the Savoy Theatre, and his American debut in *Just Suppose*, at the Henry Miller Theatre in 1920. The plays he'd written included *Don't Play with Fire* in 1927, *'Til the Cows Come Home* in 1936, *Black Swans* in 1937, and others. He is the father of John Kerr, the actor who played the sensitive student in *Tea and Sympathy* and the lieutenant in the film version of *South Pacific*.

Gordon, in his anticipation, kept worrying about a star even though the play was not yet written, until Kaufman finally became annoyed and told Gordon to consider the problems of the play first. "I don't want to be told," Kaufman said, "that the star is terrific, and the play is nothing." Kerr later changed the title of the play to *Say When*. But this became academic, and all the work on the play went out the window, when Kaufman and Gordon learned that Kerr had previously sold the movie rights to the novel. Kerr had sold the rights to Alexander Korda, and Kaufman at first assumed that Korda would welcome the play, since it would enhance the value of the film, so he did not expect that the prior sale of film rights would present a problem. But when Kaufman obtained a copy of the Kerr-Korda contract and forwarded it to Gordon's lawyer, the lawyer discovered an unusual clause. Kerr had signed away all rights to Korda so that if Gordon and Kaufman produced the play, they would not share in any film, radio, television, or other subsidiary income, one hundred per cent of which belonged to Korda. Gordon and Kaufman decided not to proceed.

The setback on the play was aggravated for Kaufman by health problems. He had found out about the hernia which eventually required an operation, and he wrote to Gordon, "I have just come back from having a truss fitted. This has depressed me a great deal—the whole idea of wearing an appliance—but I'll get over it." He also developed backaches. "Laid up with my damned back again," he wrote to Gordon. "I thought it had been cured, but apparently having to wear a truss has thrown it off again." He wrote to Ruth about his back, "I've had a corset made which I hate to wear—just hate it, but it was helping a little a few days ago, so of course I quit wearing it, and then it hurt again." He was using a cane at his time, but it was a very special one which had originally belonged to George M. Cohan's father. Cohan had willed it to Sam Harris, who in turn gave it in his will to Kaufman.

Despite his troubles, Kaufman was never without a sense of humor about them. He wrote Gordon about his difficulties in getting servants, saying that if *The Solid Gold Cadillac* closed, he'd hire Gordon. Later, Kaufman turned his irritation with the noise of Manhattan and his resulting problems in getting sleep into the poem called *New York: A Prayer*, which was published in *The New Yorker*'s issue of September 3, 1955.

After *Silk Stockings*, Kaufman found no worthwhile projects until Gordon brought him and S. N. Behrman together to write *The Legendary Mizners*, which Gordon wanted to do as a musical with a score by Irving Berlin. The show was to be based on a biography of Addison and Wilson Mizner, brothers who were Broadway celebrities in the early years of the century, by Alva Johnston. Wilson Mizner was famous for his wit, and though most witty comments are by nature topical and ephemeral, one of Mizner's survived to become a show business axiom. "Be nice to those you meet going up the ladder," he said. "They're the same people you'll meet coming back down again." He seemed to be a character made to order for Kaufman.

Behrman was born in Worcester, Massachusetts, on June 9, 1893. He attended Clark University, but switched to Harvard for his B.A., and earned his M.A. from Columbia. He was also an ex-*Times* man, having been assistant editor of the book review section when Kaufman was in the dramatic department. In 1924, Behrman wrote a one-act play called *A Night's Work*, in collaboration with Kenyon Nicholson, who later wrote *The Barker*, the hit which gave Claudette

Colbert her first successful role. *A Night's Work* was produced only at a summer hotel in Peekskill, New York, and was described by the majority of the audience as awful. Behrman's first Broadway production, *The Second Man*, did not excite playgoers, and closed after forty-four performances, despite the presence of the Lunts and Margalo Gillmore. But Behrman went on to write many hits, including *Biography*, *No Time for Comedy*, *Jacobowsky and the Colonel*, and his greatest success, *Fanny*, which was produced in 1954. His many successful books included *Duveen*, *The Worcester Account*, and *People in a Diary*, and he wrote, among other Hollywood assignments, two Greta Garbo classics, *Queen Christina* and the script of Tolstoy's *Anna Karenina*. Behrman died at the age of eighty, of a heart attack, on September 10, 1973, following a stroke which had placed him in a wheelchair three months earlier.

Gordon paid Behrman a $5000 advance and signed Irving Berlin, and Kaufman and Behrman went to work. But it soon became apparent that the basic idea of *The Legendary Mizners* lacked substance, and Kaufman began to feel that they were like authors whom Behrman himself had once dismissed as "writers who mask sterility with incessant productivity." The collaborators agreed to drop the project, and Gordon's advance was returned.

Throughout 1956, Gordon kept looking for a project good enough to interest Kaufman, but Kaufman turned them all down, and none of his negative judgments were proved wrong by anyone. In August, Gordon rushed him a play by Andy McCullough called *Benedict Arnold*. "I like a great deal of it," Gordon wrote, "and if Columbia or NBC would put up the $250,000 necessary, I would be for doing it. We would, of course, have 50 per cent of the show for nothing. I think the best thing for us to do is to have 50 per cent of every show without putting up any money. We can sell our interest on a capital gains basis under a tax decision handed down in favor of Herman Levin, who sold 20 per cent of *My Fair Lady* on a capital gains basis."

"I'm sorry," Kaufman said in reply, "that you spent $4.90 to send the McCullough play over so fast—it really could have waited. I don't think a play can be written by a scissors and a pastepot—some place the writer has to do some writing. I can't imagine this holding an audience."

Gordon next bought *Gordy* by Arthur Marx, Groucho's son, and Mannie Manheim, and rushed a copy to Kaufman with a note that Oscar Hammerstein II loved it. "I can't see it," Kaufman replied, "and am worried that you and Oscar think it's promising. If you feel strongly, you should do it, but I could never work on it." Then, after thinking over what he'd written, Kaufman became concerned that Gordon might take it as encouragement to go ahead with the play. He wrote again to Gordon, "I'm afraid I don't trust Oscar's judgment at all. As for yours, I always respect it, as you know, but I think you're making yourself see things in this play that aren't there." Gordon replied, "I will respect your wishes about the Marx play, if it's a failure. If it's a hit, I will put your share in a trunk and keep it there until I convince you to take it. I know you think there is very little chance of a quarter being made with this show, but it will surely sell for a picture, and the stock and amateur rights will be big." But Kaufman had been right in the first place, and there was no share for him to take.

Kaufman was more interested in *The Lipstick War*, a musical he began to write next with Alan Campbell, who was living for a while in London. Campbell was born in Virginia in 1905, and graduated from Virginia Military Institute, but decided before his graduation that he wanted to become an actor. His family sent him to Europe to change his mind, but he was still determined when he returned, and went to New York, where he got a job in the Shubert costume department. He then met Eve Le Gallienne, got some small parts in her company, and also played Laurette Taylor's son on Broadway in *The Furies*. Campbell then switched to writing, married Dorothy Parker, and collaborated with her on the screenplays of the original *A Star Is Born*, *Trade Winds*, *Saboteur*, and *Sweethearts*. Campbell and Miss Parker were divorced in 1947, but remarried in 1950. Campbell killed himself with an overdose of sleeping pills on June 15, 1963, at the age of fifty-eight.

The Lipstick War is a satire on big business, government regulations, advertising, and the stock market. It concerns a big lipstick firm and its struggles with a federal antitrust suit. Kaufman warned

Gordon against any publicity about his work with Campbell in London, since Kaufman's visa was a non-working one, and any work would mean he would be subject to British income tax. So Kaufman and Campbell worked in secret at 17 Blomfield Road. Gordon started to line up a team for the score, and proposed bringing in Rodgers and Hammerstein, but Kaufman vetoed the idea. "I disagree with you completely," he wrote to Gordon, "about the Rodgers and Hammerstein idea. This is not their kind of show, and I would not enjoy working with them on the terms that I know I would have to work with them. Also, it would not wind up as your show, either. Let's keep this one to ourselves . . . I don't want to divide in any way with Rodgers and Hammerstein. Just a temperamental bastard, that's me." But the discussion proved to be irrelevant, when, three days after Kaufman had sent a draft of the play to Gordon, Gordon cabled back and said that he just did not like it and couldn't produce it.

Other abortive projects in this period included a play which Art Buchwald was supposed to be writing, but which never materialized; *Jamboree*, a musical by Abel Kandel, which Gordon sent to Kaufman, but which Kaufman turned down as old-fashioned; and a musical version of *The Women*, with lyrics by Alan Jay Lerner, which Gordon talked about doing, but which never really got started.

Kaufman returned to the United States three week later, his mood very low. Shortly after he arrived, Hassard Short died, on October 9. The past two years had seen too many friends die: Irving Pichel on July 13, 1954, John Golden on June 17, 1955, Robert E. Sherwood on November 14, 1955, and Charles MacArthur on April 21, 1956. In late 1956 and early 1957, Kaufman was as depressed as he had ever been, and even reverted to his old fears of becoming another Owen Davis.

Then, in June 1957, something finally clicked. Kaufman was approached by David Merrick, who was preparing to produce Peter Ustinov's London hit, *Romanoff and Juliet*, on Broadway. Merrick, a relative newcomer to Broadway production, had previously been a successful lawyer, and had produced *Fanny* in 1954, *The Matchmaker* in 1955, and *Look Back in Anger* in 1957. He would later become the top Broadway producer of the period with such blockbusters as *Gypsy, Irma La Douce, Becket, Oliver, Stop the*

World—I Want to Get Off, Hello, Dolly, and others. *Romanoff and Juliet* had first tried out in Edinburgh, Scotland, and then been sent to Liverpool for a tryout week before opening in London. On the opening night in Liverpool, Merrick walked into Ustinov's dressing room, introduced himself, and said that he wanted to do the play in New York. Ustinov invited him to supper after the show, and the deal was closed there. Merrick was a great admirer of Kaufman and wanted him to direct the play, but Kaufman wasn't sure that he had the strength, and told Merrick that he might not be able to finish. Merrick replied that he'd take that chance. Kaufman appeared at the earliest rehearsals leaning on his cane, but put it aside within a few days and was his old self again. Merrick said, "Just getting back to the theatre has made a new man of him. He's going to be wonderful for the play."

Peter Ustinov, who was both author and star of the play, and who was making his Broadway acting debut, was not pleased with Kaufman's direction. Ustinov had directed and produced the play himself in England, and did not always see the point of Kaufman's changes. Ustinov, born April 16, 1921, was the son of a British journalist and his artist wife, and as a child showed a remarkable gift for mimicry. He made his professional debut at the age of seventeen in *The Wood Demon*, and was best known to American audiences as an actor in the films *Quo Vadis* in 1951, *The Egyptian* in 1954, and *We're No Angels* in 1955. At one point, Ustinov became so angry with Kaufman that he asked Merrick to replace Kaufman as director. Merrick refused, saying that even if it meant a flop—which he was certain it wouldn't—he would never hurt Kaufman at this stage of Kaufman's life. Ustinov bowed to Merrick, and rehearsals continued without incident. Kaufman was not offended, and in a press interview, just before the Boston tryout, called Ustinov "a gay and highly companionable fellow," and called *Romanoff and Juliet* "about the best play I've come in contact with these many years."

Kaufman wrote an article about the play called *The Tryout Blues (or Coos)*, which appeared in the New York *Herald Tribune* on September 21, 1957. Kaufman discussed the qualities of Boston, Philadelphia, Wilmington, and New Haven as tryout towns for prospective Broadway productions. He said that he couldn't explain it, but one always had a bad third act in Wilmington. Since it couldn't be the authors who were responsible, he said, it had to be the town. Philadelphia, Kaufman said, was too comfortable and pleasant. "New Haven," he wrote, "is a charming town, but so far as I am concerned, after you've seen the Yale campus, you're through for the week. It was Joe Fields who, standing in the lobby of New Haven's leading hostelry, looked about him with a baleful eye, and observed, 'They opened this hotel in New Haven twenty years ago and never did bring it in.' "

Besides Ustinov, Jack Gilford, Fred Clark, and Kaufman's old friend Natalie Shafer were in the cast of *Romanoff and Juliet*. The play opened at the Plymouth Theatre on Thursday, October 10, 1957, to a very warm critical reception, and even warmer response from the delighted first night audience. In the *Post*, Richard Watts, Jr., called the play "a quiet, genial, warmhearted satire, as charming as it is entertaining," and John Chapman in the *News* called it "a deft, funny, delightful fable." And Frank Aston in the *World-Telegram and Sun* had special praise for Kaufman. "It was comforting to know," he said, "that when speeches grew windy, relief would come soon, because George S. Kaufman had done the staging." The play was a very solid hit, and ran for 389 performances, closing on September 13, 1958.

Kaufman continued to explore new projects. During his work on *Romanoff and Juliet*, he began to collaborate with a young playwright named Helen Hunter on *Apartment to Share*, which he described in a letter to Ruth as a lightweight comedy. He told Gordon, "If I can last with *Romanoff*, I'll probably want to direct the Hunter play myself—there would be so much to explain to a director that I could find it easier to do myself." Then he talked about the hard work of interviewing actors for the Ustinov play. He said that if he and Gordon produced *Apartment to Share*, he wanted an assistant director to handle this chore for him, and he proposed his choice for his assistant. "It's Alan Campbell, who is smart as hell and also broke as hell, and altogether a charming man. I hope you'll go for this when the time comes. If I get the usual 2½ per cent for directing," he added, "I'd take 2 and give him the remaining ½." He signed the note "Old Man Kaufman." His hidden motive, a desire to help Campbell, was obvious, but remained stillborn, since the writing of *Apartment to Share* was abandoned in October.

Leueen still came to see him, and they collaborated on a one-act play called *Amicable Parting*, about an intellectual couple who decide to get a divorce but encounter difficulties in splitting up their property. The play was published, but its only performance was a five-day presentation by the Camden, New Jersey, Lunch Theatre at the Off Broadway Playhouse, during lunch hours from June 3 through June 7, 1968.

Kaufman also attempted a collaboration with Ruth Goetz, whose husband and collaborator, Augustus Goetz, had died September 30, 1957. The play was called *The Same as Before Only Worse*. The title, Kaufman decided eventually, described what they had written, and no attempt was made at production. The same fate befell *Story of a Woman*, which Kaufman wrote with Leueen. Gordon continued to read plays, interviewing and buying lunch for an army of playwrights, but developed no viable projects.

Kaufman kept writing short humor pieces. *Musical Comedy—or Musical Serious?* appeared in *The New York Times Magazine* of November 3, 1957, and has serious overtones, talking about the death of the straight-comedy musical and the trend toward plays of the style of *Oklahoma!* Kaufman wrote one piece for *The Saturday Review*'s issue of July 16, 1958, called *Here's Good News from A&P*, and another, *It's a Dirty Word*, taking Brooks Atkinson to task for having objected to the word "with" in the credits of a play by two collaborators, which appeared in *The Saturday Review* on November 15, 1958. *Mother Goose and the Golden Egg*, a satirical playlet aimed at the many restrictions and obstacles imposed in the theatre by unions, ran in *The Saturday Review*'s issue of February 21, 1959.

Despite his continued pursuit of his interests, the weakening of Kaufman's body gradually caught up with him and overtook him. He fainted at the theatre party following the opening of *My Fair Lady* on December 21, 1956. He fainted again at the premiere of John Osborne's *The Entertainer* at the Royale Theatre on February 13, 1958, falling unconscious across the lap of a woman seated near him. Sam Zolotow was in the theatre that night and rushed him home, fearing that Kaufman was nearly gone. But Kaufman was feeling fine by the time they got home, and Zolotow, enormously relieved, was suddenly so starved that he dashed to Kaufman's refrigerator and ate it virtually empty. Kaufman's doctor, Dr. Edward B. Greenspan, said that Kaufman had had a gastric attack the day before and hadn't eaten that day, and that this plus the very warm theatre were the only causes of the fainting spell. The doctor did not have to add that old age and declining strength were also involved.

In the last years of his life, Kaufman suffered a series of strokes, and lost temporarily the use of one hand and one eye. He also had three prostate operations in his last years. He even, finally, tried psychoanalysis, going to a lady doctor, Dr. Ruth C. Conkey, but he gave her up, saying, "She's asking too damn many personal questions."

Kaufman had, of course, always feared old age and death. But toward the end, he made peace with his fears, and was able to write to Ruth, who was away on a trip, on July 25, 1960, "The doctor says I'm pretty good—afraid I'll still be here when you get back." He could even write a letter cheering up Gordon on one of *his* depressions. "You sound better," Kaufman wrote, "and properly keen again. Believing in yourself is the main thing, and you have plenty of evidence to support that belief. I suffer a little in that department myself, so I understand it. Pat Weaver," he added in a reference to Sylvester Weaver, called Pat, one-time president of NBC, "will be watering the streets when you're still producing shows." To Moss Hart, he proposed a new credit listing for himself, as follows: "By George S. Kaufman, plus glucose, lecithin, bemax, serpisal, anesolysene, nutrilite, lipotaine, equanil, empirin, veganin, codeine, dramamine, Doctors E. B. Greenspan, L. S. Kubie, J. Janvrin, C. L. Johnson, Vitamins B1-2-3-4-5-6-7-8-9-10-11 and -12, laboratory staff of Mount Sinai Hospital, phenobarbital, seconal, nembutal, truian, and FUCKITALL," startling Hart with this rare use of a four-letter word. In another jest at illness, he said of Howard Lindsay, who was a year older than he: "I watch him carefully to see what I'm going to catch next."

On March 9, 1944, Kaufman had written to his brother-in-law,

Leonard Bakrow, recounting an incident which had just happened. He'd gone down in the elevator, and the operator told him that the man in Ten South had died the previous night. Since Kaufman lived in Ten South, this gave him "something of a turn." The operator meant the man in Twelve South, but Kaufman wrote Bakrow, "Naturally, this started the day off fine—and from there it was all downhill." But by 1960, with death very much closer, he would have laughed at the incident. Near the very end of his life, he ran into Peggy Leech Pulitzer one day, and realized that they had both grown very old. "My God, Peggy," he was able to say. "I thought we were both dead."

He was also able to joke about doctors, as when a friend recommended a doctor on the grounds that he was an expert on the theatre. "I don't want a doctor who spends a lot of time at the theatre," Kaufman said. "The kind of doctor I want is one who, when he's not examining me, is home studying medicine."

32. THE END

AS THE DOCTORS who attended him could testify, Kaufman's spirit and style were strong until the very last day of his life. The first time that Kaufman was examined by his new physician, Dr. Menard Gertler, a specialist in geriatrics, he argued forcefully when told that he had to give up smoking. Kaufman stubbornly insisted that he had to have at least two cigarettes a day to calm his nerves, but Gertler remained adamant. Kaufman was relieved; he had no strong desire to smoke, but had wanted to test his doctor's firmness. On another occasion, he called the doctor, who rushed over, thinking from Kaufman's manner that his patient might be close to dying. But he found Kaufman in better shape than he had been in weeks. "I just wanted to see how long it would take you to get here if I really was sick," Kaufman said.

Kaufman remained fully engaged with his friends and with his writing. His interest in the health of his friends was no longer tainted with morbid fears for himself. Many years before, when George Gershwin had died, Kaufman started having severe headaches. Beatrice told him, then, "George, it's remarkable that you should have the same ailments as your friends, but it's even more remarkable that you should have them in the same order." But now his hypochondria faded, and when his friends were ill, or when they had died, Kaufman's feelings were for them alone. He suffered the loss of Herbert Bayard Swope on June 21, 1958, and John P. Marquand on July 17, 1960, and lost an especially close friend when Franklin P. Adams died on March 24, 1960. Kaufman also admired and liked Dashiell Hammett, author of *The Maltese Falcon, The Thin Man,* and other mystery classics, and phoned Lillian Hellman, author of *The Little Foxes,* daily when Hammett was near death at her home.

Kaufman grew progressively weaker, but he never lost his sharp intelligence, as his essays and other writing projects demonstrate. His last piece for *The New Yorker, Memoir,* which appeared in the June 11, 1960, issue, pokes fun at one of Kaufman's favorite targets, songwriters, in particular taking to task his old friend Irving Berlin for writing *When the Midnight Choo-Choo Leaves for Alabam.* Kaufman points out that he went over to Pennsylvania Station one day and learned that the southbound train actually leaves at 12:19. "Ever since then," Kaufman says, "I have not quite believed everything I heard in a song lyric."

Leueen came to see him frequently and often stayed at his place while they worked together. In the year before his death, they collaborated on a play, *I Give It Six Months,* a title which was a gift from Dorothy Parker. On a trip to Hollywood, Mrs. Parker saw a picture which a press agent had rigged up as a publicity stunt. It showed two elephants dressed as bride and groom. "I give it six months," Mrs. Parker said. Kaufman's and Leueen's play is about a woman from abroad who falls in love with a New York cabdriver. The play's hero was surprising, considering Kaufman's well-known dislike of cabdrivers, and caused his friends to conclude that he really was mellowing; he occasionally said, later in life, that

Colbert her first successful role. *A Night's Work* was produced only at a summer hotel in Peekskill, New York, and was described by the majority of the audience as awful. Behrman's first Broadway production, *The Second Man,* did not excite playgoers, and closed after forty-four performances, despite the presence of the Lunts and Margalo Gillmore. But Behrman went on to write many hits, including *Biography, No Time for Comedy, Jacobowsky and the Colonel,* and his greatest success, *Fanny,* which was produced in 1954. His many successful books included *Duveen, The Worcester Account,* and *People in a Diary,* and he wrote, among other Hollywood assignments, two Greta Garbo classics, *Queen Christina* and the script of Tolstoy's *Anna Karenina.* Behrman died at the age of eighty, of a heart attack, on September 10, 1973, following a stroke which had placed him in a wheelchair three months earlier.

Gordon paid Behrman a $5000 advance and signed Irving Berlin, and Kaufman and Behrman went to work. But it soon became apparent that the basic idea of *The Legendary Mizners* lacked substance, and Kaufman began to feel that they were like authors whom Behrman himself had once dismissed as "writers who mask sterility with incessant productivity." The collaborators agreed to drop the project, and Gordon's advance was returned.

Throughout 1956, Gordon kept looking for a project good enough to interest Kaufman, but Kaufman turned them all down, and none of his negative judgments were proved wrong by anyone. In August, Gordon rushed him a play by Andy McCullough called *Benedict Arnold.* "I like a great deal of it," Gordon wrote, "and if Columbia or NBC would put up the $250,000 necessary, I would be for doing it. We would, of course, have 50 per cent of the show for nothing. I think the best thing for us to do is to have 50 per cent of every show without putting up any money. We can sell our interest on a capital gains basis under a tax decision handed down in favor of Herman Levin, who sold 20 per cent of *My Fair Lady* on a capital gains basis."

"I'm sorry," Kaufman said in reply, "that you spent $4.90 to send the McCullough play over so fast—it really could have waited. I don't think a play can be written by a scissors and a pastepot—some place the writer has to do some writing. I can't imagine this holding an audience."

Gordon next bought *Gordy* by Arthur Marx, Groucho's son, and Mannie Manheim, and rushed a copy to Kaufman with a note that Oscar Hammerstein II loved it. "I can't see it," Kaufman replied, "and am worried that you and Oscar think it's promising. If you feel strongly, you should do it, but I could never work on it." Then, after thinking over what he'd written, Kaufman became concerned that Gordon might take it as encouragement to go ahead with the play. He wrote again to Gordon, "I'm afraid I don't trust Oscar's judgment at all. As for yours, I always respect it, as you know, but I think you're making yourself see things in this play that aren't there." Gordon replied, "I will respect your wishes about the Marx play, if it's a failure. If it's a hit, I will put your share in a trunk and keep it there until I convince you to take it. I know you think there is very little chance of a quarter being made with this show, but it will surely sell for a picture, and the stock and amateur rights will be big." But Kaufman had been right in the first place, and there was no share for him to take.

Kaufman was more interested in *The Lipstick War*, a musical he began to write next with Alan Campbell, who was living for a while in London. Campbell was born in Virginia in 1905, and graduated from Virginia Military Institute, but decided before his graduation that he wanted to become an actor. His family sent him to Europe to change his mind, but he was still determined when he returned, and went to New York, where he got a job in the Shubert costume department. He then met Eve Le Gallienne, got some small parts in her company, and also played Laurette Taylor's son on Broadway in *The Furies*. Campbell then switched to writing, married Dorothy Parker, and collaborated with her on the screenplays of the original *A Star Is Born*, *Trade Winds*, *Saboteur*, and *Sweethearts*. Campbell and Miss Parker were divorced in 1947, but remarried in 1950. Campbell killed himself with an overdose of sleeping pills on June 15, 1963, at the age of fifty-eight.

The Lipstick War is a satire on big business, government regulations, advertising, and the stock market. It concerns a big lipstick firm and its struggles with a federal antitrust suit. Kaufman warned his nature was that he felt deeply, yet he sheered from any display of emotion. Almost always, it remained unexpressed."

Then Hart told about the time that he had been about to go on that journey and Kaufman had appeared unconcerned. "I did not spend that last evening in New York with my family," Hart said. "I spent it with George, for George in many ways was more father to me than my own father. We had dinner together and talked through the evening—and not once did he mention my leave-taking or the reason for my going. When it came time to go, he saw me to the door, and lifted that inevitable finger of his in his gesture of goodbye. That was all. I walked home bitterly—and there on my desk was a three-page, single-spaced, typewritten letter, hand-delivered while he sat opposite me saying nothing of what he felt—the letter saying what he found himself incapable of saying to me face-to-face. How sad that he should have known that he could not say the words to me himself, but how marvelous that he should have written that letter beforehand.

"Finally, there was George the playwright. We all sat at his feet. My own debt to him is incalculable, but he would be astonished and disbelieving even now if he were told that the theatre, too, is in his debt. He was never really aware of the position he held (he had pride, but no vanity whatever), and he completely under-estimated the contribution he made to the theatre of his time. Yet no history of that time in the American theatre can be written with-out George S. Kaufman's name and influence on it looming large and clear.

"The people who worked with him in the theatre, and all of us, his friends, owe him a different kind of debt, a very special one. He was a unique and arresting man, and there are few enough unique people in anyone's time. Nature does not toss them up too often. And part of our loss is that we will not know again the uniqueness and special taste and flavor that was George. But part of our solace is that we were lucky enough to have known him—that he lived in our time."

With Kaufman's death, a great deal of material appeared in the press recounting his wit. Among many, many other incidents, it was recalled that, when *Vanity Fair* had asked a number of celebrities to write their own epitaphs, Kaufman had suggested "Over My Dead Body!" matched only by Dorothy Parker's "Excuse My Dust!" Ruth Friedlich recalled the seventeenth birthday of her twin children, and Kaufman's telegram to them beginning, NOW THAT YOU ARE 34 . . . And Ruth Gordon remembered the time that Kaufman was trying out a play in Atlantic City when she was there appearing in a drama. Her audience, she told Kaufman unhappily, laughed during her tragic scenes. Kaufman suggested that since his audiences weren't laughing during his funny ones, the thing for them to do was change audiences.

Among the serious tributes to Kaufman was Charles Martin's statement that "he was easily one of the greatest dramatists who ever lived, and a master constructionist." And Groucho Marx said, "There should be a permanent theatrical memorial to George S. Kaufman. Kaufman was no two- or three-play wonder. He made America laugh for over forty years."

Kaufman was gone personally, but he was not forgotten. His humor and art remained impressive, unlike the wit of contemporaries who sparkled for a few seasons and then faded. More than five years after his death, on October 1, 1966, the New York *Times* reported, "The late George S. Kaufman will be the best represented writer this season, on or off Broadway. Four of his plays, three of them collaborations, are scheduled for presentation between now and March." Three of these were revivals, *Dinner at Eight, You Can't Take it with You,* and *The Butter and Egg Man.* In addition to these, *Sherry,* the musical version of *The Man Who Came to Dinner,* was also presented that season. A columnist reported that the income from the revivals "could run into the millions, and George S. Kaufman is obviously the season's hottest playwright." *Life* magazine, reporting on the revivals, spelled Kaufman with two n's, which probably would have drawn a comment from Kaufman about his fleeting fame. But Richard Barr, one of the producers of *The Butter and Egg Man,* said, "His plays will be done for generations to come."

During Kaufman's last days, Leueen refused to take the lead in a revival of Ibsen's *Ghosts,* in order to be with her ex-husband. Then, when Kaufman died, she told David Ross, the producer, that she just didn't feel like working at all. She went to Europe, and returned in August, somewhat recovered, to play the Ibsen role at the 4th Street Theatre. She was set to appear in *The Cherry Orchard* in October 1962, but was replaced by Signe Hasso after she disagreed with the director about the execution of her role. She remained inactive after that, despite occasional announcements that she would be returning in a play, until September 1970, when she took the part of Lady Nelson in Terence Rattigan's *A Bequest to the Nation* in London.

The Kaufman circle grew smaller with the passing of the years. Moss Hart, Kaufman's greatest collaborator, lived only six months after delivering his eulogy, and died in Palm Springs, California, on December 20, 1961. A memorial service for Hart was held a short time later, in the Music Box Theatre.

Alan Campbell's suicide followed on June 14, 1963. Ben Hecht died on April 18, 1964. Bernard Hart, Moss Hart's brother and stage manager, died on August 28, 1964. Harpo Marx died on September 28 of the same year, and Groucho said sadly to a friend of his and Harpo's, Betty Comden, "I worked with Harpo for forty years, which is longer than most marriages, so his death leaves quite a void in my life. He was a nice man in the fullest sense of the word. He was worth all the wonderful adjectives that were used to describe him."

Joseph Fields's death came on March 4, 1966. Dorothy Parker was next, dying of a heart attack on June 7, 1967. She was seventy-three. Howard Lindsay died on February 11, 1968, and Laurence Stallings died on February 28.

Then, on April 16, 1968, Edna Ferber died, at the age of eighty-two. Her funeral service was at Campbell's, where Kaufman's funeral had been held. One of the eulogists, Ken McCormick, formerly editor-in-chief of Doubleday and now senior editorial consultant to the firm, read four passages from her book, *A Kind of Magic*, including a final section in which Miss Ferber said to the world, "I want to say I love you. I have always loved you—or almost always."

John Steinbeck died on December 20, 1968, and Robert B. Sinclair was murdered on January 2, 1970.

Next to die, on April 27, 1970, was Gypsy Rose Lee. Oscar

Levant died of a heart attack on August 14, 1972. S. N. Behrman died following a stroke on September 9, 1973. Samuel Goldwyn died on January 31, 1974. Harry Ruby died on February 24, 1974, in Beverly Hills. And Margaret Leech Pulitzer died on the same day in New York.

The simplest and saddest statement of what had happened to the circle was made by Dorothy Parker, toward the end of her own life. "So many of them died," she said. "My Lord, how people die."

APPENDIX

DRAMATIC WORKS*

The Failure (with Irving Pichel)
  1903
  (*never produced*)

Going Up, sketch
  1916
  (*never produced*)

Someone in the House (with Larry Evans and Walter C. Percival)
  Knickerbocker Theatre
  September 9, 1918
  Produced by George C. Tyler
  37 performances

Jacques Duval
  Blackstone Theatre (Chicago, Illinois)
  November 10, 1919
  Produced by George C. Tyler
  (*closed out of town*)

Dulcy (with Marc Connelly)
  Frazee Theatre
  August 13, 1921
  Produced by George C. Tyler and H. H. Frazee
  246 performances

To the Ladies (with Marc Connelly)
  Liberty Theatre
  February 20, 1922
  Produced by George C. Tyler and A. L. Erlanger
  128 performances

---

* Except where otherwise noted, all theatres, opening dates, producers, and performance totals refer to first New York runs.

No, Sirree! (with Marc Connelly)
    49th Street Theatre
    April 30, 1922
    Produced by The Vicious Circle of the Hotel Algonquin
    1 performance

The 49ers (with Marc Connelly)
    Punch and Judy Theatre
    November 7, 1922
    Produced by George C. Tyler
    15 performances

Merton of the Movies (with Marc Connelly)
    Cort Theatre
    November 13, 1922
    Produced by George C. Tyler and Hugh Ford
    248 performances

Helen of Troy, New York (with Marc Connelly)
    Selwyn Theatre
    June 19, 1923
    Produced by Rufus LeMaire and George Jessel
    191 performances

Beggar on Horseback (with Marc Connelly)
    Broadhurst Theatre
    February 12, 1924
    Produced by Winthrop Ames
    144 performances

Beggar off Horseback, sketch (with Marc Connelly)
    (used in revue, *'Round the Town*)
    The Century Roof
    May 21, 1924
    Produced by S. Jay Kaufman and Herman J. Mankiewicz
    14 performances

Just a Corner of Old Hyde Park, London, England, song lyric
    (used in revue, *'Round the Town*)

Moron Films, Educational, Travel, and Topical, sketch (with Herman J. Mankiewicz)
    (used in revue, *'Round the Town*)

Be Yourself (with Marc Connelly)
    Sam H. Harris Theatre
    September 3, 1924
    Produced by Wilmer and Vincent
    93 performances

Minick (with Edna Ferber)
    Booth Theatre
    September 24, 1924
    Produced by Winthrop Ames
    141 performances

The Butter and Egg Man
    Longacre Theatre
    September 23, 1925
    Produced by Crosby Gaige
    243 performances

The Cocoanuts (with Morrie Ryskind)
    Lyric Theatre
    December 8, 1925
    Produced by Sam H. Harris
    218 performances

Business Is Business, short film (with Dorothy Parker)
    1925
    Produced by Paramount Pictures

The Good Fellow (with Herman J. Mankiewicz)
    Playhouse Theatre
    October 5, 1926
    Produced by Crosby Gaige
    7 performances

The Royal Family (with Edna Ferber)
    Selwyn Theatre
    December 28, 1927
    Produced by Jed Harris
    345 performances

Animal Crackers (with Morrie Ryskind)
    44th Street Theatre
    October 23, 1928
    Produced by Sam H. Harris
    191 performances

The Still Alarm, sketch
    (used in revue, *The Little Show*)
    Music Box Theatre
    April 30, 1929
    Produced by William A. Brady, Jr. and Dwight Deere Wiman
    55 performances

June Moon (with Ring Lardner)
    Broadhurst Theatre
    October 9, 1929
    Produced by Sam H. Harris
    273 performances

The Channel Road (with Alexander Woollcott)
    Plymouth Theatre
    October 17, 1929
    Produced by Arthur Hopkins
    60 performances

If Men Played Cards as Women Do, short film
    1929
    Produced by Paramount-Famous-Lasky
    (also used as sketch in film, *Star-Spangled Rhythm*, 1943, produced by Paramount Pictures)

Strike Up the Band (with Morrie Ryskind)
    Times Square Theatre
    January 14, 1930
    Produced by Edgar Selwyn
    191 performances

Once in a Lifetime (with Moss Hart)
    Music Box Theatre
    September 24, 1930
    Produced by Sam H. Harris
    305 performances

The Band Wagon (with Howard Dietz)
    New Amsterdam Theatre
    June 3, 1931
    Produced by Max Gordon
    260 performances

Eldorado (with Laurence Stallings)
  Shubert Theatre (New Haven, Connecticut)
  October 26, 1931
  Produced by Isadore Polisuk and Sam H. Harris
  (*closed out of town*)

Of Thee I Sing (with Morrie Ryskind)
  Music Box Theatre
  December 26, 1931
  Produced by Sam H. Harris
  441 performances

Dinner at Eight (with Edna Ferber)
  Music Box Theatre
  October 22, 1932
  Produced by Sam H. Harris
  232 performances

Let 'Em Eat Cake (with Morrie Ryskind)
  Imperial Theatre
  October 21, 1933
  Produced by Sam H. Harris
  90 performances

The Dark Tower (with Alexander Woollcott)
  Morosco Theatre
  November 25, 1933
  Produced by Sam H. Harris
  57 performances

Roman Scandals, film (with Robert E. Sherwood, George Oppenheimer, Arthur Sheekman, Nat Perrin, and W. A. McGuire)
  1933
  Produced by Samuel Goldwyn and United Artists

Merrily We Roll Along (with Moss Hart)
  Music Box Theatre
  September 29, 1934
  Produced by Sam H. Harris
  155 performances

Spring Song by Sam and Bella Spewack (*served as play doctor*)
  Morosco Theatre
  October 1, 1934
  Produced by Max Gordon
  40 performances

Bring on the Girls (with Morrie Ryskind)
  National Theatre (Washington, D.C.)
  October 22, 1934
  Produced by Sam H. Harris
  (*closed out of town*)

First Lady (with Katharine Dayton)
  Music Box Theatre
  November 26, 1935
  Produced by Sam H. Harris
  238 performances

Tomorrow's a Holiday by Romney Brent (*served as play doctor*)
  Golden Theatre
  December 30, 1935
  Produced by John Golden and Joseph Schildkraut
  8 performances

A Night at the Opera, film (with Morrie Ryskind and James Kevin
    McGuinness)
  1935
  Produced by Metro-Goldwyn-Mayer

Stage Door (with Edna Ferber)
  Music Box Theatre
  October 22, 1936
  Produced by Sam H. Harris
  169 performances

You Can't Take It with You (with Moss Hart)
  Booth Theatre
  December 14, 1936
  Produced by Sam H. Harris
  837 performances

I'd Rather Be Right (with Moss Hart)
    Alvin Theatre
    November 2, 1937
    Produced by Sam H. Harris
    266 performances

Save Me the Waltz by Katharine Dayton (*served as play doctor*)
    Martin Beck Theatre
    February 28, 1938
    Produced by Max Gordon
    8 performances

Sing Out the News by Harold Rome and Charles Friedman
    (officially conceived and directed by Charles Friedman, but the
        program adds "with a bow to George S. Kaufman," and Kauf-
        man and Hart purportedly contributed two sketches, though
        they are not credited)
    Music Box Theatre
    September 24, 1938
    Produced by George S. Kaufman, Moss Hart, and Max Gordon
    105 performances

The Fabulous Invalid (with Moss Hart)
    Broadhurst Theatre
    October 8, 1938
    Produced by Sam H. Harris
    65 performances

The American Way (with Moss Hart)
    Center Theatre
    January 21, 1939
    Produced by Sam H. Harris and Max Gordon
    244 performances

The Man Who Came to Dinner (with Moss Hart)
    Music Box Theatre
    October 16, 1939
    Produced by Sam H. Harris
    739 performances

George Washington Slept Here (with Moss Hart)
　　Lyceum Theatre
　　October 18, 1940
　　Produced by Sam H. Harris
　　173 performances

The Land Is Bright (with Edna Ferber)
　　Music Box Theatre
　　October 28, 1941
　　Produced by Max Gordon
　　79 performances

Sleeper Jump, screenplay (with Herman J. Mankiewicz)
　　1942
　　(*never produced*)

Dream on, Soldier, sketch (with Moss Hart)
　　Madison Square Garden
　　April 5, 1943
　　Produced by the American Red Cross
　　1 performance

The Late George Apley (with John P. Marquand)
　　Lyceum Theatre
　　November 21, 1944
　　Produced by Max Gordon
　　357 performances

Local Boy Makes Good, sketch
　　(used in revue, *The Seven Lively Arts*)
　　Ziegfeld Theatre
　　December 7, 1944
　　Produced by Billy Rose
　　183 performances

Hollywood Pinafore
　　Alvin Theatre
　　May 31, 1945
　　Produced by Max Gordon and Meyer Davis
　　52 performances

Park Avenue (with Nunnally Johnson)
  Shubert Theatre
  November 4, 1946
  Produced by Max Gordon
  72 performances

School for Waiters, basic material for sketch
  (used in revue, *Inside U.S.A.*)
  Century Theatre
  April 30, 1948
  Produced by Arthur Schwartz
  399 performances

Bravo! (with Edna Ferber)
  Lyceum Theatre
  November 11, 1948
  Produced by Max Gordon
  44 performances

The Small Hours (with Leueen MacGrath)
  National Theatre
  February 15, 1951
  Produced by Max Gordon
  20 performances

Fancy Meeting You Again (with Leueen MacGrath)
  Royale Theatre
  January 14, 1952
  Produced by Chandler Cowles and Ben Segal
  8 performances

And Baby Makes Two (with Leueen MacGrath)
  1952
  (*never produced*)

United Nations (with Howard Teichmann)
  1952
  (*never finished*)

The Solid Gold Cadillac (with Howard Teichmann)
  Belasco Theatre
  November 5, 1953
  Produced by Max Gordon
  526 performances

The Hat, television play (with Leueen MacGrath)
   1953
   (*never produced*)

Under the Influence (with Geoffrey Kerr)
   1954
   (*never finished*)

Story of a Woman (with Leueen MacGrath)
   1954
   (*never produced*)

Exile (with Howard Teichmann)
   1954
   (*never produced*)

In the Money (with Howard Teichmann)
   1954
   (*never finished*)

Silk Stockings (with Leueen MacGrath and Abe Burrows)
   Imperial Theatre
   February 24, 1955
   Produced by Cy Feuer and Ernest Martin
   478 performances

The Lipstick War (with Alan Campbell)
   1956
   (*never produced*)

Apartment to Share (with Helen Hunter)
   1957
   (*never finished*)

Amicable Parting, sketch (with Leueen MacGrath)
   Off Broadway Playhouse (Camden, New Jersey)
   1957; first performance June 3, 1968
   Produced by Off Broadway Playhouse
   5 performances

The Same as Before Only Worse (with Ruth Goetz)
   1958
   (*never produced*)

APPENDIX

I Give It Six Months (with Leueen MacGrath)
    1961
    (*never produced*)

Labor Leader (with Marc Connelly)
    1961
    (*never finished*)

PUBLISHED WORKS

Short Humor and Humorous Poetry, many items
  (The Passaic, New Jersey, *Herald*, 1909)

Short Humor and Humorous Poetry, many items
  (In Franklin Pierce Adams's columns, first in the New York *Mail*, then in the New York *Tribune*, then in the New York *World*, 1909–1922)

This and That and a Little of the Other, humor column
  (The Washington *Times*, first six times weekly and then seven times weekly, from December 9, 1912 to December 1, 1913)

On the Value of a College Education, humor
  (*Princeton Tiger*, Spring 1914)

"Kick-In" Scores Field Goal at Republic Theatre, article
  (*Gotham Weekly Gazette*, January 17, 1915)

Be That as It May, humor column
  (The New York *Mail*, six times weekly, from February 5, 1915 to June 28, 1915)

The Mail Chute, humor column
  (The New York *Mail*, six times weekly, from June 29, 1915 to July 16, 1915)

Wringing in the New Year, article
  (*Harper's Weekly*, January 1, 1916)

Point and Counterpoint, article
  (*Musical America*, January 23, 1916)

The Theatrical Business Is Good, But—, article
  (*Dramatic Mirror*, March 1919)

APPENDIX

Collective Bargaining for Actors' Wages, article
  (*The New York Times Book Review and Magazine*, July 13,
  1919)

"Erminie": Thirty-five Years After, article
  (*The New York Times Book Review and Magazine*, January 2,
  1921)

The Other Side of Al Jolson, article
  (*Everybody's Magazine*, April 1921)

Ballade of the Unfortunate Fisherman, poem
  (*Life*, June 1921)

Life's Calendar (with Marc Connelly)
  (*Life*, monthly, January through December, 1922)

A Christmas Carol (with Marc Connelly), humor
  (*The Bookman*, December 1922)

Revelations on the Making of 'Merton' (with Marc Connelly), humor
  (The New York *Herald*, December 24, 1922)

An Explanation (with Edna Ferber), introduction to book
  (from *Old Man Minick and Minick* by Edna Ferber and George
  S. Kaufman, Doubleday, Page and Company, 1924)

Notes on an Infamous Collaboration, article
  (*Theatre Magazine*, December 1929)

How I Became a Great Actor, humor
  (*Theatre Magazine*, December 1930)

Jimmy the Well-Dressed Man, humor
  (*The Nation*, June 15, 1932)

With Gun and Camera in London, article
  (The New York *Times*, January 22, 1933)

Socratic Dialogue (with Morrie Ryskind), humor
  (*The Nation*, April 2, 1933)

The Green, White and Blue, humor
  (*The New Masses*, May 11, 1935)

All We Need Is Horse Sense, humor
  (*The New Yorker*, May 25, 1935)

Lines Upon Looking Through a Pile of Old Checks, poem
(*The New Yorker,* May 1, 1937)

God Gets an Idea, humor
(*The Nation,* February 19, 1938)

Music to My Ears, humor
(*Stage,* August 1938)

Einstein in Hollywood, humor
(*The Nation,* August 6, 1938)

The Meek Inherit the Earth, humor
(*The Nation,* October 1, 1938)

Interpretation, humor
(*The Nation,* May 13, 1939)

The Great Caviar Riots, humor
(*The Nation,* February 10, 1940)

Expectant Playwrights Saved, humor
(The New York *World-Telegram,* February 15, 1941)

Notes of a Co-Author, article
(The New York *Times,* November 2, 1941)

Untitled, introduction to book
(from *Better Bridge for Better Players* by Charles Goren, Doubleday, Doran and Company, 1942)

Forked Lightning, introduction to book
(from *Six Plays* by George S. Kaufman and Moss Hart, The Modern Library, 1942)

A Playwright Tells Almost All, humor
(*The New York Times Magazine,* September 17, 1944)

On Getting "Mr. Apley" Straight, article
(The New York *Times,* November 26, 1944)

In Nineteen Fifty-four, poem
(*Playbill,* February 4, 1945)

By the Way, humor
(*The Saturday Review of Literature,* August 11, 1945)

Notes for a Film Biography, humor
　　(*The New Yorker*, August 11, 1945)

Untitled, humor
　　(*The New Yorker, Department of Amplification*, June 29,
　　1946)

School for Waiters, humor
　　(*The New Yorker*, August 2, 1947)

That Morning Mail, poem
　　(*The New York Times Magazine*, April 18, 1948)

The Great Kibitzers' Strike of 1926, humor
　　(*The New Yorker*, November 26, 1949)

Amazing Anecdotes, humor
　　(The New York *Times*, February 11, 1951)

My Book and I, humor
　　(*The New Yorker*, May 26, 1951)

Does Newark Have to Be Where it Is?, humor
　　(*The New Yorker*, September 19, 1953)

Lines Written After Four Weeks in a Hospital, poem
　　(*The New Yorker*, May 1, 1954)

New York: A Prayer, poem
　　(*The New Yorker*, September 3, 1955)

The Tryout Blues (or Coos), humor
　　(The New York *Herald-Tribune*, September 21, 1957)

Musical Comedy—or Musical Serious?, article
　　(*The New York Times Magazine*, November 3, 1957)

Annoy Kaufman, Inc., humor
　(*The New Yorker*, December 21, 1957)

When Your Honey's on the Telephone, humor
　　(*The New Yorker*, February 22, 1958)

Here's Good News from A&P, humor
　　(*The Saturday Review*, July 16, 1958)

It's a Dirty Word, humor
　　(*The Saturday Review*, November 15, 1958)

Mother Goose and the Golden Egg, humor
    (*The Saturday Review,* February 21, 1959; reprinted in *Reader's Digest,* March, 1961)

Memoir, humor
    (*The New Yorker,* June 11, 1960)

Big Casino Is Little Casino, humor
    (*never published*)

NOTE: The thousands of news stories and reviews written by Kaufman as a staffer on the *Tribune* and *Times* have not, of course, been included. On the listed items, the choice of descriptive word or phrase has been fairly arbitrary. If a piece seemed more factual than funny, it's been called an article; and if a piece seemed to contain more fun than facts, it's been called humor.

DIRECTED BY GEORGE S. KAUFMAN

The Good Fellow by George S. Kaufman and Herman J. Mankie-
    wicz
  (co-directed with Howard Lindsay)
  Playhouse Theatre
  October 25, 1926
  Produced by Crosby Gaige
  7 performances

The Front Page by Ben Hecht and Charles MacArthur
  Times Square Theatre
  August 14, 1928
  Produced by Jed Harris
  276 performances

June Moon by Ring Lardner and George S. Kaufman
  Broadhurst Theatre
  October 9, 1929
  Produced by Sam H. Harris
  273 performances

Joseph by Bertram Bloch
  Liberty Theatre
  February 12, 1930
  Produced by John Golden
  13 performances

Once in a Lifetime by Moss Hart and George S. Kaufman
  Music Box Theatre
  September 24, 1930
  Produced by Sam H. Harris
  305 performances

Of Thee I Sing by George S. Kaufman and Morrie Ryskind
  Music Box Theatre
  December 26, 1931
  Produced by Sam H. Harris
  441 performances

Face the Music by Irving Berlin and Moss Hart
  (directed only the book; Hassard Short was general director)
  New Amsterdam Theatre
  February 17, 1932
  Produced by Sam H. Harris
  165 performances

Here Today by George Oppenheimer
  Ethel Barrymore Theatre
  October 8, 1932
  Produced by Sam H. Harris
  39 performances

Dinner at Eight by George S. Kaufman and Edna Ferber
  Music Box Theatre
  October 22, 1932
  Produced by Sam H. Harris
  232 performances

Let 'Em Eat Cake by George S. Kaufman and Morrie Ryskind
  Imperial Theatre
  October 21, 1933
  Produced by Sam H. Harris
  90 performances

The Dark Tower by Alexander Woollcott and George S. Kaufman
  (co-directed with Alexander Woollcott)
  Morosco Theatre
  November 25, 1933
  Produced by Sam H. Harris
  57 performances

Merrily We Roll Along by George S. Kaufman and Moss Hart
  Music Box Theatre
  September 19, 1934
  Produced by Sam H. Harris
  155 performances

Bring on the Girls by George S. Kaufman and Morrie Ryskind
    National Theatre (Washington, D.C.)
    October 22, 1934
    Produced by Sam H. Harris
    (*closed out of town*)

First Lady by Katharine Dayton and George S. Kaufman
    Music Box Theatre
    November 26, 1935
    Produced by Sam H. Harris
    238 performances

Tomorrow's a Holiday by Romney Brent
    Golden Theatre
    December 30, 1935
    Produced by John Golden and Joseph Schildkraut
    8 performances

The Postman Always Rings Twice by James M. Cain
    (billed as "consulting director"; Robert B. Sinclair was the of-
        ficial director)
    Lyceum Theatre
    February 18, 1936
    Produced by Jack Curtis
    72 performances

Stage Door by George S. Kaufman and Edna Ferber
    Music Box Theatre
    October 22, 1936
    Produced by Sam H. Harris
    169 performances

I'd Rather Be Right by George S. Kaufman and Moss Hart
    Alvin Theatre
    November 2, 1937
    Produced by Sam H. Harris
    266 performances

Of Mice and Men by John Steinbeck
    Music Box Theatre
    November 23, 1937
    Produced by Sam H. Harris
    207 performances

The Fabulous Invalid by Moss Hart and George S. Kaufman
Broadhurst Theatre
October 8, 1938
Produced by Sam H. Harris
65 performances

The American Way by George S. Kaufman and Moss Hart
Center Theatre
January 21, 1939
Produced by Sam H. Harris and Max Gordon
244 performances

The Man Who Came to Dinner by Moss Hart and George S. Kaufman
Music Box Theatre
October 16, 1939
Produced by Sam H. Harris
739 performances

George Washington Slept Here by George S. Kaufman and Moss Hart
Lyceum Theatre
October 18, 1940
Produced by Sam H. Harris
173 performances

My Sister Eileen by Joseph A. Fields and Jerome Chodorov
Biltmore Theatre
December 26, 1940
Produced by Max Gordon
865 performances

The Land Is Bright by George S. Kaufman and Edna Ferber
Music Box Theatre
October 28, 1941
Produced by Max Gordon
79 performances

The Doughgirls by Joseph A. Fields
Lyceum Theatre
December 30, 1942
Produced by Max Gordon
194 performances

The Naked Genius by Gypsy Rose Lee
    Plymouth Theatre
    October 21, 1943
    Produced by Michael Todd
    36 performances

Franklin Street by Ruth and Augustus Goetz
    Playhouse Theatre (Wilmington, Delaware)
    November 8, 1943
    Produced by Max Gordon
    (*closed out of town*)

Over 21 by Ruth Gordon
    Music Box Theatre
    July 8, 1944
    Produced by Max Gordon
    197 performances

While the Sun Shines by Terence Rattigan
    Lyceum Theatre
    September 19, 1944
    Produced by Max Gordon
    39 performances

The Late George Apley by John P. Marquand and George S. Kauf-
        man
    Lyceum Theatre
    November 17, 1945
    Produced by Max Gordon
    357 performances

Hollywood Pinafore by George S. Kaufman
    Alvin Theatre
    May 31, 1945
    Produced by Max Gordon and Meyer Davis
    52 performances

The Next Half Hour by Mary Chase
    Empire Theatre
    October 24, 1945
    Produced by Max Gordon
    8 performances

Park Avenue by Nunnally Johnson and George S. Kaufman
Shubert Theatre
November 4, 1946
Produced by Max Gordon
72 performances

The Senator Was Indiscreet, film (screenplay by Charles MacArthur)
1947
Produced by Nunnally Johnson and Universal-International Pictures

Town House by Gertrude Tonkonogy
National Theatre
September 23, 1948
Produced by Max Gordon
12 performances

Bravo! by Edna Ferber and George S. Kaufman
Lyceum Theatre
November 11, 1948
Produced by Max Gordon
44 performances

Pretty Penny by Harold Rome and Jerome Chodorov
Bucks County Playhouse (New Hope, Pennsylvania)
June 13, 1949
Produced by Leonard Field
(*closed out of town*)

Metropole by William Walden
Lyceum Theatre
December 6, 1949
Produced by Max Gordon
2 performances

The Enchanted by Jean Giraudoux
Lyceum Theatre
January 15, 1950
Produced by David Lowe and Richard R. Davidson
45 performances

Guys and Dolls by Jo Swerling and Abe Burrows
  46th Street Theatre
  November 24, 1950
  Produced by Cy Feuer and Ernest Martin
  1,200 performances

The Small Hours by George S. Kaufman and Leueen MacGrath
  National Theatre
  February 15, 1951
  Produced by Max Gordon
  20 performances

Fancy Meeting You Again by George S. Kaufman and Leueen Mac-
    Grath
  Royale Theatre
  January 14, 1952
  Produced by Chandler Cowles and Ben Segal
  8 performances

The Solid Gold Cadillac by Howard Teichmann and George S.
    Kaufman
  Belasco Theatre
  November 5, 1953
  Produced by Max Gordon
  526 performances

Romanoff and Juliet by Peter Ustinov
  Plymouth Theatre
  October 10, 1957
  Produced by David Merrick
  389 performances

FILMS BASED ON PLAYS

1920   *Someone in the House* (Metro)

1923   *Dulcy* (Joseph M. Schenck)

1923   *To the Ladies* (Famous Players-Lasky)

1924   *Merton of the Movies* (Famous Players-Lasky)

1925   *Beggar on Horseback* (Famous Players-Lasky)

1925   *Welcome Home* (based on *Minick*) (Warner Brothers)

1928   *The Butter and Egg Man* (First National)

1929   *The Cocoanuts* (Paramount-Famous-Lasky)

1930   *Not So Dumb* (based on *Dulcy*) (M-G-M)

1930   *The Royal Family of Broadway* (based on *The Royal Family*) (Paramount-Publix)

1931   *Animal Crackers* (Paramount-Publix)

1931   *The Front Page* (United Artists)

1931   *June Moon* (Paramount-Publix)

1932   *The Tenderfoot* (based on *The Butter and Egg Man*) (First National)

1932   *Make Me a Star* (based on *Merton of the Movies*) (Paramount-Publix)

1932   *The Expert* (based on *Minick*) (Warner Brothers)

1932   *Once in a Lifetime* (Universal)

1933   *Dinner at Eight* (M-G-M)

1934 *Elmer and Elsie* (based on *To the Ladies*) (Paramount)

1934 *The Man with Two Faces* (based on *The Dark Tower*) (First National)

1937 *Dance, Charlie, Dance* (based on *The Butter and Egg Man*) (Warner Brothers)

1937 *Blonde Trouble* (based on *June Moon*) (Paramount)

1937 *First Lady* (Warner Brothers)

1937 *Stage Door* (RKO-Radio)

1938 *You Can't Take It with You* (Columbia)

1939 *No Place to Go* (based on *Minick*) (Warner Brothers)

1939 *Of Mice and Men* (United Artists)

1940 *An Angel from Texas* (based on *The Butter and Egg Man*) (Warner Brothers)

1940 *Dulcy* (M-G-M)

1940 *His Girl Friday* (based on *The Front Page*) (Columbia)

1942 *The Man Who Came to Dinner* (Warner Brothers)

1942 *George Washington Slept Here* (Warner Brothers)

1942 *My Sister Eileen* (Columbia)

1943 *Good Fellows* (based on *The Good Fellow*) (Paramount)

1944 *The Doughgirls* (Warner Brothers)

1945 *Over 21* (Columbia)

1946 *Doll Face* (based on *The Naked Genius*) (Twentieth Century-Fox)

1946 *The Postman Always Rings Twice* (M-G-M)

1947 *Merton of the Movies* (M-G-M)

1947 *The Late George Apley* (Twentieth Century-Fox)

1947 *While the Sun Shines* (Associated British)

1950 *Dancing in the Dark* (based on *The Band Wagon*) (Twentieth Century-Fox)

APPENDIX

1954 *Three Sailors and a Girl* (based on *The Butter and Egg Man*)
      (Warner Brothers)

1955 *Guys and Dolls* (Samuel Goldwyn)

1955 *My Sister Eileen* (Columbia)

1956 *The Solid Gold Cadillac* (Columbia)

1957 *Silk Stockings* (M-G-M)

1961 *Romanoff and Juliet* (Universal)

BIBLIOGRAPHY

The following books were consulted for insights into and information about George S. Kaufman, his family, friends, associates, and times:

Abbott, George: *Mr. Abbott*
   Random House, Inc., 1963

Adams, Franklin Pierce: *The Diary of Our Own Samuel Pepys* (2 volumes)
   Simon and Schuster, Inc., 1935

——: *F.P.A. Book of Quotations*
   Funk and Wagnalls, 1952

——: *Half a Loaf*
   Doubleday, Page and Company, 1927

——: *Nods and Becks*
   Whittlesey House, 1944

——: *Overset*
   Doubleday, Page and Company, 1922

——: *Something Else Again*
   Doubleday, Page and Company, 1920

——: *So Much Velvet*
   Doubleday, Page and Company, 1924

——: *So There!*
   Doubleday, Page and Company, 1923

——: *Tobogganing on Parnassus*
   Doubleday, Page and Company, 1911

Adams, Samuel Hopkins: *The American Heritage History of the 20s and the 30s*
American Heritage Publishing Company, 1970

———: *A. Woollcott, His Life and His World*
Reynal and Hitchcock, 1945

Amory, Cleveland, editor: *Celebrity Register*
Harper and Row, 1963

Arliss, George: *George Arliss*
John Murray, 1940

———: *Up the Years from Bloomsbury*
Little, Brown and Company, 1938

Astor, Mary: *My Story: An Autobiography*
Doubleday and Company, Inc., 1959

Atherton, Gertrude Franklin: *Black Oxen*
Boni and Liveright, 1923

Atkinson, Brooks: *Broadway*
The Macmillan Company, 1970

———: *Broadway Scrapbook*
Theatre Arts, Inc., 1947

Bankhead, Tallulah: *Tallulah*
Harper and Brothers, 1952

Baragwanath, John: *A Good Time Was Had*
Appleton-Century-Crofts, Inc., 1962

Beckwith, J. A. and Coope, G. G., editors: *Contemporary American Biography*
Harper and Brothers, 1941

Benchley, Nathaniel: *Robert Benchley*
McGraw-Hill Book Company, Inc., 1955

Birmingham, Stephen: *The Late John Marquand*
J. B. Lippincott Company, 1972

Block, Maxine, editor: *Current Biography 1941*
The H. W. Wilson Company, 1941

——: *Current Biography 1942*
The H. W. Wilson Company, 1942

——: *Current Biography 1943*
The H. W. Wilson Company, 1944

Blum, Daniel: *A Pictorial History of the American Theatre*
Crown Publishers, Inc., 1969

——, editor: *Screen World 1957*
Greenberg: Publisher, 1957

——, editor: *Screen World 1958*
Greenberg: Publisher, 1958

——, editor: *Theatre World, Season 1947–48*
Theatre World, 1948

——, editor: *Theatre World, Season 1948–49*
Greenberg: Publisher, 1949

——, editor: *Theatre World, Season 1951–52*
Greenberg: Publisher, 1952

——, editor: *Theatre World, Season 1952–53*
Greenberg: Publisher, 1953

——, editor: *Theatre World, Season 1953–54*
Greenberg: Publisher, 1954

——, editor: *Theatre World, Season 1954–55*
Greenberg: Publisher, 1955

Brockett, Oscar G.: *The Theatre: An Introduction*
Holt, Rinehart and Winston, Inc., 1964

Brown, Catherine Hayes: *Letters to Mary*
Random House, Inc., 1940

Brown, Ivor: *Theatre 1955-56*
Max Reinhardt, 1956

Brown, John Mason: *The Art of Playgoing*
W. W. Norton and Company, Inc., 1936

——: *Broadway in Review*
W. W. Norton and Company, Inc., 1940

[683]

———: *Dramatis Personae*
   The Viking Press, 1963

———: *Seeing Things*
   Whittlesey House, 1946

———: *Still Seeing Things*
   McGraw-Hill Book Company, Inc., 1950

———: *Two on the Aisle*
   W. W. Norton and Company, Inc., 1938

———: *Upstage*
   W. W. Norton and Company, Inc., 1930

———: *The Worlds of Robert E. Sherwood*
   Harper and Row, 1962

Busfield, Roger M., Jr.: *The Playwright's Art*
   Harper and Brothers, 1958

Candee, Marjorie Dent, editor: *Current Biography 1955*
   The H. W. Wilson Company, 1955, 1956

Capote, Truman: *The Dogs Bark*
   Random House, Inc., 1973

Capra, Frank: *The Name Above the Title*
   The Macmillan Company, 1971

Case, Frank: *Do Not Disturb*
   Frederick A. Stokes Company, 1940

———: *Tales of a Wayward Inn*
   Frederick A. Stokes Company, 1938

Cerf, Bennett A. and Cartmell, Van H., editors: *Sixteen Famous American Plays*
   The Modern Library, 1941

———, editor: *Thirty Famous One-Act Plays*
   Random House, Inc., 1943

———, editor: *24 Famous One-Act Plays*
   Doubleday and Company, Inc., 1958

Chapman, John: *Broadway's Best 1960*
   Doubleday and Company, Inc., 1960

———, editor: *The Best Plays of 1947–48*
Dodd, Mead and Company, 1948

———, editor: *The Best Plays of 1948–49*
Dodd, Mead and Company, 1949

———, editor: *The Best Plays of 1949–50*
Dodd, Mead and Company, 1950

———, editor: *The Best Plays of 1950–51*
Dodd, Mead and Company, 1951

———, editor: *The Best Plays of 1951–52*
Dodd, Mead and Company, 1952

———, editor: *Theatre '54*
Random House, Inc., 1954

———, editor: *Theatre '55*
Random House, Inc., 1955

———, editor: *Theatre '56*
Random House, Inc., 1956

Chase, Ilka: *Past Imperfect*
Doubleday, Doran and Company, 1942

Churchill, Allen: *The Literary Decade*
Prentice-Hall, Inc., 1971

Clark, Barrett H. and Davenport, William H., editors: *Nine Modern American Plays*
Appleton-Century-Crofts, Inc., 1951

——— and Freedley, George, editors: *History of American Drama*
Appleton-Century-Crofts, Inc., 1947

Clurman, Harold: *The Fervent Years*
Alfred A. Knopf, Inc., 1945

Cohn, Art: *The Nine Lives of Michael Todd*
Random House, Inc., 1958

Cole, Toby and Chinoy, Helen Krich, editors: *Directing the Play*
The Bobbs-Merrill Company, 1953

Connelly, Marc: *Voices Offstage*
Holt, Rinehart and Winston, Inc., 1968

Coward, Noël: *Present Indicative*
Doubleday, Doran and Company, Inc., 1937

Dickinson, Thomas H.: *Playwrights of the New American Theatre*
The Macmillan Company, 1925

Downer, Alan S.: *Fifty Years of American Drama*
Henry Regnery Company, 1951

———, editor: *The American Theatre Today*
Basic Books, Inc., 1967

Drennan, Robert E., editor: *The Algonquin Wits*
The Citadel Press, 1968

Driscoll, Charles B.: *The Life of O. O. McIntyre*
The Greystone Press, 1938

Eastman, Max: *The Enjoyment of Laughter*
Simon and Schuster, Inc., 1936

Eells, George: *The Life That Late I Led*
G. P. Putnam's Sons, 1967

———: *Hedda and Louella*
G. P. Putnam's Sons, 1972

Eisenstaedt, Alfred: *Witness to Our Time*
The Viking Press, Inc., 1966

Egri, Lajos: *The Art of Dramatic Writing*
Simon and Schuster, Inc., 1946

Elder, Don: *Ring Lardner*
Doubleday and Company, Inc., 1956

Encyclopedia Dello Spetta Colo Fondata da Silvio D'Amico
Casa Editrice La Maschere, 1959

Engel, Lehman: *The American Musical Theatre*
CBS Legacy Collection Books, 1967

Eustis, Morton: *B'way, Inc.!*
Dodd, Mead and Company, 1934

Ewen, David: *Journey to Greatness*
Henry Holt and Company, 1958

[686]

——: *New Complete Book of the American Musical Theatre*
Holt, Rinehart and Winston, Inc., 1970

——: *Richard Rodgers*
Henry Holt and Company, 1937

Fadiman, Clifton: *American Treasury*
Harper and Brothers, 1955

Ferber, Edna: *A Kind of Magic*
Doubleday and Company, Inc., 1963

——: *A Peculiar Treasure*
Doubleday, Doran and Company, Inc., 1939

—— and Kaufman, George S.: *Old Man Minick and Minick*
Doubleday, Page and Company, 1924

Flexner, Eleanor: *American Playwrights: 1918–1938*
Simon and Schuster, Inc., 1938

Ford, Corey: *The Time of Laughter*
Little, Brown and Company, 1967

Freedley, George and Reeves, John A.: *A History of the Theatre*
Crown Publishers, Inc., 1968

Gagey, Edmond M.: *Revolution in American Drama*
Columbia University Press, 1947

Gaige, Crosby: *Footlights and Highlights*
E. P. Dutton and Company, Inc., 1948

Gallaway, Marian: *The Director in the Theatre*
The Macmillan Company, 1963

Gassner, John: *Directions in Modern Theatre and Drama*
Holt, Rinehart and Winston, Inc., 1966

——: *Dramatic Soundings*
Crown Publishers, Inc., 1968

——: *Masters of the Drama*
Random House, Inc., 1940

——: *Producing the Play*
The Dryden Press, 1941

——: *Theatre at the Crossroads*
    Holt, Rinehart and Winston, Inc., 1960

——: *The Theatre in Our Times*
    Crown Publishers, Inc., 1954

—— and Allen, Ralph G.,: *Theatre and Drama in the Making*
    Houghton Mifflin Company, 1964

——, editor: *The Best American Plays, 1951–57*
    Crown Publishers, Inc., 1958

——, editor: *Best Plays of the Modern American Theatre*
    Crown Publishers, Inc., 1947

Geisinger, Marion: *Players and Playwrights*
    Hart Publishing Company, 1971

Gershwin, Ira: *Lyrics on Several Occasions*
    Alfred A. Knopf, 1956

Gibbs, Wolcott: *More in Sorrow*
    Henry Holt and Company, 1958

Gilder, Rosamond, Issacs, Hermine Rich, and MacGregor, Robert M., editors: *Theatre Arts Anthology*
    Theatre Arts Books, 1950

Gillette, William: *The Illusion of the First Time in Acting*
    Dramatic Museum of Columbia University, 1915

Goldman, William: *The Season*
    Harcourt, Brace and World, Inc., 1969

Gordon, Ruth: *Myself Among Others*
    Atheneum, 1971

Goren, Charles H.: *Better Bridge for Better Players*
    Doubleday, Doran and Company, 1942

Gottfried, Martin: *A Theatre Divided*
    Little, Brown and Company, 1967

Gottlieb, Polly Rose: *The Nine Lives of Billy Rose*
    Crown Publishers, Inc., 1968

[688]

Gould, Jean: *Modern American Playwrights*
  Dodd, Mead and Company, 1966

Graham, Sheilah: *The Garden of Allah*
  Crown Publishers, Inc., 1970

Grant, Jane: *Ross, The New Yorker, and Me*
  Reynal and Company, Inc., 1968

Grebanier, Bernard: *Playwriting*
  Thomas Y. Crowell Company, 1961

Green, Abel and Laurie, Joe, Jr.: *Show Biz from Vaude to Video*
  Henry Holt and Company, 1951

Green, Stanley: *The World of Musical Comedy*
  Ziff-Davis Publishing Company, 1960

Griffith, Richard and Mayer, Arthur: *The Movies*
  Simon and Schuster, Inc., 1957

Gruen, John: *Close Up*
  The Viking Press, Inc., 1968

Guernsey, Otis L., Jr., editor: *The Best Plays of 1964–65*
  Dodd, Mead and Company, 1965

———, editor: *The Best Plays of 1965–66*
  Dodd, Mead and Company, 1966

———, editor: *The Best Plays of 1966–67*
  Dodd, Mead and Company, 1967

———, editor: *The Best Plays of 1967–68*
  Dodd, Mead and Company, 1968

———, editor: *The Best Plays of 1968–69*
  Dodd, Mead and Company, 1969

———, editor: *The Best Plays of 1969–70*
  Dodd, Mead and Company, 1970

Hall, James B. and Ulanov, Barry: *Modern Culture and the Arts*
  McGraw-Hill Book Company, Inc., 1967

Harriman, Margaret Case: *Blessed Are the Debonair*
  Rinehart and Company, Inc., 1956

————: *Take Them Up Tenderly*
Alfred A. Knopf, 1944

————: *The Vicious Circle*
Rinehart and Company, Inc., 1951

Hart, Moss: *Act One*
Random House, Inc., 1959

Hartnoll, Phyllis, editor: *The Oxford Companion to the Theatre*
Oxford University Press, 1967

Hatlin, Theodore W.: *Orientation to the Theatre*
Appleton-Century-Crofts, Inc., 1962

Hayes, Helen and Dody, Sanford: *On Reflection*
M. Evans and Company, Inc., 1968

Hecht, Ben: *Charlie*
Harper and Brothers, 1957

Hellman, Lillian: *An Unfinished Woman*
Little, Brown and Company, 1969

Hewes, Henry, editor: *The Best Plays of 1961–62*
Dodd, Mead and Company, 1962

————, editor: *The Best Plays of 1962–63*
Dodd, Mead and Company, 1963

————, editor: *The Best Plays of 1963–64*
Dodd, Mead and Company, 1964

Hewitt, Barnard: *Theatre U.S.A. from 1668 to 1957*
McGraw-Hill Book Company, Inc., 1959

Hirschfeld, Al: *Show Business Is No Business*
Simon and Schuster, Inc., 1951

Houghton, Norris: *Advance from Broadway*
Harcourt, Brace and Company, 1941

Houseman, John: *Run-Through*
Simon and Schuster, Inc., 1951

Hoyt, Edwin P.: *Alexander Woollcott: The Man Who Came to Dinner*
Abelard-Schuman, 1968

Hudson, Lynton: *Life and the Theatre*
Roy Publishers, 1954

Hughes, Glenn: *A History of the American Theatre, 1700–1950*
Samuel French, 1951

Jablonski, Edward and Stewart, Lawrence D.: *The Gershwin Years*
Doubleday and Company, Inc., 1958

Jessel, George: *So Help Me*
Random House, Inc., 1943

Kahn, E. J., Jr.: *The World of Swope*
Simon and Schuster, Inc., 1965

Kanin, Garson: *Remembering Mr. Maugham*
Atheneum, 1966

Kaufman, Beatrice and Hennessey, Joseph, editors: *The Letters of
Alexander Woollcott*
The Viking Press, Inc., 1944

Keats, John: *You Might As Well Live*
Simon and Schuster, Inc., 1970

Kernodle, George R.: *Invitation to the Theatre*
Harcourt, Brace and World, Inc., 1967

Kerr, Walter: *Thirty Days Hath December*
Simon and Schuster, Inc., 1969

Kouwenhoven, John: *The Columbia Historical Portrait of New
York*
Doubleday and Company, Inc., 1960

Kramer, Dale: *Ross and the New Yorker*
Doubleday and Company, Inc., 1951

Kronenberger, Louis: *No Whippings, No Gold Watches*
Little, Brown and Company, 1970

———, editor: *The Best Plays of 1952–53*
Dodd, Mead and Company, 1953

———, editor: *The Best Plays of 1953–54*
Dodd, Mead and Company, 1954

———, editor: *The Best Plays of 1954–55*
Dodd, Mead and Company, 1955

——, editor: *The Best Plays of 1955–56*
Dodd, Mead and Company, 1956

——, editor: *The Best Plays of 1956–57*
Dodd, Mead and Company, 1957

——, editor: *The Best Plays of 1957–58*
Dodd, Mead and Company, 1958

——, editor: *The Best Plays of 1958–59*
Dodd, Mead and Company, 1959

——, editor: *The Best Plays of 1959–60*
Dodd, Mead and Company, 1960

——, editor: *The Best Plays of 1960–61*
Dodd, Mead and Company, 1961

Krutch, Joseph Wood: *American Drama Since 1918*
Random House, Inc., 1939

Kunitz, Stanley J. and Haycraft, Howard, editors: *Twentieth Century Authors*
The H. W. Wilson Company, 1942

Lahr, John: *Notes on a Cowardly Lion*
Alfred A. Knopf, 1969

Langner, Lawrence: *The Magic Curtain*
E. P. Dutton and Company, Inc., 1951

Laufe, Abe: *Anatomy of a Hit*
Hawthorn Books, Inc., 1966

Lawson, John Howard: *Theory and Technique of Playwriting and Screenwriting*
G. P. Putnam's Sons, 1936, 1949

Lembke, Russell W.: *The Esthetic Values of Dissonance in the Plays of George S. Kaufman and His Collaborators*
Doctoral Dissertation for the State University of Iowa, January 1946

Levant, Oscar: *The Memoirs of an Amnesiac*
G. P. Putnam's Sons, 1965

——: *A Smattering of Ignorance*
Doubleday, Doran and Company, Inc., 1940

———: *The Unimportance of Being Oscar*
G. P. Putnam's Sons, 1968

Levin, Martin: *The Phoenix Nest*
Doubleday and Company, Inc., 1960

Lewis, Allan: *American Plays and Playwrights of the Contemporary Theatre*
Crown Publishers, Inc., 1965

Lewis, Emory: *Stages*
Prentice-Hall, Inc., 1969

Ley, Maria Piscator: *The Piscator Experiment*
Alfred A. Knopf, 1933

Little, Stuart W. and Cantor, Arthur: *The Playmakers*
W. W. Norton and Company, Inc., 1970

Loos, Anita: *A Girl Like I*
The Viking Press, Inc., 1966

Lumley, Frederick: *New Trends in 20th Century Drama*
Oxford University Press, 1967

———: *Trends in 20th Century Drama*
Essential Books, 1956, 1960

MacCarthy, Desmond: *Humanities*
Oxford University Press, 1954

Macgowan, Kenneth: *Footlights Across America*
Harcourt, Brace and Company, 1929

———: *A Primer of Playwriting*
Random House, Inc., 1951

——— and Melnitz, William: *The Living Stage*
Prentice-Hall, Inc., 1955

Maney, Richard: *Fanfare*
Harper and Brothers, 1957

Mantle, Burns: *American Playwrights of Today*
Dodd, Mead and Company, 1929

———: *Contemporary American Playwrights*
Dodd, Mead and Company, 1941

————, editor: *The Best Plays of 1919–20*
Dodd, Mead and Company, 1920

————, editor: *The Best Plays of 1920–21*
Dodd, Mead and Company, 1921

————, editor: *The Best Plays of 1921–22*
Small, Maynard and Company, 1922

————, editor: *The Best Plays of 1922–23*
Small, Maynard and Company, 1923

————, editor: *The Best Plays of 1923–24*
Dodd, Mead and Company, 1924

————, editor: *The Best Plays of 1924–25*
Dodd, Mead and Company, 1925

————, editor: *The Best Plays of 1925–26*
Dodd, Mead and Company, 1926

————, editor: *The Best Plays of 1926–27*
Dodd, Mead and Company, 1927

————, editor: *The Best Plays of 1927–28*
Dodd, Mead and Company, 1928

————, editor: *The Best Plays of 1928–29*
Dodd, Mead and Company, 1929

————, editor: *The Best Plays of 1929–30*
Dodd, Mead and Company, 1930

————, editor: *The Best Plays of 1930–31*
Dodd, Mead and Company, 1931

————, editor: *The Best Plays of 1931–32*
Dodd, Mead and Company, 1932

————, editor: *The Best Plays of 1932–33*
Dodd, Mead and Company, 1933

————, editor: *The Best Plays of 1933–34*
Dodd, Mead and Company, 1934

————, editor: *The Best Plays of 1934–35*
Dodd, Mead and Company, 1935

——, editor: *The Best Plays of 1935–36*
Dodd, Mead and Company, 1936

——, editor: *The Best Plays of 1936–37*
Dodd, Mead and Company, 1937

——, editor: *The Best Plays of 1937–38*
Dodd, Mead and Company, 1938

——, editor: *The Best Plays of 1938–39*
Dodd, Mead and Company, 1939

——, editor: *The Best Plays of 1939–40*
Dodd, Mead and Company, 1940

——, editor: *The Best Plays of 1940–41*
Dodd, Mead and Company, 1941

——, editor: *The Best Plays of 1941–42*
Dodd, Mead and Company, 1942

——, editor: *The Best Plays of 1942–43*
Dodd, Mead and Company, 1943

——, editor: *The Best Plays of 1943–44*
Dodd, Mead and Company, 1944

——, editor: *The Best Plays of 1944–45*
Dodd, Mead and Company, 1945

——, editor: *The Best Plays of 1945–46*
Dodd, Mead and Company, 1947

——, editor: *The Best Plays of 1946–47*

—— and Gassner, John, editors: *A Treasury of the Theatre*
Simon and Schuster, Inc., 1935

—— and Sherwood, Garrison P., editors: *The Best Plays of 1909–
1919*
Dodd, Mead and Company, 1933

Marquand, John P.: *Thirty Years*
Little, Brown and Company, 1954

Marx, Arthur: *Life with Groucho*
Simon and Schuster, Inc., 1954

——: *Son of Groucho*
David McKay, Inc., 1972

Marx, Groucho: *The Groucho Letters*
Simon and Schuster, Inc., 1967

Marx, Harpo and Barber, Rowland: *Harpo Speaks*
Bernard Geis Associates, 1961

Melchinger, Siegfried: *The Concise Encyclopedia of Modern Drama*
Horizon Press, 1964

Meredith, Scott, editor: *The Fireside Treasury of Modern Humor*
Simon and Schuster, Inc., 1963

Mersand, Joseph: *The American Drama Since 1930*
Kennikat Press, Inc., 1949, 1968

——: *Traditions in American Literature*
The Modern Chapbooks, 1939

Middleton, George: *The Dramatists Guild*
Authors League of America, Inc., 1953

——: *These Things Are Mine*
The Macmillan Company, 1947

Millett, Fred B.: *Contemporary American Authors*
AMS Press, 1940

Morehouse, Ward: *Forty-five Minutes from Broadway*
The Dial Press, 1939

——: *Just the Other Day*
McGraw-Hill Book Company, Inc., 1953

——: *Matinee Tomorrow*
Whittlesey House, 1949

Moritz, Charles, editor: *Current Biography 1960*
The H. W. Wilson Company, 1960, 1961

——, editor: *Current Biography 1961*
The H. W. Wilson Company, 1961, 1962

——, editor: *Current Biography 1965*
The H. W. Wilson Company, 1965, 1966

Morley, Robert and Stokes, Sewell: *Robert Morley*
Simon and Schuster, Inc., 1966

Morris, Lloyd: *Curtain Time*
Random House, Inc., 1953

——: *Postscript to Yesterday*
Random House, Inc., 1947

Moses, Montrose J.: *The American Dramatist*
Little, Brown and Company, 1925

—— and Brown, John Mason, editors: *The American Theatre as
Seen By Its Critics, 1752–1934*
W. W. Norton and Company, Inc., 1934

Murray, Nicholas and Gallico, Paul: *The Revealing Eye*
Atheneum, 1967

Nannes, Casper: *Politics in the American Drama*
The Catholic University of America Press, Inc., 1960

Nathan, George Jean: *Encyclopedia of the Theatre*
Alfred A. Knopf, 1940

——: *The Intimate Notebooks of George Jean Nathan*
Alfred A. Knopf, 1932

——: *The Morning After the First Night*
Alfred A. Knopf, 1938

——: *Passing Judgments*
Alfred A. Knopf, 1935

——: *Since Ibsen*
Alfred A. Knopf, 1933

——: *Testament of a Critic*
Alfred A. Knopf, 1931

——: *The Theatre Book of the Year 1944–1945*
Alfred A. Knopf, 1945

——: *The Theatre Book of the Year 1945–1946*
Alfred A. Knopf, 1946

——: *The Theatre Book of the Year 1946–1947*
Alfred A. Knopf, 1947

———: *The Theatre Book of the Year 1947–1948*
Alfred A. Knopf, 1948

———: *The Theatre Book of the Year 1948–1949*
Alfred A. Knopf, 1949

———: *The Theatre Book of the Year 1949–1950*
Alfred A. Knopf, 1950

———: *The Theatre Book of the Year 1950–1951*
Alfred A. Knopf, 1951

———: *The Theatre in the Fifties*
Alfred A. Knopf, 1953

———: *The Theatre of the Moment*
Alfred A. Knopf, 1936

Novick, Julius: *Beyond Broadway, The Quest for Permanent Theatres*
Hill and Wang, 1968

O'Brien, Pat: *The Wind at My Back*
Doubleday and Company, Inc., 1964

O'Connor, Richard: *John Steinbeck*
McGraw-Hill Book Company, Inc., 1970

O'Hara, Frank Hurburt: *Today in American Drama*
The University of Chicago Press, 1959

Oppenheimer, George: *The View from the Sixties*
David McKay, Inc., 1966

———, editor: *The Passionate Playgoer*
The Viking Press, Inc., 1958

Paar, Jack: *My Sabre Is Bent*
Simon and Schuster, Inc., 1961

Perelman, S. J.: *The Dream Department*
Random House, Inc., 1943

Phelps, William Lyon: *Autobiography with Letters*
Oxford University Press, 1939

Phillips, Cabell: *From the Crash to the Blitz 1929–1939*
The Macmillan Company, 1969

Play, James H. and Crempel, Daniel: *The Theatrical Image*
McGraw-Hill Book Company, Inc., 1967

Quinn, Arthur Hobson: *A History of the American Drama*
Appleton-Century-Crofts, Inc., 1927, 1936

Rascoe, Burton: *We Were Interrupted*
Doubleday and Company, Inc., 1947

Reed, Joseph Verner: *The Curtain Falls*
Harcourt, Brace and Company, 1935

Rice, Elmer: *The Living Theatre*
Harper and Brothers, 1959

Rigdon, Walter, editor: *The Biographical Encyclopedia and Who's Who of the American Theatre*
James H. Heineman Company, 1965

Roberts, Vera Mowry: *On Stage, A History of Theatre*
Harper and Row, 1962

Rogers, Agnes and Allen, Frederick Lewis: *I Remember Distinctly*
Harper and Brothers, 1947

Rosmond, Babette: *Robert Benchley: His Life and Good Times*
Doubleday and Company, Inc., 1970

Rothe, Anna, editor: *Current Biography 1946*
The H. W. Wilson Company, 1947

———, editor: *Current Biography 1948*
The H. W. Wilson Company, 1949

——— and Lohr, Evelyn, editors: *Current Biography 1952*
The H. W. Wilson Company, 1952

Sardi, Vincent, Sr., and Gehman, Richard: *Sardi's*
Henry Holt and Company, 1953

Saylor, Oliver M.: *Our American Theatre*
Brentano's, 1923

Schorer, Mark: *Sinclair Lewis*
McGraw-Hill Book Company, Inc., 1961

Seldes, Gilbert, editor: *The Portable Ring Lardner*
The Viking Press, Inc., 1946

Shadegg, Stephen: *Clare Boothe Luce*
Simon and Schuster, Inc., 1970

Sievers, W. David: *Freud on Broadway*
Hermitage House, 1955

Sillman, Leonard: *Here Lies Leonard Sillman*
The Citadel Press, 1959

Smith, Cecil: *Musical Comedy in America*
Theatre Arts Books, 1950

Smith, Harry B.: *First Nights and First Editions*
Little, Brown and Company, 1931

Sobel, Bernard: *Broadway Heartbeat*
Hermitage House, 1953

———: *The New Theatre Handbook and Digest of Plays*
Crown Publishers, Inc., 1959

Sobol, Louis: *The Longest Street*
Crown Publishers, Inc., 1968

Spaeth, Sigmund: *Fifty Years with Music*
Fleet Publishing Company, 1959

Stambler, Irwin: *Encyclopedia of Popular Music*
St. Martin's Press, 1965

Stagg, Jerry: *The Brothers Shubert*
Random House, Inc., 1968

Talese, Gay: *The Kingdom and the Power*
The World Publishing Company, 1969

Taubman, Howard: *The Making of the American Theatre*
Coward-McCann, Inc., 1965

Taylor, Deems, Peterson, Marcelene, and Hale, Bryant: *A Pictorial History of the Movies*
Simon and Schuster, Inc., 1943

Teichmann, Howard: *George S. Kaufman, An Intimate Portrait*
Atheneum, 1972

Thomas, Bob: *King Cohn*
  G. P. Putnam's Sons, 1967

———: *Thalberg: Life and Legend*
  Doubleday and Company, Inc., 1969

Thurber, James: *Credos and Curios*
  Harper and Row, 1968

———: *The Years with Ross*
  Little, Brown and Company, 1958

Toohey, John L.: *A History of the Pulitzer Prize Plays*
  The Citadel Press, 1967

Trewin, J. C.: *The Turbulent Thirties*
  Macdonald and Company (Publishers), Ltd., 1960

Tyler, George C. and Furnas, J. C.: *Whatever Goes Up*
  The Bobbs-Merrill Company, 1934

Untermeyer, Louis, editor: *A Treasury of Laughter*
  Simon and Schuster, Inc., 1946

Vardac, A. Nicholas: *Stage to Screen*
  Harvard University Press, 1949

Veiller, Bayard: *The Fun I've Had*
  Reynal and Hitchcock, 1941

Watson, E. Bradlee and Pressey, Benfield, editors: *Contemporary
    American Plays*
  Charles Scribner's Sons, 1931

Whiting, Frank M.: *An Introduction to the Theatre*
  Harper and Row, 1954

Witham, W. Tasker: *Living American Literature*
  Stephen Daye Press, Inc., 1947

Wodehouse, P. G. and Bolton, Guy: *Bring on the Girls*
  Simon and Schuster, Inc., 1953

Wright, Edward B. and Downs, Lenthiel H.: *A Primer for Playgoers*
  Prentice-Hall, Inc., 1958

Yates, Norris W.: *Robert Benchley*
  Twayne Publishers, Inc., 1968

Ohio University Press, 1970
Yurka, Blanche: *Bohemian Girl*

Zimmerman, Paul D. and Goldblatt, Burt: *The Marx Brothers at the Movies*
G. P. Putnam's Sons, 1968

Zolotow, Maurice: *Stagestruck: The Romance of Alfred Lunt and Lynn Fontanne*
Harcourt, Brace and World, Inc., 1964

plus the published and unpublished works of George S. Kaufman and his collaborators, friends, and associates.

In addition, more than ten thousand clippings were collected from the following periodicals:

American Heritage, The American Mercury, Arts and Decorations, The Baltimore (Maryland) *Evening Sun, The Bookman,* The Boston (Massachusetts) *Advertiser,* The Boston (Massachusetts) *Globe,* The Boston (Massachusetts) *Journal,* The Boston (Massachusetts) *Transcript,* The Brooklyn (New York) *Daily Eagle, The Catholic Digest,* The Chicago (Illinois) *Evening Post,* The Chicago (Illinois) *Herald-Examiner,* The Chicago (Illinois) *Journal of Commerce,* The Chicago (Illinois) *Tribune, Commonweal, Coronet, Current Opinion, The Dial, The Diners' Club Magazine, Drama League Review, Dramatic Mirror, Everybody's Magazine,* The Fargo (North Dakota) *Forum, The Freeman, Gotham Weekly Gazette, Harper's Magazine, Harper's Weekly, The Independent, The Jewish Criterion, The Journal of Commerce and Commercial Bulletin, Judge,* The Kansas City (Missouri) *Star,* The Kansas City (Missouri) *Times,* The Keanstrong (New Jersey) *News, Life, The Literary Digest, Modern Drama,* The Montreal (Quebec, Canada) *Gazette, Musical America, Musicians Club Monthly, The Nation, The New Masses, The New Republic, Newsday, Newsweek,* The New York (New York) *American,* The New York (New York) *Commercial,* The New York (New York) *Evening Post,* The New York (New York) *Globe,* The New York (New York) *Herald,* The New York (New York) *Herald-Tribune,* The New York (New York) *Journal,* The New York (New York) *Journal-American,* The New York (New York) *Mail,* The New York (New York) *Mirror,* The New York (New York) *Morn-*

ing Telegraph, The New York (New York) *News*, The New York (New York) *PM*, The New York (New York) *Post*, The New York (New York) *Star*, The New York (New York) *Sun*, The New York (New York) *Telegram*, The New York (New York) *Times*, *The New York Times Book Review and Magazine*, *The New York Times Magazine*, The New York (New York) *Tribune*, The New York (New York) *World*, The New York (New York) *World-Journal-Tribune*, The New York *World-Telegram*, The New York (New York) *World-Telegram and Sun*, *The New Yorker*, *The North American Review*, *The Outlook and Independent*, The Passaic (New Jersey) *Herald*, The Pittsburgh (Pennsylvania) *Post*, The Pittsburgh (Pennsylvania) *Post-Gazette*, *The Players Magazine*, *The Playgoer*, *Princeton Tiger*, The Providence (Rhode Island) *Sunday Journal*, *Publishers' Weekly*, *Puck*, *The Quarterly Journal of Speech*, *Reader's Digest*, The Rochester (New York) *Democrat*, The Rochester (New York) *Herald*, The Rochester (New York) *Post-Express*, The Rochester (New York) *Times-Union*, *The Saturday Evening Post*, *The Saturday Review*, *The Saturday Review of Literature*, *Scribner's Magazine*, *The Spectator*, *The Stage*, The Stillwater (Minnesota) *Gazette*, *Theatre Arts Monthly*, *Theatre Magazine*, *This Week*, *Time*, *Town and Country*, *Town Topics*, *Vanity Fair*, *Variety*, *Vogue*, The Washington (D.C.) *Times*, The Winona (Minnesota) *Independent*, *Women's Wear Daily*.

Most of the pictures in the book were provided by the people in the pictures or by their relatives or friends, and I'd like to express my appreciation to Amy Adams, Nathaniel Benchley, Irving Berlin, Eileen Bransten, Heywood Hale Broun, Marc Connelly, Howard Dietz, Clifton Fadiman, Cy Feuer, Gertrude Tonkonogy Friedberg, Ruth Friedlich, Charles Friedman, Ira Gershwin, Max Gordon, Kitty Carlisle Hart, George Hughes, Dorothy Stickney Lindsay, Ernest Martin, Arthur Marx, Groucho Marx, George Oppenheimer, Richard Rodgers, Morrie Ryskind, Madeline Sherwood, Howard Teichmann, Helen Thurber, and William Walden. I'm also very grateful for pictures and drawings given to me by Doubleday and Company, Inc., Little, Brown and Company, Metro-Goldwyn-Mayer Studios, *The New Yorker*, G. P. Putnam's Sons, *Reader's Digest*, Charles Scribner's Sons, and The Wisconsin Center for Theatre Research. And I'm especially grateful to George Oppenheimer, who should win the Extraordinary Courtesy Award for using his encyclopedic knowledge of the theatre (and just about everything else) to check the manuscript line by line for accuracy.

There's one other debt which can never be repaid, but which certainly must be listed. I mentioned this project casually one day to an old friend, Mrs. Charles Penchansky, who is an Assistant Professor and head of the Interlibrary Loan Department at Queens College, New York, and found myself the beneficiary of a level of research assistance rarely available to writers of books. For several years, merely because she found the project interesting and because she's that kind of person, Mrs. Penchansky tracked down literally hundreds of books, magazines, newspapers, pictures and documents containing details essential to the telling of the Kaufman saga, some of it material which other people had assured me no longer existed. So if there are facts, figures, and other details in the book which surprise friends and associates of George S. Kaufman because they're things they didn't remember or didn't know themselves, it's only because Mimi Black Penchansky has a talent for detection and discovery which would arouse envy and even awe in the heart of Sherlock Holmes.

S.M.

SCOTT MEREDITH says he is always mildly surprised to find himself visible as the author of a book, since he works mostly behind the scenes. He is president of a large firm of authors' representatives with principal offices in New York and London, handling the literary and business affairs of a great many major authors and public figures.

He started out as a writer, however, selling his first story to a magazine at the age of fourteen, and had sold more than four hundred stories, serials, and articles before he was twenty-one. He also once undertook a contract with a small paperback publishing house and wrote nineteen novels for the firm in ten months.

He is the author of a textbook on fiction techniques, *Writing to Sell*, which is required reading in courses at over thirty colleges. He has also edited eleven anthologies (one of which, *The Fireside Treasury of Modern Humor*, is a thousand pages long), written the article on humor for three editions of the Encyclopaedia Britannica and the article on fiction for two editions of the Oxford Encyclopaedia, and appears occasionally as an expert witness in copyright cases. He lives on the north shore of Long Island with his wife, Helen, his son, Steve, his daughter, Randy, and two gigantic German shepherd dogs, Chloe and Archie. The Merediths collect Impressionist and post-Impressionist art, and nearly every wall of their house is covered with paintings and drawings; even the kitchen area contains a Picasso, a Dali, a Magritte, a Laurencin, an Orozco, and a Dufy.

INDEX

Auerbach, Arnold, 600
Authors' League of America, 389–90, 400

Babbitt, 96
Bakrow, Beatrice. *See* Kaufman, Beatrice (*née* Beatrice Bakrow)
Bakrow, Leonard, 644
Bakrow, Sarah, 590
Bakrows (Bakrow family), 53–54, 142, 386. *See also* individual members
Baldwin, Walter, Jr., 306
Bancroft, George, 101
Band Wagon, The, 10, 60, 114, 508–13, 515
Bankhead, Tallulah, 64, 103, 150, 233
Barbier, George, 132, 359–60
Barker, Jess, 535
Barnes, Clive, 69
Barnes, Howard, 583, 607
Barr, Richard, 650
Barrat, Robert, 60
Barry, Philip, 451, 452
Barrymore, Ethel, 231, 233–34, 235–36, 344, 351, 506
Barrymore, John, 58, 231, 232–33, 234, 236, 244, 497, 502, 561
Barrymore, Lionel, 231, 233, 502, 541
Barrymore family, 231–36, 244, 247. *See also* individual members
Barthelmess, Richard, 587
Barton, Ralph, 285
Baruch, Bernard, 152, 153, 506, 592, 596
Battle, George Gordon, 365
Baxter, Warner, 229
Beau Brummell, 389
Beck, Martin, 265–66
Becky Sharp, 116
Beebe, Lucius, 546
Beery, Wallace, 502
Beggar off Horseback, 136
Beggar on Horseback, 6, 128–35, 140, 258, 273, 307
Behrman, S. N., 189, 241, 288, 351, 354, 366, 443, 636–38; biography, described, 636–38; collaboration with GSK, 636–38; death of, 652
Belasco, David, 102
Belasco Theatre (New York City), 630
Bel Geddes, Norman, 77, 192
Bellamy, Francis R., 312
Belmont, Eleanor (Mrs. August Belmont), 116
Benchley, Robert, 63, 103–4, 105, 124, 136, 139, 251, 438–39, 500; death of, 590; described, 103–4, 154–55; and Ross and *The New Yorker* magazine, 285, 288; and Round Table group, 150, 152, 154–55, 157, 158, 166

Benedict Arnold, 637
Bennett, Joan, 504
Benny, Jack, 467, 555
Benson, Sally, 288, 580
Berlin, Ellin Mackay, 183
Berlin, Irving, 9, 75, 115, 183, 270, 276–77, 278, 280, 292, 336, 399, 432, 449, 465, 483–84, 487, 636, 637, 646
Berman, Pandro S., 504
Best Plays, 45; *1922–23*, 109; *1923–24*, 229; *1924–25*, 133; *1925–26*, 258; *1927–28*, 247; *1928–29*, 366; *1929–30*, 338; *1930–31*, 478; *1932–33*, 498; *1935–36*, 518, 587; *1936–37*, 503, 536, 566; *1939–40*, 552; *1940–41*, 580; *1942–43*, 581; *1943–44*, 584; *1944–45*, 595
Be That as It May, 44
Better Bridge for Better Players (Goren), 584
Be Yourself, 76, 137
Bibesco, Prince Antoine, 166
Bigley, Isabel, 610
Bijou Theatre (New York City), 229
Billboard (magazine), 34, 240
Biltmore Theatre (New York City), 200, 580
Birch, Reginald, 32
Birchall, Frederick T., 298
Black Oxen, 156
Blackstone Theatre (Chicago, Ill.), 60, 71
Black and White Club, 142–43
Blaine, Vivian, 583, 610
Blind Mice, 503
Bloch, Bertram, 584, 585
Blondell, Joan, 582, 583
Blonde Trouble, 339
Bloomingdale, Alfred, 1–2
Boasberg, Al, 526
Bogart, Humphrey, 496
Bogdanovich, Peter, 478
Bolger, Ray, 137, 608
Bolitho, William, 330, 420
Bolton, Whitney, 601
Boni and Liveright, 191, 193
Booth, Mr. and Mrs. Enos, 350, 351
Booth, John, 210–11
Booth, Shirley, 579, 597
Booth Theatre (New York City), 229, 536, 537
Born Yesterday, 630–31
Boule de Suif, 310–11
Bower, Roger, xiv, 255
Bowery After Dark, The, 269
Bradford, Roark, 137
Brady, Alice, 172
Brady, William A., 396–97
Brando, Marlon, 611